Learning to Teach in the Secondary School

Overall, a complete benefit to all PGCE students – an absolute must!

PGCE student's response to the second edition.

Learning to teach might sound easy but the reality involves hard work and careful preparation. To become an effective teacher requires subject knowledge, an understanding of your pupils and the confidence to respond to dynamic classroom situations. This edition has been updated to include changes to the National Curriculum for England and Wales that came into force in September 2000. It covers changes in the organisation of, and curriculum for, Initial Teacher Training and Continuing Professional Development.

With even more useful strategies and ideas, *Learning to Teach in the Secondary School* covers the range of situations and potential problems faced by the student teacher and the newly qualified teacher.

The book contains 29 units, organised into nine chapters each covering a key concept or skill, including:

- Managing classroom behaviour
- Ways pupils learn
- Planning lessons and schemes of work
- Differentiation, progression and pupil grouping
- Assessment, including public examinations
- Inclusion and Special Educational needs
- Using ICT in teaching and learning
- Getting your first teaching post

This text offers a sound and practical introduction to the skills needed to gain Qualified Teacher Status, and will help you to develop those qualities that lead to good practice and a successful future in education. This book is the core text for the subject-specific *Learning to Teach* series, also published by RoutledgeFalmer, and is an essential buy for every student teacher.

Susan Capel is a Professor in the Department of Sports Science at Brunel University. **Marilyn Leask** is a Principal Research Officer at the National Foundation for Educational Research. **Tony Turner** has recently retired from the Institute of Education, University of London.

Learning to Teach Subjects in the Secondary School Series

Series Editors

Susan Capel, Brunel University, London; Marilyn Leask, National Foundation for Educational Research; and Tony Turner, formerly of the Institute of Education, University of London.

Designed for all student teachers learning to teach in secondary schools, and particularly those on school-based initial teacher training courses, the books in this series complement *Learning to Teach in the Secondary School* and its companion, *Starting to Teach in the Secondary School*. Each book in the series applies underpinning theory and addresses practical issues to support student teachers in school and in the training institution in learning how to teach a particular subject.

Learning to Teach English in the Secondary School
Jon Davison and Jane Dowson

Learning to Teach Modern Foreign Languages in the Secondary School, 2nd Edition
Norbert Pachler and Kit Field

Learning to Teach History in the Secondary School, 2nd Edition
Terry Haydn, James Arthur and Martin Hunt

Learning to Teach Physical Education in the Secondary School
Edited by Susan Capel

Learning to Teach Science in the Secondary School
Tony Turner and Wendy DiMarco

Learning to Teach Mathematics in the Secondary School
Edited by Sue Johnston-Wilder, Peter Johnston-Wilder, David Pimm and John Westwell

Learning to Teach Religious Education in the Secondary School
Edited by Andrew Wright and Ann-Marie Brandom

Learning to Teach Art and Design in the Secondary School
Edited by Nicholas Addison and Lesley Burgess

Learning to Teach Geography in the Secondary School
David Lambert and David Balderstone

Learning to Teach Design and Technology in the Secondary School
Edited by Gwyneth Owen-Jackson

Learning to Teach Music in the Secondary School
Edited by Chris Philpott

Learning to Teach in the Secondary School, 3rd Edition
Edited by Susan Capel, Marilyn Leask and Tony Turner

Learning to Teach in the Secondary School

A companion to school experience

Third edition

**Edited by Susan Capel, Marilyn Leask
and Tony Turner**

London and New York

First published 2001
by RoutledgeFalmer
11 New Fetter Lane, London EC4P 4EE

Simultaneously published in the USA and Canada
by Routledge
29 West 35th Street, New York, NY 10001

RoutledgeFalmer is an imprint of the Taylor & Francis Group

Typeset in Bembo by Keystroke, Jacaranda Lodge, Wolverhampton
Printed and bound in Great Britain by Bell & Bain Ltd, Glasgow

British Library Cataloguing in Publication Data
A catalogue record for this book is available from the British Library

Library of Congress Cataloging in Publication Data
A catalog record for this book has been requested

ISBN 0–415–25976–2

CONTENTS

List of figures   ix
List of tables   xi
List of tasks   xiii
Notes on contributors   xvii
Foreword   xxi

Introduction   1

CHAPTER 1   BECOMING A TEACHER   6

1.1   What do teachers do?   8
Marilyn Leask

1.2   The student teacher's role and responsibilities   18
Marilyn Leask

1.3   Managing your time and preventing stress   29
Susan Capel

1.4   Teaching and learning with ICT: an introduction   37
Marilyn Leask

CHAPTER 2 BEGINNING TO TEACH   49

2.1   Reading classrooms   50
Tony Turner

2.2   Schemes of work and lesson planning   65
Marilyn Leask and Jon Davison

2.3   Taking responsibility for whole lessons   77
Marilyn Leask

CHAPTER 3 CLASSROOM INTERACTIONS AND MANAGING PUPILS   88

3.1   Communicating with pupils   89
Susan Capel, Roger Strangwick and Margaret Whitehead

3.2 Motivating pupils   103
Susan Capel

3.3 Managing classroom behaviour   116
Jon Davison

CHAPTER 4 PUPIL DIFFERENCES   128

4.1 Pupil grouping, progression and differentiation   130
Tony Turner

4.2 Growth, development and diet   147
Tony Turner

4.3 Cognitive development   160
Tony Turner

4.4 Responding to diversity   178
Tony Turner

4.5 Moral development and values   203
Tony Turner

4.6 An introduction to inclusion and special educational needs   218
Nick Peacey

CHAPTER 5 HELPING PUPILS LEARN   234

5.1 Ways pupils learn   235
Diana Burton

5.2 Active learning   250
Tony Turner

5.3 Teaching styles   268
Marilyn Leask

**5.4 Improving your teaching: an introduction to action research and
reflective practice**   278
Marilyn Leask

CHAPTER 6 ASSESSMENT   286

6.1 Assessment and accountability   287
Terry Haydn

6.2 External assessment and examinations   313
Bernadette Youens

CHAPTER 7 THE SCHOOL, CURRICULUM AND SOCIETY   326

7.1   Aims of education   327
Graham Haydon

7.2   The school curriculum   338
Graham Haydon

7.3   The National Curriculum   347
Gill Watson

CHAPTER 8 YOUR PROFESSIONAL DEVELOPMENT   362

8.1   Getting your first post   363
Susan Capel and Alexis Taylor

8.2   Developing further as a teacher   381
Susan Capel and Alexis Taylor

8.3   Accountability, contractual and statutory duties   395
Marilyn Leask

CHAPTER 9 AND FINALLY   402

APPENDICES

Appendix 1 Glossary of terms   404

Appendix 2 Guidance for writing, *Susan Capel and John Moss*   418

Appendix 3 Discipline in schools (The Elton Report)   427

Appendix 4 Useful addresses   431

Bibliography   435
Name index   448
Subject index   453

FIGURES

1.1.1	The work in the classroom – the tip of the iceberg	11
1.1.2	Subject knowledge is just part of the effective teacher's professional tool kit	13
1.2.1	Phases of development of a teacher	23
1.2.2	Becoming an effective teacher	23
1.3.1	How to avoid working around the clock	32
1.4.1	Example of 'WebQuest'	44
2.1.1	Classroom observation guide	56
2.1.2	Teacher–pupil interaction	57
2.1.3	Monitoring teachers' questions	62
2.2.1	Scheme of work pro forma	68
2.2.2	Planning a lesson: one possible approach	70
2.2.3	The structure of a lesson	72
4.1.1	Scheme for developing differentiated activities	136
4.1.2	Forms of differentiation: a contrast	144
4.2.1	Mean height of children, 5–16 years	149
4.2.2	Mean height of children, 10–16 years	149
4.2.3	Mean weight of children, 5–16 years	150
4.2.4	Mean weight of children, 9–16 years	150
4.3.1	The pendulum: variables	166
4.3.2	Fifty percent of what?	168
4.3.3	A bicycle for a postman	174
4.4.1	Population changes in England and Wales, 1901–1999	181
4.4.2	Sylvia's story	182
4.4.3	Differences in GCSE achievement, by class, gender and ethnicity (five or more GCSE passes at grade A–C)	186
4.4.4	Differences in achievement by ethnicity (five or more GCSE passes at grade A–C)	187
4.4.5	GCSE/SCE Standard Grade Examination entries and results 1996/97	190
4.4.6	GCE A level and SCE Higher Grade Examination, entries and results 1996/97	190
4.4.7	Examination achievements 1996/97: Great Britain	191
4.4.8	Modern apprenticeships 1999 in England and Wales	192
4.4.9	Employment by occupation and gender, 1998, Great Britain	192
4.4.10	The gendered occupations of men and women, 1998, Great Britain	193
4.4.11	Equal opportunity policy of Nonesuch School	196
4.5.1	A set of values	206
5.1.1	Kolb's experiential learning cycle (1985)	246

5.2.1	An active learning model	256
5.2.2	A pupil's meaning of fruit	257
5.2.3	Concept map: weather	257
5.2.4	Preparing for reporting back	262
6.1.1	The planning/teaching/assessment/planning loop	288
6.1.2	Effect of context on assessment	292
6.1.3	A pupil's school report, circa 1960	295
6.1.4	A pupil's physical training report, 1962–1968	296
6.1.5	A school report, 1999	297
6.1.6	Assessment: from the receiving end	299
6.1.7	Why am I marking this work?	300
6.1.8	How might ICT help to reduce the burden of assessment, reporting and recording?	309
6.2.1	Processes involved in setting and marking an external examination	323
8.2.1	The planning cycle for school development planning	391
8.3.1	Structure of the education system	396

TABLES

1.1.1	Some of the activities which teachers undertake in their academic and pastoral roles	14
1.2.1	The school's expectations of the student teacher	21
1.2.2	Attributes of effective teachers	24
1.4.1	Elements of ICT in various subject areas	40
1.4.2	Evidence from research about the way IT supports teaching and learning	41
1.4.3	Checklist for planning ICT projects with other schools	45
3.2.1	Theories of motivation and their implications for you as a teacher	106
4.2.1	A guide to reporting ethnicity	154
4.3.1	Data on different pendulums obtained by pupils (for Task 4.3.3)	167
4.3.2	Pupils' performance on questions involving ratio	169
4.6.1	Important legislation relating to the provision of SEN	221
5.3.1	Defining a teaching style	268
5.3.2	Examples of learning outcomes from a lesson	270
5.3.3	Identifying teaching styles	272
5.3.4	Mosston's continuum of teaching styles	274
5.3.5	An observation grid	275
5.4.1	An action research framework	279
5.4.2	OFSTED: criteria for judging the quality of teaching	280
5.4.3	Principles of effective learning	281
5.4.4	An ethical approach to action research	283
6.1.1	Aspects of achievement	294
6.2.1	Framework of national qualifications	320
7.3.1	The four Key Stages of the National Curriculum	348
7.3.2	Expectations of pupil performance in the National Curriculum	348
7.3.3	Summary of changes introduced into the National Curriculum beginning 2000	356
7.3.4	The structure of the subject Orders in the National Curriculum	358
8.3.1	Statutory duties of teachers	399

TASKS

1.1.1	Focusing on competences/standards	9
1.1.2	Subject knowledge competences/standards	12
1.1.3	Health and safety procedures	15
1.1.4	Health and safety – what should you know?	15
1.2.1	Professional accountability	22
1.2.2	What kind of teacher do you want to be?	24
1.2.3	'The average child'	26
1.2.4	What have the pupils learned?	26
1.3.1	How you spend your time in lessons	30
1.3.2	Planning how to use lesson time	31
1.3.3	Balancing your work and leisure time	33
1.3.4	Causes of stress for student teachers	34
1.3.5	Systematic observation of aspects of your teaching	34
1.4.1	Auditing your skills and knowledge	39
1.4.2	Identifying ICT resources for your subject area	39
1.4.3	How does ICT help teaching and learning?	42
1.4.4	Exploring the potential of the internet to support the work in the classroom	45
1.4.5	Using ICT for administration and monitoring	46
2.1.1	Observing the start of a lesson	53
2.1.2	Teacher–pupil talk	57
2.1.3	Teacher movement	59
2.1.4	What do classrooms look like?	60
2.1.5	Teachers' questions	61
2.1.6	Pupil–teacher contact time	63
2.2.1	How do you learn?	66
2.2.2	Record keeping and assessment	69
2.2.3	Drawing up a scheme of work	69
2.2.4	Writing objectives	71
2.2.5	Planning and giving lessons	73
2.3.1	Classroom norms	78
2.3.2	Sanctions and rewards	79
2.3.3	Checking your lesson plan	81
2.3.4	Swearing	83
2.3.5	Procedures for dealing with poorly equipped pupils	83
2.3.6	Defusing difficult situations	85

3.1.1	The quality of your voice	91
3.1.2	The language of your subject	92
3.1.3	Explaining	93
3.1.4	Questioning	96
3.1.5	Improving your verbal and non-verbal communication	97
3.1.6	Conveying enthusiasm 1	98
3.1.7	Conveying enthusiasm 2	99
3.1.8	Confidence	100
3.1.9	Using eye contact	101
3.2.1	Theory x and theory y	105
3.2.2	Achievement motivation	105
3.2.3	Attribution theory of motivation	105
3.2.4	Expectation theory and your teaching	108
3.2.5	Hierarchy of needs theory	109
3.2.6	Using rewards	109
3.2.7	Whole-part-whole teaching	110
3.2.8	The language of praise	110
3.2.9	Teaching styles	114
3.3.1	Misbehaviour 1	117
3.3.2	Misbehaviour 2	117
3.3.3	School rules	119
3.3.4	Coping with misbehaviour	121
3.3.5	Analysing misbehaviour	123
3.3.6	The whole school behaviour policy	124
3.3.7	The pastoral role	125
3.3.8	Bullying	125
3.3.9	Your personal values	125
3.3.10	Implications of the Elton Report	126
4.1.1	How are pupils grouped in your school?	134
4.1.2	Lesson planning for differentiation 1	137
4.1.3	Using the case studies of pupils	139
4.1.4	Using case studies to guide lesson planning	139
4.1.5	Writing your own case study	139
4.1.6	Recall	140
4.1.7	Lesson planning for differentiation 2	141
4.2.1	Pupil growth and development	151
4.2.2	What will your pupils be like?	152
4.2.3	The pupils in your class	153
4.2.4	School meals	157
4.3.1	Design and Technology (D and T)	164
4.3.2	Sorting variables 1	165
4.3.3	Sorting variables 2	165
4.3.4	Sorting variables 3	168
4.3.5	Responding to test data	169
4.3.6	Your pupils' understanding of percentages	170
4.3.7	Are pupils all-rounders?	172
4.3.8	Design a bicycle for postmen	174

4.4.1	Raising standards	188
4.4.2	Examination performance and job opportunities by gender	189
4.4.3	Men and women in higher education	191
4.4.4	Policies towards equal opportunities (EO)	195
4.4.5	Responses to gender: classroom observation	196
4.4.6	Responses to ethnicity: classroom observation	197
4.4.7	Bias and stereotyping in teaching resources	197
4.4.8	The role of the form tutor: some dilemmas	198
4.4.9	The role of the form tutor: Personal and Social Education	199
4.4.10	Setting and streaming by gender	200
4.4.11	Setting and streaming by ethnic group	200
4.4.12	Who is recruited to post-16 courses?	200
4.5.1	Aims of the school and how they are interpreted	208
4.5.2	The place of subject work in promoting moral development and values education	209
4.5.3	Class control	210
4.5.4	Your response to cheating in class?	211
4.5.5	Critical incidents	212
4.5.6	Responding to ethnic diversity	213
4.6.1	Your school's policy and the Code of Practice on the identification and assessment of Special Educational Needs	221
4.6.2	Working with support teachers or teaching assistants in your classroom	223
4.6.3	Pupil assessment on entry to the school	224
4.6.4	How does a statement come about in your school?	225
5.1.1	Analysing learning activities	237
5.1.2	Scaffolding pupils' learning	242
5.1.3	Structuring topics for effective learning	244
5.1.4	Your own learning style	245
5.1.5	Determining types of learners	247
5.1.6	Your own approaches to learning	247
5.2.1	What makes for a good performance?	253
5.2.2	Rote learning	255
5.2.3	Using a learning model	256
5.2.4	Developing guidelines for the use of a video	264
5.2.5	What makes a good worksheet?	264
5.2.6	The advantages of active learning methods	266
5.3.1	Pupil participation and teaching styles	273
5.3.2	Mosston's continuum of teaching styles	273
5.3.3	Analysing aspects of your teaching style	275
5.4.1	Focusing on effectiveness	279
5.4.2	A mini-action research project	282
5.4.3	School-based action research	283
6.1.1	Your own experience of assessment	289
6.1.2	The effect of context on performance	292
6.1.3	School reports pre-National Curriculum	297
6.1.4	Formative and summative assessment	305
6.1.5	Assessment tensions	306
6.1.6	Encouraging weaker pupils	307

6.2.1	Your personal experience of external examinations and assessment	314
6.2.2	GCSE coursework	317
6.2.3	Using examination papers in your teaching	324
6.2.4	Study skills	324
7.1.1	School aims: a comparison	329
7.1.2	The governing body: aims for a new school	330
7.1.3	Why teach Information and Communication Technology (ICT)?	333
7.1.4	Aims and education – the NC for England and Wales	336
7.2.1	School curricula: a comparison	339
7.2.2	Linking curriculum content to aims	343
7.2.3	Justifying your subject in the school curriculum	345
7.3.1	Evaluating the National Curriculum	355
7.3.2	Implementing the cross-curricular dimensions of the National Curriculum	359
8.1.1	Where do you want to teach?	364
8.1.2	What type of school do you want to teach in?	364
8.1.3	Your curriculum vitae	371
8.1.4	Mock interviews	378
8.2.1	Diary of effective practice and professional portfolio	382
8.2.2	Preparing for induction	386
8.3.1	Moral accountability and professional accountability	397
8.3.2	Statutory duties	398

APPENDICES AT END OF UNITS

4.3.1	Answers to Task 4.3.2 Sorting variables 1	177
4.3.2	Commentary on Task 4.3.3 Sorting variables 2	177
4.5.1	Handling discussion with classes	215
4.5.2	Simulations	217
5.2.1	Active learning methods	267

NOTES ON CONTRIBUTORS

Diana Burton is Institute of Education co-ordinator at the Crewe Campus of Manchester Metropolitan University's Institute of Education. She has taught education studies to students and serving teachers and has been involved in the re-design of school-based teacher education courses, leading developments in mentor training and researching the subsequent changes in the role of university tutors. She taught humanities and social science in an urban comprehensive school for twelve years, developing a particular interest in pastoral care and educational psychology. She has a PhD from Birmingham University, the subject of which was the potential of cognitive style for developing differentiated approaches to learning. Current research interests include the application of learning-style measurements to aspects of pupil behaviour and learning.

Susan Capel is Professor and Head of the Department of Sport Sciences at Brunel University. She was previously Reader in Education and Director of the Academic Standards Unit at Canterbury Christ Church University College. Prior to that she was programme director for a PGCE course. Before entering higher education she taught physical education and geography in the UK and Hong Kong. She has a PhD in Physical Education and has published widely in a range of areas. She is the editor of *Learning to Teach Physical Education in the Secondary School: A Companion to School Experience*, and co-editor of *Starting to Teach in the Secondary School: A Companion for the Newly Qualified Teacher*, both of which are companions to this book. She is also co-editor of *Issues in Physical Education*.

Jon Davison is Professor and Head of the School of Education at University College Northampton. After teaching English and media studies for seventeen years in inner London, he became an advisory teacher at the English and Media Centre, London, and went on to become Head of the Department of Secondary Education at Canterbury Christ Church University College. He has published widely on teaching and teacher education. His recent publications include *Subject Mentoring in the Secondary School* (Routledge, 1997), *Learning to Teach English in the Secondary School* (Routledge, 1998), *Issues in English Teaching* (Routledge, 2000) and *Social Literacy, Citizenship Education and the National Curriculum* (RoutledgeFalmer, 2000).

Terry Haydn is a Senior Lecturer in Education at the School of Education and Professional Development at the University of East Anglia, where he is Director for the secondary PGCE course. He was formerly Head of Humanities at an inner-city school in Manchester. He later became lecturer in education at the Institute of Education, University of London where his roles included PGCE Curriculum Tutor in history. His research interests include the use of new technology in education, citizenship and values education and the working atmosphere in the classroom.

Graham Haydon is a lecturer in the philosophy of education at the Institute of Education, University of London. He has experience of initial teacher education at the Institute over many years and through several changes of format of teacher education: at the receiving end as a student there himself; as a course tutor in professional studies and in optional courses; and for several years as co-ordinator of the Issues in Education component of the Institute PGCE. He now runs a professional development course at Masters level in Values in Education, including PSHE and citizenship issues, and much of his recent publication has been in these areas.

Marilyn Leask is a Principal Research Officer at the National Foundation for Educational Research. For ten years prior to this she was involved in all aspects of initial teacher education as a Principal Lecturer at De Montfort University. Her recent work focuses on the use of information and communication technologies for teacher professional development. As part of a professional commitment to disseminate findings from research directly to teachers, she has published a number of texts in initial teacher education, management and quality issues. Recent texts include *Issues in Teaching with ICT, Learning to Teach with ICT in the Secondary School*, with Norbert Pachler, and, with John Meadows, *Teaching and Learning with ICT in the Primary School*. These report the work of innovative teachers, as well as the outcomes relevant to the teachers' work in the classroom of various research projects. She has directed and been adviser to a number of national and international projects in this area for agencies such as the Department for Education and Skills (DfES), British Council, European School Net, and Department for International Development (DfID).

John Moss is Head of Secondary Education and Director of the secondary PGCE programme at Canterbury Christ Church University College. His publications include co-authorship of *Subject Mentoring in the Secondary School* (Routledge, 1997) and joint editorship of *Issues in English Teaching* (Routledge, 2000). He is currently editing a series of books on citizenship education.

Nick Peacey is currently co-ordinator of the Special Educational Needs Joint Initiative for Training (SENJIT), Institute of Education, University of London. He recently returned to this post from a one-year secondment as Principal Manager, Equal Opportunities and Access at the Qualifications and Curriculum Authority. SENJIT is a staff and project development consortium which carries out work on all aspects of special educational needs, involving all difficulties and disabilities, in partnership with thirty-one Local Education Authorities, individual schools and services and the Institute of Education. Nick Peacey taught for many years in comprehensive schools throughout the age range and later moved on to set up and manage LEA secondary special provision supporting the needs of youngsters whose behaviour caused concern. He is a member of the National Advisory Group on Personal, Social and Health Education and other DfEE steering groups. He is a governor of a primary school and chair of governors of a school for pupils with emotional and behavioural difficulties.

Roger Strangwick is a Principal Lecturer at De Montfort University Bedford. After studying mathematics and physics at university, he lived for a while in Spain. He learnt Russian during National Service then spent some time in advertising before qualifying as a teacher. He worked in schools in Liverpool, Lincolnshire, Swindon and Hitchin. While teaching, he took an external degree in English. He is co-author of two textbooks and has also written plays and poems. He has an MA in Education and an MA in Linguistics.

Alexis Taylor is a Lecturer in Education at Brunel University, where she is Director of the Division for Initial Teacher Education. Prior to this, she held positions of Head of the Religious

Education Department and Head of Year in a secondary school in south-west London. Current research interests include recruitment into initial teacher education; student teacher perceptions of special education; and, at doctoral level, learning and teaching in initial teacher education.

Tony Turner until retirement in September 2000 was Senior Lecturer in Education at the Institute of Education, University of London, based in Science and Technology. He has been involved in PGCE since 1976 both at subject level and in the reorganisation of the Institute's secondary initial teacher education courses. More recently he has been involved in induction courses for NQTs and pre-service courses for intending teachers. He is co-author of *Learning to Teach Science in the Secondary School* (Routledge, 1998). His research has focused recently on issues of equity for graduates seeking entry to initial teacher education and he has written on issues in the secondary science curriculum.

Gill Watson is currently a Principal Lecturer in Secondary Education at Canterbury Christ Church University College. She worked for thirteen years as a secondary teacher and became involved in a number of national curriculum development initiatives before moving into higher education. She spent three years as a Principal Subject Officer at QCA before deciding to return to work in initial teacher education in 1999.

Margaret Whitehead recently retired from full-time work at De Montfort University Bedford, where she was Head of Quality for the Faculty of Health and Community Studies. She now works part-time at the University, contributing to Physical Education Initial Teacher Education courses. Margaret taught physical education in school, lectured at Homerton College and in 1980 moved to Bedford College of Higher Education. She has devised, led and taught on a range of initial teacher education courses. In addition, Margaret studied philosophy of education and completed a PhD on the implications of existentialism and phenomenology to the practice of physical education. Margaret is currently President of the Physical Education Association of the United Kingdom. She served on the implementation group for the Government Sports Strategy – 'A Sporting Future for All', and is also a member of the Professional Development Board (PE) England.

Bernadette Youens is a Lecturer in Science Education at the School of Education, University of Nottingham where she teaches on the PGCE (secondary) course. She taught science in comprehensive schools in Nottinghamshire for six years before moving into initial teacher education in 1998. Her current research interests include mentoring in initial teacher education and pupil perspectives on science and science teaching.

FOREWORD

Education is under the spotlight. In many countries throughout the world, governments, parents and members of the teaching profession are pondering the methods used in schools in the light of advancing technology and the impact of globalisation. Because work is increasingly taking place in more complex organisations – and many peoples' social and emotional lives are becoming more complicated – intelligent decision-making has become crucially important. Since parents, employers and governments are all looking to teachers to prepare pupils for this world, teachers, therefore, need to become even more effective than before.

In my experience, effective secondary teachers are able to engender a love of their chosen subject amongst their pupils and, through this love, convince them of the desire to learn more about it. She or he seems to do this through a combination of their own enthusiasm, knowledge of subject matter and pedagogical skills alongside their respect for, and liking of, their pupils.

To be effective, therefore, teachers have themselves to be good learners. They have to learn how to present information clearly, to diagnose misunderstandings perceptively and to reinforce success enthusiastically. Furthermore, effective teachers have also to relate well to a wide range of pupils, many of whom may well be radically different to themselves in their backgrounds, talents and value systems.

People aspiring to become effective secondary teachers require to build up a repertoire of successful practice from their observations, their reading and from the accumulation of their knowledge and understandings. In order to develop the skill of reflection which will enable them to keep improving, they also need challenge and ongoing evaluation.

The third edition of *Learning to Teach in the Secondary School* provides excellent self-teaching material. It has been revised in the light of comments about the two earlier versions and takes account of changes introduced to the National Curriculum, Initial Teacher Education Programmes and the New Code of Practice for Special Educational Needs. The approach of the book stems from careful analysis of the classroom behaviour of both teachers and pupils. As a result the authors introduce their readers to a range of ways to teach and to learn. Most importantly, the book is immensely practical and provides ways to retrieve lessons which have gone wrong.

The tone of the book is informative rather than prescriptive, on the principle that no single method can ever be appropriate in all situations. It is the individual teacher who is best placed to diagnose the needs of pupils and to select an appropriate response. One of the major strengths of the book is the way the implications of many common responses are so clearly set out. This allows a teacher to establish insights into their own classroom behaviour and to appreciate its potential consequences.

I recommend *Learning to Teach in the Secondary School*, compiled by practitioners and teacher trainers, as a daily manual for new teachers: use it and learn from it. I also advocate its use, as a source of new ideas and refreshment, by more experienced teachers. I am confident that its impact – even among those who are already well suited to teaching – will be beneficial.

Professor Peter Mortimore
London
June 2001

INTRODUCTION

Teaching is both an art and a science. In this book we show that there are certain essential elements of teaching that you can master through practice which help you become an effective teacher. However, there is no one correct way of teaching, no one specific set of skills, techniques and procedures that you must master and apply mechanically. Every teacher is an individual and brings something of their own unique personality to the job. We hope that this book helps you to develop skills, techniques and procedures appropriate for your individual personality and style, and provides you with an entry to ways of understanding what you do and see. An effective, reflective teacher is one who can integrate theory with practice. We also hope that it provides the stimulus for you to want to continue to learn and develop throughout your career as a teacher.

DEVELOPING YOUR PHILOSOPHY OF TEACHING

There have been many changes in initial teacher training over recent years, and the most significant of these has been the shift from higher education-based to more school-based training. We would argue that an initial teacher training course provides not merely **training** but also the further **education** of intending teachers. What we mean by this is that teacher training is not an apprenticeship but a journey of personal development in which your skills of classroom management develop alongside an emerging understanding of the teaching and learning process. This is a journey of discovery which begins on the first day of your course and may stop only when you retire. Thus, we should refer to initial teacher **education** rather than initial teacher training. We use the term initial teacher education throughout this book.

The advantage of a school-based course is the opportunity it gives for student teachers to appreciate at first hand the complex, exciting and contradictory events of classroom interactions without the constant immediacy of having to teach all the time. It should allow student teachers time to make sense of experiences, both in the classroom and the wider school, that demand explanations. Providing such explanations requires you to have a theory of teaching and learning.

By means of an organised course, which provides for practical experience, structured observation and reflective activity suitably interwoven with theoretical inputs, student teachers can begin to develop their own theory of teaching and learning. Theoretical inputs can come from tutors and teachers, from lectures and from libraries, and we hope from using this book. Theory also arises from practice, the better to inform and develop practice.

Everyone who teaches has a theory of how to teach effectively and of how pupils learn. The theory may be implicit in what the teacher does and the teacher may not be able to tell you what their theory is. For example, a teacher who is a disciplinarian is likely to have a different theory about the conditions for learning than a teacher who is liberal in their teaching style. Likewise, some teachers may feel that they do not have a philosophy of education. What these teachers are really saying is that they have not examined their views, or cannot articulate them. What is your philosophy? For example, do you consider that your job is to transfer the knowledge of your subject to pupils? Or are you there to lead them through its main features? Are you 'filling empty vessels' or are you the guide on a 'voyage of discovery'? On the other hand, perhaps you are the potter, shaping and moulding pupils.

It is recognised that an initial teacher education course allows only a start to be made on developing your own personal understanding of the teaching and learning process. There are a number of different theories about teaching and learning. You need to be aware of what these are, reflect on them and consider how they help you to explain more fully what you are trying to do and why. Through the process of theorising about what you are doing, reflecting on a range of other theories as well as your own, you understand your practice better and develop into a reflective practitioner, i.e. a teacher who makes conscious decisions about the teaching strategies to employ, and who modifies their practice in the light of experiences.

An articulated, conscious philosophy of teaching emerges only if a particular set of habits is developed. In particular, the habit of reviewing your own teaching from time to time. It is these habits that need to be developed from the start of your initial teacher education course. This is what many authors mean when they refer to 'the reflective practitioner'. This is why we (as well as your course tutors) ask you to evaluate your own teaching, to keep a diary, and to develop a professional portfolio to record your development and carry that forward from your initial teacher education course to your first post. Part of this reflection is included in your career entry profile if you are learning to teach in England.

HOW TO USE THIS BOOK

Structure of the book

The book is laid out so that elements of appropriate background information and theory introduce each issue. This theory is interwoven with tasks designed to help you identify key features of the behaviour or issue. A number of different enquiry methods are used to generate data, e.g. reflecting on the reading and observation or on an activity you are asked to carry out, asking questions, gathering data, discussing with a tutor of another student teacher. Some of the tasks involve you in activities that impinge on other people, e.g. observing a teacher in the classroom, or asking for information. If a task requires you to do this, **you must first of all seek permission of the person concerned**. Remember that you are a guest in school(s); you cannot walk into any teacher's classroom to observe. In addition, some information may be personal, or sensitive and you need to consider issues of confidentiality and professional behaviour in your enquiries and reporting.

The main text is supported by a number of appendices that provide further guidance to you as a student teacher. The glossary of terms is included to help you interpret the jargon of education. An appendix on writing and reflection is included to help you with the written assignments on your initial teacher education course. There are also extracts from two documents, which are referred to in the main body of the book, and some useful addresses.

Developing your competence

The range and type of competences/standards you are expected to become aware of and develop during your initial teacher education course will have been derived from those for student teachers in the country in which you are learning to teach. The units in this book are designed to help you work towards developing these competences/standards. Your tutors in school and in your institution help you identify levels of competence appropriate to your status as a student teacher and as a newly qualified teacher. We ask you at appropriate points in the text to relate the work directly to the specific competences/standards to which you are working.

In addition to the competences/standards required of newly qualified teachers, there are competences/standards that are unlikely to be developed until into your first post, e.g., developing and sustaining working relationships with pupils at Key Stage 4, as they are unlikely to be achieved adequately without more experience than school experience can give. You will develop such competences/standards as you gain experience in your first post.

Your diary of reflective practice

As you read through the book and complete the tasks, we ask you to keep a reflective diary. This diary can be used to record the outcomes of tasks and your thoughts on the reading, analyses undertaken as part of that reading, or other activities that arise as part of your course. The diary can also be used to record your reactions to events, both good and bad, as a way of letting off steam! It provides a record of your development which can be very useful in developing your professional portfolio and writing the relevant sections of your career entry profile.

Your professional portfolio

Your professional portfolio provides a selective record of your development as a teacher and is something that you continue to develop throughout your teaching career. At the end of your initial teacher education course it contributes directly to your career entry profile. It is likely that your institution has a set format for a professional portfolio, in which case you will be told about it. If not, you should develop your own. You can use any format and include any evidence you think appropriate.

This portfolio should contain selective evidence of your development, your strengths as well as areas for further development. At a minimum this can be provided through evidence of completion or otherwise of the competences/standards required as part of your course. However, to be truly beneficial, it should contain much other evidence. This further evidence could be work of value to you, a response to significant events, extracts from your diary of reflective practice, good lesson plans, evaluations of lessons, teaching reports, observations on you made by teachers, outcomes of tasks undertaken, assessed and non-assessed coursework.

Try to develop your portfolio during your course, using evidence from learning experiences on the course. At the end of your course you can use your portfolio as the basis for completing your career entry profile. To help you with this you might write a personal statement describing aspects of your development as a teacher during your teacher education course. This would include reference to teaching reports written by teachers, tutors and yourself. The portfolio can be used to enable you to reflect on your learning and achievements; to help you complete applications for your first post; and to take to interview. It can help provide the basis of your continued professional development as it enables you to identify competences/standards in need of development and thus targets for induction and continuing professional development in your first post, first through your career entry profile then as part of the appraisal process you will be involved with as a teacher. It describes strengths and weaknesses, hopes for the future, and identifies elements of your emerging personal philosophy of teaching and learning. Thus, we strongly recommend that you start to keep a diary of reflective practice now to form the basis for this professional portfolio.

Ways you might like to use this book

With much (or all) of your course being delivered in school, you may have limited access to a library, to other student teachers with whom to discuss problems and issues at the end of the school day, and, in some instances, limited access to a tutor to whom you can refer. There are likely to be times when you are faced with a problem in school which has not been addressed up to that point within the course you are following and you need some help immediately – for example, before facing a class the next day or next week. This book is designed to help you address some of the issues or difficulties you are faced with during your period of initial teacher education, by providing supporting knowledge interspersed with a range of tasks to enable you to link theory with practice.

The book is designed to be used in a number of ways. It is designed more for you to dip in and out of, to look up a specific problem or issue that you want to consider, rather than for you to read from cover to cover (although you may want to use it in both ways, of course). You can use it on your own as it provides background information and supporting theory about a range of issues you are likely to face during your initial teacher education course. Reflecting on an issue faced in school with greater understanding of what others have written and said about it, alongside undertaking some of the associated tasks, may help you to identify some potential solutions. The book can also be used in association with your tutors (higher education and/or school staff responsible for overseeing your learning and development). The tasks are an integral part of the book and you can complete most individually. Most tasks do, however, benefit from wider discussion, which we encourage you to take part in whenever possible. However, some tasks can be carried out only with other student teachers and/or with the support of a tutor. You should select those tasks that are appropriate to your circumstances.

However, this book will not suffice alone; we have attempted to provide you with guidance to further reading by two methods: first, by references in the text, the details of which appear at the end of the book; second, by readings related to the units. These further readings, to direct and develop understanding, appear at the end of the units. There is an increasing amount of educational material available on the World Wide Web. We make reference to this throughout the book and we urge you to keep a record of useful websites. The governmental sites are a useful start (www.teachernet.gov.uk), as are those of subject associations. Addresses are also given to provide easy access to further information. In addition, you should use this book alongside your course handbook, which outlines specific course requirements, agreed ways of working, roles and responsibilities.

If you see each unit as potentially an open door leading to whole new worlds of thought about how societies can best educate their children, then you will have achieved one of our goals – to provide you with a guidebook on your journey of discovery about teaching and learning. Finally, we hope that you find the book useful, and of support in school. If you like it, tell others; if not, tell us.

We have tried to mix, and balance, the use of gender terms in order to avoid clumsy he/she terminology. We call school children 'pupils' to avoid confusion with students, by which we mean people in further and higher education. The important staff in your life are those in school and your higher education institution; we have called all these people tutors. Your institution will have its own way of referring to staff.

CHAPTER 1   **BECOMING A TEACHER**

Through the units in this chapter, the complexity and breadth of the teacher's role and the nature of teaching are explored. You are posed questions about your values and attitudes because these influence the type of teacher you become. Society is constantly changing and so the demands society places on teachers change. Consequently you can expect to carry on learning not only about teaching and learning (pedagogy) but, as your career progresses, you will find you need new skills and knowledge. Professional development is a lifelong process for the teacher which is aided by regular reflection on practice and continuing education, e.g., through continuing professional development.

Each unit in this chapter examines different facets of the work of student teachers and experienced teachers.

Unit 1.1 covers wider aspects of the teacher's role, including academic and pastoral roles, and we consider the necessity for continual curriculum review.

In Unit 1.2 we discuss the expectations which your higher education and school tutors have of you. The meaning of professionalism is discussed and the idea that you will have your own philosophy of teaching is introduced. Phases which mark your development as a teacher are identified. We suggest that, as your own confidence and competence in managing the classroom grow, you can expect the focus of your work to move from your self-image and the mechanics of managing a lesson, to the learning taking place generally and, as you become more experienced, to the learning for the individual pupil.

Unit 1.3 provides advice for managing time, both inside and outside the classroom, and for preventing stress. There are a variety of competing demands made on your time, and if you learn to use your time effectively, you will have more time to enjoy your work as a teacher, and more leisure time.

Unit 1.4 provides an introduction to ways in which information and communications technology can be used to support teaching and learning.

To become a teacher you need to supplement your subject knowledge with professional knowledge about teaching and learning, and to develop your professional judgement, e.g. about managing situations that arise with pupils. Ways of developing your professional knowledge and judgement provide themes running throughout the book. In the UK, you can find a wealth of material on government-supported websites to support you as a teacher. Starting places are:

- for England, http://www.teachernet.gov.uk
- for Scotland, http://www.scotland.gov.uk
- for Wales, http://www.cymru.gov.uk
- for Northern Ireland, http://www.deni.gov.uk

International curricula are available on http://www.inca.org.uk European and Commonwealth education networks can be found on http://www.eun.org and http://www.col.org/cense.

You may come to recognise your situation in the following poem, called 'Late'.

You're late, said miss
The bell has gone,
dinner numbers done
and work begun.

What have you got to say for yourself?

Well, it's like this, miss
Me mum was sick,
me dad fell down the stairs,
the wheel fell off my bike
and then we lost our Billy's snake
behind the kitchen chairs. Earache
struck down me grampy, me gran
took quite a funny turn.
Then on the way I met this man
whose dog attacked me shin —
look, miss you can see the blood
it doesn't look too good,
does it?

Yes, yes sit down —
and next time say you're sorry
for disturbing all the class.
Now get on with your story
fast!

Please miss, I've got nothing to write about.
Judith Nicholls in Batchford (1992) *Values: Assemblies for the 1990s*

UNIT 1.1 WHAT DO TEACHERS DO?

MARILYN LEASK

INTRODUCTION

The answer to this question depends on where and when the question is being asked. You will be teaching in the twenty-first century. We'd like to take you back in time, just for a moment, to English schools in the Middle Ages.

Curtis writes that in England in the twelfth century:

> theology was considered the queen of studies, to which philosophy served as an introduction. The studies which led to the supreme study of theology were known generally as the Seven Liberal Arts. The Arts (or sciences) were termed liberal from liber, free and constituted the course of study suitable for the freeman as contrasted with the Practical and Mechanical Arts which were learned and practised by slaves in the classical period. The arts were divided into the Trivium and Quadrivium. . . . The subjects of the Trivium consisted of Grammar, Rhetoric and Dialectic (logic); and of the Quadrivium, Arithmetic, Geometry, Astronomy and Music – the subjects of the Trivium were taught to younger pupils and the Quadrivium to older pupils. There were grammar schools (providing preparation for university work), song schools (for teaching singing in Latin at church services) and reading and writing schools (effectively providing a primary education). The three schools were often housed under the one roof and the language of instruction changed with political changes – from Latin to Norman-French to the vernacular.
>
> (1967, pp. 23–24)

Clearly what teachers teach reflects the times in which they live, so change is essential in education. Without change, we would have a fossilised, out-of-date curriculum – what Peddiwell (1939, cited in Goddard and Leask, 1992) called the 'sabre-toothed curriculum'. Peddiwell describes a prehistoric community which successfully taught its youngsters how to deal with sabre-toothed tigers. Unfortunately, the curriculum wasn't updated when the sabre-toothed tigers died out, with the result that the pupils' education didn't prepare them for the new challenges facing the community. This illustrates the necessity for regular review of the curriculum, and, for similar reasons, teachers' knowledge and skills should be regularly updated. So what teachers do depends on what is happening in the wider community. The way society develops an appropriate curriculum is discussed in more detail in Chapter 7.

OBJECTIVES

By the end of this unit you should:

- be aware of the range of skills and forms of knowledge which a teacher uses in planning and giving lessons;
- have considered the relationship between subject knowledge and effective teaching;

- have an understanding of various aspects of a teacher's role and responsibilities including academic and pastoral roles, administration and health and safety;
- be developing your own philosophy of teaching.

CLASSROOM PRACTICE – AN INTRODUCTION TO HOW TEACHERS TEACH

The teacher's job is first and foremost to ensure that pupils learn. To a large extent, what (i.e. the lesson content) pupils should learn in maintained (state) schools in England and Wales is determined through legislation, and the requirements are set out in various National Curriculum documents. Other countries may give schools and teachers much more autonomy. On the other hand, in many education systems, how you teach so that the pupils learn effectively (i.e. the methods and materials used) is left to the professional judgement of the individual teacher, department and school.

Task 1.1.1

FOCUSING ON COMPETENCES/STANDARDS

To understand what is expected of newly qualified teachers you need to be familiar with the competences/standards you are required to reach by the end of your course. These can be found in your course handbook and other documentation provided by your institution and we suggest you look at them now.

Teaching is a very personal activity and while certain teaching styles and strategies might suit one teacher, they might not be appropriate for another. However, although there exists a core of good practice to which most teachers would subscribe, there are differences between teachers which relate to personality, style and philosophy. Moreover, observers of the same teacher might well disagree about the strengths and weaknesses of that teacher. In your first days in school, it is likely that you will spend time observing a number of experienced teachers. It is highly unlikely that you will see two teachers who teach identically. Perhaps you will see teaching styles that you feel more at home with, while others do not seem as appropriate to your own developing practice. Of course, there is no one way to teach. Provided effective teaching and learning take place, a whole range of approaches, from didactic (formal, heavy on content) to experiential (learning by doing), is appropriate – often in the same lesson. Unit 5.3 provides more details about teaching styles.

Learning to manage the classroom is similar in many ways to learning to drive. At the outset there seems so much to remember. How do you manage to: depress the clutch, brake, change gear, be aware of oncoming traffic and cars following you, look in the mirror, indicate; obey the speed limit; observe traffic signs and signals, be aware of and sensitive to changing road and weather conditions, anticipate problems and steer simultaneously? After a short time, however, such skills become part of subconscious patterns of behaviour.

Much of what many experienced teachers do to manage their classes has become part of their unconscious classroom behaviour. Their organisation of the lesson so that pupils learn is implicit in what they do rather than explicit. So much so, that often teachers find it hard to articulate exactly what it is they are doing or why it is successful. This situation, of course, does not help the student teacher. It also gives weight to the spurious notion that teachers are born rather than made and that nobody can tell you how to teach.

Undoubtedly some teachers may well begin teaching with certain advantages such as a 'good' voice or organisational skills. Nevertheless there are common skills and techniques to be learned which, when combined with an awareness of, and sensitivity to, the teaching and learning contexts, enable student teachers to manage their classes effectively.

Teaching is a continuously creative and problem-solving activity. Each learner or each group of learners has their own characteristics which the experienced teacher takes into account in planning the relevant learning programme. For example, if there has been recent controversy over environmental issues in the local area or the school has taken refugees fleeing from civil war, an effective teacher will adapt their approach to the discussion of such matters to make lessons more relevant and to allow the pupils to draw on their experience. Although lessons with different groups may have similar content, a lesson is rarely delivered in the same way twice. Variations in interactions between the pupils and the teacher affect the teaching strategy chosen.

THE WORK IN THE CLASSROOM – THE TIP OF THE ICEBERG

On the surface, teaching may appear to be a relatively simple process – the view that the teacher stands in front of the class and talks and the pupils learn appears to be all too prevalent. (Ask friends and family what they think a teacher does.)

The reality is somewhat different.

Classroom teaching is only the most visible part of the job of the teacher. The contents of this book are designed to introduce you to what we see as the invisible foundation of the teacher's work: **professional knowledge** about teaching and learning and **professional judgement** about the routines, skills and strategies which support effective classroom management. Your **subject knowledge** comes from your degree and from your continuing professional development. An effective teacher draws on these three factors in planning each and every lesson; and the learning for a particular class is planned ahead – over weeks, months and years – so that there is continuity and progression in the pupils' learning. Each lesson is planned as part of a sequence of learning experiences.

The following analogy may help you understand what underpins the work in the classroom. Think of a lesson as being like an iceberg – 70 to 80 per cent, the base, is hidden (Figure 1.1.1). The work in the classroom represents the tip of the iceberg. Supporting this tip, but hidden, are many elements of the teacher's professional expertise. These include:

- evaluation of previous lessons;
- preparation for the lesson;
- planning of a sequence of lessons to ensure that learning progresses;
- established routines and procedures which ensure that the work of the class proceeds as planned;
- personality – including the teacher's ability to capture and hold the interest of the class, to establish their authority;
- subject knowledge;
- professional knowledge about effective teaching and learning;
- professional judgement built up over time through reflection on experience.

CLASSROOM PRACTICE

EVALUATION
ROUTINE
PREPARATION
PLANNING
PERSONALITY
PROFESSIONAL JUDGEMENT
SUBJECT KNOWLEDGE
PROFESSIONAL KNOWLEDGE

Figure 1.1.1   The work in the classroom – the tip of the iceberg

Acknowledgement: Simon Beer

During your course, you will often see experienced teachers and student teachers teaching. But what are you really seeing? You need to learn to 'read the classroom' – to train yourself to look beyond what is readily visible so that you come to understand the variety of skills and strategies which the teacher brings to bear in order to maximise the learning taking place. Some of these skills and strategies are easily identifiable; others require you to observe more carefully. Any classroom observation you undertake must have a purpose, be focused, generate information and provoke thought. We hope to sensitise you to what happens behind the scenes of the classroom so that you can build on that knowledge in your own classroom work.

Throughout your course, you should expect to develop confidence and new levels of competence in all the areas in Figure 1.1.1.

SUBJECT KNOWLEDGE AND EFFECTIVE TEACHING

A common misunderstanding about teaching is that if you know your subject then automatically you can teach it well. In the same way that delivering milk to the doorstep provides no guarantee that it will be taken into the house, so too is it with the subject content of a lesson. You cannot assume that pupils will automatically take in what you had hoped to teach them. The fact that you are an expert in a subject is no guarantee that you can help others learn that subject.

It is usually assumed that student teachers on a one-year postgraduate course have an appropriate level of subject knowledge, and their initial teacher education course usually concentrates on subject application to the classroom. These student teachers often find they have to relearn aspects of their subject which they may not have thought about for years, as well as material which is new to them. You can expect to have to widen your knowledge base so that you have a deeper understanding of the subject than is required by the syllabus. Wider knowledge enables you to develop differentiated tasks for pupils with differing abilities much more easily, and gives you confidence that you will be able to answer questions.

Teaching requires you to transform the knowledge you possess into suitable tasks which lead to learning. Acquiring appropriate up-to-date knowledge requires some effort on your part and this is just part of the work of the teacher. The English National Curriculum (http://nc.uk.net) provides a useful starting point for student teachers in England, and most subject associations produce relevant materials and run annual conferences which help you keep up with developments. Addresses of subject associations can be found in *The Education Year Book* (published annually).

However, to teach effectively, you need more than good subject knowledge.

Task 1.1.2

SUBJECT KNOWLEDGE COMPETENCES/STANDARDS

Identify the competences/standards in subject knowledge required by your course. You will see that some of these relate to the National Curriculum. Now look at the National Curriculum for your subject. Analyse it to identify the areas of knowledge that you can cope with now, those you could learn with some effort, and those areas that require totally new learning. Where there are areas that are unfamiliar to you, set yourself goals for improving this aspect of your knowledge.

You may find it helpful to discuss these goals with more experienced colleagues. Make sure to check your progress regularly, e.g. before school experience and after your final school experience. For those teaching in England, a profile of your developing knowledge of subject matter could be included in your Career Entry Profile, which you take to your first post. Your knowledge needs may be able to be further addressed in your first post as a newly qualified teacher through continuing professional development.

As already indicated, **personality and personal style** influence your effectiveness as a teacher but many skills and strategies can be learned and practised until they become part of your professional repertoire. We introduce you to theories underpinning educational practice and ideas which can provide a foundation for your development as an effective teacher, whatever your subject. But what do we mean by effective teaching?

Effective teaching occurs where the learning experience structured by the teacher matches the needs of the learner, i.e. tasks develop the individual pupil's knowledge, skills, attitudes and/or understanding in such a way that the pupil is applying past knowledge as appropriate and laying the foundation for the next stage of learning. A key feature of effective teaching is balancing the pupils' chance of success against the level of difficulty required to challenge them. Effective teaching depends on complex interrelationships of a whole range of factors, a major one of which is the teacher's understanding of the different ways in which pupils learn. Chapter 5 provides further information about pupil learning. Understanding about the ways in which learning takes place is essential to your work as a teacher of a subject, and this understanding provides the foundations on which to build your professional knowledge about teaching and learning. The more closely the teaching method matches the preferred learning style of the pupils, the more effective the teaching will be.

As a student teacher you have the opportunity to develop a repertoire of teaching styles and strategies and to test these out in the classroom. The information in various chapters should help you in this process. It may take you considerable time before you can apply the principles of effective teaching to your classroom practice but you can monitor your development through regular evaluation of lessons (see Unit 5.4). We aim to provide a basic introduction to what are complex areas and it is up to you to develop systematically your professional knowledge and judgement through analysing your experience (i.e. through reflection) and wider reading. Figure 1.1.2 illustrates what we see as the interconnections between effective teaching, subject knowledge, professional knowledge and professional judgement.

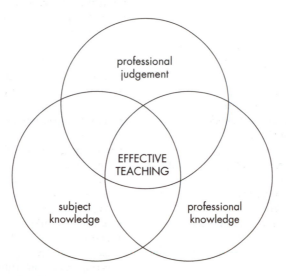

Figure 1.1.2 Subject knowledge is just part of the effective teacher's professional tool kit

THE WIDER ROLE

The success of a school depends on the qualities and commitment of the staff as well as the pupils. A teacher's work is very varied and probably no one teacher's job is exactly the same as another's.

Most staff have responsibilities beyond their subject specialism. They may become involved in: cross-curricular issues; personal, social and health education; school development planning; work experience; liaison with primary schools; careers advice; links with industry; planning educational trips and social events; curriculum planning and development; pupil performance monitoring; assessment; planning and implementing school policies; extra-curricular activities. In addition, teachers have a role to play in supporting the school ethos by reinforcing school rules and routines, e.g. on behaviour, dress and in encouraging pupils to develop self-discipline so that the school can function effectively and pupils can make the most of opportunities available to them.

Under the 1988 Education Reform Act, teachers in England and Wales have responsibility for implementing the National Curriculum and for the spiritual and moral welfare of their pupils (Unit 8.3 sets out statutory duties), so most teachers have both a specialist academic role and a pastoral role. Both roles encompass administrative as well as teaching responsibilities. Some of these features are described in Table 1.1.1.

Table 1.1.1 Some of the activities which teachers undertake in their academic and pastoral roles

The academic role	*The pastoral role and spiritual and moral welfare*
The academic role of the teacher encompasses a variety of activities including: • subject teaching • lesson preparation • setting and marking of homework • assessing pupil progress in a variety of ways including marking tests and exams • writing reports • recording achievement • working as part of a subject team • curriculum development and planning • undertaking visits, field courses • reporting to parents • keeping up to date (often through work with the subject association) • implementing school policies • extra-curricular activities • examining for GCSE and A level boards	Pastoral duties vary from school to school. They often include: • working as part of a pastoral team • teaching pastoral, social and health education • taking part in the daily act of worship required by legislation • getting to know the pupils as individuals • helping pupils with problems • being responsible for a form; registering the class, following up absences • monitoring sanctions and rewards given to form members • reinforcing school rules and routines, e.g. on behaviour • writing reports, ensuring records of achievement and/or profiles are up to date • house/year group activities (plays/sports) • liaising with parents • ensuring that school information is conveyed to parents via pupils • giving careers and subject guidance • extra-curricular activities

There are a number of administrative responsibilities which are part of a teacher's job: for example, record keeping (marks for homework, tests, classwork, attendance), marking, producing pupils' profiles and helping with records of achievement, writing references, attending meetings and planning. From the beginning of your school experiences, it is worth trying to develop efficient ways of dealing with this administration, otherwise you will waste a lot of time. Developing your word-processing and spreadsheet skills will be useful in helping you prepare teaching materials and record and monitor progress. Some teachers keep their mark books electronically using spreadsheets, and many schools have Management Information Systems, which are used to monitor pupil performance and assessment. Unit 1.3 on time management provides further advice. Later units provide more detailed information on a variety of aspects of the academic and pastoral roles.

HEALTH AND SAFETY

All teachers are responsible for the health and safety of the pupils in their charge. Legally, as a student teacher you cannot take on that responsibility. Whenever you are teaching, the ultimate responsibility lies with the class teacher.

Nevertheless in planning your lessons you must take into account the health and safety of your pupils by appropriate planning: e.g. identifying activities that do not endanger pupils, e.g. climbing on chairs; or for science and related subjects following the COSHH (Control Of Substances Hazardous to Health) regulations. Sharing your lesson plans in advance with your class teacher is an essential feature of your responsibility to both the pupils and your teachers. If you have any doubts about the safety of the lesson, ask for advice. If advice is not available, then don't use that strategy.

Whilst you are teaching, an experienced teacher must always be available in the classroom or nearby. If the lesson has special safety considerations, e.g. in physical education or science, then if the class teacher or a suitably qualified teacher is not available, you must not proceed as if they were. Have an alternative lesson up your sleeve which does not require specific subject specialist support but could be carried out with the support of another teacher. Sometimes you may have to cancel your planned lesson.

It follows from this situation that, legally, you cannot act as a supply teacher to fill in if the regular teacher is absent.

Task 1.1.3

HEALTH AND SAFETY PROCEDURES

Find out who is responsible for health and safety in your school-experience school. Find the school and departmental policies on health and safety.

Check the procedures you will be expected to apply. For example, in science, find out how you should check the safety of the chemicals or other equipment you may use, locate the eyewash bottle and gas, water and electricity isolating taps/switches; in physical education check that you know how to test the safety of any apparatus pupils might use. Find out the names of the First Aiders in the school, where the first aid box is, what you are permitted to do if an incident occurs and what forms have to be filled in to record any accident.

We suggest that you take a first aid course and find out how to deal with, for example, faints, nose bleeds, fits, asthma attacks, epilepsy, diabetic problems, burns, bleeding and common accidents. But you should not administer first aid yourself unless qualified and, even then, only the minimum necessary. You should report any incident and make a written record. There will usually be a record book in school for this purpose. Your subject association should be able to provide you with subject-specific safety information, and local branches of the British Red Cross or St John Ambulance have information about first aid courses. St John Ambulance produces a first aid text for schools.

Teachers also have a wide range of statutory duties which are further discussed in Unit 8.3.

Task 1.1.4

HEALTH AND SAFETY – WHAT SHOULD YOU KNOW?

What should you know and be able to do if you are to discharge your duties as a student teacher and as a teacher in your subject area? Discuss this with your tutor and other student teachers in your specialist area. To what extent do school and department rules help staff and pupils understand their duties in the area of safety?

SUMMARY AND KEY POINTS

In the UK, while the curriculum is to a large extent determined centrally, the choice of teaching strategies and materials is largely in the hands of the individual teacher. Your own philosophy of teaching affects the way you approach your work – this philosophy will develop over time as you acquire further professional knowledge and your professional judgement develops.

Clearly there are certain skills which an effective teacher possesses, and you can identify many of these by skimming through the contents of each chapter. As a student teacher, you have to move from knowing about these skills to being able to exercise them flexibly so that the planned learning can take place. The lists of competences/standards for newly qualified teachers are best regarded as highlighting areas for development in which you will improve your capability. There are no ready-made patterns for success in teaching. Key elements in becoming a successful teacher, i.e. ensuring your pupils learn, include:

- adequate, secure subject and pedagogic knowledge;
- attention to planning;
- awareness of pupil needs;
- concern for the welfare of pupils;
- careful monitoring of pupil achievement.

A range of different solutions can be employed in most situations and different strategies succeed with different pupils.

FURTHER READING

Bramall, S. and White, J. (2000b) *Will the New National Curriculum Live up to its Aims?* Philosophy of Education Society of Great Britain, London: Institute of Education.
   This provides a useful analysis of the National Curriculum in England.

Desforges, C. (ed.) (1999) *An Introduction to Teaching – Psychological Perspectives*, Oxford: Blackwell.
   This text complements the book you are reading now, exploring in more depth many of the issues which we have touched on. Chapters cover personal, social and moral education, ethnic and gender differences, different ways of teaching, including management of group work and teaching through discussion.

Fisher, R. (1995) *Teaching Children to Think*, Cheltenham: Stanley Thornes.
   An important role of the teacher is to give the pupils intellectual tools for learning. These include the ability to problem-solve, to think creatively, to understand the difference between stating a fact, creating hypotheses and testing out hypotheses in valid ways. We also recommend the work by Phillip Adey on cognitive acceleration for the same reasons.

Hay McBer Report (2000) 'Research into Teacher Effectiveness' London: DfEE. See the DfEE website www.dfee.go.uk/teachingreports
   This comprehensive report into effective teaching proposes a model of teacher effectiveness comprising teaching skills and professional characteristics. The early sections are particularly useful in relation to the preparation and planning of lessons.

Kyriacou, C. (1997) *Effective Teaching in Schools: Theory and Practice* (2nd edn), Cheltenham: Stanley Thornes.
This book is aimed at student teachers and more experienced teachers who wish to examine and develop their practice. The text covers the key areas that student teachers should understand.

MacGrath, M. (1998) *The Art of Teaching Peacefully: Improving Behaviour and Reducing Conflict in the Classroom*, London: David Fulton.
In the author's words 'this book provides a new approach since its emphasis is not so much on behaviour management as on the cultivation of co-operative behaviour through school, classroom behaviour management techniques, strategies to make work accessible to all, effective communication and the development and maintenance of positive relationships with pupils'. The author provides tested strategies for teachers to use in enabling pupils who might be difficult and not apparently interested in learning to achieve more than they expect of themselves. It recognises the teacher's role in encouraging and supporting teenagers in their school work, whilst at the same time recognising the emotional turmoil that many young people find themselves in.

McNamara, E. (1999) *Positive Pupil Management and Motivation: A Secondary Teacher's Guide*, London: David Fulton.
This text is packed with advice and guidelines for the positive management of adolescent behaviour.

Marland, M. (1997) *The Art of the Tutor: Developing your Role in the Secondary School*, London: David Fulton.
This text provides practical advice for the beginning teacher. Michael Marland has written many texts for teachers which are now out of print. You may find these in a library.

Matheson, D. and Grosvenor, I. (eds) (1999) *An Introduction to the Study of Education*, London: David Fulton.
This text provides an overview of aims and purposes of education from a range of perspectives. It provides a useful foundation for understanding education today.

St John Ambulance (1999) *Emergency Aid in Schools* (7th edn), St John Supplies, Priory House, St John's Lane, London WC1M 4DA (Tel: 020 7235523).
This is a useful text for all teachers, providing basic information about incidents and accidents which many teachers come across. St John Ambulance also produce training CD-ROMs and a range of other texts.

Shaffer, R. H. (1997) *Making Decisions About Children* (2nd edn), Oxford: Blackwell.
Teachers, by the fact that they are teachers, have been successful in various learning environments. From a privileged position it is easy to lack understanding of the difficult lives that many pupils lead. This books provides a useful framework for teachers to understand the different emotional issues which pupils may be facing. It discusses the impact of divorce and marital conflict, the relationship with step-parents, the relationship between poverty and psychological development and issues of vulnerability in general. Teachers can have a critical impact on pupils' self-esteem at vulnerable points in their lives.

Stephens, P. and Crawley, T. (1994) *Becoming an Effective Teacher*, Cheltenham: Stanley Thornes.
This is another text providing guidance for the beginner.

TEACHERLINE – a 24-hour confidential counselling, support and advice service (0800 562561).
This service is supported by the Teachers Benevolent Fund, London, WC1H 9BE.

UNIT 1.2 **THE STUDENT TEACHER'S ROLE AND RESPONSIBILITIES**

MARILYN LEASK

INTRODUCTION

The school-based experiences of the student teacher depend on a three-way partnership between the school, the student teacher and a higher education institution, except in those cases where the school is undertaking teacher education on its own. These experiences include the periods of whole class teaching as well as those occasions when direct class teaching is not the main purpose of the exercise.

In most partnerships between the school and the student teacher, roles and responsibilities have previously been agreed and worked out. It is important that the student teacher is aware of what those are. The same principle applies when two institutions are in partnership with the student teacher. Agreed roles and responsibilities can usually be found in the handbook for the course.

In this unit we discuss your tutors' expectations of you and your professional responsibilities. We then go on to discuss the phases of development through which a student teacher is likely to pass.

OBJECTIVES

By the end of this unit you should:

- have clarified your own role and that of your tutors in the partnership;
- have an understanding of your working role within the school;
- be aware of your responsibilities and your tutors' expectations of you;
- have developed an understanding of the professional responsibilities and behaviour required of a newly qualified teacher;
- recognise the phases of development you are likely to be going through in the transition from student teacher to effective teacher, including taking on a pastoral role.

THE SCHOOL TUTOR

Schools identify members of staff to support and advise student teachers, often from the student teacher's subject department. Increasingly schools are appointing a general school tutor to oversee the work of student teachers in the school. You can expect to meet regularly with school staff to discuss your progress, any lessons observed and wider school issues.

ARRANGEMENTS FOR SCHOOL EXPERIENCE

What is expected of you in school?

Your school-based work is usually built up through a series of structured activities:

- detailed observation of experienced teachers, where you look at specific aspects of teaching in a lesson, e.g. how teachers use questions to promote learning;
- team teaching, where you share the lesson with others – planning, giving the lesson and evaluating together;
- micro-teaching: this is a short teaching episode where you teach peers or small groups of pupils – it can be useful to videotape your micro-teaching so that an analysis of different aspects of your teaching can be carried out;
- whole class teaching with the class teacher present;
- whole class teaching on your own. (As a student teacher, you should always have an experienced teacher nearby.)

An important issue for student teachers on school experience is the way feedback is given on lessons. The amount of feedback student teachers get from teachers watching their lessons varies. If you wish to have feedback on every lesson, ask if this can be done. Some student teachers prefer a small amount of very focused feedback; others can cope with a page or more of comments. Written feedback is essential because it provides a record of your progress and ideas for your development. In practice, your course will have agreed conventions governing this aspect of your work. These take into account how you are to achieve the competences/standards required to complete your programme successfully.

You will probably find comments on your teaching divide into those relating to tangible technical issues, which can be worked on relatively easily, and those relating to less tangible issues relating to pupils' learning. Technical problems, such as your use of audio-visual aids, the quality and clarity of your voice, how you position yourself in the classroom, managing transitions from one activity to another in a lesson, are easy to spot, so you may receive considerable advice on these issues. Problems with these aspects of your work are usually resolved early in your course, whereas less tangible issues which are directly related to the quality of pupil learning require ongoing reflection, attention and discussion – e.g. your approach to the explanation of lesson content, your style of questioning, your evaluation of pupil learning. More detailed advice related to the teaching of your specific subject is given in the subject-specific texts in the RoutledgeFalmer 'Learning to Teach in the Secondary School' series.

THE STUDENT TEACHER ROLE

You are expected to play a full part in the life of the school – gradually taking on as many aspects of a teacher's work as possible – and you should take advantage of any opportunities to extend your experience. As well as the structured teaching activities identified above, you can expect to undertake a wide range of activities. Table 1.2.1 provides a list illustrating the range of activities teachers undertake.

Teachers have other roles and responsibilities such as planning the curriculum and liaising with outside agencies but these are not usually undertaken by student teachers. However, you may have the opportunity to help to write course materials if your department is developing new areas of work.

In addition to these general responsibilities, staff have expectations relating to:

1 your organisation and teaching approach;
2 your professionalism;
3 your social skills.

Table 1.2.1 summarises the expectations staff may have of you in these areas.

PROFESSIONAL ATTITUDES AND RESPONSIBILITIES

Part 2 of Table 1.2.1 provides some guidance about professional behaviour but professionalism extends beyond personal behaviour.

What does it really mean to be a professional?

The hallmarks of a profession are that there is a substantial body of knowledge which the professional needs to acquire, that substantial training is required before an individual can be accepted into the profession and that the profession is self-governing as well as publicly accountable. On the basis of this definition, for you, becoming a member of the teaching profession means that you make the following commitments, that you will:

- reach an acceptable level of competence and skill in your teaching by the end of your course. This includes acquiring knowledge and skills which enable you to become an effective teacher and which enable you to understand the body of knowledge about how young people learn and how teachers can teach most effectively.
- continuously develop your professional knowledge and professional judgement through experience, further learning and reflection on your work.
- be publicly accountable for your work. Various members of the community have the right to inspect and/or question your work: the head, governors, parents, inspectors. You have a professional duty to plan and keep records of your work and that of the pupils. This accountability includes implementation of school policies, e.g. on behaviour, on equal opportunities.
- set personal standards and conform to external standards for monitoring and improving your work.

There is a professional code of ethics which is currently unwritten in the UK but which you are expected to uphold. For example, you are expected to treat information about individuals with confidentiality; provide equal opportunities for the pupils in your care; deal with pupils in an objective, professional manner regardless of your personal feelings; keep up to date in your subject; reflect on and develop your teaching; adopt appropriate language and a professional demeanour. From time to time, there is debate in the profession about adopting a code of ethics but no code has been accepted in the UK.

In some countries teachers must have their qualifications accepted and registered with a national or state teachers' council before they are allowed to teach. Their names may be removed from this register if, for example, they are found guilty of professional misconduct. In England and Wales recognition of qualifications by the Department for Education and Employment (DfEE) is required before you can teach in government-funded schools, and teachers are required to register with the General Teaching Council for England.

Table 1.2.1 The school's expectations of the student teacher

1 Organisation and teaching approach

You will be expected to:

- be well organised.
- arrive in plenty of time. And that doesn't mean arriving just as the bell goes. It means arriving considerably earlier in order to arrange the classroom; check the availability of books and equipment; test out equipment new to you; talk to staff about the work and the children's progress; and clarify any safety issues.
- plan and prepare thoroughly. Be conscientious in finding out what lesson content and subject knowledge are appropriate to the class you are teaching. In many cases, you will be teaching material which is new to you or which you last thought about many years ago. Staff will expect you to ask if you are not sure but to work conscientiously to improve your subject knowledge. They will not be impressed if you frequently show you have not bothered to read around the subject matter of the lesson.
- keep good records. Have your file of schemes of work and lesson plans, pupil attendance and homework records up to date. Your evaluations of your lessons are best completed on the same day as the lesson.
- know your subject.
- try out different methods of teaching. Teaching practice is your opportunity to try out different approaches without having to live with the results of failures, but you have a duty to the class teacher not to leave chaos behind you.

2 Professionalism

You will be expected to:

- act in a professional manner, e.g. with courtesy and tact; and to respect confidentiality of information.
- be open to new learning. Seek and act on advice.
- be flexible.
- dress appropriately (different schools have different dress codes).
- become familiar with and work within school procedures and policies. These include record keeping, rewards and sanctions, uniform, relationships between teachers and pupils.
- accept a leadership role. You may find imposing your will on pupils uncomfortable, but unless you establish your right to direct the work of the class, you will not be able to teach effectively.
- recognise and understand the roles and relationships of staff responsible for your development.
- keep up to date with your subject.
- take active steps to ensure that your pupils learn.
- discuss pupil progress with parents.

3 Social skills

You will be expected to:

- develop a good relationship with pupils and staff.
- keep a sense of humour.
- work well in teams.
- be able to communicate with children as well as adults.
- learn to defuse difficult situations.

Task 1.2.1

PROFESSIONAL ACCOUNTABILITY

As a teacher, you are held professionally accountable for your own work. What does this mean in practice? Discuss this question with other student teachers and make a note of the standards which you would wish to govern your own professional conduct.

As a student teacher you gradually take on the responsibilities of a teacher and develop as a professional. To do this you go through three main phases of development. In the following section, we discuss these so that you can get a sense of progression in your development.

PHASES OF DEVELOPMENT

Initially most student teachers are concerned with class management issues, how they come across as teachers (self-image), how they are going to control the pupils, if there is sufficient material for the lesson and whether the pupils will ask difficult questions. It is only when you have achieved some confidence in your classroom management skills that you are able to focus on whether the learning outcomes you have planned for have been generally achieved. Your initial focus is on yourself as a teacher, after which you focus on whole class learning, then the individual pupil and their learning.

During your initial teacher education course, and in your early teaching career, you can expect to pass through three broad overlapping stages which we identify as:

- Phase 1: focus on self-image and class management
- Phase 2: focus on whole class learning
- Phase 3: focus on individual pupils' learning

Many student teachers are six or eight weeks into their school experience before they feel a level of confidence about their image and the management of the class (phase 1). They can then start to focus on whether the learning taking place is what was intended (phase 2). Once a student teacher feels reasonably competent in classroom management and in achieving global objectives, they should be able to shift their focus to the needs of individuals (phase 3). Figure 1.2.1 shows how the focus of your work may change over time as you become more effective as a teacher.

As you move to phase 3 we would expect you to become aware of your pupils' personal development as well as their academic development. On school experience you can initially expect to assist the form tutor, who introduces you to this area of work.

PHASE 1: SELF-IMAGE AND CLASS MANAGEMENT

How do I come across?

Do you see yourself as a teacher? Student teachers can find it quite hard to change their self-image from that of learner, in which they may have had a passive role, to the active, managing, authoritative image of a teacher. Up until now, you may have been a learner in most classrooms

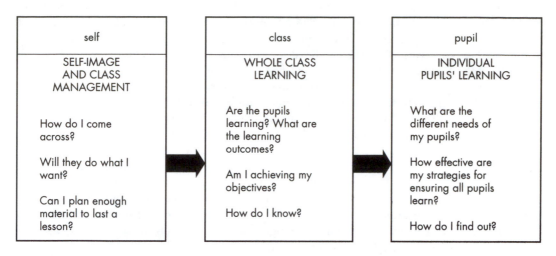

Figure 1.2.1 Phases of development of a teacher

you've been in and now you have to make the transition from learner to teacher. This requires a change in self-image. Teaching is sometimes likened to acting, and thinking of this comparison may enable you to assume a new role more easily. Accompanying this role is a need to change your perspective. As a learner, the teachers were 'in charge'; as a student teacher, teachers and tutors are also 'in charge' of you but, as a class teacher, you now become 'the person in charge'. Your role and your perception of it change during your school experience.

As your experience increases, your professional judgement should develop alongside your store of professional knowledge, but confidence and self-belief are also needed to help you carry off the part. Figure 1.2.2 illustrates the interdependency of these different aspects.

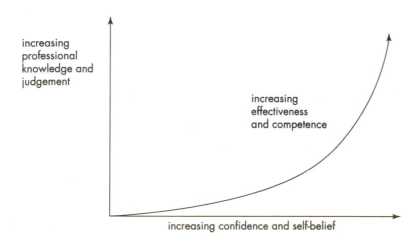

Figure 1.2.2 Becoming an effective teacher

There has been much research on what makes teachers effective, and the various texts on teaching skills and classroom management listed throughout this book provide a wide range of perspectives on effectiveness (e.g. the subject-specific texts in this 'Learning to Teach in the Secondary School' series; Bleach, 2000; Kyriacou, 1997; Marland, 1997a; Robertson, 1996). A summary of the attributes of effective teachers drawn from these texts is listed in Table 1.2.2.

When pupils' perceptions of teachers were researched as part of a wider study on discipline in Scotland (Munn, Johnstone and Holligan, 1990), pupils identified over 75 per cent of their teachers as being effective in terms of getting the class to work well, although, as the authors point out, getting the class to work well is not the same as ensuring that the pupils learn what was intended. Humour as well as use of sanctions and threats were perceived by pupils as important characteristics of effective teachers. The amount of talk between pupils in lessons is usually of concern to staff. Yet pupil comments about the effect of the level of talk were mixed, i.e. some felt a high level of talk was a sign that the teacher wasn't in control, while others did not suggest this link. Making it clear to pupils what types of talk you allow in the classroom can be helpful to pupils. 'Partner talk' is an example of what you might allow when pupils are working together, i.e. a soft voice which only one other person can hear.

It is unlikely that any one teacher will have all the attributes listed below. In any case, you could probably have many of the attributes listed below but still lack authority in the classroom. Neither the attributes themselves nor relationships between teachers and pupils can be developed by checking off attributes on a checklist. However, you can monitor and evaluate their development. We have included this list in order to give you ideas to consider when you are undertaking your own self-evaluation.

Table 1.2.2 Attributes of effective teachers

humorous	enthusiastic	enjoys the subject
relaxed	organised	makes the work relevant
imaginative	supportive	is active in helping pupils learn
warm	cheerful	uses a variety of methods
firm	flexible	has high expectations
listens	encourages	explains clearly
fair	sympathetic	gives praise
friendly	responsive	applies sanctions fairly and doesn't make empty threats

Task 1.2.2

WHAT KIND OF TEACHER DO YOU WANT TO BE?

What image do you want to create? What role do you see yourself assuming? How would you like others to see you as a teacher? If you are at the beginning of your course, write a profile for the 'sort of teacher I want to be' in about 500 words. Base this on your own education and educational experiences.

Repeat the activity at the end of the course when you have had experience. If you are learning to teach in England, you might use this to write a summary statement for your Career Entry Profile at the end of your course. The purpose of a Career Entry Profile is described in the introduction and in Unit 8.2.

Will they do what I say? Classroom management and control

Controlling adolescents is one of the biggest worries student teachers have initially. Unit 2.3 provides a considerable amount of information to prepare you for this aspect of your work and Unit 2.1 contains guidelines about observing teachers and classrooms. Developing an aura of authority takes time, effort and reflection on what has happened in order to modify your behaviour. The tasks in Unit 2.1 are designed to help you analyse the routines and expectations which appear to be operated, often effortlessly, by the teachers whose classes you take.

To see how these routines and expectations are established you would have to shadow a teacher new to a school from the beginning of the school year. The early weeks that teachers new to a school spend with their classes are crucial to setting up the working relationship, as is the way new teachers conduct themselves in the corridors and playground. The pupil grapevine is a powerful means of spreading a teacher's reputation. Teachers who have been at the school for some time are automatically treated in a certain way by pupils because their reputation has gone before them. So you need to work at establishing your reputation.

PHASE 2: WHOLE CLASS LEARNING

Teaching is not the same as learning, nor is telling pupils the same as them learning. Teaching means organising experiences and activities which cause pupils to engage actively with the material and thus learn. Copying notes, for example, does not, in our experience, lead to active engagement, whereas constructing notes with help and guidance is good practice. The teacher's role is then to monitor the outcomes from these experiences and activities. Chapter 5 provides further details about learning.

As you become more competent in classroom management, your concerns shift from asking 'Will I survive?' to 'Are the pupils learning anything from me?' The way you present your lesson and explain the material (the exposition) and the methods you use for asking questions about it become the focus of your attention as you try to improve the learning taking place for the whole class. In Unit 2.2 on lesson planning, the importance of setting clear objectives for each lesson is stressed. These identify the learning outcomes that you expect from that lesson, such as skill development, mastery of content, development of attitudes, understanding of processes. However, what is important is that the objectives are clear enough for you to identify when the pupil has achieved those objectives, by action or other behaviour. Individual lesson objectives give a cumulative picture of the outcomes that you expect your class to achieve. Assessment is then based on the achievement (or otherwise) of outcomes.

Your lesson evaluations help you monitor the learning of the class. They provide an analysis of what went well and what could have been improved. You can expect your class teachers and tutor to discuss your evaluations. In this second phase of your development, such post-lesson discussions focus more on the learning taking place rather than on the image and management issues which will have preoccupied you initially.

PHASE 3: INDIVIDUAL LEARNING

Later, as your analytical and planning skills develop and you build your confidence and professional knowledge about learning, you become able to design your lessons so that the academic needs of individual pupils are better catered for, i.e. you can more easily build differentiation into your teaching.

Effective teachers help individual pupils to grow. If a teacher can manage, in spite of the pressures of time, to give individuals a sense of achievement and self-worth then their pupils' motivation is usually increased. The converse is also true.

Task 1.2.3

'THE AVERAGE CHILD'

In your classroom observations and evaluations, focus on an 'average child' for a number of sessions. Plan your interactions with a small group of these pupils so that you leave them feeling 'special'. Discuss your perceptions with other student teachers.

Whilst student teachers are expected to analyse their effectiveness in achieving their lesson objectives, the skills and experience required to be able to provide differentiated work usually take longer to develop, and opportunities should arise to develop this understanding further after your initial teacher education course. Differentiated work is work which is designed to allow pupils with different abilities to achieve preset goals, i.e. it provides the opportunity for pupils to undertake different tasks or to achieve different outcomes depending on ability. Unit 4.1 provides further information about how you may differentiate work.

Task 1.2.4

WHAT HAVE THE PUPILS LEARNED?

Towards the end of your school experience, arrange to interview a small group of pupils before you teach them about what they know and understand about a topic. Have specific questions in terms of knowledge and understanding that you expect them to achieve through their work on the topic. Then interview them after the lesson to find out what they know and understand about it after being taught. Consider the implications of the findings for your teaching.

SUMMARY AND KEY POINTS

In this unit we have introduced you to some of the complexities of your role as a student teacher. The role of a teacher is diverse but with practice, support, increasing experience and ongoing learning you can expect your level of competence to rise and with it satisfaction.

Because of the dynamic nature of educational practice you should expect to go on learning throughout your career. Your initial teacher education course only provides a foundation on which to build your professional knowledge and your professional judgement.

In becoming a teacher, you can expect to move through the three phases (self-image and class management, class learning, individual learning) as your experience, confidence and competence increase. We hope, by identifying each phase, that we have helped you understand the task ahead of you. Evaluation through critical reflection is one of the tools in your professional tool kit which you can use to analyse your effectiveness in helping pupils learn (see Unit 5.4). The professional knowledge and judgement of experienced teachers with whom you work also provide a rich resource on which to draw in developing your own knowledge and judgement about how to support pupil learning effectively.

FURTHER READING

Allsop, T. (1994) 'The language of partnership' in M. Wilkin and D. Sankey (eds) *Collaboration and Transition in Initial Teacher Courses*, London: Kogan Page, pp. 42–55.
This article contains an interesting discussion of the arrangements for looking after student teachers, expectations and some school responses in the Oxford Internship scheme. It identifies 'language' as an important factor in identifying and setting roles. By language, the authors mean the definitions of roles and expectations written into the agreements between the school and higher education institution or school and student teacher.

Bleach, K. (2000) *The Newly Qualified Secondary Teacher's Handbook*, London: David Fulton.
This text focuses specifically on helping student teachers in England to meet the standards required to achieve qualified teacher status.

Cole, M. (ed.) (1999) *Professional Issues for Teachers and Student Teachers*, London: David Fulton.
This text contains chapters on conditions of service, legal liabilities and responsibilities, child protection and other important aspects of a teacher's role.

Frobisher, L., Monaghan, J., Orton, A., Orton, J., Roper, T. and Threfall, J. (1999) *Learning to Teach Numbers – A Handbook for Students and Teachers in the Primary School*. Cheltenham: Stanley Thornes.
Many teachers, whatever their subject, will use number work in their teaching. This text provides a useful understanding of how to teach numbers and can provide valuable underpinning to the work of a secondary teacher.

Howe, M. J. A. (1998) *A Teacher's Guide to the Psychology of Learning* (2nd edn), Oxford: Blackwell.
The more a teacher understands about the process of learning, remembering and the acquisition of knowledge and skills, it could be argued that the more likely they will be able to benefit individual pupils. This book is of particular value in covering a range of learning experiences from the earliest years upwards. It addresses the issues of the importance of rehearsing and practising activities as well as the importance of a teacher providing material of personal relevance. It goes on to talk about the structuring of information in ways that aid learning and deals with issues such as motivation, intelligence and extending writing skills. This is a valuable text to add to a teacher's professional toolbox.

Kyriacou, C. (1997a) *Effective Teaching in Schools: Theory and Practice* (2nd edn), Cheltenham: Stanley Thornes.
This text extends the advice in this unit.

Marland, M. (1997) *The Art of the Tutor: Developing your Role in the Secondary School*, London: David Fulton.
This provides practical advice for the student teacher about the pastoral role.

Munn, P., Johnstone, M. and Holligan, C. (1990) 'Pupils' perceptions of effective disciplinarians', *British Educational Research Journal*, 16 (2), 191–198.
This article provides interesting data from a three-year research project on discipline in schools in Scotland. The pupils' perceptions of the characteristics of the effective teacher are interesting to consider in the light of your own teaching experience.

Robertson, J. (1996) *Effective Classroom Control* (3rd edn), London: Hodder and Stoughton.
Robertson provides advice and strategies for student teachers to use in developing good relationships with pupils. He focuses particularly on analysing and dealing with unwanted behaviour and establishing and expressing authority.

Voice Care Network. Their booklet 'More Care for your Voice' is available from the following address: 29 Southbank Road, Kenilworth, Warwickshire CU8 1LA. (Tel: 01926 864000) Website: http://www.voicecare.org.uk Email address: vcnuk@btconnect.com
This organisation began in 1984 and is a registered charity with subscribing members. They focus on teachers' problems and encourage teachers to contact them for advice. They also provide training sessions.

UNIT 1.3 MANAGING YOUR TIME AND PREVENTING STRESS

SUSAN CAPEL

INTRODUCTION

Although teaching can be rewarding and exciting, it can also be stressful and demanding. You may be surprised by the amount of time and energy you use while on school experience (and later as a teacher), inside and outside the classroom and outside the school day. There is little time within a school day in which you can relax. Even your breaks are often disrupted. This means that you must plan to use your time and energy effectively and efficiently over the week. You must not spend so much time preparing one lesson that you do not have time to prepare others well (there are, of course, times when you want to take extra time planning one particular lesson, e.g. for a difficult class with whom the last lesson did not go well or if you are less familiar with the material). Likewise, you must use your energy wisely, so that you have enough energy to teach each lesson well.

Undoubtedly you will be tired. Many student teachers have told us that they are so tired when they get home from school that they have to force themselves to stay awake to plan and prepare lessons in the evening. If your teaching commitment is not to take over your whole life, you need to use your time and energy to advantage. You also need to manage stress associated with your school experience and teaching.

Although you are unlikely to find competences/standards on your course related to time and stress management, if you can put the ideas in this unit into practice, you are more likely not only to manage effectively your school experience and teaching itself, but also to enjoy the job and develop as a teacher.

OBJECTIVES

By the end of this unit you should be able to:

- identify ways you can use your time more effectively in the classroom;
- develop ways to manage your time more effectively;
- identify factors that may cause you stress;
- develop methods for coping with stress.

MANAGING YOUR TIME

Managing your time in the classroom

To use classroom time effectively and economically requires you to plan how you are going to use time in each lesson. Ways of managing your time in the classroom include:

- allocating a high proportion of available time for academic work;
- maintaining a good balance in the use of time on teaching, supervisory and organisational activities;
- spending a high proportion of time in 'substantive interaction' with pupils (i.e. explaining, questioning, describing, illustrating);
- regularly reviewing the conduct of lessons in terms of effective use of your own and pupils' time;
- devising simple, fast procedures for routine events and dealing with recurring problems;
- eliminating unnecessary routines and activities from your own performance;
- delegating (to classroom assistants or pupils) responsibilities and jobs that are within their capability (adapted from Waterhouse 1983, p. 46).

This should enable pupils to:

- spend a high proportion of their time actually engaged on their tasks;
- experience a high degree of success during their engaged time.

These time management principles can be applied in many ways in the classroom. For example:

- using classroom assistants or pupils to help give out and collect textbooks, pupils' books or equipment, to mark straightforward homework tests in class, and to make sure the classroom is left ready for the next class with the chairs tidy, floor clear, board clean and books tidied away;
- carrying a marking pen with you as you move around the class checking the work that is going on. As you skim pupils' work and comment to them, you can make brief notes on the work. It is easier to pick up mistakes and check work when it is fresh in your mind. This saves you having to go back to the work at a later stage which, in itself, wastes time;
- collecting in books which are open at the page where you should start marking;
- ensuring that work is dated and that homework is clearly identified so that it is easy for you to check what work has been done and what is missing. Ruling off each lesson's work helps you to check this;
- keeping one page of your mark book for comments about progress (folding the page over ensures that comments are not seen inadvertently by pupils). As you see pupils' work in class or when you are marking, you can make brief notes which are then immediately at hand for discussions with parents, head of year, report writing, etc.

You can spend a lot of class time on discipline. Establishing rules for behaviour in the classroom early in your first few lessons with a class can save time later on (see Unit 3.3 on managing pupil behaviour).

Task 1.3.1

HOW YOU SPEND YOUR TIME IN LESSONS

Observe how several experienced teachers use their time effectively and economically in lessons. Use a series of checklists, each with something specific to look for, e.g. how they divide time between teaching, supervisory and organisational activities, how much time is spent disciplining pupils, how much time is spent on explaining and questioning, how much time is spent on procedures for routine events such as collecting in homework or giving back books, or which responsibilities and jobs are delegated to classroom assistants or pupils. Ask another student teacher or your tutor to observe how you use time in the classroom in one lesson or over a series of lessons. Discuss with the observer the findings and possible ways of using your or the pupils' lesson time more effectively and economically. Record these ideas in your diary and try them out systematically in your teaching.

Planning outside the classroom

Careful planning for a series of lessons and for each individual lesson enables lesson time to be used most effectively. It is helpful to allocate time for each activity in a lesson (e.g. use a time line in your lesson plan, as described in Unit 2.2). This enables you to see what you have planned to do in each lesson and to evaluate the lesson later. It is important that you plan for such things as pupils moving from one part of the school to another for the lesson, changing time for physical education or getting the class settled, particularly at the beginning of the day, after a break or after lunch. You may find initially that you under- or over-estimate the time tasks take to accomplish. At the end of each lesson you can compare the time taken for each activity with that allocated. In this way you gradually become realistic about how long different activities in a lesson take.

You also need to plan for a series of lessons. You have a certain amount of work to cover over a given period of time. If you do not plan carefully, you may find yourself taking too long over some of the content and not leaving yourself with enough time to complete everything required in the time available. Pupils' knowledge and understanding develop over a period of time; therefore if they do not complete the content required, their learning may be incomplete. Unit 2.2 provides more information about lesson planning and schemes of work.

Task 1.3.2

PLANNING HOW TO USE LESSON TIME

When planning your lessons, deliberately think about how best you can use the time available. Determine what proportion of time to allocate to each activity and indicate, next to each activity, the amount of time to be allocated to it. When you evaluate the lesson and each activity in it, look specifically at how the time was used. Ask yourself how you can organise pupils and establish routines to make more time available for teaching and learning. Include these in future lesson plans.

Managing your own time effectively

However well you use time in the classroom, you may not be using the time you put into your work and your own time to best advantage. Some people naturally use their time more effectively than others. Some people always seem to work long hours but achieve little, whereas others achieve a great deal but still appear to have plenty of time to do things other than work. One explanation for this could be that the first person wastes time through, for example, being unsystematic in managing time or handling paperwork, putting off work rather than getting on and doing it, trying to do it all rather than delegating appropriately, or not being able to say no to jobs; whereas the second person uses time well by, for example, having clear objectives for work to be done, prioritising work, completing urgent and important jobs first, and writing lists of jobs to be done during the day. Which of these descriptions fits you? To check, you need to analyse the way you work and, if necessary, try to make changes. Compiling a time log showing how you spend your time over a given period will help with this.

Fontana (1993) stressed that if we could use our time effectively at work we would be more efficient and more productive, be better able to plan long term, be more satisfied with our work and our job, be less stressed, have more time for ourselves and more opportunity to switch off out of work. There are many different techniques you can use to manage your time effectively. Figure 1.3.1 highlights some of these.

Figure 1.3.1 How to avoid working around the clock

PREVENTING STRESS

Studies of stress in student teachers (e.g. Capel, 1996, 1997, 1998; Hart, 1987; Kyriacou and Stephens, 1999; Morton, Vesco, Williams and Awender, 1997) have shown that major causes of stress for student teachers include:

- not being regarded as a real teacher;
- control and discipline and dealing with disruptive behaviour;
- motivating pupils and maintaining pupils' interest;
- conflict with pupils;
- coping with the ability range of pupils within a class;
- practical skills of teaching, techniques of lesson preparation and getting the teaching and/or planning right;

- disagreement with the tutor;
- personality disagreement with the tutor;
- coping with a heavy workload;
- observation, evaluation and assessment of teaching by the supervisor, particularly receiving the supervisor's or class teacher's opinion of classroom competence;
- role conflict, role overload and role ambiguity.

There are, of course, many other aspects of your teaching that may cause you stress or anxiety, e.g. delivering material with which you are not very familiar or reprimanding a pupil. Later units in this book identify practical ways to help you overcome many of these anxieties. The last two on the list above are considered briefly below.

When you are being observed, evaluated and assessed, you are 'on show'. You are vulnerable because your developing skills are analysed and constructively criticised. This may be exacerbated where school teachers take on the role of tutors in initial teacher education. Pateman (1994) indicated that the role of teachers in assessing the teaching competence of student teachers means that many student teachers feel unable to talk freely and openly to teachers about other concerns. Thus, the role of the teacher-tutor in assessment does not take account of student teachers' needs for friendship, counselling and tutoring. This may cause stress for student teachers. This finding is supported in other research on stress in student teachers, e.g. Capel (1994).

Role conflict can result from carrying out a number of different activities within your job, each requiring different responsibilities, demands and skills, e.g. teaching, form tutoring, talking to parents, administration (clerical work and committee duties), other jobs within the department, in-service training and professional development (inter-role conflict), or from trying to meet the different expectations of a number of people with whom you are working, e.g. pupils, your tutor, other teachers, head of department, senior managers, parents, OFSTED (intra-role conflict). Often you are not quite sure how to perform in the role of a student teacher as your role is ambiguous.

Role overload can occur because there are so many things for you to do as a teacher and too little time in which to do them. This can mean working very long hours to get the job done and not having enough time mentally and physically to relax for work the following day or week.

Task 1.3.3

BALANCING YOUR WORK AND LEISURE TIME

Over the course of a week on school experience, list the time you spend on school-related activities other than teaching your classes and the amount of leisure time that you have. Why is the balance as it is? Is this balance acceptable? If not, is it because of, for example, inefficiency, lack of experience or overload? How can you improve it? Discuss the balance of work and leisure with other student teachers.

Role conflict and overload may affect student teachers more than qualified teachers for a number of reasons, e.g. student teachers take longer to prepare each lesson than more experienced teachers; student teachers may be unsure of their role in a lesson, a department or the school as a whole (role ambiguity) and they may, at any one time, be answering to and trying to please a number of people, who expect different things.

It may be that stressors outside work, e.g. tensions of home and family, are brought to and add to stress at work and make a person more vulnerable to stressors at work. Job stress may vary during the year according to the demands of a job, personal circumstances and/or other factors at any one time. A significant stressor at a particular time could account for differences in stress experienced by people at different times of a school year.

Task 1.3.4

CAUSES OF STRESS FOR STUDENT TEACHERS

In your diary write a list of factors that cause stress for you in your role as a student teacher. Compare these with causes of stress identified by another student teacher. Discuss similarities and differences. After reading the next section of this unit identify ways you can prevent or alleviate the stress. Try out methods of prevention as soon as you can.

Task 1.3.5

SYSTEMATIC OBSERVATION OF ASPECTS OF YOUR TEACHING

You should be getting regular feedback on your teaching from your tutor. However, you may want to ask your tutor to focus specifically on one aspect of your teaching that is causing you most anxiety and then give you feedback on this, along with ideas about how you might be able to improve in this area, e.g. giving feedback to pupils, giving praise, working with individuals in the class. It may help to develop an observation schedule for each specific aspect. You can find examples of lesson observation schedules in subject texts in the 'Learning to Teach (subjects) in the Secondary School' series, which are listed at the front of this book. Plan your next lesson taking these points into account. Ask your tutor to observe another lesson a couple of weeks later to see if there is any difference in your performance. Try this again with another aspect of your teaching.

How can you cope with your stress?

Many different strategies have been identified to prevent or alleviate stress. However, as there are different causes of stress for different people and for the same person at different times, there is no one way to cope with stress; you have to find out what works for you or for you in particular situations. Different ways of preventing and/or alleviating stress, therefore, are appropriate for different people.

Those identified below have been drawn from a number of sources (e.g. Cains and Brown, 1998; Cockburn, 1996; D'Arcy, 1989; Dean, 1993; Head, Hill and Maguire, 1996; Kyriacou, 1989). The strategies listed for managing your time may also be useful, as not using your time effectively may cause stress. These lists are by no means exhaustive and you may find other strategies useful.

- **Prepare for stressful situations when you are not under pressure**, e.g. prepare lessons before the day on which you are teaching them.

- **Role-play a situation that is causing you anxiety and/or visualise what you can do to overcome the problem**. This helps you to focus on the problem and can be used to rehearse how you are going to cope.

- **Actively prepare for a situation**, e.g. if you are anxious about a particular lesson prepare it more thoroughly than normal. Plan thoroughly how you can reduce the likelihood of a problem occurring or deal with a particular problem. This strategy can help you to identify the reasons for a problem and focus on possible ways of preventing or dealing with it.

- **Develop effective self-management techniques**, e.g. establish routines so that you can do things automatically, particularly when you are tired.

- **Recognise and try to develop your strengths as well as your weaknesses** so that you can rely on your strengths as you work on improving any weaknesses.

- **Do not worry about incidents that have happened in school, and keep problems in proportion**. Try not to take problems home.

- **Identify where you can get help**. You should get regular feedback on your teaching, but identify other people who may be able to help.

- **Develop support systems which provide a network of people with whom you could talk through problems**, e.g. other student teachers, your tutor, other teachers, a partner or friend. You may want to talk to different people for help with different problems. You may form a group with other student teachers to provide mutual support, talk about your anxieties/concerns, develop a shared understanding of a problem and provide possible alternative solutions and practical help to address a problem, e.g. through a lesson being observed then discussed with another student teacher.

- **Take account of the amount and variety of work you are doing, to reduce both role overload and conflict**. This may mean, for example, that you need to try to take work home less often or take on fewer extra-curricular activities. You may need to work on this over a period of time.

SUMMARY AND KEY POINTS

We would be very surprised if, as a student teacher on school experience, you are not tired. Likewise, we would be very surprised if you are not anxious when someone comes in to watch your lessons, particularly if that person has a say in whether you become a qualified teacher, or if you are not worried about other aspects of your school experience. It may help to know that you are not going to be alone in being tired or feeling anxious or worried about your school experience, and that many of the causes of tiredness and stress are the same for other student teachers. Where you are alone is in developing effective techniques for managing your time and for preventing or coping with stress. There are no ready answers for managing time or preventing or alleviating stress. They are complex processes. Other people can help you with this, but nobody else can do it for you because what works for someone else may not work for you. Finally, you must work at managing your time and stress over time; there are no short-term, one-off solutions to these problems.

FURTHER READING

Child, D. (1997b) *Psychology and the Teacher* (6th edn), London: Cassell.
Chapter 3, 'Human motivation', includes a section on stress in teachers and pupils.

Dunham, J. (1995) *Developing Effective School Management*, London: Routledge.
This book is designed to help teachers to identify and develop knowledge and skills to become effective middle managers. It includes chapters on time management and stress management, which should be helpful to you as student teachers.

Fontana, D. (1993) *Managing Time*, Leicester: British Psychological Society Books.
This book is based on the premise that good time management can be learned. It combines text and a series of exercises to help you better understand different aspects of time management, including the qualities of a good time manager, determining how you currently use your time and planning how you can use your time better.

Handy, C. (1993) *Understanding Organisations* (4th edn), London: Penguin.
This book includes a section on stress, which provides a broader perspective of stress than that found when looking only at stress in teachers.

Kyriacou, C. (2000) *Stress-Busting for Teachers*, Cheltenham: Stanley Thornes.
This book aims to help teachers to develop a range of strategies for coping with stress at work. It looks at what stress is; sources of stress; how to pre-empt stress; how to cope with stress; and what schools can do to minimise stress.

Maitland, I. (1995) *Managing your Time*, London: Institute of Personnel and Development.
This book helps you to analyse your use of the following components of time management: analysing your workload; getting organised; delegating successfully; tackling paperwork; handling meetings; controlling time-wasting activities; and making the most of free time.

UNIT 1.4 **TEACHING AND LEARNING WITH ICT: AN INTRODUCTION**

MARILYN LEASK

INTRODUCTION

This unit introduces ways in which the communication opportunities supported by Information and Communications Technology (ICT) can be used for curriculum, administration and professional development purposes. (The term ICT is now widely used instead of the term Information Technology (IT) to indicate that the communication technologies, e.g. internet and email, are included.) Teacher Training Agency (TTA) documentation defines ICT as including 'computers, the internet, CD-ROM and other software, television, radio, video, cameras and other equipment' (TTA, 1998, p. 1).

The ideas in this unit are based on practice in innovative schools. There is considerable variation between schools. Although student teachers in England are required to demonstrate competence in basic skills in word processing, databases, spreadsheets, email and internet use, we do not cover basic skills here. If you are just beginning to use computers, there are many materials providing this information – for example, Leask *et al.* (2000); Trend *et al.* (1999); Warren *et al.* (1998). You may wish to take your 'European Computer Driving Licence (ECDL)(1)'. This provides a structured way of developing your skills supported by material freely available from the British Computing Society. Details of the ECDL can be found on http://www.bcs.org.uk/ecdl/

In this unit we focus deliberately on pedagogical applications of ICT because the new knowledge about curriculum applications being created by innovative teachers in schools is not yet widely disseminated.

The rapid pace of development in ICT software and hardware is forcing everyone who uses the technology to undergo a process of continual learning and regular adjustment of working practices. 'Just-in-time learning' where the learner learns just enough to go to the next stage and 'experiential learning' (learning through doing) are familiar patterns of learning for those working with ICT. A working environment where staff are mutually supportive and can work collaboratively to solve ICT challenges is essential if teachers are to keep up with change.

In this unit you will find references to software and to websites which are recommended by teachers as well as references to texts which may provide you with further ideas. But these ideas only provide starting points. Websites change regularly, with new ones developing and old ones disappearing daily. The resources we reference are those that we consider are providing a professional service and are likely to have a permanent presence on the internet. The situation with regard to the quality and type of equipment available in schools is also rapidly changing. Some schools and Local Education Authorities (LEAs) already have useful websites and intranets (closed networks) well established. If you work in organisations with these resources then you will be able to integrate internet and email applications easily into your teaching programme. For example, you may be able to ask for websites which you want to use for your teaching to be downloaded and hosted on the school or LEA server (a computer dedicated to internet/intranet work). This means that access to the materials is reliable and not limited by the slowness of internet connection. Or you may be able to join in existing initiatives running in your department. Some teachers have access to 'electronic white boards' where images and texts stored in or accessed using the computer can be projected on to a large screen and manipulated by the teacher to emphasise points made during the lesson, e.g. in English literature lessons snippets of video recordings of plays can be projected alongside the text. In the best-equipped schools, teachers have their own personal computer or laptop, and multimedia projectors (projecting the computer screen image on to a large screen) or interactive whiteboards are commonly available.

OBJECTIVES

By the end of this unit you should:

- understand a range of ways in which ICT can be deployed for educational purposes;
- have explored a number of these options through visiting various educational websites;
- have identified specific applications relevant to your subject area and used those available to you;
- have audited your skills and knowledge in this area against those demanded by your course and developed an action plan for improving these.

BACKGROUND

Computers became widely available in schools in the mid-1980s. Initially these offered basic word-processing, spreadsheet and database capabilities. Whilst electronic networking was available between some schools at this time, such a resource did not become widely accessible to all schools until the middle to late 1990s when access to the internet (through a World Wide Web of networked computers) became available at prices individual schools could afford. In the meantime, CD-ROM technology also developed together with software (2) which made it easy for pupils and teachers to develop multimedia applications and from this, using low-cost CD-ROM writers, to produce inexpensive CD-ROMs. However, it was access to the internet in particular which changed computers from being machines which were used for quite specific purposes in specialist rooms, to machines which provided a medium which combined the attributes of video machines, telephones, television and radio and which could be employed for a range of purposes in all classrooms.

In many countries around the world, teachers are under increasing pressure to demonstrate that they can use ICT for teaching and learning as well as for professional development. Acquiring knowledge about the educational applications of ICT is not therefore an optional activity. Traditional approaches to teaching, where teachers often taught their pupils in the ways they had been taught themselves, must be reviewed in the light of what technology can now offer. However, as with any changes in classroom practice, the one question must always be asked: 'What is the most effective approach to take to achieve the desired learning outcomes?' ICT should only be used where its use is justified as a method of achieving the stated learning outcomes for any lesson.

THE SKILLS AND KNOWLEDGE REQUIRED OF STUDENT TEACHERS

In England, TTA (1998) states that student teachers must demonstrate that they have acquired a range of ICT competences. They must be able to use word-processing, desktop publishing, and spreadsheet or database software as well as being able to demonstrate that they understand how ICT can support their own professional development and teaching and learning in their subject area. They need to know how ICT can help pupils with particular special educational needs. Student teachers must also demonstrate an understanding of ethical issues (e.g. pupils' personal details such as names and photographs should not be placed on the web), health and safety legislation (e.g. pupils should not be required to use workstations that are poorly designed), and legal issues such as data protection and copyright (e.g. that the strict limits on the reproduction of materials authored by others include placing such material on school websites; that personal details of individuals are not held on computers without appropriate authorisation). Student teachers in other parts of the UK must also demonstrate similar competences.

As a useful starting point, we suggest that you check the requirements of your course for your ICT skills and that you audit your strengths and weaknesses. You may find it helpful to write an action plan setting out how you are going to become familiar with the ways that ICT can support the work in your own subject.

Task 1.4.1

AUDITING YOUR SKILLS AND KNOWLEDGE

Your school or higher education institution will provide you with the criteria you have to satisfy in terms of ICT competences. We suggest you use these to identify the areas in which you are competent and those in which you need to develop further competence. When you have undertaken Task 1.4.2, we suggest you draw up an action plan which identifies the areas on which you are going to work, the ways in which you are going to develop competence and the timescales you set yourself.

Table 1.4.1 illustrates how the various facets of ICT, as defined by the English National Curriculum for IT (applications, communicating information, modelling, handling data, control and measurement) can be applied in different subjects.

As indicated earlier in this unit, there are many materials, courses and programmes which individuals can use or undertake if they wish to learn how to use word-processing, desktop publishing, spreadsheet or database software and, increasingly, training will become available in the application of the communicative aspects of the technology to particular subjects.

Task 1.4.2

IDENTIFYING ICT RESOURCES FOR YOUR SUBJECT AREA

Find out what ICT resources are available to you in your school/higher education institution to support your subject area. Discuss the application of these to the lessons you are taking with your tutor and fellow student teachers. Use these resources in lessons and evaluate your success in achieving the learning objectives you set. Identify your strengths and weaknesses in using ICT and draw up and implement an action plan which sets out a strategy for ensuring that your weaknesses are addressed.

Table 1.4.1 Elements of ICT in various subject areas

Art and Design

Applications	–	Commercial art
Communicating	–	Multimedia for students' portfolios
Modelling	–	Spreadsheet to model design specs
Handling data	–	Surveys
Control	–	Embroidery

Business and Commercial Studies

Applications	–	Commercial packages, administration systems
Communicating	–	Business letters, email, internet
Modelling	–	Business modelling
Handling data	–	Pay packages, databases

Drama, Dance and Music

Applications	–	Ticket booking, lighting control, recording studios
Communicating	–	Multimedia for students' portfolios, internet and email projects, sound files
Modelling	–	Lighting sequences
Control	–	Lighting sequences, MIDI interfaces

English

Applications	–	Publishing, news services, advertising
Communicating	–	Word processing, multimedia, email, internet
Handling data	–	Class surveys, database of books/reading

Humanities

Applications	–	Weather stations, archiving, museums
Communicating	–	Multimedia, word processing, posters, projects related to culture and belief
Modelling	–	Spreadsheet modelling, building design packages, simulations
Handling data	–	Surveys, database, internet
Measurement	–	Weather, wind speed, rainfall

Maths

Applications	–	Space programme
Communicating	–	Multimedia, email projects
Modelling	–	Number patterns, algebra
Handling data	–	Class database, graph work
Control	–	Programming language, e.g. Turtle, Logo
Measurement	–	Accurate short/long period measurements

Technology

Applications	–	Industrial production, engineering, electronics
Communicating	–	Health and safety posters, design (logos, packaging)
Handling data	–	Product survey/comparisons
Modelling	–	Building design
Control	–	Lathes, textiles, embroidery

Physical Education

Applications	–	Recording, timing
Communicating	–	Events leaflets, posters
Handling data	–	Personal/group performance database/spreadsheet
Measurement	–	Accurate timing, recording

Modern Foreign Languages

Applications	–	internet, Teletext, translation services
Communicating	–	Multimedia, D. T. P., word processing, email
Modelling	–	Cafe bills
Handling data	–	Class surveys, topic database

Science

Applications	–	Nuclear power stations
Communicating	–	Safety posters, word-lists
Modelling	–	Experiment results modelling
Handling data	–	Graph work, data logging
Control	–	Experiment control
Measurement	–	Accurate short/long period measurement

Source: Leask and Pachler, 1999, with thanks to Dave Maguire.

The requirements of teachers listed in Table 1.4.1 are demanding and need you to take an active role in your own professional development. There is research evidence (e.g. BECTa, 2000) which indicates that when ICT is effectively deployed, pupil motivation and achievement are raised in a number of respects. Some of the evidence is introduced in the next section.

WHY USE ICT?

Research carried out for the National Council for Educational Technology (NCET) in the mid–1990s provided evidence of the following positive reasons for using IT in schools. (Note: this work was done before the opportunities offered by ICT were widely available, so the term IT is used.) Table 1.4.2 summarises these findings.

Table 1.4.2 Evidence from research about the way IT supports teaching and learning

1 Children who use a computer at home are more enthusiastic and confident when using one in school
2 Video games can be educational if they are well managed
3 IT can provide a safe and non-threatening environment for learning
4 IT has the flexibility to meet the individual needs and abilities of each student
5 Students who have not enjoyed learning can be encouraged by the use of IT
6 Computers give students the chance to achieve where they have previously failed
7 Computers can reduce the risk of failure at school
8 IT allows students to reflect on what they have written and to change it easily
9 Using a computer to produce a successful piece of writing can motivate students to acquire basic literacy skills
10 IT gives students immediate access to richer source materials
11 IT can present information in new ways which help students to understand, assimilate and use it more readily
12 IT removes the chore of processing data manually and frees students to concentrate on its interpretation and use
13 Difficult ideas are made more understandable when information technology makes them visible
14 Interactive technology motivates and stimulates learning
15 Computing programs which use digitised speech can help students to read and spell
16 IT gives students the power to try out different ideas and to take risks
17 Computer simulations encourage analytical and divergent thinking
18 IT is particularly successful in holding the attention of pupils with emotional and behavioural difficulties
19 IT can often compensate for the communication and learning difficulties of students with physical and sensory impairments
20 Pupils with profound and multiple learning difficulties can be encouraged to purposeful activity and self-awareness by IT
21 Using IT makes teachers take a fresh look at how they teach and the ways in which students learn
22 Computers help students to learn when used in well-designed, meaningful tasks and activities
23 Students make more effective use of computers if teachers know how and when to intervene
24 IT offers potential for effective group working
25 Giving teachers easy access to computers encourages and improves the use of IT in the curriculum
26 Headteachers who use computers raise the profile of IT in their schools
27 Management Information Systems can help save money and time in schools

Source: NCET (1994).

Task 1.4.3

HOW DOES ICT HELP TEACHING AND LEARNING?

Consider the list in Table 1.4.2 in the light of your experiences in schools. What evidence have you come across of the potential of computer-supported activity, as outlined in this table, being realised? Is there any scope within your school situation for testing some of the findings listed in this table and examining how various forms of ICT could support teaching and learning in your subject area?

It is worth noting that a number of the points in the table relate specifically to the support that IT provides for pupils with special educational needs (SEN). Franklin (1999) provides detailed advice about particular forms of ICT which support pupils with SEN. He recommends that teachers interested in SEN issues join the online forum run within the Virtual Teacher Centre by the British Educational Communications Technology Agency (BECTa) (3). BECTa also produce a number of publications providing detailed advice, including subject-specific advice, to teachers about ICT issues. Much of this information is available on their website, including reviews of CD-ROMs (4). This is listed in the further reading at the end of this unit.

Motivation and classroom management

Cox (1999) provides a detailed examination of motivational theories and their application to ICT. She also gives the following advice on the teaching of word processing which you may wish to use as a checklist against your own practice when using computers.

In planning a series of lessons using word processing there are a number of pitfalls to avoid which are too commonly seen in classrooms. The following advice applies to many uses of ICT which, if not carefully planned, provide no motivation and very little learning benefit either:

- tasks must be relevant;
- pupils should be prepared for their tasks before being assigned computers;
- don't let pupils sit at computers while you are talking to them at the introduction of the lesson;
- don't leave pupils for the whole lesson just working on their task with no intervention to remind them of the educational purpose;
- don't expect pupils to print out their work at the end of every lesson;
- end each lesson by drawing pupils together to discuss what they have achieved;
- don't rely on the technology to run the lesson.

As mentioned earlier in this unit, the rapid development of technology means that it may be hard for any individual to claim expert status across a whole range of software and hardware. Selinger suggests the following solution to the problem of pupils knowing more than you do yourself:

Classroom dynamics with ICT alters considerably especially when teaching takes place in a computer room. There will be an increase in noise level and pupils may need to move freely around the classroom. It is also not always easy to be sure pupils are on task or not, and you have to find ways of ascertaining this through questions and summing up sessions at the end of the lesson. You may well find yourself in the unusual position of knowing less than your pupils about hardware or software. There is no need to feel threatened by this situation; use it as an opportunity to increase your own knowledge, and to give pupils an opportunity to excel. Some software requires independent learning, but do not feel as though you are no longer teaching, your role as a mediator between the pupils and the machine is often crucial in developing their understanding. Questioning pupils about what they are doing, and why they are doing it in that way, demands that they have to articulate their understanding and in so doing can consolidate their learning.

(Selinger, 1999)

Selinger also provides advice about how to manage ICT in the classroom with varying numbers of machines (Leask and Pachler, 1999). Increasingly the use of wireless technology will give teachers flexibility in their use of ICT.

PEDAGOGIC AND PROFESSIONAL APPLICATIONS OF THE INTERNET

Ways of using the capability of the internet for pedagogic and professional purposes are still developing. The internet provides educators with the following:

1 **Access** to a huge range of free and high-quality information sources including the rapid and inexpensive publication of the latest research findings from researchers around the world in all disciplines (5), as well as access to museums, galleries, newspapers, radio stations (6) and libraries. These resources are often available in a variety of languages. In the UK, the National Grid for Learning (7) and the Virtual Teacher Centre within it are intended to provide resources to support teachers. Various government-supported sites all have information of potential use to teachers (8, 9, 12). Unfortunately information of dubious quality and information inappropriate for pupils is also easily available. Teaching strategies and procedures in schools related to access to the internet need to take these issues into account by considering the location of computers, rules for access and use and strategies for effective searching of the internet.

2 For teachers and schools the opportunity to **publish information** about their work. School websites and intranets provide opportunities for publishing material for a range of purposes. For example, pupils are sometimes set projects to publish material which they have researched themselves. In doing this, both pupils and teachers are developing their knowledge about the use of this technology. Parents can be kept informed more fully about the work their children are doing through website publications and, of course, parents who are seeking schools for their children may find such sites of value in guiding their choice. In addition, the school website can provide a useful departmental resource as colleagues pool ideas and use the website as a form of departmental filing cabinet for resources.

3 **Synchronous** (e.g. video conferencing and online chat/discussion groups) **and asynchronous communication** (e.g. email) with single or multiple audiences, e.g. with other teachers, pupils, parents and experts in particular fields regardless of their location. Some schools tap the expertise of parents and local companies to provide experts online for short periods. These are specialists who are able to answer pupils' questions in areas relevant to their expertise. Teachers are using these facilities for a range of purposes, both curriculum-based and for professional development. For example, joint curriculum projects with classes in other countries can be easily maintained through the use of email. Results of such collaboration can also be posted on the school website

for participants in both countries to see. The European SchoolNet site (http://www.eun.org) provides a partner finding service. If you are interested in undertaking such projects then starting with something small and achievable will enable you to develop strategies that work for you in your particular subject. For example, survey work carried out by pupils in two countries can be done over a very short time span, perhaps a couple of weeks. This enables you to avoid problems with clashes of holidays. Funding for collaborative work may be available from UK or European Union sources. Details are available on the European SchoolNet website. Table 1.4.3 provides some guidelines for the running of email projects.

But these ideas are just a beginning; there are many **other possibilities**. For example, Lord Grey School in Bletchley has undertaken sustained ICT curriculum projects across subjects and involving many countries. Holy Cross Convent School in Surrey has undertaken innovative cross-curricular video-conferencing projects with a school in Japan. This work is described further by Lawrence Williams, the director of studies (Pachler and Williams, 1999). Further examples of projects with other schools, e.g. Virtual field trips (10, 11) Virtual art galleries, are given in Leask and Pachler (1999). Figure 1.4.1 provides an example of a 'WebQuest'.

A WebQuest is a framework made by teachers for pupils for stimulating educational adventures on the Web and to help pupils in the acquisition of problem-solving and searching skills. Taking account of curricular goals, the teacher sets up a few guidelines, with a simple structure:

- Introduction – context information related to the task/problem/adventure/questions to be completed by the pupils;
- The task/problem/adventure/questions – what has to be done by the pupils;
- Internet resources – location of internet resources such as websites, databases, live video cameras for educational purposes (e.g. vulcanology);
- Reporting results and final discussions.

Figure 1.4.1 Example of 'WebQuest'

FINDING PARTNERS FOR EMAIL/VIDEO-CONFERENCING/INTERNET-BASED PROJECTS

There are a number of ways of finding partners. These include the following:

- by using existing contacts, through, for example, exchanges or through the local community and teachers in the school;
- by emailing schools direct. Various sites provide lists of schools' email addresses, e.g. European SchoolNet (http://www.eun.org);
- by advertising your project, e.g. by registering it on a site such as one of those mentioned below;
- by searching sites listing school projects and finding projects which seem to fit with your curriculum goals.

Table 1.4.3 Checklist for planning ICT projects with other schools

1 What learning outcomes do you want the pupils to achieve in terms of: knowledge/concepts, skills, attitudes?

2 What is the timescale of the project and how does that fit with school holidays and other events in the partner school?

3 What languages can you work in? (Don't forget that parents, other schools and the local community may be able to help here.)

4 What resources – staff, equipment, time – are involved?

5 Does anyone need to give their permission?

6 How are you going to record and report the outcomes?

7 Do staff need training?

8 Can you sustain the project within the staff, time and material resources available to you?

9 What sorts of partners are you looking for?

10 How are you going to find the partners?

11 How are you going to evaluate the outcomes?

Sites such as the Global School House (13) in the USA, OzTeacherNet (14) in Australia, European Schoolnet, and Internet Scuola in Italy (15) provide all three options. The Central Bureau for Exchanges and Visits may also be able to help (16). Table 1.4.3 provides advice about issues to consider when setting up such projects.

It is too early to predict the extent to which teaching processes are likely to change in response to the opportunities discussed above. In the UK at secondary level, change would accelerate if the examination boards incorporated ICT-based work into assessment requirements. Clearly pupils have to be taught skills of critical appraisal of material but good teachers will be doing this already. Issues related to plagiarism, as pupils download sections of text and incorporate these into assignments, are likely to be more problematic for teachers. Whilst teacherless classrooms are unlikely to occur, certainly the positive motivation which some learners feel when using technology is not to be under-estimated, but this does depend on the context for learning which the teacher establishes.

Task 1.4.4

EXPLORING THE POTENTIAL OF THE INTERNET TO SUPPORT THE WORK IN THE CLASSROOM

If you have not already done so, we suggest you take this opportunity to find out how teachers of your subject are using the internet to support teaching and learning. You may, for example, ask other teachers for ideas in a chat area. You may wish to undertake a general search for curriculum projects in your area using the TeacherNet site or the Virtual Teacher Centre. It may be of use to know that the term K-12 (kindergarten to year 12) is used on websites in the USA to refer to the years of compulsory schooling. Ideas are sometimes published on school websites. If you are going to be looking for jobs shortly it may be useful to explore the local education authority website for those areas in which you wish to work, as well as the inspection and league table information on maintained schools which is available on the DfES and OFSTED sites.

Task 1.4.5

USING ICT FOR ADMINISTRATION AND MONITORING

Schools and teachers use a variety of systems for recording, monitoring and analysing pupil progress and teacher effectiveness against targets, and predictions. Find out what systems are in use in the school in which you are placed and compare these, if possible, with those used in other schools. This information may be found by talking to teachers or student teachers from other schools.

SUMMARY AND KEY POINTS

In this unit, it has only been possible to touch on some of the classroom practice and professional development opportunities available through ICT. We recommend that you extend your understanding beyond the guidance here by reading more widely in this area, by experimenting with different types of software of particular use in your subject, by spending some time surfing the internet to identify high-quality resources and educational websites which are specifically relevant to your interests, and by talking to teachers and student teachers who are themselves exploring the possibilities offered by new technologies. Make sure you know what your subject association website offers.

However, it is important to remember that ICT use in the classroom should be directly related to the achievement of specified learning outcomes. As Cox (1999) points out, using ICT in your classroom provides no guarantee that learning takes place.

FURTHER READING

The subject-specific texts in the 'Learning to Teach in the Secondary School' series all contain chapters about the use of ICT (or IT) in the specific subject area. You may find further ideas for the application of ICT in your subject areas in these texts. The RoutledgeFalmer text *Learning to Teach using ICT in the Secondary School* (Leask and Pachler, 1999) provides detailed guidance, and the website linked to this book lists a number of sites recommended by the teachers and other contributors to the book.

BECTa (2000) *A Preliminary Report for the DfEE on the relationship between ICT and Primary School Standards*, Coventry: BECTa.
This report indicates that the use of ICT leads to higher pupil achievement in primary schools.

Collins, J., Hammond, M. and Wellington, J. (1997) *Teaching and Learning with Multimedia*, London: Routledge.
This book provides ideas for teachers in the use of multimedia.

Crook, C. (1994) *Computers and the Collaborative Experience of Learning*, London: Routledge.
A useful overview of the benefits of computer use.

Leask, M. (ed.) (2001) *Issues in Teaching with ICT*, London: RoutledgeFalmer.
   Issues related to the use of ICT for professional development and pedagogy are raised in this text.

Leask, M., Dawes, L. and Litchfield, D. (2000) *Keybytes for Teachers*, Evesham: Summerfield Publishing.
   This is a text and CD-ROM for teachers wishing to practise basic ICT skills.

Leask, M. and Pachler, N. (1999) *Learning to Teach using ICT in the Secondary School*, London: RoutledgeFalmer.
   This text provides an overview of the use of ICT in secondary schools.

National Council for Educational Technology (1994) *Information Technology Works! Stimulate to Educate*, Coventry: National Council for Educational Technology.

Papert, S. (1993) *The Children's Machine: Rethinking School in the Age of the Computer*, New York: Basic Books.

Papert, S. (1996) *The Connected Family: Bridging the Digital Generation Gap* (includes CD-ROM and web-site links), Atlanta, Ga.: Longstreet Press.
   Papert is one of the foremost thinkers about the use of computers with pupils.

Sandholtz, J.H., Ringstaff, C. and Dwyer, C.D. (1996) *Teaching with Technology: Creating Pupil-Centred Classrooms*, New York: Teachers College Press.
   This text sets out some of the challenges facing teachers in using ICT in classrooms.

Somekh, B. and Davis, N. (eds) (1997) *Using Information Technology Effectively in Teaching and Learning*, London: Routledge.
   This text provides useful guidance about ensuring that learning takes place when ICT is used.

Trend, R., Davis, N. and Loveless, A. (1999) *QTS Information Communication Technology*, London: Letts Educational.
   This text provides guidance for student teachers in England who have to demonstrate ICT competence.

Warren, A., Brunner, D., Maier, P. and Barnett, L. (1998) *Technology in Teaching and Learning: An Introductory Guide*, London: Kogan Page.
   This text provides detailed guidance on basic ICT terminology and use.

WEB ADDRESSES

Many of these web addresses have been recommended by Ed Baines, Glendon (Ben) Franklin, David Litchfield, Norbert Pachler and Christina Preston who all contributed to Leask and Pachler (1999). Their contribution is gratefully acknowledged.

1   The European Computer Driving Licence is supported by the British Computing Society and details can be found on http://www.bcs.org.uk/ecdl/
2   Hyperstudio is software which is very easy for pupils to use to produce multimedia presentations. Free demonstrations are available from TAG Developments Ltd, 25 Pelham Green, Gravesend, Kent DA11 0HU.
3   Specific information relating to special educational needs is scattered across the Web so a starting point that gathers many of them together is useful. Such a site is http://www.becta.org.uk/SENCO/. This site will lead you inevitably to the SENCO forum in the VTC. Further help and advice for teachers

working with gifted pupils can be obtained from the National Association for Gifted Children: http://www.rmplc.co.uk/orgs/nagc/. BECTA, formerly NCET, is at the Science Park, Milburn Park Road, Coventry. (Tel: 02476 416994).

4   See, for example, BECTA CD-ROM reviews available at http://www.becta.org.uk/info-sheets/cdrom.html

5   The British Educational Research Association provides access through websites to research papers from conferences around the world (http://www.bera.ac.uk). It is now common practice for papers presented at conferences to be put on the website so that, at the touch of a couple of buttons, you can find out the latest research news.

6   Searching through the news and media categories in the Yahoo search engines on the Web provides access to thousands of news sites around the world. Ones you may find useful include:

http://www.reuters.com
http://www.bigissue.com
http://www.telegraph.co.uk
http://www.guardian.co.uk

The BBC news site is excellent: http://www.bbc.co.uk. If you have Realplayer on your computer (available free from http://www.realplayer.com) you can access radio and video news of the day.

7   National Grid for Learning can be found on http://www/ngfl.gov.uk. The UK government-funded Virtual Teacher Centre can be found through the NGFL as can the DfEE and OFSTED websites.

8   The Teacher Training Agency (TTA) is at http://www.teach-tta.gov.uk

9   General Teaching Council: http://www.gtce.org.uk

10 Access to European http://www.field-guides.com/

11 Mirandanet is on http://www.mirandanet.com

12 TeacherNet (DfEE) is on http://www.teachernet.gov.uk. TeacherNet UK, an organisation lobbying for the coherent provision of internet resources for teachers, is on http://teachernetuk.org.uk

13 Global School House: http://www.gsh.org/. Projects are on http://www.gsh.org/pr/index.html

14 OzTeacherNet: http://www.owl.qut.edu.au/oz-teachernet.
Projects are on http://www.owl.qut.edu.au/oz-teachernet/projects/projects.html

15 Internet Scuola: http://www.quipo.it/internetscuola/homeing.html

16 See, for example, 'ePALS Classroom Exchange' available at http://epals.com/ and 'Windows on the Worlds' by the Central Bureau for Educational Visits and Exchanges available at
http://www.wotw.org.uk/

17 Scottish Consultative Council on the Curriculum electronic forum on Teaching for Effective Learning: http://claudius.sccc.ac.uk. Click on Forums.

Note: A new theory about how ICT is changing the process of teaching and learning is emerging as this book goes to press. The thoery is called 'communal constructivism' and in classrooms where teachers are employing a communal constructivist pedagogy, pupils will be drawing on the knowledge of different types of communities around the world to gain up-to-date relevant information. They will be publishing their work for other pupils to read and build on, for example, via the school intranet.

'Communal constructivism (is) an approach to learning in which students not only construct their own knowledge (Constructivism) as a result of interacting with their environment (Social Constructivism), but are also actively engaged in the process of constructing knowledge for their learning community'. (Holmes *et al.*, 2001, p. 1). See Leask, M., Ramos, J-L. and Younie, S. 'Communal Constructivist Theory, ICT pedagogy and internationalisation of the Curriculum', *Journal for IT in Teacher Education*, (forthcoming). See also Holmes, B., Tangney, B., Fitzgibbon, A., Savage, T. and Mehan, S. (2001) 'Communal Constructivism: students constructing learning for as well as with others', Society for IT in Education (SITE) 2001 conference proceedings.

CHAPTER 2 **BEGINNING TO TEACH**

The last chapter was concerned with the role and responsibilities of the teacher and how you might manage those. In this chapter, we look first at how you might learn from observing experienced teachers and then move on to consider aspects of planning and preparing lessons.

For most students there is a period during which you observe other teachers working, take part in team teaching and take part of a lesson before taking on a whole lesson. During this period, you use observation and critical reflection to build up your professional knowledge about teaching and learning and your professional judgement about managing learning. Unit 2.1 is therefore designed to focus your attention on how to observe the detail of what is happening in classrooms.

It is also difficult for a student teacher to become fully aware of the planning that underpins each lesson, as planning schemes of work (long-term programmes of work) is usually done by a team of staff over a period of time. The scheme of work then usually stays in place for some time. The extent of the actual planning for each lesson may also be hidden – experienced teachers often internalise their planning, so their notes for a lesson are brief in comparison with those that a student teacher needs. Unit 2.2 explains planning processes. Unit 2.3 combines much of the advice of the first two units in an analysis of the issues you probably need to be aware of before taking responsibility for whole lessons.

The quality of lesson planning is crucial to the success of a student teacher in enabling the pupils to learn. Defining clear and specific objectives for the learning in a particular lesson is one aspect of planning that many student teachers initially find difficult.

We hope that by the end of this chapter you will be able to plan lessons in which both you and the pupils know exactly what they are meant to be learning. Explicitly sharing your lesson objectives with pupils provides them with clear goals and potentially a sense of satisfaction from your lesson as they achieve the goals set. You can expect to find processes in place in most schools for the setting of personal targets for pupils.

UNIT 2.1 **READING CLASSROOMS**

TONY TURNER

INTRODUCTION

The following true story appears in 'Teachers' first encounters with their classes' (Wragg, 1984, pp. 62–75).

> A chemistry graduate once arrived at his school experience school in January. Before commencing his own teaching he watched a third year class's regular chemistry teacher take a double period of practical work. After a brief exposition delivered whilst seated on the front bench, one or two shared jokes and asides, the experienced chemistry teacher signalled the start of the practical phase with 'Right 3C you know what to do, so get the gear out and make a start.' The class dispersed quickly to the cupboards and far recesses for various pieces of equipment and an hour of earnest and purposeful experimental work ensued.
>
> The following week the chemistry graduate took the class himself and began by lolling on the front bench in imitation of the apparently effortless and casual manner he had witnessed only seven days earlier. After a few minutes of introduction he delivered an almost identical instruction to the one given by the experienced man the week before 'Right 3C, get the gear out and do the experiment.' Within seconds pupils were elbowing their fellows out of the way, wrestling each other for Bunsen burners, slamming cupboard doors. He spent most of the practical phase calling for less noise and reprimanding the many pupils who misbehaved.

The point of this story is that mimicry is an inadequate basis for building your own teaching style. By January of that academic year, this experienced teacher would have moulded the class to his own way of working. The pupils and teacher know how to respond to each other; they know the boundaries of behaviour and work within them, most of the time. What the student teacher had not seen was the process which had led to this situation. Consequently attempting to copy the practice of another, albeit successful, teacher failed because there was no shared background of expectation or understanding.

In this unit you are introduced to ways of observing other teachers at work and suggestions as to how to focus on some important teaching skills. You should take every opportunity throughout your school experience to watch teachers, focusing on your current needs. We hope this introduction gives you confidence to develop your own strategies for observation and encourages you to reflect on your own and others' practice. Monitor your progress in relation to the competences/standards for your course of initial teacher education. The series 'Learning to Teach (Subjects) in the Secondary School' gives you subject-specific support (see p. ii).

OBJECTIVES

Observing other teachers teach is an important part of developing your own teaching skills. This activity is needed by all teachers, student, newly qualified or experienced. At the end of this unit you should have:

- considered ways of observing teachers and pupils in classrooms with a purpose in mind;
- learned to recognise and record information from observations so that analysis can take place;
- gained some insights into the complex nature of teaching and learning;
- be aware of some advantages and limitations to methods of observing others teach;
- begun to evaluate your own teaching as well as that of others against the competences/standards expected for a newly qualified teacher.

In Unit 1.1 we asked the question 'What do teachers do?' In this unit we help you look for some answers.

OBSERVATION

Why observe?

The situation described in the introduction to this unit suggests that copying the good practice of other teachers is not the way to learn to teach. Observing experienced teachers informs your own teaching, especially if you observe skilful teachers, are able to identify practices and behaviours that are of use to you and can account for their success. The range of what counts as good teaching is wide, encompassing a variety of personalities, strategies and methods contributing to personal teaching style. You should endeavour to observe teachers from many subject areas in the course of your school experiences. Through observation, reflection, reading, experimentation and discussion with others about those activities, what it means for you to teach well emerges and develops. Observing other people do things you want to do yourself can be frustrating. Quite rightly the beginner wishes to get stuck in and learn how to do it 'on the job'. This is well and good but, although practice makes perfect, bad practice consolidates imperfection. It would be wise to watch competent teachers, alongside gaining 'hands-on' experience.

Observation is the act of looking with a purpose. Simply watching an activity may not tell you much about what is going on. Watching a sports event may give pleasure and excitement but you may not be able to say what factors contributed to the final result. Good commentators on sports events analyse the action and afterwards are able to offer an analysis of the performance of participants and their contribution to the result. Learning to observe is an important skill which is part of your professional repertoire. Observation activities are a necessary part of the transition from student teacher to experienced teacher and may help you to see classrooms and teachers as you haven't experienced them before.

Ways of observing

Observation can be conducted through a fly-on-the-wall approach or through direct involvement. These are referred to respectively as the **systematic approach** and the **participatory approach**. Both approaches yield valuable but different information about classroom events and behaviours.

The systematic observer has predetermined goals and criteria for identifying valid examples of the behaviours in which they are interested. The observer does not interact with the teacher or the pupil and so does not influence events (other than through her presence).

The participant observer has a less clear notion of what counts as evidence but seeks to collect information about many events in the classroom. He talks to pupils directly about what they are doing, he may be involved in discussion and even be part of the teaching arrangements. Such observers gain information about some pupils and the ways they respond to the teacher as well as insights into the many social interactions that occur. As in the systematic approach the observer gains knowledge of the content of the lesson. Analysis of the data is more difficult and the criteria on which validity of evidence is accepted emerge *after* the event. The participatory observer influences the data they collect. Systematic observers collect more quantitative evidence which can be analysed by psychometric methods. By contrast, participant observation generates largely qualitative evidence.

All observation develops descriptions of events, either holistic accounts arising from participatory involvement or focused accounts of particular events or practice in the classroom. The description of what happens is an important outcome of classroom observation. Without this knowledge analysis cannot take place.

Observing other teachers involves selecting, looking, listening, recording and analysing. You need to focus on events, strategies, responses or other circumstances of interest to you, observe those and then **do something** with the results. After evaluation, some of what you have seen, heard or concluded may be incorporated tentatively into your own teaching.

Observing other people's lessons is also about feelings: your own because of the task ahead of you; the teachers' because they are under scrutiny; and the pupils' because they are wondering what you are there for and what you might be like next week! The observer is observed.

What we see and hear we have to **interpret**. You are likely to be familiar with classrooms having spent many years of your life, literally hundreds of hours, in classrooms as pupil and student, and you have a good idea of what you think makes a good classroom. You are biased as a result of that experience, not a neutral observer nor one who necessarily brings a fresh eye to teaching. You may need to unlearn some of what you know about the classrooms of your adolescence and undergraduate days before you can start to understand today's secondary classrooms. Your experience was probably that of a successful learner, perhaps a keen learner, not a reluctant one. Like many other adults you feel that you know what good teaching is and how classes should be conducted. You may be right in your assumptions but many features of your background may have to be examined and their relevance re-assessed for teaching today's pupils in your classroom.

General preparation

Most observation takes place in classrooms, occasionally in a corridor, dining hall or outside. We suggest that before undertaking any observation you should:

1 obtain the agreement of the class teacher to attend her lesson;
2 tell her what data you plan to collect, why, and what you intend to do with it;
3 discuss with her how you plan to collect the data, and seek her advice;
4 discuss issues of confidentiality, e.g. that pupils and teacher not be named in any written report arising from your observations;
5 agree your role, as a participatory observer or as a systematic one (see above). The role of

systematic observer may be difficult to accomplish because you may see pupils needing help. One way forward is to decide to collect information for a set period about a particular event and then take part in the lesson as a helper. Alternatively you can agree to stand back from events throughout the whole lesson.

6 Identify, if you can, a time when you can talk with the class teacher about your data.

There are some obvious things you must check. You need to:

7 have pens, pencils, notebook, watch and any pro forma needed for recording information;
8 arrive about five minutes in advance to check seating, last-minute planning, etc.;
9 know where to sit or stand in the classroom;
10 have details of the class – see checklist at the top of Figure 2.1.1;
11 know what the lesson is about so that you can help pupils (if that has been agreed);
12 know which pupils you can talk to, when and for how long;
13 be willing to answer pupils' questions about yourself and why you are there.

It is important that immediately after the lesson you spend a little time recording additional information which explains events in the lesson and allows you to interpret the lesson some time after the event. List questions you need to ask the teacher. Trying to recall events several hours afterwards leads to uncertainty and even confusion. Finally, the observation of other teachers is designed to gain information and explanations to help your own teaching and not to provide material with which to criticise the teachers you observe.

OBSERVATION TASKS

Starting a lesson

At the start of school experience your main concerns may be whether you can stand in front of the class and have pupils listen to you, control their behaviour *and* remember enough of the subject matter to get through the lesson smoothly. Other skills, such as effective questioning and managing pupils with different abilities and attitudes, follow but are equally essential to developing good management skills, maintaining effective learning and motivating pupils. Before your first lesson you should observe your pupils being taught by their regular teacher. What might you look for in that lesson?

One of the first jobs of a teacher is to get the class into the room, settled and on to task as quickly as possible – the preparing and beginning phases of a lesson. How do different teachers do that? You need to prepare for this observation and plan systematically to monitor particular events; see Task 2.1.1.

Task 2.1.1

OBSERVING THE START OF A LESSON

You are about to observe a class being taught and it is one you haven't seen before. You know the teacher, having met her once already. Read through all sections of this task before embarking on it. In Unit 2.2 we discuss 'constructing a lesson' and 'beginnings to lessons' (pp. 72–75).

Preparing yourself

a **Write a list of questions** that interest you about how she will start the lesson. Do this on your own for about five minutes.

b If possible, **share your ideas** with another student teacher. Agree a set of questions – use about ten minutes for this exercise.

c **Categorise** the questions by using these features of beginning a lesson:

1 outside the classroom
2 entrance and settling
3 introducing the lesson

Your list may include the following questions:

- Were the children left outside until the teacher came or did they have entry without the teacher?
- Did they enter quietly, in silence or in what manner?
- Did the teacher stand at the door or did she start sorting out her own books and materials while the pupils came in?
- Do pupils have their own seats or do they sit anywhere?
- Do pupils bring bags and coats into the lesson? Where do they put them? Who organises this?
- Did the teacher take a register?
- How many pupils did the teacher speak to before the lesson started?
- Was it public conversation or was it small group/individual conversation?
- What was the talk about?
- At what point did the lesson begin? How did you know; what was the signal?
- At what point did the pupils know what the lesson was about?
- How long did it take for the lesson proper to start?

Plan how you are going to observe the class. Use the checklist under **general preparation** on pp. 52–53. The pro forma in Figure 2.1.1 may be helpful in planning how to record your data.

If you intend to observe the start of the lesson, beginning in the corridor outside the classroom, check where you can stand, decide whether you are going to write notes as you wait. It may be sensible to keep a mental note of these outside events and record them later inside the classroom.

Note: Once the lesson is under way you may wish to participate in the lesson, supporting the teacher. In this way you may supplement your earlier notes and gain new insights.

Making use of the data

Relate your data to the categories of questions 1–3 above.

1 How does the teacher deal with the pupils in the corridor outside the classroom and get them into the classroom? Compare your notes with those of other student teachers. For example:

- Did the pupils line up in silence and enter in a formal manner? Or was entry to the room a casual affair? How did the teacher gain quiet? What did she say? Was it something like 'come in 3B, bags on the side and stop chewing, Billy', or a more formal greeting? How will you expect your pupils to enter your classroom?

- Once in the classroom what did the teacher say to the class? Was it about the pupils themselves; about the work in hand; or about outside events? What atmosphere does she create?
- Was a register taken? Was registration used as a control exercise? Was talking allowed? Did this event mark the transition from the informal to the formal part of the lesson (i.e. when teaching began)? How will you use the registration time in your lessons?
- Were any pupils praised or reprimanded? What words or phrases were used for reprimand; for praise? List these remarks.
- How was the transition, moving from the informal phase of the lesson to the formal, handled? How did the pupils know when this change of focus took place? What was said or done? Was it change of language, voice or body language? Was it where the teacher stood?

2 What other issues arise from this observation task? Identify and record them for discussion with your tutor and other student teachers. Check what you have learned against the competences/standards for your course.

The flow of a lesson

It is sometimes helpful in the analysis stage to try to summarise the data. One way to do this is using a flow diagram. The start of a lesson may be summarised like this:

1 Class outside, talking quietly. The teacher in class organising resources. Comes outside to class.	2 Class told to go in, talking quietly and making friendly comment to teacher.	3 Teacher chats to some pupils as they enter, mainly about other events in school and outside school.
4 Note on board for pupils to copy while register is taken. Pupils get out books and begin writing.	5 Teacher reviews last lesson by question/answer. Writes key words on board.	6 Teacher outlines purpose of today's lesson, linking it to previous work.

Using your data, draw up your own sequence; annotate the diagram with your notes from the lesson. Discuss the flow of events with the class teacher and compare your observations with the teacher's view of the effectiveness of her actions and her reasons for them. Compare your 'start of a lesson' sequence with that of other student teachers.

Observer.............. Date............ Room..............

Class name............... Year group.............. Boys/girls/mixed..............

Class time(s) .... Teacher.............. Topic ....

real time	place	pupil actions	teacher action	pupil talk	teacher talk	notes

Figure 2.1.1 Classroom observation guide

Using other people's data

Information about classroom behaviour and practice can be gained quickly by visitors to a classroom, provided they are primed in advance and have a focus for their observation. In this example we consider gaining numeric information about an event.

An example of data collected by observation of teacher talk is shown in Figure 2.1.2. In the part of the lesson observed, the teacher was preparing pupils to carry out a practical task. The purpose of the observation task was to identify the number and type of oral interactions between pupils and teacher at the beginning of the lesson. Information was collected about who was talking and what the talk was about.

The data in Figure 2.1.2 show information gained by an observer over a period of twenty minutes by identifying, at one-minute intervals, who was talking and what they were talking about. This data represents a snapshot of a classroom and may, or may not, reflect the teacher's usual style of teaching.

Data from a twenty-minute period at the start of a lesson

Activity	Talking: who initiates?		Purpose of talk					
	Teacher	Pupil	Discipline	Give information	Seek information	Give instructions	Check understanding	Seek clarification
Total instances	15	2	2	8	3	0	1	0

Figure 2.1.2 Teacher–pupil interaction

Task 2.1.2

TEACHER–PUPIL TALK (see Figure 2.1.2)

What can you infer from the data about the way the lesson was set up? Use the following questions (or others of your choice) to interrogate the data.

- What is the talk about?
- Who initiates the talk?
- Who does the most talking?
- What is the nature of the talk?
- Comment on the length of the introduction.
- How would you judge the effectiveness of this part of the lesson? What further evidence would you need to collect?

When discussing your responses bear in mind the limited amount of information you have about the class, the teacher and the topic.

1 Discuss the nature and extent of pupil participation in the initiation of the lesson and how this might affect their motivation and learning.
2 How do the data in Figure 2.1.2 compare with your observation of teachers in similar circumstances?
3 Consider the occasions or circumstances when this teaching approach could be used.

Check the outcomes of this task against the competences/standards for your course.

MOVING ON: MORE OBSERVATIONS

How might the technique used in Task 2.1.2 be used to gather different information about classrooms? Some suggestions are given below. Identify the objectives of your task and agree them with the class teacher. Draw up an observation schedule for yourself. Decide if you plan to be a systematic observer or to collect evidence while you support the class teacher. Keep notes of events which allow you to interpret your findings. After the observation period share your information with the class teacher. He may be very interested in your data and may be able to help explain some observations. You may find *Classroom Observation* (King, 1996) helpful in designing your observation tasks.

Transitions between phases of lessons

Lessons often contain three to four discrete activities or phases. How does the teacher:

- decide when to move from one phase to the next?
- signal this change of activity?
- deal with pupils who are not ready to move on?
- signal awareness to those pupils ready to move on?
- maintain pupils on task?
- limit the amount of time used to effect the transition?
- ensure most pupils understand (rather than just complete) the work?

On-task talk

Listen to pupil conversation in class and find out:

- the time they spend talking to each other;
- the time given to 'on task' talk;
- the nature of the on-task talk; is it about procedure (how) or about ideas or concepts (what or why);
- if pupils understand what they are doing and why they are doing it;
- which pupils, if any, have no conversations?

Closing down a lesson

Observe an end-of-lesson phase in which the teacher is bringing together what has been learned. You may find that this information is best gained by standing back from events and recording systematically. Gather information about:

- how a summary of learning is brought together. Is it by telling, by discussion, by questioning or in other ways?
- who makes the summary and how it is recorded;
- who did most of the talking in the summary phase of the lesson;
- how the teacher checked if pupils had learned anything;
- evidence that learning has taken place;

- the match between the aims of the lesson and what was learned;
- homework and how it relates to the lesson content.

Where is the teacher during a lesson?

The movement of teachers in the classroom may say a lot about their relationship with pupils and how they keep an eye on pupil activity and behaviour. See Task 2.1.3.

Task 2.1.3

TEACHER MOVEMENT

Draw an 'A4 map' of the classroom in which you are observing. Mark on it key points: teacher's desk, pupils' desks, blackboard, overhead projector, etc. Have several copies of the map available. Throughout the lesson mark on your map where the teacher stands and where she has moved from. Do this at regular intervals, e.g. one-minute, and so build up a picture of position and movement. At the same time record the time and what is going on in the lesson, which enables you to interpret teacher movement (King, 1996, p. 21). Analyse your map to see:

- where the teacher is most likely to be found during the lesson. Explain the teacher's movements in terms of her actions and pupil activity;
- the purpose of movement. Is it to encourage work or to maintain discipline?
- whether any pupils were off-task for most of the lesson and if the teacher was aware of the situation;
- whether some pupils were given more attention than others;
- how the teacher keeps an eye on all the events in the room.

Share your information with other student teachers. Does the nature of the subject or the topic dictate teacher movement? What differences might you expect between teachers of different subjects? Or are the differences related more to individual teaching styles?

Check the competences/standards for your course.

Some experienced teachers can control some pupils by eye contact or a raised eyebrow and do not need to be physically close to the pupil. A few teachers keep pupils at a distance and sometimes use their desk or equipment as a barrier between themselves and the pupils, especially if they lack confidence. Sometimes we use body language to distance ourselves from others, such as folding our arms in front of us.

Investigating the displays in classrooms

A feature of some schools is the lively, attractive displays of children's work, from a project, a school event or classwork. What advantages does displaying pupils' work have for the teacher? Discuss with other student teachers the advantages of this practice. It is prominent in primary schools, less so in secondary schools. Why might this be so? The best work often greets you in the foyer as you enter the school. Are the classrooms equally as attractive? See Task 2.1.4.

Task 2.1.4

WHAT DO CLASSROOMS LOOK LIKE?

What is the impression classrooms convey as you look about you? Pupils spend most of their time in classrooms and this may affect the way they view and value what is taught in them. In this activity try to find out what is visible in the room, what it is for, and if, and how, it supports teaching and learning.

What to do

You need several sheets of plain A4 paper, folded to make two facing A5 pages. Draw a rectangle on one side, leaving a margin of 2–4 cm at the edges. On this side sketch one wall and mark on the diagram what is on the wall. In the margin of the sketch add other points of interest such as general decorative order, plants, aquarium, statue, notice-board. Annotate the sketch on the facing A5 side, to help interpret what you see. Repeat for as many walls as you have time for. For each item consider the following features:

origin	other teachers, class teacher, pupil, commercial, other
purpose	decoration, relevant to lesson, left over from previous lessons, information, e.g. fire exit, purpose not clear
is it looked after?	new, old, dusty, defaced, tatty and soiled (check dates)
attractively presented?	yes, no, care taken, colourful, eye-catching
been there ages?	yes, no, can't tell
technical?	name it, does it look used?
made reference to?	yes, no, not sure
notice board	does it have notices? recent? for pupils? for other teachers?
safety/conduct	purpose clear, obscure, clear instructions
language used	suitable for school use? Does the item recognise English second language or special educational needs pupils?

What to do with the observations

Share your findings with other student teachers in your school or higher education institution and together discuss the image of the school revealed by this information. Discuss your findings in terms of:

- who 'owns' the classroom and who teaches in there;
- what encouragement the classroom environment gives to pupils to learn (to look, read, engage, play, interact);
- the cultural diversity of the school;
- how images of boys and girls are portrayed;
- valuing of pupils' work.

Is the rest of the school like this classroom? Several student teachers could, as a group, study other rooms and areas of your school. **A short report could be made for the school**; check with your school tutor about the best way to do this.

TEACHERS' QUESTIONS

Types of questions

A characteristic of teachers is to ask questions; they are, it seems, forever probing pupils' knowledge and understanding. But what types of questions do teachers ask and what is their focus? Are the questions about management, behaviour, factual recall, understanding or something else? What proportion of teachers' questions are about thinking and understanding? Is the focus of questioning about learning? Recent research into the questions asked by primary teachers showed that 57 per cent of questions were about management, 35 per cent about recall of information, and 8 per cent about higher-order thinking (Wragg, 1993). We suggest you find out how many questions teachers ask in a lesson and then try to classify them. Suggestions for classifying them appear in Task 2.1.5. We discuss 'questioning' in Unit 3.1 'Communicating with pupils'; see Task 3.1.4. A short but useful discussion on 'asking questions' is given by Kyriacou in Desforges, 1995, p. 124.

Task 2.1.5

TEACHERS' QUESTIONS

Investigate in a systematic way the types of questions used by a class teacher. Observe a lesson and every time the teacher asks a question record it and categorise it as one of three types:

1   about management, control and behaviour;
2   requiring simple recall of factual information, about subject or procedure;
3   inviting opinion, speculation, analysis of data given in words or diagrammatically, or answers requiring recognition of acceptable alternatives.

Questions that demand a type 2 response are often **closed questions** to which there is one right answer, or a specific answer the teacher wants. Questions which require a type 3 response are often more **open-ended** and require the pupil to think about the topic more deeply, i.e. involve higher-order skills.

Draw up a grid like that in Figure 2.1.3.

Collect data for the first 15–20 minutes and analyse that. Then continue the exercise again later when the teacher is, for example, drawing the lesson together at the end, summarising learning.

Which type of question is asked most frequently? Explain the number and type of questions asked in relation to the nature of the lesson. Discuss the nature of the learning going on in the class as revealed by the types of questions used and answers received.

Check the competences/standards for your course in relation to questioning.

Pupil ability and open questions

Teachers sometimes explain that open questions involving higher-order thinking can only be used with higher-performing pupils. The implication is perhaps that lower-performing pupils, especially many with special educational needs, cannot use higher-order thinking. This suggestion has strong implications for the way teachers use questions in mixed ability classes. What evidence

Time/min.	Type of question		
	Type 1 Management	Type 2 Recall	Type 3 Open
0–1			
1–2			
2–3			

Figure 2.1.3 Monitoring teachers' questions

Acknowledgement: Chris Kettle.

is there that teachers do not use higher-order questioning with lower-performing classes or pupils? Devise a way of investigating this assertion in your school.

Recently, attention has been focused on the development of 'thinking skills' in pupils as part of the government's drive to raise standards. All teachers teaching the National Curriculum in England and Wales from 1999 onwards are expected to promote a number of generic skills in their curriculum subject, including a range of 'thinking skills' (DfEE/QCA,1999a, pp. 23–24). This development has been, in part, activated by the Cognitive Acceleration in Science Project (CASE) (Adey and Shayer, 1994). CASE has provided evidence that radical intervention by teachers in the curriculum to stimulate pupils' thinking skills has had lasting, beneficial effects on pupil achievement both in and beyond science lessons. In many cases pupil performance in GCSE English and mathematics has shown marked increases, as well as in science. The findings suggest that if pupils are given the right mental stimulation they can achieve higher levels of performance than at first thought. Appropriate questioning is part of developing pupils' thinking.

How do teachers respond to pupils' answers?

Do they accept only correct answers and how do they respond to incorrect answers? The classroom is a public place and pupils can be wary of responding if they are unsure of their answer. Many pupils are reluctant to risk the embarrassment of a wrong answer. How do teachers encourage pupils to answer questions or volunteer information?

By using structured observation of a class, identify the ways in which the teacher responds to pupils' answers.

Asking questions

How long does the teacher wait for an answer? Research in the United States has shown that the 'wait time' – the time spent after asking a question before the teacher intervenes – is one second (Rowe, 1972). More recently, research has provided evidence that allowing pupils adequate 'wait time' leads to better-quality answers, especially if the questions are of the open kind (Cruikshank, 1990); see type 3 questions in Task 2.1.5. The older research may be a comment on the dominant type of question asked by the American teachers on those occasions.

Devise a way of recording the time period elapsing between the teacher asking a question and expecting an answer. Does the period depend on the type of question asked, e.g. open or closed (see Task 2.1.5 above)? What does the 'wait time' tell you about the sort of thinking needed by pupils to answer the question?

How much involvement with the teacher does a pupil have during a lesson?

This feature of teaching can be measured by how much time is actually spent by the teacher in personal contact with any one pupil. It has been reported that primary teachers spend, on average, 56 per cent of their time reacting with individual pupils (Cockburn, in Desforges, 1995, p. 78). In a class of thirty pupils this reduces to quite a short period of time. Thus, during a five-hour day, the teacher may spend all together about five minutes with any individual child. This situation may apply equally to pupils in secondary school, where pupils may see four or five different teachers a day. If the transactions are largely about management, how much 'quality time' is spent on promoting learning?

Task 2.1.6

PUPIL–TEACHER CONTACT TIME

Devise a way of finding out:

- which pupils answer the teacher's questions and how long that contact is;
- on how many other occasions the pupil has the personal attention of the teacher, and for how long.

Discuss with other student teachers the implications of your findings, if any, for:

- individual pupil learning;
- any particular group of pupils;
- the role of the teacher in promoting learning.

SUMMARY AND KEY POINTS

Observation is a research exercise. Research enables you to gather data on teacher behaviour, action and performance and pupil learning. The type of observation you undertake affects the nature of the information you get. Systematic observation, standing back from events, and participant observation, being part of the unfolding events, are two ways to collect information.

By analysing your data, you can begin to identify factors that contribute to effective teaching and learning, and so place them in the framework of your own emerging skills. Analysis, however, has to consider the background and viewpoint of the observer and try to detect any bias. Discussion with your tutor and other student teachers helps that process.

Observing other teachers working should be a continuing exercise; as your own teaching develops you need to refine and widen your skills, and observing others with purpose can aid your development. The checklist of competences/standards for your course and, later, those required of newly qualified teachers are useful ways to monitor that development.

This unit has introduced you to some features of classroom observation and addressed a small number of topics. We have not addressed all the skills needed by teachers and we suggest that you adapt and modify these approaches to meet your individual needs – for example, managing disruptive pupils, organising practical activities, using a visual aid to support teaching or the internet to support learning. The art of explaining has not been addressed in this unit but is referred to in Unit 3.1 'Communicating with pupils'; see Task 3.1.3. The further reading section at the end of this unit may help you to plan other investigations of interest to you and draws attention to the value of research in improving teaching skills and pupil learning.

FURTHER READING

Hopkins, D. (1993) *A Teacher's Guide to Classroom Research* (2nd edn), Buckingham: Open University Press.
Contains practical ideas for teachers wanting to investigate their own classroom practice.

King, S. (1996) *Classroom Observation*, London: Institute of Education, University of London. A booklet in the series 'Occasional Papers in Teacher Education and Training', available from Academic Services, Initial Teacher Education, Institute of Education, University of London, 20 Bedford Way, London WC1H OAL.
Observing others teaching is not an instinctive skill but one that can be learned. Ways for the student teacher to observe are discussed with detailed examples. There is a substantial section in support of tutors observing student teachers.

Stoll, L. and Fink, D. (1996) *Changing our Schools*, Buckingham: Open University Press. See 'Teachers as learners', particularly pp. 152–157.
The authors provide a discussion about the role of teachers in the 'learning community' and the need for teachers to be learners throughout their teaching career.

Wragg, E. (1994) *An Introduction to Classroom Observation*, London: Routledge.
Contains useful perspectives on life in the classroom and how to record and analyse observational data, with evidence from in-depth research of classrooms.

UNIT 2.2 SCHEMES OF WORK AND LESSON PLANNING

MARILYN LEASK AND JON DAVISON

INTRODUCTION

Our lesson observations revealed that in classes run by effective teachers, pupils are clear about what they are doing and why they are doing it. They can see links with their earlier learning and have some ideas about how it could be developed further. The pupils want to know more.

(Hay McBer, 2000: para. 1.2.4)

If your time with the pupils is to be used effectively, you need to plan carefully for each lesson – taking account of how pupils learn, the requirements of the curriculum, the most appropriate methods of teaching the topic and the resources available as well as the evaluations of previous lessons.

There are two levels of planning particularly appropriate to your work in the classroom – the scheme of work and the lesson plan. Examples of lesson plans are available on the web – for example, on the sites listed in the introduction to Chapter 1, p. 6. You will quickly gain experience of planning as you plan lessons and schemes of work on your school experience. However, planned activities do not have to be followed through rigidly and at all costs. Because planning is integrally linked to evaluation and development, evaluation of plans for a specific situation may point to the need to change or develop your plans.

OBJECTIVES

By the end of this unit you should be able to:

- explain what is meant by the terms, 'aims', 'objectives', 'progression', 'differentiation';
- construct schemes of work (also known as programmes or units of work);
- construct effective lesson plans.

Check the competences/standards for your course which relate to lesson planning and schemes of work to make sure you understand what is required of you.

PLANNING WHAT TO TEACH

What should you teach and how should you teach it?

The factors influencing what should be taught (lesson content) are discussed in Unit 1.1, but how much you teach in each lesson and how you teach it (teaching methods) are the teacher's own decisions.

Lesson content

Recall the 'sabre-toothed curriculum' of the Stone Age and the 'queen of studies' from medieval times (Unit 1.1). Similarly, the knowledge, skills, understanding and attitudes appropriate for a young person entering the world of work in the twenty-first century are vastly different from those that were considered appropriate even fifteen years ago. Ideas about what teachers should teach change regularly and the curriculum is under constant scrutiny by those responsible for education.

As a student teacher, you are usually given clear guidelines about what to teach and the goals for pupils' learning within your subject. These goals are in part usually set out in government-produced documents, e.g. the National Curriculum documents, school documents and syllabuses prepared by examination boards. If you teach in England and Wales, you need to become familiar with the National Curriculum requirements and the terminology (see Chapter 7). However, before you plan individual lessons you need an overall picture of what learning is planned for the pupils over a period of time. This overall plan is called a scheme of work and most departmental schemes of work cover between half a term's work and a couple of years' work.

Teaching methods

However constraining the guidelines on content are, the decision about which teaching methods to use is usually yours. As you become more experienced as a teacher, you acquire your own personal approach to teaching. But as people learn in different ways and different teaching methods are suitable for different types of material, you should become familiar with a range of ways of structuring learning experiences in the classroom. For example, you might choose to use discussion, rote learning, discovery learning, role play and so on to achieve particular objectives. Chapter 5 gives you detailed advice on teaching styles and strategies appropriate to different approaches to learning.

Task 2.2.1

HOW DO YOU LEARN?

Spend a few minutes making notes of the methods that you use to help you learn and the methods of teaching used by teachers from whom you felt you had learned a lot. Then make notes about those situations from which you did not learn. Compare these notes with those of other student teachers. People learn in different ways and different areas of learning require different approaches. You need to take account of such differences in planning your lessons, and to demonstrate that you can use a range of teaching methods in order to take account of such differences.

SCHEMES OF WORK AND LESSON PLANS

There are two main stages to planning for pupil learning:

1 Preparing an outline of the work to be covered over a period – the scheme of work.
2 Planning each individual lesson – the lesson plan.

A number of formats for both schemes of work and lesson plans are in use. We suggest you read the advice given for the teaching of your subject in the subject-specific texts in this 'Learning to Teach' series. However, whilst the level of detail may vary between different approaches, the purpose is the same – to provide an outline of the work to be done either over an extended period (scheme of work) or in the lesson (lesson plan) so that the planned learning can take place. Try different approaches to planning in order to find those most appropriate to your situation. The best plans are ones which support you in your teaching so that your pupils learn what you intend them to learn. The illustrations in this unit are intended to provide examples with which you can work and later modify.

The scheme of work

This might also be called the 'programme of work' or the 'unit of work'. Different terms may be used in your school or in your subject but the purpose is the same – to devise a long-term plan for the pupils' learning. So a scheme of work sets out the long-term plans for learning and thus covers an extended period of time – this could be a period of years, a term or half a term, or weeks, e.g. for a module of work. A scheme of work should be designed to build on the learning that has gone before, i.e. it should ensure continuity of pupil learning.

Schemes of work should be designed to ensure that the knowledge, skills, capabilities, understanding and attitudes of the pupils are developed over a particular period in order to ensure progression in learning. The term 'progression' means the planned development of knowledge, skills, understanding or attitudes over time. In some departments, the schemes of work are very detailed and include teaching materials and methods as well as safety issues.

Using a scheme of work

Usually, you are given a scheme of work. In putting this together, the following questions have been considered:

1 What are you trying to achieve? (Aims for the scheme of work and objectives for particular lessons – see the definitions in the numbered paragraphs below.)
2 What has been taught before?
3 How much time is available to do this work?
4 What resources are available?
5 How is the work to be assessed?
6 How does this work fit in with work pupils are doing in other subjects?
7 What is to be taught later?

The scheme itself may be quite brief (Figure 2.2.1 shows a pro forma used by student teachers on one course) but it will be based on the above information. Each of these areas is now discussed in turn. To start with, think about what learning should be taking place.

1 What are you trying to achieve? The aims of a scheme of work are general statements about the learning that should take place over a period.

Objectives are specific statements which set out what pupils are expected to learn from a particular lesson in a way that allows you to identify if learning has occurred. Objectives are prepared for each lesson and further detail is included under lesson planning later in this unit.

Scheme of work for x topic

Area of work			Ref:

Class	No. in class	Age	Key stage
No. of lessons	Duration	Dates	

Aims (from the National Curriculum programmes of study)

(Objectives are listed in each lesson plan)

Framework of lessons	NC reference

Assessment strategies

Other notes (safety points)

Figure 2.2.1 Scheme of work pro forma

In devising each scheme of work a small aspect of the whole curriculum has been taken and a route planned through this which provides the best opportunities for pupils to learn. Progression in pupil learning should be considered and built into schemes of work.

2 What has been taught before? This information should be available from school documentation and from staff. In the case of pupils in their first year of secondary education, there is usually a member of staff responsible for liaising with primary schools who may have this information.

3 How much time is available to do this work? The length of lessons and the number of lessons devoted to a topic are decided by the department or school in which you are working. Don't forget that homework has a valuable role to play in enhancing learning and that not all the lessons you expect to have are available for teaching. Some time is taken up by tests, revision, fire drill, special events, lateness.

4 What resources are available? Resources include material resources as well as human resources, and what is available depends on the school where you are working. You need to find out the procedures for using resources in the school and what is available. You may find there are resources outside the school to draw upon – parents, governors and charities. Many firms provide schools with speakers on current topics. There may be field studies centres or sports facilities nearby. You need to check if there are any safety issues to consider when choosing appropriate resources.

5 How is the work to be assessed? Teaching, learning and assessment are interlinked. Most of the work you are doing with pupils is teacher-assessed, although some is assessed by outside agencies. A main purpose of teacher assessment is formative – to check pupils' progress, e.g. in relation to lesson objectives. In any case, you should keep good records of the pupils' progress (homework, classwork, test results) in your own record book as well as providing these in the form required by the school or department. Chapter 6 focuses on assessment issues.

Task 2.2.2

RECORD KEEPING AND ASSESSMENT

Ask staff in your department how they expect pupil assessment records to be kept and what forms of assessment you should use for the work you are doing.

---

6 How does this work fit in with work the pupils are doing in other subjects? There are many areas of overlap where it is useful to discuss the pupils' work with other departments. For instance, if pupils are having difficulty with measurement in technology, it is worth checking if and when the mathematics department teaches these skills and how they teach them. Cross-curricular dimensions to the curriculum (see Units 7.2 and 7.3) will have been considered by the school and responsibilities for different aspects shared out among departments. Ask staff in your department what responsibilities the department has in this area.

7 What is to be taught later? *Progression* in pupil learning has to be planned for and a scheme of work has to be drawn up for this purpose. From this scheme of work you know what work is to come and the contribution to pupil learning that each lesson is to make.

Task 2.2.3

DRAWING UP A SCHEME OF WORK

In consultation with your tutor, draw up a scheme of work to last about six to eight lessons. Focus on one particular class you are teaching. Use the format provided for your course (or the one we provide in Figure 2.2.1) or one which fits in with the planning methods used in the department.

The lesson plan

The lesson plan provides an outline of one lesson within a scheme of work. In planning a lesson, you are working out the detail required to teach one aspect of the scheme of work. To plan the lesson you use a framework and an example of a lesson planning framework, is given in Figure 2.2.2.

Date: . . . . Class: . . . .

Area of work: . . . .

Aim: . . . .

Objectives: . . . .

. . . .

Time	Teacher activity	Pupil activity	Notes/Equipment needed
0–5 min	Class enter and settle	Coats and bags put away	
5–10 min	Homework discussed/ recap of work so far/task set/new work explained		
10–25 min	Teacher supports groups/individuals	Pupils work in individual groups to carry out the task	
. . . and so on			
Ending	Teacher summarises key points/sets homework		

Evaluation: Were objectives achieved? What went well? What needs to be addressed next time? How are individuals responding?

Figure 2.2.2 Planning a lesson: one possible approach

The following information is required for you to plan effectively.

1 Overall aim(s) of the scheme of work and the specific objectives for this lesson. Defining objectives which clarify exactly what learning you hope will take place is a crucial skill for the effective teacher. It helps you to be clear about exactly what the pupils should be achieving and it helps the pupils understand what they should be doing. However, drawing up effective objectives requires thought.

At this stage in your career, if you ensure that your lesson objectives focus on what should be achieved from the lesson in terms of pupils' learning, then you have made a good start. Listing objectives after the following phrase

By the end of this lesson, pupils will be able to . . .

may help you to devise clear goals and to understand the difference between aims (general statements) and objectives (specific goals).

Words that help you be precise are those such as **state, describe, list, identify, prioritise, solve, demonstrate an understanding of**. These words force you to write statements which can be tested. If you think your objectives are vague, ask yourself whether the objective makes it clear what the pupils must do to achieve it. When you tell the pupils what your objectives are, do they understand what is expected of them? Objectives may be related to **knowledge, concepts, skills, behaviours and attitudes**.

Task 2.2.4

WRITING OBJECTIVES

There is different terminology in use – some people refer to behavioural objectives, some to learning objectives. These are the same things and they refer to the observable outcomes of the lesson, i.e. to what pupils are expected to be able to do. Discuss the writing of objectives with other student teachers and your tutor. Choose a particular lesson and, as a group, devise appropriate objectives which relate to changes in pupils' learning or behaviour. Pay particular attention to the quality and type of objectives you are setting – are they focused on the pupils' learning?

---

2 Range of abilities of the pupils As you develop as a teacher, you are expected to incorporate differentiation into your planning. This refers to the need to consider pupils' individual abilities when work is planned, so that both the brightest pupils and those with lesser ability are challenged and extended by the work. Differentiation can be achieved in different ways depending on the material to be taught. Differentiation may, for example, be achieved by outcome, i.e. different types or qualities of work may be produced, or by task, i.e. different tasks may be set for pupils of differing abilities. (Unit 4.1 provides further information.) You provide continuity of learning for the pupils by taking account of and building on their existing knowledge, skills, capabilities and attitudes.

3 Time available On the examples of a lesson plan provided (see Figure 2.2.2), a time line is drawn on the left-hand side. If you refer to this in the lesson, you are quickly able to see if it is necessary to adapt the original plan to fit the time available.

4 Resources available Staff usually go out of their way to help students have the appropriate resources. But don't forget that others may be needing them, so ask in good time for the resources you require. Check how resources are reserved in your department.

5 Approaches to classroom management These should be suitable to the topic and subject (see Chapters 3 and 4).

6 Teaching strategies and the learning situation These should be set up as appropriate to the work being covered (see Chapter 5). Explaining and questioning are two key skills which you should work to improve. It is a good idea to write out questions in advance which you may want to use to test the pupils' grasp of the topic and which develop thinking. Phrasing appropriate questions is a key skill for a teacher (Unit 3.1 has further details).

7 Assessment methods Decide which ones to use in order to know whether your objectives have been achieved (see Chapter 6).

8 Any risks associated with the work Safety is an important issue in schools. In some subjects, the assessment of risk to the pupils and incorporation of strategies to minimise this risk are a necessary part of the teacher's planning. Departmental and national guidelines are provided to ensure the safety of the pupils and should be followed. Student teachers should consult their head of department or tutor for guidance on safety issues. If you are in doubt about an activity and you cannot discuss your worries with the class teacher or your tutor, do not carry out the activity.

9 What do the pupils know now? As your experience of the curriculum and of pupils' learning develops, you will find it easier to answer this question. You need to consider what has been taught before as well as the experience outside school which pupils might have had. It may be appropriate to do some form of testing or analysis of knowledge, skills and understanding, or to have a discussion with pupils to discover their prior experience and attitudes to the work in question. As a student teacher you should seek advice from the staff who normally teach your classes.

Lessons have a structure and a rhythm to them. As you read this next section, think about the overall pattern to a lesson and the skills you use at each stage.

Constructing a lesson

Initially, you might find it difficult to see exactly how teachers manage their classes. In order to help you see the underlying structure of a lesson, we have divided the lesson and its planning into five key stages:

- preparation;
- beginning;
- moving on;
- ending;
- evaluation.

Figure 2.2.3 illustrates this rhythm. Each stage is discussed below.

Preparation

The most successful lessons are thoroughly planned and structured beforehand, and you manage a class more effectively if you carefully consider how to organise yourself and the pupils beforehand.

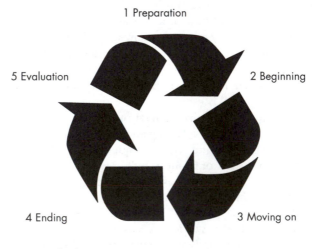

Figure 2.2.3 The structure of a lesson

Acknowledgement: Chris Kettle

Task 2.2.5

PLANNING AND GIVING LESSONS

As you read about the five stages of a lesson, make notes in your diary to remind you of key points to pay attention to when you are planning and giving lessons. Unit 2.3 provides more details.

Make sure you have enough of the necessary materials, equipment and resources. Know the exact number of the items you are using so that you know if something has been lost and can take steps to find it immediately. Most departments have developed their own systems of stock control – e.g. a useful technique for textbooks is to number them and, when you give them to pupils, record the textbook number in your mark book.

Ensure that you know how to operate any equipment you plan to use (e.g. television monitors, videos, computers or subject-specific equipment) and that it is in working order. If you are carrying out a science experiment, you should do it yourself before the lesson. This enables you to anticipate problems pupils might encounter.

Plan a variety of appropriate teaching and learning activities (see Chapter 5). Remember, the concentration span of adults is about twenty minutes and that of most pupils is shorter. Plan extra, related activities in case your chosen approach does not work or pupils complete tasks more quickly than you anticipate.

Give advance warning to pupils of any books, materials, etc. that they need for the lesson. If you have asked them to collect particular items or materials, don't rely on them remembering – bring enough yourself in order for the lesson to proceed, just in case, or have alternative plans.

Beginning

A good beginning is a crucial part of a successful lesson as it sets the tone, motivates pupils and establishes your authority. There are a number of key points to be kept in mind when you think about beginning your lessons.

Be in the classroom before the pupils arrive and ensure equipment is ready. Undoubtedly, the school you are in has established rules about pupil movement around the school and entry to classrooms. However, in the lower years in particular, it is common to line up pupils outside your teaching room and to usher them inside in an orderly manner.

Settle the class as quickly as possible and ensure that all pupils are facing you – even when they are seated in groups around tables – and are listening in silence before you begin the lesson. Do not begin the lesson when any pupil is talking, but wait calmly, confidently and expectantly for quiet. You will get it! Do not press on until you have established quiet. It is worth taking the time to do so.

Class management is much easier when you know the pupils by name. So make a determined effort to learn their names as quickly as possible. It does not happen by osmosis, so you have to work at it. Seating plans are useful, as is the practice, in the early stages, of asking pupils to raise their hands when you register them. Although it might appear time-consuming, giving out exercise books to pupils individually quickly allows you to put a face to a name.

If you are unable to address pupils by name, address them by their class/form designation. For example, 'Right 7G, I want everyone looking this way.' This is far better than 'Right girls/boys/ladies/lads, etc.' Never resort to 'Oi you, blondie!' or some equally unprofessional outburst.

Similarly, impersonations of deflating a balloon through continued 'Sshh-sshh-ing' do nothing to enhance your authority.

Pupils like to know what is expected of them. They relax and have a far more positive approach if you explain what you plan to do in the lesson, with a brief rationale of how it fits in with previous and future work, and if you let them know what you want them to achieve in the lesson.

Establish a crisp, but not rushed, pace from the beginning. Never stand in one place in the room for more than a matter of a few minutes. Some teachers suggest that, as a student teacher, you don't sit at the teacher's desk during the lesson except *in extremis*. Use eye contact, vary the pace and tone of your voice (see Unit 3.1) and monitor pupil reaction continually.

Moving on

Smooth, seamless transitions between one part of the lesson and the next are vital if there is to be overall continuity and coherence. Having introduced the lesson, you need to explain the purpose of the first (and thereafter any subsequent) pupil task. Be very clear about what you want the pupils to do and tell them exactly how long they are to spend on the activity. They then have an idea of the pace they need to work at and how much you expect them to 'produce', and what quality of work you require.

Before they begin the activity, check that all pupils understand exactly what they are expected to do. Deal with any queries before the class begins work. This saves endless repetition of the task to individuals.

Have a definite routine for distributing books and materials. Will you give out equipment? Will pupils come out to collect it row by row, table by table? Will one pupil per table/row collect it? In any event, it is essential that this activity is carried out in a controlled and orderly manner in any classroom. Moreover, if you are teaching a physical education or science subject, the safety aspect of this area of class management is of vital importance.

When the pupils are engaged in the activity, move around the room monitoring pupil progress and dealing with questions; but do not interfere unnecessarily. Let them get on with the task. Effective class management depends upon your active involvement. Key skills are: circulation; monitoring progress; the use of proximity to pupils; sensitivity to, and awareness of, pupil needs. Even when the whole class is engaged in a task, it is rarely appropriate to sit at the teacher's desk and 'switch off'.

Give one or two minutes' warning of the end of the activity. Be vigilant about keeping to the time limit you imposed at the beginning of the activity. Do not let things 'slide'. Be aware that not every pupil will finish the task set. Use your judgement in assessing whether, while a few may not have finished within your deadline, most are ready for the next stage. If, however, it becomes clear that the whole class needs longer than you anticipated for an activity, be flexible enough to adjust your planning.

At the end of the activity, settle the class and expect all pupils to be sitting quietly, facing you, before you proceed to the next stage of the lesson. Be sure to maintain your businesslike manner and the crisp pace you established earlier.

Ending

It is important that any learning experience is rounded off, so that pupils experience a sense of completion. Similarly, pupils need some mental space between lessons. They need to 'come down' from one lesson in order to prepare themselves for the next. Remember, depending upon the timetable, pupils may need to negotiate the conceptual intricacies of between four and eight subjects in a day. Your lesson, therefore, needs to be completed in an organised manner.

Plan enough time at the end of the lesson to: sum up what has been achieved; set homework where appropriate; give a brief idea of what the next lesson will comprise and (if necessary) explain what pupils need to bring to it.

As with the distribution of materials (see the section on 'Beginning'), have a definite, orderly routine for collection.

Before pupils leave, make sure the classroom is neat and tidy, and remember that the pips or bell are signals for you, not the pupils. Dismiss the pupils by table or row and ensure that they leave the room in a quiet, controlled fashion. Enforcing a quiet orderly departure also adds to the pupils' experience of the standards you expect, i.e. that your classroom provides an orderly and calm learning environment. Take a well-earned ten-second breather before beginning the whole process again with the next class!

Evaluation and planning future lessons

As soon as you can after the lesson, evaluate its success. What went well? What didn't go well? What evidence do you have which allows you to answer with some degree of certainty? (See Unit 5.4.) What should you change next time on the basis of this evaluation and how does this fit in with the scheme of work? If you develop the practice of reflecting on your work as a matter of course, then modifying future practice on the basis of this reflection becomes second nature. In this way, you use your experience systematically to build up your professional knowledge and to develop your professional judgement.

SUMMARY AND KEY POINTS

You should now be able to explain the following terms: aims, objectives, progression, differentiation. And you should have considered how to construct schemes of work and lesson plans which are comprehensive and useful.

At this point, you may like to reflect on criteria used by the Office for Standards in Education (OFSTED) inspectors for judging teaching quality. Although teaching methods vary, the criteria to judge a teacher's effectiveness which are used by OFSTED are standard. Table 5.4.2 (see p. 280) lists these criteria.

FURTHER READING

Canter, L. and associates, *Assertive Discipline Programme*, available from www.behaviour-learning.com
Teachers speak highly of this programme which focuses on positive behaviour management strategies. Behaviour Management Ltd, HMA House, 78 Durham Road, London SW20 0TL. (Tel: (020) 8944 6161).

Cohen, L., Manion, L. and Morrison, K. (1996) *A Guide to Teaching Practice* (4th edn), London: Routledge.
A useful, comprehensive book dealing with central issues of classroom practice. Readable and aimed specifically at those with no teaching experience.

Hay McBer (2000) *Research into Teacher Effectiveness*, London: DfEE.
This comprehensive report into effective teaching proposes a model of teacher effectiveness comprising teaching skills and professional characteristics. The early sections are particularly useful in relation to the preparation and planning of lessons.

Kyriacou, C. (1997) *Essential Teaching Skills* (2nd edn), Cheltenham: Stanley Thornes.
An excellent and readable overview of the key skills which underpin effective teaching.

Mager, R. (1997) *Preparing Instructional Objectives – A Critical Tool in the Development of Effective Instruction* (3rd edn), London: Kogan Page.
Mager provides a transatlantic perspective on training. He has written many books around the theme of goal setting and teaching techniques. Although this book is focused on skills-based objectives, nevertheless the exercises in it will help you develop your skills in setting objectives.

Scottish Consultative Council on the Curriculum (1996) *Teaching for Effective Learning*, Dundee; see the website: http://claudius.sccc.ac.uk
The SCCC have produced a very readable booklet on the principles of effective teaching and learning. Discussion forums are available via the website.

UNIT 2.3 TAKING RESPONSIBILITY FOR WHOLE LESSONS

MARILYN LEASK

INTRODUCTION

This unit draws attention to issues which have particular relevance to you when you are just starting to take responsibility for whole lessons.

Recall the iceberg image of a teacher's work from Unit 1.1. The delivery of the lesson in the classroom represents the tip of the iceberg, whilst the bulk of the teacher's work for a lesson – routines, preparation, subject knowledge, professional knowledge and judgement, previous lesson evaluations – is hidden. This unit focuses on particular aspects of planning and teaching which initially cause many student teachers problems.

OBJECTIVES

By the end of this unit you should have considered the following:

- routines for good class management;
- how your personal attributes contribute to your effectiveness;
- lesson preparation;
- how to avoid common problems.

Concerns common to student teachers who are beginning to teach are also discussed.

ROUTINES FOR CLASS MANAGEMENT

Routines for class and lesson management provide a structure so that learning can take place within a classroom where the rules are understood by all. In time, these routines become instinctive for you. Establishing rules decreases the likelihood of having to waste lesson time disciplining pupils at a later stage.

But your routines are not established in a vacuum. The pupils you teach have been in schools for at least seven years – they expect the teacher to establish 'norms' for classroom work, talk and movement, and most pupils are conditioned to accept such classroom routines. This doesn't mean that they won't resist you when you insist on certain types of behaviour but it does mean that they have certain expectations that you will set the rules. Three types of routines in operation are:

- for managing work and movement;
- for managing relationships and reinforcing expectations of attitudes and behaviour;
- for gaining attention – for both the pupils and the teacher.

Routines for managing work and movement

For your early lessons, one of your main goals is to get the pupils down to work fairly promptly by providing them with clear tasks and clear instructions. Your concern is to establish yourself as an organised teacher who sets clear objectives for a lesson and provides work which allows students to achieve those objectives. These lessons will probably go more easily if you can fit in with established routines.

Task 2.3.1

CLASSROOM NORMS

Make a list of your expectations for the presentation of work, talk and movement for pupils in your classroom. Find out through observation and discussion what the expectations of the experienced teachers are, especially the teachers of the classes you are taking. Update and amend your list as you gain experience with what works for you.

Routines for managing relationships and reinforcing expectations

Adopting a firm, fair, friendly approach may help you develop good relationships with pupils. Pupils have certain expectations of you. They expect the teacher to be consistent and fair in applying rules. They expect those who do well to be rewarded and/or acknowledged, e.g. through praise, even just a quiet word, or by letting them go first at the end of the lesson. Those who don't abide by your rules expect to be reprimanded. A quiet individual reprimand at the end of a lesson may be sufficient to establish your authority with many pupils. Confrontations in front of the whole class are to be avoided. Remember, the role of routines is to make your lessons run smoothly – everyone should know what your expectations are for classroom behaviour.

It takes time for the student teacher, and for any teacher new to a school, to find out about influences on classroom relationships which come from the community. Information about the range of group 'norms' of behaviour for teenagers in the local area and background information about other social relationships (e.g. which pupils are cousins, stepsisters or stepbrothers) may help you understand more easily your pupils and their expectations.

Experienced teachers can often sense that trouble is brewing between pupils and defuse the situation. They use their voice sparingly – drawing on a range of other controls, e.g. placing themselves near pupils who need more encouragement to stay on-task and using non-verbal gestures to remind pupils to keep working. If needed, there are a number of sanctions which all teachers can use. Beware of giving pupils detentions as a first step. Time is precious to you so don't waste it, and in any case establishing your authority can be just as easily achieved by using one of a range of other sanctions. For example:

- the pupil is required to apologise (or face sanctions);
- a verbal warning is given – a brief reprimand or keeping the pupil for a moment at the end of the lesson to indicate your displeasure;
- a couple of pupils tidy up after the others have gone (teachers are wise to protect their professional reputations by not remaining alone in closed classrooms with individual pupils);
- additional work is given.

Task 2.3.2

SANCTIONS AND REWARDS

Find out about the policies on sanctions and rewards at the school where you are teaching. Make notes of the key issues which affect your work. Check your understanding of the application of these policies with experienced staff.

Routines for gaining attention

Getting the attention of the whole class at points during the lesson is a skill which experienced teachers practise effortlessly. First, act as though you believe the pupils will obey you. One technique teachers often practise is to call for attention ('Stop what you're doing and just look here for a minute'). They then follow this with a focus on an individual ('Paul, that means you too') which acts as a reminder to all pupils that if they don't want to be the focus of the teacher's attention they need to stop what they're doing. The time to call the class to attention is not when they're all working well but when the work is flagging and they need to be spurred on or they've come to a difficult point – unless, for example, you wish to draw their attention to a point on safety.

One of the fundamental rules of the classroom is that pupils should not speak when the teacher is speaking. Spending a few minutes in a lesson waiting for silence until you speak saves a lot of time later, as pupils know what you expect. Pupils may need reminding of your expectations and you probably need to reinforce the idea that this is one of your basic rules. You must be able to get the class's attention when you require it. When observing classes, the following questions may help you see some of the strategies used by teachers to establish this aspect of their authority.

1 **What verbal cues does the teacher use to establish quiet?** Key phrases such as 'Right then', 'Put your pens down now' establish that the teacher requires the class to listen. Some students make the mistake of thinking that the words 'quiet' or 'shush' repeated over and over will gain the required effect. Experienced teachers tend to use more subtle or strident methods, e.g. 'QUIET!' – said once with great emphasis. Units 3.2 and 3.3 provide further advice.
2 **What non-verbal cues does the teacher use to gain attention?** Look at the way teachers use gestures – eyes, face, arms, hands – to establish that they require the class to listen. They may stand still and just wait. Their pupils know that if they keep their teacher waiting they will be penalised. Unit 3.1 contains more ideas.

There are also routines related to the way pupils gain the teacher's attention. The usual routine is that the pupil puts up their hand and doesn't call out. Again, we suggest you find out what the current practice is for the classes you are teaching. If you decide to change established practices then you have to put in considerable effort to establish the new rules.

YOUR PERSONAL ATTRIBUTES

Body language plays an important role in your communication with others and is an aspect of the way you present yourself which you should consider. Some personal attributes which may interfere with your teaching may only reveal themselves once you are teaching. For this reason, it is worth keeping this aspect of your interaction with pupils and staff under review.

Try to establish early in your teaching experience:

- whether your voice can be heard at the back of a classroom;
- whether you have any particular habits which may interfere with the developing of a relationship with a class, e.g. do you rattle coins in your pocket as you speak; do you play with your hair; are you able to use facial expressions effectively to indicate enthusiasm; do you speak in a monotone; do you look at people when you speak to them; what do you communicate through your smiling (some people inadvertently smile when they are angry)?
- what messages your posture and your movement in classrooms and corridors convey;
- what gestures you normally use when speaking.

We suggest you ask for feedback occasionally on these aspects in order to check whether you are inadvertently presenting yourself in an unfavourable manner. Unit 3.1 on communication provides more detail.

LESSON PREPARATION

'I spent days preparing my first lesson on my first teaching experience – geography with a group of 15-year-olds who weren't exactly enamoured with the subject. Educationally it was a disaster! I was so nervous that I rushed through my carefully prepared 40-minute lesson and at the end of 10 minutes I had nothing more to say. I panicked and told them to draw a map – any map – for the rest of the lesson.'

This true story, from a (now) very successful teacher, highlights the nervousness that many student teachers experience when faced with their first lessons. Such nervousness is natural. You are assuming an unfamiliar role – as a teacher – but there are no set lines which you can learn to carry you through the scene. Over time, you build your professional knowledge about teaching and learning and your professional judgement about how to manage the work in the classroom so that the situation described above does not arise. In the meantime, you are having to learn from each situation you face.

When you are spending hours planning for your first lessons, you may wonder whether you've made a sound choice of career, but recall the learner driver mentioned in Unit 1.1. In time, many aspects of driving become automatic; so it is with some features of teaching. In your first lessons, it is a good idea not to try to do anything too ambitious. Limited success is better than unlimited disaster!

It is, of course, possible for a teacher to be in a classroom with a class and for no effective teaching or learning to take place! Effective teaching requires some planned learning to occur in those being taught. Therefore, for your pupils to learn effectively, you must plan carefully.

We suggest you skim through Units 2.2, 5.2 and 5.3 of this book as they provide ideas about the basic teaching skills and planning approaches that you need to employ in your first lessons. You should, of course, be building on your experience of group work, micro-teaching and on the observations you have made.

Following the steps outlined below should ensure that you start your first lessons from a position of being well prepared.

1 **Plan the lesson and ask for advice about your plan**.

Task 2.3.3

CHECKING YOUR LESSON PLAN

Look at your plan for one of your lessons.

- Are you making your expectations of the pupils clear at each stage?
- Are the pupils actively engaged at each point or are they wasting time waiting for you to organise books or equipment?
- Are you expecting them to concentrate on you talking for too long; to take in too much new information without the chance to discuss it and assimilate it?
- Is there scope for pupils to feed back to you what they've learned this lesson, e.g. through question and answer?

As a trial run, try to explain the main points of the lesson to another student teacher. The quality of explanation you are able to give affects the learning which takes place, as does the nature of the questions you ask. Ask another student teacher, your tutor or the teacher whose class you are teaching to keep these points in mind when they observe the lesson and to give you feedback afterwards.

---

2 **Check that you have adequate extension and alternative work.** Anticipate that additional work may be needed. You may find that equipment you had planned to use stops working or the specialist in your subject is not available to supervise you.

3 **Know the class if possible, through your observations, and have a strategy for using and learning names.** Try to learn names quickly – making notes beside the names in the register may help you remember. Drawing up a seating plan can help; pupils may always, or at least usually, sit in the same places. In any case, you can ask them to sit in the same seats until you know their names.

Tony Buzan (1984, 1995) writes extensively on developing memory and he suggests a number of strategies for remembering faces:

- try to link the faces or characteristics of people new to you with existing friends with the same names;
- try to use images to make a mental link between the name and the face of the new person;
- try to repeat the person's name several times during your conversation with them ('That's an interesting piece of work, David. David, what do you enjoy most about . . . ?'). Unit 2.2 provides additional advice on learning names.

If you have the opportunity to observe the class beforehand, look at how the teacher deals with the potentially noisy or the very quiet pupils.

AVOIDING COMMON PROBLEMS

By this point, you know the routines you will use, your lesson is planned. You have also given some thought to where you will stand, when and how you will move around the room. You know to keep scanning the class and, when you talk to children, not to have your back to most of the class.

Judging the timing during a lesson is one of the most difficult problems initially and following a time line on your lesson plan can help you to see at a glance how the lesson is progressing in relation to the time allowed.

Unavoidable incidents will occur to interrupt the flow of your carefully prepared lesson but other incidents can be anticipated or at least dealt with effectively if you are prepared. It is as well to anticipate problems so that you are not too distracted from the lesson you planned to deliver. We discuss below some of the more common incidents and possible solutions so that you are not taken by surprise.

1 One or more pupils won't settle to the work. When some pupils are being disruptive, it is essential to get the bulk of the class working, preferably on work that requires less input from you than normal. This allows you time to deal quietly and firmly with those resisting your authority and thus to establish your authority over them. Ignoring deliberately provocative remarks such as 'This is boring' can help you avoid confrontation. Try to motivate uninterested pupils by linking the work with their interests if possible. Letting them feel you are interested in them as people can promote positive relationships but you still should expect them to work. Ask your experienced colleagues for advice if particular pupils constantly cause you trouble. It is likely that they are also causing some other staff difficulties.

2 You are asked a question and you don't know the answer. This is bound to happen. You can admit you don't know – 'What an interesting point, I've not thought of it that way'; 'I just can't remember at the moment' – but make arrangements for the answer to be found. The pupil can follow it up for homework, use the library to look for the answer or write to those who might know. You may also be able to find out from other teachers or student teachers or your subject association.

3 You are asked personal questions. At some point you'll be asked 'Have you got a boyfriend/girlfriend? Are you a student?' (Ask the school if you are to be introduced as a member of staff or a student.) 'Have you ever done this before? How old are you?' Or comments may be made about your car (or lack of one) or what you are wearing.

Don't allow yourself to be distracted from the work in the lesson. You can choose whether or not to answer personal questions but set boundaries beyond which you won't go. Often a joke deflects the questioner – 'Mine is the Rolls parked around the corner.' Offering to answer the question in the pupil's time, after the lesson, can lead to loss of interest on the part of the questioner.

4 A pupil swears. As a student teacher, you cannot solve all the problems of the pupils and the school. Usually if a pupil is asked to repeat what they said, they omit the offensive word and feel sufficiently rebuked. You have indicated that swearing is unacceptable.

What you do need to do is to establish a line about what is acceptable and stick to it. Make it clear to your classes what your rule is and link it to school policy which should be 'no swearing'.

However, swearing at teachers or abusing other pupils are serious offences and you must take action. There are different ways in which you might react – depending on the pupils, the context, the school. You may require an apology or you may wish to take the matter further. Take advice from experienced teachers. Act in haste and repent at leisure is good advice for a student teacher. Take a little time to decide on the response. Letting a pupil know that an act was unacceptable and that you are thinking about how to respond can be more effective than an ill-considered response from you at the time.

Consistency in your approach to discipline is an important facet of establishing your reputation. You want the pupils to know that if they do X, which is unacceptable, some form of action, Y, always follows. (This approach is an application of behaviourist learning theories (see Unit 3.2) – you are teaching the pupils to understand that a certain negative action on their part always gets a certain negative response from you. Thus it is perfectly clear to them how to avoid a negative response.)

Task 2.3.4

SWEARING

Discuss the following two scenarios with the teachers with whom you're working. What is an appropriate response for you in each case?

1 You overhear a pupil use swear-words in conversation with another pupil. The word is not used in an abusive way.
2 A child swears at another child or at you!

What are the routine responses for dealing with these incidents in your school?

---

5 Pupils are not properly equipped to do the work. They lack PE kit, pens, books, maths equipment. You should aim to get most of the class working so that you can then direct your attention to those who require individual attention. Many departments have systems in place for dealing with pupils' lack of kit and equipment. In the early days of your teaching, it can be less disruptive to your lesson for you simply to supply the missing item (pencil/paper) so that you can keep the flow of the lesson going. But make sure you retrieve what you have loaned and indicate firmly that you expect pupils to provide their own.

Task 2.3.5

PROCEDURES FOR DEALING WITH POORLY EQUIPPED PUPILS

Find out whether there is a system in the department in which you are working for dealing with pupils who are not properly equipped. Plan how you can avoid this problem interfering with the smooth running of your lesson.

---

6 Equipment doesn't work. You must check equipment beforehand and, in any case, have an alternative lesson planned if your lesson is dependent on equipment working.

7 You have too much material. Pupils have to get to their next lesson on time and have to have their break on time. So you must let them go on time! Five minutes or so before the end of a lesson (more if they have to change or put equipment away), pull the lesson together, reminding them of what's been achieved and what's expected in the way of homework, and perhaps what's coming next. They then pack away and are ready to go at the correct time.

8 The pupils finish the work earlier than you had anticipated. Inevitably there will be occasions when you have time with a class which you didn't expect. The work may have been finished early or changes in arrangements meant you couldn't do what you had planned. This can be a worrying experience for a student teacher; however, such time can be used to educational advantage in a number of ways:

1 Have questions prepared relating to recent work in the area under study.

2 Do a quick test of the issues covered in the lesson or a spelling test of new words.

3 Use your lesson objectives to devise questions about the work.

4 Ask pupils to work in pairs or teams to devise questions to be put to the rest of the class or to other teams. Answers can be written in rough books with the pupils swapping books to mark them.

5 Work coming up in subsequent lessons can be introduced so that pupils can see the purpose in what they are doing now – remember repetition is an aid to learning. Introducing concepts briefly in one lesson means they will be more familiar when you go over them in depth later. (This is an example of constructivist learning theory in action – new knowledge is 'scaffolded' on existing knowledge.)

6 Pupils' existing knowledge on the next topics could be ascertained by question and answer. (Learning is more certain where you, as the teacher, build on pupils' existing knowledge and experience.)

7 You may take the opportunity to check the pupils' ability to apply a range of study skills. There are excellent books on this topic available through the major bookshops. Plan together with the pupils ways of learning the work you've been covering, e.g. developing a spider diagram for summarising the key points in a topic in history or geography, producing a mnemonic to aid the recall of key issues (see Unit 5.2 for more ideas).

8 Homework (either past or just set) can be discussed in more detail. You may allow the pupils to discuss this together.

Or, in practical subjects:

9 You may ask pupils to repeat a sequence they've been working on in PE, perhaps extending it to incorporate another skill; to observe each other performing the sequence and to comment on the performance; or to demonstrate what is coming up in the next lesson.

10 Alternatively, if the class is new to you, you may take the opportunity to learn their names. With experience, you acquire the skill of fitting work to the time available, so the problem ceases to cause you anxiety.

MORE GENERAL CONCERNS

There are a number of more general concerns which most students feel at some point or another. We discuss these here so that, by anticipating problems and posing solutions, you may be better prepared for dealing with them.

   1 **Maintaining good behaviour**. This is cited as an area of concern by student teachers more often than any other area and Units 3.2 and 3.3 provide more detailed guidance. Various books listed in the further reading at the end of each unit also provide valuable advice. Pupils are influenced by your confidence, the material, the demands of the work and your ability to enforce rules. The first lesson may be a honeymoon period, where the pupils are sizing you up; or, on the other hand, they may test you out. If you insist (in a quiet, firm way) that you are in charge of what happens in the classroom, then the vast majority of pupils give way – as long as you are seen as fair and reasonable. Whilst it is important not to see the class as 'them' against 'you', adopting a 'divide and rule' strategy can pay dividends: praise those who work well and reward them – for example, with privileges or house points or merit slips – using the systems established within the school. Do not expect to win over all pupils immediately; some may take months; a few may never be won

over. Discuss any difficulties you have with other teachers – it may be that they have effective strategies for dealing with the pupils who are giving you concern.

2 Defusing situations. Inexperienced teachers tend to reprimand pupils much more frequently than experienced teachers, probably because they have less well developed subtle control mechanisms (e.g. body language).

Techniques used by teachers to defuse situations include:

- Anticipating changes of mood and concentration and moving the lesson on and perhaps increasing the pace of the lesson, e.g. 'Right, let's see what you've understood already . . .'
- Scanning the class regularly, even when helping individuals or groups, so that potential problems are prevented: 'That's enough, Julia' or 'Have you got a problem over there?' is usually sufficient to remind pupils to keep on-task. Pupils are impressed if you can see what they are doing without them realising you are looking at them. Standing in position at a pupil's desk perhaps towards the back of the room allows you to monitor the work of pupils close to you as well as scan the rest of the class without them seeing you.
- Using humour to keep pupils on-task – a knowledge of adolescent culture and local activities is useful: 'You're too busy thinking about what you'll be doing on Friday night to concentrate.'
- Using a whole range of non-verbal cues – posture, facial expressions, gestures, positioning in the classroom – to reinforce your authority. The children recognise these and you need to recognise them too (see Unit 3.1).

Notice that none of these techniques requires the teacher to shout or to be angry in order to keep the children on-task.

Task 2.3.6

DEFUSING DIFFICULT SITUATIONS

We suggest that when you are observing experienced teachers you look specifically at how they defuse situations so that reprimands are not required. Note these in your diary.

---

3 Retrieving situations. You may have a poor lesson with a class. This doesn't mean that all lessons with that class will be like that. What it does mean, however, is that you must analyse the situation and put into place strategies for ensuring that the next lesson is better. Experienced colleagues should be able to give you advice. Observing an experienced teacher, even if in another discipline, teaching a group that you have difficulty with can be eye-opening and can provide you with ideas for the way forward. Discuss what you've seen with the teacher. Ask someone to watch you teach the class with whom you are having difficulty and ask for suggestions about how you can improve.

4 Personal vulnerability, lack of self-belief and confidence. In becoming a teacher, you are more vulnerable than when being educated for many other professions, as you are exposed to a discerning audience (the class) early on. So much of your performance in the classroom depends on your own personal qualities and your ability to form good relationships with pupils from a wide range of backgrounds. Your performance is analysed and commented on by those who observe you teaching. You are forced to face your own strengths and weaknesses as a result of this scrutiny. This can be stressful, particularly when you may be given apparently conflicting advice from different observers. As you become more experienced and you develop more analytical skills for use in appraising your performance, you should build your self-belief and confidence.

5 Dealing with your feelings. Incidents will occur which leave you feeling deflated, unsure or angry. Try to adopt a problem-solving reflective approach to your work so that you maintain some objectivity and can learn from any difficult experiences you have. One group of PGCE students was asked, at the end of their year of initial teacher education, what advice they would give to new student teachers. Above all else, they said, keep in touch with other students so that you can discuss your concerns with others in the same situation. It is likely that your concerns are also the concerns of other student teachers.

6 The challenge to your own values. Most people mix with people who hold similar values and attitudes. As a teacher, you are dealing with children from different backgrounds and with different expectations about education and different values from your own. You need to consider how you can best provide equal opportunities in your classroom and what strategies you might use to motivate disaffected pupils. Chapter 4 provides further advice in these areas.

7 Loss of books or equipment and breakages. Schools have different approaches to dealing with loss and breakage of equipment by pupils should it occur. Seek advice from those with whom you are working. Anticipating and thus avoiding problems makes your life easier. The simple strategy of managing your lesson so that there is sufficient time at the end to check that equipment and books are returned saves you time in the long run.

8 Having a ready answer. There are a number of routine situations which can throw you off balance in the lesson, e.g. 'Someone's taken my pen/book', 'Sir, she did it too', 'Miss, he started it', 'But Miss, you let her go to the toilet', 'Do you like . . .' (and here they name a pop group about which they all know but of which you've never heard). Discuss these situations with other students and make notes for yourself about how you might deal with them. See how other teachers deal with these situations.

9 Time and stress management. These are important enough issues that Unit 1.3 is devoted to them. Here we want to raise three points:

- giving the lesson is only one part of a teacher's job;
- preparing your first lessons takes you a long time;
- if you skimp on lesson preparation, then the stress level you experience in the lesson will be high, as you will not feel in control.

SUMMARY AND KEY POINTS

Your first encounters with the pupils are important in setting the tone for your relationships with them. It is worth carefully considering the image you wish to project in these early lessons and planning your work to help reinforce this image. If you want to create the image that you are a disorganised teacher who doesn't know what the lesson is about any more than the pupils do, then this is relatively easy to achieve. Your image is something you should create deliberately and not just allow it to happen.

Most student teachers have to work on controlling their nerves and developing their self-confidence. Covering the following points in your preparation should prevent some of the difficulties you would otherwise encounter:

- set clear, simple objectives for the lesson which are likely to be achieved;
- plan the lesson carefully and have extension work ready;

- know the class and obtain pupil lists;
- check the room layout: are things where you want them? What about safety issues?
- know the school, class and lesson routines;
- be on time;
- prepare board work beforehand if possible (check that it won't be rubbed off if there is a lesson before yours), or use a prepared overhead projector transparency, or computer projector presentation worksheet;
- act as though you are in charge although you probably won't feel that you are;
- know the subject and/or make crib notes, and put key points on the board, on a transparency, or on a computer worksheet if you're unsure;
- plan the rhythm of the lesson to give a balance between teacher talk and pupil activity;
- include a time line in your lesson plan so that you can check during the lesson how the plan is working. Try not to talk too quickly;
- be prepared to clamp down on misbehaviour. It is easier to reprimand one pupil who is misbehaving than to wait until they have goaded other pupils into following suit or retaliating;
- visualise yourself being successful;
- have a fallback plan for the lesson.

From the observations you've done, you should have established how other teachers deal with minor infringements of school rules – remember there are a number of types of reprimand you can use before you give out detentions.

One of your major problems may be believing that you are indeed a teacher. This is a mental and emotional transition which you need to make. The pupils, parents and staff usually see you as a teacher, albeit a new one, and expect you to behave as such.

FURTHER READING

The subject-specific texts in the 'Learning to Teach (subject) in the Secondary School' series provide you with further advice.

Some teachers join chat rooms or discussion groups on the internet to discuss issues related to their teaching. You should be aware that these discussions may be public and may be archived. See Unit 1.4.

Buzan, T. (1995) *Use Your Memory*, London: BBC Books.
    This is just one of Tony Buzan's books which are packed with ideas for improving memory. Why not draw them to the attention of your pupils?

Hay McBer (2000) *Research into Teacher Effectiveness*, London: DfEE.
    This comprehensive report into effective teaching proposes a model of teacher effectiveness comprising teaching skills and professional characteristics. The early sections are particularly useful in relation to the preparation and planning of lessons.

Wragg, E.C. (1999) *An Introduction to Classroom Observation* (2nd edn), London: Routledge.
    Wragg has written many texts on aspects of teaching and learning, e.g., questioning, classroom management, assessment, explaining.

CHAPTER 3 **CLASSROOM INTERACTIONS AND MANAGING PUPILS**

Effective classroom management is essential to effective learning. Classroom management refers to arrangements made by the teacher to establish and maintain an environment in which learning can occur, e.g. effective organisation and presentation of lessons so that pupils are actively engaged in learning. Classroom management skills and techniques are addressed throughout this book in a number of different chapters and units. This chapter includes three units about different aspects of classroom management related to interacting with pupils. Together they give an insight into the complex relationships that are developed between teachers and pupils, and emphasise the need for well-developed skills and techniques that you can adapt appropriately to the demands of the situation. They reinforce the fact that, although you must plan your lessons thoroughly, not everything you do in the classroom can be planned in advance, as you cannot predict how pupils will react in any situation on any given day.

Classroom interactions are based on verbal and non-verbal communication. Unit 3.1 is designed to help you communicate effectively in the classroom. It considers verbal communication, including listening skills, and then non-verbal communication, both on its own and in how it enhances or detracts from verbal communication. Non-verbal communication is addressed largely by considering how teachers present themselves to pupils.

In Unit 3.2 we consider aspects of motivating pupils. The unit starts by asking what motivation is and presents a number of theories of motivation. It then considers factors affecting motivation in the classroom, concentrating on the use of praise and punishment, feedback and, finally, motivating individuals.

We recognise student teachers' concerns about managing behaviour and misbehaviour. Our objective in Unit 3.3 is to help you address these concerns by focusing on managing pupils' behaviour. The unit emphasises the importance of preventing misbehaviour as far as possible (recognising that teachers cannot prevent all misbehaviour), but also being prepared to deal with misbehaviour that does occur. Thus, the unit also includes sections on managing behaviour problems and developing effective classroom management skills to prevent misbehaviour. We also consider the Elton Report, *Discipline in Schools* (DES/WO, 1989), as this important document contains much valuable information and recommendations about all aspects of behaviour in schools.

UNIT 3.1   **COMMUNICATING WITH PUPILS**

SUSAN CAPEL, ROGER STRANGWICK AND MARGARET WHITEHEAD

INTRODUCTION

> A teacher opens up unknown or only half suspected areas of skill or knowledge; he makes things clear; he makes things as simple as possible. He enables pupils to do more things and to do them better, to understand more things and to understand them better.
>
> (Marland, 1993, p. 11)

We can all think of teachers who achieved this and from whom we have learned a lot. These teachers may have been very different as people and as teachers, with different personalities and styles. Whatever their differences, they all had in common the ability to communicate effectively with pupils.

Communication is a two-way process involving the mutual exchange of information and ideas. This unit focuses on communication between the teacher and pupils. However, classroom communication can also be between pupil and pupil. Communication between pupils is also very important, as it can enhance or hinder learning in the classroom. Pupils can learn from communicating with each other, e.g. by talking about a task. Equally, such communication can be irrelevant to the lesson and may interfere with the progress of the lesson, therefore detracting from pupils' learning.

Most of us tend to think we communicate well. However, we may never have analysed our communication skills. When we study them systematically, most of us can find room for improvement. You cannot predict how pupils will react to an activity, a conversation or a question asked. In order to respond appropriately you need well-developed communication skills and techniques, combined with sensitivity and judgement. Your response, both verbally and non-verbally, in any classroom situation influences the immediate and, possibly, long-term relationship with the class.

Communication is a complex process which can occur in many different ways, e.g. written, verbal and non-verbal. In this unit we consider both verbal and non-verbal communication. First we consider aspects of verbal communication, including using your voice (volume, projection, pitch, speed, tone, clarity and expressiveness), the language you use and the importance of active listening. We then consider aspects of non-verbal communication, e.g. appearance, gesture, posture, facial expression and mannerisms, particularly in relation to how you present yourself as a teacher. Further aspects of communication are addressed in Unit 5.2 'Active learning'.

OBJECTIVES

By the end of this unit you should be able to:

* appreciate the importance of effective verbal and non-verbal communication skills;

- vary your voice consciously to enhance your teaching;
- appraise your use of language and use questioning more effectively as a teaching tool;
- understand the relationship between verbal and non-verbal communication;
- be aware of and have control over your own self-presentation in order to present yourself effectively.

By meeting these objectives you will have addressed competences/standards related to effective communication identified in your course handbook. Refer to these as you work through this unit.

VERBAL COMMUNICATION

Gaining attention

You need to establish procedures for gaining pupils' attention at the beginning of a lesson and also when you want the class to listen again after they have started an activity. This latter skill is especially important if there is a safety risk in the activity or lesson. Before you start talking to a class, make sure that all pupils can see and hear you, that you have silence and that they are paying attention. Establish a means of getting silence – e.g. say 'quiet please', clap your hands, blow a whistle in physical education or bang on a drum in music – and use this with the class each time. Wait for quiet and do not speak until it is calm. Once you are talking, do not keep moving around. This distracts pupils, who may pay more attention to the movement than to what you are saying.

Using your voice

A teacher's voice is a crucial element in classroom communication. It is like a musical instrument and, if you play it well, then your pupils will be an appreciative and responsive audience. Some people have voices that are naturally easier to listen to than others. Certain qualities are fixed and those give your voice its unique character, but there are many variations available and those variations lend impact to what you say. It is important to stress that you can change the way you talk. There are many different aspects of your voice that you can alter in order to use it more effectively, including volume, projection, pitch, speed, tone, clarity and expressiveness. You can practise each of these.

The most obvious way you can vary your voice is by altering the **volume**, by talking very quietly or very loudly. It is useful to have the whole volume range available but it is rarely a good thing to be loud when it is not needed. Having achieved silence, do not shout into it. Loud teachers have loud classes. If you shout too much, you may get into the habit of shouting all the time. It happens and sometimes people know that somebody is a teacher because of their loud voice. Also, if you shout too much, you may lose your voice every September! Of course, you have to be heard, but this is done by projection more than by volume.

You **project** your voice by making sure it leaves your mouth confidently and precisely. This needs careful enunciation and breath control. If your voice is projected well, you are able to make a whisper audible at some distance. Equally, good projection brings considerable volume to your ordinary voice without resort to shouting or roaring.

Everybody varies the **pitch** of their voice naturally. Each group of words spoken has its own 'tune' that contributes to the meaning. A person may have a naturally high or low voice but that 'natural' pitch can be varied with no pain. Generally speaking, deep voices sound more serious and significant; high voices are more exciting and lively. To add weight to what is being said, the pitch should be dropped; to lighten the tone, the pitch should be raised. A lower voice can create a sense of importance. A voice with a lower pitch comes across as more authoritative and confident than a high-pitched voice. It can also be raised more easily to command attention, whereas raising a naturally high-pitched voice may result in something similar to a squeak, which does not carry the same weight.

Speed variations give contrast to delivery. You can use pause to good effect. It shows confidence if you can hold a silence before making a point or answering a question. Equally, have the patience to wait for a pupil to respond. Research suggests that three seconds is a reasonable time for any such pause. Speaking quickly can be a valuable skill on occasion. You need concentration and careful enunciation to speak quickly.

Task 3.1.1

THE QUALITY OF YOUR VOICE

Record your voice. You may want to read from a book or a newspaper or to record yourself in natural monologue or conversation. Play the recording back and listen to it with a friend or another student teacher. If you have not heard yourself before, the experience may be a little shocking! Your voice may sound different from the way you hear it and a common response is to blame the recording equipment. This is probably not at fault. Remember that you hear your voice coming back from your mouth. Most of your audience hear it coming forward. As you become used to listening to yourself, try to pick out the good points of your voice. Is it clear? Is it expressive? Is the basic pitch pleasant? When you have built up your confidence, consider areas for improvement. Do you normally speak too fast? Is the tone monotonous?

Repeat the task, but this time trying to vary your voice. For example, try reading at your normal speed, then faster, then as quickly as you can. Remember to start each word precisely and to concentrate on what you are saying. Then try varying the pitch of your voice. You will be surprised at how easy it is. Ask another student teacher to listen to the tape with you, comment on any differences and provide helpful advice for improving.

To use your voice effectively you need to consider the factors above together. For example, you do not communicate effectively if the pitch of your voice is right, but you are not speaking clearly or the volume is wrong, e.g. you are shouting, or pupils at the back cannot hear what you are saying. It is also important to put feeling into what you say. Often, pupils respond to HOW you say something rather than WHAT you say. If you are praising, sound pleased; if you are disciplining, sound firm. If you deliver all talk in the same way, do not be surprised if pupil response is undifferentiated.

Language of the teacher

A teacher's language must be accessible. There is no point in talking to pupils in language they do not understand. That does not mean that subject vocabulary cannot be introduced, only that you must not assume that everybody knows the words or constructions that you do. All teachers are teachers of language; you gradually introduce your class to the language of the subject, but to do this you must start with a simple direct language that makes no assumptions. Do not assume that pupils understand simple connecting phrases, e.g. 'in order to', 'so that', 'tends to', 'keep in proportion', etc.

It is easier for pupils to understand a new concept if you make comparisons or use examples or references to which they can relate. As a teacher your language must be concise. When you are speaking, you stress or repeat important words or phrases. That is important in teaching too. If they help learning, repetition and elaboration are valuable, but filling silence with teacher talk is generally unproductive. It is too easy for you to inflict your increasing eloquence on a captive audience. You take longer to deliver the same information and pupils' time may not be used most effectively. However, it is generally accepted that pupils understand something and learn it better if they hear it a number of times. Therefore, as the Chinese proverb says, you should:

- tell them what you are going to tell them,
- tell them,
- then tell them again what you have told them.

Task 3.1.2

THE LANGUAGE OF YOUR SUBJECT

Write down a list of specialist words and phrases used in your subject or in a particular topic in your subject that you may be teaching. Think how many of these might be in the normal vocabulary of an average pupil at your school. Consider this aspect of your lesson planning carefully. How might you introduce and explain these words and phrases? How might you allow pupils opportunities to practise their use of the words in the lesson? Tape the lesson that you are teaching. After the lesson replay the tape and consider your use of language in the lesson, particularly those aspects identified above. It can be particularly helpful to listen to this with a student teacher learning to teach another subject, who does not have the same subject knowledge and language that you are using and who therefore may be nearer to pupils' experience of the subject. Then consider whether you could have given the pupils the same information in a shorter time and whether you could have used the pupils' time more effectively.

A teacher's language is not just used to convey the subject. It is also used to create individual relationships with pupils which make them more interested in learning. Using pupils' names; showing interest in their lives outside the classroom; valuing their experience; all these are important in building a positive atmosphere for classroom learning (see Unit 3.2 on motivating pupils for further information).

Teachers also use language to impose discipline. Often, negative terms are used for this. This is not inevitable and a positive approach may have more success. For example, can you suggest a constructive activity rather than condemning a destructive one? Could earlier praise or suggestion have made later criticism unnecessary? It is also important when disciplining a pupil to consider who else can hear, as a rebuke in public can have a negative influence on the pupil concerned (see Unit 3.3 on managing classroom behaviour).

Types of communication

There are many different ways in which verbal communication is used in teaching. Three of these – explaining, questioning and discussion – are considered briefly below.

Explaining

Teachers spend a lot of time explaining to pupils. In some teaching situations it can be the main form of activity in the lesson. Explaining provides information about what, why and how. It describes new terms or concepts or clarifies their meaning.

Being able to explain something effectively is an important skill for teachers to acquire because pupils expect teachers to explain things clearly and become frustrated when they cannot understand an explanation. A good explanation is clear and well structured. It takes account of pupils' previous knowledge and understanding, uses language that pupils can understand, relates new work to concepts, interests or work already familiar to the pupils. A good explanation actively engages pupils in learning and therefore is able to gain and maintain the pupils' attention. Use of analogy or metaphor can also help an explanation. Pupils learn better if they are actively engaged in the learning process. You must plan to involve pupils, e.g. mix an explanation with tasks, activities or questions, rather than relying on long lectures, dictating notes or working out something on the board.

Task 3.1.3

EXPLAINING

Observe an experienced teacher and another student teacher explaining an idea, concept or topic in their subject to a group of pupils. Write down in your diary the techniques they use, e.g. relating the new work to something pupils have learned previously, using analogies or metaphors, or actively involving pupils by such techniques as questioning. Also write down how pupils respond to the explanation. Compare the outcomes of the two observations and discuss your notes with the teacher and student teacher.

Questioning

One technique for actively involving pupils in their learning is questioning. Teachers use a lot of questions in their teaching. Research suggests that it may be as many as 400 in an average day, which can be as much as 30 per cent of teaching time (Wragg, 1984). We introduced aspects of questioning in Unit 2.1, 'Reading classrooms', and elaborate further below.

Asking questions effectively

In order to use questioning effectively in your classes, you need to plan for this in your lessons and prepare the questions beforehand (see Unit 2.2 on lesson planning). To use questioning effectively you need to consider:

- why you are asking a question(s);
- what types of question(s) you are going to ask;
- when you are going to ask questions;
- how you are going to ask questions;
- of whom you are going to ask a question, how you expect the question to be answered, how you are going to respond if the pupil does not understand the question or gives an inappropriate answer, and how long you are going to wait for an answer.

However, you cannot plan this rigidly; you must be flexible, adapting your plan during the lesson to take account of pupils' responses.

Asking questions is not a simple process. Questions are asked for many reasons, e.g. to gain pupils' attention or check that they are paying attention, to check understanding of an instruction or explanation, to reinforce or revise a topic, to increase understanding, to encourage thinking or to develop a discussion. Perrott (1982) suggested that questions are asked to develop the six levels of thought processes described by Bloom (1956, see Perrott, 1982), i.e. knowledge (recalling such things as facts, terminology, conventions and generalisations), comprehension (calculating, translating, interpreting, extrapolating and making deductions to solve problems with familiar solutions), application (apply knowledge and information in unfamiliar situations), analysis (breakdown of material into its constituents in order to find the relationship between them), synthesis (putting together of the constituents by rearranging and combining them to give an arrangement not apparent before) or evaluation (value judgements about materials, ideas, methods, etc.).

Questions can be categorised in different ways. One common way of categorising them is into open and closed questions.

Closed and open questions

The most common reason for asking questions is to check that pupils have learned what they are supposed to have learned or that they have memorised certain facts or pieces of information. These are questions like: what is the capital of Peru? What is the atomic weight of nitrogen? How many people are in a netball team? What do we call the main artery leading from the heart? How do you spell 'geranium'? These are called **closed** questions. There is only one correct answer to each of those questions. The pupil either knows the answer or not. No real thought is required. Pupils recall information rather than think about the answer. Closed questions might be given to the whole class, with answers coming instantaneously. A short question–answer session like that might reinforce learning, refresh pupils' memories or make a link to new work.

On the other hand, **open** questions may have several possible answers and it may be impossible to know if an answer is 'correct'. These questions are often used to develop understanding. Examples of open questions are: how could we reduce vandalism in cities? What sort of man is Hamlet? Why did the Roman Empire decline and fall? How might you defeat the offside trap in football? What words could you use to describe a wood in spring?

These questions are much more complex than the first set. The respondent has to think and manipulate information, e.g. reason or apply the information and use knowledge, logic and imagination to answer them. Open questions cannot usually be answered quickly. Pupils probably need time to gather information; sift evidence; advance hypotheses; discuss ideas; plan answers.

You can ask closed or open questions or a combination of the two as **a series of questions**. The questions in the series can start with a few relatively easy closed questions and then move on to more complex open questions. A series of such questions is designed to extend pupils' understanding of a topic. Such series of questions take time to build up if they are to be an integral part of the learning process, and therefore they must be planned as an integral part of the lesson. If they are put at the end of the lesson as a time-filler, their effect is lost. Questions at the end of the lesson are much more likely to be closed-recall questions to help pupils remember what they have been taught in the lesson.

Questions can be asked to the whole class; to specific named individuals; or to groups. The questions can be spoken; written on a board; or given out on printed sheets. The answers can be spoken or written. They can be given at once or produced after deliberation. For example, you may set a series of questions for homework and either collect the answers in to mark or go through them verbally with the class at the start of the next lesson.

Effective questioning is a skill you must develop as a teacher. It requires you to be able to ask clear, appropriate questions; use pause to allow pupils to think about an answer before responding; use prompting to help pupils who are having problems to answer a question; and use follow-up questions to probe further, encourage pupils to develop their answers, extend their thinking, change the direction of the questioning and involve the whole class by distributing questions around the class. Your non-verbal communication – e.g. eye contact, manner, tone of voice – is important in being able to question effectively.

Wragg (1984, p. 116) studied errors in questioning by student teachers. Errors of presentation – e.g. not looking at pupils when asking a question, talking too fast, at the wrong volume or not being clear – were identified by teachers as the most common errors. Wragg considered that the ease of detection and of improvement of these errors may have contributed to them being identified as the most common errors. The second most common type of error was the way student teachers handled replies to questions, e.g. they only accepted answers that they wanted or expected. You must avoid the guessing-game type of question-and-answer session where the teacher has a fixed answer in mind and is not open to possible alternative answers. Pupils then spend their time guessing what the teacher wants. Other errors identified by teachers in this study were: pupils not knowing why particular questions were being asked; student teachers not giving enough background information to enable pupils to answer questions; asking questions in a disjointed fashion rather than a logical sequence; jumping from one question to another without linking them together; and tending to focus on a small group of pupils and ignoring the rest of the class. Teachers tended to focus on those pupils sitting in a V-shaped wedge in the middle of the room. Some aspects of questioning were not identified as common errors, but Wragg felt that this might be because they are difficult to detect and to correct, e.g. whether the vocabulary is appropriate for the pupils' level of understanding or whether the questions are too long, complex or ambiguous. It is as important to think about and develop these aspects of questioning as it is those that are more obvious.

The use of questioning in a lesson should not be considered in isolation; rather it should be considered in relation to the use of other teaching techniques. For example, you can encourage pupils to participate actively in questioning by listening and responding appropriately to answers, praising good answers, being supportive, and respecting answers, and not making pupils feel they will be ridiculed if they answer a question incorrectly (see Unit 3.2 on motivating pupils for further information).

Task 3.1.4

QUESTIONING

Plan a lesson that incorporates a series of questions as described above, i.e. why, what, when, how, of whom you are going to ask the question, how you expect the question to be answered (write down as many appropriate and inappropriate answers as you can), how you are going to respond if the pupil does not understand the question or gives an inappropriate answer, and how long you are going to wait for an answer. Ask your tutor to observe the lesson when you teach it, looking particularly at the effectiveness of the questioning. You may want to devise a list of questions for the observer, e.g. did the pupils understand the questions? Did a number of different pupils respond? Did the questions lead the pupils to a deeper level of understanding? Discuss the lesson with your tutor afterwards. Try to take account of that discussion when planning your next series of questions.

Discussion

Questioning and discussion overlap, and questioning may lead naturally into discussion in order to explore a topic further. The teacher is still in control of a discussion but, as pupils generally have some control over the direction of a discussion, they have more control over the material to be included than in many teaching situations. The relatively less structured atmosphere of a discussion can be used to encourage pupils to contribute more freely, as can suggestions or questions interjected by the teacher, as appropriate. The atmosphere of the class and the response of the teacher and other pupils all contribute to the success or otherwise of a discussion. To develop an effective discussion in a lesson takes planning, e.g. of seating arrangements, questions to stimulate discussion, and how you are going to respond to different potential developments of the discussion so that as many pupils as possible are able to make a contribution. Before you use discussion in your classes, it is wise to observe another teacher using this technique in their teaching. See also the Appendix to Unit 4.5, 'Handling discussion with classes'.

Listening

Communication with pupils is not effective if you do not listen to and take account of the response. **Being able to listen effectively** is as important as being able to send the message effectively. Learn to recognise and be sensitive to whether or not a message has been received properly by the other person, e.g. you get a bewildered look or an inappropriate answer to a question. Be able to react appropriately, e.g. repeat the same question or rephrase the question. However, also reflect on why the communication was not effective, e.g. was the pupil not listening to you? If so, why? For example, the pupil had 'switched off' in a boring lesson or the question was worded poorly. It is all too easy to blame a pupil for not listening properly, but it may be that you had a large part to play in the breakdown of the communication. Do not assume that pupils have your grasp of meaning and vocabulary.

It is too easy to ask a question and then 'switch off' or think about the next question or the next part of the lesson while an answer is being given. This lack of interest conveys itself to the person speaking. It is distracting to know that the person you are talking to is not listening and not responding to what is being said. Good listening is an active process, with a range of non-verbal and verbal responses that convey the message to the person speaking that you are listening to what is being said. These include looking alert, looking at the person who is talking to you, smiling, nodding and making verbal signals to show you have received and understood the message or to encourage the person to continue, e.g. 'yes', 'I see what you mean', 'go on', 'Oh dear', 'mmmm', 'uh-huh'.

NON-VERBAL COMMUNICATION

Much teacher–pupil communication is non-verbal. Non-verbal communication includes your appearance, gestures, posture, facial expression and mannerisms. Non-verbal communication supports or detracts from verbal communication, depending on whether or not verbal and non-verbal signals match each other; for example, if you are praising someone and smiling and looking pleased or if you are telling them off and looking stern and sounding firm, you are sending a consistent message and are perceived as sincere. On the other hand, if you are smiling when telling someone off or are looking bored when praising someone, you are sending conflicting messages that cause confusion and misunderstanding. Robertson expresses this well:

> When non-verbal behaviour is not reinforcing meaning . . . it communicates instead the speaker's lack of involvement. Rather than being the message, it becomes the message about the messenger.
>
> (1989, pp. 70–71)

Effective communication therefore relies not only on appropriate content, but also on the way it is presented.

Non-verbal communication can have a considerable impact without any verbal communication; e.g. by looking at a pupil slightly longer than you would normally, you indicate your awareness that they are talking or misbehaving. This may be enough to make the pupil stop. You can indicate your enthusiasm for a topic by the way you use gestures. You can probably think of a teacher who stands at the front of the class leaning against the board with arms crossed waiting for silence, the teacher marching down between the desks to tell someone off, or the teacher who sits and listens attentively to the problems of a particular pupil. The meaning of the communication is clear and there is no need to say anything. Thus, non-verbal communication is important for good communication, classroom management and control.

Task 3.1.5

IMPROVING YOUR VERBAL AND NON-VERBAL COMMUNICATION

Develop two lists, one of matching verbal and non-verbal communications, the other of ones that do not match. There are some examples given above to help you start on these lists. Practise those that are matching and then ask your tutor or another student teacher to observe whether your verbal and non-verbal communication match in your teaching. You can give the observer the list generated above as a starting point. After the lesson discuss the outcome with the observer and then try to identify areas where you can overcome problems of non-matching verbal and non-verbal communication. Practise these and then ask the observer to observe another lesson to see if you have improved.

PRESENTING YOURSELF EFFECTIVELY

There might seem to be some contradiction in including this section as it could indicate that there is a correct way to present yourself as a teacher. However, the title clearly refers to you as an individual, with your own unique set of characteristics. Herein lies one of the keys to effective teacher self-presentation: while there are some common constituents, it is also the case that every teacher is an individual and brings something of their own unique personality to the job.

Initial impressions are important and the way you present yourself to a class on first meeting can influence the class and their learning over a period of time. A teacher's appearance is an important part of the impression created, as pupils expect all teachers to wear clothes that are clean, neat and tidy, and certain teachers to wear certain types of clothes, e.g. it is acceptable for a physical education teacher to wear a tracksuit but not a history teacher. Thus, first impressions have as much to do with non-verbal as with verbal communication, although both are important considerations.

How teachers follow up the first impression is equally important, e.g. whether you treat pupils as individuals, how you communicate with pupils, whether you have any mannerisms, such as constantly flicking a piece of hair out of your eyes or saying 'er' or 'OK' frequently when you are talking, which reduce or prevent effective communication (pupils tend to focus on any mannerism rather than on what is being said and they may even count the number of times you do it!). It is generally agreed that effective teaching depends on and is enhanced by self-presentation that is **enthusiastic**, **confident** and **caring**. Why are these attributes important? How can you work towards making these part of your self-presentation as a teacher?

Enthusiasm

One of the tasks of a teacher is to enable pupils to learn to do or understand something. Before many young people will make an effort to get to grips with something new, the teacher needs to 'sell' it to them as something interesting and worthwhile. Your enthusiasm for your subject is infectious.

Task 3.1.6

CONVEYING ENTHUSIASM 1

Think back to teachers you have worked with and identify some whose enthusiasm for their subject really influenced your learning. Discuss your recollections with another student teacher and consider how these teachers' enthusiasm was evident. Try out some of these teachers' strategies with classes you are teaching.

There are perhaps three principal ways in which you can communicate enthusiasm. These include both verbal and non-verbal communication. The first is via **facial expression**, once described like this:

> An enthusiastic speaker will be producing a stream of facial expressions which convey his excitement, disbelief, surprise or amusement about his message. Some expressions are extremely brief, lasting about one fifth of a second and may highlight a particular word, whereas others last much longer, perhaps accompanying the verbal expression of an idea. The overall effect is to provide a running commentary for the listener on how the speaker feels about the ideas expressed. In contrast, a speaker who is not involved in his subject shows little variation in facial expression. The impression conveyed is that the ideas are brought out automatically and are failing even to capture the attention of the speaker.
>
> (Robertson, 1989, p. 64)

The second way is via the **use of your voice**. The manner in which you speak as a teacher gives a clear indication of how you feel about the topic under debate and is readily picked up by pupils. The voice needs to be varied and to indicate your feelings about what you are teaching. As mentioned above, you are engaged in something akin to a 'selling job', and your voice has to show this in its production – it has to be persuasive and occasionally show a measure of excitement. A monotone voice is hardly likely to convey enthusiasm. See the section above for more information about using your voice.

A third way to convey enthusiasm is via your **poise and movement**. An enthusiastic speaker has an alert posture and accompanies speech with appropriately expressive hand and arm gestures. Sometimes these gestures can emphasise a point, and at other times they might reinforce something that is being described through indicating relevant shape or direction – for example, of an arrangement of apparatus or a tactical move in hockey. If you are enthusiastic, you are committed and involved, and all aspects of your posture and movement should display this.

Task 3.1.7

CONVEYING ENTHUSIASM 2

Ask your tutor or another student teacher to observe a lesson and grade you A, B or C for enthusiasm in self-presentation, looking at facial expression, voice, poise/movement in turn. You may like to use an observation table as shown in the example below:

	Facial expression	Voice	Poise/ movement
e.g. Welcome to the class	B	B	C
Lesson introduction	C	C	C
Instruction for first task	B	B	C

Remember that your enthusiasm should be evident at all times, not only when you are presenting material but also when you are commenting on a pupil's work, particularly perhaps when the pupil has persevered or achieved a goal. Enthusiasm should be sustained throughout the lesson. Discuss the results and try to improve your rating in two or three further lessons.

Confidence

It is of paramount importance that as a teacher you present yourself with confidence. This is easier said than done because confidence relates both to a sense of knowledgeable mastery of the subject matter being worked on and to a sense of assurance of being in control over the classroom conduct of the pupils.

There is an irony in pupils' response to teacher confidence. For pupils this expression of authority is part of the role they expect of a teacher, and where this confidence is in evidence pupils feel at ease and reassured. In fact, pupils prefer the security of a confident teacher. However, it is in young people's nature to attempt to undermine authority if they sense at any time that a teacher is unsure or apprehensive.

The key to confident self-presentation is to be well planned, both in respect of material and in all areas related to organisation (see Unit 2.3 on taking responsibility for whole lessons for further information). Of course, in many cases it is experience that brings confidence, but sadly pupils seldom allow that to influence their behaviour. Without the benefit of experience it is of course true that all your excellent plans may not work, for one reason or another, and you may have no alternative 'up your sleeve'. Whatever happens you need to cultivate a confident exterior, even if it is something of an act and you are feeling far from assured inside.

How is confidence conveyed? Confidence can be conveyed verbally and non-verbally. Verbally it is displayed in clear, purposeful instructions and explanations that are not disrupted by hesitation. Instructions given in a direct and businesslike manner, such as 'John, please collect the scissors and put them in the red box', convey a sense of confidence. On the other hand, the same instruction put in the form of a question, such as 'John will you collect the scissors and put them in the red box?', can convey a sense of your being less assured, not being confident that, in fact, John *will* co-operate. There is also the possibility of the pupil saying 'No'! Your voice needs to be used in a firm, measured manner. A slower, lower, well-articulated delivery is always more authoritative and displays more confidence than a fast, high-pitched method of speaking. Use of voice is particularly important in giving key instructions, especially where safety factors are involved and in taking action to curtail inappropriate pupil behaviour. This is perhaps the time to be less enthusiastic and animated and more serious and resolute in your manner.

Task 3.1.8

CONFIDENCE

Tape-record a lesson in which you are involved in a variety of verbal inputs. After the lesson, listen to the tape yourself and decide if you sound confident and enthusiastic and if your voice is appropriate. Discuss with a colleague whether the principal message you are giving on the tape is one of confidence and enthusiasm. Remember also that there could be a danger of 'going over the top' when showing enthusiasm. If you are over-excited it can give the episode a sense of triviality, so the enthusiasm has to be measured.

Non-verbally, confidence is expressed via tone of voice, posture, movement and eye contact, both in their own right and as an appropriate accompaniment to verbal language. There is nothing agitated about the movement of confident people. They tend to stand still and to use their arm gestures to a limited extent to reinforce the message being conveyed.

Eye contact is a crucial aspect of conveying confidence to pupils. A nervous person avoids eye contact, somehow being afraid to know what others are thinking, not wanting to develop a relationship that might ultimately reveal their inability or weakness. Clearly it is your role as a teacher to be alert at all times to pupil reaction and to be striving to develop a relationship with pupils that encourages them to seek your help and advice. Steady, committed eye contact is usually helpful for both of these objectives. You must also recognise that the use of eye contact is regarded differently by people of different cultures, e.g. some members of some cultures avoid use of eye contact (this also applies to other aspects of non-verbal communication, such as proximity to another person). You should therefore take into account cultural sensitivities. Take advice from your tutor, a staff member of that culture, staff at the local multicultural centre, or the Commission for Racial Equality (see Appendix 4 for details).

Task 3.1.9

USING EYE CONTACT

During one day of teaching make a conscious effort to look pupils in the eye while you are giving whole class instructions or explanations, taking account of cultural differences in relation to eye contact. Ask your tutor or another student teacher to observe this aspect of your teaching and give you feedback as to how successful you are being.

Caring

It is not surprising perhaps that young people feel that a caring approach is important in developing an effective relationship with teachers. In a piece of research reported by Wragg (1984, p. 82), children were found to favour teachers who were 'understanding, friendly and firm'. Many more pupils indicated that this was their preference over 'efficient, orderly and firm' and 'friendly, sympathetic and understanding'. It is interesting to note that firmness is also a preferred characteristic.

Notwithstanding young people's preferences, interest in pupils as individuals and in their progress is surely the reason most teachers are in teaching. Your commitment to pupils' well-being and learning should be evident in all aspects of your manner and self-presentation. While this attitude goes without saying, it is not as straightforward as it sounds, as it demands sensitivity and flexibility. In a sense it is you as the teacher who have to modify your behaviour in response to the pupils (rather than it always being the pupil who has to fall into line with everything asked for by the teacher). There is a potential conflict between firm confidence and flexible empathy. There is a balance to be struck and it is one of the challenges of teaching to find this balance and to be able to respond suitably at the appropriate time.

A caring approach is evident from a range of features of teaching, from efficient preparation through to sensitive interpersonal skills such as listening. Those teachers who put the interests of the pupils above everything have taken the time and trouble to prepare work thoroughly in a form appropriate to the class. Similarly the classroom environment shows thoughtful design and organisation.

In the teaching situation, caring teachers are fully engaged in the task at hand, observing, supporting, praising, alert to the class climate and able to respond with an appropriate modification in the programme if necessary. Above all, however, caring teachers know pupils by name, remember their work, problems and progress from previous lessons and are prepared to take time to listen to them and talk about personal things as well as work. In other words, caring teachers show a real sensitivity to pupils' individual needs.

SUMMARY AND KEY POINTS

As teachers you can improve your ability to communicate, as the techniques and skills can be learned and practised. Good communication is essential for developing good relationships with pupils, a positive classroom climate and effective teaching and learning. This unit has aimed to help you identify both the strengths and weaknesses in your communication and to provide the basis for further development. Your developing professional knowledge and judgement should enable you to use these skills sensitively and to best advantage.

FURTHER READING

Kyriacou, C. (1997) *Effective Teaching in Schools: Theory and Practice* (2nd edn), Cheltenham: Stanley Thornes, chapter 4.
This chapter looks at setting up the learning experience, including giving an explanation, questioning and discussion as part of teacher exposition.

Ogborn, J., Cress, G., Martins, I. and McGillicuddy, K. (1996) *Explaining Science in the Classroom*, Buckingham: Open University Press.
This is a report of a research project into the way science teachers try to explain ideas to pupils (although the context is science, the focus is communication). Conducted by scientists and linguists, it is suitable for those becoming secure in their teaching and who wish to read more deeply.

Perrott, E. (1982) *Effective Teaching*, London: Longman, chapters 4 and 5.
Chapter 4 looks at lower-order questions which require pupils to recall information and higher-order questions which require pupils to manipulate information for some purpose. Chapter 5 builds on this by looking at a questioning strategy needed to help pupils develop skills in higher-order thinking.

Robertson, J. (1989) *Effective Classroom Control: Understanding Pupil–Teacher Relationships* (2nd edn), London: Hodder and Stoughton.
This book looks at relationships between teachers and pupils. It considers this in different ways, but includes sections on expressing your authority, establishing authority in first meetings and conveying enthusiasm. The sections consider effective non-verbal communications in these relationships.

UNIT 3.2 **MOTIVATING PUPILS**

SUSAN CAPEL

INTRODUCTION

Pupils' attitudes to school and motivation to learn are a result of a number of factors, including past experiences, future expectations, peer group, teachers, school ethos, gender, family background, culture, economic status and class (see also Unit 4.4 'Responding to diversity'). The link between motivation and educational performance is complex.

Some pupils have a more positive attitude to school and to learning, e.g. it is valued at home or they see a link between education and a job. These pupils are therefore more likely to work hard, behave in the classroom and succeed in education. Many pupils want to learn but depend on teachers to get them interested in a subject at school. Even though some pupils may not be inherently motivated to learn, the school ethos, teachers' attitudes, behaviour, personal enthusiasm, teaching style and strategies in the classroom can increase their motivation to learn (see Unit 3.1 on 'Communicating with pupils'). Pupils not motivated to learn are more likely to misbehave. If the teacher does not manage the class and their behaviour effectively, the learning of all pupils in the class can be negatively affected.

Thus, a central aim for you as a teacher is to motivate pupils to learn. There are a range of techniques you can use to increase pupils' motivation to learn, for example:

- showing your enthusiasm for a topic, subject or teaching;
- treating each pupil as an individual;
- providing quick feedback by marking work promptly;
- rewarding appropriate behaviour.

In order to use such techniques effectively you need to understand why each technique is used. A study of motivation is therefore crucial to give you some knowledge and insight into ways of motivating pupils to learn. There is a wealth of material available on motivation. This unit tries to draw out some of the material we feel is of most benefit to you as a student teacher.

OBJECTIVES

By the end of this unit you should be able to:

- understand the role and importance of motivation for effective teaching and classroom management;
- appreciate some of the key elements of motivation for effective teaching;
- understand how to motivate pupils effectively.

By completing this unit you will have addressed some of the competences/standards expected of you as a newly qualified teacher. Refer to the competences/standards for your course now and identify those implicitly or explicitly related to motivation of pupils.

WHAT IS MOTIVATION?

Motivation 'consists of internal processes and external incentives which spur us on to satisfy some need' (Child, 1997b, p. 44). Motivation can be intrinsic (motivation from within the person rather than from someone else, e.g. a sense of achievement at having completed a difficult piece of work), or extrinsic (motivation from someone else, e.g. praise from a teacher for good work). Research has shown that intrinsic motivation is generally more motivating than extrinsic motivation and is therefore to be encouraged in learning.

A teacher's job would certainly be easier if all pupils were motivated intrinsically. However, pupils are asked to do many activities at school which are new to them, which are difficult, at which they may not be immediately successful or which they may perceive to be of little or no relevance to them. In order to become intrinsically motivated, pupils need encouragement along the way, e.g. written or verbal praise for effort, making progress or success, feedback on how they are doing or an explanation of the relevance of the work. Teachers can deliberately plan such extrinsic motivators into their lessons. Developing motivation is part of good formative assessment (see Units 6.1 and 6.2).

What motivates people?

The activities that people start and continue and the amount of effort they put into those activities at any particular time are determined by their motivation. Pupils may be motivated by a number of factors. These include:

- achievement (e.g. completing a piece of work which has taken a lot of effort);
- pleasure (e.g. getting a good mark or praise from a teacher for a piece of work);
- preventing or stopping less pleasant activities (e.g. avoiding getting a detention);
- satisfaction (e.g. feeling that you are making progress);
- success (e.g. doing well in a test).

It is often difficult for a teacher to identify what is motivating a particular pupil at a particular time or indeed for a pupil to identify exactly what is motivating them. As a teacher you can often only infer whether or not pupils are motivated by observing their behaviour; for example, a pupil who is not motivated may not be listening to what you are saying, is talking, looking bored or staring out of the window. Low motivation may result from a number of factors, e.g. boredom or a task being too difficult.

Theories of motivation

There are a number of theories of motivation. In addition, we adopt our own, often unconscious, theories. Examples of theories of motivation, along with some of their implications for you as a teacher in determining learning activities, are given in Table 3.2.1. Below are several tasks to help you think about the application of these theories. Record the outcomes in your diary so that you can compare these theories of motivation.

Task 3.2.1

THEORY x AND THEORY y

In two columns, write down your general assumptions about (i) people you work with and (ii) pupils in classes you teach, using assumptions in Table 3.2.1 from the entry called theory x and theory y. Do you have the same assumptions for both sets of people? Which theory do you tend towards? Write down in the same two columns anything you can about your approach to people you are working with or to your teaching. Reflect on these as you read through this unit to see if you are using the most appropriate and effective methods of motivation.

Task 3.2.2

ACHIEVEMENT MOTIVATION

Discuss with your tutor how you can differentiate work so that all pupils in a mixed ability class can perceive that they can succeed approximately 50 per cent of the time, in line with achievement motivation theory. How is the work modified to enable each pupil to be able to succeed? What can you do to prevent loss of motivation if pupils are not successful in this work?

Task 3.2.3

ATTRIBUTION THEORY OF MOTIVATION

Reflect on one aspect of your educational performance in which you had success and one in which you were not as successful. In relation to attribution theory, for each of these, reflect on (i) to what you attribute your success or lack of it, (ii) whether you expected certain grades from assignments, and (iii) to what you attribute unexpected grades: ability, effort, difficulty of the task or luck.

It is generally accepted that pupils are more likely to try harder if they can see a link between the amount of effort they put in and success in the activity. Therefore, as a teacher you should design activities which encourage pupils to attribute success or failure to effort. However, this is not always easy. Postlethwaite (1993) identified the difficulty of determining how much effort a pupil has put into a piece of work (especially that done at home) and hence the problems of marking the work. You can no doubt think of occasions where one person has put in a lot of effort on a piece of homework, but missed the point and received a low mark, whereas another person has rushed through the homework and managed to achieve a good mark. In 'norm-referenced' marking a mark is given solely for the level of performance on a piece of work in relation to the level of performance of the rest of the group. A certain percentage of the class get a designated category of mark, no matter how good each individual piece of work. This encourages success or failure to be attributed to ability or luck. In 'criterion-referenced' marking, pupils' work is not compared to allocate marks. Rather, pupils are given a mark which reflects how closely the criteria for the assessment have been met, irrespective of the performance of other pupils. Thus, all pupils

Table 3.2.1 Theories of motivation and their implications for you as a teacher

Theory	Author and date	Main points	Implications for teachers
Theory *x* and theory *y*	McGregor, 1960	**Theory *x*** managers assume that the average worker is lazy, lacks ambition, is resistant to change, self-centred and not very bright.	You may treat pupils differently, depending on whether inherently you believe in theory *x* or theory *y*.
		Theory *y* managers assume that the average worker is motivated, wants to take responsibility, has potential for development and works for the organisation. Any lack of ambition or resistance to change comes from experience.	A **theory *x*** teacher externally motivates pupils by directing, controlling their actions, persuading, rewarding and punishing them to modify their behaviour.
			A **theory *y*** teacher encourages intrinsic motivation by allowing pupils to develop for themselves.
Achievement motivation	Atkinson, 1964 McClelland, 1961	Motivation to perform an achievement-orientated task is related to (i) the need to achieve on a particular task, (ii) expectation of success on the task, and (iii) the strength of the incentive after the task has been successfully completed.	Plan tasks that are challenging but attainable with effort. Work should be differentiated according to individual needs. Tasks on which pupils expect to achieve approximately 50 per cent of the time are the most motivating. You also need to plan for the loss of motivation if pupils fail (up to 50 per cent of the time).
Attribution theory	Weiner, 1972	Success or failure is attributed to ability, effort, difficulty of task or luck, depending on (i) previous experience of success or failure on the task, (ii) the amount of work put in, or (iii) a perceived relationship between what is done and success or failure on the task.	Reward effort as well as success, as pupils are more likely to try if they perceive that success is due to effort, e.g. you can give two marks for work: one for the standard of the work, the other for effort. Use teaching and assessment which are individualised rather than competitive.

Table 3.2.1 continued

Theory	Author and date	Main points	Implications for teachers
Expectation theory	Rogers, 1982	Teachers' expectations of pupils' performance can influence the way pupils perform, their motivation to learn and how they attribute success or failure. Pupils perform in the way they are expected to perform by teachers.	Pupils perform according to expectations of them. Do not prejudge pupils on their past performance so that you convey your expectations (high or low) of them. Rather, encourage pupils to work to the best of their ability all the time.
Hierarchy of needs theory	Maslow, 1970	Hierarchy (highest to lowest): 1 Self-actualisation (need to fulfil own potential) 2 Self-esteem (need to feel competent and gain recognition from others) 3 Affiliation and affection (need for love and belonging) 4 Need for physical and psychological safety 5 Physiological needs (e.g. food, warmth) Energy is spent meeting the lowest level of unmet need.	If basic needs, e.g. sleep, food, warmth, are not met, a pupil concentrates on meeting that need first and is unlikely to benefit from attempts by teachers to meet higher-level needs. Try to create a classroom environment to fulfil basic needs first, e.g. rules for using dangerous equipment provide a sense of physical safety, routines give a sense of psychological security, group work can give a sense of belonging (affiliation) (Postlethwaite, 1993).
Behavioural learning theories	Skinner, 1953	Activity or behaviour is learned and maintained because of interaction with the environment. An activity or behaviour reinforced by a pleasurable outcome is more likely to be repeated.	Positive reinforcement (reward), e.g. praise, generally increases motivation to learn and behave. This has a greater impact if the reward is relevant to the pupils, they know how to get the reward and it is given fairly and consistently.

who meet stated criteria for a particular category of mark are marked in that category. Although this overcomes some of the disadvantages of norm-referenced marking, it does not reflect how much effort the pupil has put into the work (see also Units 6.1 and 6.2 on assessment).

Postlethwaite went on to say that effort can best be judged by comparing different pieces of the same pupil's work, as the standard of work is likely to reflect the amount of effort put in. Giving two marks for the work – one for content and standard of the work and one for effort and presentation – can encourage effort. Thus, even if the content and standard are poor, it may be possible to praise the effort. This praise can motivate the pupil to try harder, especially if pupils value the mark for effort. Postlethwaite suggested that another way of encouraging pupils to attribute success to effort is to ask them to write about the way they tackled the task.

Expectation theory says that a teacher forms an impression of a pupil on which expectations of that pupil are based; the teacher's verbal and non-verbal behaviour is based, consciously or unconsciously, on those expectations; the pupil recognises, consciously or unconsciously, the teacher's expectations of them from the teacher's behaviour, and responds in a way that matches the teacher's behaviour and expectations of them (Rogers, 1982). It is generally accepted that, if a teacher expects high achievement and good behaviour, pupils perform to the best of their ability and behave well. If, on the other hand, teachers have low expectations of pupils' work and behaviour, pupils achieve little and behave badly. In the same way, teachers can develop stereotypes of how different groups of pupils perform or behave; stereotypes can direct expectations (see Unit 4.4 'Responding to Diversity'; Gillborn and Gipps, 1996, chapter 4; and Gillborn and Mirza, 2000, for further information).

One aspect of the organisation of a school that may particularly influence teachers' expectations of pupils is the way pupils are grouped. If pupils are streamed by ability, they remain in the same group throughout the year, whatever their ability in different subjects. Whatever the labels attached to each stream, pupils are perceptive and judge their abilities by the stream they are in. This may be partly because teachers' verbal and non-verbal behaviour communicates clearly their expectations. Teachers expect pupils in the 'top' stream to do well; therefore they behave accordingly, e.g. actively encouraging pupils, setting challenging work. Teachers expect pupils in the 'bottom' stream not to do as well; therefore they behave accordingly, e.g. constantly nagging pupils, setting easy work (or none at all). Both groups of pupils tend to fulfil the expectations of teachers. No doubt many of you have heard of the notorious 'bottom' stream in a school. Setting pupils for different subjects can overcome problems of streaming, i.e. recognising pupils' ability in different subjects and changing the grouping of pupils according to their ability in a specific subject. Grouping pupils in mixed ability classes and providing differentiated work within the class to enable pupils of different abilities to work alongside each other can also overcome the problems (for further information about this, see Unit 4.1 on 'Pupil grouping, progression and differentiation').

Task 3.2.4

EXPECTATION THEORY AND YOUR TEACHING

Reflect on whether your expectations of, and behaviour towards, pupils have been influenced by previous knowledge (given to you by the teacher) about the ability or behaviour of particular pupils in a class you are teaching. Ask someone to observe a class you are teaching, looking specifically to see if your behaviour indicates that you might have different expectations of pupils. Discuss their observations.

Task 3.2.5

HIERARCHY OF NEEDS THEORY

Consider some of the home and school conditions that are likely to leave pupils with unmet needs when they come to school and which prevent effective learning (according to the hierarchy of needs theory (Maslow, 1970)). Discuss with your tutor or another student teacher what you can do in your lessons that may help pupils to meet these basic needs, to provide a foundation for effective learning. Discuss when and to whom you should report if you suspect pupils' most basic needs are not being met, as this may require the skills of other professionals.

Rewards

Four types of **reward** (positive reinforcements) have been identified (Bull and Solity, 1987). These are listed below in the order in which they are used most often:

- social rewards (social contact and pleasant interactions with other people, including praise, a smile to recognise an action or achievement or to say thank you, encouraging remarks or a gesture of approval);
- token rewards (house points, grades, certificates);
- material rewards (tangible, usable or edible items);
- activity rewards (opportunities for enjoyable activities).

Task 3.2.6

USING REWARDS

Develop an observation schedule which has sections for the four types of reward listed above. Observe a class and mark in the appropriate category any reward used by the teacher in the class. Discuss with the teacher the variety and frequency of use of the different possible methods of reward. Ask your tutor or another student teacher to undertake the same observation on one of your lessons. Discuss the differences in variety and frequency of reward used. As you plan your lessons consider how you might use reward in the lesson. Ask the same person to observe a lesson a couple of months after the first one and see if you have changed your use of reward in your lessons. Relate this to what you know about behavioural learning theories.

Factors influencing motivation to learn

Success

Success is generally motivating in itself. Some pupils struggle to succeed, whereas others succeed much more quickly. There are many ways to help pupils succeed, e.g. using a technique often called whole-part-whole teaching. In this, pupils are shown the whole activity first so that they know what they are trying to achieve. The activity is then broken down into small, self-contained, achievable parts, which allow pupils to receive reinforcement for each small, successful step. Pupils gradually build up the whole from these small steps; therefore when they attempt the whole, they are most likely to succeed. You may relate to this by thinking about when you learned (or tried to learn) front crawl in swimming. You probably practised your arms, legs and breathing separately before you tried to put it all together. What other techniques can you use to help pupils succeed?

Task 3.2.7

WHOLE-PART-WHOLE TEACHING

As part of your normal lesson planning with a class, select one activity which you can break down into small, self-contained, achievable parts, which can be put together to build up gradually to the whole. Ask your tutor or another student teacher to observe you teaching this activity. Show the class the whole activity first and then gradually teach the separate parts of the activity, giving pupils appropriate feedback at each stage (see below for more information about giving feedback), until you have built up the whole activity. At the end of the lesson discuss how this went with some of the pupils. Discuss with the observer how the pupils responded and how well they learned the task.

Praise

Research findings show that pupils generally respond more positively to praise and positive comments about their work or behaviour than to criticism and negative comments. This, in turn, may produce a more positive atmosphere, in which pupils work harder and behave better. If pupils do misbehave in such an atmosphere, Olweus (1993, p. 85) suggested that the use of praise makes pupils feel appreciated and relatively well-liked, which may make it easier for them to accept criticism of inappropriate behaviour and attempt to change.

Research has also shown that teachers give relatively little praise. OFSTED (1993a) reported that teachers' vocabulary is generally more negative than positive. Praise is given more often for academic work than social behaviour and social behaviour is more likely to be criticised than praised, maybe because teachers expect pupils to behave appropriately in the classroom.

Some teachers use very few different words to praise pupils, e.g. 'good', 'well done', 'OK'. What other words can you use to praise someone or give feedback? Try to develop a list of such words, because if you use the same word to praise pupils all the time, the word loses its effect. The range of words must be accompanied by appropriate non-verbal communication signals (see Unit 3.1 on 'Communicating with pupils' for more information about non-verbal communication).

Task 3.2.8

THE LANGUAGE OF PRAISE

Draw up an observation schedule, such as the one below, which has categories for praise given to an individual, a group or the whole class, and negative comments to an individual, a group or the whole class, for both academic work and social behaviour.

	Tick each time praise or negative comment is given in each category								
Praise to individual for academic work									
Praise to group for academic work									
Praise to whole class for academic work									
Praise to individual for social behaviour									
Praise to group for social behaviour									
Praise to whole class for social behaviour									
Negative comments to individual for academic work									
Negative comments to group for academic work									
Negative comments to whole class for academic work									
Negative comments to individual for social behaviour									
Negative comments to group for social behaviour									
Negative comments to whole class for social behaviour									

Observe a class taught by an experienced teacher. Sit in a place where you can hear everything that is said. Record the number of times praise is given and the number of times negative comments are made in each of the twelve categories given above. Observe the same experienced teacher in another lesson. This time write down the different words, phrases and actions the teacher uses to give praise and negative comments in each of these categories and the number of times each is used.

Ask someone to conduct the same observations on your lessons. You might be surprised to find that you use a phrase such as 'good' or 'OK' very frequently in your teaching. Discuss the differences with your tutor and, if appropriate, develop strategies to help you improve the amount of praise you give and the range of words, phrases and actions you use to give praise. Record these strategies in your diary and gradually try to incorporate them into your teaching.

Although it is generally accepted that praise aids learning, there are dangers in using praise. There are times when it may not be appropriate to use praise. For example, pupils who become lazy about their work as a result of complacency may respond by working harder if their work is gently criticised on occasion. If praise is given automatically, regardless of the work, effort or behaviour, pupils quickly see through it and it loses its effect. Praise should only be used to reward appropriate work, effort or behaviour.

Some pupils do not respond positively to praise, e.g. they are embarrassed by praise, especially if they are praised in front of their peers. Others perceive praise to be a form of punishment, e.g. if they are teased or rejected by their peers for 'being teacher's pet' or for behaving themselves in class. Other pupils do not know how to respond to praise because they have not received much praise in the past; for example, because they have continually received low marks for their work or because they have been in the bottom stream, they have therefore learned to fail. Some of these pupils may therefore want to account for their failing as a result of not caring or not trying to succeed. One way they may do this is by misbehaving in the classroom.

Thus, pupils respond differently to praise. In the same class you may have some pupils working hard to get praise from the teacher or a good mark on their homework, whilst others do not respond well to praise or are working hard at avoiding praise. You have to use your judgement when giving praise; for example, if you praise a pupil who is misbehaving to try to encourage better behaviour, you may be seen to be rewarding bad behaviour, thereby motivating the pupil to continue to misbehave in order to get attention. If you are not immediately successful in your use of praise, do not give up using praise, but consider whether you are giving it in the right way, e.g. would it be better to have a quiet word, rather than praise pupils out loud in front of their peers? As your professional knowledge and judgement develop, you become able to determine how best to use praise appropriately to motivate pupils in your classes.

Punishment

Teachers use both praise and punishment to try to change behaviour. However, reward, most frequently in the form of praise, is generally considered to be more effective because it increases appropriate behaviour, whereas punishment decreases inappropriate behaviour. If pupils are punished they know what behaviour results in punishment and therefore what not to do, but they may not know what behaviour avoids punishment.

However, there are times when punishment is needed. At such times, make sure that you use punishment to best effect; for example, avoid punishing a whole class for the behaviour of one or a few pupil(s); always make it clear which pupil(s) are being punished for what behaviour; always give punishment fairly and consistently and in proportion to the offence. Do not make idle threats to pupils, by threatening them with punishment that you cannot carry out. In order to increase appropriate behaviour, identify to the offender any positive aspects of the behaviour being punished and explain the appropriate behaviour. Unit 3.3 provides further information on reprimanding pupils and managing behaviour problems and Unit 4.5 addresses some ethical and moral dimensions of behaviour.

Feedback

It may be that pupils who do not respond positively to praise are under-performing and have been doing so for a long time. You may be able to check whether they are under-performing by referring to the standard assessment data held on pupils when they enter the school. Such pupils and others benefit from being given feedback on how they are doing, as it helps pupils to know whether they are on the right track when learning something. Feedback gives pupils information about how they are doing and motivates them to continue. A pupil is more likely to learn effectively or behave appropriately if feedback is used in conjunction with praise. A sequence in which feedback is sandwiched between praise, i.e. praise–constructive feedback–praise, is designed to provide encouragement and motivation, along with information to help the pupil improve the activity. Giving praise first is designed to make pupils more receptive to the information and, afterwards, to have a positive approach to try again. Try combining feedback with praise in your teaching.

Feedback can be used effectively with the whole-part-whole teaching method described above. If you give feedback about how a pupil has done on each part, this part can be improved before going on to the next part. If you give feedback immediately (i.e. as an attempt is being finished or immediately after it has finished, but before another attempt is started), pupils can relate the feedback directly to the outcome of the activity. Thus, pupils are more likely to succeed if they take small steps and receive immediate feedback on each step. This success can, in turn, lead to increased motivation to continue the activity.

One problem with giving immediate feedback is how you can provide feedback to individual pupils in a class who are all doing the same activity at the same time. There are several methods which you can use to provide feedback to many pupils at the same time, e.g. getting pupils to work through examples in a book which has the answers in the back; setting criteria and letting pupils evaluate themselves against the criteria; or having pupils assess one another against set criteria (see the reciprocal teaching style of Mosston and Ashworth (1994) in Unit 5.3 for more information about this and other teaching styles). If they have been properly prepared for it, pupils are generally sensible and constructive when responsibility for giving feedback is placed on them.

Not all feedback comes from another person, e.g. the teacher or another pupil; feedback also comes from the activity itself. The feedback from the activity may be easier to identify for some activities than others; for example, a pupil gets feedback about their success if an answer to a mathematics problem matches that given in the book, or the wicket is knocked down when bowling in cricket. In other activities, right or wrong, success or failure, is not as clear-cut, e.g. there is often no right or wrong answer to an English essay. In the early stages of learning an activity, pupils find it hard to use the feedback from the activity, e.g. they may notice that they were successful at the activity, but not be able to identify why. Normally, therefore, they need feedback from another person. This immediate, external feedback can be used to help pupils become more aware of what they are doing and how they are improving, and to help them identify why they were successful or not at the activity and therefore to help them make use of feedback from the activity. Later in the learning, e.g. when refining an activity, pupils should be able to benefit from feedback from the activity itself, and therefore it is better not to give immediate feedback.

Finally, to be effective, feedback should be given about pupils' work or behaviour, not about the pupils themselves. It must convey to the pupils that their work or behaviour is satisfactory or not, not that they are good (or bad) *per se*.

You need to observe pupils very carefully in order to spot small changes or improvements. This allows you to provide appropriate feedback. See Unit 2.1 on 'Reading classrooms' for more information about observation techniques, and Units 6.1 and 6.2 on formative assessment. Your developing professional knowledge and judgement will help you to know when and how to use feedback to best effect.

Task 3.2.9

TEACHING STYLES

As an integral part of your lesson planning, select one activity where pupils can observe each other and provide feedback. Devise a handout with the main points to be observed. Plan how you are going to introduce this activity into the lesson. Discuss the lesson plan with your tutor. Ask your tutor to observe the lesson. Discuss the effectiveness of the strategy afterwards, determining how you can improve its use. Also try to observe teachers who use this strategy regularly. Try the strategy at a later date in your school experience. Think of other ways in which you can get more feedback to more pupils when they are doing an activity. Include these in your lesson plans, as appropriate. Teaching styles are discussed in Unit 5.3.

Motivating individuals

As the discussion above has highlighted, there is no one correct way to motivate pupils to learn. Different motivation techniques are appropriate and effective in different situations, e.g. pupils of different ages respond differently to different types of motivation, reward, punishment or feedback. Likewise, individual pupils respond differently. Further, any one pupil may respond to the same motivator differently at different times and in different situations.

Pupils need to feel that they are individuals, with their needs and interests taken into account, rather than just being a member of a group. If pupils are not motivated, do not let them avoid doing the task, but try to find ways of motivating them; for example, if pupils are bored by work that is being done, try to stimulate their motivation by relating it to something in which they are interested. You can motivate pupils most effectively by using motivation techniques appropriate for a particular pupil in a particular situation.

Thus, you need to try to find out what motivates each pupil in your class. As a student teacher you are at a disadvantage here because you can only know what motivates each pupil and what rewards they are likely to respond to if you know your pupils well and know something about their needs and interests. As a student teacher, you do not usually spend enough time in one school to get to know the pupils well and therefore you can only try to motivate individual pupils by using your knowledge and understanding of pupils of that age. Learning pupils' names quickly gives you a start in being able to motivate pupils effectively (see Unit 2.3 on 'Taking responsibility for whole lessons', for strategies you can use to learn pupils' names). As you get to know pupils, you can identify what motivates them by finding out what activities they enjoy, what they choose to do and what they try to avoid, what types of reward they work for and to what they do not respond (e.g. by observation, talking to pupils, discussing a pupil with the form tutor or other teachers). The sooner you can relate to pupils individually, the sooner you can manage a class of individuals effectively. However, this does not occur at an early phase in your teaching (see 'Phases of development' in Unit 1.2, pp. 22–26).

SUMMARY AND KEY POINTS

This unit has identified some general principles and techniques for motivation. However, you need to be able to use these appropriately. For example, if you praise a group for working quietly while they are working you may negatively affect their work. It is better in this situation to let the group finish their work and then praise them. In addition, pupils are individuals and therefore respond differently to different forms of motivation, reward, punishment and feedback. Further, the same pupil responds differently at different times and in different situations. To motivate each pupil effectively therefore requires that you know your pupils so that you can anticipate how they will respond. Motivation is supported by good formative assessment techniques. Your developing professional knowledge and judgement enable you to combine theory with practice to motivate pupils effectively in your classes, which raises the standard of their work.

FURTHER READING

Child, D. (1997b) *Psychology and the Teacher* (6th edn), London: Cassell.
Chapter 3 provides in-depth consideration of motivation in education. It starts by considering three broad types of theories of motivation, then looks specifically at how motivation applies in education and describes how some of the theories of motivation impact on you as a teacher.

Entwistle, N.J. (1993) *Styles of Learning and Teaching* (3rd edn), London: David Fulton.
Chapters 5 and 9 contain extended discussion about the relationship between personality and motivation and styles of learning.

Kyriacou, C. (1998) *Essential Teaching Skills* (2nd edn), Cheltenham: Stanley Thornes.
This book contains chapters on lesson management and classroom climate, both of which consider aspects of motivation, e.g. whether lesson management helps to maintain pupils' motivation and whether the opportunities for learning are challenging and offer realistic opportunities for success.

UNIT 3.3   MANAGING CLASSROOM BEHAVIOUR

JON DAVISON

INTRODUCTION

'Good behaviour and discipline in schools are essential to successful teaching and learning' (DFE, 1994a, p. 1). Misbehaviour prevents pupils from learning effectively. It is easier to prevent misbehaviour in the classroom than it is to deal with it afterwards. There is no easy answer to preventing misbehaviour. However, there is less misbehaviour and more effective teaching and learning in classes in which there is effective class management. The Elton Report (DES/WO, 1989, p. 69) concluded that:

> teachers' group management skills are probably the single most important factor in achieving good standards of classroom behaviour; . . . those skills can be taught and learned.

Thus, behaviour in the classroom is directly affected by the quality of your classroom management skills. However, behaviour may also be influenced by other factors, e.g. demotivated pupils are more likely to misbehave than motivated pupils. The demotivation may be the result of a number of factors, only one of which is classroom management. There are some principles on which effective classroom management techniques are based and these principles identify ways of coping with any misbehaviour that does occur, although you must adapt these according to your preferred teaching style, the class and the circumstances.

This unit is designed to enable you to reflect on whether your management is contributing to the incidence of misbehaviour in the classroom, and to identify some possible strategies for improving this; and consequently to help you manage your classroom to prevent misbehaviour and to enable effective teaching and learning to take place. As you cannot prevent all misbehaviour in class, we also consider ways of dealing with misbehaviour. In this unit we also consider briefly misbehaviour outside the classroom.

Although relatively old, the Elton Report (DES/WO, 1989), *Discipline in Schools*, is considered to be a key text, providing valuable insight into behaviour and recommendations about how to improve discipline in schools. We therefore look at aspects of this report in this unit. The key recommendations relating to you as a student and newly qualified teacher are reproduced in this book as Appendix 3, but we recommend that you also look at the full report to develop further understanding of this area. This should be in the library in your institution.

OBJECTIVES

By the end of this unit you should be beginning to:

- understand common causes of misbehaviour in the classroom;
- develop a variety of class management skills designed to prevent misbehaviour;
- develop techniques to deal with behavioural problems that you might encounter.

By doing this you address competences/standards related to managing behaviour and discipline required on your course. Refer to your course competences/standards at this point and identify the specific competences/standards you are addressing.

WHAT IS MISBEHAVIOUR?

Misbehaviour is usually defined as behaviour which causes concern to teachers (Elton Report, DES/WO, 1989). There are many types of pupil misbehaviour, ranging from minor irritation or disruption such as talking in class or not settling down to work, to major confrontations or disruption in the class or school, including bullying and racial harassment.

Teachers' perceptions vary as to what constitutes misbehaviour. While teachers generally agree about types of misbehaviour, there is less agreement about what constitutes minor and major disruption and how any misbehaviour should be dealt with. These differences are mainly due to differences in personality, e.g. some teachers are more tolerant and some more strict than others. However, there should be some guidelines in your school experience school as to what is considered appropriate behaviour and what is not.

Task 3.3.1

MISBEHAVIOUR 1

Spend a few minutes brainstorming the types of pupil misbehaviour that you believe might occur in the classroom. You may recall misbehaviour which occurred in classes you have taught or observed or classes in which you were a pupil. Try to group these into categories of misbehaviour (you may want to start with the four main sources of misbehaviour given by Francis (1975, in Smith and Laslett, 1993, p. 34): noise, equipment, movement and chatter). Then try to list these in rank order of misbehaviour, from very minor disruption to major confrontation. Ask another student teacher to do this activity at the same time and then compare your notes. See if you can agree the rank order. As you gain experience, write down how you plan to deal with each type of misbehaviour.

Task 3.3.2

MISBEHAVIOUR 2

Discuss with your tutor: (i) types of behaviour that are inappropriate in the classroom (e.g. talking); and (ii) how the behaviour is controlled (e.g. by the teacher, by the school rules and expectations). If you are learning to teach a practical subject, e.g. design technology, physical education or science, discuss with your tutor the implications of misbehaviour in relation to safety in lessons and how such misbehaviour is controlled. Consider these in relation to the types of misbehaviour identified in Task 3.3.1 above.

MISBEHAVIOUR IN THE CLASSROOM

Causes of misbehaviour

The three most common causes of misbehaviour in the classroom are: boredom; an inability to do the work a teacher has set; and effort demanded for too long a period without a break. Misbehaviour can also be a means of seeking attention. Clearly, these factors can be anticipated and avoided by careful lesson planning and considered class management. Another factor to be borne in mind is that school life for pupils is as much (some argue more) a social experience as an academic one, and the complex web of social interaction between pupils undoubtedly underpins classroom interaction. Pupils come into the classroom continuing conversations begun on the way to school, in the playground or corridors. This is not to say that the social nature of a pupil's school life should be allowed to dominate the classroom, rather that it should be acknowledged and kept in mind.

Some pupils are more predisposed to misbehave than others, e.g. low academic self-esteem sometimes affects pupils' behaviour in the classroom. Much can be done if you anticipate this factor and plan the lesson to take account of it. The few pupils that you encounter with real emotional difficulties (as opposed to those 'difficulties' that are part of adolescence), and pupils whose sets of values are completely different from those of the school, may cause you problems. However, the school will have identified them and you should discuss these problems with colleagues to identify the support you might be offered and successful strategies which others use with particular pupils.

Class management skills designed to prevent misbehaviour

Remember that the best judges of teachers are pupils. They are experts because they spend at least five hours a day for eleven years observing them. What a pupil thinks is a 'good teacher' might not conform to your model, but pupils do have certain expectations of teachers. Pupils expect teachers to **establish and conform to certain routines**, e.g. going in and sitting down quietly when they arrive, collecting and returning books, getting equipment out or moving around the classroom. They know what they have to do and that there are not going to be any surprises; therefore it makes them feel safe. See Unit 2.3, 'Taking responsibility for whole lessons', for further information about establishing routines.

Pupils 'test out' any new teacher, however experienced; for example, they may test the routines you try to establish. Your response to this is very important. If you over-react, are too harsh or respond in a way that rewards pupils, e.g. you become flustered or angry, the pupils continue to try to find out how far they can go. If, however, you do not rise to any bait given by pupils, but respond coolly, calmly, firmly and fairly, the pupils soon become bored with testing you out and get on with the task of learning.

Perhaps the key skill to develop concerning general class management is the ability to **anticipate problems before they arise**. As with health care, where the most positive and successful form is preventative medicine, the most successful way of managing pupil behaviour is to prevent misbehaviour. If you cannot prevent misbehaviour entirely, the next best thing is to try to contain it as much as possible, to prevent minor disruptions from escalating into major confrontations.

Whatever teaching style you begin to adopt in the classroom, the key to teaching effectively is to **establish your authority**. If you do not establish your authority, e.g. because you are anxious or tense, the atmosphere in the class may be affected and your attempts to manage the class undermined. Your authority in the classroom is founded upon four main aspects, which are:

- conveying your status;
- teaching competently;
- effective class management;
- dealing effectively with pupil misbehaviour.

In Unit 1.2, the section on phases of development considers establishing your authority in greater depth. In addition, Robertson (1989) considers authority in great detail in his book *Effective Classroom Control*, and you may wish to refer to this for further information.

Laying the ground rules

Perhaps the most important factor in classroom management in the prevention of misbehaviour is **the establishment of ground rules to prevent misbehaviour**.

Any school in which you teach has its set of rules and code of conduct to which pupils are expected to conform. Similarly, it has a clearly defined system of rewards and punishments. The pupils are aware of these systems. It is essential that you are very clear about these systems too and that you enforce and employ them equally, even if you personally disagree with some aspects of them. Do not try to court favour with pupils by expressing disagreement. It is unlikely to earn their respect.

Even if the school has rules about classroom behaviour, it is worth spending some time with a new class establishing an agreed set of rules for behaviour in your classroom. The rationale for these rules needs to be established. You may be surprised at how sensible pupils are when engaging in this exercise. Once you and the class have drawn up your rules, display them in the classroom. At the first sign of a minor infringement, draw attention to the agreed set of rules. Likewise, give positive reinforcement to those pupils who keep to the rules, by, for example, remembering to raise a hand rather than calling out (see Unit 3.2 on motivation which looks in more detail at reinforcement).

Task 3.3.3

SCHOOL RULES

Obtain a copy of the rules and code of conduct to which pupils in your school experience school are expected to conform, both inside and outside the classroom, and the system of rewards and punishments available to teachers in order to maintain these rules or to deal with breaches of the rules. If the rules and code of conduct are not written down, discuss with your tutor what they are and make sure you are clear about them. Compare similarities and differences between these rules and code of conduct and those collected by a student teacher from another school. Observe lessons taught by experienced teachers to see how these rules and code of conduct operate in the school. Ask each teacher how they would deal with any rules which you did not see being implemented during your observation. Compare how different teachers interpret and operate the rules and code of conduct. Do teachers interpret them in the same or in their own way? Do teachers develop their own set of rules for their own classroom? Discuss your findings and the implications for your teaching with your tutor.

In a study of secondary teachers, Wragg and Wood (1989) identified eleven classroom rules. In order of occurrence these were:

- pupils must not talk when the teacher is talking;
- pupils should not make disruptive noises;
- rules for entering, leaving and moving around the classroom;
- pupils must not interfere with the work of others;
- work must be completed in a specified way;
- pupils must raise a hand to answer or speak – not shout out;
- pupils must make a positive effort in their work;
- pupils must not challenge the authority of the teacher;
- respect must be shown for property and equipment;
- rules to do with safety;
- pupils must ask if they do not understand.

Smith and Laslett (1993) described four rules of effective classroom management: get them in (greeting, seating, starting); get them out (concluding, dismissing); get on with it (content, manner); and get on with them (who's who; what's going on). These 'rules' may help you to remember the broad range of activities you need to address in order to manage your classroom effectively to prevent misbehaviour. Sections in Unit 2.2 on thorough planning (preparation of schemes of work, lesson planning, having enough of the needed equipment), an effective beginning to the lesson, smooth, seamless transitions and a successful completion of the lesson, address these issues in more detail. We suggest that you refer to these sections at this point and consider these particularly in relation to pupil behaviour in class.

Managing behaviour problems

Effective class management, then, comprises a variety of skills and techniques used with awareness and sensitivity. A well-managed class is much less likely to cause behaviour problems. However, you cannot stop all misbehaviour through effective class management, so how do you cope when pupil behaviour does give cause for concern?

As you may have discovered in the discussion with another student teacher while attempting Task 3.3.1 above, one teacher might regard a particular behaviour as trivial, while another deems it serious. Of course, any pupil misbehaviour might be regarded as being in some way serious if it interferes with the smooth flow of a lesson or with the pupil's or another pupil's work. However, it is interesting to note that in the Elton Report (DES/WO, 1989), HMI reported the following to be the most frequently cited forms of misbehaviour:

- arriving late for the lesson;
- not paying attention to the teacher;

- excessive talking – talking out of turn;
- being noisy – both non-verbally and verbally;
- not getting on with the work;
- pupils being out of their own seats without good reason;
- hindering others.

Your own list of misbehaviour developed in Task 3.3.1 may have included the violent or indeed homicidal, so it is comforting to note that all examples of the most common misbehaviour are, in effect, trivial. This is not to say that serious misbehaviour does not occur but, like violent crime, it is in reality extremely rare – it is just that it makes the headlines. There is also some comfort to be drawn from the fact that if thirty pupils wish to stand up and walk out of the classroom, there is nothing that even the best teacher in the world can do to stop them. We have never known it to happen.

Task 3.3.4

COPING WITH MISBEHAVIOUR

Write down how incidents of the most frequently cited forms of misbehaviour from the Elton Report (DES/WO, 1989) above have been dealt with, by you if they have occurred in your classroom, and by experienced teachers you have observed. How did your handling of these compare with that of experienced teachers? Try to identify specific areas where you need to improve your class management techniques to deal with misbehaviour and discuss with your tutor what you can do to improve in these areas.

Strategies to prevent misbehaviour

It is important to be vigilant in class and constantly monitor the mood, atmosphere, attitude and behaviour of any class you are teaching – what the Hay McBer Report (2000) refers to as the 'lighthouse effect' – that is, being aware of all that is going on around you by developing 360-degree vision. Even if you are reading aloud to a class, it is necessary to scan the class frequently to gauge from, say, body language the pupils' level of attention to your reading. Make eye contact with pupils. Eye contact held just slightly longer with a pupil who is whispering to another is usually enough to silence the miscreant without the need to stop reading.

Circulate around the classroom even when reading. It is not necessary to wander continually like a lost soul, but spending a few minutes in each part of the room ensures that the pupils are very aware of your presence quite close to them. Again, if a pupil is misbehaving as you are addressing the class, your moving towards them and standing by them are often enough to quieten them without the need to break your flow or even to mention their behaviour.

Being very aware of the class enables you to notice pupil misbehaviour. Noticing misbehaviour and responding calmly, quickly, effectively and good-humouredly prevent such behaviour from escalating. The same is true of pupils' disrespect. If pupils do not experience negative consequences, they continue to push the boundaries of accepted behaviour.

Changing the pace of a lesson by providing a variety of tasks and activities does much to prevent boredom, which is, perhaps, the major cause of misbehaviour. If you become aware that a pupil is experiencing difficulty with a task, be on hand to give academic help. Of course, you are not there to do the work for them, but you are there to facilitate their learning; for example, a pupil may misbehave because of frustration at not being able to do the work set, and therefore you must help the pupil to understand the work and solve the problem, thus reducing the frustration. You must not let the pupil avoid doing the work because they find it difficult. Such action compounds the problem later when the pupil cannot do the next piece of work because it is based on the current work.

If a pupil continues to misbehave, move her. You need to have articulated your intention to do so to the whole class at the laying down of the ground rules and to have warned the pupil that this action might be a consequence of her current behaviour. Warning miscreants clearly gives them an opportunity to avoid sanctions. In doing this you allow them not to lose face. However, always do what you have promised or threatened to do. Never make idle threats because pupils soon learn that you do not follow through with your threats and therefore they take no notice of them. Not only do the threats lose their effect but also you lose your credibility. Empty threats create a downward spiral in which it becomes continually more difficult to prevent misbehaviour.

Reprimanding pupils

Your main objective in noticing misbehaviour or in reprimanding a pupil must be to allow the class to continue in a productive manner. Therefore, you should express concern and, possibly, disappointment, as this may cajole the pupil into responding appropriately. At all costs avoid anger: **the throbbing, protruding veins and bulging eyes of an angry teacher make a highly entertaining diversion for even the most well-motivated pupil**.

A major objective in reprimanding a pupil should be to avoid confrontation. The use of private rather than public reprimands negates the need for a pupil to save face in her social sphere. Do not enter into a debate with a pupil, but firmly inform her that you will discuss the matter at a time convenient to you, such as after the lesson. Then immediately carry on with the lesson.

Avoid unfair comparisons and never insult or criticise a pupil; rather, criticise the behaviour. For example, 'Stop being so stupid, Michael!' can be guaranteed to prompt a face-saving response, whereas 'All right Michael, it's time to be getting on with the work' makes the same point. However, do avoid the 'You wouldn't do that at home, would you Michael?' as it allows even the slowest of wits to reply 'Yes, I would!' and raise a laugh at the teacher's expense.

Direct your comments to the work, as in 'Is there a problem with this piece of writing, Michael?', to show that you are aware of his misbehaviour, but which allows him to reply 'No' and then get on with the task. It also allows you to emphasise what is required of a pupil rather than dwelling on the negative. Following up such an interchange by looking through what has been produced thus far also allows the teacher to praise some aspect of the work and reinforce a pupil's positive behaviour.

Remember that a correctly targeted reprimand delivered firmly, fairly and without anger is effective. Try to avoid reprimanding the whole class, as it is guaranteed to be unfair to some and may well alienate those who were thus far sympathetic towards you. For similar reasons never denigrate pupil(s) in public or belittle an individual or a whole class.

It is essential that you are seen to be consistent and fair in your reprimands. Pupils possess a finely tuned sense of justice. A punishment should be in proportion to the offence committed. Do not make empty threats, and resist the temptation to 'up the stakes' from sanctions such as 100 to 1,000 lines or a detention to detention every night for a week – you destroy any credibility you might have. All schools have their own systems of sanctions, but if you do have recourse to detentions, remember that you are normally required to give parents at least twenty-four hours' notice of your intention. You need to check with the school the policy on detentions.

It should not need to be said, but never, under any circumstance, even in the face of the severest provocation, physically punish a pupil. That way lies litigation and a very short career in teaching.

If, despite all efforts, a pupil's behaviour is impossible to manage, seek support. Avoid classroom confrontation with the pupil at all costs. Be very aware of the school support system and obtain the necessary support from a colleague. Most schools operate some system of 'parking' extremely difficult pupils in order that a teacher can get on with the job of teaching a class. For example, pupils may be 'parked' at the head's or deputy head's office or sent to the head of year. Check if such a system operates in your school experience school. Remember, if you have effective class management skills, have made every attempt to pre-empt and deal effectively with misbehaviour, have avoided anger and confrontation, and the pupil is still extremely difficult – then the problem lies elsewhere.

Task 3.3.5

ANALYSING MISBEHAVIOUR

This task invites you to reflect upon an incident that may have occurred in your own classroom in the light of what you have learned from this unit. You may have experienced an example of pupil misbehaviour towards you, however trivial. Briefly note down details of what happened. In the light of what you now understand about management of pupil misbehaviour, record in your diary:

- what you believe were the causes of the misbehaviour;
- how this misbehaviour might have been anticipated and prevented;
- how you would deal with such misbehaviour now.

The Elton Report concluded that the most effective schools seem to be those in which there is a positive atmosphere. This is based on consensus about:

> standards of behaviour among staff, pupils and parents. Staff, pupils and parents should have clear guidance about these standards and their practical application; staff should be encouraged to recognise and praise good behaviour as well as deal with bad behaviour. Pupils should be clear about the distinction between the punishment given for minor and more serious misbehaviour and these punishments should be applied fairly and consistently.
>
> (DES/WO, 1989, p. 13)

Misbehaviour outside the classroom

Teachers have a key role to play in maintaining standards of behaviour in school. You have the major responsibility for control and discipline in your classroom. In addition, you must do your part to prevent or deal with, if they should occur, other serious incidents of misbehaviour in the school, including bullying and racial harassment. The Elton Report recommended that:

headteachers and staff should be: alert to signs of bullying and racial harassment; deal firmly with all such behaviour; and take action based on clear rules which are backed by appropriate sanctions and systems to protect and support victims.

(DES/WO, 1989, p. 26, recommendation 28)

The report then indicated that schools should not allow such behaviour to occur and that everyone (including pupils) must take responsibility to prevent it or deal with it when it does occur. In order to do this effectively a whole school approach to dealing with such problems is needed. Some schools have constructed a whole school approach to discipline which centres on the reinforcement of the positive aspects of pupil behaviour. *Assertive Discipline* (see Canter and Canter, 1977) described one such whole school approach.

The Elton Report also highlighted the need for concerted action at classroom, school, community and national levels, i.e. a concerted effort by a number of professionals working as a team, plus governors, LEAs and government (as well as teachers and parents), in influencing the effectiveness of discipline in schools. The school policy should recognise the need for the school to work as part of the wider community and to call on other professionals such as counsellors, educational welfare officers, educational psychologists or education social workers, as appropriate. The Elton Report emphasised 'the importance of the pastoral role of class teachers and form tutors and the need for the school to maintain regular contact with the education welfare service and other agencies rather than calling them in as a last resort' (DES/WO, 1989, p. 13, recommendation 15). See chapter 4 in Capel, Leask and Turner (1997) for more information about the role of the education social worker and educational psychologist.

An effective whole school policy supports teachers in their responsibility for control and discipline in their classroom, in the wider school and in their pastoral role. One purpose of the pastoral role is to ensure that there is a member of staff who has an overview of an individual pupil's progress and is able to provide support. One aspect of pastoral work which may be of immediate concern is bullying, which, as indicated above, is a major factor affecting pupils' ability to learn at school. It was recognised in the Elton Report (DES/WO, 1989, p. 107) that often pupils are aware of serious bullying and racial harassment before staff are aware, because they occur outside the classroom, in corners of the playground, on the way home from school or in other out-of-the way places. It is important that pupils feel able to tell staff about such incidents because, beyond any physical injury, the misery caused to individual pupils can be very damaging to their self-esteem, motivation and achievement. The school's behaviour policy should also make it clear that pupils have a responsibility to share this knowledge with staff in confidence. An effective pastoral system should enable this to operate effectively.

Task 3.3.6

THE WHOLE SCHOOL BEHAVIOUR POLICY

One of the recommendations of the Elton Report was that headteachers and teachers, in consultation with governors, develop whole school behaviour policies which are clearly understood by pupils, parents and other school staff. Ask your tutor for a copy of this policy. Study it carefully and discuss its origins, implementation and effectiveness with your tutor and other school staff. Compare this policy with one from another school collected by another student teacher, or with the examples of behaviour policies contained in the Elton Report. Record the differences in your diary and reflect on these in the light of your continued development as a teacher.

In their pastoral role teachers have a range of responsibilities for the individual pupil. Haydon and Lambert (1992, p. 35) identify three dimensions of pastoral care:

1 *pastoral casework*: work with individual pupils on any aspect which affects their development and achievement;
2 *pastoral curriculum*: all aspects of work with groups (not just tutorial groups) which contribute to their personal and social development;
3 *pastoral management*: the planning, monitoring, reviewing and communication systems required amongst the various teams and individuals. This supports the overall orderly climate required for pupils' learning and development.

The importance of the pastoral role in influencing pupil behaviour was specifically mentioned in the Elton Report. The committee stressed 'the importance of personal and social education as a means of promoting the values of mutual respect, self discipline and social responsibility which underlie good behaviour'. They recommended 'that personal and social education should be strengthened both inside and outside the National Curriculum' (Elton Report, DES/WO, 1989, p. 13, recommendation 14).

Task 3.3.7

THE PASTORAL ROLE

Discuss with your tutor the pastoral role undertaken by teachers in your school, especially in relation to discipline in the school. How is pastoral care organised? What is the role in pastoral care of the individual teacher as a class teacher and as a form tutor? What support is there for teachers in these roles? Observe teachers working with a form. Discuss their role with your tutor and compare this with the role of a form tutor recorded by another student teacher working in another school.

Task 3.3.8

BULLYING

Discuss with your tutor what you can do to prevent bullying in your school. Who can you turn to for help? How does the whole school policy for behaviour, rules and codes of conduct both inside and outside the classroom support teachers in this task? Is bullying covered as an issue in pastoral work? If so, how? When? Discuss this with your tutor.

Task 3.3.9

YOUR PERSONAL VALUES

Your personal values and beliefs on, for example, politics, marriage, family life, gender roles, may be at odds with those of some pupils and could influence your response to the demands of the pastoral role. Consider situations where your personal values and beliefs might be different from those of your pupils. What do you say to a pupil who complains about another member of staff being a poor teacher? or who argues about conforming to school rules which you yourself do not feel are vitally important? Discuss these issues with other student teachers and your tutor and identify what might be appropriate responses to situations in which pupils' actions contradict your personal values and beliefs.

Task 3.3.10

IMPLICATIONS OF THE ELTON REPORT

Discuss with another student teacher what the information in Appendix 3 means for your work in school, in terms of your work in the school as a whole, in your classroom and your pastoral role.

SUMMARY AND KEY POINTS

The key to managing classroom behaviour effectively is effective class management. Well-planned, well-prepared and well-managed lessons are far less likely to promote behaviour problems in pupils. Likewise, an awareness of, and sensitivity to, pupil mood and motivation prevent much problem behaviour about which student teachers are most concerned. Active participation in lessons minimises disruption (see also Unit 5.2 on 'Active learning').

To maintain effective learning in your classroom you need to read this unit in conjunction with others that relate to managing your classroom, and work on developing effective classroom management techniques. Also remember that you are part of a team and can draw on the support and advice of the team as and when you need it.

You also have responsibility for pupils' behaviour beyond your classroom. You have a pastoral role but, further, a role across the school. In effective schools, teachers are supported in managing behaviour by school policies and procedures. In return, teachers must support fully the school policies and procedures.

FURTHER READING

Canter, L. and Canter, M. (1977) *Assertive Discipline*, Los Angeles: Lee Canter Associates.
This is a training pack including video and workbook. Although the materials were designed for INSET purposes to facilitate a school-wide approach to discipline, there is much to be gained from an investigation of the use of positive reinforcement in class management. Available only from Behaviour Management Ltd, UK.

Department for Education (DfE) (1994b) *Bullying: Don't Suffer in Silence. An Anti Bullying Pack for Schools*, London: DfE.
This pack is part of a series of measures by the government to combat bullying. It contains a video which shows the steps some schools have taken to combat bullying. The video is accompanied by a training pack. This should be available in all schools.

Department of Education and Science and the Welsh Office (DES/WO) (1989) *Discipline in Schools. Report of the Committee of Enquiry Chaired by Lord Elton* (The Elton Report), London: HMSO.
This report was the outcome of an inquiry into discipline in schools in response to concern about the problems facing the teaching profession. It covers a wide range of aspects of the problem and contains examples of behaviour policies from schools.

Hay McBer (2000) *Research into Teacher Effectiveness: A Model of Teacher Effectiveness*, London: DfEE.
This report contains within it a dictionary of professional characteristics, which includes a section on 'Managing Pupils'.

Office for Standards in Education (OFSTED (1993b) *Achieving Good Behaviour in Schools. A Report from the Office of Her Majesty's Chief Inspector of Schools*, London: HMSO.
This is a short booklet which reports on 'the evidence of inspection to examine some of the means by which schools with high standards of behaviour and good discipline achieve them' (p. 1), in order to identify some principles of good practice and suggest a possible code of practice for schools.

Smith, C.J. and Laslett, R. (1993) *Effective Classroom Management: A Teacher's Guide*, London: Routledge.
This book considers many aspects of discipline in the classroom, from minor disruption to confrontation. It includes some very good case studies of how confrontations can occur and how they can be managed well or, alternatively, how they can get out of hand. It includes a section on working with pupils with emotional and behavioural difficulties in mainstream classrooms.

CHAPTER 4 **PUPIL DIFFERENCES**

It is a truism to say that each pupil in your class is different but from time to time it is important to remind ourselves of this fact. A class of same-age pupils is likely to contain individuals at different stages of development. These differences may be physical, mental or cultural or some combination of all three. Prominent differences occur in the abilities shown by a class of pupils, especially in a mixed ability class. Other differences arise from the cultural, religious and economic backgrounds and affect strongly the response of pupils to schooling. Some pupils are gifted and need special attention, as do many pupils with learning or behavioural difficulties. Some pupils are at ease with adults whilst others find the experience less comfortable

This chapter, comprising six units, invites you to consider several aspects of the background and development of your pupils. In practice most features discussed interact giving the complex and varied behaviours which characterise human beings. For ease of discussion, some factors have been separated out; we hope this approach helps you subsequently to integrate your understandings and develop better relationships with your pupils.

One response of schools in recent years has been to acknowledge the differences between pupils in their response to school subjects, especially differences in cognitive development, and to develop appropriate courses of action. Thus Unit 4.1 addresses **differentiation and progression**; the unit also addresses **pupil grouping**. Central to successful differentiation is the identification of pupil needs; thus case studies invite you to enquire more deeply into the background and response of individual pupils and plan differentiated work. You may want to return to this unit after dipping into other units.

Unit 4.2, 'Growth, development and diet', focuses on physical characteristics of pupils as they develop and mature in adolescence and young adulthood, and draws attention to the range of 'what is normal'. There is concern in society about the diet and health of young people and so we address diet, growth and health towards the end of this unit.

In Unit 4.3 Cognitive development is discussed alongside concepts of intelligence, including the theory of 'multiple intelligences'. Some examples of teaching material from secondary school curricula are discussed in terms of their cognitive demand on pupils. You are invited to look specifically at the cognitive differences in performance between pupils of different ages. There are opportunities for you to work with pupils and to see for yourself how pupils respond to different tasks; we address the importance of teaching pupils how to learn.

In Unit 4.4, 'Responding to diversity', the cultural background of pupils is considered, including class, gender and ethnicity. The focus here is differences in performance of different groups of pupils from different backgrounds, using research evidence. These differences in performance are linked to the implementation of equal opportunities policies in schools and issues of access to the curriculum and career opportunities.

Unit 4.5, 'Moral development and values' links the development of values in young people, particularly moral values, with the new curriculum structure for schools in England and Wales, operating since September 2000. While not stressing differences between pupils, the focus of the chapter does acknowledge the range of values and beliefs in our society, and how schools have in the past and continue today to contribute to the spiritual, moral and cultural development of pupils as well as to their mental and physical development.

Unit 4.6, on special educational needs, addresses the ways in which those pupils with special physical, behavioural and learning needs may be supported by the new Code of Practice for schools and LEAs in England and Wales, expected in late 2001. The classroom teacher remains in the front line of identification of need and response to need through choice of curriculum and teaching strategy.

UNIT 4.1 PUPIL GROUPING, PROGRESSION AND DIFFERENTIATION

TONY TURNER

INTRODUCTION

Education systems have responded to the differences in pupil attainment by adopting methods of selecting pupils into schools, such as academic entrance examinations, parental interview or the ability to pay. The 11+ system in England and Wales, which was used to select the more able pupils for grammar school until the mid-1960s, was an academic test. Many independent fee-paying schools use all three methods.

In the academic year 1998/99 there were 3,788 state-maintained secondary schools in England and Wales, the majority of which were comprehensive, i.e. non-selective. Some comprehensive schools are 'creamed' by neighbouring selective schools, upsetting the balance of their intake (Davies, 2000, pp. 23–38). Of these, 164 were grammar (selective) schools which admitted pupils by academic examination (Crook, Power and Whitty, 1999, p. 2). In addition, about 7 per cent of secondary pupils in England and Wales attend fee-paying independent schools. In the period 1980–2000 a small but increasing number of maintained schools admitted some pupils by selection, on academic achievement or parental interview, e.g. some Foundation schools. This procedure has, unsurprisingly, led to a rise in the proportion of pupils getting high grades in public examinations in those schools.

Schools have traditionally sought to cope with differences in pupil performance either through setting, banding and streaming or by setting work at appropriate levels for pupils in **wide ability** classes (unstreamed or mixed ability classes). **Streaming** places the best performers in one class for all subjects, the least able performers in another class, with graded classes in between. **Banding** places pupils in broad performance groups for all subjects and tries to avoid producing classes comprising only pupils showing low attainment or unwillingness to learn. **Setting** describes the allocation of pupils to classes by attainment in each subject, i.e. streaming or banding for each subject. Broad streaming and banding support the notion of a general intelligence whereas setting acknowledges that pupil attainment may be different across subjects and contexts.

Differentiation is about raising the standards of all pupils in a school, not just those under-achieving, and is conceived within a whole school policy, as set out in *Better Schools* (DES, 1985b). Differentiation is a planned process of intervention by the teacher in the pupil's learning. The purpose of a differentiated approach is to maximise the potential of the pupil and to improve learning by addressing the pupil's particular needs.

This unit addresses issues about selecting pupils for schools and pupil grouping in school, and discusses differences between pupils and how best to provide appropriate learning environments for pupils. Strategies for developing differentiated units of work are provided, building on the subject specialist focus of the reader. See also Units 2.2 and 3.2.

OBJECTIVES

By the end of this unit you should be able to:

- discuss teaching methods which allow for differentiation;
- apply principles of differentiated learning and progression to lesson planning;
- evaluate differentiated learning in wide ability grouping and other forms of pupil grouping;
- appreciate that strategies adopted for teaching and learning reflect fundamental views about the purpose of education;
- relate your progress in planning and teaching for differentiation to the competences/ standards expected of a newly qualified teacher.

GROUPING PUPILS

Across schools: comprehensive and selective

The selection of above-average-ability pupils for grammar schools was a feature of the English educational system enshrined in the 1944 Education Act. (See also p. 175.) The gradual abandoning of selection has left a handful (164) of grammar schools across England and Wales. The question of whether a selective system or a comprehensive system of schooling is the more effective has been the subject of much research. A recent survey of that research, prompted by the government's decision in 1998 to decide the future of remaining local grammar schools by a ballot of parents, has suggested that it is not obvious which is the better system (Crook, Power and Whitty, 1999, pp. 50–56). The differences in the effectiveness of schools within a category (selective or comprehensive) are as great as the differences in the effectiveness of categories of school. At the system level, it is not possible to say which system is better. In other words, some schools are more effective than others, irrespective of category. It is increasingly difficult to investigate this issue, because of the decreasing number of selective schools and the fact that many comprehensive schools are either creamed of the most able pupils by local selective schools, or themselves operate some form of selection.

In schools: wide ability, setting and streaming

Prior to the Education Act of 1988 (ERA, 1988), many state schools grouped their pupils in wide ability classes for teaching purposes. The backgrounds, aptitudes and abilities of pupils, coupled with differences in interest and motivation, can lead to large differences in achievement between pupils which, by age 11, are substantial and widen as pupils grow older. Recognising these differences without prematurely labelling pupils as successes or failures was regarded as an essential prerequisite for organising the teaching of secondary pupils. The moves towards de-streaming were most strongly evident in the 1960s, following the Plowden Report (DES, 1967) into primary schooling, some of the recommendations of which spilled over into secondary schooling. The abandonment of selection in schools by the introduction of comprehensive schooling in the 1950s and 1960s caused mixed ability grouping to be seen as the logical way to group pupils in secondary school, thus avoiding selection under one roof and the labelling that selection implied.

There was strong opposition to this form of grouping, especially from parents and teachers of able pupils. Evidence accumulated in the 1970s suggested that differences in the academic performance of pupils in mixed ability groups, compared with those in other groupings, could not be attributed solely to the differences in grouping, especially given the other variables affecting pupil performance (HMI, 1978; Newbold, 1977). The Newbold study and a later one (Postlethwaite and Denton, 1978) both identified gains for low ability pupils in the mixed ability setting while the performance of able pupils was not reduced.

The research carried out over many years into grouping pupils by ability has been reviewed recently (Hallam and Toutounji, 1996). The authors suggest that turning the clock back and introducing selective education or highly structured systems of streaming would not provide an effective solution to the under-achievement of some pupils in our schools. They note too the great emphasis placed on ability in Western educational systems, as opposed to emphasising effort on the part of pupil, parent and teacher, as, for example, occurs in the Japanese educational system (Hallam and Toutounji, 1996, p. 22). The same authors suggest that attention should be given to semi-structured forms of pupil grouping, responding to the different strengths and interests of pupils in various areas of the curriculum; and to moving away from a notion of one single intelligence (Gardner, 1983, 1993a). The use of differentiated materials focused on individualised instruction is suggested also as a way forward.

Despite the uncertainty in the research evidence concerning the factors affecting the academic performance of pupils, there was evidence that all pupils gained socially from working in wide ability groups. Such groupings allowed pupils from a variety of backgrounds, as well as abilities, to work together, strengthening social cohesion. These arguments were strongly supported in inner city environments where selection processes often led to separation of pupils along class and ethnic dimensions.

A comparative study of pupils in two comprehensive schools has rigorously documented their differences in knowledge and understanding of mathematics and their motivation and attitude towards the subject (Boaler, 1997). The 'progressive' school – which offered more open-ended project work, linked mathematics to the lives of the pupils and encouraged pupils to identify problems in which they were interested – achieved outcomes as good as, and in many cases better than, the school which adopted 'traditional' rule learning and application as the main teaching strategy. The 'progressive' mathematics department did not group pupils in streamed sets, unlike the department working on 'traditional' lines (Boaler, 1997, chapter 10). There was evidence that in the traditional teaching structure able pupils were anxious, especially those pupils in the top set, and under-performed in the GCSE examination. Many girls were disadvantaged by the traditional teaching approach of this school (Boaler, 1997, chapter 9). The author points out that the current dismay in government circles at the low standard of mathematics performance by English pupils in international comparative studies has occurred when most mathematics teaching in classrooms is of the 'traditional' type (citing inspection reports as evidence) (OFSTED, 1994b).

Following the introduction of the Education Reform Act (ERA, 1988), wide ability grouping has been in retreat. Indeed, government advice from both left and right of the political spectrum has advocated a return to grouping by ability, together with increased whole class teaching. The response of the late 1990s under the New Labour government was to lay down policy on pupil grouping into the next century. The White Paper *Excellence in Schools* (DfEE, 1997b) states that mixed ability grouping has not proved capable of playing to the strengths of every pupil (p. 38, para. 3) and that, by setting, advantage can be taken of whole class teaching to maintain the pace and challenge of lessons; furthermore, that by 2002 'we will have all schools setting pupils by ability' (p. 7, para. 4). The year-on-year growth during the 1990s, continued in 2000, in the number of pupils gaining grades A–C in GCSE, especially in the state sector, does not support the contention that the comprehensive system has failed (Wintour, 2000) or provide evidence that setting will improve the standards of those not yet achieving adequately.

The same White Paper introduces the idea of 'target grouping' (DfEE, 1997a, p. 39), in which pupils are grouped by ability for part of the week and the composition of the groups is changed in line with regular assessment. It is not clear what type of grouping is expected for the remaining part of the week. The consequences of moving pupils in and out of groups as the result of regular testing are not discussed. Movement of pupils between groups has implications for teachers setting appropriate work for pupils, which is based, in part, on their knowledge of pupils built up over time. Target grouping may also have implications for pupil friendship grouping; meeting friends is a powerful incentive for many pupils to go to school.

Teachers are expected to organise teaching to maximise the potential of all pupils in their classes, to differentiate to meet the needs of pupils and ensure progression in learning. Such demands in effect require teachers to acknowledge that their classes, however grouped, are mixed ability, but clearly, when 'setted', classes contain a narrower spread of ability than when organised around wide ability groupings. It is said to be less demanding on teachers to prepare lessons for a narrow spread of ability, and this assertion may apply to classes comprising able pupils. Nevertheless a very bright, able but bored pupil is potentially as disruptive as any other pupil, and this circumstance can arise in a setted class or a wide ability class. The pressures on schools to maximise performance can lead to streamed classes taught as though the pupils are a homogeneous set, treating pupils as 'all the same'.

Streamed classes, however they are formed, are usually based on achievement, not on potential, ability or motivation, and so contain pupils with a range of attitudes and approaches to learning. Under-performing pupils with high IQs and hardworking pupils with average IQ can easily be placed in the same achievement group. Some streamed classes must contain many pupils who, for one reason or another, under-achieve – for example, because of learning difficulties, or behavioural or emotional problems. Teachers working with classes formed in this way may have a daunting task. The existence of such classes in the 1960s was one reason why wide ability grouping was first introduced.

The best way to group pupils has been a vexed question for many years. The raising of the school leaving age in 1972 required schools to cater for a wide range of ability, behaviour and motivation in pupils up to 16 years of age, and, more recently, beyond 16 as more pupils have sought post-16 education. The emphasis on schools and their teachers to raise standards, measured through SAT and GCSE results, has led to greater demands for setting or streaming and whole class teaching. The emphasis has been on results (summative assessment) and not on learning and development (formative assessment). Although standards of achievement may rise for many, but not all, pupils (DfEE, 1998a, appendix), one wonders whether the raised achievements of pupils taught in this pressured way will have any lasting effect on real educational standards. What will be their capacity as future adults to participate in the 'learning society' (DfEE, 1998d)? 'For further discussion see the further reading section at the end of this unit; see also Bourne and Moon, 1994.)

Task 4.1.1

HOW ARE PUPILS GROUPED IN YOUR SCHOOL?

Find out the ways in which pupils are grouped in your school experience school, the reasoning behind that grouping and how it works in practice. These enquiries could form the basis for written coursework or be part of your portfolio.

The following questions may be helpful, but first talk to your tutor in school. Information may be found in your staff handbook, school policy documents and the school's publicity materials.

1 How are pupils grouped for teaching purposes on entry to your school?
2 Is this grouping changed after a period of teaching, e.g. a term?
3 What criteria are used for grouping pupils?
4 Are primary records, e.g. NC Achievement Levels used to group pupils?
5 Are any tests, such as the Cognitive Abilities Test (NFER-Nelson), used to assess pupils and assign pupils to groups? In what other ways are these tests used?
6 Are pupils grouped differently for some subjects? Why is this? Are pupils grouped differently for English, mathematics and science compared to other subjects?
7 Is there a change of grouping policy between KS3 and KS4? Identify reasons for any change. Does the change affect teaching and learning?

How do staff in the school respond to the grouping policy in operation in your school? Is the grouping policy successful in promoting learning?

Write a short account (one to two sides of A4) of the grouping policy in your school. This account could be, for example, in preparation for a group seminar with other student teachers, to discuss 'grouping pupils for teaching'.

LEARNING AND PROGRESSION ACROSS ABILITIES

By far the greatest challenge to teachers is to maintain progression in the learning of all pupils in their class. Each pupil is different, whether in streamed, banded or wide ability classes. The teacher must take account of personal interest, ability and motivation in setting work which challenges and interests pupils but, at the same time, ensures for each a measure of success. Differentiating the work for pupils depends on teachers knowing their pupils, being secure in their own subject knowledge and having access to a range of teaching strategies. There is no one right way to differentiate the work for pupils. Effective differentiation is a demanding task, difficult to realise when classes are large, the subject curricula overloaded and taught two to three times a week in teaching periods of thirty to sixty minutes.

Each pupil brings to school unique knowledge, skills and attitudes formed by interaction with parents, peers, the media and their everyday experience of the world. Pupils are not blank sheets on which new knowledge is to be written. Many pupils may have skills of which the school is not aware: some pupils care for animals successfully; others play and adapt computer games; yet others may work with parents in the family business. Some pupils may know more arithmetic than we dream of, as the following parody of stock market practice suggests:

> *Teacher:* What is two plus two, Jane?
> *Jane:* Am I buying or selling, Sir?

Diversity of background and culture is in your classrooms; planning for differentiation has to take account of differences in culture, expectation, knowledge and experience. This 'cultural inheritance' that each pupil has interacts with their 'genetic potential for learning', both of which are moulded by experience and affected by the particular learning context. Each pupil responds to the curriculum in a different way. The values placed by the school on a broad, largely academic education may not be shared by some parents and their children who may value a vocational, relevant education more highly because it is immediately applicable to earning a living.

It is the teacher's job to make the curriculum interesting, relevant, cognitively digestible, culturally acceptable but challenging. We know little about the potential of each pupil; wide ability grouping is one way of promoting learning for all, while avoiding the premature and perhaps inaccurate labelling of pupils, providing that ways and means can be found to ensure **progression**. Progression is the result of guiding the pupil from where they are towards a number of possible goals and, we hope, reaching them. Each step in that progression needs some guarantee of success, a recognised aim, understood and agreed by the pupil. Progress must be monitored by assessment tasks, purpose-built into the curriculum.

Developing differentiated work

The curriculum involves the syllabus, objectives, methods, resources and assessment tools. The syllabus is usually laid down, as in England and Wales through the National Curriculum, and expressed through the school's scheme of work. The teacher has freedom to identify objectives for his pupils and to choose the teaching methods and resources most applicable to his circumstances. Teachers are assessing pupils all the time, mostly informally, and this is an important part of your teaching skills. The feedback from all assessment should direct the choice of future learning activities.

It is unrealistic to expect one teacher to plan differentiated work separately for each pupil; it is better perhaps to identify groups of pupils who can work to a given set of objectives using methods suitable to those pupils and the topic in question. It is helpful to some teachers to have a framework within which to plan work. One such plan is shown in Figure 4.1.1.

Figure 4.1.1 assumes that you know the teaching topic and its place in the school's scheme of work. The diagram draws attention to factors to be considered in preparing lesson plans (see also Unit 2.2). The aims and short-term objectives must be broad enough to apply to most pupils in your class. There are often a number of ways of achieving the same goal; Step 2 requires you to consider which activities to give pupils, linking them to what the pupil already knows and identifying outcomes. Achievable outcomes are one way of ensuring motivation but goals must set pupils a challenge, i.e. not be too easy. By identifying achievable outcomes for different groups of children, the process of differentiation is set in motion. The final selection of activity, Step 3, reminds you of some practical issues to consider in selecting or preparing resources, again introducing another feature of differentiation. Step 4 addresses assessment issues. Assessment is achieved in a number of ways: for example, by question-and-answer sessions, taking part in small group discussions, responding to queries in class, asking questions of pupils working on an activity, listening to pupils discussing their work, as well as marking books or short tests. This information helps you identify the next steps for the pupil.

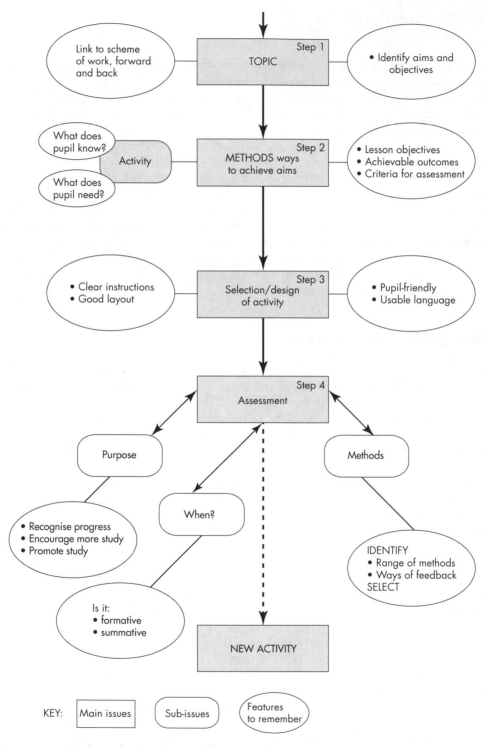

Figure 4.1.1 Scheme for developing differentiated activities

Assessment must reflect your objectives. Step 4 in Figure 4.1.1 draws attention to purpose, timing and methods of assessment. If you have different objectives for different pupils, the assessment must reflect those differences. The objectives may focus on knowledge, or on how pupils gain that knowledge, or on procedures of investigation, or on how pupils communicate their knowledge or understanding. Each of these objectives requires a particular type of assessment. Some aspects of learning (objectives) can be tested after submission of the work (mainly summative) whereas other aspects require monitoring throughout the teaching–learning process – formative assessment. Both forms of assessment should be teaching activities, leading to improved learning. On occasions summative assessment is used to check learning or to grade pupils. See Units 6.1 and 6.2 for discussion of assessment.

Task 4.1.2

LESSON PLANNING FOR DIFFERENTIATION 1

Select a topic for a class you teach. Use Figure 4.1.1 to develop an outline for your lesson. Consider whether the main activity is for all pupils or whether the aim of the lesson is best achieved using a small number of different activities. Prepare notes for Steps 1 to 4. If you plan a small number of different activities, identify how many different activities you can manage safely and effectively; check the resource implications.

We suggest you approach this task either:

- in a group of specialist student teachers, sharing ideas as they evolve;
- or on your own, later sharing your ideas with other student teachers and tutors who know the class you are about to teach.

Check your understanding of differentiation against the competences/standards for your course.

However well you plan your activities on paper the response of the pupils is your yardstick of success. This response depends on how well you know your pupils and how that knowledge translates into devising activities that are achievable but challenging. We suggest you look at the case histories of some pupils below and then attempt Task 4.1.3 and Task 4.1.4.

Case studies of pupils

Peter

Peter is a popular member of his group and has an appealing sense of humour. He can use this in a disruptive way to disquiet teachers while amusing his peers.

He appears very bright orally but when the work is of a traditional nature, i.e. teacher-led, he often avoids the task in hand; it is at such times that he can become disruptive. His disruption is not always overt; he employs a range of elaborate avoidance tactics when asked to settle to work and often produces very little. His written language and numeracy attainments are significantly lower than those he demonstrates orally.

When given responsibility in groups, Peter can sometimes rise to the challenge. He can display sound leadership ability and, when he is motivated and interested in a group project, can encourage his peers to produce a good team effort. His verbal presentations of such work can be lively, creative, humorous and full of lateral thinking. At such times Peter displays an extensive general knowledge.

Peter's tutor is concerned about Peter's progress. He fears that Peter will soon begin to truant from those subjects in which teaching is traditional in style. He is encouraging Peter's subject teachers to provide him with as much problem-solving work as possible.

Tina

Tina is under-achieving across the curriculum in her written work, although orally she appears quite bright. Her concentration span on written work is short. In basic skills she is falling behind her peers. In lessons she can appear quite demanding, as she often appears to need work to be individually set and she finds it difficult to get started and then to sustain and complete pieces of work. She can appear to spend significant amounts of lesson time disrupting the work of other learners. She seems to have a knack of knowing just how to provoke and 'wind up' other learners, so disputes are not unusual. She has been known to be rather confrontational towards teachers, who perceive this to happen when Tina feels threatened.

At the same time, Tina has got what some people describe as 'charm'. Others describe this as being good manipulation. This makes her quite difficult to deal with in school; different teachers develop very different approaches and boundaries in relation to her.

She has a clique of peers who seem to follow her lead. She has a paradoxical relationship with others in the class, who seem to be wary of her, yet also rather courteous towards her.

Filimon

Filimon arrived a year ago from Ethiopia via the Sudan. He had not been at school for at least a year due to his country's war. He speaks Sunharic at home, as well as some Arabic, but knew no English on arrival. Eight months of the year he has spent at school here have been a 'silent period' during which time he was internalising what he was hearing. Now he is starting to speak with his peers and his teacher. He has a reading partner who reads to him every day and now Filimon is reading these same stories himself.

Joyce

Joyce is a very high achiever. She always seems to respond to as much extension activity as she can get. She puts in a lot of effort and produces very well presented work (capably using IT, for example), amply demonstrating her ability to understand, evaluate and synthesise. Joyce's achievements are maximised where she is able to work on her own or in a pair with one of a couple of other girls in the class. In other groups she tends to keep herself to herself. Some teachers are concerned that she is not developing her social and leadership potential.

Joyce's parents put a lot of pressure on her and are keen for Joyce to follow an accelerated programme wherever this is possible. Should she achieve her ambitions for higher education, Joyce will not be the first in her family to make it to Oxbridge.

(Case studies are provided by Paul Greenhalgh, adapted by him from Greenhalgh, 1994.)

Task 4.1.3

USING THE CASE STUDIES OF PUPILS

Identify the skills and abilities of each pupil. Identify those factors that you think you particularly need to take account of in planning lessons generally in your subject. Share your analysis with other student teachers.

Check your ability to plan lessons against the competences/standards for your course.

Task 4.1.4

USING CASE STUDIES TO GUIDE LESSON PLANNING

Select one of the pupils described in the case studies and consider ways in which the plans you outlined in Task 4.1.2 would need to be modified to take account of this pupil.

Consider the implications of the presence of several of these pupils in your lessons.

Developing and using your own case studies

The following task asks you to focus your attention on one or two pupils in your class and on their learning needs, and subsequently to redesign the lesson to take these pupils into account.

Task 4.1.5

WRITING YOUR OWN CASE STUDY

Identify two pupils in your class, the same class you used in Task 4.1.2. Use the examples of case studies above to help you identify the information you need to collect. Do not use the pupil's real name in any report you make or discussion outside the school.

Collect information from the class subject teacher and the form teacher. The form teacher can give you background information about the pupils, as much as is relevant to your study.

After collecting the information and writing your report ask the class teacher to read it and comment on it. Finally, use the information to amend Task 4.1.2 or plan a new lesson.

If there are other student teachers in your school, share your case studies with them. Use the case studies to identify some learning needs of these pupils and plan teaching strategies to take account of these needs. The study can contribute to your professional portfolio.

More about differentiation: 'stimulus–task–outcome' flow diagrams

The outcome of any particular task depends on the way it is presented to the pupil and how they respond. Teaching methods can be restricted by our own imagination; we are inclined to present a task in just one way with one particular outcome in mind, rather than to look for different ways to achieve our goals or to accept a range of sensible responses.

A traditional teaching goal is to ensure that pupils remember things, such as Mark Antony's speech on the death of Caesar. This activity may be described as follows:

STIMULUS	TASK	OUTCOME
Play the role of Mark Antony in a class presentation of excerpts from Julius Caesar	Learn by heart the relevant text	Complete oral recall

Or as a flow diagram:

$$X \quad \rightarrow \quad X \quad \rightarrow \quad X$$

Stimulus   Task   Outcome

Much learning depends on recall methods: for example, learning the names of element symbols in science; preparing vocabulary in a language lesson; recalling formulae or tables in mathematics; learning to spell. Recall is necessary, if unexciting.

Task 4.1.6

RECALL

Select two recall tasks for your teaching subject, identifying the appropriate age and level. Suggest ways of helping pupils accomplish the activity successfully.

In Figure 4.1.1 we suggest you look for different methods of achieving the same ends (see Step 2). For example, to stimulate pupils to punctuate a piece of text which includes reported speech you could:

- Engage in a discussion with pupils, tape it and ask pupils to transcribe it.
- Use an interview from a newspaper report; read it out loud and discuss it with the class; give out a report with the punctuation removed and ask for the punctuation to be inserted.
- Ask pupils to gather opinions about a topic of interest and write a report which includes verbatim examples of opinion, e.g. interviewing other pupils about proposed new school uniforms.
- Suggest pupils write their own play.

These strategies are examples of *active learning*; see Unit 5.2. Suggest other ways of teaching punctuation. The flow diagram below may represent the way this piece of work was set:

             X

             X $\rightarrow$ X $\rightarrow$ X

             X

Stimuli   Task   Outcome

It suggests that the outcome is the same. In the punctuation exercise, are the task and outcome the same no matter which activity is chosen?

Consider circumstances from your own teaching subject in which different stimuli could be used to achieve the same ends. In the example you choose, are the task and outcome the same no matter which activity is given to the pupils?

Can the same stimulus, or activity, generate different outcomes. Identify a teaching example from your own subject and explore the possibility of different outcomes arising from the same activity.

				X
X	$\rightarrow$	X	$\rightarrow$	X
				X
Stimulus		Task		Outcomes

Task 4.1.7

LESSON PLANNING FOR DIFFERENTIATION 2

You have a set of photographs showing the interiors of domestic kitchens covering the period 1850 to the present. Describe two or more ways in which you could use these photographs to teach your subject. Confine your discussion to a class you teach, covering one to two lessons.

For each example, identify:

- how you use the photographs;
- the activities you set your pupils;
- the objectives (outcomes);
- how you assess outcomes;
- the ways in which the activity can be differentiated.

Analyse your plan in terms of stimulus, task and outcome for the differentiated approaches you develop. If you do not like the choice of photographs, choose your own stimulus, e.g. an astronaut working in a space lab; a Salvador Dali painting such as *Persistence of Memory*, 1931 (Schneede, 1973). Increasingly websites are available providing images for teachers to use; see, for example: http://www.scran.ac.uk

Check your understanding of differentiation against the competences/standards for your course.

Beyond task and outcome

The discussion of differentiation in terms of setting tasks or assessing outcomes suggests that work is given to pupils and they get on with it. In practice, of course, you support pupils while they are working. Thus differentiation also takes place at the point of contact with the group or individual. Differentiation is not simply a case of task and outcome.

Your response to pupils working in class includes:

- checking that they understand what they are supposed to do;
- listening to a discussion and prompting or questioning when needed;
- helping pupils to brainstorm an idea or problem;
- asking questions about procedure or techniques;
- suggesting further action when difficulties arise or motivation flags;
- giving pupils supporting worksheets or other written guidance appropriate to the problem in hand. The guidance might explain the topic in simpler terms or simpler language;
- checking pupils' notebooks and noting progress;
- marking pupils' work;
- encouraging pupils by identifying success;
- setting targets for improvement;
- increasing the demand of an existing task;
- noting unexpected events or achievements for a plenary session.

Discuss this list of strategies with other student teachers and identify those strategies appropriate to the teaching of your subject; add to the list of responses.

The different ways in which you respond to your pupils' activities affect the quality of their performance; your response to pupils is an important feature of a differentiated approach and knowing how to respond is part of the repertoire of all good teachers. Thus the dichotomy of differentiation, discussed above as 'task vs. outcome', hides a host of other ways by which you support your pupils. Knowing how to set such tasks depends on how well you know your pupils.

Identifying different activities, or levels within one activity and around the same theme, requires some ingenuity. The activity needs to be challenging yet achievable. The ways in which activities can be differentiated include:

- their degree of open-endedness;
- the degree of familiarity with the resources;
- whether the activity is a complete piece of work or a contributory part of a larger exercise;
- the amount of information you give pupils;
- the language level at which it is presented;
- whether the activity is set orally or by means of written guidance;
- the degree of familiarity with the concepts needed to tackle the activity;
- the amount of guidance given to pupils; for example, in science lessons, the guidance given on making measurements, recording data or drawing a graph.

Discuss this list and rewrite it in terms of strategies appropriate to your subject and the context of your teaching.

Differences in outcome may be recognised by the amount of help given to pupils and by:

- the extent to which all aspects of the problem have been considered;
- adoption of a suitable method of approaching the activity;
- the use of more difficult concepts or procedures in planning;
- recognition of all the factors involved in successful completion of the activity and limiting the choice appropriately;
- thoroughness and accuracy of recording data in a quantitative exercise;
- appropriateness and selection of ways to present information and the thoroughness and depth of analysis;

- the use of appropriate ideas (or theory) to discuss the work;
- accuracy and understanding of conclusions drawn from an activity, e.g. are statements made appropriate to the content and purpose of the activity;
- the distinction between statements supported by evidence and speculation or opinion;
- the way the report is written up, the selection of appropriate style for the target audience;
- the ability of pupils to express themselves in an increasingly sophisticated language;
- the use of imagination or insight;
- the selection of appropriate diagrams, sketches or pictures;
- sensible use of ICT to support a task;
- recognition of the limitations of the approach to a problem and awareness of ways to improve it.

Differentiation is good teaching and requires that you know your pupils, enabling you to judge the extent to which pupils have given an activity their best shot. Left alone, pupils may settle for the easy option. Your role is to persuade the pupil, or group of pupils, to maximise their effort and to judge what is an appropriate outcome. In assessing your pupils, attitudes are as important as cognitive skill. You will find the discussion of the work of Vygotsky and Piaget on learning theory of importance and interest here; see Unit 5.1. Both authors identify the importance of relating activities to the experience of the learner and setting targets for pupils which are achievable. Further help on lesson objectives and differentiation may be found in Kerry, 1999.

DIFFERENTIATION AND AIMS

The 1988 Education Reform Act required schools to address afresh the question of standards. The National Curriculum for England and Wales is an entitlement; despite changes in its structure and some erosion of the notion of entitlement in the wake of revisions (Dearing, 1994; DfEE/ QCA,1999a), there remains for all pupils a substantial curriculum entitlement; see also Unit 7.3.

How can this entitlement be realised given the diversity of performance, experience and motivation displayed by pupils? Schools either establish broad groups of pupils of similar attainment or try to treat pupils as individuals. Establishing broad groups of pupils by streaming leads to a class of low-attaining pupils in each year group. Such groups may be taught on a regular basis using a restricted syllabus, less rich, narrow in focus and, perhaps, lacking balance. On the other hand, if pupils are treated more as individuals, their needs have to be diagnosed and their teaching structured to take account of those needs within the framework of a common syllabus.

Whichever policy is adopted, however, at the heart of the problem there lies a deeper question. This is:

Do the same basic goals apply to all pupils across the whole ability range?

In the course of their review of and research into the educational provision for raising the attainment of pupils, the National Foundation for Educational Research identified broad differences between schools in setting goals for pupils. Some schools identified the same goals for most of their pupils whilst other schools were less clear about this issue (Stradling, Saunders and Weston, 1991). Other schools made similar curriculum provision for all their pupils which implied a common core. Modification (i.e. differentiation) of the common core in these schools might, for example, include a modular course with a common core of modules. Options outside the common core might include pre-vocational work, enrichment activities and units of work of a cross-curricular nature.

By contrast, schools which focused on differentiation by grouping pupils by ability were seen to be less sure about whether the same goals of education applied to all pupils. Different tasks set to different groups of pupils frequently reflected different content and curriculum aims. Breadth and balance in the curriculum were less likely to be found in schools which streamed pupils. A thinner curriculum was offered to low-achieving pupils which was justified by arguing that retaining breadth and balance might drive some 14–16-year-old pupils away from school. Allowing pupils to specialise successfully in a few activities will encourage them, it was said, to attend, raising their interest in school and lowering truancy rates. All schools emphasised the importance of a regular assessment and regular review of progress, through teacher–pupil discussion.

The NFER research identifies two broad model types of school, as shown in Figure 4.1.2. One model differentiates pupils by grouping, the other by individuals.

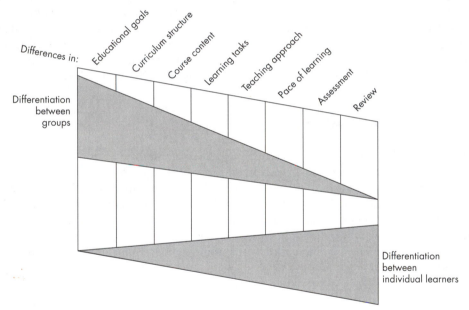

Figure 4.1.2 Forms of differentiation: a contrast

Source: Stradling, Saunders and Weston, 1991, p. 10.

The upper section of Figure 4.1.2 identifies the broad features of a school which separates its pupils into streams or bands. The striking characteristic of this model is difference in the aims, or goals, set for different groups of pupils. By contrast the second model achieves differentiation by concentrating on the individual; the goals remain the same but differences appear in teaching approaches and the pace of learning. Another difference lies in the review of pupils' work (see right-hand side of the diagram). For the schools which 'differentiate between groups', the same method of reviewing progress is used for all pupils, whereas 'differentiation between individual learners' is accompanied by an individual review of pupils' work.

The diagram in Figure 4.1.2 indicates trends and is not meant to imply that the practice of schools is one of either of the two models. The diagram shows that both models overlap in the emphasis on learning tasks and teaching approaches. Whichever method of grouping pupils is adopted, the choice of task and the range of teaching strategies are seen to be important for the successful implementation of a differentiated approach to the curriculum.

Aims

At the heart of the debate about standards and differentiation of work for pupils are educational aims. Should all pupils work towards common goals for most of their time in school? Or should the differences between pupils, as measured by their achievement in school, be acknowledged by developing curricula appropriate to their needs? Both courses of action can be justified education-ally. The willingness of society to structure and resource these alternative curriculum decisions is a political decision, resting on values and beliefs. The choice of educational aims for our pupils is a political one but the implementation of those aims through the curriculum, choice of teaching methods and the grouping of pupils in a school must be an educational one. We are in danger of more decisions about implementation being made outside the school. This process de-skills teachers.

When comprehensive schools were first introduced in the 1960s teachers tried to respond by developing teaching methods suited to wide ability classes, often through resource-based learning. The comprehensive principle has been eroded, significantly through the Education Reform Act, 1988 and subsequent legislation. Setting by achievement is the expectation, with differentiation to be exercised within that context. Target setting is the new language of differentiation (DfEE, 1997a; SCAA, 1997). Target setting for pupils and grouping by setting create a tension. Teachers are expected to set targets for individual pupils based on regular testing and personal knowledge of the pupil. At the same time whole class teaching is advocated to maintain the pace and challenge of lessons. Thus recommended teaching methods and class organisation are directed at groups while target setting is aimed at the individual.

SUMMARY AND KEY POINTS

Children learn in different ways at different speeds. Some pupils have learning barriers related to behavioural, emotional and cognitive needs. Teachers should plan their lessons to take account of these differences, as far as is practically possible. In the past, schools have responded to pupil differences by grouping pupils, through setting, banding, streaming and wide ability groupings. Many education systems have recognised these differences; the education system of England and Wales has moved from a mix of grammar, technical and secondary modern schools arising from the 1944 Education Act towards a system of comprehensive schools which now account for over 80% of schools. Recently specialist schools have appeared in England and Wales designed to cater for the different interests and abilities of pupils, involving some selection. Some evidence about the effectiveness of different types of schools suggests that there is no clear cut academic advantage of one system of schooling over another, or the ways pupils are grouped. The skill of teachers and the motivation of pupils may be more important than grouping.

Pupils need to be stimulated, have work set that interests them and is within their grasp, but sufficiently challenging to provide progression in learning. Differentiation supports progression. Differentiation can be achieved through the choice of activities given to pupils and the teachers' expectations about outcomes. Much more, however, depends on the way you respond to your pupils, giving support, encouragement, stimulation and providing feedback on their progress. Differentiation is embedded in these teaching skills.

Developing those skills depends on getting to know your pupils, both as individuals and as members of a class. 'Getting to know pupils' is difficult to achieve in a one-year teacher education course involving, usually, experience in two schools; it is essential to realise the importance of this factor when you start your first post. Pupils need to learn to trust your ability to teach them and develop confidence in your willingness to help; in these circumstances most pupils grow and develop and, most importantly, learn to take responsibility for their own progress.

Monitor your progress in developing these skills through the standards/competences which apply to your course of initial training and during your NQT year. The section on further reading enables you to widen your knowledge of differentiation, grouping and selection.

FURTHER READING

Bourne, R., Davitt, J. and Wright, J. (1995) *Differentiation: Taking IT Forward*, Coventry: National Council for Educational Technology.
A useful book which identifies ways in which IT can support teachers introducing differentiation into their lessons.

Crook, D., Power, S. and Whitty, G. (1999) *The Grammar School Question: A Review of Research on Comprehensive and Selective Education*, London: Institute of Education. A monograph in the series 'Perspectives on Education Policy'.
This review gives an outline of policy on grammar schools and reviews the research into the advantages and disadvantages of each system of schooling. The review identifies the ideologies underpinning the research, case by case. An important read before offering opinions on an emotive topic.

Hallam, S. and Toutounji, I. (1996) *What Do We Know about the Grouping of Pupils by Ability? A Research Review*, London: Institute of Education, University of London.
Essential reading for those seeking to understand arguments about grouping pupils in school. Carries an extensive bibliography (c. 250 references) which reviews the research carried out in this country and overseas into the effects of pupil grouping on academic performance. See also Hallam, 1996.

Hart, S. (ed.) (1996) *Differentiation and the Secondary Curriculum: Debates and Dilemmas*, London: Routledge.
For those wishing to dig deeper into the purposes and practice of differentiation.

Kerry, T. (1999) *Learning Objectives, Task Setting and Differentiation*, London: Hodder and Stoughton.
This short book contains very useful chapters on differentiation in practice and evidence of research into classroom practice (chapters 8 and 9). Full of practical ideas.

Lambert, D. (1994) *Differentiated Learning*, London: Institute of Education, University of London, Initial Teacher Training (Occasional papers in teacher education and training).
A short, 24-page, booklet specially written for the student teacher which addresses the issues met by a new teacher attempting to put differentiation into practice.

UNIT 4.2 **GROWTH, DEVELOPMENT AND DIET**

TONY TURNER

INTRODUCTION

Adolescence is a period of growth and of physical, mental and emotional change. These changes take place against a background of family life, within a particular society and culture that has expectations of its young people. Young people often bring to school the expectations of their family, which may carry both advantages and disadvantages. These disadvantages include parents living on low wages, or who are unemployed, or instability within the family, any of which may portend poor career prospects (Child, 1993, p. 302). Some adolescents bring family pressures to succeed and a burden of high expectation. Yet others have disabilities, some mild and supportable by technology, e.g. wearing glasses, while other young people carry more serious disadvantages, such as dyslexia, less easily overcome.

The Life of Adrian Mole (Townsend, 1982) offers an often amusing but insightful commentary on the pains of growing up. The onset of changes in adolescence comes at a time when society demands that young people attend school and be in continual close contact with their peers, where they are reminded constantly of the differences between themselves and others. This extended proximity can place a strain on the adolescent's self-perception.

Balancing family and peer pressures is important during adolescence. Parents are anxious that any physical shortcoming should be treated properly, whereas adolescents themselves are likely to shy away from drawing attention to themselves. Thus, wearing glasses or dental braces, for example, becomes an issue for teenagers, because the image they give to others is one of 'difference' and, perhaps, defect. Teachers need to be aware of these difficulties in order to respond sensitively in the classroom and be prepared to initiate remedial action when necessary.

Most young people want to be normal, to conform to what they see in others of their peer group. This gives rise to pressure to conform to peer norms and to question or reject family norms. Conforming, in part, concerns appearance; personal appearance becomes a highly sensitive consideration during adolescence for two reasons. One concerns the notion of normality, shape, size, etc. The second concerns sexuality and emerging relationships.

Many adolescents are trying to 'find their feet', develop an identity and develop new relationships with adults, especially parents. Within this context the academic pressures of school demand that pupils make far-reaching choices about careers. Pressures to make this choice come from home and school, such as through the commonly asked question 'what do you want to do when you leave school?' Many young people, often with good reason, just don't know how to respond, or how to choose.

Schools have a vital part to play in this developmental period. They exist unequivocally to further the development of pupils and must try to provide the environment in which personal autonomy can grow. At the same time, and to cope with several hundred young people in a confined space, schools must provide a disciplined context not just for the healthy growth of the individual, but for everyone. Having many young people all together means that these conditions are not necessarily compatible with those for the emergence of the autonomous individual.

This unit enables you to consider the phenomenon of physical growth and development, to consider the range of development that encompasses the 'normal pupil', and to do this in part by observing the pupils in your school. The unit addresses, too, the diet and health of young people and the promotion of healthy eating in school. Some implications of these factors for your teaching are raised, as is the influence of peer pressure on behaviour.

OBJECTIVES

At the end of this unit you should be able to:

- discuss the meaning of normal growth and development in relation to adolescence;
- describe and understand some of the physical differences between school-age pupils;
- appreciate the effect of external pressures and influences on pupil behaviour and identify some implications of these influences for teaching and learning;
- discuss healthy eating and the role of the school in promoting this ideal;
- identify the competences/standards for your course relevant to teachers' responsibilities for growth, development and diet.

ABOUT PHYSICAL GROWTH AND DEVELOPMENT

Variation in the height and weight of humans depends on genetic, health and nutritional factors. In the case of young people, the period from birth to the start of adulthood is critical if the genetic potential of the individual is to be realised. Information about the growth and health of individuals is best obtained by a study of changes in body measurements of individuals and comparing those to reference standards. Patterns of change in height and weight of young people are shown in Figures 4.2.1–4.2.4 and include measurements on young people from the age of 5 to 15-plus (Whitehead, 1991). See also Tasks 4.2.1 and 4.2.2.

The data are based on observations of a large number of individuals of different age groups, i.e. a cross-sectional study, and they show the 50th percentile. The 50th percentile corresponds to the mean value and so the graphs in Figures 4.2.1 to 4.2.4 show the average height and weight of pupils in the age groups. Boys and girls are shown separately to contrast their rate of physical development. Figures 4.2.2 and 4.2.4 show in closer detail the mean changes around the period of adolescence.

Children who receive enough energy and nutrients in their diet should grow adequately; the growth curve of such a person may be close to the average growth, as shown in Figures 4.2.1–4.2.4. The data in Figures 4.2.1 to 4.2.4 are mean figures; in practice there is considerable spread in the height and weight of children of a given age; see Whitehead (1991, pp. 198–201) for more detailed information. Consistent and large departures from the normal pattern of development may need monitoring. Sudden departures from a regular pattern of growth usually have a simple explanation, related to illness or nutritional factors, to which we return later in this unit.

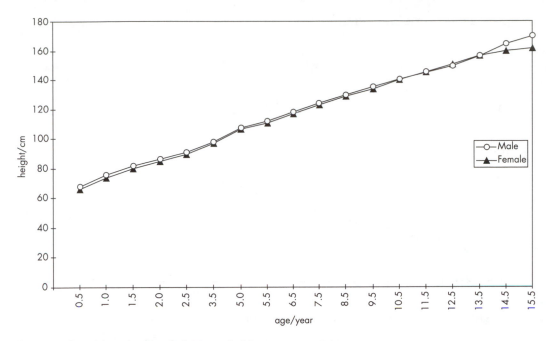

Figure 4.2.1 Mean height of children, 5–16 years

Source: Whitehead, 1991, p. 200.

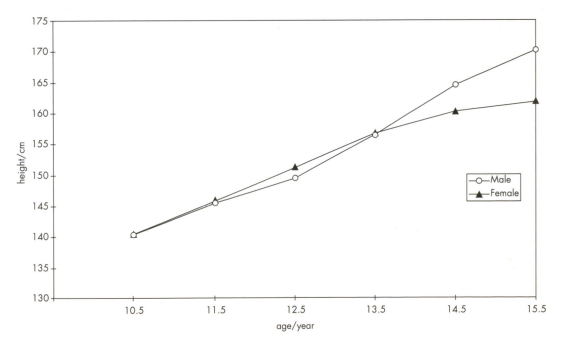

Figure 4.2.2 Mean height of children, 10–16 years

Source: Whitehead, 1991, p. 200.

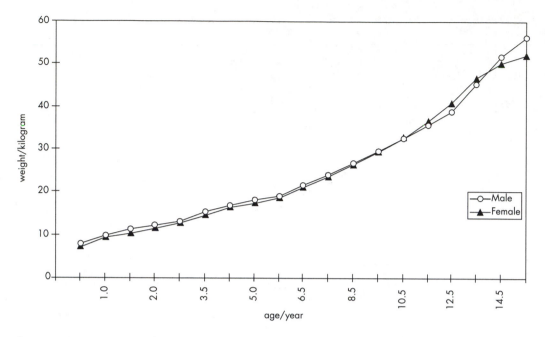

Figure 4.2.3 Mean weight of children, 5–16 years
Source: Whitehead, 1991, pp. 201–202.

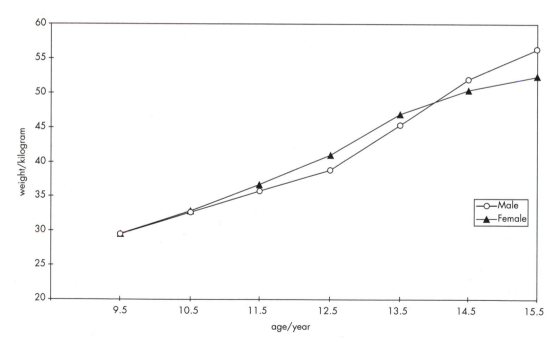

Figure 4.2.4 Mean weight of children, 9–16 years
Source: Whitehead, 1991, pp. 201–202.

Task 4.2.1

PUPIL GROWTH AND DEVELOPMENT

Using Figures 4.2.1 and 4.2.2 describe the different rate of height increase in boys and girls and identify the probable ages at which these are most obvious. Repeat the exercise to compare weights of boys and girls as they grow older. Do the differences in height and weight occur at the same ages, on average?

Further data can be found on the Department of Health (DoH) website or in Whitehead (1991, pp. 198–201). The DoH website address is: http://www.doh.gov.uk/dhhone.htm

---

Young people tend to have growth spurts, particularly after puberty, the point at which the sex glands become functional; see Figures 4.2.2 and 4.2.4. Most girls mature physically earlier than most boys. There are differences in growth rates between boys and girls at the onset of puberty, some girls showing a growth spurt at an earlier age than most boys. However, there is little difference in mean height of boys and girls up to age 13, but after 16 years boys on average are over 13 cm taller than girls. Height increases appear earlier than weight increases and this has implications for physical activity. The differential rate of height and weight development is the origin of clumsiness and awkwardness in some adolescent pupils. As well as obvious gender differences between pupils in a coeducational context, the differences between individuals within a group of boys, or a group of girls, can be quite large and obvious. These differences in development can be worrying for the individual and may affect pupils' attitudes to and performance in academic work. For example, it can happen that some pupils who have developed physically earlier than their peers may dominate activity in a class causing a number of pupils to reduce their involvement for fear of being ridiculed by more grown-up members of the class.

Some research suggests that pupils physically maturing faster score better on mental tests than pupils developing more slowly. Girls develop physically and mentally faster than boys on average, and it was because of this factor in the 1940–50s that the 11+ examination was adjusted to give equal opportunities for boys to gain places in grammar schools in the face of girls' earlier maturation.

There is evidence that environmental factors affect growth (Tanner, 1990). These factors include:

- the size of the family; many larger families have children of below-average height;
- where the pupil is raised; urban-reared children are often taller and heavier than those raised in a rural society;
- the socio-economic status of the family (parents); lower social class, defined by the employment status of the parents, correlates with having shorter children;
- prolonged unemployment has a similar effect to socio-economic factors.

There is some evidence, cited above, that physical size and development are linked to social class and economic factors (Tanner, 1990). There may be evidence in your school of a link between 'growth and development' and socio-economic factors such as free school meal provision. The uptake of free school meals is used, for example, by OFSTED in school inspections as a proxy measure of deprivation. The link between health and diet and academic performance is also recognised in those schools that make available free breakfast for pupils.

These issues of difference in physical development, taken together with the large differences in performance in school subjects, have raised the question of whether pupils should be grouped in classes by age, as they are now, or whether some other method should be used to group pupils for teaching purposes, e.g. by achievement. Some other educational systems require pupils to reach a certain academic standard before proceeding to the next grade, leading to mixed-age classes. Thus under-performing pupils are kept back a year to provide them with an opportunity to improve their performance. This practice has a big impact on friendship groups and on personal esteem.

The environmental factors, listed above, by themselves do not have a direct causal relationship but reflect complex underlying influences on growth and development. These factors also affect the onset of puberty. It is of interest to consider that any 12-year-old girl might be in a pre-pubertal, mid-pubertal or post-pubertal state; and any 14-year-old boy similarly. Thus it is not sensible to talk of a 14-year-old group of children as though they represented a homogeneous cohort.

Task 4.2.2

WHAT WILL YOUR PUPILS BE LIKE?

The school at which you were a pupil may be quite different from your school experience school. This task is intended to reveal some of those differences and provide you with an opportunity to discuss their implications for your teaching.

In what ways do the pupils in your school experience school resemble or differ from:

- pupils from your own school days?
- your expectations prior to your initial teacher education course?

You might consider:

- family sizes, and extended families in the school;
- socio-economic classes into which most of your pupils' families may fit;
- physical appearance such as height, weight and physical maturity;
- employment rates of parents;
- achievement, as measured by standardised national tests; for example, Standard Assessment Tasks (SATs) levels or tests of cognitive ability.

Other factors which may help in describing the pupils in your school include:

- how pupils are dressed and adherence to school uniform;
- self-confidence, willingness to talk to teachers and to each other;
- attitude to authority, including respect for other pupils and for teachers.

Collect your own impressions of the pupils in your school, for discussion with other student teachers and your tutor. It may be interesting to repeat this exercise after a period in the school and see how familiarity with the pupils and school has altered first impressions. Keep a record of your work in your professional portfolio.

The variation in physical development of pupils shown, for example, in any year cohort has implications for your management of secondary school classes. These differences are particularly apparent in Years 7–9 and may stand out in activities which prosper on physical maturity or physical control. Boys in early adolescence who develop late often cannot compete with their peers in games; and girls who mature earlier than their friends can be advantaged in physical education and games but, at the same time, feel embarrassed. Thus competitive activities such as running or throwing, or physical confrontation games such as association football, hockey and rugby, favour faster-developing pupils. Equally important is physical control, the ability to co-ordinate hand and eye and control tools and equipment properly and safely. In the past, some adolescents have been regarded as clumsy, which may be related to growth spurts, described earlier. Activity in subjects such as physical education, art and design, technology, science and computing depends, in part, on good co-ordination and psychomotor skills.

Task 4.2.3

THE PUPILS IN YOUR CLASS

Select a class you teach and:

1 Find out as much as you can about the background of your pupils.
2 Shadow the class for a day and try to relate your findings to the ways pupils respond to teachers and different subjects.

Some information for this task may be obtained in Task 4.2.2.

Respect the confidentiality of information you acquire in any written or oral report. Reports should not quote names. Discuss your plan with your tutor who can direct you to appropriate sources of information such as the form tutor. The school physical education staff may well be able to provide information on physical development There may be special provisions for some pupils in your school which may provide additional information, e.g. homework club or provision for pupils unable to work at home.

When you visit classrooms, get permission from the teacher, tell him what you are doing, what is to happen to the information and what is expected to emerge. Be prepared to share your findings with him.

The list of suggestions, **A to D**, following this task, indicates the type of information you could gather, but you may need to **select** from this list an appropriate **focus** for your task. **Section E** below suggests ways to use the information. Write a short report for your tutor. The report may contribute to your professional portfolio.

Record in your diary your personal response to this work and any implications it has for you.

The following notes, sections A to D, refer to Task 4.2.3 and suggest the nature and possible sources of information about your pupils.

A Background and attendance

Use the attendance register and personal files to collect information on your pupils. Talk first to the form tutor about your task. Include:

- the names and the numbers of boy and girls;
- the ethnicity of pupils; check the way the school reports ethnicity. If there is no guide to this available, then use the guide in Table 4.2.1;
- the religious or cultural background of pupils, e.g. Seventh-day Adventist, travellers' children;

- recent immigrants or children of asylum seekers;
- patterns of absences and whether absences are supported by notes from parents or guardians;
- the regularity of completing homework, and its quality (the class teacher should have such a record).

Table 4.2.1 A guide to reporting ethnicity

Not known	Asian – Indian
white	Asian – Pakistani
black – African	Asian – Bangladeshi
black – Caribbean	Asian – Chinese
black – other	Asian – other

Source: Graduate Teacher Training Registry, 2000, table I.

B   Physical characteristics

Gather data about:

- the height and weight of pupils; are any pupils deemed overweight or obese (see later in this unit)?
- the number of pupils who wear glasses all the time;
- the number who use glasses for reading or board work (it can be instructive to find out, perhaps from the form teacher, those who should use glasses, but don't. Young people don't usually wear contact lenses but ask about this as well);
- how many use a hearing aid; some pupils may be seated near the front of the class for this reason. Find out if any should wear a hearing aid, but don't;
- any pupils who are undergoing prolonged dental treatment, e.g. wearing tooth braces;
- the number of pupils who suffer from anorexia nervosa, asthma, diabetes or epilepsy;
- any other disabilities, but see C below.

C   Special needs

Collect data about the number of pupils in the class who have:

- statements of special need and the reason for this;
- specific learning difficulties, e.g. dyslexia;
- a support teacher, and why;
- no support teacher, but need one. Identify the special need and why it cannot be supported.

D   School meals

Gather data about the number of pupils in the class who are entitled to free school meals. This information is also confidential. If the school provides breakfast, how many pupils use this service?

E   Using the information

The data may focus on a particular area of interest. Gather together all the data collected

- read it through;
- identify points of interest;
- identify issues which need clarification.

Check your findings with the form tutor. Meet with your tutor to discuss your findings. Questions which could be addressed in this meeting include:

- How representative is the information of the class or group investigated?
- How do the data compare with your impressions of the class? What information or perspective has been added?
- How useful is this information in your future lesson preparation, classroom organisation and management?
- Does the sample you have used represent the school? How far does this survey give you a snapshot of all pupils in the school?

This task may help you to be alert to possible hearing or other physical handicaps in your pupils; it may also improve your sensitivity to signs of distress in pupils and help you to be alert to pupils at risk.

We have discussed the physical development of pupils and drawn attention to the differences in development both within a gender group and between boys and girls. A large influence on physical development is diet, lifestyle and attitude to exercise and games. There is concern about the dietary habits of some young people, in part about risk of disease and in part about the level of fitness of many young people. Others draw attention to the increased use of computers in entertainment and the accompanying sedentary habits this entails. Thus we turn to consider diet, growth and development and the role of schools.

DIET AND THE CURRICULUM

In the past one hundred years the average height and weight of children and adults have increased. At the same time the age at which puberty arrives has decreased. Such average changes are due in part to increased nutritional standards, better conditions of health and sanitation as well as better economic circumstances for the majority. The nutritional status of most children in England and Wales, in 1989, does not appear to be a cause for concern, as judged by height, weight and obesity (Coles and Turner, 1995, p. 17). The body mass index (BMI) for most pupils suggests that in this respect their diet is appropriate. However, the BMI was designed for adults and is defined as the weight/height^2 (units: kg/m^2). Overweight adults have a BMI of between 25 and 30 units and obese people have a BMI of over 30 units. For children aged 5–15 there is no agreed definition of overweight or obesity (Health Education Authority, 1998) and thus it is not clear, in these situations, how to apply the BMI to children who are growing and developing.

By contrast with the nutritional status of children, both the HEA report above and a more recent report identified overweight and obesity as a rapidly growing problem in adults; in 1998, 21 per cent of women and 17 per cent of men were obese (National Audit Office, 2001). By contrast, surveys of eating habits (as opposed to nutritional status) suggest that there may be cause for concern for some of our pupils. A recent report says that 'less than a fifth of children or young adults of either sex reported eating fruit or vegetables more than once every day, compared with the recommendation of five portions★ a day' (Health Education Authority, 1998, see summary: eating habits).

★ A portion is about 80 g, i.e. a peeled orange or two to three carrots (Rodwell, 2000, p. 81).

The low rate of consumption of fruit and vegetables by this group of people was matched by an increasing proportion of this group consuming more crisps, sweet foods and soft drinks than many other young people. Eating habits appeared to be linked to social class and household income for children up to age 15. In the case of young adults, social class was again relevant but the economic factor did not apply to them; that is, the factor is choice not price. Further details of this survey may be found on the Department of Health website (http://www.doh.gov.uk/dhhone.htm). At the same time as promoting healthy eating, by emphasising the importance of fresh fruit and vegetables as part of a balanced diet, it must be recognised that in growing people there is a need for fats as part of that balanced diet, different in quantity from that required by many adults.

The teaching of nutrition and diet through food technology, physical education and personal, social and health education is important for the future health of our pupils. The role of the school, in its attitudes to school meals and towards promoting the sale of food on the premises in various other ways, is very important because of the example it sets. This factor has been recognised by a recent government inquiry into the school meals service (Great Britain, Education and Employment Committee of the House of Commons, 1999). The report of the inquiry acknowledges that young people today are heavier, taller but fatter than previous generations. The inquiry showed that the diet of young children does not contain a healthy balance between the different kinds of foods available.

The report reminds us that the central control of nutritional standards for school meals was removed by the 1980 Education Act. The effects of that Act were monitored and revealed a deterioration in the diets of school children. A survey in 1989 clearly indicated that many children were eating an unbalanced diet too high in fats and sugar; further, that socio-economic grouping was an important factor in determining the type of diet chosen. In particular those pupils on free school meals had a poorer and less varied diet (Department of Health, 1989). That situation remains today for many pupils, and the high incidence of heart-related disease in adults is attributed, in part, to the type of diet identified above and associated lifestyle. Being overweight or obese in teenage years increases the likelihood of carrying that condition into adulthood, which in turn may lead to increased susceptibility to coronary heart disease (Which? 2000).

One consequence of the 1980 Act was the contracting-out of school meals services to commercial organisations. These contractors may provide a range of meals with an acceptable dietary balance but they often have to compete with out-of-school suppliers who provide the high-cholesterol foods and sugary drinks that many young people prefer. Dinner money may often have been channelled to the high street rather than the school meals service. The policy of the school on the nutritional level of school meals, their control of the movement of pupils during the lunch break, and the provision of casual snack foods are all important factors in the influence of the school on the diet of pupils.

The recent report (Great Britain, Education and Employment Committee of the House of Commons, 1999) describes draft regulations for the re-introduction of national standards for school meals for the under-fives and additional regulations for children in primary and secondary school. Schools negotiating contracts with catering organisations must now specify minimum standards related to those regulations. The report identifies further the responsibility of headteachers and governing bodies to monitor the effect of vending machines and 'tuck shops' on the provision of an adequate and balanced diet in school. Task 4.2.4 invites you to investigate aspects of meals in your school.

> ### Task 4.2.4
>
> ## SCHOOL MEALS
>
> Find out at first hand as much as you can about school lunch. We suggest you spend one or two lunchtimes gathering the information. Talk to some pupils about what they eat at lunchtime and how they choose their meals. Talk first to your tutor about what you intend to do. You could:
>
> * collect a set of menus for a week and look at the choice and balance of the menus over that period;
> * read the school policy document about school meals provision and compare that policy with what is served or chosen in the dining hall;
> * observe how free school meals are provided for pupils.
>
> Write a short account of how pupils appear to respond to the meals provided and the way the lunch is provided. Discuss the findings with your school tutor. Information about the dietary requirements of school meals can be found in Coles and Turner, 1995, pp. 8–9.

The National Curriculum (NC) for England and Wales includes aspects of diet under the programme identified for Personal, Social and Health Education (PSHE), although these guidelines are non-statutory. The complete advice appears in the section 'Developing a healthy, safer lifestyle'; see the Qualifications and Curriculum Authority website at: http://www.qca.org.uk/menu.htm.

The guidelines for PSHE include, at Key Stage 3, that pupils should be taught:

* how to keep healthy and what influences health, including the media;
* that good relationships and an appropriate balance between work, leisure and exercise can promote physical and mental health;
* to recognise and manage risk and make safer choices about healthy lifestyles, different environments and travel.

Diet and health are also addressed in PSHE at Key Stage 4. The NC suggests that pupils should be taught:

* to think about the alternatives and long- and short-term consequences when making decisions about personal health;
* to use assertiveness skills to resist unhelpful pressure;
* about the link between eating patterns and self-image, including eating disorders;
* about the health risks of alcohol, tobacco and other drug use, early sexual activity and pregnancy, different food choices, and sunbathing, and about safer choices they can make.

More detailed guidance on health and diet is given in subject-specific contexts of the NC for England and Wales, such as science, physical education and food technology (Owen-Jackson, 2000, chapter 3). Detailed information about diet, the chemical composition of food and its metabolism is given in the Attainment Target 2 of the Programme of Study for science at Key Stages 3 and 4 (DfEE/QCA, 1999a). For a discussion of health education and its place in the curriculum, see Turner and DiMarco, 1998, chapter 11. An outside view of what schools teach about food is given in Which? 1998, pp. 14–17.

The crucial factor in the teaching of diet in the context of healthy growth and development is the way in which the school curriculum integrates and links the various components of the subject, taught at different points in the curriculum. Schemes of work, for example, need to be cross-referenced and the PSHE programme constructed with these contributions in mind.

SUMMARY AND KEY POINTS

Adolescence sees dramatic physical changes in young people. These changes cause nervous introspection: 'am I growing normally, am I too tall, too short, too fat? Will I be physically attractive to others?' Comparison with others becomes the main yardstick of development. Personal appearance assumes a growing importance and causes sensitivity. Muscles are flexed in relation to contemporaries and to teachers and parents. On the other hand, some young people seek direction and guidance from parents and teachers to be sure they act appropriately.

Girls mature physically earlier than boys, but the range of development of both sexes is wide. Adolescence involves physical, mental and emotional changes leading towards maturity. In terms of physical development, the range of differences between pupils means that, at the same age, pupils respond quite differently to tasks and situations in school. Some pupils are awkward in the way they handle their rapid growth which may be seen as clumsiness.

Young people are taller and heavier than previous generations, in part due to improved diets. At the same time, dietary concerns have arisen, due in part to the growth of the availability of 'fast foods', increased advertising and the 'snacking and grazing' approach to eating. There are increasing numbers of overweight pupils and adults; this phenomenon is linked to diet and perhaps to change in exercise patterns. The role of schools in raising awareness of the importance of healthy eating and exercise remains to be fully developed.

A number of issues affecting diet and health have not been raised For example, the increasing prevalence of asthma and diabetes in the population, and the cultural differences in attitudes towards health, food and exercise all contribute to important differences between pupils and the way they respond to schooling. These and other issues are discussed in, for example, Coles and Turner, 1995, and the government report on school meals (Great Britain, Education and Employment Committee of the House of Commons, 1999).

Schools have a big role in helping young people to move through adolescence with minimum disruption, to understand the changes in their bodies, to be comfortable with themselves as they are and how they look. Schools play a part in ensuring that pupils have access to a balanced diet and that they understand its importance to them both now and in the future. Schools can engender the self-confidence in young people to take control of this aspect of their lives and to resist fashion and peer pressure. The new NC for England and Wales recognises this role for schools such that the sum of the teaching and learning makes a difference to pupils' development and life chances both physically and academically.

You should now identify the competences/standards for your course relevant to teachers' responsibilities for growth, development and diet.

FURTHER READING

Coles, A. and Turner, S. (1995) *Diet and Health in School Aged Children*, London: Health Education Authority.

A survey of research findings on the diet and health of the nation's children. Discusses the work of schools in health education, their provision of meals and what might be done to improve the diet of young people. A short and useful booklet for all teachers concerned with teaching healthy eating.

Rutter, M., Maughan, B., Mortimore, P. and Ouston, J. (1979) *Fifteen Thousand Hours: Secondary Schools and their Effects on Pupils*, London: Open Books.

A research report which describes in detail how schools affect teaching and learning. The case is made that 'how schools are organised matters for pupils' success'. Worth reading in this context are chapter 3, 'Schools and the area they serve', and chapter 8, 'Ecological influences'.

Tanner, J.M. (1990) *Foetus into Man*, Cambridge, Mass.: Harvard University Press. Revised and enlarged edition.

An excellent resource for those interested in the detail of growth and development of humans. The chapters on 'Puberty' and 'Heredity and Environment' are particularly useful.

UNIT 4.3 **COGNITIVE DEVELOPMENT**

TONY TURNER

INTRODUCTION

Our everyday common-sense experience tells us that individuals differ in their capacity to cope with problems. Some children are more advanced than others from an early age. Some learn to walk before others; some children, not necessarily the same ones, learn to talk before others. Later some children learn to read earlier than other children and appear, at least temporarily, to benefit more from school. We often refer to this behaviour as intelligence. Such differences are important for parents who are concerned that their child is developing normally and is able to respond to the demands of school work.

By cognition we mean the exercise of skills with understanding, such as map reading, following instructions to make something, carrying out a task, problem-solving or assessing evidence of various kinds. Cognition is distinguished from conditioned learning or reflex actions.

Cognitive development describes the capacity for logical reasoning as found, for example, in legal, linguistic, moral, mathematical or scientific contexts. Many school subjects require the exercise of such skill, e.g. handling evidence, making judgements, understanding when and how to apply rules, untangling moral dilemmas or applying theories. Most Western societies in their schooling of children privilege the cognitive and linguistic intelligences over other ways of knowing about the world. The tests of ability used by some schools to select new entrants or to allocate pupils to teaching groups are often problem-solving exercises involving pattern seeking, pattern recognising and pattern using and the capacity to think logically.

We consider some ways in which pupils' cognitive abilities develop and are identified, and discuss briefly the idea that there are a number of discrete intelligences that can be used. This unit is a continuation of Unit 4.2 which considered physical development. Unit 5.1 addresses in more detail theories of how children learn and develop and can be read in conjunction with this unit.

OBJECTIVES

By the end of this unit you should:

- be able to appreciate the differences in academic performance of pupils in terms of intelligence and development;
- have met some tests of pupil attainment and tried them out with pupils;
- have considered the implication for curriculum planning of a developmental model of learning;
- be aware of discussions about the nature of intelligence;
- have identified this aspect of understanding pupil attainment with the competences/ standards expected of newly qualified teachers.

DIFFERENCES BETWEEN PUPILS

Differences in young children, often siblings, are usually noted through play and games, e.g. card games, board games, etc. Games also help children to socialise, to learn to take turns, to appreciate others' viewpoints. Success encourages greater participation, enhances skills and encourages the winner. In families with more than one child, it soon becomes evident that some children learn to play board games more quickly than others. Such learning may result in some children being labelled brighter than others from an early age. These children may be more intelligent than other children, have greater drive to succeed or both.

It can be argued that school work is a game which pupils have not chosen to play, but which others, teachers and society, have chosen for them. If this assumption is correct, then it is likely that some pupils may not be highly motivated by the content and focus of lessons and, therefore, these pupils may not be successful at school. For such pupils extrinsic motivation is the spur, such as praise, good examination results or avoidance of unpleasant consequences of failure. It is well documented that both young and adult learners work best at tasks which they themselves identify as worthwhile. It would appear that they have the intrinsic motivation that accompanies self-chosen tasks, and a key task for teachers is to generate intrinsic motivation in pupils; see Unit 3.2.

From the pupil's first day in primary school, both parents and teachers are able to recognise that some pupils are better at school tasks than others. Their daily achievement is better than that of other pupils; they produce more work or achieve better quality of writing, tackle harder tasks or are able to read a wider range of books. Some pupils can solve harder sums than other pupils or achieve higher scores in tests. From a young age it is clear that some pupils are more advanced than others.

It might be said that some pupils are 'more intelligent' than others or, more accurately, display more intelligent behaviour. A different way of describing such differences is that some pupils have developed cognitively faster than others. The first description suggests that there is a limiting factor or factors, called intelligence, which allows some pupils to respond to tasks and challenges in a different way from other pupils. The second description looks upon mental alertness as a developing quality which 'grows faster' for some pupils than for others. A developmental model carries with it the potential for change, which teaching can do something about. Intelligence, however that is described or measured, is something that limits the performance of its possessor.

The capacity for intelligent behaviour may be imagined as something with which we are born; the realisation of intelligent behaviour is the response of the individual to the environment, including school. Intelligent behaviour is the product of genetic factors and environmental factors. The extent to which one factor dominates the other in determining final performance is an age-old debate, referred to as the 'nature–nurture debate'. The appearance of intelligent behaviour requires situations in which such skills can be revealed; to improve intelligent behaviour pupils need the opportunity and encouragement to exercise and hone such skills. Evidence has accumulated to suggest that lack of stimuli in early childhood limits the capacity of pupils to profit from school and other learning situations and so limits the development of intelligent behaviour. In the same way, unless pupils are given the opportunity to think, their thinking skills do not develop. It is of interest that in the most recent renewal of the National Curriculum in England and Wales, all subjects are expected to contribute to the development of thinking skills (DfEE/QCA, 1999a, pp. 22–23).

In a recent discussion about the teaching of art and design in secondary school the authors describe cognition in terms of the acquisition, assimilation and application of knowledge (Addison and Burgess, 2000). Acts that lead to the achievement of these steps include:

- perception: observation based on experience;
- intuition and reason: both the unconscious and conscious making sense of experience which are transformed into ideas and values. These activities require the use of imagination and thinking skills.

Whereas mathematics and science, for example, are regarded as involving the application of logical and mathematical thinking, art and design is less often discussed in these terms, and for some people the subjects lie towards opposite ends of a spectrum or are 'different cultures', as they were once described (Snow, 1960). Nevertheless the work of artists and designers involves similar skills to those of scientists, requiring the manipulation of materials for some prior purpose or need. It may be that artists do more of their thinking in the process of manipulation of their medium, in contrast to scientists. Furthermore, it appears that the importance of cognitive processes in developing visual and aesthetic literacy is not often stressed in current secondary art and design curricula (Addison and Burgess, 2000 p. 29).

The point of this discussion is not to polarise views about artistic or scientific thinking or practice; neither is the intention to suggest, by omission, the demands of other subjects in the curriculum, but to suggest that intelligent behaviours may be manifest in many ways and that privileging the linguistic and logical-mathematical modes of thinking in school does not give scope to the full range of human potential. However, the way in which pupils are selected for some schools involves reasoning tasks, numerical, verbal and non-verbal, all of which rely on linguistic skills or logico-mathematical reasoning. The IQ tests (see pp. 163 and 175) used by some schools or Local Education Authorities to select pupils are examples of such tests. On the other hand, some schools use scores on mathematics and English tests to allocate pupils to classes.

In schools, the appreciation and judgement of the products of artistic activity are more likely to be acceptable through a cognitive, analytical process rather than through the senses; at the same time non-cognitive modes of appreciation are deemed acceptable for pupils with special needs (Addison and Burgess, 2000, pp. 26–29). Nevertheless, the products of artistic endeavour and design can be appreciated through a holistic view in which the overall impact and impression of the product are considered, instead of through an atomistic, analytical approach.

Imagination and imaginative thinking play a part in the capacity of individuals to solve problems, both intellectual and practical. A pupil's ability to develop such skills demands an 'oiled intelligence', that is one which has been nurtured and exercised, backed by positive attitudes. By attitude we include, for example, the willingness to engage with tasks, perseverance, open-mindedness and the strength to withhold judgement in the face of inadequate evidence. Imaginative thinking is essential for progress in many disciplines and activities, and it is essential to the solution of many problems in our lives.

We have suggested that, although intelligence is most often linked to the pupil's capacity to exercise linguistic skills and logical mathematical reasoning, there are other ways of displaying intelligent behaviour. In his 'theory of multiple intelligences', Gardner suggests that humans display a number of discrete, autonomous intelligences (Gardner, 1983; and later revised, Gardner, 1993a). He describes intelligence as 'the ability to solve problems or fashion products that are of consequence in a particular culture, setting or community'. Gardner identified seven intelligences:

- **linguistic**: use and understanding of speech sounds, grammar; meaning and the use of language in various settings;
- **musical**: needs training or exposure over many years to be able to appreciate pitch, rhythm and timbre;

- **logico–mathematical**: use and appreciate abstract relationships;
- **spatial**: perceive visual or spatial information, to be able to transform and modify this information, to re-create visual images even when the visual stimulus is absent;
- **bodily kinaesthetic**: use all or part of one's body to solve problems or fashion products;
- **intrapersonal**: knowledge of self and personal feelings. This knowledge enables personal decision making;
- **interpersonal**: awareness of feelings, intentions and beliefs of others.

Gardner proposes that there is not one underlying mental capacity, or intelligence, but a number of intelligences each of which can be exerted alone or combined in different contexts at different times. A number of intelligences may be needed in order to carry out some tasks. In the case of art and design, discussed above, clearly spatial intelligence and bodily-kinaesthetic intelligence must contribute to learning in this curriculum area. More recently, Gardner has proposed, somewhat tentatively, an eighth intelligence, termed the naturalist's intelligence, which is described as 'the kind of skill at recognising flora and fauna that one associated with biologists like Darwin' (Gardner, Kornhaber and Wake, 1996, p. 203). The intelligences referred to above are different from the ways in which pupils learn, or the learning styles they prefer (see Unit 5.1, 'Ways pupils learn').

Some of the ideas behind the theory of multiple intelligences have been adopted by some teachers and advisers (White, 1998, pp. 2–3) but it is by no means widely accepted and has received critical reviews (White, 1998). However, the recent consultative document on 'creative and cultural education' has referred specifically to the theory of multiple intelligences in support of its advocacy of a broader approach to education than currently exists under the NC for England and Wales (Robinson, 1999, pp. 34–37).

It has been pointed out recently that, although it is unlikely that there exists a 'monolithic intelligence' responsible for all our actions, there is good correlation between the scores on a number of the intelligences proposed by Gardner (Adey, 2000, p. 165). Adey suggests that a likely model of intelligence is one which operates through a general underlying intelligence backed up by a small number of special abilities such as the numerical, spatial and verbal.

Nearly twenty-five years ago, HM Inspectorate reviewed the state of the secondary curriculum and published a forward-looking document outlining ways of thinking about what pupils might learn in school. They identified eight 'areas of experience' to which pupils should be exposed. These areas were the aesthetic and creative, the ethical, the linguistic, the mathematical, the physical, the scientific, the social and political, and the spiritual (HMI, 1977, p. 6). This publication prompted much debate and several years of discussion about the school curriculum in England and Wales. But the 1988 Education Act did not reflect any of that thinking. You might like to consider the correlation between the newly emerging theory of multiple intelligences referred to above and the near-forgotten 'areas of experience'.

The use of intelligence tests to identify pupils with different levels of ability has led to the widespread use of the concept of the 'Intelligence Quotient' (IQ). The IQ is reported as a number which is derived from test scores and shows the extent to which the pupil is below or above an average score based on a large sample of pupils. The test is norm-referenced and the average score is given an arbitrary value of 100. The widespread use of IQ tests gives rise to belief in a general intelligence factor. For further discussion on intelligence see the further reading section at the end of this unit, especially White and Adey; also see Unit 5.1 'Ways pupils learn'.

Because of the importance attached to the area of logical reasoning, in this unit we concentrate on some examples of logical reasoning taken from the school curriculum. By means of tasks for you to carry out, we consider now some evidence obtained from activities set for pupils, which allow us to learn something about how pupils respond to thinking tasks and thereby gain some insight into aspects of cognitive development. In considering the information we gain about pupils as a result of them engaging in these tasks, we should bear in mind that the judgement should relate only to the context in which they were set; whether the knowledge, understanding or skills displayed can be transferred to other situations is less certain.

Task 4.3.1

DESIGN AND TECHNOLOGY (D AND T)

Read the following introductory notes and respond to the questions below.

D and T is a relative newcomer to the secondary subject curriculum although the constituent disciplines have long been taught in schools, e.g. home economics. **D and T** embraces the teaching of resistant materials, food technology, control systems and textile technology, and draws on other curriculum areas in its implementation, including ICT. Learning to be successful at **D and T** involves a number of skills, most of which may be summarised as 'learning by doing' and 'developing capability', achieved by addressing the solving of problems of a practical nature. Two key elements involved in learning **D and T** are:

1 **Product analysis**: this involves comparing, analysing, investigating, evaluating. These are skills of enquiry and require pupils to organise and carry out research, develop criteria for analysis, be selective, gain and use information, and work alone and in teams.
2 **Design and make**: this involves investigating, generating ideas, planning and making, and evaluating.

These two elements encompass the notion of 'capability', which has been described as 'the purposeful, active application of knowledge and skills, the movement of thought into action and the use simultaneously of thought and action'. Capability is an action-based concept involving 'knowing how' and 'knowing that'. An essential feature of capability is the integration of thought and skills into a holistic exercise, rather than a piecemeal exercise of isolated skills (Owen-Jackson, 2000, p. 115).

Discuss the skills and intelligences demanded by **D and T** by responding to these questions:

1 In what ways do the demands of **D and T** link to the importance attached by school to linguistic and logico-mathematical aptitude?
2 Using Gardner's theory of multiple intelligences, discuss the teaching and learning of **D and T** as the development and utilisation of different intelligences.
3 Develop arguments to support the place of **D and T** as a required foundation subject in schools for all pupils aged 11–16.

Further background to **D and T** is in Owen-Jackson (2000), chapters 1 and 8.

COGNITIVE DEMANDS ON PUPILS

We turn now to consider some of the cognitive demands made on pupils through the curriculum, but initially we have selected a task from a quiz book, a group of books popular with secondary pupils and many adults: see task 4.3.2 (Brandeth, 1981). The problems in these types of books are often abstract, they lack a real context, but demand reasoning skills – perhaps not too far from the situation commonly found in school.

Task 4.3.2

SORTING VARIABLES 1

Try out the following problem on your own; then share your answer with other student teachers and discuss how you set about solving the problem.

When Amy, Bill and Clare eat out, each orders either chicken or fish, according to these rules:

a   *If Amy orders chicken, Bill orders fish:*
b   *Either Amy or Clare orders chicken, but not both;*
c   *Bill and Clare do not both order fish.*

Who could have ordered chicken yesterday and fish today? (See Appendix 4.3.1, p. 177 for solution.)

The problem in Task 4.3.2 is essentially about handling information according to rules of the type 'If A, then B', commonly found in intelligence tests. In this example the rules are arbitrary and it is not a real-life problem because people don't behave in this way. The problem cannot be solved by resort to practical activity; it is a logico-mathematical task requiring abstract thinking. The puzzle can be done 'in the head', but many people need to devise a way of recording their thinking as they develop their answer and check solutions.

We turn next to an exercise commonly given to pupils in science lessons, often during Key Stage (KS) 3 or early KS4. Task 4.3.3 illustrates not just abstract thinking but the handling of real data, identifying a pattern in the data and making deductions. The exercise illustrates, too, the ways in which pupils respond to data. The task is abstract but has real-life connections, e.g. pendulums are used to control timepieces; a longcase clock contains a pendulum, with a heavy weight at one end, which controls the escapement. The length of the pendulum is adjusted to control the accuracy of the timepiece.

In this example, pupils are set a problem-solving exercise in which they are invited to identify the factors that affect the frequency of a pendulum, that is, the number of swings it makes in a given time. The activity is a familiar task in a science lesson and concerns **understanding** and **how understanding is gained** rather than knowing and recall. The analysis of the data requires abstract thought and the ability to handle a complex situation. The term complex in this context refers to the fact that several factors (variables) have to be considered.

Task 4.3.3

SORTING VARIABLES 2. WHICH FACTORS (VARIABLES) AFFECT THE SWING OF A PENDULUM?

Background information

(If you know about pendulums, go to the pupil's task.)

A pendulum is essentially a rod pivoted vertically at one end and free to swing from side to side.

A simple example of a pendulum is a piece of string suspended at one end with a weight at the other; see Figure 4.3.1. Pupils are sometimes expected to use experimental data to deduce 'rules of the pendulum'; they may be given the data, or derive the data for themselves. The extent to which pupils can rationalise the data into rules explaining how a pendulum is controlled is one measure of their intellectual development. The task is not to learn the rules, but to understand how the rules derive from observation. What follows is an example of an experimental situation set up by a teacher for pupils. The exercise for the pupils, and you, is to work out what can, or cannot, be deduced from the data.

The pupils' task

Two pupils were given a task to find out which factors affected the time period of a pendulum. They were not told exactly what to do but the teacher had suggested investigating the effect of length, weight and push. They decided to measure the number of swings made by a pendulum in half a minute. They changed variables of the pendulum each time, by varying:

- the length of the pendulum; they had one short pendulum and one long pendulum (Figure 4.3.1a and b);
- the size of the weight on the end of the pendulum; they had a heavy weight and a light weight (Figure 4.3.1b and c);
- the height it was raised to set it going – the push; one 'push' was high up, the other 'push' low down (Figure 4.3.1c and d).

In their work, pupils sometimes changed one thing at a time but occasionally changed more than one variable at a time. They collected some readings (Table 4.3.1) and then tried to sort out what the readings meant.

Your task

From the evidence in Table 4.3.1 *alone*, what do you think the data tell you about the effect of **length**, of **weight** and of **position of release** on the number of swings per half-minute of the pendulum? (See Appendix 4.3.2, p. 177, for further information.)

Refer to the competences/standards for your course about helping pupils analyse data with several variables.

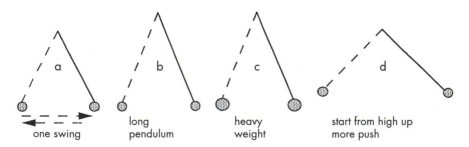

Figure 4.3.1 The pendulum: variables

Table 4.3.1 Data on different pendulums obtained by pupils (for Task 4.3.3)

Investigation number	Length of the pendulum	Size of weight on the end	Push at start	No. of swings in half-minute
1	long	heavy	large	17
2	short	heavy	large	21
3	long	light	small	17
4	short	light	large	21

From a **cognitive developmental point of view** the interesting features of this problem include:

1 Intuitively pupils expect the size of the weight and the 'push' to have an effect on the results. The results are contrary to common sense and pupils often think they have obtained a wrong result. This effect can cause cognitive conflict. In particular, many pupils expect heavy weights to 'do more' than light weights.

2 In the data, the evidence is not always clear-cut and so judgements may have to be withheld. This situation may cause mental conflict because pupils expect experiments to yield positive information.

3 In this example, some further information can be obtained from the data once a decision is made about the effect of weight on the time period of the pendulum; see Appendix 4.3.2.

Research again suggests that many pupils by age 16 in secondary school do not acquire the skills necessary either to sort out the data or to plan and carry out such an activity. By contrast, if pupils are told the factors that affect the time period of a pendulum, or are given a formula, they can apply that information to routine problems. The key factor here is that pupils have difficulty in generating evidence for themselves and analysing evidence correctly. It is the difference between learning and recall (which we, as teachers, do a lot of) and understanding what we have learned (which we do less of).

For example, when pupils are faced with the need to get evidence for themselves, they frequently choose trial-and-error methods rather than logically constructed enquiries. Trial-and-error-methods often lead to data which do not provide clear-cut answers to questions, which can be demotivating; this factor can often lead pupils to make unwarranted inferences from the data in an attempt to get an answer. Recognising that sometimes no clear inference can be made is a measure of cognitive maturity. Many pupils develop these skills as they get older but nevertheless pupils need to be taught these skills if they are to be exercised.

Pupils and adults find some evidence harder to accept than other evidence. Thus evidence that the magnitude of the weight at the end of the pendulum has no effect on the time period is often rejected intuitively or put down to error. Common-sense notions are in powerful opposition to logical thinking. Some pupils do not accept, for example, that, if two variables are changed at the same time, then it is not possible on that evidence alone to make a deduction. In this situation, some pupils may then bring in evidence external to the investigation to support their argument, instead of using the data they have. There is a powerful expectation by pupils, and many adults, that 'experiments' yield positive information, and that saying 'this enquiry tells us nothing about the question' is not an acceptable answer, especially if the teacher has set up the enquiry. Such feelings are powerful motivating forces; and attitudes of persistence and honesty are critical for the generation of real understanding. Such studies as these suggest that, without direct teaching, handling situations which contain several variables is a difficult task for many pupils. Teaching can improve pupils' achievement in these skills, as has been shown by the Cognitive Acceleration in Science Project (CASE) (Adey and Shayer, 1994, chapters 5 and 8). (Note: the acronym for the Campaign for State Education is also CASE.)

We note finally that the influence of life outside the classroom is powerful, especially if it is an established part of the social structure in which pupils live. For example, despite evidence that the 'star sign' under which you are born has no effect on our daily lives, the use of astrological forecasts is an important feature of some people's lives. Evidence is not always used as a basis for decision making, or action; sometimes custom or belief are more powerful factors.

Task 4.3.4

SORTING VARIABLES 3

Working with pupils

If you want to try the pendulum task with pupils, details can be found in *Science Reasoning Tasks* (Whylam and Shayer, 1978) or the CASE materials (Adey, Shayer and Yates, 1989). The CASE project materials and strategies may have important implications for teaching and learning because the effects of using them suggest that cognitive development can be accelerated by the same intervention strategies for pupils in English and mathematics (Adey, 2000, p. 169).

Pupils' understanding of ratio

A different sort of cognitive skill, for example, is the development, understanding and application of ratio and proportion. Ratio is a relationship between a pair of numbers usually written as **a:b**. An interesting number is $\prod$, called pi, the ratio of the circumference of a circle to the diameter. Proportion is the equality between two ratios, written formally as **a:b = c:d**. An interesting ratio is percentage (c) where the proportion is compared to parts in one hundred, thus **a:b = c:100**. For example, if there are six boys in a class of thirty pupils the percentage of boys is twenty, where 6:30 = 20:100; the answer is usually written as 20%. The percentage is often calculated by writing and solving the sum $(6 \div 30) \times 100$ without formal recourse to the proportionality above.

Percentage is an important part of economic life, in retail, mortgages, investment and cost of living generally. It is an area of understanding where considerable confusion reigns for both pupils and adults. See Figure 4.3.2.

A supermarket offered olive oil for sale labelled '50% free'. The bottle contained 750 cm^3 and was priced £2.99, the same price as a regular bottle of oil containing 500 cm^3. A group of adult customers were arguing that this offer was wrong because the price was not cheaper, i.e. £1.50. Despite having the nature of the offer explained to them several times by another customer, most of the group refused to buy the item because it did not cost less than the regular item.

Figure 4.3.2 Fifty percent of what?

A further example of a common confusion is financial inflation; many adults expect the cost of living to come down when the inflation rate is reduced from 3 per cent to 2 per cent. There is evidence, too, that not all adults can calculate real costs when sales advertising offers percentage discounts; see question c in Table 4.3.2. When pupils are faced with problems involving ratio, it appears that context is as important as the numbers themselves. In addition, the understanding of what constitutes a right answer is confused with 'what answer is good enough, given the context'. We might sympathise with this last point – for example, when preparing a dish for four people and faced with a recipe which requires two-thirds of a pint of cream for six people. (If metric units were used then the problem would be simpler because the recipe might say 'use 350 cm^3 of cream'.) The following example and the discussion that follows illustrate the influence of context on the way questions can be tackled.

Pupils were given three questions on percentages, together with an introduction which explained the meaning of the symbol '%'; the questions (a, b and c) and the number of pupils getting the right answer (the success rate) for each of three year groups are shown in Table 4.3.2. Read through the questions and answers and then do Task 4.3.5.

Table 4.3.2 Pupils' performance on questions involving ratio

Q. 8: % means per cent or per 100 so 3% is 3 out of every 100		

a 6% of pupils in school have free dinners. There are 250 pupils in the school. How many pupils have free dinners?

age/years	13	14	15
success rate/%	36	45	57

b The newspaper says that 24 out of 800 Avenger cars have a faulty engine. What percentage is this?

age/years	13	14	15
success rate/%	32	40	58

c The price of a coat is £20. In the sale it is reduced by 5%. How much does it now cost?

age/years	13	14	15
success rate/%	20	27	35

Source: Hart, 1981, p. 96. For further studies on the performance of pupils see Keys, Harris and Fernandes, 1996.

Task 4.3.5

RESPONDING TO TEST DATA

In Table 4.3.2 are the responses of one group of pupils to three questions on percentages set in different contexts.

1 Discuss possible reasons for the variation in performance of this group of pupils across the three questions.

2   Common wrong answers to questions are given below. Suggest ways in which pupils may have reached these incorrect answers and discuss what this says about their understanding.

- A popular answer to question b was 192. How might this wrong answer be obtained?
- Common wrong answers to question c were 15 or 16 (40 per cent of 13-year-old pupils gave this answer and 27 per cent of 15-year-olds).

Discuss how data like this contributes to your wider role of teaching numeracy skills.

You might like to investigate the understanding of pupils in your class or classes by using these same questions; see Task 4.3.6. See also Task 6.1.2 for further effects of context on assessment.

Task 4.3.6

YOUR PUPILS' UNDERSTANDING OF PERCENTAGES

Carry out a survey to sample pupils' understanding of ratio and proportion. Use the set of questions in Table 4.3.2. By sharing the work with other student teachers, Years 7, 9 and 11 in your school could be sampled. Analyse the results of your survey to see:

- how many succeed;
- what sorts of wrong answer you obtain and how they might be explained.

Interview some pupils and ask them to show you how they did the sum. Use the discussion following this task to help interpret the pupils' responses.

The sample of questions shown in Table 4.3.2 was part of a battery of questions designed to investigate pupils' ability to handle ratio and proportion and to investigate the strategies used by pupils when solving these problems. The author of the report of this investigation (Hart, 1981) concluded that when faced with ratio or proportion sums:

- pupils can often handle problems that involve doubling or halving;
- some pupils can handle harder problems which use doubling or halving strategies to construct an answer, which she called 'the building up approach' to number problem solving;
- if doubling and halving and then 'adding bits on' don't work, then a subtractive strategy is used (see question c in Table 4.3.2, where the answer 15 can arise from calculating $(20 - 5)$; and 16 arises as an answer by calculating $(20 - 20/5)$;
- only a minority of pupils in this age group can handle ratio in terms of multiplying by a fraction;
- when additive strategies give nearly right answers then there is seen to be little need for a new strategy. Being *nearly right* is often seen as acceptable.

The last point is interesting. The fact that some pupils can accept a nearly right answer suggests perhaps that it is the answer itself which is the important factor, rather than the understanding of how a right answer can be obtained. The fact that some answers can be fundamentally wrong (e.g. 192% for question b, Task 4.3.5) indicates an unawareness of what is possible or reasonable. This problem arises, too, with the use of calculators by many pupils where any answer on the readout may be accepted.

When adults discuss mathematics they are often quite happy to reveal their ignorance and incapacity to do sums – the numerical aspect of mathematics. Much greater reticence is found in the incapacity to read and write adequately and, for many, the absence of these skills is a cause for shame. The drive by government agencies to redress innumeracy and illiteracy in the population is a recognition of the importance of these skills.

The Teacher Training Agency (TTA), the body responsible in England for teacher supply and qualification, has, from 2000, demanded that all trainee teachers be tested in aspects of numeracy as a condition of gaining qualified teacher status, and it has provided considerable support for teachers (TTA, 2000b, 2000d; Patmore, 2000).

IMPLICATIONS OF A DEVELOPMENT MODEL

The results of activities and tests, examples of which were described above, suggest that as pupils get older there is a corresponding development in understanding. More older pupils are more capable of abstract thought than younger pupils. This finding may suggest that as pupils mature they are capable of an increasingly higher level of thinking (cognitive processing). Such a model of progressive development may be the result of biological maturation, of the quality of their experiences, including teaching, or both. The same results suggest, too, that some older pupils may not be able to solve certain types of problems. The data accumulated by these and other tests of performance all point to the fact that a considerable number of pupils are unable to cope with such demands. This situation may be attributed as much to faulty teaching or lack of motivation, as to any lack of intelligence; or it may be due to lack of biological maturation. In this context you might wish to find out how some of your pupils resolve moral dilemmas (i.e. do they try to work it out for themselves or appeal to higher authority?); or if they can solve murder mysteries in the popular genre of 'whodunits' of films or books.

Biological maturation may be another way of saying that the full genetic potential of the pupil becomes available. It implies, we suggest, that the conditions for the emergence of potential, the maximum intelligent behaviour of which the individual is capable, have been realised. What might those conditions be? The realisation of potential implies a home life in which the pupil has been encouraged in her play and schooling; where the emotional, linguistic and cognitive needs of the pupil have been met as the pupil grows and develops. It may include, too, exposure to good nursery and primary schooling and supportive parents who recognise and support the needs of the growing child. In other words, to what extent has the nurturing of the child allowed the child full expression of his potential? The performance we see in school, in class, on tests such as those above is, at least, a balance between nature and nurture, referred to earlier. This balance is unique for each child; knowledge of the individual child's progress and background is essential before we can discuss the intelligence or otherwise of individuals.

Two ideas have been introduced so far: one suggests that performance is a product of inheritance and nurture; the second idea is that as pupils grow and develop so does their capacity to handle complex situations. If this second idea is accepted it provides a rationale for structuring learning experiences for pupils or classes and so contributes to curriculum planning. If the demand made by a piece of work is carefully analysed and the current performance of the pupil or a group of pupils is identified by reference to relevant knowledge and skills needed to do the task, then future learning activities for a pupil can be planned so as to guarantee some success for the pupil. Curriculum development, in this model, becomes a process of matching the curriculum demand to pupil development.

A number of issues arise from proposing such a model. These include:

1 The efficiency of the model depends on being able to analyse teaching material sufficiently accurately in order to match material to pupil.
2 Does the cognitive demand made by the teaching material depend on its 'intrinsic' concepts, or does it depend on the way the material is presented? Put another way, can most concepts be taught to most pupils if suitably packaged and presented?
3 If matching 'curriculum to pupil' is the goal of the exercise, how might you build in development, going beyond the current level of performance? How would pupils progress and is there a danger that reducing the chance of failure may remove challenge?
4 Records of pupil performance and development are needed in order to match material to pupil. How should such records be kept?
5 If each pupil develops differently, how can a teacher cope with a class full of pupils at different stages of development? See Unit 4.1.
6 If pupils cannot cope with certain concepts because they are not yet ready for them, does this mean that some areas of the curriculum cannot be taught? Is rote learning an acceptable way to overcome this problem? See Unit 4.1 on differentiated learning, Unit 5.1 on theories of learning, and Unit 5.2 on active learning.
7 Can pupils be taught to think in generic ways that will help them to learn better across a range of subjects and contexts? See the section on multiple intelligences earlier in this unit and the CASE Project (Adey, 2000).
8 How well does a developmental model fit with a prescribed curriculum, such as the mandatory National Curriculum in England and Wales?
9 If pupils perform well at some tasks, can they be expected to perform well at other tasks? Can the demonstration of one set of skills be used to predict success at new skills? Do the same pupils perform well at most subjects at school? See Task 4.3.7. Is there a 'generalised cognitive skill'? For further discussion see 'Describing and measuring cognitive development' in Adey and Shayer (1994, chapter 2).

You may wish to add your own ideas to this list.

Task 4.3.7

ARE PUPILS ALL-ROUNDERS?

We asked, above, the question 'Do the same pupils perform well at most subjects at school?' Investigate this hypothesis.

In a year group draw up a class list of pupils and allocate them to a number of performance bands; use three to five bands. Talk to teachers of other subjects for this class and ask them to draw up a similar banding for their subject. Repeat this exercise for as many subjects as possible, drawing on the range of subjects offered in the school. Alternatively the school may have this information already on a database.

Compare the placement of pupils in this list to answer the opening question. You could take this comparison further and compare the placement of pupils in your lists with their scores on any national test of intelligence the school may use for predictive purposes, e.g. the *Cognitive Abilities Test* (NFER, 1996).

Identify any patterns in your data and discuss your findings with your tutor. Can any general explanation(s) be made for your findings, or must each pupil be discussed separately?

ANOTHER WAY OF LOOKING AT COGNITIVE SKILLS

Earlier in this unit we put forward a description of cognition in terms of the 'acquisition, assimilation and application of knowledge' (p. 161). Elsewhere we cited the claims for Design and Technology as fostering capability which is 'the integration of thought and skills into a holistic exercise, rather than a piecemeal exercise of isolated skills' (p. 164).

A good example of holistic problem solving is shown in a collection by Edward de Bono of children's responses to problems set by adults. The collection shows the spontaneous work by pupils (upper primary, lower secondary) in response to problems related to everyday events (de Bono, 1972). The tasks include:

- 'how would you stop a cat and a dog fighting?'
- 'design a machine to weigh an elephant'
- 'invent a sleep machine'
- 'how would you build a house quickly?'
- 'how would you improve the human body?'
- 'design a bicycle for postmen'.

In this work pupils need knowledge of the context from which the problem is drawn and also use knowledge and skills from both inside and outside the classroom. The work of pupils is occasionally unusual and the solutions sometimes impractical. The responses show much imagination and insight into their everyday world. Figure 4.3.3 is the response of one lower secondary school pupil to the task of designing a bicycle for postmen. The details for setting this task were:

Brief: Design a special bicycle for postmen. Pupils were asked to write and/or draw their answer in any way they liked (you could provide pupils with a sheet of sugar paper, say 0.5m square).

Rationale Bicycles are very familiar objects to pupils and the purpose of giving this problem was to see how pupils would alter what was already a familiar object in order to make it better. The question was how would pupils decide to improve the bicycle? What would be added? The problem was posed in such a way as to direct the improvements towards the postman's bicycle and not just bicycles in general.

In the author's discussion of the many sketches and solutions made in response to the task, he noted that children quickly identified what the postmen's problems were. These problems included nasty dogs, getting wet and getting the bike up steep hills. Children recognised that postmen spent a lot of time getting on and off the bike; so solutions were directed to delivery in the saddle. Pupils acknowledged that postmen spent a lot of time outside delivering the post, so some solutions provided the postman with food and drink, even hot drinks. The solutions were usually additive, leading to complexity, without elegance or aesthetic appeal. The important criterion was effectiveness.

You may wish to set a task for your pupils; see Task 4.3.8.

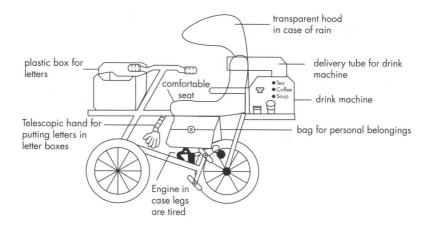

Bicycle – 6

Further refinements such as a transparent hood over the rider so that he doesn't get wet in the rain, and also a drink machine, where you put a coin in the slot and then choose whether you are going to have tea, coffee or soup. To save the postman's energy there is a telescopic hand for putting letters in letter-boxes. There is also an engine in case his legs get tired, but if there is going to be an engine it is hard to see why the postman should not use it all the time. But perhaps the designer thought that, if the bicycle was motorized throughout, then it would no longer be a postman's bicycle but a postman's motorcycle, so the engine is only provided as a sort of reserve, just as yachts have little reserve engines without ceasing to be yachts.

Figure 4.3.3 A bicycle for a postman

Source: De Bono (Viking, 1996) copyright © McQuaig Group Inc

Task 4.3.8

DESIGN A BICYCLE FOR POSTMEN

Set this task to one of the classes you teach. Alternatively choose a different task from the list above; or invent your own topic. It is important that the task is seen to be relevant to your teaching topic, otherwise it may not be treated seriously. Your choice of task should consider the pupils' environment; urban pupils may not see postmen on bicycles. The pupils' responses may give you an insight into their thinking as well as providing an imaginative homework task. You should consider how you will deal with the product; how is it to be marked and what are the criteria for your response? You could display the work in your classroom and invite pupils to identify the interesting, imaginative and useful solutions generated. Your pupils could develop criteria for assessing the work.

Write a short account of carrying out this task and discuss it with your tutor. File it in your professional portfolio.

MEASURING COGNITIVE DEVELOPMENT AND INTELLIGENCE TESTS

Much work has been carried out to measure children's responses to problem situations, as a means of 'getting a handle' on cognitive development; for example, Piaget and others following his seminal research – see, for example, Donaldson, 1978, 1992; Child, 1997b, chapter 7.

When an individual is tested or her performance is measured in some way, the information gained is only really about the individual's ability to perform that skill. It may be possible to generalise further but other factors intervene, e.g. motivation, culture. Intelligence tests are constructed in different ways, e.g. verbal, non-verbal and numerical, and so the aspect of 'intelligence' being measured is different in each case.

The study of intelligence and intelligence testing has been the focus of study for the last century. It assumed great importance in the UK post-Second World War due to the 1944 Education Act. Pupils were selected for grammar, technical or 'modern' schools by means of intelligence tests, the 11+ examination. Despite being developed into a reliable, sophisticated tool, IQ testing for selection purposes failed to take account of late developers or the variation in the social background of pupils. The tests also favoured pupils with good linguistic skills, those who had a good vocabulary and were familiar with middle-class culture, and girls. Girls on average mature faster than boys and the 11+ entry had to be modified to ensure equal access to grammar school for boys and girls. It was shown, too, that performance on the tests could be improved by training, which suggested that, in part at least, learned skills were being tested rather than any innate intelligence. In due course, the IQ test was rejected by arguments of justice and equity.

Assessment may be carried out for a number of reasons. IQ testing is used now by educational psychologists to assist in monitoring pupil progress and to assess pupils who, in various ways, find school difficult. It is also used in various selection procedures outside education. The assessment may be used to place pupils in particular schools through the LEA. Some LEAs retain selection to grammar schools, e.g. Kent, Buckinghamshire (Crook, Power and Whitty, 1999, pp. 1–3). Other reasons for assessment may be for research purposes as part of monitoring a population.

Many different sorts of tests exist, both general tests and tests which explore specific skills, e.g. spatial skills, while other tests use non-verbal methods. IQ tests, like most tests, are not culture-free; that is, they make assumptions about the testee's familiarity with the society in which the tests are to be applied (Gould, 1984).

Testing is a skilled process and tests cannot be used by just anyone. Many tests are supplied commercially, such as through the National Foundation for Educational Research (NFER). For example, if your school uses NFER tests to measure pupil abilities, usually they have to be carried out by approved persons. Your school may use these tests to help identify the abilities of pupils as part of a monitoring process or as a predictive tool. One test is the Cognitive Abilities Test (CAT); see Unit 6.1. Pupils are tested on entry to secondary school and again at the end of Key Stage 3. Data are provided on groups and individuals. The CAT is one means of monitoring progression and contributes to 'value added'. Find out about the tests used in your school and see how they are applied. In the first instance seek the advice of the special educational needs co-ordinator or the examination officer in the school. See, for example, Child, 1997b, p. 251 and Unit 6.1, p. 301, para. 6.

Intelligence testing is used to measure people's ability to carry out certain tasks or to predict success in further education. Usually the reporting is in terms of comparison of one group with another; or of one person against a standardised sample. This method of reporting intelligence is very different from that adopted by developmental psychologists who are interested in the type and sequence of thought process adopted by learners; see, for example, Piaget (Donaldson, 1978). Nevertheless both types of study lead to notions of norm-referencing for comparison purposes, whether it be scores on an intelligence test or quality of thought processes revealed by interview.

SUMMARY AND KEY POINTS

In this unit we have raised the issue of cognitive development and discussed the ways in which cognition may be defined. We have drawn attention to the priority given by schools in Western society to linguistic skills and logical reasoning, especially that used in developing the sciences and mathematics. At the same time we have drawn attention to the knowledge skills and attitudes needed by arts, design and technology courses and asked you to consider their contribution to cognitive development.

Within this discussion we have raised the issues around intelligence, the nature of intelligence and intelligence testing. Examples of testing for cognitive development have been drawn from science and mathematics. We ask you to consider to what extent such situations are reflected elsewhere in the school curriculum. What are the corresponding cognitive situations in geography, English, and language learning? For example, you might identify the different ways of punctuating the following statement and the different meanings that result:

The constable said the manager was not doing his job

In the same way that pupils develop ways of understanding the natural world, so pupils show a range of ways of tackling problems. There is a variation in abilities of pupils at the same age, as well as some increase in the numbers of those successful with increasing age. As pupils mature there is an increased capacity to perform cognitively more complex tasks. However, by the time pupils leave school, many pupils have not shown the ability, or willingness, to attempt some problems. By listening to pupils, and studying their responses to tasks, we can know more about their understanding and this can help us to match tasks to help their development. We need to adopt ways to encourage thinking, and we have drawn attention to a project which is endeavouring to promote thinking in the curriculum (Adey and Shayer, 1994).

We refer you to Unit 5.2 'Active learning', Unit 3.2 'Motivating pupils' and Unit 5.1 'Ways pupils learn' for further discussion of those related topics. You should check the competences/standards for your course as they relate to pupil learning and development.

FURTHER READING

Child, D. (1997b) *Psychology and the Teacher*, London: Cassell.
   The 6th edition of a classic text. Useful review of cognitive development, theories of learning and intelligence; includes research into classrooms, practice, management and special needs. Source of references.

de Bono, E. (1972) *Children Solve Problems*, London: Penguin Education.
   An amusing and informative study of children's responses to problem situations. A rich source of ideas to follow up in class or to probe pupils' understanding of ideas.

Donaldson, M. (1978) *Children's Minds*, Glasgow: Collins.
   Essential reading for anyone interested in developmental psychology and Piaget's work on cognitive growth. Review of work of Piaget. See also *Human Minds* (Donaldson, 1992).

Gardner, H. (1994) 'The theory of multiple intelligences' in B. Moon and A. Shelton-Mayes (eds) *Teaching and Learning in the Secondary School*, London: Routledge.

Readers interested in this model of intelligence might read this introductory paper before tackling his other writing (Gardner, 1993a, 1993b).

APPENDIX 4.3.1

Answers to Task 4.3.2 Sorting variables 1

From rules a and b, if Amy orders chicken, Bill orders fish and Clare orders fish. This contradicts rule c. So Amy orders only fish. Then, from rule b, Clare can order fish or chicken. Clare orders chicken, then Bill orders fish or chicken. If Clare orders fish then Bill can order only chicken. So Clare could have chicken yesterday and fish today.

APPENDIX 4.3.2

Commentary on Task 4.3.3 Sorting variables 2

The time period of a pendulum depends on the length of the pendulum; neither the magnitude of the weight nor the position from which the pendulum starts swinging (high or low) affects the time period.

From the pupil readings in Table 4.3.1, it follows:

- Investigations 1 and 2 tell you the length has an effect on the time period, since only length was changed, weight and position of release being held the same.
- Investigations 2 and 4 tell you that weight has no effect on the time period, since length and position of release are held the same.
- Finally, from 1 and 3, *if weight has no effect*, then, since the length is constant in both experiments, the position of release has no effect on the number of swings per half-minute.

UNIT 4.4 **RESPONDING TO DIVERSITY**

TONY TURNER

INTRODUCTION

In a report from the Organisation for Economic Co-operation and Development it was stated that:

> Fifteen to thirty percent of pupils and students in many countries of the OECD are at risk of failing school.
>
> (OECD, 1994, p. 1)

The term 'at risk' was identified in the following way. Being at risk:

> would lead to low educational attainment and self esteem, dwindling participation in school activities, truancy, dropping out, behavioural problems and delinquency.

The authors of the report tried to identify factors which could be used to predict some or all of these outcomes. They acknowledged that many of the factors are interactive and do not act in isolation. Nevertheless, the factors include:

> family poverty; ethnic minority status; single parenthood, uneducated parents, cramped housing, no relations between home and school, physical and mental abuse; poor grasp of the language of instruction; the type and location of the school and community failings.

Such a list makes depressing reading and the factors identified may contribute to alienation from school and even truancy. However, the report made an encouraging, positive statement by identifying education as a way of tackling the 'at risk' population:

> Schools can cope with the diverse demands and expectations presented by multi-cultural and pluralistic communities.

The OECD report echoes the findings of an influential report on school effectiveness in the UK which, although dated, is still highly relevant. It concluded that 'schools make a difference' to the life chances of pupils (Rutter, Maughan, Mortimore and Ouston, 1979). Recent studies support this view, e.g. Smith and Tomlinson, 1989; Myers, 1996; and Mortimore and Whitty, 1997.

Equality of opportunity has long been the aim of educators. In the last two decades, rapid strides have been made in identifying the cultural issues that affect the academic performance of pupils. Cultural issues include factors such as family background, social class, gender and ethnicity. These factors rarely operate in isolation; performance and behaviour are the result of a set of influences on the child. The OECD report indicates that social class is not a useful predictor of disadvantage unless causative factors are identified. It is easier to consider predictive factors separately even though we know that the overall effect on pupils is due to a combination of factors. In this unit we address issues of class, gender and ethnicity in schooling. We consider the different school performances of boys and girls as well as those of pupils from different ethnic groups in the community, and ways you might respond to this diversity in school.

OBJECTIVES

At the end of this unit you should be able to:

- review evidence about the relative academic performance of pupils in relation to class, ethnicity and gender;
- understand some of the cultural pressures on boys and girls which influence achievement;
- assess the power of teachers and schools to increase or ameliorate those pressures;
- discuss issues of discrimination and bias in relation to gender and ethnicity;
- review some classroom procedures to promote better opportunities for learning in all pupils;
- consider school policies which can be adopted to promote equality of access to the curriculum;
- relate these skills and attitudes to the competences/standards expected of a newly qualified teacher.

LANGUAGE AND DEFINITIONS

Sometimes the term 'ethnic' is used inappropriately to refer to minority groups, often black. Everyone belongs to an ethnic group; it has been customary to refer to numerically smaller ethnic groups as ethnic minorities, such as people of African/Caribbean origin in the UK. However, for some citizens that origin is distant, particularly if they are second or third generation British nationals. The term ethnic minority is offensive to some people, implying minority rights. In this book we use the phrase 'minority ethnic group' to identify ethnic groups numerically smaller than the white ethnic group. Another misuse of the word 'ethnic' occurs when ethnic foods are identified with, for example, jerk pork and dhal and not with fish and chips or black pudding.

For many purposes, e.g. in a national census or on an application form to enter a PGCE course, the ethnicity of all individuals is requested. One such list of ethnic categories can be found in Unit 4.2, Table 4.2.1. We use the term 'black' to refer to people of African or Caribbean origin unless the context requires a more specific description or we quote from sources.

At the heart of much discussion about cultural and gender issues lie notions of discrimination. We shall use the following definitions of 'discrimination' and 'prejudice' in this unit.

Discrimination can be defined as:

- to perceive or note the difference in or between; to distinguish;
- to make a distinction, especially on grounds of race or colour or sex; to select for unfavourable treatment.

Prejudice can be described as:

- a feeling, favourable or unfavourable, towards any person or thing, prior to or not based on, actual experience. An unreasoning predilection or objection. (Adapted from Klein, 1993, p. 13.)

With these ideas in mind we first look at issues of equal opportunities.

Why do equal opportunities matter?

For many people it is self-evident that the implementation of equal opportunities policies is a reflection of basic human rights. An absence of effective equal opportunities policies wastes human talent and deprives both the individual of the satisfaction of realising their full potential and society of their skills. Of equal importance, the discrimination that lies beneath unfulfilled ambitions of many children sours families and communities and leads to anger and frustration. Such feelings are evident in our multiethnic society, in school, in the workplace and on the streets. In the 1980s and earlier there was concern about the under-achievement of West Indian pupils (Short, 1986). At the begining of the twenty-first century there is growing concern about the low performance of many white working-class boys and pupils from some minority ethnic groups. Although much progress has been made in the last three decades as regards equal opportunities for men and women in the workplace and boys and girls at school, there remain substantial differences in the perceived role of men and women in society (Myers, 1987, 1990). In many cases, concerns about under-achievement focused on the shortcomings of the pupil or their families, the 'deficit model' explanation. More recently the focus has shifted to addressing the educational system as one of the factors contributing to under-achievement.

BACKGROUND 1: OUR MULTIETHNIC SOCIETY

The presence of small numbers of people from other cultures, faiths and backgrounds has been a feature of British society for many centuries. 'Britishness' is neither a clearly defined concept nor a fixed quantity. Attempts to define Britishness are either narrowly conceived, such as that based on a particular section of society, or merely trivial (such as the Tebbitt cricket test★). It was recently suggested that the term 'British' had, historically, largely 'white' connotations, and a broader view of being British needed to emerge to embrace the multiethnic nature of our society (Parekh, 2000). Britishness has been described also as 'dynamic and ever changing, adapting and absorbing new ideas and influences' – a view, we suggest, in sympathy with that expressed by Parekh (DES, 1985a).

Immigration into the British Isles has come in waves. A few examples draw attention to the changing ethnic mix that contributes to present day society. The Roman conquest of England at the dawn of the Christian era lasted some six centuries, the end of which saw invasion by Germanic peoples. About two centuries later the Viking invasion brought Danes and Norwegians to the mix of peoples. In 1066, the Normans took over much of England and many French people stayed and were assimilated. In the sixteenth century many people fled mainland European countries to escape, for example, religious persecution.

The ethnic mix was added to by Jewish immigration following their persecution at the end of the nineteenth century. Two world wars saw a further migration of people in mainland Europe away from conflict. As independence has been gained by many former colonial countries post-Second World War (1939–45), so has immigration from Africa and Asia altered the ethnic mix in the UK. The important difference associated with this latter wave of immigration was the visibility of newcomers. Prior to 1948 there was only a trickle of black immigrants; the 1950s in the UK

★ Which country would a member of a minority ethnic group support in the event of a cricket match between England and their country of origin?

saw the active recruitment of black and Asian families to fill the gaps in the workforce (Briggs, 1983, pp. 310–312).

Throughout the twentieth century the population of England and Wales grew steadily, from 35.5 million in 1901 to nearly 49 million in 1991; see Figure 4.4.1. The data shown in Figure 4.4.1 describe a steady population increase over the century with larger growth occurring in the decades ending 1921, 1941, 1951 and 1971.

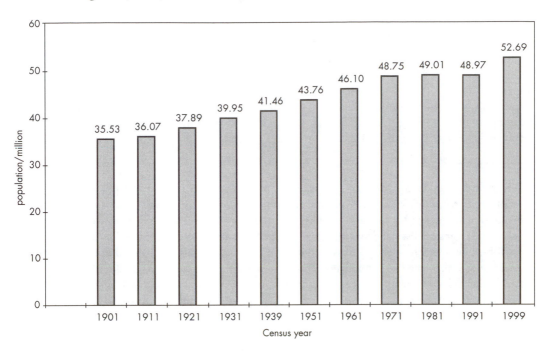

Figure 4.4.1 Population changes in England and Wales, 1901–1999

Note: 1999 figure is an estimate

Source: Office for National Statistics

The 1991 census showed that the population of Great Britain was almost 54 million, of whom nearly 6 per cent were Asian and black (Ballard and Kalra, 1994, p. 10). It would appear that steady population growth has been supplemented by immigration. Much of this underlying population growth can be attributed to improved health and sanitation. The minority ethnic population is expected to grow to some 10 per cent of the population by 2020; today the proportion of school-aged minority ethnic pupils approaches 11 per cent (adapted from Ballard and Kalra, 1994, p. 11).

Up to the early 1950s immigration was largely white. Many immigrants prior to that date were assimilated into the host culture, although a few immigrant groups maintained their distinctive lifestyle, for example the Jewish community. At first, the host community adopted the same attitude towards the black and Asian immigrants and expected them to adopt the values and lifestyle of the host nation. That this policy did not work may be attributed to the influence of racism – black people were not accepted in the same way as white immigrants of the past. Despite shared Christian values, the after-effects of colonialism and slavery may have affected the attitudes of many English people towards people of African and Asian origins (Klein, 1993, p. 17).

The eugenics movement of the early twentieth century may also have been influential. This movement was supported by some scientists, who claimed to supply 'evidence' of a hierarchy of intelligence among the 'races', as well as between men and women; this hierarchy placed whites above all other ethnic groups and men above women (Gould, 1984; Wersky, 1988, pp. 26–37). The influence of this movement may, at that time, have supported the racist views of some of the host population towards the new immigrants.

BACKGROUND 2: THE EDUCATIONAL EXPERIENCE

As the new immigrants settled in and the first generations of pupils of minority ethnic groups entered schooling, it became evident that many of these pupils were under-achieving (Coard, 1971). The experiences of many black and Asian pupils in school reflected in part the experiences of their parents in settling in the UK, that is, one of being marginalised (Carter, 1986). The story of Sylvia, described in Figure 4.4.2, may be typical.

Sylvia had been to a grammar school in Jamaica. She had earned her place through a scholarship, a considerable achievement in a highly competitive situation. Yet when she came to England at the age of 14 (in the 1960s) her school assigned her to the low-ability stream. When her family protested, the head told them that it was because she would be behind in the things that English schools taught. But Sylvia was convinced that what pupils were learning in the higher stream was well within her capabilities. When she made this known to her teachers she was told that if she did well during her first year at school they would reconsider her streaming the following year. This was not a school that pushed its low-ability stream classes and for a year she learned little. By the following autumn she had fallen badly behind in her studies, and she left school as soon as she could. She had ultimately studied her O levels and A levels in the evenings, while working in the daytime. She is now a senior nurse.

Source: Klein, 1993, p. 57

Figure 4.4.2 Sylvia's story

Explanations for under-achievement by pupils at first focused on a deficit model of the pupils and their culture. Thus the under-achievement of West Indian children was identified with poor linguistic skills, or with a poor self-image (Milner, 1975; Brittan (1976), in Klein, 1993, p. 56), in which the problem lies within the person or family and not the education system. These explanations for under-achievement were strongly attacked – for example, by Stone, 1981. During the 1970s, government-led research into the performance of all pupils was focused on identifying under-achievement – for example, through the Assessment of Performance Unit.

From the mid-1970s, teachers and LEAs began to address the issues raised by the presence of significant numbers of minority ethnic groups in schools, particularly in large conurbations. An approach that acknowledged and celebrated cultural diversity developed, known as multicultural education. This strategy, while raising the self-esteem of pupils, did little to address the issue of academic under-performance, and at times the celebration of culture may have replaced attention to the requirements of formal education. The importance of raising awareness in the mainly white pupils of the various cultures in society was a positive step and the first, it seems, to acknowledge the need of the indigenous population to understand the new cultures in their midst. The main drawback of multicultural education was the switch in focus from achievement in terms of the education system to a celebration of culture and diversity. Unless carefully handled this approach may have left minority ethnic pupils behind in terms of examinations and academic achievement. The aspirations of parents of minority ethnic pupils were high academically and frequently expressed as one of the reasons for migration to the UK (Klein, 1993, p. 57).

Multicultural education did not adequately address racism in society. It has been suggested that it is not possible to integrate minority ethnic families into a racist society (Klein, 1993, p. 32). The Rampton Report (Rampton, 1981) and the more substantial Swann Report (DES, 1985a) identified both overt and institutional racism as factors in the poor performance of minority ethnic pupils. The latter report drew attention as well to the need for all sections of the population to address issues of cultural diversity, not only to improve the life chances of all pupils but to avoid the problems of civil unrest emerging in Britain (Scarman, 1982). The succeeding two decades saw the growth of anti-racist policies both in education and more widely. The introduction of the National Curriculum (NC) for England and Wales in 1988 gave entitlement to all pupils to a broad and balanced curriculum and was an important step towards implementing equal opportunities policies. At the same time the NC diverted much energy away from the ethnic dimension of education and issues of access (as opposed to entitlement).

The Swann Report drew attention to under-achievement of minority ethnic pupils but made the important point that achievement varied from group to group. The report also emphasised the fact that many pupils were first or even second generation English-born. Thus the factors that might have operated in the circumstances of new arrivals no longer were relevant. Some pupils of Asian background, such as Indians, were achieving much more than, for example, pupils of Bangladeshi origin. The reasons for under-achievement are complex and not attributable to a single causative factor.

A report in the mid-1990s (Gillborn and Gipps, 1996) showed that considerable progress had been made by many, but not all, groups of minority ethnic pupils. That situation remains today. Two current reports identify the serious under-achievement of Afro-Caribbean pupils and show that these pupils have not shared in the rise in standards and achievement shown by many other pupils, especially white pupils (Fitzgerald, Finch and Nove, 2000; and Gillborn and Mirza, 2000). Many pupils of Pakistani background have failed to keep up with the improvements of most pupils in the last ten years. The researchers point out that governments, both central and local, have failed to address adequately the issue of under-achievement of particular groups of pupils. As a consequence, the gap between the high and low achievers widens with time. The under-performance of many white working-class boys serves to emphasise the importance of addressing ethnic group differences in performance and culture directly. In the population as a whole, girls now achieve better results than boys in public examinations (Gillborn and Mirza, 2000, p. 22); this change in performance over the last ten to fifteen years serves to emphasise that schools can make a difference to pupils' life chances (Smith and Tomlinson, 1989, p. 76; OFSTED, 1999, paras 93–95).

BACKGROUND 3: LEGISLATION

Understanding and awareness of the role of bias and discrimination in work, education, law, taxation, etc. have been growing in the past two decades. The concerns of society for the opportunities for all pupils to be realised have been supported by national legislation, all of which applies to schools and schooling. The Sex Discrimination Act of 1975 made both direct and indirect sex discrimination illegal. An example of direct discrimination would be refusing to allow a pupil to study a subject because of their gender. Indirect discrimination might occur where a condition was applied which made it unlikely that boys (or girls) could comply. There is no national policy on anti-racist education. The legal protection for anyone who feels discriminated against because of their ethnicity is the Race Relations Act, 1976. As regards employment, at an establishment in Great Britain it is unlawful for a person to discriminate against another in relation to employment by him:

- in the arrangements he makes for the purpose of determining who should be offered that employment; or
- in the terms on which he offers him that employment; or
- by refusing or deliberately omitting to offer him that employment.

(The male pronoun is used here to denote both men and women.)

Section 17 of the Race Relations Act specifies that discrimination in education is unlawful. It is concerned with the access to educational institutions in the terms on which pupils are offered admission; it is unlawful to refuse or deliberately omit to accept an application on the grounds of race.

Further, if limited, support for equal opportunities practices in school is the Children Act of 1989. Although it applies to the protection of children up to 8 years of age, it sets a precedent for further legislative protection. It has been described as a genuine advance in providing child care and an education service founded upon anti-discriminatory practice and principles of race equality (Klein, 1993, p. 99). The 1989 Act asserts the children's 'right' to an 'environment which values the religious, cultural, racial and linguistic background of the child and which is free of racial discrimination'.

Furthermore the Act describes a fit person to care for children to include one who has:

- 'knowledge of and a positive attitude to multicultural issues and people of different racial origins';
- 'commitment and knowledge to treat all children as individuals and with equal concern'.

It is to be hoped that similar appropriate legislation can follow for schools and colleges. For further discussion on the legal issues, see Klein, 1993, chapter 6.

The real problems in society are subtle; overt discrimination is relatively easy to recognise and often to confront. Attitudes of parents, peers, teachers and others all influence behaviour, choice and hence performance. Attitudes are hard to identify and explain and are more difficult to change and thus less responsive to legislation. Attitudes have been shown to be responsible for discrimination in the curriculum, e.g. Wright (1994). In her study of subject choices made by pupils at 13 years old, it appeared that teachers directed pupils into lower-achieving sets on behavioural grounds, in spite of the fact that these pupils had good enough examination results to enter the top sets. Such practices in this case prejudiced the chances of black pupils. Equally the attitude of some parents towards the education of girls can limit their aspirations (Taher, 2000).

If, for example, girls are not allowed to opt out of science or mathematics before 16 years of age, or boys are required to study home economics as well as a foreign language, then at least, it is hoped, gender divisions are delayed until 16 plus. This is one reason why the National Curriculum was welcomed by many people – because it was an entitlement for all pupils. Removing choice in this way eventually gives a wider educational opportunity to all. The recent softening of the demands of the National Curriculum has re-introduced the opportunity for schools to offer options at the end of Key Stage 3, in many ways a return to pre-National Curriculum practice.

DISCRIMINATION AND PREJUDICE

Secondary schools can have a positive effect in countering pupils' negative attitudes towards themselves and others. A secondary school policy has over 6,000 hours in which to counteract the prejudices of the environment and earlier conditioning. This can be achieved through curriculum planning and the development of good practice and can be used to tackle racism in school. This ideal can be supported by positively promoting cultural sharing and understanding (Robinson, 1999, p. 5). However, getting it wrong means that 6,000 hours are used to ignore or, worse, to perpetuate prejudicial attitudes.

Deep-seated prejudice contains the dimension of insularity; that is, although new facts might become available to a person which logically should change their views, the basic prejudice is maintained. In other words, the belief is held in the face of evidence to the contrary. When such prejudice occurs in a situation between unequal partners and concerns differences in ethnicity then this leads to a definition of racism as 'prejudice plus power'. The teacher–pupil relationship is one such position of inequality and contains the potential for racist behaviour.

Anti-racist education attempts to address not just discrimination, but the power relations involved. Equally, any antipathy between the sexes is exacerbated in a power relationship; such situations occur widely in our society, e.g. in some marriages and partnerships. Sexist behaviour can occur as a result of stereotypical views about gender roles, e.g. career guidance when an officer directs boys or girls into stereotyped jobs; or headteachers encouraging girls to study biology at A level rather than another science.

ACHIEVEMENT

The achievement of many pupils in the GCSE examination has grown in recent years as judged by the benchmark of five GCSE passes at grade A★–C. In 1988, 33 per cent of all 16-year-old pupils gained five GCSE passes at grade A★–C; in 1997 the figure was 45 per cent and it has continued to rise. Not all pupils have shared in the rising standards. In Figure 4.4.3★ the change in the proportion of pupils achieving this benchmark since 1988 has been plotted for years between 1988 and 1997. The graphs are plotted relative to the national average, as a difference between the group score for that year and the national average for the same year. The national average for each year is shown by the line (mean = zero) on the graph. The line for white pupils is nearly coincident with the mean because white pupils constitute some 93 per cent of all pupils.

The data introduce the categories of social class, ethnicity and gender which have become available from the Youth Cohort Study (DfEE, 1999). These data suggest:

- not all groups of pupils have shared in the rising standards of achievement; some groups achieve consistently below average;

★ Figures 4.4.3 and 4.4.4 are adaptations of those presented by Gillborn and Mirza, 2000, redrawn using the original data (DfEE, 1999, table B, p. 9).

- the biggest difference in achievement is found between the children of unskilled workers and professional management workers. This difference has widened since 1988 and in 1997 was 49 percentage points;
- the difference between the performance of boys and girls has widened in the period under study, more girls achieving the benchmark than boys;
- the difference between the performance of boys and girls is small (9 percentage points) compared with the difference between the two social classes (49 percentage points);
- pupils of African-Caribbean background under-achieve in comparison with the white cohort of pupils. The difference has fluctuated in the period studied but the gap had widened in 1998 to 15 percentage points. This difference is larger than the gender gap in achievement.

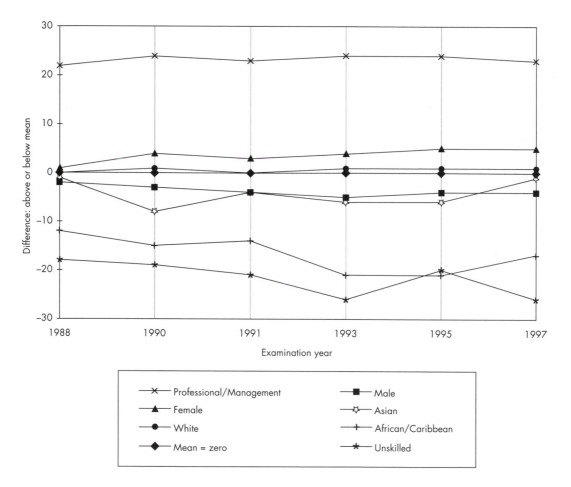

Figure 4.4.3 Differences in GCSE achievement, by class, gender and ethnicity (five or more GCSE passes at grade A–C)

Ethnicity

The Youth Cohort Study (DfEE, 1999) does not have data for the whole period, 1988 to 1997, because minority ethnic data were not available in the first two studies, 1988 and 1990. Using data only from the Youth Cohort Study, Figure 4.4.4 compares the examination achievements of the several ethnic groups during the period 1991 to 1997; the graphs are presented in the same way as in figure 4.4.3.

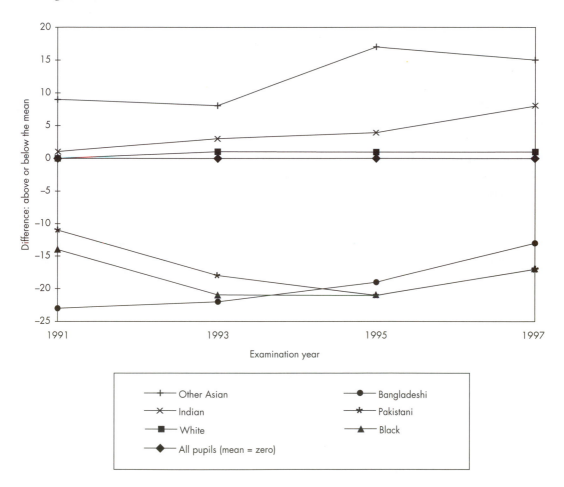

Figure 4.4.4   Differences in achievement by ethnicity (five or more GCSE passes at grade A–C)

Figure 4.4.4 shows that some groups of minority ethnic pupils consistently under-achieve and that Indian pupils as a group outperform most other ethnic groups, except for the mixed group 'other Asian'. African-Caribbean, Pakistani and Bangladeshi pupils do not appear to have enjoyed equal opportunities. We suggest you study this data further through Task 4.4.1. Further data are available covering the period 1988–97, using information from more than one source (Gillborn and Mirza, 2000, pp. 22–23). Using this wider range of data, a similar picture emerges, over the longer time period, to that revealed by Figure 4.4.4.

Task 4.4.1

RAISING STANDARDS

The graph in Figure 4.4.4 shows the achievement of different groups of pupils as measured by the proportion of pupils achieving five or more GCSE passes at grade A*–C. In the period studied the overall achievement of pupils in England and Wales has risen. In 1988, 33 per cent of all 16-year-old pupils gained five or more GCSE passes at grade A*–C; in 1997 the figure was 45 per cent and it has continued to rise.

Discuss the data by responding to these questions:

1 Which minority ethnic groups have shown improving rates of achievement?
2 Comparing the groups with each other, in 1997 and 1991, describe the differences between the achievements of each group as they changed over time?
3 Which groups, if any, may not have benefited from the improved overall achievement of pupils demonstrated nationally?
4 Suggest reasons for the under-achievement suggested by Figures 4.4.3 and 4.4.4 .

These data and information from other sources are discussed in greater detail by Gillborn and Mirza, 2000, pp. 13–17, 22–26. The data may be downloaded from the Web: www.ofsted.gov.uk

The data from the Youth Cohort Study and other data have been analysed further to look at the effect of gender on performance in each ethnic group. When this is done, the number of pupils in each subgroup becomes small and in some cases falls to about thirty pupils (Gillborn and Mirza, 2000, p. 24, footnote 75). The trends emerging need to be treated with caution but suggest that:

- girls are more likely to achieve a higher number of grades than boys in all ethnic groups;
- under-achievement is linked with ethnicity for both girls and boys;
- girls from Indian and white ethnic groups are more likely to achieve five GCSE grade passes at A*–C than any other group of pupils;
- African-Caribbean boys show a small decline in an already low relative achievement over the period 1991–5 (Gillborn and Mirza, 2000, figure 8, p. 23); and their achievement is marginally lower than in 1988.

In 1985, the evidence accumulated by the Swann Inquiry (DES, 1985a) suggested that many minority ethnic pupils were under-achieving. The recent research described above and that by Gillborn and Gipps (1996) show that, although achievement has been raised for most pupils, under-achievement persists and is linked to class and ethnicity.

In eight out of ten LEAs that took part in the Youth Cohort Study, and monitored the performance of all their pupils by ethnicity, it was shown that, as a group, Indian pupils attain higher outcomes than their white counterparts. This finding indicates that having English as a second language may not hinder academic achievement. A recent study has shown that 88 per cent of Indians, 92 per cent of Pakistanis and 97 per cent of Bangladeshis speak a second language (Modood, 1997, quoted in Gillborn and Mirza, 2000, p. 10).

Although some groups of pupils appear to under-perform, the research showed that each ethnic group outperforms all other ethnic groups in at least one LEA responding to the Youth Cohort Study (Gillborn and Mirza, 2000, p. 9). That is, pupils from all ethnic groups can achieve.

These facts remind us that the performance of pupils is related to many factors including ethnicity, gender and class. Academic performance and success at school depend on many interlocking factors, and success or under-achievement cannot be linked simply to a single variable or attributed to one cause. The variables used here – class, ethnicity and gender – are not causes; these variables hide causative factors which contribute to under-achievement. One such factor is poverty, the effect of which has been described graphically by Davies (2000, pp. 3–22). Many of these factors were identified in the OECD report referred to in the introduction to this unit. Many more pupils than at present are capable of raising their achievement given the right conditions, support and encouragement, and this assertion is borne out by the rise in standards nationally.

Under-achievement in school may be a factor in the higher unemployment rate suffered by many minority ethnic adults. In 1998, 13 per cent of women and 14 per cent of men from minority ethnic groups were unemployed in Great Britain, compared to 5 per cent of female and 6 per cent of male white adults. The national unemployment rate in 1998 was 7 per cent (Equal Opportunities Commission, 2000, p. 9).

Gender

Girls have been steadily improving their performance in school examinations over the past twenty years. In 1997 girls outperformed boys in all but one subject at GCSE level; in mathematics the same proportion of boys and girls achieved at least five passes at grade A★–C (Figures 4.4.5 to 4.4.7). At GCE A level, girls as a group now perform better than boys; more girls achieve passes at grade C and above than boys in business studies, chemistry, mathematics and physics; see Figures 4.4.6 and 4.4.7. The number of girls entering for some subjects, e.g. physics, is much lower than the number of boys. It is important to recognise that the able girl achieves just as good examination results as do able boys.

This development in the increased performance of girls in public examinations has not yet fed through into the workplace. In 1998, for example, the professional and managerial groups were male-dominated (Figures 4.4.8 to 4.4.10). The earnings of men and women remain very different although some progress towards equality has been made in the last twenty years. The *hourly earnings* of women in Great Britain in full-time work rose from 148 pence per hour in 1978 to an average of 822 pence per hour in 1998, compared to the equivalent male earnings of 205 and 1,026 pence per hour respectively (Equal Opportunities Commission, 2000, p. 12). The ratio of earnings, women to men, expressed as a percentage has increased from 72 per cent in 1978 to 80 per cent in 1998. When the same measure is calculated for *weekly earnings*, the ratio of earnings is about 10 percentage points lower but has moved in the same direction as the hourly rate.

Task 4.4.2 and Task 4.4.3 invite you to respond to the data about gender, education and employment in Figures 4.4.5 to 4.4.10.

Task 4.4.2

EXAMINATION PERFORMANCE AND JOB OPPORTUNITIES BY GENDER

Examine Figures 4.4.5 to 4.4.10. Discuss with other student teachers the implications of these data for the education of boys and girls. How might schools respond through, for example, the curriculum or the careers service?

Subject	Women		Men	
	Entries thousands	% passes at grade C or above ^	Entries thousands	% passes at grade C or above ^
English	325	64	333	48
French	204	57	178	42
Mathematics	342	47	345	47
Single Award Science	38	22	39	18
Double Award Science*	235	49	234	48
Design and Technology*	69	54	78	39
Craft, Design and Technology	23	55	96	41
Business studies	70	56	63	48
Home economics	95	45	18	26
Art and Design	121	70	113	52
Geography	133	58	171	51
History	125	61	118	53
Any subject	380	78	384	70

Figure 4.4.5 GCSE/SCE Standard Grade Examination entries and results 1996/97 (entries for all ages in schools and FE sector colleges)

Source: Education and Training Statistics for the UK 1998, DfEE, in 'Equal Opportunities Commission Fact Sheet, *Facts about men and women*' (www.eoc.org.uk)

Notes
* England and Wales only
^ SCE Standard grades 1–3

Subject	Women		Men	
	Entries thousands	% passes at grade C or above	Entries thousands	% passes at grade C or above
English	43	58	25	57
French	21	63	8	63
Mathematics	33	66	54	63
Biological sciences	40	56	26	53
Chemistry	24	64	29	62
Physics	10	68	33	61
Business studies	23	57	20	51
Art and design	26	70	16	61
Geography	22	64	27	56
History	27	56	21	57
Social studies	52	46	25	42

Figure 4.4.6 GCE A level and SCE Higher Grade Examination, entries and results 1996/97 (entries for all ages in schools and FE sector colleges)

Source: Education and Training Statistics for the UK 1998, DfEE in, 'Equal Opportunities Commission Fact Sheet, *Facts about men and women*' (www.eoc.org.uk)

	England	Wales	Scotland	Great Britain
GIRLS **GCSEs and SCE Standard Grades***				
5 or more grades A–C or 1–3	50.0	49.9	60.8	51.0
1–4 grades A–C or 1–3	26.0	23.6	24.6	25.8
1 or more grades D–G or 4–7, no higher grades	17.4	19.0	10.2	16.8
no graded results	6.5	8.5	4.4	6.4
2 or more GCE A levels or 3 or more SCE Higher^	32.5	30.4	35.0	31.6
BOYS **GCSEs and SCE Standard Grades***				
5 or more grades A–C or 1–3	40.5	38.6	48.9	41.2
1–4 grades A–C or 1–3	24.8	22.9	30.7	25.2
1 or more grades D–G or 4–7, no higher grades	26.0	26.4	15.4	25.0
no graded results	8.8	12.2	4.9	8.6
2 or more GCE A Levels or 3 or more SCE Higher^	26.7	23.1	25.4	25.5

Figure 4.4.7 Examination achievements 1996/97: Great Britain

Source: DfEE, The National Assembly for Wales and the Scottish Executive in 'Equal Opportunities Commission Fact Sheet, *Facts about men and women*' (www.eoc.org.uk)

Notes

* Examination achievements of pupils in their last years of compulsory schooling; the proportion (%) achieving grades specified

^ Examination achievements of pupils in schools and students in FE aged 17–19 at the end of the aademic year in England and Wales as a percentage of the 18-year-old population; and of pupils in years S5/S6 in Scotland as a percentage of the 17-year-old population

---

Task 4.4.3

MEN AND WOMEN IN HIGHER EDUCATION

Which subjects do men and women study in higher education? Talk to pupils about their aspirations for a career and whether they would consider going into higher education. Identify which subjects they would study and whether any subjects or career areas are favoured more by boys or girls. Ask for reasons for their preferences.

Select a number of pupils, getting a balance of boys and girls representative of the social and cultural mix in your school.

Use your data as the basis for discussion with your tutor. Sources of further data include:

1 Figures 4.4.5 to 4.4.10.
2 Students in higher education institutions, from the Higher Education Statistics Agency.
3 The Equal Opportunities Commission publication *Facts about Women and Men* which can be downloaded from the EOC website at: www.eoc.org.uk

Selected sectors	Women		Men	
	Thousands	**% of sector**	**Thousands**	**% of sector**
Engineering manufacture	0.9	4	19.4	96
Business administration	12.8	79	3.4	21
Motor Industry	0.3	3	10.4	97
Construction	0.2	2	9.2	98
Retailing	5.6	59	3.9	41
Hotel and catering	3.7	46	4.4	54
Electrical installation engineering	0.1	1	8.0	99
Hairdressing	7.4	92	0.6	8
Health and social care	6.0	89	0.7	11
Childcare	3.9	97	0.1	3
Accountancy	2.3	58	1.7	42
Customer service	2.7	68	1.3	32
Travel service	2.3	86	0.4	14
Information technology	0.9	43	1.9	71
TOTAL for these sectors	49.0	43	65.5	57

Figure 4.4.8 Modern apprenticeships 1999 in England and Wales

Source: Technician Education Council delivered government-supported training: work-based training for young people and adults – England and Wales, Statistical First Release 14/1999, DfEE, in 'Equal Opportunities Commission Fact Sheet, *Facts about men and women*' (www.eoc.org.uk)

Major occupational group	Women		Men	
	Thousands	**% of group**	**Thousands**	**% of group**
Managers/administrators	1,385	33	2,816	67
Professionals	1,082	39	1,669	61
Associate professional and technical	1,305	50	1,314	50
Clerical and secretarial	2,892	75	984	25
Craft and related	281	9	2,877	91
Personal and protective	1,906	67	938	33
Sales	1,299	64	736	36
Plant and machine operatives	468	19	1,993	81
Other occupations	1,000	45	1,064	52
All occupations *	11,618	45	14,394	55

Figure 4.4.9 Employment by occupation and gender, 1998, Great Britain (employees and self-employed aged 16 and over)

Source: Equal Opportunities Commission analysis of Labour Force Survey, Spring 1998, Office for National Statistics, in 'EOC Fact Sheet *Facts about men and women*' (www.eoc.org.uk)

* Includes those not stating occupation

Selected occupations	Women		Men	
	Thousands	% of employees	Thousands	% of employees
Drivers of road goods vehicles	16	3	451	97
Production, works and maintenance managers	30	8	361	92
Warehouse and storekeepers	49	13	323	87
Computer analyst/ programmers	52	21	193	79
Technical and wholesale reps.	55	25	166	75
Marketing and sales managers	137	26	388	74
Chefs and cooks	127	52	119	48
Secondary teachers	180	53	159	47
Sales assistants	896	74	307	26
Waiters and waitresses	154	75	51	25
Bookkeepers and financial clerks	519	75	169	25
Computer and records clerks	231	77	69	23
Counter clerks and cashiers	252	78	69	22
Cleaners and domestics	555	81	129	19
Catering assistants	189	82	41	18
Retail checkout operators	167	82	36	18
Primary and nursery teachers	302	86	48	14
Nurses	418	89	51	11
Care assistants and attendants	461	92	40	8

Figure 4.4.10 The gendered occupations of men and women, 1998, Great Britain (employees and self-employed aged 16 and over)

Source: Equal Opportunities Commission analysis of Labour Force Survey, Spring 1998, Office for National Statistics, in 'EOC Fact Sheet *Facts about men and women*' (www.eoc.org.uk)

Under-achievement in school may be more to do with school expectations, tradition and ethos than with any intellectual inadequacy (Wright, 1994; Eggleston, 1985, p. 219). In the past, data on the performance of pupils in public examinations have not been gathered nationally by the DfEE in relation to their ethnicity by ethnic grouping, although some LEAs do so, as the Youth Cohort Study above has shown.

Evidence has shown that young people from minority ethnic groups are more likely to stay on in full-time education after the age of 16 than young whites (National Commission for Education, 1993). For example, one reason why pupils from minority ethnic groups have a high profile in further education may be poor examination results, especially in the case of Afro-Caribbean boys. This situation may lead them to seek qualifications outside school. The numbers involved suggest that such people are determined to succeed and value education. This finding echoes earlier in-depth studies, in a small number of schools in England, of the educational and vocational experiences of pupils from minority ethnic groups (Eggleston, 1985).

Among young people in the age group 16–24, people from minority ethnic groups are more likely than whites to have a degree or other higher education qualification. There is no marked difference in the availability of job-related training for people from minority ethnic groups as compared with whites, although in general the former are more exposed to unemployment. This evidence, together with the under-performance of some pupils in the school system, raises questions about what goes on in school. There has been a shortage of teachers from minority ethnic groups in schools for many years, which in part has led to under-representation of these teachers in positions of responsibility. Not long ago the Law Society wrote to all firms of solicitors about discrimination against black applicants to train as solicitors (Dyer, 1994; Institute of Policy Studies, 1994). One important outcome of the Swann Report (DES, 1985a) was the realisation that no single causal factor was responsible for the under-achievement of pupils from minority ethnic groups in school, but the report identified racism and racist practices as one contributing factor. This factor may still operate.

ASPECTS OF SCHOOL PRACTICE

The period 1970 to 1990 saw the development of school policies on multicultural and anti-racist education, as teachers, school managers and many LEA personnel gained a deeper understanding of the issues at stake (Klein, 1993, p. 95). The massive upheaval in the school curriculum caused by the introduction of the National Curriculum, new examination procedures and the government inspection system (OFSTED) has pushed the ethnic dimension of education to the background. OFSTED has commissioned research into the achievements of minority ethnic pupils, for example, Gillborn and Gipps, 1996 and Gillborn and Mirza, 2000, although they were reluctant to publish the latter (Smithers, 2000). The DfEE have not monitored the progress of minority ethnic pupils as closely as other groups of pupils and the LEAs and OFSTED need to add an ethnic dimension to their inspection and monitoring systems.

Policies are only as effective as the extent to which people understand them and put them into practice. There is a great difference between intention and practice. The tasks below are designed to enquire into the equal opportunities policies in your school. There are a number of tasks from which you can select those that interest you or are more applicable to your situation.

Each task requires you to collect some facts during your school experience, using the ideas below as a starting point. A tactful summary of your thoughts on any of these matters might well be of interest to the school. However, you should seek the advice and guidance of your school tutor for both the enquiry and the format and distribution of any subsequent report. Inevitably the work that you do in this unit touches only the surface of the issues involved. Any one area could be explored in greater depth to form the basis for an academic assignment.

School policies

Many schools have developed policies concerning aspects of equal opportunities, including gender and anti-racism; there may be policies about behaviour, including bullying which carries with it issues of equal opportunities of a different nature. In addition, many equal opportunity issues are central to other policies, such as assessment or pastoral care. In the following task we focus on equal opportunity policies; we address pastoral care later in the unit.

Task 4.4.4

POLICIES TOWARDS EQUAL OPPORTUNITIES (EO)

1   Obtain a copy of the EO policy in your school. Read it and try to identify:
   - who wrote the policy? Were parents or pupils involved?
   - how old is it?
   - are there any later documents, e.g. working party reports?
   - what areas of school life does it cover ? Does it cover the curriculum, playground behaviour, assembly or other aspects of school life? Are any areas of school life omitted from its brief?
   - what is the focus of the policy? Is it gender, ethnicity, social class or disabilities?

2   Who knows about the policy? Devise a way of sampling knowledge, understanding and opinion of pupils and staff about the policy. For example:
   - are copies of the policy displayed in the school?
   - how many staff know about it; have read it?
   - how many pupils know about it; have read it?
   - who is responsible for EO in the school?

3   Is the policy treated seriously in the school? For example:
   - has any in-service programme been devoted to EO issues?
   - does the school EO policy influence departmental policy or classroom practice?

4   Widen your study by examining another school's policy on equal opportunities. Try to obtain one from a nearby school, or from another student teacher. An example of a recent policy from a school, called Nonesuch School, is given in Figure 4.4.11.

   In what ways:

   - is this policy different from the policy in your school?
   - does the policy correspond to that in your school?
   - do the policies go beyond intentions into practice? How can the aims of the policies be implemented?

See Klein, 1993, pp. 103–110 for further discussion.

How are policies implemented in your school?

No matter how concerned the school is to promote equal opportunities through good policies, implementing them in the classroom is not an easy matter. It is instructive to use lesson observation time to look at specific aspects of teaching and then to report back to your tutor or tutor group. Some ideas are listed below in Tasks 4.4.5 and 4.4.6.

Nonesuch School is a comprehensive school; that means it is for everybody. In this school we believe that everyone has a right to equal chances and each individual is valued and respected for who they are.

- There are at least 15 languages spoken in the homes of students and staff at Nonesuch.

- Students' families and staff have links with many parts of the world.

- People at Nonesuch are glad that it is a multicultural school.

- You will study many different cultures and countries.

- You also find out and discuss why people pre-judge others often through their own ignorance or lack of understanding.

- If anyone tries to offend you because of your race or colour, religion, nationality, language or culture, the school will support you.

- At Nonesuch, all subjects are equally important; there are no 'girls'' subjects and no 'boys'' subjects.

- In the first year, everybody studies the same subjects. After that there is a choice. When choices are made for subjects or careers, you will be given help; this will make sure that boys and girls all have the same opportunities.

- Many people grow up thinking that women are not as good as men; at Nonesuch you learn that this is not true.

- If anyone tries to offend or limit you because of your sex, the school will support you.

- Please report sexist comments or behaviour to a teacher or Head of Year or the Head(teacher)

No one should suffer prejudice or discrimination against them.

Figure 4.4.11   Equal opportunity policy of Nonesuch School

Task 4.4.5

RESPONSES TO GENDER: CLASSROOM OBSERVATION

Ask a class teacher if you can observe her lesson. Explain the purpose of your enquiry, which is to find out which pupils participate in the lesson more than others; and which pupils the teacher invites to answer questions or volunteer information. Be prepared to share your findings with her.
      Keep a tally of the frequency of attention to, and the time given to, boys and girls. Devise a recording sheet to collect information about one or two of the following behaviours:

- who puts their hand up to answer a question?
- who does the teacher select?

- in class activities, how much time is spent by the teacher with boys, with girls?
- does the teacher respond to a pupil with praise, criticism or further questioning?
- when pupils are reprimanded, is there any difference in:

  - the nature of the misdemeanour? That is, what is tolerated, or not, by the teacher?
  - the action taken by the teacher?

You might consider whether different messages are conveyed to boys, and to girls, by the teacher through her response to classroom interactions.

Task 4.4.6

RESPONSES TO ETHNICITY: CLASSROOM OBSERVATION

Redesign the record sheet you used in Task 4.4.5 to collect data about teachers' responses to pupils of different ethnicity. Use the same questions as listed under Task 4.4.5 and observe the same protocols about observing classrooms. You may wish to add to the list of questions:

- did racist behaviour occur in the class?
- what was the nature of the racism? Was it name calling, inappropriate language or metaphors, stereotyping, inappropriate book or other visual resources (see Task 4.4.7)?
- how was the racist incident dealt with?

Read 'Race and racism as a classroom topic' in Klein, 1993, pp. 139–145.

When you first start teaching your concern is to promote learning through well-ordered lessons; when you feel more confident ask a colleague to observe one of your lessons, focusing on the questions above.

Books and attitudes

Equal opportunity policies must influence the material placed in front of pupils. Pupils, like us, are heavily influenced by the words and pictures, particularly moving ones. Access to the World Wide Web has opened up all sorts of material to pupils.

Task 4.4.7

BIAS AND STEREOTYPING IN TEACHING RESOURCES

Interrogate a resource used in teaching in your school for bias and stereotyping. Resources include books, worksheets, wallcharts, CD-ROMs, video recordings and internet material. Some questions you could use to address this issue include:

- how accurate are the images shown of people and of places?
- are women and girls shown in non-traditional roles?

- are men shown in caring roles?
- who is shown in a position of authority? Who is the employer, the decision maker, the technologist? Is it always a man? What are the roles of women?
- are people stereotyped, e.g. black athletes, male scientists, female social workers, male cricketers?
- how and why are people in the developing world depicted? Is it to illustrate malnutrition, or their living conditions or the technology employed? Are the images positive or negative?
- what assumptions, if any, are made concerning minority ethnic citizens in the UK?
- what assumptions, if any, are made concerning under-development in the developing world?

Read 'Printed and published materials in schools' in Klein, 1993, pp. 167–180.

THE PASTORAL ROLE

In many schools new teachers are often expected to act as form tutors to a class. In this role it is likely that they will be asked to deal with human relationships including issues of gender and race. You should take the opportunity to work alongside a form teacher throughout your initial teacher education year so as to become aware of the demands on and responses by form teachers. Many schools expect involvement of the student teacher in pastoral matters, including participation in aspects of Personal and Social Education courses. Some examples of situations met by teachers in this role have been identified in Unit 4.5. You will, no doubt, in a short time in school have begun to gather examples of incidents rooted in sexist or racist issues; you might wish to discuss these in a tutor group. We include Tasks 4.4.8 and 4.4.9 which may alert you to issues that may soon confront you.

Task 4.4.8

THE ROLE OF THE FORM TUTOR: SOME DILEMMAS

Here are some situations to which some teachers may have had to respond. If you are working in a group of student teachers, agree between yourselves that one of you will be responsible for giving their reactions to the dilemma to the rest of the group. Allow time for all of you to read through one chosen example at a time and formulate your own reaction. Take it in turns to make the first response. As a group, identify the wider implications for the school of any one incident.

1 A pupil tells a racist joke during tutor time. How do you react? If this incident had happened either in a lesson or in the playground would you have responded differently? If so, in what way? If it were a sexist joke how would this alter your response?
2 A girl in your class is crying. She tells you, eventually, that a group of boys in the class have been calling her names and had tried to 'touch her up' on the way to school. She does not tell you who is involved. What do you do?
3 A group of girls in your form are making a young male teacher's life misery by calling out after him, following him around and never leaving him in peace. What would you do?

4 Graffiti, calling a girl in your class a 'slag', have appeared in the girls' toilets. The person you think might be involved denies all knowledge of it. What might you do next? How would you tackle the issue with:

- the pupil targeted by the graffiti?
- the whole class?

5 One of your class finds racist slogans written on his books and on bits of papers passed to him during lessons. The pupil is upset and asks you to do something about it. What course of action might you take?

6 You are a PE teacher and you want to introduce a dance unit into the curriculum for boys. In spite of the requirements of the National Curriculum your suggestion meets with disbelief from some of your staffroom colleagues as well as the boys concerned. How do you respond?

Other examples of problem situations appear in Unit 4.5, Tasks 4.5.5 and 4.5.7.

Task 4.4.9

THE ROLE OF THE FORM TUTOR: PERSONAL AND SOCIAL EDUCATION

Examine your school Personal and Social Education (PSE) programme; in what ways does it address relations and attitudes towards the opposite sex? Does it suggest ways of identifying and combating bias, stereotyping and discrimination? How is the programme related to whole school policies, such as those addressing equal opportunities and anti-racism? Identify the contexts in the programme in which these issues are raised.

Write a short report on your findings and show it to your tutor. For further reading see Klein, 1993, chapter 7.

SCHOOL POLICIES ON PUPIL GROUPING AND ACCESS TO FURTHER STUDY

Many schools organise their teaching by placing pupils into mixed ability groupings or by adopting a policy of setting or streaming. Access to examination classes of a higher or lower status is achieved by reference to achievement in SAT tests or internal school examinations. Access to higher grades in GCSE is governed by teachers selecting pupils for entry to the appropriate tier of papers suited to their achievements. Selection is again expected to be based on achievement rather than potential or other features, such as behaviour or attitude.

Examine the practices in your school by which pupils are identified and placed in teaching classes and entered for examinations, such as SATs and GCSE. The following tasks will help you to organise your enquiry.

Task 4.4.10

SETTING AND STREAMING BY GENDER

If your school operates a streaming, setting or banding system, collect data about the numbers of boys and girls in different teaching groups. Sort the information by ability and selected school subjects, e.g. two core subjects and your teaching subject. You may find it helpful to focus on one year group, e.g. the transition from Year 9 to Year 10, when GCSE subject choices are made.

Task 4.4.11

SETTING AND STREAMING BY ETHNIC GROUP

If your school operates a streaming, setting or banding system, collect data about setting and streaming and the distribution of pupils from minority ethnic groups across the classes. Several student teachers could share out the work, enabling a wider picture of one year group to emerge. Collect the data in a form that allows comparison between the several ethnic groups. See Table 4.2.1 for information about ethnic classification.

Task 4.4.12

WHO IS RECRUITED TO POST-16 COURSES?

If your school has a sixth form, compare the number of pupils in the first year academic and vocational courses, by gender and ethnicity, and compare those numbers with the numbers in the previous year's Year 11 cohort. Identify the subject preferences.
How many pupils left school to carry on education in another institution and what are their gender and ethnic characteristics?

RESPONDING TO DIVERSITY IN THE CLASSROOM

Your immediate concerns are focused on the classroom but much of what goes on in the classroom has its origins outside the classroom. These origins include the cultural background of the pupils; the teachers' expectations of pupils; the externally imposed curriculum; and the school's ethos realised through its policies and practices.

Expectations of academic performance are often built upon both evidence of what the pupil has done in the past and their social position: male/female; white/black; Irish/Afro-Caribbean; working/middle-class; stable/unstable family background. A perceived social position is sometimes, if unconsciously, used by teachers to anticipate pupils' progress and their capacity to overcome difficulties. For example, 'Jimmy is always near the bottom of the class, but what do you expect with his family background?' Or 'The trouble with Verma is her attitude, she often seems to have a chip on her shoulder and doesn't respond well to discipline even when she is in the wrong. She never gives herself a chance; I'm always having a go at her.'

The interaction of the teacher with pupils in the classroom is often revealing. Some teachers may subconsciously favour asking boys, rather than girls, to answer questions. Once established, the reasons for this behaviour can be explored. Similar questions can arise about the way teachers responds to pupils' answers. Whereas one pupil might make a modest and partly correct response to a question, to which the teacher's response is praise and support, another pupil, offering the same level of response, may find a more critical attitude adopted by the teacher.

Are these different responses justified? Is the pupil who received praise gaining support and encouragement from praise; or is the pupil being sent a message that low-level performance is good enough? It is teacher expectations that direct and control such responses. If, as has been documented in the past about the performance of girls, the praise is implicitly saying 'you have done as well as can be expected because you are a girl', and the critical response is implying 'come on now, you're a boy; you can do better than this', then there is cause for concern.

Such interpretations depend very much on the context. A comparison of teacher behaviours in different lessons might reveal the influences on teaching and learning of the subject and the gender, age and social and cultural background of teachers and pupils.

SUMMARY AND KEY POINTS

Equal opportunities are about maximising the aspirations of all pupils, and not about trying to make pupils of all ethnic backgrounds more like each other, any more than they are about trying to make girls behave like boys. The task of the school is to create a learning environment in which all pupils can thrive. A compulsory curriculum supports equal opportunities policies but access must be ensured.

Sometimes you hear a teacher say 'I didn't notice their colour, I treat them all the same.' Learning opportunities are enhanced by *not* being 'gender blind' or 'colour blind'. We suggest that not recognising pupil differences, including culture, is as inadequate a response to teaching demands as the stereotyping of pupils. Pupils learn in different ways and a key part of the differentiated approach to learning is to recognise those differences without placing limits on what can be achieved (see also Unit 4.1 and Unit 4.2). This brings us back to the expectations of the teacher. If you expect most Asian girls to be quiet and passive and good at written work, then that is not only what they do, but also perhaps all they do. Individuals respond in different ways to teachers; you should try to treat each person as an individual and respond to what they do and say, making positive use of your knowledge of the pupil's culture and background.

You should check the competences/standards for your course about the issues raised in this unit.

FURTHER READING

Davies, N. (2000) *The School Report: Why Britain's Schools are Failing*, London: Vintage Books.
A critical review of the state of some schools in the UK. It reveals the difficulties faced by some teachers, schools and LEAs caused by poverty and under-funding. It is not a balanced review of schooling in the UK but describes aspects of the background of life in some schools.

Gillborn, D. and Mirza, H.S. (2000) *Educational Inequality: Mapping Race, Class and Gender; a Synthesis of Research Evidence*, London: OFSTED. (This material can be downloaded from the World Wide Web on: www.ofsted.gov.uk)

This report says that black children failed to share in the dramatic rise in attainment at GCSE which took place in the 1990s, to the same degree as their white peers. Black and minority ethnic youngsters are disadvantaged in the classroom by an education system which perpetuates existing inequalities. Differences in the achievements of boys and girls and children of professional and working-class parents are compared and contrasted.

Klein, G. (1993) *Education Towards Race Equality*, London: Cassell.

An important book which gives an overview and background to the development of anti-racism in schools It tackles the issue of 'all-white' schools. Attention is given to the role of subject teaching in tackling inequality, which is useful for classroom teachers.

Weiner, G. (1994) 'Ethnic and gender differences' in C. Desforges, *An Introduction to Classroom Teaching: Psychological Perspectives*, Oxford: Blackwell.

The author analyses some of the ways in which teachers talk about ethnicity and gender in schooling. She addresses factors including achievement, curriculum, classroom processes, language and teacher expectations. The chapter helps to identify current controversies, issues and debates.

UNIT 4.5 **MORAL DEVELOPMENT AND VALUES**

TONY TURNER

INTRODUCTION

Schools have always had a broad vision of their purpose, beyond the delivery of subject knowledge. This vision is expressed in a number of ways, ranging from the school motto to a set of school aims; these aims often include personal and social targets for pupils. The personal targets are about developing the whole person through their skills and talents; the social aims include concern for others, responsibility to and for others and contributing to the welfare of society; see Units 7.1 and 7.2.

Manifestations of these aims are often found in school policies, such as those for equal opportunities, bullying and dress codes; or through the ways in which parents are invited to contribute to the school. A key factor in the affirmation of many of those aims is the way the teachers behave with, and respond to, pupils through subject teaching, their pastoral role and through extra-curricular activities. The teacher sets the example; if the school is concerned about punctuality, then teachers must be punctual.

The way a school conducts itself, the standards it sets and the relationships it nurtures are sometimes referred to as the ethos of the school. Ethos is often intangible and can be a feeling you get about what is valued when you spend time in the school. Ethos can be expressed in the way parents are welcomed into the school; or the relationship of teacher to pupil outside as well as inside the classroom; or staff sensitivity to cultural and faith differences in the school; or how the school celebrates the success of its pupils. Some authors refer to the hidden curriculum: the values a school upholds implicitly and nurtures in all its dealings with young people. The ethos of a school contributes as much to values education as does the prescribed curriculum of subjects.

In England and Wales, the National Curriculum sets out to:

(a) promote the spiritual, moral, cultural, mental and physical development of pupils at the school and of society; and
(b) prepare pupils at the school for the opportunities, responsibilities and experiences of adult life (DfEE/QCA, 1999a, p. 12);

through the framework of the 1988 Education Act (ERA, 1988) and re-affirmed in the 1996 Education Act (Great Britain, 1996, para. 31).

It is within this framework of values and aims that teachers are expected to teach their subject and promote the spiritual, moral, cultural, mental and physical development of their pupils. The focus of much of this unit is on the opportunities in your daily work with pupils to foster and develop values and moral judgement and to help pupils understand the need for a set of common values and what those values might be. We do not address in depth theories of moral development or their origin but the further reading section at the end of this unit offers that opportunity, e.g. Langford, 1995. See also Unit 5.1 'Ways pupils learn', which introduces you to theories of how learning happens.

OBJECTIVES

By the end of this unit you should:

- know the legal responsibility of the school towards pupils in the area of moral, spiritual and cultural development;
- be aware of the opportunities in school to promote these aims;
- be able to try out some methods of teaching towards these aims and evaluate them;
- be able to place moral and values education in a subject and school context;
- be able to relate these aspects of a teacher's role to the standards/competences expected of a newly qualified teacher.

A FRAMEWORK FOR VALUES EDUCATION

Morals and ethics

Ethics may be described as a process of rational enquiry by which we analyse and decide on issues of right and wrong and thus good and bad. Ethics are linked to action and underpinned by morals. Ethics applied to people and their actions enable us to determine what we should do, as opposed to what we can do. Some professions have a code of ethics which prescribes the behaviour of its members; thus ethics are contextualised, e.g. the Hippocratic oath of the medical profession.

What we can do, in contrast with what we should do, is limited by many factors. These factors include the means and resources to effect change and the attitudes of people or organisations both to carrying out change and to the consequences of change. The attempt to implement the Kyoto agreement on the environment through a reduction in the use of carbon-based fuels is a good example of the contrast between knowing what society should do, can do and is willing to do.

Morals are more general and linked to belief systems and values. All societies have a code of conduct which was, in the past, frequently related to a belief system. Thus moral development is linked for many with religious belief. Humanists and agnostics would argue otherwise. By moral development we refer to changes in the individual in relation to their personal and social behaviour. The development of moral judgement and a system of values is, ultimately, a personal choice. However, it is not simply a matter of personal choice. Both the development and exercise of moral judgement and the acquisition of a set of personal values are influenced by the home and school, culture and faith, people and society.

A study of how moral judgement and values develop has been made by Piaget and Kohlberg; for an introduction to their work see, for example, Langford, 1995, p. 69. Piaget linked the development of moral judgement with cognitive capability, i.e. mature moral judgement is dependent on a capacity to reason logically. Both writers describe features of the development of moral judgement. They point out that not everyone appears to attain the higher levels of moral judgement, and, moreover, if they do, may not practise them. Whereas these researchers place emphasis on maturational factors, others focus on moral development through social learning. Theories about the origin, as opposed to a description, of moral judgement have been attempted by Freud (Langford, 1995, p. 13).

Moral development is reflected often in the response of pupils to authority. A first response may be through obedience, leading to conforming to accepted standards as pupils understand the need for rules. Later there may develop a personal code of behaviour generated by logical argument within a framework of personal autonomy. The school has a potential for influence in this development and may, for many pupils, be the only place where value systems are raised to consciousness, debated and challenged.

Schools are, and always have been, concerned with developing young people who value themselves and have a good personal self-image. This self-image includes many things, such as self-confidence and the willingness to tackle new ideas and problems. Equally important is the confidence to listen to the contribution of others and be able to respond, knowing that that their own contribution is valued. Values are about self and one's relation to other people.

The National Curriculum

The values underpinning, and the purposes of, the National Curriculum in England and Wales are described in the following terms:

> Foremost is a belief in education, at home and at school, as a route to the spiritual, moral, social, cultural, physical and mental development, and thus the well-being, of the individual. Education is also a route to equality of opportunity for all, a healthy and just democracy, a productive economy, and sustainable development. Education should reflect the enduring values that contribute to these ends.
>
> (DfEE/QCA, 1999a, p. 10)

These values and purposes are to be achieved through two key aims. The first describes its hopes in relation to pupil learning. The second aim is:

> to promote the pupils' spiritual, moral, social and cultural development and prepare all pupils for the opportunities, responsibilities and experiences of life
>
> (DfEE/QCA, 1999a, p. 11)

which adds little to the statement of the hopes of the 1996 Education Act, cited in the introduction to this unit – (a) and (b). However, this second aim is elaborated further by stating that pupils should:

> in particular, develop principles for distinguishing between right and wrong. It [the achievement of the aim] should develop their knowledge, understanding and appreciation of their own and different beliefs and cultures, and how these influence individuals and societies. The school curriculum should pass on enduring values, develop pupils' integrity and autonomy and help them to be responsible and caring citizens capable of contributing to the development of a just society.
>
> (DfEE/QCA, 1999a, p. 11)

These aims are to be achieved through the opportunities of the statutory subject curriculum, including religious education together with a programme of Personal, Social and Health Education (PSHE), including Citizenship (DfEE/QCA, 1999b). For further discussion of the National Curriculum see Unit 7.3.

When the new National Curriculum for England and Wales was in preparation, the government set up a Working Party (see Figure 4.5.1) to give guidance to teachers and managers on values education. An extract from their report is included in the National Curriculum handbook for teachers (DfEE/QCA, 1999a, pp. 195–197).

The Report of this Working Party produced a 'Statement of values' which sets out to identify common values in society, to which most people would agree, irrespective of culture or belief: see Figure 4.5.1 The values identified in Figure 4.5.1 may be examples of the 'enduring values' referred to above. For further discussion on enduring values see Warnock, 1998, pp. 122–124.

The National Forum moved from the broad general statement of values (Figure 4.5.1) to the translation of those values into practice. For example, under the heading of 'The self', the National Forum team listed the following goals for pupils:

- develop an understanding of our own characters, strengths and weaknesses;
- develop self-respect and self-discipline;
- clarify the meaning and purpose in our lives and decide, on the basis of this, how our lives should be lived;
- make responsible use of our talents, rights and opportunities;
- strive, throughout life, for knowledge, wisdom and understanding;
- take responsibility, within our capabilities, for our own lives (DfEE/QCA, 1999a, p. 196).

A statement of values

1 The self
We value ourselves as unique human beings capable of spiritual, moral, intellectual and physical growth and development.

2 Relationships
We value others for themselves, not only for what they have or what they can do for us. We value relationships as fundamental to the development and fulfilment of ourselves and others, and to the good of the community.

3 Society
We value truth, freedom, justice, human rights, the rule of law and collective effort for the common good. In particular, we value families as sources of love and support for all their members, and as the basis of a society in which people care for others.

4 The environment
We value the environment, both natural and shaped by humanity, as the basis of life and a source of wonder and inspiration.

Figure 4.5.1 A set of values

Source: National Forum for Values in Education and the Community (DfEE/QCA, 1999a, p. 196).

The values identified by the National Forum can provide a basis for action to be used by the individual or by the teacher as goals for teaching. Similar detailed statements of values for 'relationships', 'society' and the 'environment' were produced by the National Forum.

Successive Education Acts since 1988 have required OFSTED to inspect the contributions which schools make to pupils' spiritual, moral, social and cultural education. In the most recent framework for the inspection of schools OFSTED requires its inspectors to identify 'how well the school cultivates pupils' personal – including the spiritual, moral, social and cultural – development' (OFSTED, 1999, p. 39).

The inspection framework also requires inspectors to judge the extent to which the school 'promotes the principles which distinguish right from wrong'. However, there is no guidance to teachers on identifying these principles and one presumes that these are taken to be self-evident truths. The values identified by the National Forum, referred to above, do not specifically include distinguishing 'right from wrong', presumably an area in which general agreement would not be expected across society, which was the criterion the Forum used to identify their published set of values. At the same time the National Forum were careful to point out that 'these values were not exhaustive' (DfEE/QCA, 1999a, p. 195).

In his Annual Report for 1998/99, the Chief Inspector of Schools gave just seven lines to comment on the moral development of pupils; he noted that moral development continues to improve and is now 'good' in nine out of ten schools. The Inspector links the presence of a strong moral emphasis to good behaviour and a clear disciplinary policy and to the fact that the school is 'civilised and well run' (OFSTED, 2000b, para. 139). The correlation between a moral 'emphasis' and 'behaviour' is not explored further in the report. The brevity of comment on moral development seems to give short shrift to a key feature of the National Curriculum and may indicate that both teachers and the Inspectorate have, in the past, seen the curriculum subjects as the most important dimension to the curriculum. It remains to be seen how the new NC, with clearly stated aims and values, fortified by the introduction of a strong PSHE programme, including Citizenship, fosters moral development and values.

THE RESPONSE OF SCHOOLS

Schools have always paid attention to moral education but curriculum demands in the last decade have created a heavily loaded timetable, in which opportunities to develop a values dimension to education have been limited. In the curriculum, values have been implicit rather than explicit, perhaps 'caught' rather than 'taught'; but pupils don't just acquire values or the capacity to make moral judgements by some 'academic osmosis'; the process needs to be made explicit, nurtured and practised.

We turn now to consider opportunities for teachers to develop in pupils a sense of moral judgement in school, and ways to help young people integrate values into a personal philosophy. The contexts in which you teach, the topics and your choice of examples give rise to opportunities to discuss values. In this unit we identify issues of a generic nature rather than those arising from curriculum subjects which are raised in the companion subject books in this series. Our approach is to make suggestions for tasks from which you select those appropriate to your school and your needs. It is not intended that all tasks be undertaken.

Aims of schools

Aims are discussed also in Units 7.1 and 7.2; see Task 7.1.1.

Task 4.5.1

AIMS OF THE SCHOOL AND HOW THEY ARE INTERPRETED

This task contains several sub-tasks which focus on the aims of the school. Carry out one or more sub-tasks, either alone or in pairs, and discuss your findings with other student teachers or your tutors.

1 Collect together the aims of your placement school and, if possible, that of another school. Compare and contrast the aims of each school.

- Does the school in its aims express a responsibility for the moral development of pupils?
- How are these aims expressed and in what ways do the school statements differ?
- How do your school's aims meet the aims of the National Curriculum, described above?

2 Consider these statements of broad aims for a school curriculum. The curriculum should:

- allow pupils to make decisions and act on them;
- expose pupils to situations in which their contribution is necessary for the success of a project;
- foster pupils' self-image, or self-esteem;
- help pupils develop independently but without losing contact with their peers;
- enable pupils to interact with teachers as young adults with adults.

Respond to these statements under these two headings:

- In what ways do the statements contribute to the moral and values education of pupils?
- How might the aims of this school curriculum be translated into opportunities for the pupil to achieve them?

3 In what ways does the Personal, Social and Health Education (PSHE) programme contribute to the moral and values education of your pupils? Select a topic, for example:

- practices and attitudes towards marriage;
- acceptable and unacceptable food, and the different practices for its preparation;
- the celebration of festivals and holidays across cultures and nations;
- preparation for careers, job applications and interviews;
- identifying bias and stereotyping and developing strategies to deal with it;
- care of the environment.

4 How does school assembly contribute to the moral and values education of pupils? You could:

- attend assembly; keep a record of its purpose, what was said and the way ideas were presented. After an assembly interview some pupils and compare your perception of the session with theirs. Did they understand the message? or believe the message? In what way is the message relevant to their life and their family?
- help plan an assembly with a teacher and with the support of other student teachers.

You may find these questions helpful in planning your enquiry:

- Does the school have a programme for assemblies? How are the content and approach agreed within your school?
- Does assembly have a Christian bias, a requirement of the 1988 Education Act?
- How do the content and messages of assemblies relate to the cultural mix of your school?
- Does assembly develop a sense of community or is it merely authority-enhancing?
- How is success celebrated and whose success is mostly recognised?

5 Is any part of in-service education (INSET) for staff devoted to moral, ethical and values education? How is such work focused and by whom? Your school tutor can direct you to the staff responsible for INSET. See also Cowie and Sharp, 1992; Haydon, 1997.

Subject teaching

Task 4.5.2

THE PLACE OF SUBJECT WORK IN PROMOTING MORAL DEVELOPMENT AND VALUES EDUCATION

1 Identify a social, ethical or moral issue that forms part of teaching your subject. Review the issue as a teaching task in preparation for discussing it with other student teachers. Your review could include:

- a statement of the subject matter and its place in the curriculum;
- the moral focus for pupils, e.g. the decriminalisation of drugs; use of animals for research purposes; road building through the green belt;
- a sample of teaching material;
- an outline teaching strategy, e.g. a draft lesson plan;
- any problems that you anticipate in teaching it;
- any questions that other student teachers might help you resolve.

2 In what ways do the curriculum resources of your department (books, videos, films, CD-ROMs, worksheets, tests) encourage a moral dimension to the teaching of your subject curriculum? Explore and discuss.

This task could be tackled alone or with other student teachers on a subject basis, later pooling and comparing information. For example, choose a topic for which you have to prepare lesson plans and consider what might be the moral dimensions of that topic. What visual aids are there to support that topic in this way?

Make a summary of your response to this task and use it to check the standards/competences for your course.

Class management

We have drawn attention earlier to the importance of teachers setting an example for pupils. If values are preached but not practised, pupils attach little significance to them, much less uphold them. Task 4.5.3 illustrates the problem of acting fairly. See also Unit 3.3 on classroom management.

Task 4.5.3

CLASS CONTROL

Pupils dislike being punished for offences which they did not commit or the misdemeanours of others. Under stress, it is easy to respond inappropriately to a misdemeanour.

A class is reading from a set text; from time to time there is a pause in the reading in order to discuss a point. As the lesson progresses, some children get bored and seek distraction by flicking pellets at other pupils seated towards the front. The teacher knows it is happening but is unable to identify the culprit. One or two pupils take offence at being hit by pellets and object noisily. The teacher asks for the action to stop but it continues; noise rises and the teacher threatens to keep the person in when they are identified. The lesson is stopped and the culprit is asked to own up. No one volunteers; the class is given five minutes to sort this out; no one owns up and the whole class is kept in after school for fifteen minutes.

    Some pupils object to detention on the grounds that they did not offend. Some walk out of the detention and refuse to stay.

How might the teacher:

- deal with this situation for those left in detention?
- deal with those who walked out?
- deal with any complaint of unfair practice?
- have responded differently to the whole incident?

How have your responses to this task helped you meet the standards/competences for your course?

Assessing pupils

Cheating – in tests, for example – is rare but when spotted involves either collusion (with other pupils) or answers being hidden on the person. This situation may be recognised by direct observation during the test, by comparing pupil scripts or by recognising a familiar phrase likely to have been copied.

    One cause of cheating is fear. The fear may be of the teacher's wrath or punishment in response to poor marks. Some teachers may, for example, give a roll-call of marks when the scripts have been marked; or make public comment on individual performances. If mistakes are treated with anger, with punishment or humiliation, pupils are not encouraged to think freely or attempt solutions. Cheating often means that the pupil gets the task correct, instead of wrong. This denies the pupil access to feedback from the teacher about the source of error and it denies them the opportunity to learn from mistakes.

Another cause of pupil anxiety may arise through trying to maintain personal esteem. This situation can occur when the pupil tries to 'keep their end up' at home. Some parents regularly ask their children how they are getting on and a pupil does not like admitting to low marks. On the other hand, the source of anxiety could be about being moved to a lower set. Where streaming is the method of grouping pupils, failure may lead to demotion, losing friends and having to make new ones; or having to join the class of an unpopular teacher.

Cheating may be a sign that the pupil cares. The misdemeanour may not entirely be their fault; children who don't care are less likely to cheat than those who do. The 'don't care' attitude is a different issue with which to contend. In Task 4.5.4 we invite you to share with others your response to pupils caught cheating in examinations.

Task 4.5.4

YOUR RESPONSE TO CHEATING IN CLASS?

How might teachers respond to a pupil caught cheating? It is not possible to condone the action but at the same time pupils are not mature adults.
Draw up some school guidelines to:

* prevent cheating;
* publicly deal with cheating;
* help the pupil concerned.

Check if there are guidelines in your school about cheating in school work or public examinations? How do these guidelines relate to your views? In what ways does this task help to develop an understanding of values for the pupil? How have your responses to this task helped you meet the standards/competences for your course?

Critical incidents

Many incidents which arise in school have at their heart moral judgements. We mentioned one above, about cheating. How we respond to them taxes our notions of right and wrong; our decisions may guide pupils towards establishing their own moral position. Two examples of incidents are presented in Task 4.5.5; your experience in school will furnish you with others. The incidents attempt to show different aspects of moral judgement that need to be exercised by the teacher and the pupil. The first problem concerns personal morality; the individual has to wrestle with their own conscience and decide what to do. In the second example the teacher is put into a position where their decision is likely to be widely known. The teacher is faced by a situation in which there is a conflict of responsibilities, towards the parents on one hand and the pupils on the other.

Task 4.5.5

CRITICAL INCIDENTS

Read through the following extract and respond to the questions below. You may wish to prepare your response to these situations prior to talking with other student teachers and your tutor. This procedure may help you get a focus on the legal responsibilities you face as a teacher.

1   *Wayne is in school during break in order to keep an appointment with a teacher. On the way, he has to walk past his own form room. As he does so he sees a pupil from his class, whom he recognises, going through the desk of a classmate. The pupil is not facing Wayne but it seems obvious to him that items are being removed from the desk and pocketed, but he can't identify the items. Wayne walks away unseen by the other pupil. Wayne decides to tell his class teacher.*

2   *Serena is 15 years old, the daughter of practising Muslim parents, and attends the local girls' comprehensive school. Her parents do not approve of her mixing, at her age, with other pupils outside school hours and expect her to return home promptly after school. Nevertheless, in the company of other girls, Serena sometimes walks home part of the way with boys from the adjacent boys' school. Under pressure from peers, she agrees to meet one boy after school. She arranges an alibi with another girl. On the proposed day of the meeting, the girl friend panics at the prospect of having to lie to Serena's parents and backs out of the agreement. That afternoon the two girls argue in class to the extent that they are kept back by the teacher after school. The teacher becomes unwittingly privy to the arrangements.*

For each case:

• Identify the issues.
• Describe the advice you would give in each situation to the teacher and the pupils.

How have your responses to this task helped you meet the standards/competences for your course?

Valuing diversity

Some schools draw their pupils from families of widely differing backgrounds and ethnicity. This rich mix of pupils can be an opportunity for the school through its curriculum and its policies to help pupils understand the differences between people. In this way, schools can help pupils make judgements about other people based, for example, on knowledge rather than hearsay, on how they behave rather than on racial origin. The importance of recognising the differences between pupils in preparing lessons has been recognised in the current National Curriculum for England and Wales; see the section on inclusion in Unit 7.3, p. 359 and Unit 4.6.

   The same argument can apply to schools in which the ethnic mix of pupils is much more narrow, but is the aim of valuing diversity altered because of this difference? A writer on minority ethnic issues made the following remarks:

If children see only white people around them in their school and locality, they are in danger of acquiring the outdated, inaccurate and racist view that only white people are of account. Schools that do not actively counteract such impressions are misleading and misinforming their pupils, neglecting the cross-curricular themes in the National Curriculum of 'multi-cultural issues' and 'citizenship', and failing to prepare them for their place in multicultural Europe and in a shrinking and independent world in which most people are not white. And the learning materials selected for the school are a major source of information.

(Klein, 1993, p. 169)

The cross-curricular themes to which the writer refers no longer exist in that form and the knowledge, skills and attitudes embedded in them have been incorporated into the new National Curriculum, as described earlier in this unit. See also Task 7.3.2. The message given by the statement and the context it describes remain valid today. How do you respond to this statement by Klein? See Task 4.5.6.

Task 4.5.6

RESPONDING TO ETHNIC DIVERSITY

Read the extract from a statement by Klein, above, which is about the importance of educating pupils for life in an ethnically diverse society. Use the following questions to respond to that statement. We suggest that first you consider this statement on your own and then bring your responses to a seminar, either with other student teachers or with your tutor.

1 What evidence have you in your daily life that people living in an all-white community develop the views described in the first sentence?
2 What evidence have you in your school experience school that pupils recognise the views expressed in the first sentence?
3 How and in what ways do the aims of your school address the challenges posed by the statement?
4 What evidence do you have that your school experience school adopts a positive approach to ethnic diversity as advocated in the statement?
5 To what extent do assemblies, PSHE, and extra-curricular activities in your school experience school contribute towards fostering positive cross-cultural attitudes?
6 How does the teaching of your subject allow you to contribute to the development in pupils of positive attitudes towards people of other cultures?
7 How do you select teaching material for pupils which contributes to the development in your pupils of positive attitudes towards people of other cultures?

MORAL DEVELOPMENT, VALUES AND THE CURRICULUM

Moral judgement, moral behaviour and the values they represent derive from personal, social, cultural, religious and political viewpoints. Societies have norms which are essential for their cohesion and continuity. These norms guide both interpersonal behaviour and national attitudes towards others. Societies in which the norms of some groups of people differ from those of the main group have the potential for enrichment or friction. In this respect, the statement of values from the National Forum, cited earlier, is an important step towards local and national harmony.

Very largely, moral standards of the young come from parents, peers and teachers. Eventually some individuals are able to make their own judgement about values, to see the broader picture and consider all the variables in a situation. When individuals reach this mature stage of development, many may view justice as problematic, i.e. to be worked at, not just as the acceptance of authority. This position may lead to questioning the values they have grown up with. Values are not necessarily useful for all time; they need to be reviewed periodically and modified if no longer valid. For example, in the case of sexual morality, by the end of the twentieth century there was a more open approach to the discussion of sexual behaviours and what is and is not acceptable, than was possible at the start, but the emphasis on love, care and the well-being of one's partner remains an enduring value.

One purpose of education is to enable young people to work towards the mature level of response, described above, in their private lives and public faces. Nevertheless, some young people (and not a few older ones) have not reached such a stage and may refer to rules for authority as a means of avoiding difficult issues; or flout agreed rules or conventions because the rules interfere with personal freedom or wants of the moment. Such a response may show a lack of concern for others.

It can be argued that values are relative, subjective and subject to change over time. Values alter with the generations and practice has to be re-examined in order that the values remain appropriate to the culture. At the same time, as we have described above, some values may be enduring. Society changes through the effect of different cultures entering and leaving the society. Our views change by exposure to catastrophe such as war or fatal illness; our values are constantly questioned through exposure to developing technology, extended travel, interaction with others, legislation, science, spiritual experience and, we hope, through education.

We see beliefs and conventions (moral standards and behaviour) changing as we follow and contribute to debates about behaviour (homosexual rights, abortion); about improving humans (genetic engineering); maintaining the environment (saving natural organisms, conservation of land and global warming); and balancing the good of society with that of the individual (road-building programmes). The decision in the English courts in 2000 to separate conjoined twins, leading to the death of one twin, was resolved legally in the face of conflicting moral viewpoints.

The first decade of the National Curriculum in England and Wales has seen the emphasis in teaching and assessment on the subjects of the curriculum. Only recently has the emphasis begun to shift towards linking the aims with the means. Following the inception of the NC in 1988, it was never made clear how a subject-based curriculum was expected to achieve its broad aims, those related to the spiritual, moral, social and ethical development of young people (O'Hear and White, 1991). It appeared as self-evident that the realisation of the aims of the NC was best achieved by the traditional route of English, mathematics, science, etc. Schools found it difficult to address the underlying purposes of the NC while at the same time implementing a subject-based curriculum (and responding to frequent changes in the content and organisation of that curriculum).

The new NC for England and Wales (DfEE/QCA, 1999a), described earlier in this unit (see p. 205), shows that it has now a respectable set of aims. It remains unclear how the subject-based curriculum is expected to achieve those aims (Bramall and White, 2000b). The link between the aims of the NC and the compulsory teaching of some subjects remains tenuous. The loosening of the domination of compulsory subjects at Key Stage 4 may lead to more choice for pupils and their parents, perhaps a move back to pre-NC days when choice was a feature of secondary education at 13 plus. However, as choice is introduced, the notion of a balanced curriculum recedes and it is not clear how the promotion of 'the spiritual, moral, cultural, mental and physical development of pupils at the school and of society' can be achieved in both a looser structure and a curriculum of subjects. We refer the reader to the discussion of the aims and means of the new NC by Bramall and White, 2000b.

The situations described in this unit have used a variety of contexts. They include interactions which are teacher–teacher, student teacher–student teacher, student teacher–pupil, student teacher–class and student teacher–school. The most common interaction is the student teacher–class relationship. Whereas moral and ethical issues can arise by accident, e.g. dealing with tale telling, there are occasions when moral and ethical issues provide the explicit aim of the lesson. Your subject work may have given rise to such opportunities (Task 4.5.2). To be effective in classroom subject teaching, you need to plan carefully for the introduction of these issues. The use of simulations is a good way of introducing such issues, as are organised discussions. We give advice on handling discussion and using simulations in Appendices 4.5.1 and 4.5.2 respectively at the end of this unit.

SUMMARY AND KEY POINTS

Teachers have a responsibility in law for the promotion of 'the spiritual, moral, cultural, mental and physical development of pupils at the school and of society'. In school there are many opportunities for developing these qualities in both subject and pastoral work. The introduction of Citizenship as a subject in the curriculum may help schools to meet these demands. The guidance on values, described earlier in this unit, provided by the National Forum on Values in Education is an important step forward in helping teachers.

Elsewhere in the unit we have identified some situations in which your judgement is called into play and which may call for the resolution of dilemmas of a moral nature. On occasions you may find it difficult to know how to respond; in your training year you should refer to experienced and qualified staff for help. These issues are likely to remain on your agenda in your induction year. It is important that you know the school policy about the issue that confronts you and the expected response of your school.

In this unit we have tried to help you become aware of the current curriculum situation nationally in relation to moral education and invited you to relate teaching situations to helping pupils develop an awareness of morals and values. The further reading section gives more detailed advice and background about the development of moral education. You should check the standards/competences for your course as they relate to the focus of this unit.

APPENDIX 4.5.1 HANDLING DISCUSSION WITH CLASSES

A common technique for raising moral and ethical issues is through discussion. Discussion activities have great potential as a vehicle for moral development through sharing ideas, developing awareness of the opinion of others, promoting appropriate social procedures and profitable debate. It can be a vehicle for learning. On the other hand, discussion can be the mere pooling of ignorance, the confirmation of prejudices and a stage for showing off.

Young people can be taught the protocols of discussion. It is necessary to help them realise that discussion may not end in a clear decision or agreement, but can lead to a deeper understanding of the issues and the position of others. For the teacher, discussion is one of the more difficult strategies to implement. Perhaps that is why it is not often used. See also Unit 3.1 on 'Communicating with pupils'.

The following notes may help you develop your strategies for conducting discussion. They adopt the neutral chairperson approach, but there are other ways: the 'balanced approach' and the 'stated commitment' (DfEE/QCA, 1998, section 10). For further help on running discussions and other ways of introducing moral issues, see Jennings (1995), Wellington (1986), and Tarrant (1981).

Four factors need to be considered. They are:

1 Rules and procedures for discussion
2 Provision of evidence – information
3 Neutral chairperson
4 Outcomes expected

1 **Rules and procedures**; you need to consider:

- choice of subject and length of discussion (young pupils without experience may not sustain lengthy discussion);
- physical seating; room size; arrangement of furniture so that most pupils have eye contact;
- protocols for discourse; taking turns; length of contribution; abusive language;
- procedures for violation of protocols, e.g. racist or sexist behaviour;
- how to protect the sensitivity of individuals; pupils may reveal unexpected personal information in the course of a discussion;
- stance of the chairperson.

2 **Provision of evidence**; in order to stimulate discussion and provide a clear basis for argument, you need to:

- know the age, ability and mix of abilities of the pupils;
- know what information is needed;
- know sources of information;
- decide at what point the information is introduced (before, during).

3 **Neutral chairperson**; a neutral stance may be essential because:

- authority of the opinions of the chair should not influence the outcome;
- the opinions of pupils are to be exposed, not those of the teacher;
- the chairperson can be free to influence the quality of understanding, the rigour of debate and appropriate exploration of the issues;
- pupils will understand the teacher's stance if it is made clear at the start.

4 **Possible outcomes**; the strategy is discussion not instruction. Pupils should:

- learn by sharing and understand the opinion of others;
- be exposed to the nature and role of evidence;
- realise that objective evidence is often an inadequate basis for decision making;
- come to know that decisions often rely on subjective value judgements;
- realise that many decisions are compromises.

Action: try out these rules by setting up a discussion with other student teachers on the topic of:

Equal opportunities for girls enable them to join the power structure rather than challenge it.

APPENDIX 4.5.2 SIMULATIONS

General and specific subject advice on simulations can be found in many of our companion subject books in the series 'Learning to Teach in the Secondary School'. For example:

Haydn, T., Arthur, J. and Hunt, M. (1997) *Learning to Teach History in the Secondary School: A Companion to School Experience*, London: Routledge, pp. 176–180. (Note: a second edition is to be published by RoutledgeFalmer in 2001.)

Lambert. D. and Balderstone, D. (1999) *Learning to Teach Geography in the Secondary School: A Companion to School Experience*, London: RoutledgeFalmer, pp. 271–288.

A fuller description of simulations and their use in science teaching is given in:

Turner, S. (1995) 'Simulations' in J. Frost (ed.) (1995) *Teaching Science*, London: Woburn Press.

FURTHER READING

Haydon, G. (1997) *Teaching about Values: A New Approach*, London: Cassell.
Sets moral education in the broader context of educational aims and values. Part 5 reviews different conceptions of values education.

Langford, P. (1995) *Approaches to the Development of Moral Reasoning*, Hove: Erlbaum.
A survey of approaches to the development of moral reasoning, including the contributions of Freud, Kohlberg and Piaget. The text provides a critical review of stage theory of moral development and alternative approaches are described.

Smith, R. and Standish, P. (eds) (1997) *Teaching Right and Wrong: Moral Education in the Balance*, Stoke-on-Trent: Trentham.
Discusses the work of the National Forum on Values in Education. Also argues for alternative approaches to values education.

Thacker, J. (1995) 'Personal, social and moral education' in C. Desforges (ed.) (1995) *An Introduction to Teaching: Psychological Perspectives*, Oxford: Blackwell.
How should we teach and what should we teach to lay a foundation of values? This reading discusses the purposeful introduction of values education in the context of school policies.

UNIT 4.6 AN INTRODUCTION TO INCLUSION AND SPECIAL EDUCATIONAL NEEDS

NICK PEACEY

INTRODUCTION

The revised National Curriculum for England and Wales (DfEE/QCA, 1999a), implemented in September 2000, sets a commitment to match the needs of all pupils, including those with special educational needs, within the commitment to the 'inclusion' of all pupils. Inclusion encompasses the right of all pupils to feel they belong and can achieve in school; it underpins the government's expectation that the mainstream school will increasingly be the place in which all pupils will be educated.

The term special educational needs (SEN) covers different learning, emotional and behavioural factors which may prevent pupils from achieving their full potential. We would expect you, as a student teacher, to be beginning to develop an understanding of issues relating to inclusion and SEN.

OBJECTIVES

By the end of this unit you should:

- have an understanding of recent legislation under what are known as *School Action and School Action Plus* of the revised *Code of Practice for the Identification and Assessment of SEN* (due to be published by the DfEE in 2001);
- understand how the terms **inclusion** and **special educational needs** are used;
- be aware of the possibility that teacher attitudes may limit pupils' achievement of their potential;
- be developing your knowledge of teaching strategies that may be used with pupils with different SEN within the whole class inclusion approach.

We suggest that you review the competences/standards related to your course to see what is required of you in the area of inclusion and SEN.

DEFINITIONS

We refer in this unit to the Consultation Draft of the revised SEN Code of Practice (DfEE, 2000) as the **draft revised COP**. All material in quotation marks, unless otherwise referenced, is taken from the same draft COP.

Inclusion has been described as follows:

Inclusion in education involves the processes of increasing the participation of students in, and reducing their exclusion from, the cultures, curricula and communities of local schools. Inclusion is concerned with the learning participation of all students vulnerable to exclusionary pressures, not only those with impairments or categorised as having special educational needs. Inclusion is concerned with improving schools for staff as well as for students.

(Centre for Studies on Inclusion in Education (CSIE), 2000)

The publication cited above (CSIE, 2000), called *Index for Inclusion*, was sent with DfEE support to every school in the country. The authors note that schools cannot remove all barriers to inclusion; there are limits, for example, to how much schools can do about the barriers created by poverty.

While the terms 'inclusion' and 'SEN' often appear together, meeting SEN is only a part of inclusion. SEN is essentially a relative term: pupils with special educational needs are said to require something additional to or different from that offered to other pupils. Some authors feel we are outgrowing the notion of SEN because it places too much emphasis on locating difficulty within the individual, the 'medical model'. This model may prevent us from seeing diversity as a resource rather than a problem: we can easily fail, the argument runs, to give proper consideration to the effects and possibilities of the policies and practice of schools in removing barriers to the learning of all.

For example, the general level of noise in the classroom (the acoustic environment) is important if you are working with students with hearing impairments. Hearing aids can distort sound: you may not be heard clearly even if the pupil is wearing one. So if you are working in a noisy classroom, you should ask colleagues what the school can do about this. For example, many schools now have what are known as sound field systems, a quad-speaker set up which provides good-quality classroom sound and ensures that people can hear what is being said, even if there is a main road outside or an airport nearby. Consideration of individual needs thus leads to benefits for all.

Much statute and regulation (including that related to funding) is still set in a SEN model and so the term 'SEN' is likely to be with us for some years. In this unit, we use the terminology of the forthcoming revised SEN Code of Practice (expected from the DfEE in late 2001) which, while not claiming that there are hard and fast categories of special educational need, groups pupils' special educational needs under four main categories:

1 Communication and interaction.
2 Cognition and learning.
3 Behaviour, emotional and social development.
4 Sensory and/or physical.

The draft revised COP suggests that 'children will have needs and requirements which may fall into at least one of the four areas, although many children will have inter-related needs which encompass more than one of these areas. The impact of these combinations on the child's ability to function, learn and succeed should be taken into account' (in planning learning).

We return later in this unit to these four categories and consider some of the classroom approaches involved.

REPORTS AND LEGISLATION RELATING TO SEN

The National Curriculum (NC) 1999

The revised NC (DfEE/QCA, 1999a) is built on aims, values and principles which support the celebration of diversity (the recognition of everything that diversity of learners brings to a school community) and the rights of all pupils to participate and be partners in their own learning.

All NC documents include what has become known as the general **inclusion statement** which has two strands:

- a demand on teachers not to ignore the three principles of curriculum inclusion (see below) in their planning and teaching;
- substantial flexibility to allow teachers to match their teaching to the needs of all pupils. For example, secondary teachers can draw on earlier Key Stage 2 Programmes of Study (or drop sections of Key Stage 3 Programmes of Study) if they feel, after proper consideration, that this is the best approach for particular pupils.

The inclusion statement is based on the following principles:

1 **The need to set suitable learning challenges**. A culture of high expectations for all is encouraged within a model of teaching and learning which can suit the approach used to pupils' abilities.
2 **Responding to pupils' diverse learning needs**. The discussion of this principle emphasises the need for thought about teaching and learning environments. This includes the physical environment – the classroom space, its use, its layout and its acoustics. It stresses also the need for all pupils to feel safe and secure, and that views – particularly stereotypical views – about disability and impairment, for example, are always challenged.
3 **The overcoming of potential barriers to learning and assessment**. This demand requires that 'Teachers must address the needs of the minority of pupils who have particular learning and assessment requirements which, if not addressed, could create barriers to learning.'

Some background to the legislation

The inclusion statement of the NC for England and Wales (DfEE/QCA, 1999a) is built on a range of legislation and regulation developed over several decades. Some important milestones of that period are identified in Table 4.6.1.

THE RESPONSE OF SCHOOLS 1

Whole school approaches

Arrangements for the education of pupils with SEN vary between schools and between LEAs. Schools are required to have policies setting out their approach to SEN. They normally appoint an SEN co-ordinator (SENCO) or SEN co-ordination team to oversee day-to-day provision throughout the school. The SENCO knows the routes to resources, information and support agencies. Senior managers (governors and headteachers) have overall responsibility for policy and practice on special educational needs. The governing body must report to parents on the implementation of policy on SEN.

Table 4.6.1 Important legislation relating to the provision of SEN

1971	Legislation in England and Wales to bring those considered 'ineducable' into education.
1981	The 1981 Act included specific duties on Local Education Authorities (LEAs) and school governors to make provision for SEN, defining responsibilities and procedures for SEN and the establishment of parents' participation in special educational assessments, along with a right of appeal.
1988	The 1988 Act introduced the National Curriculum and reinforced the duty to consider special educational needs, though many felt that proper attention was not given to the area.
1994	The *Code of Practice on the Identification and Assessment of SEN* (DfE, 1994c) came into effect on 1 September 1994. This is a statutory code of practice (approved by both Houses of Parliament) which cannot be ignored by anyone to whom it applies.
2000	The revised National Curriculum (DfEE/QCA, 1999a), containing the inclusion statement, became law.
2001	The revised OFSTED framework includes specific provisions for the inspection of inclusive practices in schools. The framework can be consulted on the OFSTED website: www.ofsted.gov.uk
2001	The revised Code of Practice

Task 4.6.1

YOUR SCHOOL'S POLICY AND THE CODE OF PRACTICE ON THE IDENTIFICATION AND ASSESSMENT OF SPECIAL EDUCATIONAL NEEDS

Obtain and read your school's policy on SEN provision. Refer also to the draft revised COP (DfEE, 2000) or the published final version; see the DfEE website: www.dfee.gov.uk

Discuss the implementation of the revised COP and school policy with your tutor and the SENCO in your school. Useful questions to guide discussion include:

- has the revised COP changed what is happening in the school?
- how does your school ensure that the requirements of the revised COP are met?
- how are all the teachers in your school involved in implementing the COP?

Discuss your findings with those of another student teacher who has undertaken the same task in another school.

The draft revised COP re-emphasises the importance of whole school approaches, including National Curriculum strategies, and suggests that 'the effective school will identify common strategies and responses across the secondary curriculum for all pupils designed to raise pupils' learning outcomes, expectations and experiences'. The curriculum available for **all** pupils directly affects the need to intervene at an individual level.

The draft revised COP goes further to identify in more detail whole school approaches to inclusion and SEN. These approaches include:

- that all teaching and non-teaching staff should be involved in the development of the school's SEN policy and be fully aware of the school's procedures for identifying, assessing and making provision for pupils with SEN;
- the importance of practice which encourages high expectations. 'All pupils should know what is expected of them. Secondary schools' general marking policies should therefore be consistent in all subjects. Schools should be similarly consistent in other areas, making clear for example how they expect all pupils to behave and to present their work. The emphasis on literacy across the curriculum will help to achieve consistency in handwriting, spelling, punctuation and presentation. Thus for all subject areas and for all pupils including those with SEN, there will be a common set of expectations across the school which are known to everyone, and a further commitment to support those pupils who have difficulty meeting those expectations;'
- that 'schools should not assume that pupils' learning difficulties always result solely, or even mainly, from problems within the young person. Pupils' rates of progress can sometimes depend on what or how they are taught. A school's own practices make a difference – for good or ill;'
- that planning for SEN should consider the views and wishes of pupils 'from the earliest possible age' as well as those of parents and carers. 'Partnership between schools, pupils, parents, LEAs, health services, social services, voluntary organisations and other agencies is essential in order to meet effectively the needs of pupils with SEN.'

The four-stage approach to meeting needs

At the heart of the draft revised COP's approach is 'a model of action and intervention designed to help pupils towards independent learning'. The draft revised COP outlines a four-stage approach to match the needs of pupils with the special education provision available to them.

School Action

The first stage, known as *School Action*, comes into play when it is clear that 'the pupil requires help over and above that which is normally available within the particular class or subject'. According to the draft revised COP, the school's SEN co-ordinator should facilitate assessment of the pupil's particular strengths and weaknesses; and plan for support and monitoring of progress.

The pupil's subject teachers remain responsible for working with the pupil on a daily basis and for planning and delivering the specified programme. Suggestions on how to do this appear in the **Individual Education Plan**. (Where a number of pupils have similar needs these are sometimes set out in a Group Education Plan.) The school may need to make additional **provision** to **support** the pupil.

Individual Education Plans (IEPs)

The IEP records that which is *additional to* or *different from* curriculum provision for all pupils. Most IEPs include information about:

- the short-term targets set for the pupil (these are typically reviewed two or three times a year);
- the teaching strategies to be used;
- the provision to be put in place (see below);
- when the plan is to be reviewed;
- the outcome of the action taken.

Good IEPs are likely also to include some details of the pupil's strengths and interests.

Support and provision on an IEP

This may include (particularly where concerns go beyond *School Action*) the deployment of extra staff to enable extra help and sometimes one-to-one tuition for the pupil. The IEP may also prescribe:
- different learning materials or special equipment;
- group support;
- cover for teacher and specialist time for planning support;
- staff development and training on effective strategies;
- support with classroom review and monitoring.

Additional staff in your classroom

Where other adults are supporting pupils in your classroom, you need to liaise closely with them to ensure the pupil gains maximum benefit from this support. The support staff should have the lesson plans well in advance. You can check with them that the materials you are providing are appropriate for a particular child.

Task 4.6.2

WORKING WITH SUPPORT TEACHERS OR TEACHING ASSISTANTS IN YOUR CLASSROOM

For a pupil to be fully supported in the classroom, the class teacher and other adults must develop an effective working relationship.

1 Ask some support teachers for advice about how best you can work together.
2 Observe support teachers working in classrooms and identify what needs to be done to ensure the pupil makes maximum progress.

School Action Plus

If the first stage of support, *School Action*, is not helping a pupil, schools need to explore the second stage, *School Action Plus*. Schools should consult specialists when they set out the strategies for a pupil at *School Action Plus*.

The draft revised COP says:

At *School Action Plus* external support services, both those provided by the LEA and by outside agencies, should advise subject and pastoral staff on new IEPs and targets, provide more specialist assessments, give advice on the use of new or specialist strategies or materials, and in some cases provide support for particular activities. The kinds of advice and support available to schools will vary according to local policies.

There is of course no reason why specialist advice cannot be taken at any other point.

The new IEP sets out revised strategies to promote the pupil's success in school. The draft revised COP indicates that 'Although developed with the help of outside specialists, the strategies specified in the IEP should usually be implemented, at least in part and as far as possible, in the normal classroom setting.'

Once again the delivery of the IEP is largely the responsibility of subject teachers, supported by their departments or faculties.

Records from transfer

When working with pupils at *School Action* or *School Action Plus* you may find useful the school records created at transfer from primary school to secondary school. These records can include:

- detailed background information collated by the primary school SENCO;
- copies of IEPs prepared in support of intervention through primary *School Action* or *School Action Plus*;
- pupil and/or parent views of what is going on;
- your school's assessments of the new entrant.

You should contact the SENCO or the pupil's form tutor if you feel such information would help your lesson planning.

Task 4.6.3

PUPIL ASSESSMENT ON ENTRY TO THE SCHOOL

Many schools assess their pupils on entry to the school; see, for example, Units 6.1 and 6.2. Find out what assessments are made of newly arriving pupils and ask if you can see examples of the tests.

Find out what use is made of the results of these assessments by subject teaching staff and the form tutor.

Multi-disciplinary assessment and the statement of SEN: the third and fourth stages of the Code of Practice for SEN

You may hear staff describe a pupil as 'statemented' or 'having a statement'. If *School Action Plus* is not succeeding, schools and parents or carers may wish to consider a full multi-disciplinary assessment to examine the possibility of a pupil having a statement of SEN. This process is called 'Statementing'.

Statementing is expensive. Assessment alone can cost several thousand pounds and LEAs have a duty to consider carefully whether to embark on the process. But the statement which can result from such assessment has been popular with parents and schools because it guarantees the resources written into its clauses. Failure to provide resources can be challenged in the tribunal for SEN and, if necessary, in the courts. The processes of statementing and implementation of the recommendations are 'high stake' operations. Unlike *School Action* and *School Action Plus* where schools have very substantial freedom these final two stages are bound in a network of statutory rules.

Task 4.6.4

HOW DOES A STATEMENT COME ABOUT IN YOUR SCHOOL?

Arrange a convenient time with the SEN co-ordinator to discuss the procedure by which a statement of special educational needs is drawn up for a pupil and how it is reviewed.

As a subject teacher you need to be aware of pupils with statements of SEN in your class and, almost certainly, need to discuss with the head of department or faculty how you can plan for their needs and ensure the resources available are used well.

THE RESPONSE OF SCHOOLS 2

English as an additional language and SEN

The draft revised COP notes:

> The identification and assessment of the special educational needs of young people whose first language is not English requires particular care. Lack of competence in English must not be equated with learning difficulties as understood in this draft revised COP. At the same time, when pupils who have English as an additional language make slow progress, it should not be assumed that their language status is the only reason; they may have learning difficulties.

This is an area where you should consult specialist help. The main points of which you should be aware include:

- pupils learning English go through well-researched stages; they may for instance say little or nothing for some time, but are learning none the less;
- pupils learning English benefit from high-quality learning environments; they do not as a rule need individual programmes;
- if the English learning stages are not proceeding as they should, the possibility of a learning difficulty may be considered.

For those wishing to take further this aspect of SEN, see Hall, 1996.

Special schools, units and resource bases

Special schools often still cater for pupils with particular needs, such as moderate learning difficulties (MLD), emotional and behavioural difficulties (EBD) and severe learning difficulties (SLD). Government plans for inclusion are likely to mean that special provision will increasingly be linked more closely to mainstream schools, and special schools will reduce in number.

Mainstream schools may have special units or resource bases attached to them. A resource base provides support within a school to pupils who are normally registered with 'ordinary' classes. A special school or unit is one step more separate: its pupils are on the roll of the unit and normally based there.

Special arrangements for examinations and assessments

All awarding bodies for public examinations and the Qualifications and Curriculum Authority (responsible for Key Stage 3 assessment) make special arrangements for pupils with SEN. If you think that a pupil you are teaching is coming up to an examination or assessment and arrangements are not in place, you should contact the SENCO or the schools examination co-ordinator to find out what is appropriate, several months before the assessment.

Concerns about a pupil not on the SEN register (i.e. not identified at one of the stages)?

You may feel concern about a pupil's progress and wonder if they have unrecognised SEN. It is worth comparing notes with another teacher to see how the pupil responds in their class. While sensory impairments of hearing or vision are sometimes not picked up until secondary age, the most frequently unrecognised issues relate to delays or difficulties in language development. The draft revised COP notes that: 'Some young people may also raise concerns about their own progress and their views should be treated seriously.'

Looking back to your time in secondary school you may reflect that this frequently requires some courage from the pupil. The issues brought to you can be the tip of the iceberg: they should certainly be taken seriously. Signs of eating disorder, particularly anorexia, whether they emerge through observation, written work or conversation, should always be reported for urgent consideration.

HELPING CHILDREN WITH SEN TO LEARN

In this section we provide some guidance on working with pupils with SEN in mainstream classrooms.

The evidence from research supporting the effectiveness of differentiated pedagogies (teaching approaches) for different groups of SEN is slender. Such evidence as there is suggests that 'good normal pedagogy' is the key (National Association for Special Educational Needs (NASEN), 2000).

The principles of the inclusion statement of the NC for England and Wales (DfEE/QCA, 1999a) can guide planning for success for all pupils. Part of this planning should involve (at a tactful moment) asking pupils with SEN how they like to be taught. A good example of how to do this is provided by the British Stammering Association which has produced an excellent video on consulting youngsters worried about speaking up in class. This resource can guide teachers into making successful approaches to pupils (British Stammering Association).

As a student teacher we suggest that you develop your teaching approaches, i.e. concentrate on good normal pedagogy. Seek advice from your tutor. We suggest you approach the issues in this way:

- concentrate on developing your overall teaching style and the best possible learning environments in classrooms you use;
- where a pupil has identified SEN, use the IEP, the knowledge of others in the school and books and websites to build your awareness of the issues in learning for him or her; do not assume that you need to teach that pupil differently or separately;
- whatever the SEN identified, motivation is a key part of learning. Special treatment can 'turn off' adolescents;
- remember that what makes a difference is often the timing and intensity of interventions rather than any difference in the pedagogy;
- have high expectations of homework and classwork. Clarity in setting homework and care in checking it has been recorded properly help those likely to find the work difficult.

The SENCO forum on the Virtual Teacher Centre website provides a space for teachers to discuss general SEN issues. The website address is http://vtc.nglf.gov.uk. Using ICT is an important way of helping some pupils with SEN: see Unit 1.4. and Leask and Pachler, 1999, chapter 8.

We turn now to discuss briefly the particular groups of children with specific educational needs. The headings are derived from the draft revised COP.

Communication and interaction

The range of difficulties encompass children and young people with speech and language delay, impairments or disorders, specific learning difficulties, such as dyslexia and dyspraxia, hearing impairment and those who demonstrate features within the autistic spectrum. These difficulties may apply also to some children and young people with moderate, severe or profound learning difficulties.

Pupils with language impairment

Pupils in this group may have receptive (i.e. limitations in comprehending what is said to them) or expressive (i.e. they find it hard to put their thoughts into words) language impairments. Obviously, the first impairment is the harder to identify. You need to be aware that:

- emotional and relationship difficulties often go with language and, less often, hearing impairments;
- language impairments need specialist attention, normally from a speech and language therapist.

When teaching these pupils you should be sure:

- to check understanding;
- to use visual aids and cues to the topics being discussed;

- that the pupil is appropriately placed to hear and see;
- that you explain something several different ways if you have not been understood the first time;
- that, like a good chairperson, you repeat what pupils say in discussion or question-and-answer sessions (in any case, others in the class may not have heard).

For further information, see Adams, Brown and Edwards (1997) or the website of the charity 'I Can' (ICAN): www.ican.org.uk. A resource pack for schools is available – see Blamires, Brookes, Lacey and Roux, 2000.

Cognition and learning

Children who demonstrate features of moderate, severe or profound learning difficulties or specific learning difficulties, such as dyslexia (reading difficulty) or dyspraxia (developmental co-ordination disorder), require specific programmes to aid progress in cognition and learning. Such requirements may also apply to some extent to children with physical and sensory impairments and those on the autistic spectrum. Some of these children may have associated sensory, physical and behavioural difficulties that compound their needs.

Learning difficulties

Pupils with learning difficulties are described as 'unlikely to reach level 2 of the National Curriculum by the age of 16' (*Guidelines for Teaching Pupils with Learning Difficulties*, DfEE/QCA, 2001) The term 'learning difficulties' thus covers a huge range of need and once again you need to check exactly what the pupil's IEP advises and seek specialist advice. The *Guidelines* referred to above should be in your school and on the website of the National Curriculum: www.nc.uk

Dyslexia

Some pupils have particular difficulty in developing their literacy skills. You should be aware that:

- the term dyslexia covers a wide range of needs;
- research suggests that many 'reading difficulties' never appear if primary teaching is of a high standard;
- the current emphasis is now on examining the individual's skills, such as phonological awareness, and working on them as a way forward.

Most schools and all LEAs have staff with specialist knowledge in this area. Help can also be sought from the major voluntary organisations working in the field. These include:

- the British Dyslexia Association, website address: www.bda-dyslexia.org.uk
- the Dyslexia Institute, website address: www.dyslexia-inst.org.uk
- the Professional Association of Teachers of Students with Specific learning difficulties (PATOSS), website address: www.patoss-dyslexia.org

There is also an email forum on dyslexia (and forums on many other areas) run by BECTa: www.becta.org.uk/inclusion/discussion/bectalists.html

Software is available to help pupils with these difficulties (Leask and Pachler, 1999, chapter 8).

Dyspraxia

Dyspraxia may be defined as difficulty in planning and carrying out skilled, non-habitual motor acts in the correct sequence. Pupils with dyspraxia need the support of whole school systems, particularly in terms of ensuring that they are taking enough exercise. If you are concerned about a pupil with dyspraxia, it may well be worthwhile talking to the PE department as well as to the SENCO.

Difficulties with handwriting are a specific co-ordination issue. The publications and conferences of the Handwriting Interest Group are helpful; further information may be found in Ripley, Daines and Barrett, 1997. The address of the Dyspraxia Foundation is: 8 West Alley, Hitchin, Herts, SG5 1EG.

Autistic spectrum disorders (ASD)

Those with autistic spectrum disorders typically lack 'mentalisation', i.e. the ability to picture what another person is thinking. This gives them particular difficulty in any social context. You may also hear of Asperger's Syndrome. While authorities differ on whether autism and Asperger's Syndrome are on a continuum, or different but overlapping conditions, it is generally agreed that they have strong similarities and that Asperger's is less of an impairment.

Pupils' absorbing interests (such as train timetables) and lack of social focus mean that co-ordinated planning is essential. You need to be aware that:

- many researchers feel the pupils' behaviour is a form of stress management for themselves; they are in a way hyper-sensitive;
- pupils with conditions on the autistic spectrum can learn 'intellectually' how to act socially, e.g. in the matter of eye contact;
- suggestions on approaches to autism vary widely; you need to be absolutely clear what agreed strategies are being used at school and home and work within them.

Further help may be obtained from the National Autistic Society; their website address is www.nas.org.uk and their telephone number is 020 7833 2299.

Behaviour, emotional and social development

The draft revised COP indicates that this category of special need includes:

Children and young people who demonstrate features of emotional and behavioural difficulties, who are withdrawn or isolated, disruptive and disturbing, hyperactive and lack concentration; those with immature social skills; and those presenting challenging behaviours arising from other complex special needs.

Emotional and behavioural difficulties (EBD)

Behavioural problems are discussed in Units 3.1, 3.2, 3.3 and 4.1 and tasks are set there to develop your skills in this area. The differentiation case studies in Unit 4.1 are relevant here.

The draft revised COP says: 'Where a pupil with identified SEN is at serious risk of disaffection or exclusion the IEP should reflect appropriate strategies to meet their need.' This brief sentence scratches a critical issue in secondary school organisation. A pupil presenting consistent problems of behaviour may, for instance:

- have special needs: a language impairment or an autistic spectrum disorder;
- have mental health needs: they may be depressed, for instance;
- be responding to an unsatisfactory school environment: bullying in the playground, or an irrelevant curriculum.

The definition 'emotional behavioural difficulties' is often applied to pupils whose behaviour is consistently poor and not obviously related to the circumstances and environment in which they find themselves. Pupils who are withdrawn also fit into this category. Traditionally, secondary schools have three management approaches to concerns about pupil behaviour. These approaches are:

1 pastoral teams (form tutor, year/house head, etc.);
2 SEN teams;
3 subject department or faculty.

The interrelationship of these management teams is critical to a school staff's success with emotional behavioural difficulties. Important points to bear in mind in your response to pupils with EBD include:

- understanding that learning, not counselling, is the teacher's contribution to resolving EBD: many heads of EBD schools talk of the 'therapy of achievement';
- being aware that 'scaffolding' success for such pupils can be demanding and you should expect support with your planning (and lessons learned) from experienced colleagues. Scaffolding is discussed in Unit 5.1.

Your lesson planning should address:

- knowing the strengths and interests of any pupils with EBD;
- knowing the levels of language and literacy of pupils with EBD;
- considering alternatives within lesson plans if one learning project is not succeeding.

Among pupils identified as having EBD you may come across some pupils known as having:

- attention deficit disorder (ADD);
- attention deficit hyperactivity disorder (ADHD).

These terms are medical diagnoses. Medication by means of stimulants is a widely used treatment. The diagnoses in themselves tell you nothing about teaching such pupils. Further help and guidance may be found in Cooper and Ideus, 1996. The website address of the ADD Information Service is www.addiss.co.uk

Sensory and/or physical needs

The draft revised COP advises that:

> There is a wide spectrum of sensory, multi-sensory and physical difficulties. The sensory range extends from profound and permanent deafness or visual impairment through to lesser levels of loss, which may only be temporary. Physical impairments may arise from physical, neurological or metabolic causes that require no more than appropriate access to educational facilities and equipment; other impairments produce more complex learning and social needs; a few children have multi-sensory difficulties. For some children the inability to take part fully in school life causes significant emotional stress or physical fatigue.

Medical conditions

The draft revised COP notes that:

> a medical diagnosis does not necessarily imply special educational needs. It may not be necessary for a child or young person with any particular diagnosis or medical condition to have a statement, or to need any form of additional provision at any phase of education. It is the child's educational needs rather than a medical diagnosis that must be considered.

A medical condition can affect a child's learning and behaviour. The effect may also be indirect: time in education can be disrupted; there may be unwanted effects of treatment; and there are the psychological effects which serious or chronic illness or disability can have on a child and their family. The school and the pupil's carers and the medical services should collaborate so that the child is not unnecessarily excluded from any part of the curriculum or school activity because of anxiety about his or her care and treatment.

Deafness and hearing impairment

If you have a deaf pupil in your class, you should be aware that:

- specialist advice is usually not difficult to come by. You should ask the SENCO for direction in the first instance;
- many of the teaching checkpoints set out under language impairment apply;
- pupils have individual communication needs: you need to know what they are.

Further advice can be obtained from the Royal National Institute for the Deaf at their website: www.rnid.org.uk. This charity has produced a valuable series of booklets on teaching deaf and hearing-impaired pupils, including material on subject teaching. The National Deaf Children's Society is also a useful source of advice; their website address is www.ndcs.org.uk

Visual impairment

If you have a pupil with visual impairment in your class, again specialist advice is usually not difficult to come by. The SENCO in your school and the individual education plan for the pupil concerned can help in the first instance. Less obvious visual problems may affect pupils' reading. Specialist optometrists sometimes prescribe overlays or tinted spectacles to help with this problem.

There is substantial support to teachers from the Royal National Institute for the Blind on their website: www.rnib.org.uk. Further information may be found in Miller, 1996.

SUMMARY AND KEY POINTS

This unit has introduced you to a range of emotional, behavioural and learning difficulties of pupils with special needs and set those needs in the context of the draft revised Code of Practice for SEN, the final version of which is expected to be published by the DfEE in 2001. We address, too, physical impairment. Understanding the requirements of that Code is important for your practice as a teacher. We have not addressed the special needs of the gifted pupil.

Every child is special. Every child has individual educational needs. A major problem that pupils with SEN have is the attitudes of others to them. For example, children who have obvious physical disabilities such as cerebral palsy often find they are treated as though their mental abilities match their physical abilities when this is not the case. How will children with special educational needs find you as their teacher?

Teachers need to ensure that all their pupils learn to the best of their abilities and that pupils with SEN are not further disabled by the lack of appropriate resources to support their learning.

In your work as a student teacher, we expect you to develop your understanding of the teacher's responsibilities for pupils' SEN so that, when you are in your first post, you are sufficiently aware of your responsibilities that you ensure that your pupils' special educational needs are met. The basic rule for you to remember is that you cannot expect to solve all pupils' learning problems on your own. You must seek advice from experienced staff.

You should check your course requirements for SEN in relation to the competences/ standards for achieving QTS.

FURTHER READING

George, D. (1992) *The Challenge of the Able Child*, London: David Fulton.

Leask, M. and Pachler, N. (1999) *Learning to Teach Using ICT in the Secondary School*, London: RoutledgeFalmer.
See, for example, the chapter in this text on the use of ICT with pupils with SEN.

OFSTED (1996b) *The Implementation of the Code of Practice for Pupils with Special Educational Needs: A Report from the Office of Her Majesty's Chief Inspector of Schools*, London: HMSO.
This is a report on monitoring by OFSTED of the implementation of the *Code of Practice on the Identification and Assessment of Special Needs* (DfE, 1994c). This report contains twelve key issues for schools to consider and some future developments. It supplements a report of OFSTED (1996a) *Promoting High Achievement for Pupils with Special Educational Needs in Mainstream Schools* (London : HMSO) which was based on a survey undertaken during the gradual implementation of the Code of Practice.

Partnership with Parents (1998) *Dealing with Dyslexia in the Secondary School*, Shepway Centre, Oxford Road, Maidstone, Kent, ME15 8AW. (Tel: 01622 755515)

Rieser, R. and Mason, M. (1992) *Disability Equality in the Classroom: A Human Rights Issue* (2nd edn), London: ILEA/Disability Equality.
This book provides case studies and covers a wide range of disabilities. It confronts the prejudice of able-bodied people.

CHAPTER 5 **HELPING PUPILS LEARN**

This chapter addresses teaching and learning. As you work through these units we hope that your knowledge about teaching and learning increases and that you feel confident to try out and evaluate different approaches to teaching.

Unit 5.1, 'Ways pupils learn', introduces you to a number of theories of how children learn and how educational theory can be used to review your own teaching. Theories about teaching and learning provide frameworks for the analysis of learning situations and a language to describe the learning taking place. As you gain experience, you develop and clarify your own theories of how the pupils you teach learn, and this unit may help you place your theories in a wider context. The unit addresses learning styles and strategies.

In Unit 5.2, 'Active learning', some teaching methods are examined which promote learning. These methods are described as active learning approaches, to distinguish them from passive, reception learning. The teaching methods you adopt may reveal something of your personal theory of how pupils learn. At this point in your development we suggest that you gain experience with a range of teaching methods, that you experiment with your teaching and widen your reading and observation, so that you are more easily able to review and select the teaching methods most appropriate to your pupils and the material to be taught.

Unit 5.3, on 'Teaching styles' provides you with details about the way in which teacher behaviour and choice of strategy interact to provide a teaching style. We suggest that as you gain confidence with basic classroom management skills you try out different styles so that you develop a repertoire of teaching styles from which you can select as appropriate.

We have talked at various points in this book about the characteristics of effective teaching. Unit 5.4, 'Improving your teaching', is designed to provide you with information about methods for finding out about the quality of your own teaching and that of others – through the use of reflection using action research techniques. These techniques include, for example, the use of observation, pupils' written work and discussion. During your initial teacher education course you are using action research skills in a simple way when you observe classes. In this unit we explain some aspects of action research.

Many of the ideas and suggestions in this chapter may help your reading of other units in this book and, more importantly, in the preparation and analysis of your teaching. We have cross-referenced units throughout the book but you may need to return to this chapter at several stages in your development.

UNIT 5.1 **WAYS PUPILS LEARN**

DIANA BURTON

INTRODUCTION

The primary aim of a teacher's work is, fairly obviously, that pupils should learn *how*, *what*, *whether* and so on in relation to the subject of study – teaching is therefore a means to an end, not an end in itself. However, the interaction between the activities of teaching and the outcomes of learning is critical. In order to develop presentation and communication techniques that facilitate effective learning a teacher must have some notions of how pupils learn. Course lectures and school experience add to and refine the ideas you already have about learning and reveal the very great differences in how individuals learn. Psychological research is concerned with this individuality of *cognition* – knowing, understanding, remembering, and problem solving. Research reveals information about human behaviour, motivation, achievement, personality and self-esteem, all of which impact on the activity of learning.

Several theoretical perspectives contribute to our understanding of how learning happens. For example:

- behaviourist theory which emphasises external stimuli for learning;
- gestalt theory which expounds principles of perception predicated on the brain's search for 'wholeness';
- personality theories which are located in psychoanalytic, psychometric and humanist research traditions.

In this unit, theories that have some direct influence on pedagogic strategy, or which are currently influential amongst educators, are considered in a little more detail. These theories include:

- Piaget's cognitive-developmental theory of maturation;
- the information-processing approach to concept development and retrieval;
- social constructivist ideas with their emphasis on social interaction and scaffolded support for learning;
- constructivist ideas about the strength of pupils' existing conceptions;
- metacognition, the way in which learners understand and control their learning strategies;
- learning style theories which serve to refute qualitative distinctions between ways of learning, stressing instead the matching of learning tasks to a preferred processing style.

In Unit 4.3 you met Gardner's (1983, 1993a) multiple intelligence theory which suggests a multi-dimensional rather than a singular intelligence. This clearly has application when considering how individuals learn. Similarly, emotional intelligence theory, which emphasises the potency of the learner's emotional state, is also of interest to teachers (Goleman, 1995).

OBJECTIVES

By the end of this unit you should have some understanding of:

- the interaction between ideas about learning and pedagogic strategies;
- a number of psychological perspectives on learning;
- your own approach to learning.

A number of the competences/standards required of NQTs are pertinent to your management of the learning process. Identify these and review how your understanding of how pupils learn helps you to meet them.

HOW IDEAS ABOUT TEACHING AND LEARNING INTERACT

Decisions you make about how to approach a particular lesson with a particular pupil or group of pupils depend on the interplay between your subject and pedagogic knowledge, your knowledge of the pupils and your various ideas about how learning happens. Let us imagine that you have spent ten minutes carefully introducing a new concept to your class but a few pupils unexpectedly fail to grasp it. You test the reasons for their lack of understanding against what you know about the pupils':

- prior knowledge of the topic;
- levels of attention;
- interest and motivation;
- physical and emotional state of readiness to learn;

and so on.

You consider also factors relating to the topic and the way you explained it, subject and pedagogic knowledge:

- the relevance of the new material to the pupils;
- how well the new concept fits into the structure of the topic;
- the level of difficulty of the concept;
- your clarity of speech and explanation;
- the accessibility of any new terminology;
- the questioning and summaries you gave at intervals during your explanation;

and so on.

Finally you draw on explanations from educational psychology which have informed your understanding of how pupils learn and provided you with questions such as:

- does the mode of presentation suit these pupils' learning styles?
- has sufficient time been allowed for pupils to process the new information?
- does the structure of the explanation reflect the inherent conceptual structure of the topic?
- do these pupils need to talk to each other to help them understand the new concept?

A teacher's ideas about learning usually derive from a number of psychological theories rather than from one specific theory. This is fine because it allows for a continual revision of your ideas as more experience is gained. This process is known as 'reflecting on theory in practice'. Some of the psychological theories from which your ideas may be drawn are reviewed in this unit. In order to contextualise that review it may be helpful to think about the types of learning activities that you engage your pupils in.

Gagné (1977) identified five main types of learning (see Task 5.1.1). Each of these types of learning is used in the teaching of all subjects of the curriculum, interacting in complex ways. It is helpful to consider them separately so that a particular pupil's learning progress and needs can be monitored and so that teachers can plan lessons that foster all types of learning. Stones (1992) has discussed the need to employ different pedagogical strategies depending on the type of learning planned.

Task 5.1.1

ANALYSING LEARNING ACTIVITIES

Draw up a table like the one below. Choose a topic you are observing the teaching of or are teaching yourself. Complete the learning activity involved in each of the five areas. An example from science has been provided to guide you.

Activity	Intellectual skills	Verbal skills	Cognitive strategy	Attitudes	Motor skills
A group activity using particle theory of matter	Discussing how to set up the activity to test a hypothesis	Defining solids, liquids and gases	Recalling previous knowledge about particles	Listening to and sharing ideas	Manipulating equipment

---

PSYCHOLOGICAL PERSPECTIVES ON LEARNING

A determining factor in lesson preparation is the knowledge that learners already possess. Unfortunately, identifying this knowledge is not as simple as recalling what you taught the pupils last time, for knowledge is, by definition, individualised. Each pupil's experiences of, attitudes towards, and methods of processing, prior knowledge are distinct. Psychologists are interested in how learners actively construct this individualised knowledge or 'meaning', and different psychological theories offer different notions about what constitutes knowledge.

Cognitive developmental theory depicts knowledge as being generated through the learner's active exploration of her world (Piaget, 1932, 1954). More complex ways of thinking about things are developed as the individual matures.

Information-processing theories view knowledge as pieces of information which the learner's brain processes systematically and which are stored as abstractions of experiences (Anderson, Reder and Simon, 1996).

Social constructivism explains knowledge acquisition by suggesting that learners actively construct their individual meanings (or knowledge) as their experiences and interactions with others help develop the theories they hold (Brown, 1994; Rogoff, 1990).

The relatively new theory of **situated cognition** does not recognise knowledge as existing outside of situations, but rather as 'collective knowledge', i.e. the shared, ongoing, evolving interaction between people (Lave and Wenger, 1991; Davis and Sumara, 1997).

The first three of these theories have been influential in shaping pedagogy. They are outlined briefly below.

Cognitive developmental theory

Piaget

Jean Piaget was a Swiss psychologist who applied Gessell's (1925) concept of maturation (genetically programmed sequential pattern of changing physical characteristics) to cognitive growth. He saw intellectual and moral development as sequential, with the child moving through stages of thinking driven by an internal need to understand the world. His theory implied an investigative, experiential approach to learning and was embraced in many European countries in the 1960s and 1970s.

According to Piaget the stages through which the child's thinking moves and develops is linked to age. From birth to about two years the child understands the world through feeling, seeing, tasting and so on. This stage of development Piaget called the **Sensory-Motor stage**. As the child grows older and matures he begins to understand that others have a viewpoint. He is increasingly able to classify objects into groups and to use symbols. This second stage, from about two to six years, Piaget termed the **Pre-operational stage**.

A third stage identified by Piaget is called the **Concrete Operational stage**. The child is still tied to specific experience but can do mental manipulations as well as physical ones. Powerful new internal mental operations become available to the child, such as addition, subtraction and class inclusion. Logical thinking develops.

The final stage of development sees the child manipulating ideas in her head and she can consider events that haven't yet happened or think about things never seen. The child can organise ideas and events systematically and can examine all possibilities. Deductive thinking becomes possible. Piaget suggested that this final stage, called the **Formal Operational stage**, began at about twelve years of age. For further information about Piaget's ideas on intellectual development see the Further Reading section at the end of this unit, e.g. Bee, 2000.

The learner's stage of thinking interacts with his experience of the world in a process called *adaptation*. The term *operations* is used to describe the strategies, skills and mental activities which the child uses in interacting with new experience. Thus adding 2 and 2 together, whether mentally or on paper, is an operation. It is thought that discoveries are made sequentially, so, for example, adding and subtracting cannot be learned until objects are seen to be constant. Progress through the sequence of discoveries occurs slowly and at any one age the child has a particular general view of the world, a logic or structure that dominates the way she explores the world. The logic changes as events are encountered which do not fit with her *schemata* (sets of ideas about objects or events). When major shifts in the structure of the child's thinking occur, a new stage is reached. Central to Piaget's theory are the concepts of *assimilation*, taking in and adapting experience or objects to one's existing strategies or concepts, and *accommodation*, modifying and adjusting one's strategies or concepts as a result of new experiences or information (see Bee, 2000, for a full description of Piaget's theory).

The influence of stage theory

Piaget's work influenced the way in which some other psychologists developed their views. Kohlberg (1976) saw links between children's cognitive development and their moral reasoning, proposing a stage model of moral development; see also Unit 4.5. Selman (1980) was interested in the way children make relationships, describing a set of stages or levels they go through in forming friendships. Stage models of development were also posited in relation to personality growth, quite independently of Piaget's work. Influenced by Freud's (1901) psychoanalytic approach, Erikson's (1980) stages of psychosocial development explain the way in which an individual's self-concept develops, providing us with important insights into adolescent identity issues, such as role confusion. Harter's research (1985) has since indicated the significance of teacher–pupil relationships for pupils' feelings of self-worth in relation to learning competence. You may be aware of the fragility of an adolescent's self-concept, of the fundamental but often volatile nature of adolescent friendships and of the increased interest adolescents show in ethical issues. It is essential to consider these factors when planning for learning since they impact so heavily on pupils' motivation for, and capacity to engage with, lesson content.

Jerome Bruner, an American psychologist, also developed a stage model of the way people think about the world. He described three stages in learning, the enactive, iconic and symbolic. **Enactive representation** is the memories of actions which become stored in our muscles, enabling actions to become automatic, e.g. we can walk, eat, drive, etc. without consciously thinking about what we are doing. The implications for teaching are to provide opportunities for practice or 'learning by doing', e.g. repetition of pronunciation, practice in craft and game skills, etc.

Iconic representation is thinking about something through concrete images in order to understand or remember it, e.g. we might think about the idea of 'nature' pictorially – a field or landscape; pupils might be aided in understanding fractions by thinking about how a cake is divided into pieces.

Symbolic representation is thinking abstractly about things, where there is no apparent connection between the object or idea and the way it is represented, e.g. language uses words to stand for objects but they have no visual correspondence – the word 'door' does not describe the physical manifestation of a door, it just stands for it. This is the most advanced form of thinking and we strive to help pupils use it in our lessons through, for example, the use of scientific formulae or grammatical terms.

Unlike Piaget's stages, learners do not pass through and beyond Bruner's different stages of thinking. Instead, the stage or type of representation used depends on the type of thinking required of the situation. It is expected, however, that as pupils grow up they make progressively greater use of symbolic representation.

The stress on the idea of 'stages' in Piaget's theory was far-reaching, especially the implication that pupils need to be at a particular developmental level in order to cope with certain learning tasks. However, research studies have substantially refuted such limitations on a pupil's thinking (Donaldson, 1978). Thus the construct of a staged model of cognitive maturation probably has less currency than the features of development described within the various stages. Flavell (1982), a former student of Piaget, has argued that, while stage notions of development are unhelpful, Piaget's ideas about the sequences learners go through are still valid. They can help teachers to examine the level of difficulty of topics and curriculum material as a way of deciding how appropriate they are for particular age groups and ability levels; see, for example, Units 4.1 and 4.3. The key task for teachers is to examine the progress of individuals in order to determine when to increase the intellectual demand on them. Bruner (1966) argued that difficult ideas should be seen as a challenge and that, if properly presented, they can be learned by most pupils.

More recent work by Adey and his colleagues has revealed that learning potential is increased if pupils are metacognitively aware, i.e. if they understand and can control their own learning strategies. These strategies include techniques for remembering, ways of presenting information when thinking, approaches to problems and so on. Shayer and Adey have developed a system of cognitive acceleration in science education (CASE) which challenges pupils to examine the processes they use to solve problems (Adey, 1992). In doing so it is argued that pupils are enhancing their thinking processes. Other researchers have found significant benefits to pupil learning where metacognitive training has been given. Kramarski and Mevarech (1997) showed that it helped 12–14-year-olds draw better graphs in mathematics. Other researchers reported that transfer of learning between tasks is enhanced where the teacher cues learners into the specific skill being learned and encourages them to reflect on its potential for transfer (Anderson, Reder and Simon, 1996). It seems, then, that the higher-order cognitive skills of Piaget's formal operations (stage) can be promoted and encouraged through a focus on metacognition. You might like to consider how you can give pupils at least one opportunity during each lesson to think about the strategies they are using.

> **Ask them, for instance, how they reached a particular conclusion, how they tackled the drawing of a 3D shape or how they would undertake a journey from point A to point B.**

Social constructivist theory

The ideas of the Russian psychologist Lev Vygotsky, and of Jerome Bruner in the USA have increasingly influenced educators in recent years. Vygotsky's work dates from between the 1920s and 1930s but was suppressed in Soviet Russia until the 1970s.

Vygotsky

Juxtaposing Piaget's and Vygotsky's theories, Kozulin describes their 'common denominators as a child centred approach, an emphasis on action in the formation of thought, and a systematic understanding of psychological functioning', and their biggest difference as their understanding of psychological activity (Kozulin, 1998, p. 34). For Vygotsky (1978), psychological activity has socio-cultural characteristics from the very beginning of development. Concepts can be generated from a range of different stimuli, implying a problem-solving approach for pupils and a facilitator role for the teacher. Whereas Piaget considered language a tool of thought in the child's developing mind, Vygotsky held that language was generated from the need to communicate and was central to the development of thinking. He emphasised the functional value of egocentric speech to verbal reasoning and self-regulation, and the importance of socio-cultural factors in its development. In communicative talk too the development is not just in the language contrived to formulate the sentence but also through the process of combining the words to shape the sentence because this also shapes the thought itself.

Thus Vygotsky's work highlights the importance of talk as a learning tool, and reports of some eminence have reinforced the status of talk in the classroom, highlighting its centrality to learning (Bullock Report, DES, 1975; Norman, 1992). Vygotsky believed that such communicative instruction could reduce a pupil's 'zone of proximal development' – the gap between her current level of learning and the level she could be functioning at with adult or peer support.

> What a child can do today in co-operation, tomorrow he will be able to do on his own.
>
> (Vygotsky, 1962, p. 67)

> **Consider how often you make opportunities for your pupils to talk in lessons – to each other, to you, to a cassette, video recorder or via CD-ROM. Listen to how the talk develops the thinking of each member of a small group of pupils. Notice how well-timed and focused intervention from you moves the thinking on.**

More recent research in this area has indicated that reciprocal peer tutoring can also promote learning (Topping, 1992). Crucially, however, children need to be given specific preparation and guidance by the teacher in order to work effectively. Brown (1994) has developed the idea of learning communities where group work and seminars provide the main vehicle for learning. Rogoff (1990) found that homogeneous student grouping and pairing, such as setting provides, have advantages in promoting argument and sharing complex ideas. However, Doise (1990) found that in pair work a slight difference in the intellectual functioning of partners was best because it promoted cognitive conflict. Unit 5.2 provides information about active learning strategies which support a Vygotskyan approach to learning.

Bruner

Bruner also placed an emphasis on structured intervention within communicative learning models. He formulated a theory of instruction, central to which is the notion of systematic, structured pupil experience via a spiral curriculum where the learner returns to address increasingly complex components of a topic. Current and past knowledge are deployed as the pupil constructs new ideas or concepts. Thus the problem of fractions in Year 5 will be tackled via many more concrete examples than when it is returned to in Year 7. Learning involves the active restructuring of knowledge through experience; the pupil selects and transforms information, constructs hypotheses, and makes decisions, relying on a developing cognitive structure to do so.

Teachers should try to encourage pupils to discover principles by themselves through active dialogue with the teacher. Thus, for Bruner, the teacher's job is to guide this discovery through structured support: for example, by asking focused questions or providing appropriate materials. Bruner termed this process '**scaffolding**' (Bruner, 1983). Maybin, Mercer and Stierer (1992) have used 'scaffolding' in relation to classroom talk. The ideas of pupils emerging through their talk are scaffolded or framed by the teacher putting in 'steps' or questions at appropriate junctures. For example, a group of pupils might be discussing how to solve the problem of building a paper bridge between two desks. The teacher can intervene when he hears an idea emerge which will help pupils find the solution, by asking a question that requires the pupils to address that idea explicitly. Bruner argued that the scaffolding provided by the teacher should decrease in direct correspondence to the progress of the learner. Wood (1988) has developed Bruner's ideas, describing five levels of support which become increasingly specific and supportive in relation to the help needed by the pupil:

- general verbal encouragement;
- specific verbal instruction;
- assistance with pupil's choice of material or strategies;
- preparation of material for pupil assembly;
- demonstration of task.

Thus, having established the task the pupils are to complete, a teacher might give general verbal encouragement to the whole class, follow this up with specific verbal instruction to groups who need it, perhaps targeting individuals with guidance on strategies for approaching the task. Some pupils need physical help in performing the task and others need to be shown exactly what to do, probably in small stages.

Task 5.1.2

SCAFFOLDING PUPILS' LEARNING

Wood's ideas can help you to think systematically about the nature of the support you should prepare for particular pupils, and to keep a check on whether the level is becoming more or less supportive. This has obvious relevance for differentiation in your classroom, workshop or gym.

For a topic you are planning to teach, use Wood's five levels to prepare the type of support you think might be needed during the first lesson. Once you start teaching the topic, choose two particular pupils who need different levels of support. Plan the support for each one, lesson by lesson, noting whether they are requiring less or more support as the topic progresses. What does this tell you about the way you are teaching and the way the pupils are learning?

Constructivism

Another theory, called 'constructivism', is that described by Driver and Bell (1986). Whilst sharing a Brunerian and Vygotskyan emphasis on the social construction of meaning, constructivism places much more importance on learners' individual conceptions and gives them responsibility for directing their own learning experiences. Constructivism is predicated on the idea that people make their own sense of things in a unique way. Driver and Bell (1986) have argued that stimuli, or knowledge, are not straightforward. New information is problematic for the learner who must examine it in relation to prior conceptions and experiences and see to what extent it fits with their existing ideas. In this approach to teaching, little emphasis is placed on instruction; the teacher must create situations which facilitate pupils constructing their own knowledge. If pupils are found to hold misconceptions the teacher must make it possible for the misconceptions to be taken apart at their root since long-held conceptions are very difficult to shake off. Some misconceptions are resistant to change even when the misunderstanding is explained. It is in the science subject area that constructivist ideas have been most influential. Naylor and Keogh (1999), for instance, have devised concept cartoons which force learners to examine the very core of their conceptions.

Information-processing theory

This approach to learning originated within explanations of perception and memory processes and was influenced by the growth of computer technology. The basic idea is that the brain attends to sensory information as it is experienced, analyses it within the short-term memory and stores it with other related concepts in the long-term memory.

Psychologists saw the functioning of computers as replicating the behaviour of the brain in relation to the processing of information. Information is analysed in the short-term memory (STM) and stored with existing related information in the long-term memory (LTM). This process is more efficient if material can be stored as abstractions of experience rather than as verbatim events. If I ask you to tell me the six times table, you recite 'one six is six, two sixes are twelve' and so on. You do not explain to me the mathematical principle of multiplication by a factor of six. On the other hand, if I ask you the meaning of the term 'economic enterprise', it is unlikely that you will recite a verbatim answer. Instead, your STM searches your LTM for your 'schema' or idea of enterprise. You then articulate your abstracted understanding of the term, which may well be different from that of the person next to you. In terms of intellectual challenge, articulating the second answer requires greater mental effort, although knowing one's multiplication tables is a very useful tool. Thus teachers need to be absolutely clear that there is a good reason for requiring pupils to learn something by rote, because rote learning is not inherently meaningful so cannot be stored in LTM with other related information. Rather it must be stored in its full form, taking up a lot of 'disk' space in the memory. Information stored in this way is analysed only superficially in STM – the pupil does not have to think hard to make connections with other pieces of information. See rote learning, Unit 5.2.

It can often be difficult in secondary schools for teachers to determine precisely the prior knowledge of their pupils. You observe that good teachers cue learners in to their prior knowledge by asking questions about what was learned last lesson or giving a brief résumé of the point reached in a topic. Such strategies are very important because, if previous learning has been effective, information is stored by pupils in their long-term memories and needs to be retrieved. Psychologists suggest that learning is more effective, i.e. more likely to be understood and retained, if material is introduced to pupils according to the inherent conceptual structure of the topic (Ausubel, 1968; Gagné 1977; Stones, 1992). This is because information which is stored using a logical structure is easier to recall because the brain can process it more easily in the first instance, linking the new ideas to ones that already exist in the memory. As a teacher, this requires you to have thought through the structure in advance, and to know how the concepts fit together; hence the importance of spending time on schemes of work even where these are already produced for you. See Task 5.1.3 and the concept maps in Unit 5.2.

This emphasis on structure and sequence can be found most readily perhaps in the teaching of modern foreign languages (MFL) and mathematics. Mitchell (1994) found that MFL teachers use a 'bottom-up' language learning theory, encouraging recognition and acquisition of vocabulary first, followed by the construction of spoken and written sentences. This approach might be described as moving from the general to the specific, but in most subjects the process is the other way around. Chyriwsky (1996) has stressed the importance of working hierarchically through mathematical knowledge. It might be argued that in mathematics we start with the general concepts of addition, subtraction and multiplication, moving to more specific computations like calculating area, solving equations, or estimating probabilities.

Concept development

Since information-processing theory is concerned with processing information it is helpful to consider briefly how that processing relates to concept development. The material held in the long-term memory is stored as sets of ideas known as 'schemata' ('schema' is the singular). A schema is a mental structure abstracted from experience. It consists of a set of expectations with which to categorise and understand new stimuli. For example, our schema of 'school' consists of expectations of pupils, teachers, classrooms, etc. As teachers, our school schema has been refined and developed as more and more information has been added and categorised. Thus it includes expectations about hierarchies, pupil culture, staffroom behaviour and so on. It is probable that our school schema is different from, and more complex than, the school schema held by a parent, simply because of our involvement in schools.

When children are young their schemata do not allow them to differentiate between pieces of information in the way that those of older pupils do. A one-year-old's schema of dog might include expectations about cats too, because she has had insufficient experience of the two animals to know them apart. As she experiences cats as furry, dogs as hairy, cats meowing, dogs barking, etc., greater differentiation is possible. Since the object of school learning is to promote pupils' concept differentiation in a range of different subjects, teachers should encourage comparison between objects or ideas and introduce new ideas by reference to concrete examples. Even as adults, whilst we can think abstractly, we find new ideas easier to grasp if we can be given concrete examples of them.

Critical thinking

Teaching in the context of information-processing theories stresses the application of knowledge and skills to new situations. The teacher's role is to help pupils find new ways of recalling previous knowledge, solving problems, formulating hypotheses and so on. Montgomery (1996) advocates the use of games and simulations because they facilitate critical thinking and encourage connections to be made between areas of subject knowledge or experience.

Task 5.1.3

STRUCTURING TOPICS FOR EFFECTIVE LEARNING

Choose a topic from your subject area. Brainstorm some of the ideas contained within it for a couple of minutes, jotting them down haphazardly on paper. Now think about how those ideas fit together and whether, in teaching the topic, you would start with the general overarching ideas and then move to the specific ones or vice versa.

You can organise your topic by drawing up a conceptual hierarchy of it like the one started below for a PSHE topic. This hierarchy moves from the general to the specific.

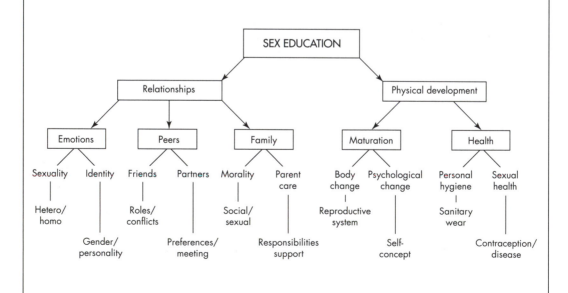

We have discussed cognitive development theories, social constructivist theories and information-processing theories. In each of these theories about how learning occurs, there has been an emphasis on the individual and the differences between them. Looking at what is known about how learners' styles and strategies differ equips us further to understand individual differences.

LEARNING STYLES, STRATEGIES AND APPROACHES

There is often confusion about what constitutes learning style as distinct from learning strategy. Psychologists argue that a cognitive or *learning style* is considered to be a fairly fixed characteristic of an individual, which may be distinguished from *learning strategies*, which are the ways learners cope with situations and tasks. Strategies may vary from time to time and may be learned and developed. Styles, by contrast, are static and are relatively in-built features of the individual (Riding and Cheema, 1991).

Learning style

Understanding how in-built features of learners affect the way they process information is important for teachers. Many researchers have worked in this area but Riding and Rayner (1998) have proposed that the various conceptualisations may be grouped into two principal cognitive styles:

1 *Wholist–Analytic style* – whether an individual tends to process information in wholes (wholist) or in parts (analytic);
2 *Verbal–Imagery style* – whether an individual is inclined to represent information during thinking verbally (verbalist) or in mental pictures (imager).

The two styles operate as dimensions so a person may be at either end of the dimension or somewhere along it.

Task 5.1.4

YOUR OWN LEARNING STYLE

Think about what your own style might be:

- do you approach essay writing incrementally, step by step, piecing together the various parts, or do you like to have a broad idea of the whole essay before you start writing?
- do you experience lots of imagery when you are thinking about something or do you find yourself thinking in words?

Discuss your style with other student teachers. In doing so you are developing your metacognitive knowledge.

Riding explains that these styles are involuntary so it is important to be aware that your classes contain pupils whose habitual learning styles vary. Teachers need then to ensure that they provide a variety of media in which pupils can work and be assessed. It would not be sensible to present information only in written form; if illustrations are added, this allows both Verbalisers and Imagers easier access to it. Similarly, Wholist pupils are assisted by having an overview of the topic before starting, whilst Analytics benefit from summaries after they have been working on information.

This is not to suggest that you must determine the style of each pupil, but that there must be opportunities for all pupils to work in the way that is most profitable for them. Unlike the way in which intelligence quotient (IQ) is used – the higher the IQ score the better the performance expected – the determination of learning style does not imply that one way of processing is better than the other. The key is in allowing learners to use their natural processing style. It is important for you to be aware of your own style because teachers have been found to promote the use of approaches which fit most easily with their own styles; see Task 5.1.4.

Learning strategy

Learning strategy describes the ways in which learners cope with tasks or situations. These strategies develop and change as the pupil becomes more experienced. Kolb's work describing two dimensions of learning strategy, perceiving and processing, is the most widely known in the area of strategy theory (Kolb, 1976, 1985). Kolb argued that these two dimensions interact and that, although learners use preferred strategies, they could be trained to develop aspects of other strategies through experiential learning. He envisaged a cyclical sequence through four stages of learning arising from the interaction of the two dimensions (see Figure 5.1.1).

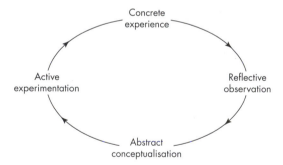

Figure 5.1.1   Kolb's experiential learning cycle (1985)

Thus Kolb suggests that learners need, at the 'concrete experience' stage, to immerse themselves in new experiences. These experiences are reflected upon from as many perspectives as possible at what Kolb calls the 'reflective observation' stage. This reflection enables the learner to create concepts which integrate their observations into logically sound theories at the 'abstract conceptualisation' stage, which are then used to make decisions and solve problems at the 'active experimentation' stage (Fielding, 1996). Learners have a predilection for one of the stages. It can be argued that learners should be provided with experiences that ensure their use of stages in the cycle additional to their preferred one, in order to extend their learning strategies (McCarthy, 1987).

Task 5.1.5

DETERMINING TYPES OF LEARNERS

Try to work out which stage of Kolb's cycle describes the way you learn yourself most of the time. Think about how you process information, e.g.:

• are you more comfortable reflecting on ideas where you have had lots of concrete experience?
• do you prefer to draw from abstract theory and experiment with it to solve problems?

Do you think Kolb's ideas could help you to process information differently? Would it be helpful to 'practise' different ways? What are the implications for your work with pupils?

Learning approaches

Other researchers are interested in the motivations and attitudes pupils and students bring to their learning. These can be described as 'approaches to learning'. Researchers have investigated how learning approaches interact with learning strategies. Biggs (1978, 1987, 1993) and Entwistle (1981) have both researched learners' approaches to study.

Entwistle described different orientations to learning, such as being oriented towards discovering the meaning of a topic or being oriented simply to scratch the surface. Combinations of these orientations with extrinsic factors, such as the need to pass examinations or the love of a subject, were thought to lead to learning strategies which characterised certain approaches to study, from 'deep' to 'surface' levels of thinking; see Unit 4.3.

Biggs explained that a student's approach is a function of both motive and strategy and that motives influence learning strategies (Biggs, 1993). Thus, a student with an instrumental (surface) motive is likely to adopt reproducing or rote-learning (surface) strategies. Deep motive results from an intrinsic desire to learn and can inspire the use of deep strategies wherein understanding and meaning are emphasised. An achieving motive might be an egotistical need to pass examinations; from this perspective the learner can derive achieving strategies which stress time management, well-ordered resources and efficiency.

Task 5.1.6

YOUR OWN APPROACHES TO LEARNING

Refer to the paragraphs on learning approaches.
Do you recognise any of these motives and strategies in relation to your own learning? Do your motives and associated learning strategies stay the same over time or do they depend on the task and the reason you are learning it?
Prepare some notes on your own ways of learning for discussion with your tutor.

Pupils whose motives and strategies are compatible with the demands made by learning tasks are likely to perform well. Pupils are likely to be less successful where motives and strategy are incompatible with task demand. For example, a pupil with a deep approach to learning is constrained by superficial task design such as a requirement for short answers, whilst a pupil with an achieving motive may be deterred if he is set very long-term, vague objectives.

Successful learning, if defined in terms of understanding and permanence, is linked with deep and deep-achieving approaches, which can be taught. The achievement-driven context within which secondary school pupils in England currently learn, however, could militate against the possibility of teaching deep approaches because of time constraints.

You should endeavour to maintain variety in the learning experiences you design for pupils, in the ways you present information, in the resources pupils use and the tasks they undertake and in the ways you assess their progress. There is a whole range of interesting work on learning style, strategy, approach and preference which we have not addressed but to which the final further reading section directs you.

SUMMARY AND KEY POINTS

The importance of teachers developing their own models of learning and refining these as they gain more experience of pupils and learning contexts has been established. The interaction between your knowledge of the pupils, of the subject and of how learning happens is continually drawn on in the teaching process. The symbiosis between theoretical positions and pedagogic practices has been emphasised. We have seen, for instance, that concept development is enhanced where pupils are introduced to new ideas via concrete examples, and that retention is aided if topics are taught according to their inherent conceptual structure.

Key features of three major psychological theories (cognitive developmental, social constructivist and information-processing) as they apply to pupil learning have been outlined, and your attention has been drawn to the implications of learning style and strategy research for teaching techniques. The benefits of teachers adopting a facilitative, interventionist approach and aiming for a variety of approaches in presentation, resource, task and assessment can be extrapolated from all the theories that have been discussed. Learning is likely to be most effective where pupils are actively involved with the material through critical thinking, discussion with others and metacognitive awareness of their own learning strategies.

You should review your learning from this unit while referring to the competences/standards for your course.

FURTHER READING

Bee, H. (2000) *The Developing Child* (9th edn), London: Allyn and Bacon.

Child, D. (1997a) *Psychology and the Teacher* (6th edn), London: Cassell.
    Both of these excellent books will take you further into theories of learning and child development.

Norman, K. (ed.) (1992) *Thinking Voices: The Work of the National Oracy Project*, London: Hodder and Stoughton.

This book provides a host of information on techniques for learning through talk. The work of Maybin *et al.* referred to in this unit appears in this book.

Riding, R.J. and Rayner, S. (1998) *Learning Styles and Strategies*, London: David Fulton.

This book provides very readable information about the research into learning styles and strategies and its implications for teachers and learners.

UNIT 5.2 **ACTIVE LEARNING**

TONY TURNER

INTRODUCTION

As we know from investigations of the process of concept formation, a concept is more than the sum of the certain associative bonds formed by memory, more than a mere mental habit; it is a complex and genuine act of thought that cannot be taught by drilling but can be accomplished only when the child's mental development itself has reached the requisite level.

Practical experience also shows that direct teaching of concepts is impossible and fruitless. A teacher who tries to do this usually accomplishes nothing but empty verbalisation, a parrot like repetition of words by the child, simulating a knowledge of the corresponding concepts but actually covering up a vacuum.

(Vygotsky, 1986, pp. 149–150)

Vygotsky uses the term concepts to mean 'word meanings'. This extract suggests that the teacher cannot do the learning for the pupil and that in order for understanding to occur the pupil has to be active in the learning process. Active learning is then meaningful learning, in which something of interest and value to the learner has been accomplished and understood. Some writers use the term 'deep learning' instead of meaningful learning, in contrast to 'shallow learning' which is learning without understanding. This unit addresses ways in which teachers help pupils to engage in meaningful learning. See also, 'Learning approaches' in Unit 5.1.

OBJECTIVES

At the end of this unit you should:

- be able to explain the term 'active learning' and discuss the advantages of active learning to the teacher and learner;
- be aware of ways of promoting active learning;
- be able to use resources to their best advantage;
- be able to link these teaching strategies to the standards/competences expected of a newly qualified teacher.

NATHAN'S STORY

The following quotation is taken from a paper which discussed the place of assessment in promoting high-quality learning. The reasons for using it in this context include:

- the degree to which the learner is involved in directing his own learning;
- the wide range of learning, including both the cognitive and affective.

The role of the teacher is understated in this short extract from the paper.

Nathan, nine years old, studies in a school which encourages pupils to research topics they take an interest in. About six hours a week are allotted to pupils' research projects. Nathan has chosen to examine the influence Golda Meir has had on the involvement of women in Israeli politics and business. He has previously researched other aspects of Golda Meir's life; in second grade he examined why this special person had decided to emigrate to Israel, so Nathan seems to have taken an interest in the famous lady. This is the research outline he presented to the teacher for approval:

- Collect information from encyclopaedia, history book, biography, Internet and previous project.
- Send a fax to famous women in business and politics asking for their views.
- Make a telephone survey to people chosen from the telephone directory asking them yes/no questions.
- Write up all the data so others and I can understand it.
- Draw conclusions from the data.

Nathan learned early on that he was flooded with information from the many sources and he needed assistance on how to make choices regarding what was relevant and of interest to his project. He presented his first version of the theoretical background to the teacher for feedback (no marking) and, based on her guidelines, he revised the first part of the project.

When he sent faxes he realised that he needed to design short questions which asked for longer answers. He learned also that people were more likely to answer if he faxed only one page. He was disappointed to learn that not all 'famous' business women or female politicians took time to answer. However, many of those who did, praised him and encouraged him to inform them of his findings. When he started with the telephone survey he panicked when he was supposed to ask strangers his pre-planned questions. So he wrote out a polite introduction and practised the interview with family and parents of friends before he started the survey. He contacted randomly chosen names from the telephone directory and quickly learned that there are various kinds of people in the world. Not everybody was interested in his project and some told him off whereas others took a keen interest in the topic, and were not only willing to spend time answering his questions but also to provide extensive advice.

Nathan collected a lot of data in various forms of which he had difficulties analysing so he turned to the math teacher to help him organise the data in tables for presentation. On this occasion he learned how to work with the suitable software. However the math teacher could not help him with the longer answers with the faxes and he received help at home on how to analyse data of a qualitative kind.

In writing up the conclusion he realised that there was not one single answer to his question and he seemed a bit disappointed at his findings. They did not agree with what he had thought when he started the project; with his hypothesis. As he said at the end "I learned something about Golda Meir that I did not know I would learn". The final version was nicely printed out and handed to the teacher for marking. The teacher did not give a score in the form of a number or letter but wrote extensive comments relating to the learning process, progress and the outcome. The bottom line was that Nathan had worked well with the task and presented a very good project. All the pupils gave a short oral presentation of their project at the end-of-year conference of the class.

(Smith, 1999, pp. 3–4)

This story is the subject of a paper about teaching, learning and assessment. Readers who are interested in the background to this story and the assessment aspect should turn to the original paper. In terms of 'active learning' the story illustrates the advantages of giving pupils the opportunities to carry out work in which they are interested. The outcomes are both predictable and unpredictable. The work gives rise to academic, social, group and individual learning and demands an unexpectedly wide range of knowledge, skills and attitudes. If carried out alongside other forms of teaching and learning, this approach can enrich the learning of most pupils.

WHAT IS ACTIVE LEARNING?

Active learning occurs when the pupil has some responsibility for the development of the activity. Supporters of this approach recognise that a sense of ownership and personal involvement is the key to successful learning. Unless the work that pupils do is seen to be important to them and to have purpose – that their ideas, contributions and findings are valued – little of benefit will be learned. Active learning can also be defined as purposeful interaction with ideas, concepts and phenomena and can involve reading, writing, listening, talking or working with tools, equipment and materials, such as paint, wood, chemicals, etc. In a simple sense it is learning by doing, as opposed to being told.

Active learning is contrasted with experiential learning (Addison and Burgess, 2000, p. 31). Experiential learning is also learning by doing but with the additional feature of reflection upon both action and the results of action. The same authors note that only where pupils are 'engaged actively and purposively in their own learning is the term experiential appropriate' (p. 31).

Active learning strategies benefit both teachers and pupils. As a teacher they enable you to spend more time with groups or individuals, which allows better-quality assessment to take place (see 'Formative assessment' in Unit 6.1). Active learning can also enhance your support of special needs pupils. For the pupils, activity methods encourage autonomous learning and problem-solving skills, important to both academic and vocationally based work. There is, of course, an extra demand on you in the planning and preparation of lessons.

The advantages of active learning to pupils include greater personal satisfaction, more interaction with peers, promotion of shared activity and team work, greater opportunities to work with a range of pupils, and opportunities for all members of the class to contribute and respond. It encourages mutual respect and appreciation of the viewpoint of others. Active learning is supportive of co-operative learning, not competitive learning; see Task 5.2.6.

It is important to realise that learning by doing, by itself, is not enough to ensure learning. The proverb 'I hear and I forget; I see and I remember; I do and I understand' can often be reformulated as 'I do and I am even more confused', (Driver, 1983, p. 9). The essential step to learning and understanding is reflection through discussion with others, especially the teacher, as Nathan's story shows. Such discussions involve 'thinking' as well as recalling.

ACTIVE LEARNING AND MOTIVATION

You support pupil learning by identifying clearly defined tasks which have purpose and relevance to them. That relevance may arise because of personal interest, i.e. it is intrinsic; or the motivation may be extrinsic, e.g. to please the teacher. Outside interests become increasingly important as the pupils get older. If the school task links with some future occupation, employment training or higher education, motivation is increased and engagement promoted. Motivation is considered in greater detail in Unit 3.2.

Upper school secondary curricula (Years 10 and 11) often aim to promote higher-order thinking. Teaching to promote higher-level intellectual skills, however laudable and desirable, cuts no ice with pupils unless the task engages with their need to know. If the task does not meet these needs then learning is on sufferance, leading to problems. Such problems may include poor recall of anything learned or rejection of learning tasks. The latter response often leads to behaviour problems, ranging from disruption to non-attendance.

LEARNING HABITS

Learning how to learn is a feature of active learning. By promoting activities which engage pupils and require them to participate in the task from the outset, you foster an approach to learning which is both skill-based and attitude-based. Active learning methods promote habits of learning which, it is hoped, are valuable in the workplace, and in the home, and which generally enhance pupils' capacity to cope with everyday life. The CASE Project sets out to promote thinking and to teach pupils how to learn (Adey, 2000, pp. 158–172).

School can be a place where pupils learn to do things well and in certain ways. Some skills are developed which are used throughout life. For example, pupils learn to consult a dictionary or a thesaurus in book form or a word-processing package, in order to find meanings or to counteract poor spelling. These skills become habits, capable of reinforcement and development. Reinforcement leads to improved performance. Many of our actions are of this sort, like dressing and eating. Important attitudes are developed, such as the confidence to question statements or to believe that problems can be solved and not to be put off by difficulties.

Many professional people depend, in part, on habits and routines for their livelihood; these include the concert pianist who may well practise time and time again a piece of music already well established in her repertoire. Practice commits the sequence of notes and pauses to memory, leaving time to concentrate on expression. Actors, too, depend on related routines for skilful performance.

Task 5.2.1

WHAT MAKES FOR A GOOD PERFORMANCE?

Discuss the performance of skilled people in terms of habits, routines and performance of their job. Compare and contrast the work of two or more of the following professional people: a surgeon, a racing driver, a teacher, an accountant. Consider:

- what constitutes a good (public) performance, or display of skill;
- the low-level skills (sub-routines) which contribute to the overall performance;
- the high-level skills (criteria for excellence) which characterise the skilled practitioner.

Identify some of the sub-routines of teaching needed for you to be a good teacher. If the sub-routines of a pianist are concerned with practice and flair, such as the interpretation of a musical score, what are the equivalents of practice and flair for teachers?

ACTIVE LEARNING, ROTE LEARNING AND DISCOVERY LEARNING

Active learning is sometimes contrasted with rote learning to suggest that rote methods do not require the learner to understand what is learned. Rote learning is an active process and often hard work. Discovery learning is active learning and attempts to motivate pupils by helping them to learn things for themselves.

Discovery learning

Discovery learning at its simplest occurs when pupils are left to discover things for themselves, but it is difficult to imagine when or where such learning ever happens and rarely in the organised classrooms of secondary schools. Much more common is the use of a structured framework in which learning can occur, sometimes called 'guided discovery'. Is the intention of guided discovery that pupils come to some predetermined conclusion or is it that learning should take place but the outcomes vary from pupil to pupil? Guided discovery as a method of teaching is a useful strategy for differentiation because the task may permit pupils to attain different end points.

You need to be clear, however, about your reason for adopting guided discovery methods. If the intention in discovery learning is to move pupils to a particular end point, then, as discovery, it could be termed a sham. This approach might preclude, for example, considering other knowledge that surfaced in the enquiry. If discovery learning focuses on how the knowledge was gained, then the activity is concerned with processes, i.e. how to discover. The question is one of means and ends. Are discovery methods concerned with:

*   discovery as 'process' – learning how to learn?
*   discovery as motivation – a better way to learn pre-determined knowledge and skills?

Rote learning

It is a fallacy, we suggest, to assume that pupils can learn everything for themselves by discovery methods. Teachers are specialists in their fields of study; they usually know more than pupils, and one, but not the only one, of their functions is to tell pupils things they otherwise might not know but need to know. You need to consider what you want to achieve and match the method with the purpose.

Pupils need to be told when they are right; their work needs supporting. On occasions you need to tell pupils when they are wrong and how to correct their error. How this is done is important but teachers should not shirk from telling pupils when they under-perform or make mistakes. See Unit 3.2 on motivating pupils, which includes a section on giving feedback; also formative assessment on pp. 310–311.

Rote learning may occur when pupils are required to listen to the teacher. There are occasions when you need to talk directly to pupils, e.g. to give facts about language, about spelling or grammar; about formulae in science; or health matters such as facts about drug abuse or safe practice in the gymnasium, etc. Other facts necessary for successful learning in school include recalling multiplication tables; or remembering vocabulary; or learning the reactivity series of metals; or recalling a piece of prose or poetry. Some facts need to be learned by heart, by rote methods. There is nothing wrong with you requiring pupils to do this from time to time, providing that all their learning is not like that. Such facts are necessary for advanced work; they contribute to the sub–routines which allow us to function at a higher level. Habits of spelling, of adding up, of recalling the alphabet are vital to our ability to function in all areas of the curriculum and in daily life. See information processing theory, Unit 5.1.

Sometimes pupils need to use a routine as part of a more important task but they may not understand it fully. You may decide that the end justifies the means and that through the experience of using the routine in different contexts understanding develops. Many of us learn that way.

Learning facts by heart usually involves a coding process. For example, recalling telephone numbers is easier if it is broken into blocks like this 0271 612 6780 and not as 02716126780. Another strategy is the use of a mnemonic to aid recall, such as recalling the musical scale E G B D F by the phrase 'Every Good Boy Deserves Fun'. Do you know any other mnemonics? What other ways are there of helping pupils to learn by rote?

Task 5.2.2

ROTE LEARNING

Describe three examples of rote learning in your subject teaching. For each example identify the content and reason(s) for adopting this strategy.

Compare your examples with those of other student teachers from the same subject group and different subject groups. Share useful mnemonics for helping recall.

What do the examples have in common? Discuss them in terms of:

- justification;
- low-level knowledge or high-level knowledge;
- essential sub-routines underlying higher-level skills.

Aids to recall

Sometimes information cannot easily be committed to memory unless a structure is developed around it to help recall. That structure may involve other information which allows you to build a picture. In other words, recall is constructed. Structures may include other words, but often tables, diagrams, flow charts or other visual models are used. Other ways of helping learners to remember ideas or facts are to construct summaries in various forms. Both the *act of compiling* the summary and the *product* contribute to remembering and learning.

In Figure 5.2.1 there is a model of learning, based on the idea that personal development proceeds best by reflection on your own actions. Reflection in the model is incorporated in the terms 'review' and 'learn'. This model is presented as a cyclic flow diagram which enables you to keep in mind the essential steps.

To develop your teaching, the key ideas in the model could be interpreted:

Do   Plan and teach a lesson to defined objectives.
Review Identify where learning took place and what contributed to successful learning. Which ideas or processes gave difficulties. Try to identify factors contributing to success and to difficulties.

Learn Clarify what has been learned about your teaching and what questions remain. Seek help about difficulties, from mentors, tutors, books and colleagues. Identify problems you can solve and those that are more deep-rooted.

Apply How can I use the new knowledge to improve future lessons? Planning and further action.

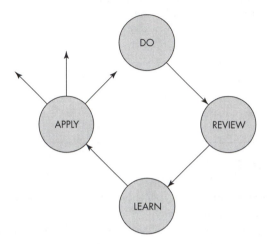

Figure 5.2.1 An active learning model

Source: Watkins, 1998, p. 6.

Task 5.2.3

USING A LEARNING MODEL (FIGURE 5.2.1)

Apply the model in Figure 5.2.1 to Nathan's story, introduced earlier in the unit (see pp. 250–252).

What did Nathan learn? Was it knowledge or skills or something else?

What were the roles of the teachers in this story?

How can the approaches described in this story be applied to your teaching?

Spider diagrams and concept maps

It is often helpful to pupils and teachers to 'brainstorm' as a way of exploring their understanding of an idea. One way to record that event is by a spider diagram in which the 'legs' identify the ideas related to the topic; it is sometimes called a burr diagram. Figure 5.2.2 shows a spider diagram of some meanings of 'fruit'.

Concept maps are examples of spider diagrams and are used to display important ideas or concepts which are involved in a topic or unit of work and, by annotation, to show the links between them. An example is shown in Figure 5.2.3.

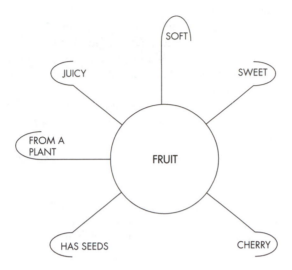

Figure 5.2.2 A pupil's meaning of fruit

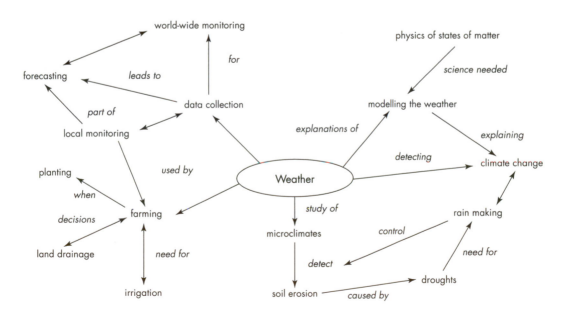

Figure 5.2.3 Concept map: weather

Concept maps can be made by pupils as a way of summarising their knowledge of a unit of work. The individual map reveals some of the pupil's understanding and misunderstandings of the topic. A good example of a Year 10 pupil's concept map can be found in Lambert and Balderstone (2000, p. 203). Making a concept map at the start of a unit helps to probe pupils' prior knowledge of the subject. In either case, you may need to provide a list of ideas with which pupils can work and to which they can add their own ideas.

Concept mapping is useful as part of your lesson preparation, particularly when beginning a new unit of work. See also Task 5.1.3 in Unit 5.1 'Ways pupils learn'. Concept mapping enables you to gain an overview of the unit, to consolidate links between several ideas and reveal any weaknesses or gaps in your own understanding. Your tutor may ask you to prepare a concept map for a unit of work as part of your preparation for teaching, using your school's scheme of work. Concept mapping is a useful way of linking topics in the curriculum so as to promote continuity and breadth of understanding in your teaching. Concept maps are difficult to make but the process of drafting one is a valuable exercise. For further discussion see White and Gunstone (1992) or Novak and Gowin (1984); and for the use of concept mapping by science teachers see Willson and Williams (1996).

We turn now to particular group of activities designed to aid recall and learning. They are familiar to many teachers but not always referred to as DARTS activities.

DARTS ACTIVITIES

The DARTS activities are ways of involving pupils in active reading, writing and listening. The term is an acronym for 'Directed Activities Related to (the use of) TextS'. A DART activity involves more than the use of textbooks, but takes in ways of using a variety of written and other visual materials. This approach can be used to address resources downloaded from the Web.

A reading exercise may require pupils to learn from a textbook; then a DARTS activity could be used to ensure that pupils interact with the text. Interaction includes, for example, underlining certain types of word; listing important words; drawing diagrams; or changing a labelled diagram into continuous prose. The level of demand is adjusted by you to meet the needs of the pupil. A listening DARTS activity may be designed to help pupils understand instructions given by the teacher.

The techniques involved in all these interactive processes are known as DARTS activities and some examples are discussed below. For further details see Gilham, 1986, p. 164; Davies and Greene, 1984.

Giving instructions

This includes activities as diverse as making bread, carrying out a traffic survey or gathering information on the effects of the Black Death.

A common complaint by teachers is that pupils do not read instructions or, if they do, are unable to comprehend them. Sometimes the language level is too high; or pupils may understand each step but not the whole, or just lack confidence to act. Sometimes it is because pupils do not have any investment in the project; it is not theirs. Ways of alleviating such problems depend very much on the ability and attentiveness of the pupils, but can include:

- Make a list of the instructions on a sheet and give to each pupil; then read it out to check understanding. As the instructional steps are completed pupils could be asked to tick off that step.
- Write the instructions on numbered cards. A set of cards can be given to a group who are instructed to put the cards into a working order. The final sequence can be checked, discrepancies discussed and the order checked against the purpose. The acceptable sequence can then be written or pasted in their books.
- Match instructions to sketches of events; ask pupils to read instructions and select the matching sketch and so build a sequence.
- A more demanding task is to discuss the task and then ask pupils to draft their own set of instructions. After checking by the teacher the pupils can begin.

The same approach can be applied to how to do something or how to explain processes. For example, helping pupils explain:

- how ice erodes rock;
- how a newspaper is put together;
- how to interrogate a database;
- how to use a thesaurus.

Listening to the teacher

Sometimes you want pupils to listen and enjoy what is being said to them. There are other occasions when you want pupils to listen and interact with the material and keep some sort of record. It may be to:

- explain a phenomenon, e.g. a riot;
- describe an event, e.g. a bore in a river;
- describe a process, e.g. making pastry;
- demonstrate a process, e.g. distillation;
- design an artefact, e.g. a desk lamp;
- give an account, e.g. of work experience or a visit to a gallery.

There are a number of ways in which you can help pupils. For example:

- Identify key words and ideas as you proceed, signalling to pupils when you expect them to record them.
- Identify key words and ideas in advance on a worksheet and ask pupils to note them, tick, underline or highlight as they are discussed. These words can be written on the board or overhead projector, for reference.
- Adopt the above strategy, but develop it as a game. Who can identify these ideas? Call out when you hear them.
- By using a diagram which pupils annotate as the lesson proceeds. This might be used to:
  - label parts;
  - describe functions;
  - identify where things happen.
- Pupils could keep their own notes and then be asked to make a summary and presentation to the class. Some pupils may need a word list to help them.

Another way to effect learning is to give pupils a depleted summary and ask them to complete it. The degree of help is a matter of judgement. For example:

- Give the summary with some key words missing and ask pupils to add the missing words.
- Give the depleted summary with an additional list of words. Pupils select words and put them in the appropriate place. The selection could include surplus words.
- Vary the focus of the omitted words. It could be on key words, or concepts, or on meanings of non-technical words, e.g. on connecting words or verbs, etc. (Sutton, 1981, p. 119).

Characterising events

You may wish to help pupils associate certain ideas, events or properties with a phenomenon. For example, what were the features of the colonisation of the West Indies; or what are the characteristics of a Mediterranean-type climate?

As well as reading and making notes:

- List ideas on separate cards, some of which are relevant to the topic and others not relevant. Ask pupils to sort the cards into two piles, those events relevant to the phenomenon and those not directly related. Pupils compare sorting and justify their choice to each other.
- A more complex task is to mix up cards describing criteria related to two phenomena. Ask pupils to select those criteria appropriate to each event. For example, compare the characteristics of the industrial revolutions of the eighteenth and twentieth centuries.

Interrogating books or websites or reading for meaning

Learners often feel that if they read a book they are learning, and don't always appreciate that they have to work to gain understanding. Learners need to do something with the material in order to understand it. There are a number of ways of interrogating the material in order to assist with learning and understanding. There are some general points to be considered. It is important that pupils:

- are asked to read selectively – the length of the reading should be appropriate;
- understand why they are reading and what they are expected to get out of it;
- know what they are supposed to be doing while they read, what to focus on, what to write down or record;
- know what they are going to do with the results of their reading; for example, write, draw, summarise, reformulate, précis, tell others, tell the teacher, carry out an investigation.

Homework which says simply 'read through this chapter tonight and I will give you a quick test on it tomorrow' is not helpful to learning because the focus is unclear. The following notes suggest ways of helping pupils read texts, worksheets, posters, etc. with purpose.

Getting an overview

Using photocopies of written material is helpful; pupils annotate or mark the text to aid understanding. Pupils read the entire text quickly, to get an overview and to identify any words they cannot understand and get help from an adult or a dictionary.

Ask pupils to read it again, this time with a purpose, such as to:

- list key words or ideas;
- underline key ideas;
- highlight key words.

Reformulating ideas

To develop understanding further, pupils need to do something with what they have read. They could:

- make a list of key words or ideas;
- collect similar ideas together, creating patterns of bigger ideas;
- summarise the text to a given length;
- turn prose into a diagram, sketch or chart:
  - a spider diagram,
  - a flow chart, identifying sequence of events, ideas, etc.,
  - a diagram, e.g. of a process or of equipment, with labels;
- turn a diagram into prose, by telling a story or interpreting meanings;
- summarise using tables, e.g. relating:
  - structure to function (organs of the body),
  - historical figures' contribution to society (emancipation of women),
  - form to origin (landscapes and erosion).

Where appropriate, pupils could be given a skeleton flow chart, spider diagram, etc., with the starting idea attached, and asked to attach further ideas.

Reporting back

A productive way of gaining interest and involvement is to ask pupils to report their findings, summaries or interpretation of the text to the class.

The summary could take one of the forms mentioned above. In addition, of course, the pupil could use the board, overhead projector, a poster or computer-assisted presentation. Pupils need to be prepared for this task. They cannot be expected to do this if not given time to prepare.

Public reporting is demanding on pupils and it is helpful if a group of pupils draft the presentation and support the reporter. The presentation could be in the form of a narrative, a poem, a poster, slides or OHP transparencies. A sequence of events is shown in Figure 5.2.4.

The feedback loop, 6 to 2 in Figure 5.2.4, can be introduced depending on the time available and the attentiveness and ability of the class.

DARTS and related types of learning activity emphasise the importance of language in learning and in assessing learning. For further discussion on the role of language in learning, see Barnes (1976), Barnes *et al.* (1972) and Bennett and Dunne (1994).

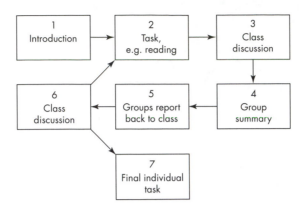

Figure 5.2.4 Preparing for reporting back

COMMUNICATING WITH PUPILS

Throughout your teaching you use many resources with your pupils. To get the best out of resources you need to consider how to use them and incorporate them into your lesson planning. The board and the overhead projector are used extensively by teachers as active teaching and learning devices. There is a growing use of multimedia projectors or electronic whiteboards connected to a computer, e.g. using Powerpoint; see Leask and Pachler, 1999, pp. 71–94.

The board

Writing on the board is not easy because we stand up to do it, whereas most writing is done sitting down. A few rules may help pupils follow your work on the board. Write on the board using joined-up script, not capital letters or printing; this is what pupils are used to. Most books use lower-case letters in their words, as we do here. You should practise handwriting on the board before you start teaching. If you want a clear style, that known as the Marion Richardson style is a useful model to work from. This style of handwriting avoids loops and the 'thick and thin lines' associated with italic or cursive script. An example of clear handwriting influenced by the Marion Richardson style is given below.

Teaching in the secondary school.

Practise keeping your writing on a straight line and big enough to be seen at the back of the class. Go to the back of the class and check your writing; better still, ask someone else to monitor your writing for legibility. Use white chalk, but colour sparingly and only then colours that can be seen, e.g. red and yellow.

Prepare important board work in advance, for choice of words, layout and headings. If you know you are going to elicit information from the class and build a set of ideas on the board, think in advance which ideas pupils are likely to suggest and those you want to introduce so that you can organise the presentation.

If you need to write on the board beforehand but don't want pupils to read it, use coloured chalk that is not easily read, e.g. blue; then in class go over it in white as you develop the ideas, e.g. when annotating diagrams.

The overhead projector, multimedia projector and whiteboard

Much the same advice applies as to the board except of course that it is not a board or a book and its purpose is not to be a substitute for a page of notes.

Some points to consider when writing materials for projection include:

- don't fill up your slide with words – they won't be read;
- use large writing, at least 'point size' 18 (Times font) on a word processor;
- draw a feint margin around each slide before you start making a transparency so that you do not lose material off the screen;
- use colour and underlining for emphasis;
- use diagrams to help minimise the number of words.

The word processor allows good-quality overheads to be made quickly. Powerpoint is helpful. Most photocopiers will produce transparencies from a paper master. Check which type of clear acetate is suitable for your school photocopier.

When you use the projector:

- consider where to stand so that you do not block the screen;
- if you are adding material to your projection, think where to stand as you write;
- when using a transparency on an overhead projector use a marker (pencil) to indicate relevant text on the transparency. Do not point at the screen or look at the screen as you talk. The advantage of projection is that you face your audience as you speak.

The various forms of projection are interactive and can be used to:

- stimulate pupils by providing ideas;
- record ideas;
- make summaries;
- bring in prepared diagrams, etc., to speak to but not read from;
- build ideas, models, diagrams, sequences, events, etc.

Another advantage of using different forms of projection is flexibility. Slides can be prepared which:

- use colour as highlight;
- have overlays – that is, several sheets of acetate/slides which successively add information. This process allows you to build a picture in stages;
- use windows; e.g. parts of an acetate are covered with an opaque material and subsequently revealed in the desired sequence. Write on the opaque material what is underneath.

If you have access to a digital camera and multimedia projector, or interactive whiteboard, you can use images from the local environment to support your lesson.

Many transparent objects can be displayed on an overhead projector. By projecting a transparent ruler on the screen, you can discuss how to use the ruler; similarly with transparent protractors and other measuring instruments. Many phenomena can be demonstrated using the OHP, such as compass movement, the pattern of a magnetic field using iron filings and a magnet, the motion of millepedes' legs, etc. Also, changes in a transparent liquid can be displayed using a clear dish. There are many good commercial sets of transparencies and Powerpoint sequences are becoming available.

The video and the worksheet

How do you use these resources in a planned way so that effective learning takes place? Tasks 5.2.4 and 5.2.5 ask you to draft guidelines for their use.

Task 5.2.4

DEVELOPING GUIDELINES FOR THE USE OF A VIDEO

Draw up a set of guidelines for using a video or video extract with a class. Identify a piece of video you plan to use. Consider questions such as:

- What advantage does the video offer over other resources?
- What do you expect pupils to learn from it?
- Is the material on the video accessible to most pupils? Is the language suitable?
- Do you need to show all the material?
- How should the video be used? Is it to be shown once or more than once?
- What are pupils expected to look or listen for?
- What do pupils do while they are watching? Should they take notes?
- What do you do in the follow-up session?
- What advance preparation do pupils need?
- What activity is planned after seeing the material?

Try out your guidelines by using them with an example. Review the guidelines after the session. Further guidance can be found in *Active Teaching and Learning Approaches in Science*, by the Centre for Science Education, Sheffield (1992), p. 120.

Task 5.2.5

WHAT MAKES A GOOD WORKSHEET?

Are there general rules about designing and using worksheets? Collect a number of worksheets used in your subject department and compare them using these broad guidelines.

Appearance – attractive, well-spaced, readable, use of images, colour.
Purpose – instructions, information, tasks, summary, to copy, temporary material to transfer to notebook.
Life – permanent, disposable, to be stuck in notebooks, easily lost.

Effectiveness – get opinions about their use from pupils and staff. Are they referred to again after the lesson?

Other factors – are there better ways of achieving your aims? Overload: how many worksheets do pupils receive per week?

Use these suggestions to draw up a checklist to guide your selection, manufacture and use of worksheets. Share your findings with other student teachers, or your mentor. See also Lloyd-Jones, 1988.

The computer

The computer can be used to support teaching and learning as a word processor, to display multimedia resources, to interrogate databases, to use spreadsheets and to design things. It is used also to collect data from the environment. Detailed support is given in:

- Unit 1.4 in this book;
- the subject books in the series 'Learning to Teach in the Secondary School' which accompany this text;
- the dedicated text on the use of ICT in the same series (Leask and Pachler, 1999). See the front of this book for details.

THE ADVANTAGES OF ACTIVE LEARNING METHODS

There are a wide range of strategies that fall into the category of active learning. These strategies are listed in Appendix 5.2.1 at the end of this unit. The **advantages** claimed for their use include:

1 Pupils co-operate with other learners
2 Group work is often used
3 Curriculum development involves the learner
4 Teachers use a greater variety of teaching methods
5 The learner 'owns' the ideas and the product
6 The learner contributes ideas to the development of the work
7 The learner is active in their own learning
8 The responsibility for learning is shifted to the learner
9 Self-discipline is needed by the learner
10 Process skills become important learning goals
11 Resource-based learning methods are used frequently
12 The teacher is a guide, not a provider.

This list draws attention to a number of features of teaching and learning, such as the way pupils learn, the role of the teacher, and what the pupils learn (knowledge, process, skills, attitudes). Task 5.2.6 asks you to review this list.

Task 5.2.6

THE ADVANTAGES OF ACTIVE LEARNING METHODS

This task may be carried out with a small group of student teachers or alone, discussing the findings with your mentor. The task refers to the list of twelve advantages of active learning, cited above. Discuss with other student teachers the usefulness of this list as a way of summarising the value and purposes of active learning. Write a short summary of your conclusions. You may find helpful the range of strategies listed in Appendix 5.2.1.

How could this list of advantages be improved? Can the list be:

- shortened?
- lengthened?
- regrouped under headings?
- made more visual using a table or diagram?

As a result of reorganising this list can you find more advantages? Discuss with other student teachers ways in which your understanding of 'active learning' has been changed by this task. How could you use the strategies identified in Appendix 5.2.1 in your teaching?

SUMMARY AND KEY POINTS

Learners learn and teachers teach; teachers guide pupils to learn but cannot do the learning for them. Teaching is an enabling process. Pupils need to engage mentally with a task if learning is to take place; thus you need to enthuse and motivate pupils, give purpose to learning tasks and provide active learning experiences. This unit has also touched on study skills, an important skill in preparing to sit public examinations.

This unit has focused on reading, writing, listening and talking, and how to help pupils get the most out of such experiences. There is much hands-on activity in practically-based subjects, such as art and design, home economics, science and technology. Working with your hands does not guarantee that learning takes place – hand and brain need to be involved. Pupils need to be involved in the design, execution and evaluation of practical work in the same way as we have stressed the need for their active involvement in reading and listening. Active learning helps you to monitor pupil progress and supports formative assessment. Active learning has been contrasted with rote learning, a smaller but important part of learning.

The key to good teaching is preparation and this is very important if you select active learning strategies. Active learning strategies are a key part of your teaching repertoire and contribute significantly to your Career Entry Profile. You should check the range of teaching strategies expected of you as an NQT, using the list of standards/competences for your course. Further advice and guidance on active learning are in the further reading section.

APPENDIX 5.2.1 ACTIVE LEARNING METHODS (FOR USE WITH TASK 5.2.6)

Brainstorming
Case studies
Computer-assisted learning
Creative writing
DARTS
Debating
Designing
Developing multimedia presentations
Diaries
Drama
Experiments
Fieldwork

Formal presentations
Games
Interviewing
Problem solving
Reports
Role play
Simulations
Small group discussion
Surveys
Teacher demonstration
Visitors
Visits

FURTHER READING

Bennett, N. and Dunne, E. (1994) 'How children learn: implications for practice' in B. Moon and A. Shelton-Mayes (eds) *Teaching and Learning in the Secondary School*, London: Routledge, pp. 50–56.

Centre for Science Education, Sheffield (1992) *Active Teaching and Learning Approaches in Science*, London: Collins Educational.
A detailed discussion of active learning methods, copiously illustrated with examples. Useful to all teachers, not only science teachers.

Child, D.(1997a) 'Learning theories and practice' in D. Child, *Psychology and the Teacher*, (6th edn), London: Cassell, pp. 112–151, especially p. 127.
A useful introduction to the ways in which learning can be explained and their application to the classroom.

Cockburn, A.D. (1995) 'Learning in classrooms' in C. Desforges, *An Introduction to Teaching: Psychological Perspectives*, Oxford: Blackwell.
Based on research evidence in classrooms, the chapter identifies classrooms as busy places, but what is learned is not always what is expected. Pupils use what they are taught in unexpected ways. A number of strategies are discussed including active learning.

Sutton, C. (ed.) (1981) *Communicating in the Classroom*, London: Hodder and Stoughton.
An older but valuable book illustrating ways of supporting pupils in their own learning. Full of practical classroom ideas and suggestions for lesson planning.

MARILYN LEASK

INTRODUCTION

In Chapter 1, you were asked to consider what kind of teacher you would like to become. In working through this unit, we hope you take the opportunity to analyse your teaching to see what has to happen if you are to achieve your goals. Everyone's 'natural' teaching style varies but you also need to be able to use other teaching styles which are more appropriate to particular lesson objectives and particular characteristics of the pupils. Thus, building your repertoire of teaching styles is a necessary part of your professional development. See also Unit 3.2, Task 3.2.9.

OBJECTIVES

By the end of this unit, you should:

- understand how teacher behaviour and teaching strategies combine to produce a teaching style;
- understand the importance of using a range of teaching styles;
- have experimented with different styles of teaching and evaluated their effectiveness.

We suggest you check the competences/standards for your course to see what is required in the area of teaching styles.

WHAT DO WE MEAN BY A TEACHING STYLE?

Teaching style is the term used to describe the way a learning experience is conducted. It is built from the behaviour of the teacher and the strategy chosen to ensure that the planned learning takes place, that the lesson objectives are achieved. Table 5.3.1 illustrates this point.

Table 5.3.1 Defining a teaching style

teaching style = teacher behaviour + teaching strategy

By **teacher behaviour** we mean the demeanour of the teacher and the way the teacher relates to pupils; for example, a teacher may choose to be distant, to be more friendly or to convey enthusiasm for their subject. The teacher indicates their expectations to pupils through their behaviour when teaching the class.

Teachers also adopt particular forms of behaviour to foster certain types of learning. For example, the teacher may see themselves as a facilitator of learning in a situation where group discussion has been chosen as the teaching method and the teacher's role is both to help individuals to contribute fully and to ensure that the group functions effectively. Or the teacher may take the role of transmitter of knowledge where knowledge acquisition is the desired outcome.

By **teaching strategy**, we mean the choice and range of teaching methods used for a lesson; for example, a teaching strategy for a drama lesson might include the methods of individual enquiry (pupil research), discussion and pupil demonstration. Unit 5.2 provides examples of a range of methods which might be used when you are devising your teaching strategies. Discussion, role play, investigational work and demonstration are among the methods from which a teacher may choose. The method chosen influences decisions about assessment, routines, pupil grouping, and choice of materials.

In any lesson you are likely to use a range of styles in order to achieve your objectives. It is, for example, common to start with a didactic style, setting out what is to be done in the lesson, and then move on to a facilitator/pupil-centred style as pupils tackle the work set, then return to a more formal style at the end of the lesson to check that the intended learning has taken place.

Precisely defining the teaching style of a particular teacher is a difficult if not impossible task as in each teaching and learning situation there are many individual variables operating.

Some of the terms often used to describe ways of teaching are: experiential, didactic, chalk and talk, teacher-directed, pupil-centred, practical, theoretical, traditional, progressive, transmission, content-based, process-based, whole-class-based. But these are general descriptions which at best give an indication of how a teacher might conduct a lesson or part of a lesson, and the boundaries implied between the styles are blurred. On their own, these descriptions provide just part of the picture of how a teacher teaches. For example, two teachers could both use 'chalk and talk' as a teaching strategy but their behaviour would influence their overall style and thus the pupils' learning. If one was very formal, the learning of pupils in that class might be more passive than for pupils of a teacher who was enthusiastic, interested in them and who actively engaged them in the material.

LEARNING OUTCOMES AND TEACHING STYLE

Teaching styles are chosen to suit the characteristics of the pupils (i.e. their attitudes, abilities, preferred learning styles) and specifically to help you achieve your lesson objectives. For example, an 'instructional' style is particularly appropriate in achieving certain types of learning – when you want to develop particular skills such as explaining how a piece of equipment is to be used. It may not be the most effective approach in other instances, such as learning about colour mixing in art, which may best be done through practical activities which reinforce the learning taking place. In choosing objectives for a particular lesson, you need to decide which of a whole range of potential learning outcomes are to be the focus of the lesson.

The style you choose should be one which best enables those objectives to be realised. Table 5.3.2 provides examples of learning outcomes. These are based on the aspects of achievement defined later on in Table 6.1.1 (see p. 294). Some people find it convenient to apply the **CASK** model to learning outcomes, i.e. learning outcomes are defined as relating to the development of pupils' **C**oncepts, **A**ttitudes, **S**kills or **K**nowledge.

If you always use a particular style then there is a danger that the learning outcomes for your pupils may be restricted to a narrow band. Your pupils may be high achievers in one aspect of achievement but low achievers in another aspect. Of course, pupils do not depend on their learning in one subject for their overall development; a school needs to ensure that across the whole curriculum there are opportunities for pupils to achieve in all of the areas outlined in Table 5.3.2.

Table 5.3.2 Examples of learning outcomes from a lesson

Aspect 1   *Acquisition of knowledge and ability to demonstrate this*, e.g. through focusing on knowledge retention, memorisation, written expression, acquiring theoretical knowledge, individual achievement.

Aspect 2   *Ability to apply knowledge*: through developing communication skills, oral skills, investigative skills, transferability of knowledge, ability to research, organise, select material.

Aspect 3   *Increased personal and social skills* such as self-confidence, leadership skills, accepting responsibility, initiative, ability to work with other people.

Aspect 4   *Improved attitudes to learning* demonstrated through increased motivation, perseverance, commitment, self-reliance.

Source: Adapted from ILEA, 1984, p. 2.

FACTORS AFFECTING CHOICE OF TEACHING STYLES

As well as taking account of the characteristics of the pupils and the desired learning outcomes, your choice of teaching style is a matter for your professional judgement. Any judgement you make about appropriate teaching styles is based on:

* your professional knowledge;
* the environment in which you teach and the resources available;
* your personal qualities.

Extent of your professional (pedagogic) knowledge

This book provides a brief introduction to the body of pedagogic knowledge available (pedagogy can be defined as the 'science of teaching'). Teacher education is considered to fall into three phases: initial teacher education, induction – which is the education and training you are given during your first year of teaching; and continuing professional development (CPD) – formerly 'in-service education and training' (INSET) – which should be available throughout your teaching life. See Unit 8.2 for further information on continuing professional development.

Your choice of teaching style is affected by your beliefs, views and assumptions as well as professional knowledge in, for example, the following areas:

* **Your theories of how teachers should teach and how pupils learn**. For example, teachers hold differing views about the place of negotiation in the classroom, appropriate teacher/pupil interaction, appropriate pupil/pupil interaction, the teacher's role (purveyor of knowledge, interpreter of knowledge, facilitator of learning) and the use of questions. Decisions you make about the balance in your lessons between the process of learning and the content influence your style. By a 'process' approach to teaching and learning, we mean an approach that focuses on teaching through activities like problem solving, skill-based learning, experiential learning, role play, simulations, collaboration. At the other end of the spectrum, content-focused teaching means that mastery of content is the focus and it is achieved through,

for example, a transmission style, chalk and talk, rote learning or didactic teaching. Your theories about learning reveal themselves in a number of ways: for example, whether you make subject matter relevant to pupil experiences and interests, in the variety of resources you use, or in the way you group the pupils.

- **Your approach to classroom management**. Your views on maintenance of discipline, including noise, movement and talk, influence the way you teach (see Unit 3.3).
- **Your confidence and competence** with the subject matter and with classroom management affect your behaviour and hence your teaching style.

The environment in which you teach

There are many environmental issues which affect your teaching – physical and mental state of the pupils, school/department decisions about pupil grouping (setting/streaming/mixed ability), type and layout of room, and the range and availability of teaching materials and equipment. Resources are usually limited and you need to adjust to the circumstances in which you find yourself. Two other influential factors are class size and your assumptions and knowledge about the pupils.

- **Class size**. There are some government ministers and officials who argue that class size has no effect on achievement. It is a convenient argument for those who allocate resources to education as the theory supports the limiting of resources. However, we believe that class size inevitably influences your choice of teaching style and so affects what can be achieved. Teaching a large group of pupils where a significant majority are demotivated is not the same as teaching the same size group of highly motivated pupils. Similarly, developing oral skills in a class of thirty is a different matter from developing them with a class of six.
- **Your assumptions and knowledge about the pupils**. Teacher expectations have a significant effect on pupil self-esteem, motivation and achievement and it is too easy for teachers to make damaging assumptions about pupils from backgrounds different from their own. This can lead to discrimination and must be avoided. This can be done by increasing your knowledge and understanding of the social and cultural influences on the pupils (see Chapter 4, especially Unit 4.4). Educational researchers such as Feuerstein, Vygotsky and Bruner have written extensively on the impact of social context on learning and their work is referred to in the texts listed at the end of this unit and Unit 5.1.

Your personal qualities

Your imagination, enthusiasm, energy, and ability to form positive relationships with pupils, as well as prejudices and assumptions about gender and race all contribute to your classroom behaviour and thus influence your teaching style. Your communication skills such as body language, voice and other issues, outlined in Chapter 3, also significantly affect your teaching style.

IDENTIFYING TEACHING STYLES

Findings of research on teaching styles are reported in Table 5.3.3 and the framework used to analyse styles may provide you with an approach to analysing your own styles. Three broad bands of style were identified:

1 **closed** – which was a more didactic and formal way of teaching with little pupil involvement in the material of the lesson;

2 **framed** – where the teacher provided a structure for the lesson within which pupils were able to contribute their own ideas and interpretations;

3 **negotiated** – where the direction of the lesson was to a considerable extent dependent on pupil ideas and contributions. This style may be appropriate, for example, for project work.

Table 5.3.3 Identifying teaching styles

	The participation dimension		
	Closed	Framed	Negotiated
Content	Tightly controlled by teacher; not negotiable.	Teacher controls the topic, frames of reference and tasks; criteria made explicit.	Discussed at each point; joint decisions.
Focus	Authoritative knowledge and skills; simplified and monolithic.	Stress on empirical testing; processes chosen by the teacher; some legitimation of pupil ideas.	Search for justification and principles; strong legitimation of pupil ideas.
Pupils' role	Acceptance; routine performance; little access to principles.	Join in teacher's thinking; make hypotheses, set up tests; operate teacher's frame.	Discuss goals and methods critically; share responsibility for frame and criteria.
Key concepts	'Authority': the proper procedures and the right answers.	'Access to skills', processes and criteria	'Relevance': critical discussion of pupils' priorities.
Methods	Exposition: worksheets (closed); note giving; individual exercises; routine practical work. Teacher evaluates.	Exposition, with discussion eliciting suggestions; individual/group problem solving; lists of tasks given; discussion of outcomes, but teacher adjudicates.	Group and class discussion and decision making about goals and criteria. Pupils plan and carry out work, make presentations, evaluate success.

Source: Adapted from Barnes *et al.*,1987, p. 25.

In Table 5.3.3, the choices that teachers make about teaching styles are analysed under the headings: content, focus, pupils' role, key concepts and methods.

Task 5.3.1

PUPIL PARTICIPATION AND TEACHING STYLES

Look at the continuum of styles identified by Barnes *et al.* in Table 5.3.3:

_____ **Closed** _____ **Framed** _____ **Negotiated** _____

and consider what the level of pupil participation in your lessons is. Check, through discussion with your tutor or other student teachers, that you understand and would recognise these different styles. With the agreement of the teacher or student teacher concerned, use the framework provided by the table to analyse the teaching styles in some lessons or parts of lessons which you are observing.

Mosston's continuum of teaching styles

Mosston and Ashworth (1994) carried out careful analytical work on teaching styles and their ideas are worthy of much more detailed consideration than is possible here. They define the components of different teaching styles in considerable detail and use a framework (the 'anatomy of a teaching style') as a basis for analysis and comparison for each one. Table 5.3.4 provides a brief outline of the styles they define. Like Barnes *et al.*, they see these styles as being part of a continuum – moving from teacher-controlled and directed learning experiences through to more independent learning.

Mosston and Ashworth describe the links between 'teaching behaviour, learning behaviour and the objectives of each style' – the T-L-O approach to use their terms. They point out that there are two aspects to objectives: intended objectives and the actual objectives observed. They also describe in detail the decisions made by teacher and learner during three phases of learning: pre-impact ('preparation'), impact ('execution and performance') and post-impact (or 'evaluation' which is ongoing throughout the lesson). A number of the styles above require the teacher to teach the pupils the style of learning they are expected to be undertaking. Developing such awareness on the part of the pupils can be seen as one of the objectives for learning.

Task 5.3.2

MOSSTON'S CONTINUUM OF TEACHING STYLES

Consider Mosston's continuum as described in Table 5.3.4. Think back to a recent lesson you taught which did not go as well as you had planned. Was the dominant teaching style you used the most suitable, i.e. did it achieve the objectives of the lesson? How else could you have tackled the lesson material? Discuss Mosston's work with other student teachers. Are his categories useful in providing you with alternative approaches? If not, why not?

Table 5.3.4 Mosston's continuum of teaching styles

The command style   This style is often described as autocratic or teacher-centred. It is appropriate in certain contexts, e.g. teaching safe use of equipment, learning particular routines in dance.

The practice style   Whilst similar to the command style, there is a shift in decision making to pupils and there is more scope with this style for the teacher to work with individuals whilst the group are occupied with practice tasks, such as writing for a purpose in English or practising skills in mathematics.

The reciprocal style   The pupils work in pairs evaluating each other's performance. Each partner is actively involved – one as the 'doer' and one observing, as the 'teacher partner'. The teacher works with the 'teacher partner' to improve their evaluative and feedback skills. This style provides increased possibilities for the 'partner' to improve their evaluative and feedback skills. It provides increased possibilities for 'interaction and communication among students' and can be applied when pupils are learning a foreign language or learning routines in gymnastics. Pupils learn to judge performance against criteria.

The self-check style   This style is designed to develop the learner's ability to evaluate their own performance. The teacher sets the tasks and the pupils evaluate their performance against criteria and set new goals in collaboration with the teacher. All pupils start at the same level and move up when the teacher deems them ready.

The inclusion style   In this style, differentiated tasks are included to ensure that all pupils gain some feeling of success and so develop positive self-concepts – for example, if an angled bar is provided for high jump practice, all pupils can succeed as they choose the height over which to jump. They decide at what level to start.

Guided discovery   Mosston sees this as one of the most difficult styles. The teacher plans the pupil's learning programme on the basis of the level of cognitive development of the learner. The teacher then guides the pupil to find the answer – reframing the question and task if necessary. Pupils with special educational needs are often taught in small groups and this approach might be used by the teacher to develop an individualised learning programme for each pupil.

Divergent style   The learners are encouraged to find alternative solutions to a problem, e.g. in approaching a design problem in art.

The individual programme: learner's design   The knowledge and skills needed to participate in this method of learning depend on the building-up of skills and self-knowledge in earlier learning experiences. A pupil designs and carries out a programme of work within a framework agreed and monitored by the teacher. Pupils carrying out open-ended investigations in science provide an example of this style.

Learners' initiated style   This style is more pupil-directed than the previous style where the teacher provided a framework. At this point on the continuum, the stimulus for learning comes primarily from the pupil not wholly from the teacher. The pupil actively initiates the learning experience. Giving homework which allows pupils freedom to work on their own areas of interest in their own way would fall into this category. The teacher acts in a supportive role.

Self-teaching style   This style describes independent learning without external support. For example, it is the type of learning that adults undergo as they learn from their own experiences.

Source: Adapted from Mosston and Ashworth, 1994.

ANALYSING YOUR TEACHING STYLE

One of our student teachers, who carried out an analysis to establish the level of her interaction with pupils during a lesson, found that over a twenty-minute period she spent only about ninety seconds supporting the work of individual pupils (there were twenty-three pupils in the class). For most of the rest of the time she was addressing the class as a whole. What surprised her was that she had intended her lesson to be much more pupil-centred and thought she had gone some way to achieving that. Unit 5.4 gives examples of ways in which you can evaluate your work. This student used another student to observe and record interactions. An observation sheet was used which required the observer to note every five seconds whether the teacher/pupil interaction was at a group level, an individual level or a whole class level. Such observation sheets need to be designed with the particular purpose in mind. Recording every five seconds is rather too often for some purposes but it worked in this case as the observer had to remember only three codes:

G – group   I – individual   W – whole class.

Table 5.3.5 shows the format these students used.

Table 5.3.5 An observation grid

Time (mins)	Type of interaction (G = group, I = individual, W = whole class) at five-second intervals										
5	G	G	G	G	G	G	G	W	W	W	W	W
6	W	W	W	G	G	G	I	G	G	G	I	I

Task 5.3.3

ANALYSING ASPECTS OF YOUR TEACHING STYLE

Arrange for another student teacher to observe two of your lessons where you try out contrasting styles. Ask them to focus on particular aspects of your work which interest you, e.g. the use of open-ended questions or giving praise. You probably need to devise your own observation schedules to record the findings. In the discussion afterwards you may find it useful to answer the following questions. Did you achieve your objectives? How successful were you in varying your teaching style? What factors influenced your success? How could you have done things differently? What could you try next? If you can repeat this exercise regularly, you will build up your repertoire of styles and your responsiveness to changing classroom situations.

SUMMARY AND KEY POINTS

In this unit, we have tried to identify factors that influence teaching style and asked you deliberately to structure some lessons in ways which allow you to explore factors influencing your teaching style. Acquiring knowledge of different teaching strategies and becoming aware of your own behaviour in the classroom are two steps on the ladder to effectiveness. However, you need to move from knowing about how these aspects influence teaching style to being able to apply this professional knowledge to your classroom teaching so that effective learning can take place. Applying a reflective approach to your teaching helps you develop your skills. The following unit, 5.4 'Improving your teaching', provides details of reflective strategies which will help you in the further analysis of aspects of your own teaching.

FURTHER READING

Coles, M.J. and Robinson, W.D. (1991) *Teaching Thinking: A Survey of Programmes in Education* (2nd edn), Bristol: Bristol Press.

This is a book which will challenge your views about what you should teach and how you should teach it. It describes a number of Thinking Skills/Critical Thinking programmes in the UK, as well as discussing international developments, such as the Philosophy for Children programme which was started in the USA by Mathew Lipman, and Feuerstein's Instrumental Enrichment programme which originated in Israel.

Dennison, B. and Kirk, R. (1990) *Do, Review, Learn, Apply: A Simple Guide to Experiential Learning*, Oxford: Blackwell Education.

This is a very practical book. It includes an introduction to the theory supporting the experiential learning approach as well as a host of ideas and practical activities which may be used in experiential learning situations.

Dockrell, J. and McShane, J. (1999) *Children's Learning Difficulties – A Cognitive Approach*, Oxford: Blackwell.

This book addresses the question 'What impedes a child's progress in acquiring new knowledge?' It takes difficulties with language, reading and numbers in turn and describes strategies for assessing learning difficulties as well as what they call ' a cognitive frame of reference' for the understanding of learning difficulties.

Fisher, R. (1995) *Teaching Children to Learn*, Cheltenham: Stanley Thornes.

This text, following Robert Fisher's work on thinking skills, focuses on current issues such as questioning, discussing, cognitive mapping, divergent thinking, co-operate learning, coaching, reviewing and creating a learning environment. Again, it is full of ideas which can help you as a teacher perform more effectively.

Jarvis. P., Holford, J. and Griffin, C. (1998) *The Theory and Practice of Learning*, London: Kogan Page.

This text provides a useful summary of a wide range of different theories of learning and approaches to the organisation of learning which are appropriate in different contexts. You are recommended to read this to gain an overview of the different theories that exist.

Joyce, B., Calhoun, E. and Weil, M. (1999) *Models of Teaching* (6th edn), Boston and London: Allyn and Bacon.

Joyce and Weil identify models of teaching and group them into four 'families' which represent different philosophies about how humans learn. This is a comprehensive text designed for those who have knowledge of teaching and learning issues. See also Mager, below.

Mager, R. (1997) *Preparing Instructional Objectives – A Critical Tool in the Development of Effect Instruction* (3rd edn), London: Kogan Page.
Mager provides a transatlantic perspective on training. He has written many books around the theme of goal-setting and teaching techniques. Although this book is focused on skills-based objectives, nevertheless the exercises in it will help you develop your skills in setting objectives.

McGuiness, C. (1999) *From Thinking Skills to Thinking Classrooms: A Review and Evaluation of Approaches for Developing Pupils' Thinking*, London: DfEE.

Mosston, M. and Ashworth, S. (1994) *Teaching Physical Education* (4th edn), New York: Macmillan College Publishing.
This text describes a continuum of teaching styles. Although written for physical education teachers, the styles described are applicable to different extents in all subjects.

UNIT 5.4 **IMPROVING YOUR TEACHING**
An introduction to action research and reflective practice

MARILYN LEASK

INTRODUCTION

How do you know your lesson went well?

This is a question you can expect to be asked from time to time and you need to be able to provide answers. The purpose of teaching pupils is that they learn. The fact that pupils are quiet and look as if they are working industriously is no guarantee that the learning you have intended is taking place.

In this unit, we introduce you to straightforward techniques which may help you to find answers to your questions about your teaching. In carrying out the tasks in this book you are engaging in 'reflective practice'. Action research is a term used to describe reflective practice. Action research is the investigation of professional practice by practitioners themselves. Action research methods encompass the methods you have been using – observation, keeping a diary, obtaining the perspectives of different interested parties (pupils, staff) and examining documentation. The work in this unit provides a brief introduction to this area and we suggest that, once you are qualified, you extend your knowledge and understanding of the tools of action research as part of your further professional development.

OBJECTIVES

By the end of this unit you should:

*   be able to demonstrate an understanding of the action research process;
*   know about different forms of evidence which you could draw on in answer to the question 'How do you know your lesson went well?'
*   have applied action research strategies to evaluate and improve aspects of your teaching;
*   understand that acquiring a high level of professional knowledge and professional judgement is a long-term learning process which can be developed by the use of reflection based on evidence gained from action research.

Check the competences/standards for your course to see which in particular relate to this unit.

THE PROCESS OF ACTION RESEARCH

Action research describes a process which teachers use to find out about the quality of teaching and learning taking place. It is based on a simple process.

In your classroom observations, you may have started with a clear focus or a question to answer (e.g. what routines does the teacher use in managing the work of the class?), and you may have collected evidence from various sources to answer that question. You may have observed and made notes about what the pupils and the teacher actually did during the lesson; you may have looked at the pupils' work and the teacher's lesson plans; you may have cross-checked your perceptions with those of the teacher as a way of eliminating bias, improving accuracy and identifying alternative explanations. Texts and lectures should have provided a theoretical framework for you to use in analysing what was happening. So, like any action researcher, you have gathered data from different sources, checked for alternative perceptions/explanations, and drawn on all of this in making your conclusions so as to improve your work in the future. Table 5.4.1 sets out the process in more detail.

Table 5.4.1 An action research framework

What do we want to know? It is important to define the question clearly – perhaps breaking the question down into several sub-questions.

- Who has or where are the data needed to answer the question?
- How much time and what other resources can be devoted to exploring this issue?
- How are we going to collect the data?
- When do we need to collect the data?
- What ethical questions arise from the collection and use of these data?
- How are we going to analyse and present the data?
- Are we prepared and able to make changes in the light of the findings?

HOW DO YOU KNOW YOUR LESSON WENT WELL?

To help you answer this question, we provide you with a set of criteria (see Tables 5.4.2 and 5.4.3). We suggest you use these data in two ways. First, in Task 5.4.1 we ask you just to reflect on your own teaching using the criteria in Table 5.4.2. Secondly, we ask you to carry out a small action research project in which you evaluate some aspects of teaching and learning (see Task 5.4.2).

Task 5.4.1

FOCUSING ON EFFECTIVENESS

Look at the criteria listed in Tables 5.4.2 and 5.4.3, or use criteria provided in your course material, and identify areas in which you feel competent already. Now consider those with which you have had difficulty. Choose one or two of these issues for further investigation. Later in this unit, you are given a task which asks you to plan a strategy for investigating these issues in the classroom.

Having listed criteria for effective teaching and learning, we move on to the question: what evidence can be collected to show that effective teaching and learning are taking place? The collection and evaluation of evidence should enable you to answer with some confidence. But what counts as evidence?

Table 5.4.2 OFSTED: criteria for judging the quality of teaching

Inspectors must evaluate and report on the quality of teaching, judged in terms of its impact on pupils' learning and what makes it successful or not. Inspectors must include evaluations of:

- how well the skills of literacy and numeracy are taught, particularly to pupils of primary age and any pupils of secondary age whose reading, writing or numeracy is poor;
- how well the school meets the needs of all its pupils, taking account of age, gender, ethnicity, capability, special educational needs, gifted and talented pupils, and those for whom English is an additional language;
- the teaching in each subject, commenting on any variations between subjects and year groups;
- how well pupils learn and make progress.

In determining their judgements, inspectors should consider the extent to which teachers:

- show good subject knowledge and understanding in the way they present and discuss their subject;
- are technically competent in teaching phonics and other basic skills;
- plan effectively, setting clear objectives that pupils understand;
- challenge and inspire pupils, expecting the most of them, so as to deepen their knowledge and understanding;
- use methods which enable all pupils to learn effectively;
- manage pupils well and insist on high standards of behaviour;
- use time, support staff and other resources, especially information and communications technology, effectively;
- assess pupils' work thoroughly and use assessments to help and encourage pupils to overcome difficulties;
- use homework effectively to reinforce and/or extend what is learned in school;

and the extent to which pupils:

- acquire new knowledge or skills, develop ideas and increase their understanding;
- apply intellectual, physical or creative effort in their work;
- are productive and work at a good pace;
- show interest in their work, are able to sustain concentration and think and learn for themselves;
- understand what they are doing, how well they have done and how they can improve.

Source: OFSTED, 2000c, p. 42.

SOURCES OF EVIDENCE ABOUT TEACHING AND LEARNING

The evidence available for drawing conclusions about teaching and learning can be divided into two types:

- qualitative data which are collected through observation, interview, questionnaires (especially open-ended questions), analysis of documents, diaries, video, photographs, discussions, focus groups, brainstorming.
- quantitative data which are collected from, for example, statistical returns, questionnaires, school management information systems, or other sources that can be reduced to numerical form.

Evidence of both types is used in action research. You need to develop a strategy for data collection which is appropriate for the issue under investigation.

Table 5.4.3 Principles of effective learning

(See also Hay McBer, 2000.)

The learners:

- clearly perceive the purpose of the lesson;
- see a practical application for what they are learning;
- solve genuine problems;
- have an active role in the processes of learning;
- use their initiative, exercise imagination and think for themselves;
- acquire knowledge and develop skills;
- develop good habits of work, including perseverance and a concern for correctness;
- derive enjoyment and satisfaction from a job well done and realise that these are related to the amount of effort they put in;
- discuss their work;
- receive constructive assessment of their efforts from the teacher and from fellow students;
- learn from their mistakes;
- perceive their own progress;
- change their ways of thinking about a subject or issue;
- improve their confidence and image of themselves.

The teaching:

- has a clear purpose and a strategy for achieving it;
- is firmly structured with a beginning, a middle and an end, yet with the possibility of being varied to take advantage of opportunities which arise unexpectedly;
- takes account of differences in learners' abilities;
- offers variety of activity and strikes a good balance between oral, practical and written work;
- involves effective use of learning aids and resources;
- proceeds at a brisk pace without sacrificing rigour;
- covers a good deal of ground in a challenging way;
- demands high standards and provides the learner with the opportunities and encouragement to achieve them;
- generates a dynamic atmosphere in which the individual can experience a shared sense of achievement.

Source: DES Conference N213, September 1988.

ACTION RESEARCH TECHNIQUES

You have already been using diaries, observation, discussions and documents to inform your thinking about teaching and learning. Questionnaires are useful for surveying pupil (or parent) views. Here we provide further advice about two areas which you may find particularly useful during your initial teacher education: observation schedules and paired observation.

Observation schedules

Unit 2.1 ('Reading classrooms') provides an example of an observation schedule, as does Unit 5.3 ('Teaching styles'). You should by now have used forms of these to observe classroom routines.

Hopkins (1993) and others listed in the further reading section provide other detailed examples of observation schedules. However, Hopkins suggests that you devise your own observation schedules to suit your particular purpose. It is not possible to record everything that happens in a classroom so you need to focus on, for example, a particular group or pupil or aspect of the teacher's work and record behaviour over time. The observation schedule provides a structured framework for recording classroom behaviours. Video recordings provide an additional way of recording data about classroom activities.

Paired observation

This is a streamlined procedure which enables you to obtain feedback on aspects of your work that are difficult for you to monitor. The example in Unit 5.3 of two students working together with one providing feedback on the topic chosen by the other is an example of paired observation in practice. Paired observation works in the following way.

Two colleagues pair up with the purpose of observing one lesson each and then giving feedback about particular aspects of the lesson or the teaching of the person observed. The person giving the lesson decides what the focus of the observation should be. The three stages of a paired observation are:

Step 1: You both agree the focus of the observation and what notes, if any, are to be made.
Step 2: You each observe one lesson given by the other. Your observations and notes are restricted to the area requested.
Step 3: You give each other feedback on the issue under consideration.

You can repeat the cycle as often as you like.

Task 5.4.2

A MINI-ACTION RESEARCH PROJECT

Look at an issue you identified in Task 5.4.1 for further investigation:

- Describe how the issue relates to your own teaching and the concerns you have about your teaching.
- List the behaviours related to the issue which you would expect to see displayed by a teacher successfully exercising this skill. For example, if you select 'clear objectives', identify:
- What is meant by 'clear' and to whom is it clear?

Discuss with your tutor how you can improve your work in this area and then evaluate your success using action research strategies described in this unit.

There is a wealth of information about your teaching which could be collected each lesson. However, you need to focus on specific aspects or you could be so swamped with information that you might feel unable to proceed. The goal is to become a more effective teacher through regular reflection, to check your skills as well as to develop your professional knowledge and judgement.

Task 5.4.3

SCHOOL-BASED ACTION RESEARCH

Find out about the types of evidence and processes used in the school to evaluate effectiveness of teaching and pupils' learning as well as to monitor pupil progress and set goals for pupils (target setting). Schools are developing increasingly detailed information systems providing data about targets and pupils' achievement. Departments may collect data to inform their development plans.

ETHICAL ISSUES

A word of warning! There are ethical considerations to be taken into account when you are collecting data from pupils and teachers. You must have agreement from those who are in a position to give this – your tutor may advise you to get the permission of the headteacher. You need to take your responsibility in this area seriously. Table 5.4.4 outlines the key areas to consider.

If you intend to develop your action research skills, then we suggest that you read several of the set texts and consult with experienced colleagues, as, in this unit, we have provided simply a brief introduction into an important area of professional practice and accountability.

Table 5.4.4 An ethical approach to action research

You must take responsibility for the ethical use of any data collected and for maintaining confidentiality. We suggest that you should, as a matter of course:

1 Ask a senior member of staff as well as the teachers directly involved with your classes for permission to carry out your project.

2 Before you start, provide staff involved with a copy of the outline of your project which includes:

- the area you are investigating;
- how you are going to collect any evidence;
- from whom you intend to collect evidence;
- what you intend to do with the data collected (e.g. whether it is confidential, whether it will be written up anonymously or not);
- who the audience for your report will be;
- any other factors relevant to the particular situation.

Check whether staff expect to be given a copy of your work.

If you store data electronically, then you should check that you conform to the requirements of the Data Protection Act. For example, you should not store personal data on computer disks without the explicit authorisation of the individual.

SUMMARY AND KEY POINTS

Developing your teaching skills is one important aspect of your professional development. But other important attributes of the effective teacher which we stress in this book are the quality and extent of your professional knowledge and judgement.

Skills can be acquired and checked relatively easily. Building your professional knowledge and judgement are longer-term goals which are developed through reflection and further professional development.

In this unit, we have opened a door on a treasure-trove of strategies which you can use to reflect on the quality of your work. We suggest that you come back to this work during the year, and again, later in your career, when you have fully mastered the basic teaching skills. The application of action research to your work at that stage opens your eyes to factors influencing your teaching and learning which you didn't know existed.

Over the early years of your teaching you acquire many teaching skills; they become part of what you could think of as your professional tool kit. But teaching skills, like tools, can become rusty or are perhaps not suitable for the job in the first place. Critical reflection aided by action research, by individuals or by teams, provides the means by which the quality of teaching and learning in the classroom can be evaluated as a prelude to improvement.

If you are seeking to understand an approach which provides you with tools to evaluate your own professional work, then we hope this has helped. You should now have ideas about how to evaluate the quality of your teaching through using a continuous cycle of critical reflection so that you can plan improvement based on evidence.

FURTHER READING

The following texts all provide a grounding in aspects of action research.

Bell, J. (1999) *Doing Your Research Project: A Guide for First-Time Researchers in Education and Social Science* (3rd edn), Milton Keynes: Open University Press.

Dillion, J.T. (1994) *Using Discussion in Classrooms*, Buckingham: Open University Press.

Hopkins, D. (1993) *A Teacher's Guide to Classroom Research* (2nd edn), Milton Keynes: Open University Press.

Lewis, I. and Munn, P. (1987) *So You Want to do Research! A Guide for Teachers on How to Formulate Research Questions*, Edinburgh: Scottish Council for Research in Education with the General Teaching Council for Scotland.

Mortimore, P. (ed.) (1999) *Understanding Pedagogy and its Impact on Learning*, London: Paul Chapman. This text provides useful background to teachers wishing to understand issues related to pedagogy across the spectrum of age and sector.

Munn, P. and Drever, E. (1990) *Using Questionnaires in Small Scale Research: A Teacher's Guide*, Edinburgh: Scottish Council for Research in Education with the General Teaching Council for Scotland.

Queensland Department of Education (1996) *Principles of Effective Learning and Teaching*, Brisbane, Australia. Reprinted as an appendix in M. Leask and T. Terrell (1997) *Development Planning and School Improvement for Middle Managers*, London: Kogan Page.

Scottish Consultative Council on the Curriculum (1996) *Teaching for Effective Learning*, Dundee: http://claudius.sccc.ac.uk

Wragg, E.C. (1999) *An Introduction to Classroom Observation* (2nd edn), London: Routledge.
Wragg has written many texts on aspects of teaching and learning, e.g. questioning, classroom management, assessment, explaining.

Yin, R. (1994) *Case Study. Design and Methods* (2nd edn), London: Sage.

CHAPTER 6 **ASSESSMENT**

This chapter addresses the purposes of assessment and their relationships to teaching and learning. We discuss briefly changes in assessment practice and reporting in the late twentieth century. Both units in Chapter 6 discuss the concepts of validity and reliability and their ongoing tensions, together with the roles of formative and summative assessment. Assessment is needed to provide information about individual pupils' progress, to help the teacher devise appropriate teaching and learning strategies, to give parents helpful information about their child's progress, and to compare pupils and schools across the country. This chapter discusses the extent to which one test can provide this information and considers the design and application of tests in relation to their purpose.

In England and Wales in the 1990s, assessment and its reporting became a central issue in teaching and learning. The 1988 Education Reform Act introduced statutory subjects and statutory assessment procedures into the curriculum for the first time, together with national tests to monitor standards.

Unit 6.1, 'Assessment and accountability', gives an overview of the principles of assessment, taking into account formative and summative assessment, diagnostic testing and important ideas of validity and reliability. In addition, the difference between norm-referenced testing and criterion-referenced testing is introduced, and the nationally set tests are discussed in the light of these principles. This unit links assessment with the classroom teacher and looks at how the results of assessment can be used to identify progress and diagnose problems. The management of assessment is addressed. The unit touches on the broader issue of what could be assessed, as opposed to what is assessed, together with the role of assessment in the public accountability of teachers, school governing bodies and LEAs.

Unit 6.2, 'External assessment and examinations', considers assessment as exemplified by the GCSE and GCE Advanced Level. This unit links national monitoring of standards with your classroom work, again raising issues of accountability. Public assessments represent vital areas of your work. These examinations grade pupils on a nationally recognised scale and exercise control over entry to both jobs and higher education. Unit 6.2 addresses how national standards are maintained and national grades are awarded. In addition, recent national developments in vocational education (NVQ and GNVQ) are discussed and contrasts made between the assessment methods used for vocational courses and academic courses.

UNIT 6.1   ASSESSMENT AND ACCOUNTABILITY

TERRY HAYDN

INTRODUCTION

If you want to give someone directions, one of the first questions you would ask is 'Where are you now?'

(Driver, 1994, p. 42)

In how many lessons do all the pupils learn everything that the teacher is trying to teach?

Assessment covers all those activities that are undertaken by teachers and others to measure the effectiveness of teaching and learning. Assessment includes not only setting and marking pupils' work, tests and examinations but also the recording and reporting of the results. The results contribute evidence to the accountability of schools to parents, the public and government. When the term assessment is used it includes that work involved in recording and reporting results.

There is some research evidence to suggest that sometimes fewer pupils understand the topic after teaching than before the teaching has taken place – all that has happened is that the teacher has slightly disturbed the pupils' misconceptions and prior understandings, and confused them. (See, for instance, the *QED* documentary, 'Simple Minds', about pupils' misconceptions in science, quoted in Dickinson, 1998, p. 17.) In many lessons, some, many or even all pupils fail to understand some of the things that the teacher is trying to teach. Since there is no direct correlation between teaching and learning, it follows that frequently we are in a position where we are trying to assess to what extent our teaching has been successful, in order to know what to do next. Do you need to go over the topic again, with some or all of the pupils, or can you proceed to the next morsel of learning? Have pupils really understood what you were trying to teach, or might they forget it in a few days? Could they only answer questions correctly if you asked them exactly the same question as in the lesson, rather than asking them in a slightly different way? Can they make appropriate connections with contingent aspects of the topic? Which bits have they grasped, and which bits are still unlearned or only partially understood?

It is important to remember that assessment is often a starting point for learning, rather than something that comes as a sort of 'terminus' of the learning process. Unless you know 'where they are up to', and what their current ideas are, how do you know where to start? A key idea here is the 'planning loop', which encompasses your learning objectives, how to achieve them, teaching, assessing and evaluating, and from which a revised set of learning objectives emerges; see Figure 6.1.1. See also Figure 5.2.1 (p. 256).

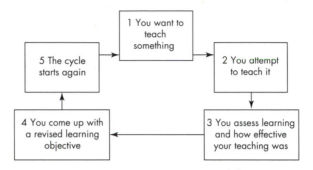

At stage 1 of the cycle, part of your thinking should be about how to assess pupil learning and the effectiveness of your teaching.

Figure 6.1.1   The planning/teaching/assessment/planning loop

There has been a revolution in assessment practice over the past twenty years. If you are to teach effectively it is important that you have a clear grasp of the key strands of assessment, including the purposes of assessment and some of the tensions between those purposes.

Assessment should not be an afterthought, or a tacked-on extra. For example, in England and Wales the National Curriculum Task Group on Assessment and Testing (TGAT) noted:

> The assessment process itself should not determine what is to be taught and learned. It should be the servant, not the master of the curriculum. Yet it should not simply be a bolt-on addition at the end. Rather, it should be an integral part of the education process, continually providing both 'feedback' and 'feedforward'. It therefore needs to be incorporated systematically into teaching strategies and practices at all levels. Since the results of assessment can serve a number of purposes, these purposes have to be kept in mind when the arrangements for assessment are designed.
>
> (DES/WO, 1988, para. 4)

to think about...

(For understandable reasons) student teachers often complete their lesson evaluations before they have marked pupils' work, following a lesson, and before the 'recap' questioning at the start of the next lesson. Keep in mind that the marking of pupils' work, and the questioning of pupils at the end of the lesson, or at the start of the next lesson, are important sources of feedback information for assessment purposes.

Task 6.1.1

YOUR OWN EXPERIENCE OF ASSESSMENT

Drawing on your own experiences as a learner, can you think of any examples of assessment that had a helpful influence on your learning? Were there any examples of assessment which were not helpful (i.e. a waste of time) or which were counter-productive in terms of your learning?

OBJECTIVES

By the end of this unit you should have:

* an understanding of the idea of the planning-teaching-assessment-planning 'loop', see Figure 6.1.1;
* an understanding of some of the ways in which teaching and learning can be assessed;
* an understanding of the differing purposes of assessment, and some of the tensions between them;
* some insight into how the present systems of assessment, evaluation and accountability have evolved;
* a knowledge of some important assessment terminology;
* an awareness of some strategies for making assessment and evaluation purposeful and manageable.

THE DISCOURSE OF ASSESSMENT

You should become familiar with some of the more important terminology which is commonly used in talking about assessment issues. We address some of this terminology below.

Formative and summative assessment

Formative assessment provides information which can aid further progress, diagnose reasons for both good and poor performance, and target particular learning needs. Summative assessment measures and reports on pupils' progress, as a 'verdict' on what has been achieved; it summarises achievement. Summative assessment occurs near the end of a piece of work, such as at the end of a Key Stage or GCSE module, or at the end of a course, such as the GCE A level or university first degree. Summative assessments are often used to determine access to further levels of education and training, or to employment opportunities where competition is fierce. As one writer said:

> Most examinations exist to distinguish better from worse. With a smaller supply of something than applicants for it – university places, training seats in racing cars, oboists' desks in a crack symphony orchestra – we need to pick out those who are to get it.
>
> (Ryan, 2000, p. 2)

This is education as 'positional goods'; there may not be enough places at University X, or Profession Y for all those who would like to enter them, even if they would be capable of completing the course, so assessment is used to decide who should get these places. Lambert makes the point that formative assessment is designed:

> primarily to serve the needs of teachers supporting individual learners, and is thus identified with professional purpose. Summative assessment can be associated more closely with bureaucratic purpose, serving the needs of the system as a whole, the administration and politicians.
>
> (Lambert, 1999, p. 289)

Norm- and criterion-referenced assessment

Norm-referenced assessment makes comparisons between a learner's performance and the performance of other learners, either within a teaching group or more widely. So to say that Alan came eighteenth out of his class of thirty pupils is to make a norm-referenced judgement. If we give Alan a mark out of ten, it does not in itself tell us what Alan can and cannot do, but we can use it to find out how Alan performed compared to the rest of the group. Commercially produced standardised tests can be used to determine where Alan stands in relation to a much broader sample of learners, placing him, perhaps, at the 40th percentile of those taking the test, which means that 40 per cent of learners of the same age scored lower than Alan on the test. Normative assessment is helpful when, for example, there are not enough places on a course of further education or not enough employment opportunities, so we have to make decisions as to who to give the places to. If there are thirty places, it may be that the places are allocated to the thirty candidates who scored most highly in the assessment.

Criterion-referenced assessment attempts to determine whether the learner has met pre-specified learning objectives. For example, the driving test tries to determine which candidates fulfil the criteria necessary to drive safely, without endangering others. It is not trying to establish a rank order. Thus:

> It wouldn't matter if nobody failed the driving test, as long as the standard of competence is high enough, and the test is conducted properly. A failure rate of 80 per cent would be fine too, if we thought the standard was right.
>
> (Ryan, 2000, p. 2)

Criterion referencing is an important part of formative assessment; teachers try to establish the criteria for 'becoming good' at a subject, and then use assessment to measure learners' progression towards expert levels in the various aspects of that subject. The information gained from assessment can be used to adjust teaching inputs, and act on emerging strengths and weaknesses.

In England and Wales, some subjects in the National Curriculum (NC) are divided into 'profile components'; the English curriculum, for example, is broken down into reading, writing, speaking and listening. The NC attainment levels attempt to establish criteria for progression in these profile components, which assists teachers in recognising and recording progression. The importance of norm-referenced and criterion-referenced assessment in public examinations is discussed in Unit 6.2.

Ipsative or 'value-added' assessment

Instead of measuring the performance of a learner against other learners (norm referencing), or against specified objectives (criterion referencing), the learner's performance can be measured against the learner's own previous levels of attainment. This is what is meant by 'ipsative assessment'. An example of ipsative assessment would be the concept of 'personal best' in athletics, where the athlete is striving to improve on previous performances.

The current emphasis on accountability in education has raised the profile of ipsative assessment because of the contribution it makes to value-added assessment. Unlike 'raw' league tables, which do not take into account pupils' prior attainment, ipsative assessment measures gains in personal learning and provides data on the extent to which the pupil, the teacher and the school have been able to improve learning. Some educationalists see 'value-added' assessment in terms of school effectiveness and as a way of making more informed comparisons between institutions; others note that if we are seriously to compare schools there are major issues of both validity and reliability in current test instruments; see, for instance, Haylock, 2001.

Validity and reliability

Validity describes the extent to which the exercise assesses exactly what it is intended to assess. If for instance the driving test was based solely on a written exercise, to what extent would we consider it a valid test of people's ability to drive safely? A history examination question, purporting to assess pupils' ability to use sources by providing a picture of Hitler stroking an Alsatian dog, asked 'Why did this man invade Poland?' (Shemilt, 1984). This might be a valid test of historical knowledge or recall, but is it a valid test of the ability to derive information from sources? Pupils who do well in the GCSE English examination are said to be 'good' at English, but what does this really mean? Validity is a complex subject because there might not even be general agreement about what it means 'to be good at' a subject. When we devise assessment exercises, we need to keep in mind the idea of validity; and, in marking the exercise, we need to keep in mind whether or not the way in which we constructed the test made it possible for pupils to provide a full and appropriate answer. Sometimes 'deficits' in responses can be the fault of poor question setting, rather than lack of knowledge and understanding on the part of pupils.

Reliability in assessment refers to the extent to which the assessment exercise is trustworthy in providing information about pupils' learning. If the assessment is repeated, does the test instrument give a similar result? Considering the reliability of an assessment helps answer questions such as:

- Is the test arbitrary and 'hit and miss' in terms of addressing the content with which the learners have worked?
- Would a different set of pupils with a similar range of abilities and backgrounds gain similar scores?
- Would you get the same result if you repeated the testing at a later date?

Haylock (2001) gives the example of bathroom scales as an instrument for measuring a person's weight, to help distinguish between validity and reliability. Bathroom scales are a valid (i.e. appropriate) way of finding out someone's weight; the scales can be reliable, that is, always respond in the same way to a given weight. However, bathroom scales may not be accurate, that is, record the true weight. In educational assessment, accuracy is subsumed into the concept of validity.

Lambert demonstrates that the way in which the question is posed can influence the outcomes of assessment (Lambert, 1999, p. 302). Figure 6.1.2 shows three ways in which pupils were tested on their ability to read information correctly from a pie chart. The number at the bottom left of the charts gives the proportion (%) of successful pupils in each case.

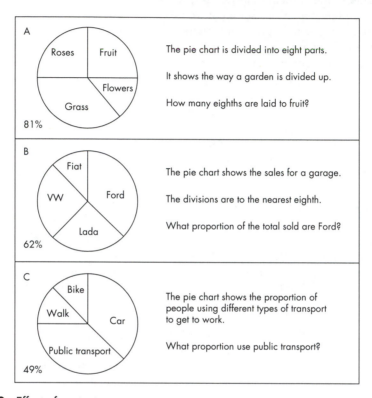

A

Roses | Fruit
Flowers
Grass

81%

The pie chart is divided into eight parts.

It shows the way a garden is divided up.

How many eighths are laid to fruit?

B

Fiat
VW | Ford
Lada

62%

The pie chart shows the sales for a garage.

The divisions are to the nearest eighth.

What proportion of the total sold are Ford?

C

Bike
Walk | Car
Public transport

49%

The pie chart shows the proportion of people using different types of transport to get to work.

What proportion use public transport?

Figure 6.1.2 Effect of context on assessment

Task 6.1.2

THE EFFECT OF CONTEXT ON PERFORMANCE

What explanations can you offer for the different success rates of pupils in reading pie charts; see Figure 6.1.2?
Is it possible to determine which is the most appropriate way of making this assessment?

It is important to remember that assessment is not an exact science. You need to be aware of the limitations and complexities involved in assessment.

'High' and 'low' stakes assessment

'**High stakes**' assessment occurs when the result is considered important, either for the learner, such as deciding the set into which the learner is placed; or for the school, such as influencing its position in league tables of school performance. This situation can have the effect of 'concentrating the learner's mind', ensuring that they revise for the test; but it can also lead to anxiety and a negative attitude to learning.

'**Low stakes**' assessment is the informal, day-to-day assessment where the results may not be formally recorded but which may set in motion a helpful dialogue between teacher and learner. One danger of this approach is that the learner may adopt a casual approach to such assessment and not really make the effort to engage with the task. Formative assessment may be seen as low-status. Some teachers claim that 'high challenge–low stress' assessment enables learners to feel free to 'have a go' and make mistakes which are helpful to the learning process in the longer term.

WHAT SHOULD BE ASSESSED?

It seems self-evident that assessment should measure what has been learned which in turn should relate to what has been taught. Teachers have to teach to a curriculum which in many cases is a statutory curriculum. The curriculum is transformed into a scheme of work and finally into lessons; lesson planning involves setting objectives. It is objectives which are assessed through formative and summative assessment methods and used to measure learning. Much emphasis is placed on cognitive skills at the expense of other equally valued qualities, such as the affective and interpersonal aspects of learning.

We often break down learning objectives into categories such as knowledge, understanding, skills and values. By far the most common categories of learning are knowledge and under-standing and it is these which are prominent in public examinations. Skills are assessed such as those needed to extract and analyse information from a range of resources. Many skills are of a practical nature related to using equipment, working with a range of materials, performing, making things or creating things.

The four categories of learning objectives identified above leave open the question of what should be tested and do not help us much to answer the question 'what counts as knowledge?' In practice the four categories of learning overlap. The four objectives do not include, for example, creativity, interpersonal relationships or self-knowledge; the development of creativity could be an important learning objective. Values is another problematical area in terms of asessment; for example, knowing and understanding the values held by different groups of people may be important in coming to an agreement on a controversial issue, e.g. the siting of a refuse site or the use of GM crops in food. Objectives such as these do not arise in most discussions of public examinations because some of these learning objectives are hard to assess, due to the difficulty of obtaining agreement on a valid and reliable test instrument. However, qualities such as values and creativity are highly rated by teachers and employers. In formulating our learning objectives, we must, therefore, be careful not to limit them to that which is easy to assess.

In an effort to draw attention to the wider dimensions of learning, the Education Committee of the Inner London Education Authority (abolished in the 1980s) drafted a broad set of aims for schools called 'Aspects of achievement' (Table 6.1.1). The set of aims was published in an attempt to counter the over-emphasis placed on some achievements through public examinations at the expense of playing down other equally important achievements.

Table 6.1.1 Aspects of achievement

'We offer these four aspects (of achievement) in order to clarify our own and our readers' thinking about achievement and we believe that such a scheme is appropriate to the educational aims of comprehensive schools and secondary school teachers.'

Aspect I
That aspect most strongly represented in GCSE: written expression, capacity to retain propositional knowledge and select from it in order to answer questions. Examinations tend to emphasise knowledge more than skills; memory more than problem solving or investigation; writing more than other forms of communication; speed more than reflection; and individual more than group achievement.

Aspect II
The capacity to interpret and apply knowledge. The emphasis here is practical rather than theoretical; oral rather than written; investigation and problem solving rather than recall. This aspect forms one part of public examinations, but one which is rarely important. It is more time-consuming and expensive to assess than Aspect I.

Aspect III
Personal and social skills. The capacity to communicate with others face to face; to work co-operatively in the interests of a wider group; initiative, self-reliance and skills of leadership. This is not an element assessed directly by traditional public examinations, including the GCSE.

Aspect IV
Motivation and commitment; the willingness to accept failure without destructive consequences; readiness to persevere and the self-confidence to learn despite the difficulty of the task.

This is often seen as a prerequisite of achievement rather than achievement in its own right, and yet motivation can be seen as an achievement in most walks of life. It is in many ways the most important aspect as it can affect outcomes in the other three.

Source: Hargreaves, 1984, p. 2.

The achievements listed were claimed to be helpful to teachers in analysing their teaching and assessing learning. However, like the four categories of learning referred to above, some aspects of achievement overlap and some are difficult to assess.

In England and Wales, the new NC now specifies a range of knowledge, understanding, skills and values that are in addition to those specified in the subject curriculum and which are expected to be taught across the curriculum (DfEE/QCA, 1999a, pp. 20–25); see also Unit 4.5 'Moral development and values'. This development may have been influenced by the ideas identified in Table 6.1.1. An important feature of learning across the NC is Key Skills, which include communication, application of number, ICT, improving one's own learning and performance, problem solving and thinking skills. Assessing the development of these areas of achievement across the curriculum has yet to be tackled.

RECENT DEVELOPMENTS IN ASSESSMENT PRACTICE IN THE UK

Assessment can seem a very complex task to student teachers. It takes time to become familiar with the battery of acronyms and the range of assessment procedures that are now part of the current educational landscape. Assessment is an integral part of your day-to-day classroom teaching, although to many it is over-bureaucratic. There are those who argue that pupils in England are being 'tested to destruction' and that assessment is in danger of becoming an unbalanced and counter-productive part of the 'planning loop'; see Figure 6.1.1.

It might be instructive, however, to look at the state of assessment before recent developments. This exercise can help you to develop some understanding of the tensions and complexities in this important area.

Figures 6.1.3 and 6.1.4 give some idea of the limitations of assessment strategies and the way they were reported in the 1960s. Figure 6.1.3 shows an end-of-year report on a pupil's progress across school subjects, and Figure 6.1.4 shows a record of a pupil's progress in physical education between the ages of 11 and 18. We ask you to discuss these reports in Task 6.1.3. Further examples of pre-NC assessment models with brief accompanying commentary can be found at the website of the University of East Anglia: http://www.uea.ac.uk/~m242/historypgce/assess

Subject	Position	Remarks	Master's Initials
English	12	Satisfactory progress.	L.S.
History	4	As usual, a very good term's work.	hcb
Geography	9	Progressing satisfactorily	TR.
French	5=	Very good this term.	HcR.
Latin	26=	Just satisfactory, but lacks confidence'.	ScB
Mathematics			
Chemistry	20	I was delighted with his Grade 3 in GCE. Possibly a little less happy with organic chemistry	Cy
Physics	27	Some progress made	cP

Figure 6.1.3   A pupil's school report, circa 1960

Name..

PHYSICAL TRAINING REPORT

Height feet ins.		Weight stns. lbs.		Chest Norm. Exp.		Physical Training	Games	Date
4	7	4	8½	23	26½	Fair work.		7.12.62
						Fair progress		27.3.63
4	7¾	4	9	22¾	25¼	Very fair		7.7.63
4	8½	4	12½	24	26¾	Fair		6.12.63
						Fair. Tries		6.3.64
4	9½	5	4			Fair progress. Keen.		13.7.64
4	9½	5	3½	24½	27½	Very fair progress.		1.12.64
						Fair.		1.4.65
						Very fair.		1.12.65
						Satisfactory term.		1.4.66
5	0½	5	10½			Has worked quite well.		7.7.66
						Satisfactory		7.12.66
						Quite good		7.7.67
						Very keen. Table-tennis & cross-country teams		6.12.67
						Keen and willing		26.6.68
						It is good to find a boy so willing to participate.		2.12.68

Figure 6.1.4 A pupil's physical training report, 1962–1968

SCHOOL REPORTS PRE-NATIONAL CURRICULUM

Figures 6.1.3 and 6.1.4 show the reports of an individual pupil, as written in the 1960s. Discuss the limitations and weaknesses of these reports as examples of summative assessment of performance and reporting.

Compare these two reports with a more recent example of an end-of-year report, shown in Figure 6.1.5. Identify the advantages and disadvantages of current school assessment and reporting procedures.

The example of a current school report for a secondary-aged pupil in Figure 6.1.5 is not designed to suggest that all developments in assessment have been positive and unproblematic in their effects.

Anytown High School

Subject:	**Science**		Date: **July 1999**
Name:	**A. Pupil**	Form:	**9Z**
Effort Grade:	**A**	Attainment Grade:	**A**
Set (if applicable):	**6 (out of 8)**		

Key:
A = Very good, B = Good, C = Satisfactory, D = Poor, E = Very poor (within the set)

Key Stage 3 Teacher Assessment: **Level 7**   Key Stage 3 NC SAT Assessment: **Level 5**

Teacher Comment:

Anthony has achieved an average of 87% in the class science tests this year; the class average is 72%. He is a bright boy who has steadily improved and worked hard. His written work is consistently good, but homeworks could be more thorough, methodical and neat. He could also ask and answer more questions in class. At the moment, physics is his weakest area; he must make sure that he puts extra effort in here so that it does not develop into a long-term weakness. His performance in the Standard Assessment Tests did not reflect his term performance. This is perhaps because he did not revise thoroughly, or with method and organisation. If he continues to work hard, he is capable of a good performance at GCSE.

Signed: A. Teacher

Figure 6.1.5   A school report, 1999

Most teachers and many schools are wrestling with the problem of how to make best use of assessment, how to ensure that the time and effort involved in assessing teaching and learning are not wasted, or even counter-productive. The moves towards 'breaking down' learning objectives into atomised 'Statements of Attainment', which occurred in the first NC, have been reversed with the recent introduction of 'level descriptors', which attempt a more holistic 'best-fit' mode of assessment. Although designed to reduce the administrative burden of assessment, the proliferation of assessment mechanisms in schools has meant that assessment remains a substantial part of teachers' workload. The range of assessments commonly in use includes: Records of Achievement, Standard Assessment Tests, Baseline Testing, Coursework, Profiling, Certificate of Achievement and World Class Tests. These terms are explained in the glossary to this book.

One student teacher is quoted as saying that 'responding to children's work is one of the most interesting and rewarding aspects of my teaching practice' (Dickinson, 1991, p. 66). However, marking sets of pupils' exercise books is not a source of unremitting pleasure; the time and effort invested in marking pupils' work can be a major drain on teachers' time and energy. There is the danger that time spent on assessment can take time away from teaching and learning; there is the danger of spending too much time 'weighing the pig instead of fattening it'.

To explore other tensions concerning assessment, it is helpful to consider the purposes behind assessing pupils' work.

THE PURPOSES OF ASSESSMENT

There are many reasons for carrying out assessment. We identify some reasons below and later ask you to discuss them in Task 6.1.4. The purposes include the following.

1 Acknowledge pupils' efforts

At a very basic level, but highly important, the purpose is to show pupils that you take an interest in their work. Even pupils who are not avid scholars are often disgruntled if they feel that you have not looked at their work, or if you are slow in returning it. Teachers are not the only ones to differentiate; pupils also differentiate, and 'rate' teachers who mark their work promptly and carefully. It is important that pupils know whether a piece of work is a vitally important assessment task, which you will scrutinise very carefully, or whether it is 'light touch' monitoring, in part to check that they have done their homework.

2 Motivate pupils

Most learners want to know how they are doing, and whether they have done well. It is an opportunity to give encouragement, to show your appreciation of their achievement or effort, and to give advice as to how to do better next time. Marking pupils' work can be a form of extrinsic motivation and can include 'rewards' such as merit marks and commendations, positive written or verbal comment, and grades and marks. But see 'Tensions and problems in assessment' in the next section, which qualifies these statements. Motivation is discussed in Unit 3.2.

3 Monitor progress

The heart of formative assessment is gaining information about pupils' progress. We assess pupils' learning in order to monitor their understanding and diagnose factors that may be blocking or

Figure 6.1.6   Assessment: from the receiving end

Why am I marking this?

Why do we have assessment?

Why are there so many different forms of assessment?

Is it helping pupils to learn more effectively?

Is it helping me to teach more effectively?

Figure 6.1.7 Why am I marking this work?

inhibiting learning. Some assessments are referred to as diagnostic assessment because they are designed specifically to probe misunderstandings or barriers to learning and so provide suggestions for ways forward. Formative assessment can give pupils an awareness of their comparative strengths and weaknesses and priorities for future learning. It is also a starting point for establishing a dialogue with a pupil about what they need to do to improve performance in your subject.

You can use the information gleaned from assessing pupils' written work, or oral responses, not just to give the work a mark or a grade, but to provide advice which helps them to respond better next time, or move on to another learning priority. In the longer term, you may be guiding pupils towards being able to monitor and evaluate their own learning and progress – learning how to learn.

4 Identify students with special educational needs (SEN)

The class teacher is in the front line of special needs diagnosis. The current SEN Code of Practice (DfE, 1994c) places responsibility on the classroom teacher to identify pupils who may have specific learning difficulties which are inhibiting them from performing to their full potential. The new Code maintains that responsibility: see Unit 4.6. Where such problems are encountered, the information is given to the school's Special Educational Needs Co-ordinator (SENCO) in order to draw up or adjust the pupil's Individual Education Plan (IEP). This aspect of your work includes identifying particularly able pupils, who may need some differentiated curriculum materials in order to make maximum progress and sustain motivation and engagement in learning.

5 Establish baseline evidence of achievement

At the start of a new phase of schooling, an audit of what each pupil can and cannot do is carried out in order to create a baseline against which future progress can be measured. This audit may be in particular subject areas, or by an intelligence test, or both. The information gained can help teachers to plan their teaching to match pupils' individual needs. These data make possible a measurement of the 'value-added' by the teacher or the school, by measuring increments in learning against the baseline score and by estimating progress over and above that expected by pupils of that ability.

Some teachers welcome baseline assessment as it takes into account pupils' prior accomplishments, in a way that 'raw' league table data do not. Others stress that the imprecision of such testing and its susceptibility to manipulation make it inappropriate for such 'high-stakes' functions. Baseline assessment is used, in part, to hold teachers to account for their pupils' progress (see point 12 on public accountability, below).

6 Detect pupil under-achievement

In order to monitor progress adequately your assessment of pupils' work should recognise pupils' ability, or potential, and previous educational performance. This process identifies pupil under-achievement, or accelerated achievement.

As well as previous school reports and SATs results there is an increasing range of commercial assessment instruments designed to provide a 'baseline' against which future performance can be calibrated. These include:

* Middle-years Information System (MidYIS);
* A Level Information System plus GNVQ (ALis+);
* Year Eleven Information System (Yellis);

all of which can be accessed from the website of the Centre for Education and Management, University of Durham; the URL is: http://cem.dur.ac.uk

A fourth instrument often used by schools is the Cognitive Abilities Test (CAT). The CAT measures a range of abilities using three tests: a verbal reasoning test, a non-verbal reasoning test and a third on number. Scores on CAT can be correlated with subsequent grades in, for example, GCSE and used to predict GCSE performance. This information contributes to value-added factors in reporting the effectiveness of schooling. The CAT is available from the National Foundation for Educational Research-Nelson; see their website for further information: www.nfer-nelson.co.uk

You should enquire whether any of these assessment systems, or others, are used in your school experience school to gain some insight into at least one of them. If a pupil has performed very well on one of these tests, but does not seem to be making appropriate academic progress, it can alert staff towards making an early intervention.

7 Report to parents

Both formative and summative assessment provide information for teachers to report to parents about their children's progress. Most parents are interested in how their children are doing in school, and good communications between parents, pupils and teachers can help pupils to learn more effectively. The 1988 Education Reform Act made it a minimum statutory requirement for schools to provide an annual report on pupils' progress. Many secondary schools also have a 'diary' system to aid communication between parents and the school. Parents are often required to sign this weekly to establish that they have seen details of homeworks set and comments on pupils' work and overall progress. Government guidance on reporting to parents makes the point that parents are not just interested in academic performance, and want to know about other aspects of their child's progress. The same guidance suggests that parents want to know about the child's performance in relation to the rest of the class and national standards, and how their child is progressing in relation to previous attainment and perceived potential. Parents should be told about their child's particular strengths and achievements, areas for development and improvement, and whether the child is behaving well, and is 'socially' adjusting to school life (QCA/DfEE, 2000).

8 Grouping of pupils

Schools have to make decisions about setting or grouping their pupils. The extent to which pupils are separated into teaching groups of similar abilities varies from school to school (see Unit 4.1 'Pupil grouping'). Where grouping strategies are used to stream or band pupils, assessment is needed to allocate pupils to groups. This is an important decision, of concern to parents, and it can have a significant impact on a pupil's own self-esteem and friendships. It is essential that there is reliable and transparent evidence to support this decision. The evidence includes an end-of-year examination or end-of-term tests. In the core subjects of English, mathematics and science, the results of end of Key Stage 2 or Key Stage 3 SATs may be used. The teacher's overall assessment of the pupil's class work and homework over the course of the year provides further evidence.

9 Measure end-of-course achievement

This summative assessment usually takes the form of an examination grade, a coursework mark, or an (NC) attainment level. Currently, all pupils are ascribed a level of attainment in each profile component of an NC subject at the end of each Key Stage. It is a formal judgement on the level of achievement in a subject, and can determine entry to subsequent stages of education, so it is important that the assessment is 'robust' in the sense of being carefully monitored for validity and reliability.

Not all countries place the same emphasis on external examinations at the age of 16 and 18 as does Britain. A visitor to Australia returning to Britain remarked:

> Of course, selection to higher education and by employers, that's what we use assessment for, and in this country, we have the public examinations system par excellence to do that. In other countries they don't use public examinations, they rely on the school's own assessment of the pupil's achievement and attainment at the end of school. I went to

Australia, where I was visiting Queensland talking to some academics, and they said 'well of course, we haven't had public exams here for 20 years', and I had to pick myself up off the floor because the thought of an education system that could function, and indeed function extremely well with no public exams whatsoever was to me, steeped in the English model, mind blowing.

(Gipps, 1995)

In the United States, special tests are used to determine university admissions; see, for example, the website of the Scholastic Aptitude Tests:

http://www.collegeboard.org/sat/center/html/answer.html

10   Compare pupils

As well as simply comparing pupils, assessment is sometimes used to place learners in a rank order. It was once common practice in some schools to rank pupils in each teaching group monthly in each subject, as well as in all subjects by combining their marks for each subject. These rank orders were displayed on a school notice-board, showing the positions of each pupil. This process did not provide information about what pupils could and could not do, but indicated only their performance relative to other pupils. As well as knowing what their children can and cannot do, parents are (understandably) concerned to know how their child is performing relative to other pupils in the class or school, and comparisons like those described above help parents; the information that they are 'doing well' does not necessarily assuage parental anxiety and concern. There is always the danger, however, that such comparisons may have a negative effect on the motivation of pupils who fare consistently badly in such assessments.

11   Monitor teaching and inform planning

The results of assessment help teachers find out the extent to which pupils have learned what they were trying to teach. This means checking for understanding, both in terms of getting to know which pupils have grasped what you were trying to teach and also those aspects of the topic learned by pupils. The results tell you also which topics need reinforcement or a change of teaching approach. The information can help to identify weaknesses in your teaching, as well as deficits in pupils' learning. Student teachers usually have to write evaluations of their lessons as part of their experience, and many student teachers gain helpful insights into their lessons from their evaluations and reflections. Advice on lesson evaluations can be found in Units 2.2 and 5.4. Your course materials will give advice on lesson evaluations, and some institutes of higher education place their advice on the World Wide Web – for example, the University of East Anglia:

http://www.uea.ac.uk/~m242/historypgce/assess

12   Account to the public

There has been increasing political concern about standards in education in England and Wales over the past twenty years. Recent governments have used the results of assessment to compare schools and LEAs. These assessments include the publication of 'league tables' of examination performance of pupils at GCSE and GCE A level, as well as the results of SATs in English, mathematics and science. League tables have been abandoned in Northern Ireland. Non-academic data about schools' such as attendance rates are used in the accountability exercise. Academic data can be used in a school to compare both departments and teachers.

Teachers, schools and LEAs are publicly accountable for the standards of education of their pupils. Accountability is a controversial area, not least because of government intentions to make gains in pupils' learning part of the performance management of teachers, affecting their professional pay and advancement. Assessments are used by schools to set targets for improvement, known as 'target setting'. All schools in England and Wales receive from the DfEE a portfolio of 'Performance and Assessment Data' (PANDA), which enables them to compare their school's performance with 'similar' schools; similarity is based on the number of pupils receiving free school meals. Target setting is designed to raise standards of educational achievement nationally (DfEE, 1998a).

- Have I thought about how I will assess pupils' grasp of what I am trying to teach?
- Do the pupils understand what they are supposed to be learning/trying to do?
- Will my assessment task provide helpful information about the extent to which they have learned, and whether my teaching has been effective?
- How does this assessment influence what and how I will teach next?
- Are they developing an understanding of what they need to do to get better in the subject?

TENSIONS AND PROBLEMS IN ASSESSMENT

Using the results of assessment

As you have seen from the previous section, assessment serves a variety of purposes. There are tensions between these purposes if the data from one test are to be used for more than one purpose, such that the results from one test are used to measure simultaneously the knowledge and understanding of pupils, the quality of teaching and the efficiency of a school. If an assessment instrument (test) is particularly effective for one purpose, it might be very weak for another purpose. It is difficult to devise 'all-purpose' assessment instruments which are valid and reliable.

The past practice of ranking pupils in a year group or class in one subject was helpful for establishing how a pupil was performing compared to the other pupils in the class, but even this information is of limited value and says nothing about the magnitude of the difference between pupils or what the difference really means. More importantly, it tells you nothing about what the pupil can and cannot do. The former practice of aggregating marks for all subjects at the end of the year and ranking pupils on this aggregate score was even less helpful.

Assessment has been one of the battlegrounds of educational policy over the past fifteen years. Arguments have raged over the comparative importance of formative and summative assessment.

Many educationalists argue that assessment could be a powerful tool for raising standards in education if the emphasis was on formative assessment, or 'assessment for learning'. This principle was the backbone of the report of the Task Group on Assessment and Testing (TGAT) (DES/WO, 1988) which directed assessment for the 1988 National Curriculum. (See also Black and Wiliam, 1998; Gipps, 1995; Murphy, 1999.)

By contrast, politicians and bureaucrats saw making teachers, schools and LEAs more accountable as the means to drive up educational standards. Accountability required some means of measuring educational outcomes beyond external examination results. The TGAT model of NC assessment in England and Wales included in its recommendations a ten-point scale of reporting progress (levels 1–10) to be used for most, but not all, subjects. For each subject written statements of expected performance were produced, called Attainment Targets (ATs), to describe progression in achievement across the period of compulsory education.

The system of 'levels of achievement', as measured by SATs, together with public examination results, is used to make comparisons of pupil performance across the curriculum. These same data were used also to compare subjects and teachers in school, schools in an LEA and LEAs nationally.

As was said at the time:

> Part of the reason for the acceptance of the TGAT Report by the DES, civil service, and politicians was the fact that it 'delivers' the required bureaucratic data, that is, pupil scores can be aggregated to show results for a class, a school and whole LEA for comparative purposes.
> (Lawton, 1989, p. 59)

Understanding why there is a complex infrastructure of assessment mechanisms in the current educational system is important. One purpose of this infrastructure is to hold teachers, schools and LEAs accountable for the progress of their pupils. The competences/standards required of all newly qualified teachers (NQTs) explicitly identify accountability as one aspect of your understanding and knowledge of assessment (DfEE, 1998b).

Task 6.1.4

FORMATIVE AND SUMMATIVE ASSESSMENT

In the previous section we described twelve purposes of assessment. Read through that list again.

- Identify those that are primarily formative in intent and those that are summative.
- Do any of the twelve purposes not fit this dual picture of assessment?
- Do any of the purposes combine both elements of assessment?
- Are there other reasons why assessment is carried out?

High-order skills and lower-order skills

A distinction can be made between skills which are relatively straightforward to identify and those which are harder to describe and identify. Thus recall is often referred to as a lower-order skill and may refer to recall of facts, of knowledge 'of' and knowledge 'how'. Lower-order skills are important and form the foundation on which many higher-order skills function. Being able to *apply knowledge* moves skills up a level but even here one can distinguish applying knowledge to familiar situations, or taught situations, from the context of a new situation which is harder for a learner (higher skill level). See also Unit 5.2, rote learning and Task 5.2.1.

Skills used in the analysis of data or of situations, and the synthesis of information into explanations of events, require even higher order skills. The use of imagination, being inventive, thinking laterally are other ways of looking at these higher-order skills. These skills are often difficult to assess.

There is often a tension between validity and reliability when making assessments of learning. It is usually easier to test for lower-order skills than for more complex areas of learning, which often need higher skills for their successful implementation. Testing a pupil's ability to do simple addition is straightforward, compared with assessing the ability to develop reasoned judgements. The more you gain validity for a test of reasoned judgement the less reliable the test. This occurs because such a test becomes complicated, longer and more subjective in its assessment. Testing ability to do addition sums requires that a pupil is either correct or incorrect.

The Key Skills of the current NC in England and Wales (DfEE/QCA, 1999a) are a good example of this tension. Key Skills include the application of number, communication and use of information and communications technology (ICT). There are a range of basic tests which can be devised to measure these skills, such as those used to test student teachers' skills in these areas, in order to gain Qualified Teacher Status (QTS). It is much harder to devise simple tests of problem solving, or working as part of a team or 'learning how to learn' (metacognition). The danger for the curriculum and efforts to raise standards is that we might drift into the trap of assessing only that which is easy to assess rather than that which is important.

Another tension in assessment arises when the economics of testing is considered. Simple pencil and paper tests are cheap and quick to administer, and use little teacher time (an increasingly precious resource). More complex assessments, such as those involved in practical work, oral testing and assessing coursework, may test other worthwhile skills and learning, but are expensive and time-consuming. It was estimated that nationally the cost of more complex NC testing was up to £1.7 billion, as against £18 million for simple pencil and paper tests (Marks, 1994). The benefits of assessing pupils need to be considered against the cost in teachers' time and the extent to which learning can be advanced at the same time as we are assessing. The time and effort involved in assessment may take time away from more creative, fulfilling lessons.

Task 6.1.5

ASSESSMENT TENSIONS

Identify, compare and discuss the advantages and disadvantages of conducting a test in these two situations, A and B.

A Pupils work individually, in silence, without recourse to textbooks or any other support materials. The finished product is a written answer to be taken in and marked by the teacher.

B Pupils are allowed to work in groups, with access to textbooks, the internet and other resources. The finished product is a group presentation, perhaps using a poster, in response to the questions posed.

Some effects of assessment

We must also be aware of possible unintended outcomes of assessment. Although we hope that the provision of constructive feedback helps to motivate pupils, there is evidence to suggest that assessment can have a negative influence on pupils' self-esteem and motivation (Barnard, 2000; Black and Wiliam, 1998). Assessment can be valid and reliable and yet have a profoundly dispiriting influence on pupils' attitude to a subject, or to school in general. It has been argued that the ways in which some assessment has been developed in recent years have contributed to disaffection and disengagement in schools (Elliott, 1998; Macdonald, 2000). Others have indicated that there is a danger that 'pupils who see themselves as unable to learn usually cease to take school seriously – many of them are disruptive within school, others resort to truancy' (Black and Wiliam, 1998, p. 4). Assessment gives teachers and schools helpful information but, if the balance between formative and summative assessment is not carefully judged, it can discourage some pupils. This may be true of those who at a young age discover that they are not performing well. Comparing pupils with their peers (normative assessment) can have the unintended outcome that those at the 'bottom of the pile' do not always respond by exhibiting a determination to get to the top.

Task 6.1.6

ENCOURAGING WEAKER PUPILS

One of the challenges you face in your teaching is how to give constructive, honest feedback to pupils who are not doing well in your subject, without discouraging them.

Talk to teachers with whom you work about how they handle the challenge of providing feedback to pupils who are trying to do well in the subject, but whose progress is limited by lack of ability rather than lack of effort.

We referred earlier to high and low stakes assessment. High stakes assessment can motivate learners to prepare diligently for the test and to invest time and effort in learning for it, as in preparation for a driving test. On the other hand, high stakes assessment can lead to a reduction in the pleasure of learning, anxiety, and 'failure avoidance' strategies. For example, some pupils say 'I'm not going to try, so no one can say that I've failed.'

The integrity of assessment

High stakes assessment can also bring into question the 'integrity' of the assessment. In view of the high stakes involved, attempts might be made to find ways around the test or to 'lean on' the assessment task to try to make it produce the desired result. One of the dangers of high stakes assessment is that the more important the assessment, the more subject it is to 'corruption processes' (Macdonald, 2000, p. 31).

An example of the adjustment of task design to produce a more favourable outcome is given below.

One country (anonymous) produced annual reports on the national testing of primary pupils' mathematical ability in 1987 and 1988, relating to pupils' ability to use a rule to continue a number sequence. The commentary on the examination results contained the following analyses:

Test question 1987
Write the next number in this sequence: 0, 7, 26, 63, . . .
Success rate: 4%
Implication: This is clearly an area of weakness to which primary schools should give more attention.

Test question 1988
Write the next number in the sequence: 1, 7, 13, 19, . . .
Success rate: 78%
Implication: This is a marked improvement on last year; primary schools have clearly responded well to our advice in last year's report.

(Haylock, 2001)

This example makes the point that, just as pupils can sometimes be tempted to 'cheat', when it comes to high stakes testing there is sometimes pressure on teachers, schools, and government agencies to try to present educational outcomes in the most favourable way possible. One facet of reliability in assessment is the extent to which it is 'honest'.

MANAGING ASSESSMENT

We discuss here two features of assessment: first, how to manage your marking and keep your marking under control; and secondly, had to identify your professional development needs now and in the longer term.

1 Keeping assessment manageable

As a student teacher or NQT, you need to think about how to manage your time, so that assessment does not detract from the rest of your teaching. Commentators who operate at some distance from the classroom sometimes bemoan the fact that not all weaknesses and mistakes in pupils' work are systematically and comprehensively corrected, including every error of spelling, punctuation and grammar. You may agree with this view. Measure how long it takes to do a comprehensive, all-embracing diagnostic dissection of a full set of thirty exercise books for a piece of extended writing and then review your position.

Teachers have to manage their time effectively; it is not practical to mark every piece of pupils' work in the same way without compromising the time available for lesson planning, etc. There are no magic answers to make assessment burdens disappear but there are ways to improve your time management.

- **Learn to mark flexibly** Some pieces of work require detailed attention and diagnosis; sometimes a light touch monitoring is more appropriate.
- **Plan marking time** When you are planning lessons, think about setting fewer written tasks that require you to mark them in a time-intensive way. Student teachers sometimes set written

tasks to take the pressure off themselves in the early stages of first placement or for class management purposes. They tend to set more written tasks than experienced teachers and this produces a heavy marking load. Since lesson planning takes a long time, extra pressure builds. In your planning, try to prepare some lessons which have as one of the objectives that they do not require marking to be done in their aftermath. Pupils can mark their own work, or that of colleagues; see below.

- **Marking codes** Develop a shorthand code for signalling marking corrections, such as symbols for omissions, development, *non sequiturs*, irrelevance, spelling errors, clumsy phrasing.
- **Common errors** Make brief notes on common errors as you are marking pupils' work so that you can report on them orally to the group as a whole, rather than writing the same comment in several books.
- **Pupil marking** On occasions it is appropriate and helpful for pupils to mark each other's work, or their own work.
- **Oral feedback** It takes more than five times as long to write something down as to say it, so sometimes provide oral feedback to pupils.
- **Pupil response to tasks** Structure tasks so that sometimes pupils present their work as a poster, a group ICT task or display work. This response may not require you to mark their books, although you need to keep records of their performance.
- **Using ICT** Consider ways in which ICT might help to reduce the administration involved in assessment, recording and reporting (see Leask and Pachler, 1999, chapter 14).

Figure 6.1.8 How might ICT help to reduce the burden of assessment, reporting and recording?

The ways to improve your management of time, listed above, are not intended to suggest that you leave yourself without marking but are intended to make room, on occasions, for you to conduct a rigorous diagnosis of your pupils' written work and provide your pupils with constructive advice. These occasions allow you to give detailed and helpful comments which encourage your pupils and provide suggestions for ways forward in their learning. All marking should let your pupils feel that you care about their progress in your subject.

2 Long-term and short-term goals

As a student teacher you should consider your immediate needs (short-term goals) and your developing needs (long-term goals). The short-term agenda is for you to become effective in your responses to pupils' work, adapting to the demands of the assessment policies of the department in which you are working. The longer-term agenda is for you to develop a sound understanding of the nature and purposes of assessment, how to use the different techniques appropriately and how to interpret assessment data. These skills are one of the hallmarks of accomplished teachers.

There is a lot to take in; you should keep in mind the problems and tensions of assessment at the same time as you get to grips with the short-term agenda. Part of getting better at assessment is questioning the model even as you are using it, thinking about the validity and reliability of your assessment system.

ASSESSMENT FOR LEARNING: IMPROVING FORMATIVE ASSESSMENT

When you are planning your lessons, you should be thinking of a range of strategies for assessing learning. Assessment does not have to be a written process, although careful scrutiny and marking of written work are often helpful. Assessment includes:

- asking pupils questions, e.g. at the end of a lesson;
- asking pupils to put their hands up if they think they understand something;
- talking to pupils one-to-one about their work;
- asking pupils to give a short oral presentation;
- pupils presenting a poster summarising the main points of their task.

You can ask pupils to make their own judgement on the extent to which they have learned something; or it can be a group exercise. Pupils can sometimes mark each other's work, or be asked to draw up a mark scheme and performance criteria themselves. All of these strategies shift assessment responsibilities towards the pupil and thus emphasise the importance to the pupil of taking more responsibility for their own learning.

Some research has found that many teachers did not ever talk to pupils about their work, or praise them when they produced good work (National Commission for Education, 1993, p. 205). Actively involving pupils in assessment through talking about learning can be one of the ways forward.

It is helpful if the assessment task is seen by pupils as part of learning, rather than as purely a check that they have learned, and if it tests what Harlen terms 'real learning' rather than simply regurgitation of information (Harlen, 1995, p. 14). Learning implies understanding which can be demonstrated by using new knowledge; as one writer has put it 'The chasm between knowing X and using X to think about Y' (Wineburg, 1997, p. 256).

Holt gives some helpful pointers to ways of assessing genuine understanding:

It may help to have in our minds a picture of what we mean by understanding. I feel I understand something if I can do some, at least, of the following:

1. state it in my own words;
2. give examples of it;
3. recognise it in various guises and circumstances;
4. see connections between it and other facts or ideas;
5. make use of it in various ways;
6. foresee some of its consequences;
7. state its opposite or converse.

The list is only a beginning, but it may help us in the future to find out what our students really know as opposed to what they can give the appearance of knowing, their real learning as opposed to their apparent learning.

(Holt, 1964, p. 176)

It can be helpful also if you are explicit about what you want pupils to learn. This can include 'modelling' or showing them what a good response might look like, and involving them in an active dialogue – talking to them, and getting them to talk about their learning. In the words of Sadler, 'How to draw the concept of excellence out of the heads of teachers, give it some external formulation and make it available to the learner is a non-trivial problem' (Sadler, in Gipps, 1995).

OFSTED inspectors have been critical of the vague and unfocused nature of some teacher assessment and of the failure to use it to any useful purpose (OFSTED, 1996c, p. 40). The time and effort involved in assessment are worthwhile when it provides clear guidance for pupils on how to improve. The term 'consequential validity' has been coined to mean 'does anything happen as a result of this assessment (and is it helpful?)':

There's an awful lot of giving smiley faces at the bottom of children's work and very elaborate praise and stars and so on. They are fine for maintaining pupils' motivation and making children feel good about it, but unless it's accompanied by more direct specific advice about what to do to make the piece of work better it's actually of very little help to pupils as a learning activity. It actually helps the pupil to be told directly but kindly, what it is they are not doing very well so that they know how to do it better.

(Gipps, 1995)

Assessment is more purposeful if you are clear about exactly what it is that you are trying to teach, and if your pupils are also aware of this. You need to make it clear to your pupils, for example, what the attributes and characteristics of a good essay are; or the qualities you are looking for in an oral presentation to the rest of the class.

It has been found that girls-only groups functioned better than boys-only and mixed groups in terms of collaboration and co-operation, until boys-only groups were told explicitly that collaboration was one of the key learning objectives, whereupon the boys-only groups made substantial progress in these areas (Underwood, 1998). To improve your assessment of pupils you need to have a clear grasp of progression in your subject – that is, to know what it means 'to get better at geography' (or whatever). In addition, you need to be aware of the full breadth of benefits which pupils might derive from the study of your subject and from being in your classroom. Some of these issues have been raised in Unit 5.2 'Active learning'.

SUMMARY AND KEY POINTS

Assessment needs to be built into your planning for teaching and learning, not tacked on as an afterthought. You should be familiar with the idea of assessment as part of the cycle of planning, teaching, and assessing, leading into revised planning and teaching.

As well as thinking about how to provide constructive and helpful comments to pupils when responding to their work, you need to become familiar with the range of assessment methods and terminology which are used in schools. You should be aware of the tensions between the different purposes and forms of assessment and of the standards and competences required of you as an NQT (DfEE, 1998b, p. 15).

Ascribing levels, marks or grades to pupils' work is not unproblematic but it is not the most difficult part of assessment. The most challenging and important part of assessment is saying and doing things which helps pupils to make progress in their learning.

FURTHER READING

Black, P. and Wiliam, D. (1998) *Inside the Black Box*, London: King's College.
A succinct introduction (20 pages) to the importance of formative assessment, and the ways in which formative assessment might lead to gains in learning.

Harlen, W. (1995) 'To the rescue of formative assessment', *Primary Science Review*, 37 (April), 14–15.
This article provides suggestions for key principles in effective assessment.

Headington, R. (2000) *Monitoring, Assessment, Recording, Reporting and Accountability: Meeting the Standards*, London: David Fulton.
This book is written specifically for trainee teachers.

Murphy, P. (ed.) (1999) *Learners, Learning and Assessment*, London: Paul Chapman/Open University.
This book is particularly helpful in terms of providing insight into subject-specific assessment issues.

Times Educational Supplement (TES) (2000) Online: http://www.tes.co.uk/online/assessit/
This *TES* website focuses on assessment issues. It is a good way of keeping up to date with recent developments.

UNIT 6.2 **EXTERNAL ASSESSMENT AND EXAMINATIONS**

BERNADETTE YOUENS

INTRODUCTION

Principles of assessment were introduced in Unit 6.1 which highlighted the importance that this aspect of education has assumed since the Education Reform Act (ERA, 1988). This Act included the publication of a report by the Task Group on Assessment and Testing (TGAT) recommending strategies for assessing and reporting pupils' progress in the National Curriculum (NC) in England and Wales (DES/WO, 1988). This unit looks at the particular role, function and nature of external assessment and examinations. Before reading this unit we suggest you work through Unit 6.1. The relationship between the NC and the subject of this unit is a key one to understand and you should refer also to Unit 7.3 which focuses on the National Curriculum of England and Wales.

This unit aims to provide you with an overview of the framework for external assessment and examinations in secondary schools. Although you are familiar with the public examinations that you took at school, in recent years there have been significant developments in assessment methods. In England and Wales this has been prominent in the post-16 sector of education where one of the most notable areas has been the growth of vocationally related courses which are taught in secondary schools alongside General Certificate of Secondary Education (GCSE) and the General Certificate of Education at Advanced level (GCE A level).

As well as looking at how pupils are assessed throughout their secondary education, it is important to be aware of the many purposes of external assessment and examinations. These purposes can be usefully divided into those associated with candidates and those that have more to do with educational establishments and public accountability; see Unit 6.1.

Two important, recurrent themes which arise when discussing external assessment and examinations are validity and reliability. These two concepts, together with the agencies, regulations and processes involved in ensuring consistency in these two areas, are discussed in this unit.

Teaching externally examined classes is a challenge for any teacher and demands particular teaching skills and strategies in addition to the routine elements of good lesson planning and teaching. This aspect of teaching is discussed in the final part of this section.

OBJECTIVES

By the end of this unit you should:

- be familiar with the range of external assessment in secondary schools and with the national framework for qualifications;
- have an understanding of the relationship between the National Curriculum in England and Wales and external examinations;

- be aware of the main purposes of external assessment;
- appreciate the processes involved in external examining and know of the institutions involved;
- have started to consider the issues relating to teaching examination classes;
- identify the competences/standards for your course related to assessment.

YOUR OWN EXPERIENCE

A good starting point is your own experience of external assessment and examinations. Task 6.2.1 invites you to recall this period of your education.

Task 6.2.1

YOUR PERSONAL EXPERIENCE OF EXTERNAL EXAMINATIONS AND ASSESSMENT

Think back to your time at school; as a pupil what did you think was the purpose of sitting exams? How did preparing for examinations impact on your motivation as a learner? Did the teaching strategies of examination classes differ from non-examination classes? Prepare some notes under each of these headings and share them with another student teacher or your tutor.

Thinking through these points provides you with a good personal starting point before going on to develop your understanding of the wider issues pertaining to external assessment and examinations.

TYPES OF ASSESSMENT

In Unit 6.1 we discussed formative and summative assessment and we remind you of those terms. Stobart and Gipps (1997) usefully define formative assessment as assessment *for* learning, and summative assessment as assessment *of* learning. External assessment and examinations are generally considered to be forms of summative assessment. There are two important methods used extensively in summative assessment with which you need to be familiar, namely, norm-referenced assessment and criterion-referenced assessment.

Norm-referenced assessment is the traditional means of assessing candidates and has been used extensively throughout the British education system. In norm-referenced assessment, the value of, or grade related to, any mark awarded depends on how it compares with the marks of other candidates sitting the same examination. The basis for this form of assessment is the assumption that the marks are normally distributed, i.e. if you plot the marks awarded against the number of candidates gaining that mark, for all candidates, a bell-shaped curve is produced, provided the sample is big enough. This curve is then used to assign grade boundaries based on predetermined conditions – for example, that 80 per cent of all those sitting the examination pass and 20 per cent fail. In this way an element of failure is built into the examination. The system of reporting by grades is essentially norm-referenced. For example, if you are awarded the highest grade (A★) in a subject at GCSE this grade does not give any specific information about what you can do in that subject, simply that you were placed within a top group of candidates.

Criterion–referenced assessment, on the other hand, is concerned with what a candidate can do *without* reference to the performance of others and so provides an alternative method to address the limitations of norm-referencing mentioned above. A simple example of criterion-referenced assessment is a swimming test. If a person is entered for a 100-metre swimming award, and swims 100 metres, then she is awarded that certificate irrespective of how many other people also reach this standard. Vocational courses use criterion-referenced assessment, to which we return later. Academic courses, such as GCSE Science, use criterion referencing when assessing practical skills. In this example, the results are reported by comparing pupils with other pupils, i.e. norm-referenced The overall assessment in this case is thus a mixture of norm and criterion referencing.

THE FRAMEWORK OF EXTERNAL ASSESSMENT IN SECONDARY SCHOOLS

We consider in turn Key Stage 3, GCSE and post-16 education in England and Wales. Different arrangements for assessing pupils are in place in Scotland and Northern Ireland.

Key Stage 3 assessment

On transfer to secondary school pupils bring with them information obtained from the end of Key Stage 2 assessment, arising from both internal teacher assessment and external assessment. This information is usually reported as National Curriculum levels; see Unit 7.3. Pupils are assessed again at the end of Key Stage 3 to determine their attainment and measure progression, again reported as levels. One of the central tenets of the National Curriculum is progression, which is a measure of pupils' personal development. At present there is considerable concern about the perceived overall lack of progress made by pupils at Key Stage 3. Indeed there have been reports about the so-called 'Key Stage 3 dip' in pupil performance (OFSTED, 2000a; QCA, 2000). Although a number of anecdotal factors are frequently cited for this apparent lack of progress – ranging from the extended summer break, or reaction to the pressures of Year 6, to a change of schools – it is clear that this area will remain an issue in the public domain for some time to come.

External assessment at the end of Key Stage 3 takes place in the form of written tests, Standard Assessments Tasks (SATs), for the core NC subjects of English, mathematics and science. The SATs now taken by pupils are far removed from the original activity-based assessment tasks advocated by the TGAT report (DES/WO, 1988). The TGAT report recommended that assessment should be embedded within classroom practice rather than being 'bolt-on' activities which eventually drive the curriculum; that is, teaching becomes test-oriented. The integration of assessment with teaching and learning is discussed also in Unit 6.1. The framework initially proposed by TGAT was of a national assessment system for all pupils up to the age of 16 based on specified criteria rather than the age-related norm-referenced system which had dominated assessment previously. Teachers were also to be involved in summative assessment and not just formative assessment. Another major change suggested by TGAT was that assessment should measure pupils' progress rather than continuously measure their relative failure. How those proposals worked out in practice is discussed below. For a more detailed discussion of the TGAT report please refer to Daugherty, 1995.

The initial NC tests were criterion-referenced, with each question being ascribed a certain level, and the tests marked by teachers. However, this system proved both unmanageable and unacceptable to the teaching profession. The system was unmanageable because of the heavy additional load on teachers and unacceptable because there was no additional financial reward. Traditionally public examinations are marked externally by paid examiners; the SATs are now set by external agencies and marked by paid, external markers. The SAT tests are written with reference to the Programmes of Study (see Unit 7.3); the questions in the tests are designed so that their demand on the pupil links closely to the level descriptions. There are two papers for each of the core subjects together with an extension paper for the award of level 8 and for the recognition of exceptional performance, i.e. above level 8. In mathematics and science there are differentiated papers designed to assess pupils across a limited range of levels. For example, in science there are two papers, one to assess pupils working within levels 3–6 and another to assess pupils working within levels 4–7. An allocation of marks is awarded to each question and grade boundaries are decided by a process known as levelling. This procedure involves deciding how many marks on the test are required for the award of each level. There is an initial process of setting draft thresholds which are confirmed later by marking a sample of papers. Thus the setting of SATs questions is criterion-referenced whilst the marking is based on normative methods. Schools are statutorily required also to provide teacher-assessed levels for separate attainment targets in each subject together with an overall assessment level for the core and foundation subjects. In this way, the progress of each pupil can be identified and reported, which was one intention of the TGAT recommendations.

The GCSE

The GCSE was first introduced in 1986 as the examination to be taken at the end of Key Stage 4. The GCSE examination was designed both to replace the GCE O level and Certificate of Secondary Education (CSE) examination and to provide certification for a much greater percentage of candidates. Historically, the GCE O level aimed to certificate 20–30 per cent of pupils in any year and the CSE a further 40 per cent. Prior to the introduction of the GCSE, up to 40 per cent of pupils therefore left school without any formal recognition of their achievements. Alternative qualifications, such as the Royal Society of Arts examination, were less prestigious. One of the aims of the new GCSE examination was to certificate 90 per cent of the cohort in any year. Seven pass grades could be awarded, from A–G, and in 1994 an additional grade, A★, was added to recognise exceptional performance. The GCSE examination also differed from the GCE O Level examination in that it was designed to test not only recall, but also understanding and skills. Because nearly all pupils take the GCSE examination, assessment techniques had to be developed to cope with such a broad range of achievement. A range of strategies was introduced to achieve differentiation and so provide all pupils with the opportunity to show what they had learnt through studying the course being examined. To achieve this aim a tiered assessment pattern was introduced to enable pupils to be entered for the paper most appropriate for their ability. This situation requires teachers to assess pupils' progress and potential and to advise pupils on which tier of the examination to enter. Tiered papers carry grade limits, thus narrowing the opportunities of pupils. For example, a higher paper may enable pupils to be awarded grades A★–D, while a foundation paper may allow only the award of grades C–G.

Furthermore if pupils fail to achieve the marks required for the lowest grade in their tier then they receive an unclassified grade. In the early years of the GCSE examination significant numbers of pupils 'fell off the bottom' of their grade range and were awarded an unclassified grade.

Another aspect of entering pupils for different tiers of entry has been the debate about the equity between a grade C awarded on the higher tier of a paper and a grade C awarded on the foundation tier. A grade C is intended to be the same value, however attained. There has been consistent evidence to indicate that it is easier to achieve a grade C on the foundation tier (Good and Cresswell, 1988). This situation of course has implications, not only for candidates but also for schools in relation to school performance – the 'league tables' – because the performance of schools, in England and Wales, is reported nationally by the number of pupils gaining five subject passes at grade A★–C.

Coursework was also introduced with the GCSE and has proved to be a great motivator for pupils. In the early days of GCSE some of the courses offered were entirely coursework-based. However, the amount of coursework is now limited by the Qualifications and Curriculum Authority (QCA) through the subject criteria and depends on the subject. In the more practically-based subjects a larger proportion of teacher-based assessment contributes to the final mark than in other subjects. In the former case the upper limit in practice is about 60 per cent, whereas in the latter case a maximum of 25 per cent of the total mark is commonly awarded for coursework. No subject is allowed to be assessed only by teacher-assessed coursework.

The introduction of coursework, though, has had implications for teachers, as Sutton reflects:

As teachers, in recent years, the task of assessing has become a greater part of our professional activity; the responsibility for assessment has shifted slowly but surely from the examination boards to schools, and the workload has increased with the growth of criterion-referencing.

(Sutton, 1991, p. 2)

Thus the GCSE examination, like the external assessment of the NC at the end of Key Stage 3, also combines norm-referenced methods with criterion-referenced methods.

Task 6.2.2

GCSE COURSEWORK

Coursework is an integral feature of the GCSE examination and it is important that you have a clear understanding of this part of the examination. Working with another student teacher in your own subject specialism, obtain a copy of a recent GCSE specification. Read the general introduction and then familiarise yourself with the aims, assessment objectives and assessment patterns of the specification. Now turn to the coursework section and find out the following information:

- how much of the overall mark is allocated to coursework?
- what form does the coursework take?
- how is the coursework assessed?
- what information about coursework criteria is given to candidates?

Once you have found out this information, discuss your findings with an experienced teacher in your school experience school. Ask if you can have access to some samples of coursework from pupils at the school, and find out:

- how the coursework is introduced to pupils;
- the range of tasks set;
- how these tasks are made accessible and relevant to pupils.

Now try assessing the coursework samples yourself using the criteria supplied by the examining body and any internal marking schemes used by the school. Discuss your marking with a member of staff and find out how the department internally moderates coursework. Find out from the coursework specifications what processes the examining authority uses to externally moderate coursework.

Check the standards/competences expected of you in your course which relate to coursework in public examinations. A record of your work could be placed in your professional portfolio.

Post–16 assessment

Of all the changes that have followed the Education Reform Act (ERA, 1988) in England and Wales the area that has still to fall into an established pattern is the provision of post-16 courses and their assessment.

GCE A level courses

GCE A level courses were first introduced in 1951 and since then have been regarded as the academic 'gold standard' by successive governments. In 1995, Dearing was commissioned to look at strategies to strengthen, consolidate and improve the framework of 16–19 qualifications. As a result of this review changes to the post-16 curriculum have been introduced from September 2000 (Dearing, 1996).

GCE A level courses remain, but each subject is now composed of six discrete units of approximately the same size. The first three units make up an Advanced Subsidiary (AS) course, representing the first half of an advanced level course of study. The other three units, which make up the second part of the GCE A level, are to be known as A2. One of the aims of the AS proposal was to provide a more appropriate and manageable 'bridge' between GCSE and GCE A level. The AS course may be taken as a qualification in itself or it may be used as a foundation to study the A2 section of the course.

GCE A levels, like GCSE examinations, may be assessed in stages, as in a modular course, or terminally. The introduction of modular assessment has proved to be very popular with candidates. Dearing listed the main advantages of modularity as:

- motivating pupils to maintain a high, constant commitment throughout their course;
- providing valuable diagnostic information from early results;
- providing the opportunity to have achievement recognised (Dearing, 1996).

He noted also that, on analysis of the examination results, candidates taking the modular route gained higher average point scores in most subjects. Concern about the fact that candidates could re-sit particular modules any number of times has been addressed and it is now possible to re-sit any particular module only once.

All GCE A2 courses must include an element of synoptic assessment designed to test a candidate's ability to make connections between different aspects of the course. There is no synoptic assessment at AS level. The synoptic element must normally contribute 20 per cent to the full A level and take the form of external assessment at the end of the course. GCE A level pass grades range from A to E with 'A' the highest grade. As with GCSE examinations there is also teacher assessment of coursework in GCE but there is no upper limit set by the QCA. In practice, the amount of teacher-assessed coursework is set by the QCA subject criteria for each subject; the most that occurs is 60 per cent; in GCE A level English (EdEXcel) there is 40 per cent teacher-assessed coursework.

Vocational courses

One of the main strands of emphasis of the Dearing Report on 16–19 qualifications was the need to provide a coherent framework for national qualifications which provides equivalent status for vocational qualifications (Dearing, 1996). The main vocational qualifications encountered in secondary schools in England and Wales are the General National Vocational Qualifications (GNVQs) which were introduced into schools in 1992 and developed from National Vocational Qualifications (NVQs).

The NVQs are work-related, competence-based qualifications and the courses were designed for people in work or undertaking work-based training. NVQ courses provide job-specific training, the assessment of which takes place in the work environment and is criterion-referenced. Central to the NVQ model is the idea of competence to perform a particular job, where competence is defined as the mastery of identified performance skills.

There are a number of GNVQ courses available both at Key Stage 4 and post-16; see Table 6.2.1. Part One GNVQ courses are made up of three units while courses composed of six units are simply referred to as GNVQs. Both qualifications are available at two levels, foundation and intermediate:

- a foundation Part One GNVQ is equivalent to two GCSEs at grades D–G;
- a foundation GNVQ is equivalent to four GCSEs at grades D–G;
- an intermediate Part One GNVQ is equivalent to two GCSEs at grades A★–C;
- an intermediate GNVQ is equivalent to four GCSEs at grades A★–C.

GNVQ foundation and intermediate qualifications are graded at pass, merit and distinction. However, there is no direct equivalence made between the pass, merit and distinction grades and the GCSE grades within each level.

After September 2000 the Advanced GNVQ course was replaced by various Vocational A levels:

- Advanced Subsidiary Vocational Certificate of Education (3 units);
- Advanced Vocational Certificate of Education (6 units);
- Advanced Vocational Certificate of Education (Double Award) (12 units).

The units assigned to each qualification are intended to be comparable to the GCE A level units described earlier in this section. Vocational A levels will be reported using the grade range A–E so that direct comparisons with GCE A level can be made (see Table 6.2.1).

Vocational courses are assessed through an internally assessed portfolio of evidence and externally set tests, projects or case study work. As with other examinations, the internal assessment is externally moderated. In general, the portfolio contributes two-thirds of the final mark and the external assessment the remaining third. Each unit is graded and these grades are aggregated to produce a mean grade for the whole qualification.

Table 6.2.1 Framework of national qualifications

Level of qualification	General qualifications	Vocationally related qualifications	Occupational qualifications
Entry	Certificate of (educational) achievement		Entry
1	GCSE grades D–G	Foundation GNVQ	Level 1 NVQ
2	GCSE grades A★–C	Intermediate GNVQ	Level 2 NVQ
3	GCE A level, awarded at levels A–E	Vocational A level awarded at levels A–E (formerly Advanced GNVQ)	Level 3 NVQ
4	Higher-level qualifications; e.g. a first degree or a BTEC		Level 4 NVQ
5	Higher-level qualifications; e.g. a postgraduate qualification or a professional qualification, such as in accountancy		Level 5 NVQ

GNVQs were introduced to provide pupils with an introduction to occupational sectors through school- or college-based courses. Indeed one of the principal aims of the GNVQ was to provide a middle road between the general academic route and occupational courses, such as NVQs described above. The framework in Table 6.2.1 shows how the three qualification strands are intended to overlap.

One of the main stumbling blocks to the uptake of vocational qualifications by schools has been the difference in assessment practice and terminology that has existed between academic and vocational courses. From September 2000 the new vocational units introduced aim to set out the knowledge, understanding and skills required in clear, jargon-free language. As this book went to press, new developments in GCSE vocational qualifications were announced for schools in England and Wales. It is intended that the GCSE vocational qualifications would be available alongside academic qualifications, with both groups of pupils maintaining their study of core curriculum subjects; see the DfEE website for further information (www.open.gov.uk/dfee). The purpose of these developments together with the other reforms outlined is to encourage Key Stage 4 pupils and post-16 students to broaden their programme of study to include vocational courses.

THE PURPOSES OF EXTERNAL ASSESSMENT

External assessment and examinations feature prominently throughout secondary school education. If the time and resources spent on this form of assessment are to be justified then it is important that the purposes of external assessment are fully understood. There is a long-standing history in the United Kingdom of externally examining pupils at particular stages in their education, which is quite different from the practice in some other countries; see the reference in Unit 6.1 to Gipps, 1995 (p. 303). In recent years this practice has extended to the external assessment of pupils at the end of Key Stages 2 and 3. The purposes of external, summative assessment can be thought of in terms of certificating candidates and the public accountability of teachers and schools.

One of the main functions of summative assessment is to categorise candidates. There are a number of reasons why we would want to categorise pupils, which include selecting candidates for higher education, employing people for particular jobs, or to recognise achievement. In the case of national examinations, categorising people means providing pupils with a grade which they and other people can use to compare them with other candidates. The grades can then be used to select or exclude pupils either for further education or for employment purposes.

A second recognised function of external assessment is that of certification. If you hold a certificate then it is evidence that competence in particular skills has been achieved. For example, if you hold a driving licence this is evidence that in a driving test you successfully performed a hill start, completed a three-point turn, reversed around a corner and so on. The significance to pupils, of both the categorising and certification purposes, is evidenced by the fact that an impending examination provides an incentive for pupils to concentrate on their studies and to acquire the relevant knowledge and skills required by the examination for which they are entered. Thus a further function of external examinations is to provide motivation for both pupils and teachers. Motivation is discussed in greater detail in Unit 3.2.

Public accountability

One reason why assessment is so high on the political agenda at present is because it is inextricably linked with the notion of raising standards and school improvement. Since 1982 schools have been statutorily required to publish examination results, with the aim of providing parents with more information and making schools more accountable. The statutory requirements were extended in 1992 to include a detailed breakdown not only of performance but additional statistics such as number of pupils on the roll with special educational needs, but without statements. This information is published each autumn in the so-called 'league tables' referred to in Unit 6.1. Although a variety of statistical information is published each autumn, currently schools in England and Wales are placed in rank order – the 'league tables' – based on just one variable, the percentage of pupils gaining five or more GCSE passes at grades A*–C.

The introduction of external assessment of pupils at the end of Key Stages 2 and 3 has had a significant impact on the teaching of pupils in this age range, providing further evidence of the effect that so-called 'high stakes' external assessment has on classroom practice. The term 'high stakes' is used to describe assessment that has significant consequences for either the candidate or the school and is discussed in Unit 6.1.

In addition to school performance tables, since September 1998, all schools in England and Wales have had to set and publish targets for all pupils aged 11–16 which demonstrate year-on-year improvements. In order to assist schools with this process, all schools in England are sent annually, in the autumn, a Package of Pupil Performance Information. This Package includes a summary of national results of assessments and value-added information to enable schools to compare the progress made by individual pupils in their school with progress made by pupils with similar prior attainment in other schools. This Package contains benchmark data so that schools can compare whole school performance with that of schools with similar intakes and profiles.

Additional information in the Package is Performance and Assessment data, usually referred to as PANDA, which are compiled on the basis of school inspection data. PANDAs are used by OFSTED in their preparation prior to school inspection and are contained in a document called Pre-Inspection and Contextual School Indicators (PICSI) (OFSTED, 1998, p. 4 and Annex 1).

Validity and reliability

We referred earlier in this unit to the concepts of validity and reliability as central to understanding the examining process. These ideas are also discussed in Unit 6.1. For all external assessment and examinations, frameworks of regulations have been developed to ensure that the examination process and the results produced are both valid and reliable. To understand this framework you need to be aware of the institutions and processes involved in this regulation.

The Qualifications and Curriculum Authority (QCA) is the government agency that approves all specifications for examinations as well as monitoring examinations through a programme of scrutinies, comparability exercises and probes. The QCA is accountable to the Department for Education and Employment (DfEE). There are three unitary awarding bodies in England which are authorised by the government to offer GCSE, GCE A and AS and GNVQ courses. These three awarding bodies, formed by the merging of a number of examination boards, are given below, together with the addresses of their websites:

- Assessment and Qualifications Alliance (AQA) (http://www.aqa.org.uk)
- EdExcel (http://www.edexcel.org.uk)
- Oxford and Cambridge Regional (OCR) (http://www.ocr.org.uk)

Following the Guaranteeing Standards' consultation (DfEEc, 1997), the formation of a single Awarding Body was considered, but a group of three was thought useful to retain a measure of competition. The key recommendations of the Standards' consultation report were:

- for each externally examined course there is a subject core that specifies the core of content that each specification must cover;
- the publication of a detailed code of practice designed to ensure that grading standards are consistent across subjects and across the three awarding bodies, in the same subject, and from year to year;
- this code of practice should also set out the roles and responsibilities of those involved in the examining process and the key procedures for setting papers, standardising marking and grading.

The processes employed by the awarding bodies to address the recommendations above and to ensure that the examinations are valid and reliable are outlined in Figure 6.2.1.

TEACHING EXTERNALLY ASSESSED COURSES

All teachers have to think beyond the particular lesson they are teaching to the end of the unit of work, to ensure that pupils can respond successfully to any assessment scheduled to take place. When pupils are assessed externally the same considerations apply – that is, how to maximise

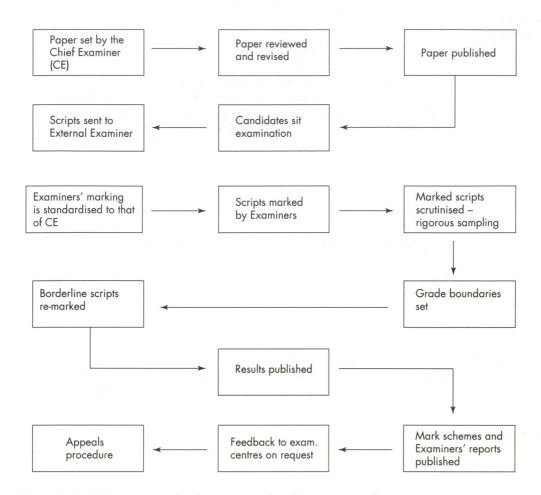

Figure 6.2.1 Processes involved in setting and marking an external examination

pupils' achievement. However, you do need to be fully aware of the nature of the external assessment for which you are preparing your pupils. It is important not just to teach to the examination but to hold on to the principles of good classroom practice.

In preparing pupils for public examinations, you need to be familiar with the subject content, the types of questions set in the examination, and, for example, the language used in setting questions. Questions are set which often employ words with a specific meaning – for example, they ask candidates to describe, or explain, or use short notes or summarise. Candidates need to know what these words mean in examination conditions. The task below is designed to help you become familiar with types of questions currently set in examination papers in your own subject and the corresponding reports of examiners.

Task 6.2.3

USING EXAMINATION PAPERS IN YOUR TEACHING

Collect together a number of GCSE examination papers for your subject together with the mark schemes and specification. Where possible also obtain the relevant examiners' reports, which are sent to all schools offering candidates to that awarding body. Read through the specification for the examination arrangements. Then address the questions in the paper in the following way:

- Answer the questions yourself.
- Mark your answers using the mark scheme.
- Evaluate your answers and marking and identify the key knowledge and concepts needed to gain maximum marks. Look back at the examination questions; identify the key words and phrases most often used in questions.
- Use the examiners' report to review and refine your findings.
- Identify any ideas that might be useful to consider in your day-to-day teaching.

Repeat the exercise for other years of the same paper; or repeat the exercise using papers set at a different level, e.g. GCE A level. A completed task could be placed in your professional portfolio.

Check the standards/competences required in your course which relate to preparing pupils for public examinations.

Once you are familiar with the structure and language used in past papers you can integrate this information into your teaching throughout the course. Another important aspect to consider is the development of study skills both in your lessons and throughout the school. For further advice on developing study skills see Balderstone and King, 1997 and Task 6.2.4.

Task 6.2.4

STUDY SKILLS

Discuss with your tutor or another experienced teacher in your school experience school what whole school and departmental approaches there are to developing pupils' study skills. These skills include, for example, managing coursework, planning and supporting revision, and time management. Use the information you gain to identify strategies to integrate into your teaching. Check the standards/competences required in your course which relate to developing study skills.

SUMMARY AND KEY POINTS

In this unit we have linked the framework for external assessment and examinations with the nature and purposes of summative assessment. Both National Curriculum assessment and external examinations utilise aspects of both norm-referenced and criterion-referenced methods, and this is an important feature of assessment of which you need to be aware and understand. Norm referencing and criterion referencing are factors used in discussions seeking to explain the steady increase in the proportion of candidates achieving A★–C grades. The changes recently introduced to the post-16 sector of education aim to encourage pupils to broaden their studies to include vocational courses alongside traditional academic courses. It will be interesting and important for you to monitor the impact of these reforms on the post-16 curriculum over the next few years. Check your course requirements for the standards/competences expected of you related to assessment and public examinations.

There are likely to be further innovations in approaches to assessment and, as long as there remains a political focus on raising standards in our schools, external assessment and examinations will maintain their present high profile and powerful influence on educational practice.

FURTHER READING

Department for Education and Employment: http://www.dfee.gov.uk/
An informative website which is particularly useful for looking at school performance tables, the autumn Package of Pupil Performance Indicators, and up-to-date information about government initiatives.

James, M. (1998) *Using Assessment for School Improvement*, London: Heinemann.
A comprehensive yet very readable book which discusses all aspects of assessment.

Stobart, G. and Gipps, C. (1997) *Assessment: A Teacher's Guide to the Issues*, London: Hodder and Stoughton.
A very accessible, readable guide to contemporary assessment issues.

CHAPTER 7 THE SCHOOL, CURRICULUM AND SOCIETY

This chapter takes you away from the immediacy of teaching to consider the aims of education, how those aims might be identified and, more importantly perhaps, how the curriculum reflects those aims. In the day-to-day urgency of teaching the given curriculum it is easy to push the 'why' into the background and simply get on with the 'how'.

By contrast, some parents do question the judgement of others who insist that their children go to school from '9 to 4', 5 days a week for 42 weeks for 11 years, and have homework. In your dealings with parents, you may wish to justify this investment in time. Pupils can bring you to a halt when, say, in the middle of a lesson, say, on the Great Depression of the 1920s and 1930s, they remark, 'Why have I got to learn this? My mum says that if I'm going to work in "Asda" down the road, knowing the economic reasons for the Depression won't help me in my job, will it?' As a prospective teacher you need an answer to this observation and similar comments in your subject.

The 1944 Education Act was a landmark in education in the UK. The Act gave a new framework for teaching and learning and it was introduced in the middle of a national crisis – the Second World War. Although the Act gave free secondary education to a wider group of pupils, the several aims of the curriculum were premised on a distinction between three groups of pupils: the academic (grammar schools), the technical (technical schools) and the rest (secondary modern schools). With hindsight we now reject such a simplistic approach.

The 1988 Education Reform Act, which replaced the 1944 Act, identified a common curriculum. The 1988 Act was premised on narrow aims and with little justification made for the connection between these aims and the subject curriculum that followed. In the decade following the 1988 Act, several reforms of the curriculum took place, and both the aims of the 1988 Act and the latest reforms are addressed in this chapter.

In Unit 7.1 'Aims of education', a comparative and analytical approach is taken to examine assumptions about education. Unit 7.2, 'The school curriculum', examines the school curriculum in terms of aims. Finally in Unit 7.3, 'The National Curriculum', we examine the structure of the 1999 NC for England and Wales which for the first time has a worked-out set of aims.

Within the general standards laid down in England for a student teacher to gain Qualified Teacher Status (QTS) (DfEE, 1998b) you are not expected to know about the aims of the National Curriculum or how your subject supports the general aims of the NC. Different criteria are laid for Northern Ireland, Scotland and Wales. An awareness that the aims of education and of subjects within a curriculum are a matter of debate and political decision does not feature in the criteria for the award of QTS. We believe that teachers should be aware of the foundations on which national policy on the school curriculum is based, because young people, between the ages of 5 and 16, spend a substantial part of the formative period of their lives in school, and a significant slice of the national budget is channelled into education. If education is 'what is left after most of what you have learned in school is forgotten', then what is education for and who decides?

GRAHAM HAYDON

INTRODUCTION

Education is very much a value-laden activity; this unit is designed to help you reflect on the values you encounter in your work and the values you yourself bring to it. People's ideas about the aims of education may, in part, be simply 'read off' from the educational traditions of their own society, which already incorporate certain shared values; and they may be formed through an individual's own reflection on their personal values. Not surprisingly, then, in a complex society there is room for differences in views about educational aims. For example, individuals with different educational and life experiences, different religious beliefs and cultural traditions, and different political tendencies may all differ in their conceptions of the aims of education. In Britain, views about the aims of education in the past have remained often more implicit than explicit, but in recent years there has been some conscious attention to aims at government level. Thus what may at first sight seem rather an abstract question – what should the aims of education be? – is in fact an unavoidable part of the context in which you are working as a teacher.

OBJECTIVES

At the end of this unit you should be able to:

* list a variety of actual and possible aims for education;
* reflect on and formulate your own aims in being a teacher;
* discuss aims of education with other teachers and with parents;
* identify the competences/standards for your course which relate to the broad aims of education.

THE SOCIAL AND POLITICAL CONTEXT OF AIMS

One difference between education systems is that the aims which teachers are expected to pursue may be decided at different political or administrative levels. Many countries today have a national education system, at least partly state-funded and state-controlled. In some cases, as once in the Soviet Union, a clearly defined ideology sets aims which the whole education system is meant to promote. Even in a more decentralised system, in which many decisions are left to local level, there may be across the whole society a more or less widely shared sense of what the aims of education should be. Thus in the USA there seems to have been in the early decades of the twentieth century a widely-shared sense that one aim of the national education system was to make a single nation out of diverse communities.

In Britain, both historically and today, the picture is mixed. Through much of the twentieth century schools had a good deal of autonomy, from a legal point of view, in setting and pursuing their aims, though in many cases the aims of a particular school were not made explicit. There was also room for some variation at local authority level. For instance, in the 1970s and 1980s there were cases where particular Local Education Authorities (LEAs) pursued more radical equal opportunities policies than were supported centrally. A case in point (though it is not relevant to go into the details here) is the political controversy over 'Clause 28', which began in the 1980s and has lasted into the present century. Some LEAs were perceived, rightly or wrongly, as aiming to promote homosexuality through programmes and curriculum materials used in schools, and legislation was brought in to rule this out. There has been a good deal of confusion in the debate over this (particularly since the influence of LEAs over individual schools has been very much reduced), but, whatever your own view of the rights and wrongs of the issue, it illustrates that the question of whether schools should or should not be pursuing certain aims is potentially controversial.

The more general question of how far there is to be scope for diversity between different localities and different schools is still being played out in Britain in the twenty-first century. A system which in some respects sets up competition between different schools, each aiming to attract and hold on to pupils, encourages each school to make its own aims clear to parents and prospective pupils, and perhaps to present itself as being in some way distinctive from other schools at the level of aims. As obvious examples, we might expect that schools labelled (and funded) as Technology Colleges, or schools labelled as Sports Colleges, would give explicit attention in their public statements of aims to the focus of their activities.

At the same time, there has been a tendency in the last two decades for attention to the aims of education to come into the political arena. It would be putting it too strongly to suggest that there has been widespread public debate about the aims of education, but politicians have tended to make statements about aims. Of course, these will not always be put explicitly in the terminology of aims, but when politicians say that schools should enable Britain to compete economically with other nations, or that schools should inculcate moral standards or should promote active citizenship, they are in effect recommending certain aims for schools.

Thus there is always a potential tension between (a) the possibility of a diversity of aims in different schools, perhaps because they are serving rather different communities, and (b) the promotion of common aims across the school system as a whole. At the time of writing, the focus on common aims is more prominent in England, largely because of the National Curriculum (NC) and other moves by government to direct and control what happens in schools. We shall pay more attention at the end of this unit and in the next unit to the explicit and ostensible aims of the NC in England and Wales.

As a student teacher, then, you are working in a context in which many expectations about aims are already in place, at least at a general level. Even if aims were not mentioned in legislation, you would still have to recognise that other teachers, your pupils, their parents, and the wider society all have their views about what you should be doing, and a legitimate interest in what you are doing. What aims you pursue as a teacher are clearly not just up to you.

Is there, in that case, much point in your doing your own thinking about the aims of education? It is a premise of this unit that there is a lot of point in this, in fact that any good teacher has some view about the aims of education. (This doesn't mean that your view is different from anyone else's, but it does mean that it is a view that you have thought through and endorsed for yourself.)

Here are two reasons why your own thinking about aims is relevant (you may well think of further reasons):

1   Within the constraints, your own thinking about aims influences the way you approach your task as a teacher of a particular subject (we discuss this aspect of aims of education further in the next unit).

2   As a citizen, you have the same right as any other citizen to form and express your own view about the aims of education in general; but at the same time other people might reasonably expect that, as a member of the teaching profession, you will be in a better position than the average citizen to make your views clear and be prepared to argue for them.

THINKING ABOUT AIMS

The following tasks, 7.1.1 and 7.1.2, are intended to give you some insight into the nature and variety of aims in education, as well as some experience in thinking about aims and their implications and discussing this with others.

Task 7.1.1

SCHOOL AIMS: A COMPARISON

When you have carried out this task by yourself, try to compare your findings with those of other student teachers. The two schools for comparison are:

1   the school in which you received your own secondary education (or the majority of it, if you changed schools);
2   your current school experience school.

For the first school, your data will be wholly or largely from your own memory. Answer the following questions as far as you can:

- Did your school have an explicit statement of its aims?
- Were you as a pupil aware of the school's aims?
- In what ways did the particular aims of your school impinge on your experience as a pupil?

For your school experience school, ask:

- Does your school have an explicit statement of aims – if so, what does it say?
- Are the pupils you are teaching aware of the school's aims?
- Does the existence of these aims appear to make any difference to the pupils' experience in the school?

If you are a parent, you could also identify the aims of your child's school, using the school's documentation and, perhaps, discussion with staff.

   Answering these questions in the case of your present school experience school gives scope for some small-scale empirical research. Depending on your subject, you may be able to incorporate some research into your teaching, e.g. in a discussion about school aims or through pupils themselves conducting a survey into how far their fellow pupils are aware of the school aims. You should discuss first with your school tutor any enquiry you plan.

Compare your findings for the two schools. Do you find that aims have a higher profile in one school or the other? Is there any evidence that the existence of an explicit policy on aims enhances the education the school is providing? Check the competences/standards for your course which relate to the aims of schools.

Task 7.1.2

THE GOVERNING BODY: AIMS FOR A NEW SCHOOL

This is a group task involving role play. It is suitable for a group of several student teachers in the same school, or for a seminar with student teachers from several schools.

With other student teachers, role-play a governors' meeting which is intended to put together a statement of aims for a new school (imagining that it is a new school allows you to start with a relatively clean sheet). Within the allotted time (say, one hour) you must try to produce a statement of aims to be included in the prospectus, to help show prospective pupils and their parents what is distinctive about the new school and its educational priorities.

Before you start the role play, you should agree on any special characteristics of the area in which the school is located. It may be best to make it a school which has to serve a wide range of interests, i.e. a comprehensive school with a socially and ethnically varied intake.

Depending on the number in your group, you can assign individuals to some of the following roles as governors. (You may think there is some stereotyping in the brief descriptions of these roles. If you have experience of role play, you should be able to distance yourself from the stereotypes.)

A Conservative-voting company director
A Labour-voting trade union leader
A Church of England vicar
A spokesperson for the main local ethnic community
A parent of a bright child, with high academic ambitions for their child
A teacher-governor
The headteacher

One of you should be elected to chair the meeting and another to take notes on the points made and record anything which is agreed.

After the role play, if you have not arrived at an agreed statement, talk about what it was that prevented agreement. In what ways does the disagreement within your group reflect the actual diversity of interests and cultures within our society?

The competences/standards of your course require you to know about the roles of the governing body of a school.

WHY BOTHER WITH AIMS?

> Education as such has no aims. Only persons, parents and teachers, etc., have aims, not an abstract idea like education.
>
> (Dewey, 1916, chapter 8, 'Aims of education')

Your experience in doing the tasks may have backed up Dewey's point. You may have seen that different people can have different aims for education. You may also have considered how much difference aims can make. A statement of aims on paper does not, of course, make any difference by itself (there is an example of this below in the context of the NC). But what people do and how they do it are certainly influenced by what they are themselves aiming at. Aims, at their different levels, can affect:

- how a whole school system is organised (for example, the movement towards comprehensive education which began in the 1960s was driven at least partly by explicit aims of breaking down class barriers and distributing opportunities for education more widely);
- how an individual school is run (for example, various aspects of a school's ethos and organisation may be motivated by the aim that pupils should respect and tolerate each other's differences);
- how curriculum content is selected and taught (there is more on this aspect of aims in the next unit).

MAKING SENSE OF THE VARIETY OF AIMS

Because aims can be so diverse, it is useful in thinking about aims to be able to categorise them in some way. There is no single right way of dividing different aims into categories; in fact it is more helpful to be able to work with different categorising schemes.

Some approaches assume that education is aiming to develop personal qualities and capacities of one sort or another, and therefore divide aims up into the categories of knowledge, attitudes and skills. A distinction between academic, personal and vocational aims is related to this, but does not coincide exactly with it. Part of the importance in practice of the academic/personal/vocational division is that it can be recognised to some extent in ways in which different types of school historically have conceived their task.

But even if you are confident that education should be developing certain qualities or capacities in individuals, there is the wider question – still one about aims – of why this should be done. Is it just for the benefit of each individual, or for the general good of society? In other words, what should be the aim of the educational system as a whole? Should it be to do the best that can be done for each individual? Or should it be to promote and maintain a certain kind of society – perhaps a democratic society, or a just society, or an economically successful society?

This question introduces another distinction which has its uses but which, like any categorisation, can be misleading if not used carefully. If you had to make a sharp choice, say between developing in people the capacities which enable each individual to lead a fulfilling life, and giving them the skills and attitudes which fit them to be cogs in an impersonal system, then there would be a real divide between aiming at the good of the individual and aiming at the good of society. But it is not necessarily like that. If, for instance, your view of a good society is that it is the kind of society in which all individuals have the capacity to lead fulfilling lives and there are no obstacles in the way of people exercising those capacities, then there need be no contradiction between aiming at the good of the individual and aiming at the good of society.

In fact, even without being idealistic, many aims do cut across the individual/society division. Giving people skills which enable them to get productive jobs, for example, is in many instances of benefit to the individuals concerned and to others in society. Other cases may be more difficult. Certain types of academic knowledge might benefit individuals who have that knowledge – if only because they happen to find it interesting – without having any spin-off for others. Certain types of moral training – such as getting people to adhere to a particular code of behaviour – might benefit others without doing anything positive for the individual concerned.

JUSTIFYING AIMS

In your role plays and discussions people have been trying to defend their own conceptions of what the aims of education should be. What sorts of argument have they been using?

One approach which used to be favoured by philosophers was to say that certain aims are incorporated into the **concept** of education. So, if someone aimed at inculcating in pupils particular religious or moral beliefs, this could be rejected on the ground that inculcating unquestioned beliefs is simply not part of our concept of education. In fact (it might be said) it is part of our concept of **indoctrination**, whereas the concept of **education** implies the promotion of rationality and critical thinking.

You may agree with this. Its limitation as an argument, though, is that it does not allow you to meet on their own ground people who might argue that what they want teachers and schools to do is to inculcate certain unquestioned beliefs. They may not mind if you don't *call* this education; it is what they want you to aim at.

In the end, argument about educational aims is not about concepts – how we use words – but about values. It is argument about the responsibilities of adult members of society towards the young members of society and towards the next generation. In some way probably almost everyone would agree that education should be seeking to improve the quality of life of individuals or of the society in general – otherwise why bother with it? – but there is room for dispute over what is important in a good quality of life. Do we do more for someone's quality of life by enabling them to earn a good income, or by developing, say, their scientific curiosity or their appreciation of art (even if these do not help them to work productively)?

Argument about the aims of education, then, may come down in the end to questions of what matters most in life. But it also has to be about the distinctive contribution that teachers and schools can make to promoting what is important in life. If we agree, for instance, that health is important in everyone's life, this does not mean that the aim of teachers in relation to health is the same as the aim of nurses and doctors, but it may be that there are particular kinds of contribution that teachers can make to improving people's chances of having a healthy life.

The individual/social dimension affects the issue of justification. If some aspect of education is seen as being of value only for (some) individuals, there may be questions about why society – people in general – should support it. If some aspect is seen as being of value only for the majority of people, but not everyone, there may be questions about whether it should be imposed on individuals if they do not freely choose it. Such questions, though, may often stem from a simplistic contrast between society and the individual; for a more sophisticated view, see John Dewey (1916).

Some writers today would argue that aims for education should be derived explicitly from a conception of the kind of society in which young people will be living. If this is to be a liberal, democratic and multicultural society, then education should be preparing people to live in that kind of society, and other more particular aims will follow from this.

The last two sections of this unit have discussed the **variety of aims** for education and ways in which aims can be **justified**. To explore further these two aspects of aims of education we suggest you address Task 7.1.3.

Task 7.1.3

WHY TEACH INFORMATION AND COMMUNICATION TECHNOLOGY (ICT)?

ICT is a relatively new subject in the curriculum but is much more influential than just a subject. ICT is conceived of as contributing to other subjects, introducing new ways of learning and influencing the way teachers teach.

Discuss the place of ICT in the school curriculum in terms of possible aims, such as the personal, academic and vocational. How might those aims be justified to the pupil, the parents or the wider society? You may wish first to re-read the previous two sections of this unit.

EQUAL AIMS FOR EVERYONE?

Through much of the history of education, it would have been an unquestioned assumption that the aims of education should be different for different people. Plato built his conception of an ideal state (*The Republic*) on the argument that the people in power would need a much more thorough education than anyone else. A similar position was apparent in Victorian Britain, where the expansion of education was driven in part by the aim that the mass of the population should be sufficiently well educated to form a productive workforce but not so well educated that they might rebel against the (differently educated) ruling classes. In the mid-twentieth century, within a system selecting by ability, there were different aims behind the education offered in different types of schools: secondary modern, technical and grammar. Also, through much of the twentieth century, differences in aims were apparent between boys' and girls' schools, and between religious foundations and schools which were effectively secular.

Today the unquestioned assumption is often the reverse: that the basic aims of education are the same for everyone, even if different methods have to be used with different people in pursuing the same aims, and even if some people go further in the process than others. This assumption underlies many important developments in the promotion of equal opportunities. One of the basic reasons for being concerned with equal opportunities is that, if what you are aiming at is worthwhile, no one should be excluded from it because of factors, such as race or gender, which ought to be irrelevant to achieving these worthwhile aims. But this basic assumption is still not without its problems.

In the area of special educational needs in England and Wales, for instance, the Warnock Committee, which was set up in the late 1970s to look into the education of pupils with physical and mental disabilities, argued that the fundamental aims of education are the same for everyone (DES, 1978). This was part of the thinking which led in the 1980s to the integration of an increasing proportion of pupils with special educational needs into mainstream schools, rather than their segregation in special schools. Schools are required, for example, to be specially equipped to respond to some needs and to appoint additional specialist staff. This requirement has led to funding problems and to inadequate provision due to a shortage of suitably trained teaching staff.

As regards gender, few people would now suggest that the aim of education for girls should be to produce wives and mothers while the aim of education for boys should be to produce breadwinners. When people today argue for single-sex schooling, it is usually not because they think there are separate aims for the education of boys and of girls, but because they think that the aims are more likely to be achieved if boys and girls are taught without the distractions or pressures present in mixed-sex groups (this is controversial, of course). Even so, some might argue that a degree of differentiation in aims is needed; perhaps, for instance, there should be an attempt to develop assertiveness in girls and sensitivity in boys.

Turning to different cultural, religious or ethnic groups, it is not surprising if governments expect the same aims to be pursued for all groups; anything else would seem grossly discriminatory. But at the same time the members of particular groups may have special aims they would like to see pursued for their own children. To some religious believers it may be more important that their children are brought up within the faith of their community, than that they are brought up as citizens of a secular society; such differences lie behind the demands that some religious groups make for separate schools.

These examples illustrate again the point made earlier, that, while at one level statements of the aims of education can appear rather platitudinous and bland, there is the potential for controversy when aims are considered in more detail and the attempt is made to see how the pursuit of certain aims can be implemented in practice.

AIMS IN THE NATIONAL CURRICULUM

You may be working within the constraints of a national curriculum, such as that for England and Wales (DfEE/QCA, 1999a). How much scope does this leave you and your colleagues in deciding on your aims?

A first stage in answering this is that you should be aware of what the documentation of your national curriculum actually says about aims. When the NC for England and Wales was first brought in, in 1988, its explicit aims were limited to the following:

- to promote the spiritual, moral, cultural, mental and physical development of pupils at the school and of society;
- to prepare pupils for the opportunities, responsibilities and experiences of adult life.

As a statement of aims, this was not very controversial (with the possible exception of the idea of spiritual development). Its problem was that it was so broad and general that it gave very little guidance. And in fact there was no indication within the rest of the original documentation of the NC for England and Wales that its content had been influenced at all by the statement of aims. That statement seemed to be an example of an error which it is easy for government agencies, and also schools, to slip into: setting out a statement of aims which looks good, but which makes no apparent difference to what actually happens.

During the late 1990s, when the NC was being reviewed, the Qualification and Curriculum Authority (QCA) decided to pay explicit attention to aims. This resulted in a much-expanded statement of aims (in Unit 7.3 on the NC, this is the 'Rationale for the Curriculum' referred to in Table 7.3.3). What does this statement say about aims?

First, the statement acknowledges that aims rest in values, and it refers to a number of values which are taken to be shared across our society. It also acknowledges that in influencing and reflecting these values schools need to work with other parts of society.

Secondly, so far as the school curriculum of England and Wales is concerned, two aims are set out and more particular statements (objectives) are made about how the curriculum can promote these aims. A summary of these aims is given below; the full statement can be found in DfEE/QCA, 1999a, pp. 11–12.

Aim 1: The school curriculum should aim to provide opportunities for all pupils to learn and achieve. The curriculum should:

promote pupils' commitment to learning and confidence in their capacities to do so – equip them with basic skills

cultivate capacity to solve problems, think rationally, critically and creatively – help pupils to become creative, innovative, enterprising and capable of leadership – develop physical skills and see the importance of a healthy lifestyle

develop pupils' sense of identity through understanding of cultural heritage and of local, national, European and international dimensions – appreciate human aspirations and achievement in aesthetic, scientific and other fields.

Aim 2: The school curriculum should aim to promote pupils' spiritual, moral, social and cultural development and prepare all pupils for the opportunities, responsibilities and experiences of life. The curriculum should:

pass on enduring social values, promote pupils' integrity and autonomy – help them become caring citizens in a just society – help them challenge discrimination – promote spiritual, moral, social and cultural development – develop knowledge of different beliefs and cultures – promote respect for environment and commitment to sustainable development at local through to global levels

promote pupils' self-esteem and emotional well-being – help them form satisfying relationships – develop their ability to work for the common good – help them respond positively to challenges and to change and adversity

prepare pupils for the next steps in learning and employment – equip them to make informed choices.

(Bramall and White, 2000b, pp. 10–12)

As a statement of aims, it could be said that this has 'something for everyone'. There is probably not much there that anyone could dissent from. At the same time there are ideas which are open to interpretation, and there is scope for balancing one aim against another in all sorts of ways.

As a teacher in schools in England and Wales, you could consider this statement of aims as a resource you can draw on. The next unit suggests ways in which you might do this in relation to your own curriculum subject.

So is this a statement of aims that actually makes a difference in schools? At least we can say at this stage that there is enough detail there to make it possible to ask whether a school is actually working in a way that helps to promote these aims. Is enough attention being paid, for instance, to different beliefs and cultures, or to the environment, or to the requirements of citizenship, or to developing pupils' self-esteem?

In the end it is for you and other teachers to determine how much difference this statement of aims makes. But the next two units in this chapter, on the curriculum in general, and on the National Curriculum in particular, give you a basis to begin thinking about how far the curriculum you are working with is likely to promote such aims as these.

Task 7.1.4

AIMS AND EDUCATION – THE NC FOR ENGLAND AND WALES

Working either from the summary above, or preferably from the full statement of values and aims for the NC of England and Wales (DfEE/QCA, 1999a; or the National Curriculum website: www.nc.uk.net), consider the following points:
Do all these aims seem to you to fit together into a coherent idea of what education is about?

Is there anything in this statement of aims which you would not have expected to see there? Is there anything which is likely to prove controversial? Is there anything you think should be mentioned which is not mentioned?

Discuss your responses with other student teachers, or with your tutor. Use the findings from your discussion to check the competences/standards for your course.

SUMMARY AND KEY POINTS

In working as a teacher you necessarily have some aims, and these are more likely to be coherent and defensible if you have thought them through. At the same time, you are operating within the context of aims set by others. Aims can exist at different levels, local or national. In Britain, in recent years, the dominant tendency has been towards a common conception of aims for everyone, and most recently in England and Wales a broad set of aims has been incorporated into the documentation for the NC. But this still leaves room for you to form your own view as to the most important priorities for education, and to discuss with others how these aims can best be realised.

It is always possible to raise questions about the justification of educational aims. Ultimately our aims for education rest on our values – our conceptions of what makes for a good life, both for individuals and for our society as a whole. Because we do not share all of our values with each other, there will always be room for debate about the aims of education.

You should review this unit to cross-check with the competences/standards of your course, particularly sections dealing with wider professional requirements.

FURTHER READING

Aldrich, R. and White, J. (1998) *The National Curriculum beyond 2000: The QCA and the Aims of Education*, London: Institute of Education.

An argument for basing the curriculum on an explicit consideration of aims, and for deriving these aims from democratic values.

Dewey, J. (1916) *Democracy and Education*, New York: Free Press.

A classic book (often reprinted) which is still well worth reading. Though Dewey is often thought of simply as an advocate of child–centred education, his educational theory is part of a well worked out theory of the relation between individual and society and of the nature of knowledge and thought. See especially chapters 1 to 4, 8 and 9.

Wringe, C. (1988) *Understanding Educational Aims*, London: Unwin Hyman.

An introductory text by a philosopher of education, reviewing a variety of positions about aims in education concerned with (i) the development of qualities and capacities in the individual for the individual's own good; (ii) what is good from the point of view of society; (iii) the pursuit of aims seen as intrinsic to education and valuable in their own right.

UNIT 7.2 **THE SCHOOL CURRICULUM**

GRAHAM HAYDON

INTRODUCTION

The curriculum is an important part of the context within which you work as a teacher. The planned or formal curriculum is the intended content of an educational programme set out in advance. We refer later to the informal and hidden curriculum. Like other aspects of the context of your work (the school buildings, say, or the administrative organisation of the school), the curriculum forms a 'frame' to what you are doing even when you are not explicitly thinking about it. But often you find that you do refer to the curriculum, in your everyday conversations with colleagues, and less frequently perhaps in meetings with parents or in talking to pupils in a pastoral role.

It might seem that the curriculum is so clearly part of the context of your work that it must be obvious what the curriculum is. In which case, why does a book of this nature need a unit on the curriculum (in fact two units, since the next unit is specifically about the National Curriculum (NC) in England and Wales)?

The purpose of this unit is to show you that, once you think about it, it is not so obvious what the curriculum is, and that it is not something you should, as a teacher, take for granted. Rather than relying on implicit assumptions about the curriculum, you should be able and willing, as part of your professional role, to think about the curriculum, about its role in education, and about ways in which it is controversial and might be open to challenge.

Similar remarks applied to the topic of aims, discussed in the previous unit. The strategy of this unit is to discuss the curriculum as one of the most important 'tools' through which educational aims can be realised. But we need first to be clearer about what the term 'the curriculum' refers to.

OBJECTIVES

At the end of this unit you should be able to:

- distinguish a number of different conceptions of the curriculum;
- discuss ways in which the curriculum may or may not help to realise educational aims;
- see why the content of the curriculum, even if often taken for granted, is potentially controversial;
- discuss the place of your particular teaching subject within the broader curriculum.

THE CURRICULUM IN GENERAL AND THE CURRICULUM WITHIN PARTICULAR SUBJECTS

It helps to avoid confusion in the rest of this unit (and we hope in your thinking more generally) if we distinguish between the curriculum of a school (or even of schools in general) and the curriculum within a particular subject. We can often mark this distinction by speaking of the 'syllabus', rather than curriculum, of a particular subject. In the way the words are actually used in professional discourse and wider debate the distinction is not clear-cut. The term 'syllabus' usually refers to a specific programme in a specific subject set out in detail in advance, possibly designed by a particular teacher, but often laid down by an examination board or other body external to the school. But people do also speak of, say, 'the science curriculum' or 'the arts curriculum', when they want to focus on a part of 'the curriculum' in general, though not necessarily at the level of the details of a specific syllabus.

The documentation of the NC for England and Wales, which is the focus for the next unit, does not make it easy to keep any sharp distinction in terminology, since in that documentation some level of detail of Programmes of Study and targets for particular subjects has always been seen as part of the NC.

For most of this unit, though, the focus is on the broad curriculum. Questions are raised about the role of particular subjects within the curriculum in general, rather than about what goes on *within* the teaching of particular subjects. But we shall have to say something about the latter point as well, because the role of a subject within the curriculum partly depends on what is done within that subject. (So far, the term 'the whole curriculum' has been avoided because that too may carry some ambiguity.)

Task 7.2 1

SCHOOL CURRICULA: A COMPARISON

(This task is deliberately parallel to Task 7.1.1 on aims in Unit 7.1.)

When you have carried out this task by yourself, try to compare your findings with those of other student teachers.

The two schools for comparison are:

1 The school in which you received your own secondary education (or the majority of it, if you changed schools);
2 Your current school experience school.

From memory, write down on one side of paper what was in the curriculum of the school you attended as a pupil. Then (without referring to documentation at this stage) write down what is in the curriculum of your school experience school. Compare the two accounts.

THE FORMAL CURRICULUM

There *could* be considerable variety in what you and other student teachers have written, because the term 'curriculum' can be used in various ways. But it is likely that what you have written down, for both schools in the comparison, is a list of subjects. What this illustrates is that when people refer to 'the curriculum' without qualification, most often they are thinking of what we can usefully label 'the formal curriculum'. This is the intended content of an educational programme, set out in advance.

At a minimal level of detail, the formal curriculum can be stated as a list of names of subjects. Thus the statement that we expect pupils to learn 'reading, writing and arithmetic' would itself be a curriculum statement (about the thinnest possible). So would be the extended and modified version adopted in the school attended by Lewis Carroll's Mock Turtle:

> "Reeling and Writhing, of course, to begin with . . . and then the different branches of Arithmetic – Ambition, Distraction, Uglification and Derision. . . . Mystery, ancient and modern, with Seaography: then . . . Drawling, Stretching, and Fainting in Coils" (but the Mock Turtle didn't do "Laughing and Grief" though they were on the curriculum; they must have been options).
>
> (Gardner, 1965, pp. 129–130, with explanations)

While the formal curriculum can be listed simply as a set of subjects (and the requirement that you write it down on one side of paper may have encouraged this approach), it is always possible to set out in more detail for each subject the content which is supposed to be taught and learned. Even when the curriculum is stated simply as a list of subjects, those who write it and those who read it have some implicit understanding of what goes into each subject. It is important to keep this in mind when comparing the curricula offered in schools at different times. It is likely that your lists contain a number of items, probably the majority, that are common to both lists. In fact we can go further. If the NC in England and Wales at the beginning of the twenty-first century is compared with the secondary school regulations for England of 1904 (Aldrich and White, 1998, p. 48), and even with the mid-nineteenth-century curriculum which Lewis Carroll was parodying, we find many items in common (the most noticeable absence from Carroll's list, which appears in all the subsequent ones, is science).

This finding does illustrate something about the extent to which the formal curriculum in schools in England has *not* gone through revolutionary changes. At the same time, it would be a mistake to conclude from the similarity of the lists that the curriculum has hardly changed at all. Even if we could set aside all changes in teaching method and concentrate solely on the content of the subjects, what is taught under the heading of history or science in 2001 is obviously going to be very different in many ways from what was taught under the same headings in 1904.

Another point to note under 'formal curriculum' is that the curriculum may contain parts which are optional. Even before the NC in England and Wales made certain subjects compulsory, it was normal for most of the curriculum in a secondary school to consist of subjects which all pupils were expected to take. But there may also be options within the curriculum, particularly in the later years of secondary school.

Related to the idea of a compulsory curriculum are the notions of a 'common curriculum' – one taken by everyone in practice, whether or not it is actually compulsory – and a 'core curriculum' – the part of a whole curriculum which everyone takes, around which there is scope for variations.

THE INFORMAL CURRICULUM AND THE HIDDEN CURRICULUM

The notion of the formal curriculum refers to the content which is, quite deliberately, taught by teachers in a school, usually in periods structured by a timetable and labelled according to subject. So the fact that something is on the curriculum means that it is taught (or at least that the intention of the curriculum planners or of the school management is that it shall be taught). But since some pupils may fail to learn what teachers are intending to teach, the fact that something is a non-optional part of the formal curriculum does not guarantee that pupils learn it.

On the other hand, pupils may learn things in school which are not taught as part of the formal curriculum. There are two ways in which this can happen. One is that the school intends that pupils should learn things which cannot be directly taught in lessons. Many of the possible aims of a school, which you were thinking about in the last unit, involve matters of this kind. If a school wants, for instance, to promote co-operation and consideration for others, then (if these are to be more than pious aspirations) it needs to do something to try to bring about co-operation and to encourage pupils to behave in considerate ways. (See also Unit 4.5 'Moral development and values' for further discussion of promoting common values.) Teachers might agree to build co-operative work into their lessons, whatever the subject; teachers and pupils might draw up a code of behaviour; there may be some system of rewards and sanctions; the school management may pay attention to the way that pupils move around the school during break-times; and so on. All such arrangements can be counted as part of the 'informal curriculum' of the school.

Taking into account both the formal and the informal curriculum, the curriculum can be defined in some way such as this:

> The school curriculum comprises all learning and other experiences that each school plans for its pupils.

> (DfEE/QCA, 1999a, p. 10)

But pupils may also learn things at school which the school does not intend them to learn. For several decades sociologists have pointed out that many pupils at school were learning, for instance, to accept passively what they were told or to see themselves as failures; while some were learning to identify with and follow the mores of a rebellious sub-culture; and some were learning racist and sexist attitudes, and so on. Such learning was not normally part of what the school was intending its pupils to learn, and the school may not have been aware of many of the things that its pupils were learning; from the school's point of view, these outcomes were side-effects of the pupils' time in school. So the term 'hidden curriculum' was invented to cover such learning.

Today, teachers are far more likely to be aware of such side-effects. In that way, what might once have been part of a hidden curriculum comes to be hidden no longer. This does not mean that schools today have no hidden curriculum; it means that a school has to be careful to try to uncover and become aware of side-effects of what it does deliberately in its teaching and its organisation. If these side-effects are unwelcome – if, say, they work against the school achieving its intended aims – then the school may make deliberate attempts to counteract them. Often a school does this by paying attention to aspects of its teaching and organisation outside of the formal curriculum. So, where the learning of racist or sexist attitudes might once have been part of the *hidden* curriculum in some schools, it is more likely today that the *informal* curriculum includes anti-racist and anti-sexist policies. And it may also be that such policies alter what is done within the *formal* curriculum, e.g. within a PSHE course or Citizenship education (an area often referred to as the pastoral curriculum).

Mention of the informal curriculum shows that the curriculum as a whole is not, for any teacher, a rigid framework within which there is no room for flexibility or planning. Even when the formal curriculum is determined largely in advance, as in the NC, there is still scope open to the school in designing the details of the curriculum and the way that links between curriculum subjects are (or are not) made; and there is space outside the National Curriculum since it is not supposed to occupy the whole timetable.

You should, then, see it as part of your professional role as a teacher that you can take an overview of the curriculum, have a sense of 'where it comes from', and be able to engage in discussion on whether it could be improved and, if so, in what ways.

CURRICULUM AS A SELECTION FROM CULTURE

A number of writers have referred to the curriculum as a selection from the culture of a society. 'Culture' here refers to 'everything that is created by human beings themselves: tools and technology, language and literature, music and art, science and mathematics – in effect, the whole way of life of a society' (Lawton, 1989, p. 17). Any society passes on its culture to the next generation, and in modern societies schooling is one of the ways in which this is done. But obviously no school curriculum can accommodate the whole of human culture; so a selection has to be made.

A natural question to ask next is: how do we make that selection? Different curriculum theories give different answers.

A first move is to recognise that since some aspects of culture are passed on or picked up independently of schools, it may make sense for schools in general to concentrate on matters which will not be learned if they are not included in the school curriculum; and secondary schools in particular have to try to build on, but not duplicate, what pupils have learned by the end of primary school. Even these points give rise to many questions. For example, many young people of secondary age pick up much of what they know about computers, sport or popular music independently of school; does this mean there is no point in including study of these areas in the curriculum?

After putting on one side things which pupils learn independently of school (if we can identify such things), there are principles by which we might try to make a selection from culture. In this unit there is space to mention just three: to select what is **best**, or what is **distinctive** of a particular culture, or what is in some way **fundamental**.

The idea of selecting, and enabling people to appreciate, what is **best** goes back at least to Matthew Arnold. Arnold was not only a Victorian poet and a commentator on the culture of his day, but also a school inspector. Historically, this principle has been linked with the idea of whole areas of culture – 'high culture', centred on arts and literature, being of greater value than the rest of culture, and also perhaps being accessible only to a minority of society. The principle does not have to be interpreted in that way. Whatever area of culture we are dealing with – including, for instance, football and rock music – we may well want people to be able to appreciate what is good rather than what is mediocre (see Gingell and Brandon, 2000 for a defence of this idea). It does not follow, though, that the school curriculum should always be focused on what is best in any area. If we suppose, for instance, that the greatest science is that of Einstein or Stephen Hawking, it does not mean we place this science at the centre of the school curriculum. In many areas, if people are ever to be able to appreciate the best, they need to start by understanding something more basic.

Another principle of selection which is sometimes favoured is to pick from the whole of human culture what is **distinctive** of a particular culture – the way of life of a particular nation, or ethnic group, or religion. This may apply more to the detailed content within areas of the curriculum than to the selection of the broad areas. We do not just learn language, we learn a particular language; and while it is possible to study historical method, any content of history is that of particular people in a particular part of the world. One question for curriculum planning, then, is how far to select from what we see as 'our' culture, and how to interpret what is 'our' culture. That question, in England, has to be resolved in a context of a multicultural society, within a world in which there is increasing interaction between different cultures.

Rather than looking to what is best, or what is distinctive, we may try to look to what is **fundamental**. This idea may apply both across the curriculum and within areas of the curriculum. Within the sciences and mathematics, for instance, the idea of what is culturally distinctive may have little application (which is not to say that these subjects as actually taught are culture-free), and the idea of teaching the best may be inappropriate. We need to think about what is fundamental. In the educational context, this does not mean what is fundamental in the whole structure of human knowledge; it means what people need to learn if they are to have a foundation on which further knowledge or skills can be built.

Thinking about the curriculum in general, we can also try to ask what is fundamental in the whole human culture in which people are living. But this question depends in turn on some particular understanding of what is important in human life. Is it the development of the capacities for rational thought and judgement? Then we might argue, as the philosopher of education Paul Hirst once did, that there are certain basic forms of human understanding – science, mathematics, interpersonal understanding, and so on – which are not interchangeable and each of which is necessary in its own way to the development of rational understanding.

Or is human life more fundamentally about providing the material necessities of life? Then we might stress what can be economically useful, and our curriculum might be primarily a vocational one. Or is the essential aspect of human life, so far as education is concerned, the fact that people live together in groups and have to organise their affairs together? Then preparing people to be citizens might turn out to be most fundamental.

So far, none of these approaches looks as if it takes us very far, by itself, in selecting which aspects of culture should make up a school curriculum. Of course, there is much more to the arguments than can be considered in detail here. But even this much discussion suggests that the attempt to select from human culture does not take us far without an explicit consideration of the aims of education. We do not, after all, have to transmit culture just as it stands (and in any case it is constantly changing). We may have views about what kind of society we wish to see, or about what kind of persons we hope will emerge from education.

RELATING CURRICULUM TO AIMS

The previous unit raised the question about the aims of education in general terms, suggested some approaches to answering it, and looked briefly at the current stated aims of the NC in England and Wales. The important point to emphasise is that the curriculum of schools is a major part of the way in which we attempt to realise educational aims. So, rationally, the planning of a curriculum should depend on how the overall aims of education are conceived. Historically, as was pointed out in the last unit, this has not always happened. Even when, as now, there is a National Curriculum incorporating an extended statement of aims, there is room to question how far the required curriculum is actually likely to realise the stated aims.

Task 7.2.2

LINKING CURRICULUM CONTENT TO AIMS

Look again at the NC of England and Wales statement of aims, as used for Task 7.1.4 (see p. 336). (You may wish to use a different national curriculum for this task.)

If you were responsible for planning a curriculum which could realise these aims, what would you think should go into that curriculum?

Look at the next unit for the details of the current NC. How far do you think the NC of England and Wales as we have it now is likely to promote its stated aims?
Discuss with other student teachers or your tutor.

Notice that this question about the National Curriculum is asking you to consider the formal curriculum with which schools in England and Wales now operate (apart from the small amount of time available to schools for pursuing activities outside the National Curriculum). But we can also think about ways in which a school's informal curriculum may further the same aims.

The aims set out in Unit 7.1 contain many that we would not expect to be realised primarily through anything in the content of the curriculum subjects. Think for instance of the promotion of self-esteem and emotional well-being; challenging discrimination; developing a sense of identity. It is clear that the informal curriculum has a large role to play here; any school which gave its attention only to the formal curriculum would be realising these other aims only incidentally if at all.

How far, then, *can* the formal curriculum promote the kinds of aims set out? It is clear that the traditional curriculum subjects have a role in promoting pupils' learning and achievement (achievement within those subjects, that is, although there are other kinds of achievement as well), and in promoting their intellectual development. What is not so clear is the role of the traditional subjects in promoting the broader aims of a moral and social kind, which were always recognised in National Curriculum documents and have now gained greater prominence than before.

The first version of the National Curriculum in England and Wales (DES/WO, 1988) attempted to address such aims by incorporating a number of cross-curricular themes: health education, citizenship education, careers education and guidance, environmental education, and education for economic and industrial understanding. These themes did not have the statutory force of the core and foundation subjects, and it was left largely to individual schools (with limited published guidance) to decide how to teach them. In fact, in many schools the cross-curricular themes were not systematically taken up at all.

In the current NC (DfEE/QCA, 1999a) a number of the stated aims relate to topics which the cross-curricular themes had been intended to address: economic understanding, careers choice and education about the environment, for instance, are clearly incorporated in the aims. But of the original cross-curricular themes, only citizenship has gained the status of a statutory subject, and the other areas are no longer there as distinct themes. It is clear from this that, in relation to the declared aims, Citizenship education carries a heavy burden, as does PSHE, even though that is not statutory. The role of Citizenship is raised also in Unit 4.5 'Moral development and values'.

What of the subjects that still form the bulk of the curriculum? It is no surprise that subjects such as English, mathematics and science have a central place in most curricula; as we saw above, they have been in the curriculum of schools in Britain (and many other countries) for a long time. But it remains true that the current National Curriculum documents do not attempt any detailed arguments to show in which ways particular subjects help to promote particular aims. Indeed some writers have questioned whether subjects such as mathematics and foreign languages do deserve the prominence they have in the curriculum if the overall purpose of that curriculum is to promote the kinds of aims set out in the documents; see Bramall and White, 2000b. More detailed arguments both for and against the prominence of mathematics in the curriculum can be found in Bramall and White, 2000a, and Tikly and Wolf, 2000. On the other hand, it may be argued that an understanding of the history of one's own society has such an important role in underpinning informed citizenship that it should not cease to be compulsory at Key Stage 4 (Bramall and White, 2000b).

How a subject relates to overall aims may affect not only its place in the overall curriculum but also how it is taught. In science and mathematics, what is the balance between equipping pupils with skills which they can put to practical use (thus furthering training and employment opportunities) and trying to show pupils something of the sheer fascination which mathematics and science can hold quite apart from their applications? In history, what is the balance between trying to promote a sense of a common British inheritance and exploring the history which has led to Britain being the multicultural society it now is?

Mathematics and history have been used as two examples here, but you may wish to think about similar questions that might be raised for other subjects.

Task 7.2.3

JUSTIFYING YOUR SUBJECT IN THE SCHOOL CURRICULUM

This can be a two-part task, with an individual stage followed by a group stage.
The task is to contribute to a school prospectus (it might be for the same imaginary school which you used in Task 7.1.2). Suppose that the school has adopted the statement of aims from a national curriculum.

Your individual task is to write a paragraph of not more than 100 words setting out for prospective parents the ways in which your teaching subject fits into the whole curriculum, and thus contributes to realising the overall aims of the curriculum. (Remember that some parents – and pupils – may wonder what the point of studying certain subjects is at all.)

The group task is for you and your fellow student teachers, representing different subjects, to make sure that the individual subject statements fit together into a coherent description of a whole curriculum, complementing and not competing with each other.

Reflect on this task and check your development against the competences/standards for your course.

SUMMARY AND KEY POINTS

The curriculum is an important part of the context in which you work as a teacher. It includes both the formal curriculum, which sets out in detail the subjects to be taught, and the informal curriculum, which covers the variety of ways in which a school can attempt to achieve the kinds of aims which cannot be captured in the content of timetabled subjects.

The curriculum is perhaps the most important means through which educational aims can be pursued. Although much of the curriculum exists already as a framework within which you work, you may well have the opportunity to contribute to discussion about the curriculum, and you should be able to take and argue a view both on the whole curriculum and on the place of your own subject within it.

Any curriculum is a selection from the culture of a society, but any way of selecting elements from culture – the attempt to select what is best, or what is distinctive or what is fundamental – may not by itself be adequate without a view of the overall aims of education.

While the current National Curriculum of England and Wales includes a statement of aims, there is still room for discussion over the contribution that individual subjects make to the achievement of those overall aims.

In this unit no more has been done than to introduce a few of the questions that can be raised and approaches that can be taken. Within educational research and theory, 'curriculum studies' has come to be a subject area in its own right on which there is a large literature; some of this literature is in the further reading below. You should refer to the statement of competences/standards for your course and check how this unit contributes to your development.

FURTHER READING

Bramall, S. and White, J. (2000b) *Will the New National Curriculum Live up to its Aims?* London: Philosophy of Education Society of Great Britain.
A short pamphlet (No. 6 in a series called IMPACT) which offers an evaluation of the content of the National Curriculum in the light of its own aims, reaching some sceptical conclusions about some of the traditional subjects.

Lawton, D. (1996) *Beyond the National Curriculum: Teacher Professionalism and Empowerment*, Sevenoaks: Hodder and Stoughton.
From one of the major British contributors to curriculum studies, this, as the title implies, considers not just the National Curriculum, but how the curriculum impinges on teachers and how teachers can be involved in curriculum planning.

GILL WATSON

INTRODUCTION

The National Curriculum (NC) in England and Wales was one of the measures incorporated within the Education Reform Act (ERA, 1988). The NC was implemented by all maintained primary and secondary schools in England and Wales in a rolling programme beginning in September 1989. Up until that point there had been very little government intervention into the curriculum taught in state schools in England and Wales. Individual schools could determine the structure and content of the curriculum with the only exception of religious education which was made a compulsory subject by the 1944 Education Act.

The 1988 Education Reform Act (ERA) was wide-ranging in its scope with far-reaching implications for the future of state education. In addition to the NC, the ERA introduced local management of schools, open enrolment, the publication of pupils' results in public examinations; and it also established entirely new types of school funded directly by central government. As student teachers you are affected most immediately and directly by the clause of the ERA that relates to the NC. If you are placed in a state-maintained school you have to ensure that your schemes of work and the lessons you teach meet the requirements of the NC and enable the pupils to make progress in line with national expectations.

OBJECTIVES

At the end of this unit you should be able to:

* define some important terms associated with the NC for England and Wales, including Key Stages, Programmes of Study, knowledge, skills and understanding, breadth of study, Attainment Targets, levels of achievement;
* explain the nature, scope and content of the NC as a whole;
* discuss the part played by the NC in the whole school curriculum experienced by pupils in maintained schools in England and Wales;
* understand the place of your subject specialism within the NC framework;
* identify the competences/standards for your course which relate to your knowledge and understanding of the school curriculum.

ESSENTIAL BACKGROUND

Concern about the decline in the standard of education in England and Wales in comparison with that of other countries was at the root of the decision to introduce a national curriculum for use in all maintained schools in England and Wales. A number of working groups were established to develop the NC. The first working group set up by the government was the Task Group for Assessment and Testing (TGAT) which made recommendations in 1988 for a complex system of teacher assessment and national tests. TGAT's recommendations were the starting point for the discussions of the working groups established for each of the NC subjects. The NC was, therefore, and still is, assessment-driven. This position runs counter to the assertion made by TGAT that 'assessment should be the servant and not the master of the curriculum' (DES/WO, 1988).

The TGAT report recommended that pupils' progress in all NC subjects should be formally assessed at four points in their school career. This assessment should take place at the end of the four **Key Stages**. The relation of Key Stage and year group to age is shown in Table 7.3.1.

Table 7.3.1 The four Key Stages of the National Curriculum

Key Stage	Age	Year group	
1	5–7	1–2	(Y1–Y2)
2	7–11	3–6	(Y3–Y6)
3	11–14	7–9	(Y7–Y9)
4	14–16	10–11	(Y10–Y11)

Pupils were to be assessed at the end of each Key Stage in relation to **Attainment Targets** (**ATs**) for each of the subjects, and progress would be measured against **Statements of Attainment** (**SoS**) – the level statements. TGAT recommended that there should be a ten-level scale against which pupils' achievement in the NC subjects would be measured, and suggested the range of levels that would normally be covered by each Key Stage. The expected range of performance, by levels, at the Key Stages is illustrated in Table 7.3.2.

Table 7.3.2 Expectations of pupil performance in the National Curriculum

Key Stage	Range of levels
1	1–3
2	2–5
3	3–7
4	4–10

While TGAT was at work and following the publication of the TGAT report, working groups of subject experts, including teachers, were set up for each of the NC subjects. The subject working parties were given the brief to determine the subject content of the NC, called the **Programme of Study** (**PoS**), appropriate for each of the Key Stages, the **Attainment Targets** for the subject, and the **Statements of Attainment** within each Attainment Target; the SoS linked progression in learning to level; see Table 7.3.2. The subject working parties worked to different timescales, as it had been decided to introduce the NC into schools as a rolling programme, which meant there were no opportunities for cross-subject discussion to ensure comparability and coherence. There were nine subjects in the NC for primary schools and ten subjects for secondary schools:

- English (Welsh in schools where Welsh was the first language)
- mathematics
- science
- art
- geography
- history
- a modern foreign language (compulsory in secondary schools only)
- music
- physical education (PE)
- technology

English, mathematics and science were designated as **core subjects** and were the first subjects to be developed, and their programmes were implemented with pupils from certain year groups on a rolling programme from September 1989; the other **non-core subjects** were implemented in phases from 1990 onwards. Thus the National Curriculum for England and Wales with its associated terminology was born. The separate subject Orders included the aspects of the discipline that subject experts considered to be vital to the development of children's understanding of their subject.

THE INTENTIONS OF THE NATIONAL CURRICULUM

The NC for England and Wales was established by the 1988 Education Reform Act and defines the minimum educational entitlement for pupils of compulsory school age. The NC applies to all pupils aged 5–16 in maintained schools. It does not apply in independent schools (i.e. private, fee-paying schools) although those schools may choose to follow it.

The 1988 ERA was reinforced by the Education Act, 1997, which required that all state schools should provide pupils with a curriculum that:

- is balanced and broadly based;
- promotes their spiritual, moral, cultural, mental and physical development;
- prepares them for the opportunities, responsibilities and experiences of adult life;
- includes, in addition to the NC, religious education and, for secondary pupils, sex education.

It is clear, therefore, that it was not the government's intention that the NC should constitute the whole curriculum for schools; rather it is a framework that schools can use to ensure that they provide a minimum curriculum entitlement for all their pupils. Every school is encouraged to create a whole school curriculum which reflects its particular needs and circumstances and that best achieves the school's aims and contributes to its ethos.

The content of each NC subject is defined in a statutory Order. Each Order consists of:

- **common requirements** which relate to access to the curriculum for all pupils, pupils' use of language, pupils' access to information technology and the Curriculum Cymreig (in Wales);
- the **Programme of Study** which sets out the minimum knowledge, understanding and skills for each subject at each Key Stage;
- **Attainment Targets** which define the expected standards of pupils; see the QCA website: www.qca.org.uk/gen5–14.htm 07/11/00

In essence the NC provided a secondary school curriculum that was very similar in number of subjects and in specified content to what had been provided for 11–14 year-olds in grammar and comprehensive schools for most of the twentieth century. However, it intended to provide a greater breadth of study than hitherto to the last two years of compulsory secondary schooling when pupils traditionally prepare for public examinations. The 1988 ERA introduced a programme of national assessment at the age of 14 (Year 9). From the outset there were concerns, in particular from headteachers and teacher associations, that there was content overload in the NC and that there would be insufficient timetable time to provide full coverage of the Programmes of Study in core and non-core subjects, never mind supplement the NC with other desirable curricular activities. However, it was the introduction of the programme of national testing associated with the NC which provoked the industrial action that led to the first review of the NC. Full-scale assessments in the core subjects of English, mathematics and science had been developed and piloted and were to be taken by all Year 9 pupils from 1993 onwards; national assessment had already been introduced at the end of Year 3 (7-year-olds) from 1991. The assessments were nationally produced but were to be administered and assessed by teachers. The results of the tests and the teachers' own assessments of their pupils were to be included on a national database. Teachers already overwhelmed by the demands of teaching the new Programmes of Study refused to take on the additional workload entailed in the setting and marking of assessments.

THE DEARING REVIEW OF THE NATIONAL CURRICULUM

Following the boycott by teachers of the national Key Stage 3 tests in 1993, the government appointed Lord Dearing (at that time Sir Ron Dearing) to:

- reduce the overall statutory content of the NC;
- review the ten-level scale originally recommended by TGAT;
- simplify the national tests;
- improve the administrative arrangements for the NC and its assessment.

When the Dearing committee produced its interim report for national consultation in 1994 the NC was still at a very early stage in its implementation. For instance, no pupils had yet studied the Key Stage 4 programme of study; there had been no national testing in any of the non-core subjects. The final Dearing proposals provided pragmatic solutions to what was perceived by primary and secondary teachers alike to be an unmanageable curriculum (Dearing, 1994). The recommendations were generally welcomed by schools and a revised set of NC Orders was completed and published for distribution to schools in January 1995. The revised Orders in all subjects for Key Stages 1, 2 and 3 had to be taught from September 1995, and the Key Stage 4 NC was to be implemented from September 1996.

A summary of the changes arising from the Dearing Review

Key Stages 1–3

The aim of the review was to free up 20 per cent of curriculum time to give schools the freedom to determine what should be taught in that time, the equivalent of one day a week. This necessitated reduction in the content of all of the subject Orders. However, the reduction was most severe in the Programmes of Study of the non-core subjects. New NC subject working groups were set up to review their curriculum, and again very little liaison took place between groups. There were clear implications for the coherence of the NC as a whole when cuts were made in a piecemeal fashion to what should be taught. One subject Order was changed more fundamentally. It was decided to separate Information Technology (IT) from the Design and Technology subject Order. The Dearing Review, therefore, in effect spawned an additional subject (IT) in the NC, which from 1996 was to form part of the core entitlement of pupils throughout all four Key Stages. This development was designed to promote an IT-literate society in the future.

Key Stage 4

Secondary schools and teacher associations had been particularly vociferous in their criticism of the original NC proposals for Key Stage 4. Pupils following the General Certificate of Secondary Education (GCSE) and its predecessors had traditionally chosen to study and sit examinations in seven to nine subjects. The NC proposals now required the study of a minimum of eleven. After much deliberation a number of subjects were made optional at Key Stage 4. This decision provoked much opposition from the subject associations representing the subjects concerned who saw the status of their subjects being diminished as a consequence.

From 1996, 14–16 year-old pupils would have to study and take a full GCSE award in the core subjects of English, mathematics and science. Additionally, pupils would be required to study one modern foreign language and design technology (as the subject was to be known) and take at least a GCSE short course (or its equivalent) in those subjects. They also had to be taught, but not examined at GCSE, physical education, religious education, personal, social and health education (PSHE), sex education and IT. History, geography, art and music were relegated to optional status. In the event, a minority of pupils did not study a modern foreign language or a course in design technology at Key Stage 4 during the period in which the Dearing proposals were in force. Certain schools decided to retain a curriculum which they felt best suited the needs of their pupils; and, in the opinion of the teachers, this did not include a modern foreign language (MFL) and/or design technology.

Assessment

The impact of the Dearing revisions was greatest in the area of assessment. This effect is not surprising as both the national tests and teacher assessment had been the object of the most severe criticisms. The whole system proposed by TGAT was reconsidered and simplified. In many subjects the number of Attainment Targets (AT) was substantially reduced, the greatest reductions being in mathematics (16 reduced to 4) and science (17 reduced to 4). Within each AT, Statements of Attainment were replaced by Level Descriptions. The original ten-level scale for use across all four Key Stages was reduced to eight levels (with the addition of an 'exceptional performance' category) to be applied only to Key Stages 1–3. Pupils' attainment at Key Stage 4 was to be assessed and reported through public examinations at 16+ (GCSE, GNVQ or, in a small number of cases, NVQ). For discussion of vocational qualifications (VQs) see Unit 6.2.

When Dearing was asked to review the NC, national tests had been developed and implemented only in the core subjects of English, mathematics and science at Key Stage 1 (1991 for Key Stages 2 and 3). Key Stage 3 national assessments had been developed and were boycotted by most secondary schools in 1993. National tests had actually been developed and piloted in some of the non-core subjects. However, the Dearing Report (Dearing, 1994) recommended that national assessments in the core subjects at Key Stages 1, 2 and 3 were to take the form of 'pen and pencil tests' rather than the more open-ended tasks used at both Key Stages 1 and 3 up to that point. The tests would be externally assessed and not marked by teachers as originally intended and no plans were made to extend national testing to the non-core subjects. However, the very controversial decision made by the government to publish the results of NC assessments for pupils aged 11 (Key Stage 2) and aged 14 (Key Stage 3) was upheld by Dearing, and it was decided that additional information on the effectiveness of schools would also be made available publicly from 1997. From that date secondary school teachers were required to assess the attainment of all their pupils in relation to the Attainment Target(s) at the end of Key Stage 3 (age 14) in all NC subjects. These data were be collected from all schools and published.

The changes recommended by the Dearing Report were consulted upon and subsequently revised and implemented by schools with a minimum of protest from teachers. The government had made an undertaking that there would be a moratorium on changes to the NC for a period of five years, until the year 2000. However, the momentum for change proved to be too great. Even before educationalists and other interested parties had time to consider the impact of the Dearing 'scissors and paste' review on the coherence and scope of the school curriculum and the extent to which it could claim to meet the aims enshrined in the 1988 ERA to provide pupils from the ages of 5 to 16 with a 'broad and balanced curriculum', other national initiatives made such an evaluation impossible.

CURRICULUM 2000

The curriculum that you are teaching is not the one arising from the implementation of the Dearing Report but a yet later version introduced in September 2000 as a result of a review commissioned by the Labour government elected in 1997 (DfEE/QCA, 1999a). The NC had been one of the flagship policies of the outgoing Conservative government. The 'New Labour' government had been elected on a manifesto pledge of 'education, education, education' and it had the reforming zeal of a party that had been out of power for nearly two decades. Very early in his period of office as Secretary of State for Education and Employment (SoS), David Blunkett made a commitment that the standards in literacy and numeracy of primary-aged pupils would rise very significantly. He said that, by 2002, a target of 80 per cent of Year 6 pupils should achieve at least NC level 4 in English and 75 per cent of Year 6 pupils should achieve level 4 in mathematics in their national tests at the end of Key Stage 2. The then Secretary of State for Education, David Blunkett, said that he would resign if these targets for these two basic skills were not reached, and this meant an increase of over 20 per cent in pupils' performance in both subjects.

A national literacy (NLS) and numeracy strategy (NNS) had been introduced into primary schools to support teachers in their work in the basic skills. These strategies were originally developed and piloted by working groups set up by the outgoing Conservative government, but the strategies were adopted and developed by the Labour government. The NLS and NNS went further than any government curriculum initiative. Not only did both strategies prescribe what was to be taught to pupils but they specified also the amount of time to be spent and the teaching approaches to be adopted. The NLS was introduced nationally in September 1998 and the NNS the following year. The strategies were not mandatory in maintained schools, but individual schools were set specific targets for achievement at Key Stage 2 and only a small minority of schools were sufficiently confident that they could achieve their target by continuing to use their established methods of teaching the basic skills.

To assist primary schools in achieving these challenging targets in literacy and numeracy the non-core subjects suffered a further loss of status between 1998 and 2000. As a result of pressure from primary schools and teacher associations, the government suspended the Programmes of Study in all the non-core subjects, including PE and design technology, to allow the curriculum in primary schools to be sharply focused on literacy and numeracy. This meant that although primary schools must continue to teach the six non-core subjects, what they taught and how much time was spent on these subjects were at the discretion of the headteachers and their governing bodies. The Qualifications and Curriculum Authority (QCA), which had been established in 1997 to advise the government on matters of curriculum and assessment, published guidance entitled 'Maintaining breadth and balance at Key Stages 1 and 2' which was issued to all primary schools (QCA, 1998). However, there was no structure in place to ensure that primary schools implemented the guidance and fulfilled the statutory requirement to provide a broad and balanced curriculum. The message was clear: the core subjects were considered to be of greater importance than the non-core. The impact of these developments for you as student teachers in secondary schools is that during 1998–2000 pupils transferring to Key Stage 3 may have done little work in six of the ten subjects. Their knowledge and progress in those subjects may have been affected and they may not have reached the NC levels expected of them.

It could be argued that the proposals of the Dearing Report created three divisions of subjects. The first division comprises the three core subjects of English, mathematics and science. These subjects are taught at all four Key Stages and are assessed by national tests at Key Stages 1–3, and they are the basis for the league tables for primary schools. Subjects in the second division are compulsory at all four Key Stages but do not have end of Key Stage national tests. These subjects include physical education, design technology, information and communications technology, modern foreign languages and religious education (although not an NC subject). The remaining subjects – music, art, geography and history – appear to have been relegated to the third division as they are only compulsory at Key Stages 1–3 and have no associated national tests. The initiatives of the Labour government since 1997 have underlined the differences between the status of core and non-core subjects. However, the picture is not so simple.

Many non-core subjects continue to be popular subjects with pupils at both GCSE and AS/A level, due in part to the flexibility of the NC at Key Stage 4. In 1998 secondary schools were reminded that they could modify the Key Stage 4 curriculum to meet the needs of pupils who might gain more from work experience and other vocational opportunities than from continued study of some of the compulsory core subjects. Pupils at Key Stage 4 have to continue with examination courses in English and mathematics but schools can apply for some pupils to take vocational studies. This alternative curriculum is achieved by removing the requirement of pupils to sit examinations in up to two of the remaining compulsory courses in science, modern foreign languages (MFL) or design technology.

In 1998 the stage was set for the review of the NC that led to the NC Orders currently in use in schools. This end-of-the-century review provided opportunities to modify the curriculum in the light of evaluation of how well the current Orders were working in practice, and to ensure the overall coherence and appropriateness of the NC for the twenty-first century. The SoS took account of the wishes of the teaching profession for curriculum continuity rather than change and identified the purpose of the review as to ensure stability. This purpose was achieved by keeping change to a minimum but creating a more flexible NC which was less prescriptive and, most importantly, 'would be at the heart of our policies to raise standards' (QCA/DfEE, 1999).

The extent and nature of the changes made to individual subject Orders for 2000 varied from subject to subject. Monitoring of the 1995 Orders, carried out by QCA (and its predecessor, the School Curriculum and Assessment Authority, SCAA), had revealed greater satisfaction and fewer concerns from teachers about some subjects than others. The opportunity was taken to align the Key Stage 1 and 2 Programmes of Study in English and mathematics with the national frameworks for teaching the basic skills of literacy and numeracy, leading to significant restructuring of the Orders for English and mathematics. The content of the Programme of Study for the non-core subjects underwent further slimming at Key Stages 1 and 2 to enable primary teachers to maintain the emphasis on basic skills and to focus on achieving the government's assessment targets for them in 2002. During the consultation process on the review, the proposals for some subjects provoked considerable media interest and the campaigns mounted by some journalists in newspapers, radio and TV made a significant impact on the content of the final version of the Orders concerned, particularly those subjects that touched closely the concept of national identity. For instance, there was sustained interest from groups outside the education profession about the authors recommended by government for study by pupils in English and about the examples of people and events that pupils might be taught about in history. The role of team games within the physical education curriculum also provoked debate in the media.

THE PLACE OF THE NATIONAL CURRICULUM WITHIN THE WHOLE SCHOOL CURRICULUM

The Curriculum 2000 review was the first occasion that discussion focused on the school curriculum as a whole and the place of the NC within it. Conferences attended by representatives from a large number of schools, subject associations and teacher associations and others with an interest in this debate were held to discuss the aims, values and priorities of the whole curriculum. The outcomes of these conferences in part set the agenda of the meetings of subject task groups established to make recommendations to the individual subject Orders. Consequently a number of whole school issues were identified for consideration and development to ensure that the NC would meet the needs of adults living in a rapidly changing world. In this context a new subject, Citizenship, was added to the curriculum. Citizenship was to be a non-statutory area of the primary school curriculum and was incorporated into the non-statutory guidelines for PSHE included within the framework of the NC. Citizenship was to become a compulsory part of the secondary school curriculum at Key Stages 3 and 4 and an entirely new subject Order was developed for these two Key Stages. Its introduction into schools was delayed until September 2002 to enable schools to restructure the curriculum and prepare resources.

Appreciation was also given in the review to the fact that freedom of access to information via the internet meant that the readership for education publications had extended beyond teachers and other professionals. Each subject Order begins with a double-page spread that contains examples of pupils' work in the subject, quotations provided by leading academics, industrialists and personalities from the media, and a statement summarising the importance of the subject. The structure and language of the Orders were scrutinised to ensure that they were clearer and more accessible, both to those who had to put the Orders into practice and to parents and governors. A consistent structure was introduced for the Orders at all Key Stages in all subjects. This consistency was intended to be helpful, particularly to teachers in primary schools, who have to teach all subjects; and it facilitates making comparisons of the content and perceived demand of different subjects at any one Key Stage.

An attempt was made to distinguish more clearly those parts of the NC Orders that are statutory and those aspects that are non-statutory and included as guidance to teachers in their planning. It had become apparent to the QCA, from their monitoring and consultations with teachers, that there was a tendency to assume that everything contained in the 1995 subject Orders had to be taught, leading to an overly prescriptive approach being taken to the curriculum.

You need to study the Order for your specialist subject(s) carefully. Those aspects that are in black typeface are statutory; those in grey are non-statutory examples or guidance. This design feature is clear enough in the published versions of the Orders but less clear when the Orders are downloaded from the internet. The non-statutory elements include the examples in the text and the marginal notes (DfEE/QCA, 1999a).

You need to be clear which content is **statutory** and which is non-statutory by reference to the Orders and your school's scheme of work. The enhanced flexibility inherent in Curriculum 2000 may be lost if these distinctions are not appreciated. In Table 7.3.3 there is an overview of the changes made to the NC for 2000; Table 7.3.4 outlines the structure of the Orders for each of the subjects. You may find further help in the subject books accompanying this text in the series 'Learning to Teach (subject) in the Secondary School'. You can find out more about the impact of the school curriculum on schools through Task 7.3.1; and more about the effectiveness of the cross-curricular dimensions by addressing Task 7.3.2.

Task 7.3.1

EVALUATING THE NATIONAL CURRICULUM

1 Interview several members of staff in your school experience school to find out:

- the impact of the NC on the school curriculum;
- their views about the content of the NC;
- their opinions about its strengths and weaknesses.

Develop a short questionnaire (5–8 questions) for use at interview. We suggest you discuss your plans with your tutor and take advice about whom to approach. Suitable staff to interview might include:

- your subject mentor;
- the teacher with responsibility for the Key Stage 3 curriculum;
- a teacher with experience of teaching your subject before the introduction of the NC;
- a teacher of a different area of the curriculum from your own.

2 Arrange a time to interview each of these teachers, using the questionnaire to structure the interview. Keep notes of the responses, particularly those relating to the impact of the NC on the achievements of the pupils.
3 Analyse the responses and write a 200-word summary for inclusion in your teaching file.
4 At the end of your first term in school, when you have planned and taught some lessons with Years 7–9, review your written summary and revise it to take account of your views.

Note: ensure that you re-read your statement before attending any job interviews.

Table 7.3.3 Summary of changes introduced into the National Curriculum beginning 2000

National Curriculum component	Change	Key issues include:
Rationale	Explicit statement of values, aims and purposes	A definition of the school curriculum (p. 10), values and purposes relating to the individual, the family, the diversity of society and the environment (p. 10). This statement reiterates the aims from the ERA, 1988 and establishes the NC as a constantly evolving and developing framework intended to establish an entitlement curriculum, establish standards, promote continuity and coherence, promote public understanding (pp. 12–13)
Scope of the NC at Key Stages 3 and 4	General and subject-specific Key Stage requirements, timescale for implementation and scope for disapplication	Outlines the government view that pupils: • should have two hours a week of **physical education** including extra-curricular activities; • should be taught food and textiles in **design and technology** at KS3; • may be taught either foundation or higher PoS at KS4 in **mathematics**; • may be taught single **science**, double science or three separate sciences at KS4. Outlines opportunities for schools to disapply aspects of the NC in MFL, design and technology and science at KS4 to meet specified needs of pupils (p. 17).
Structure	Key terms and the interrelationship of the General Teaching Requirements and the Programmes of Study and the purpose and scope of the Attainment Targets	Explains how the level descriptions should be used to provide pupils' attainment levels at the end of KS3. States that level descriptions are not designed for use in assessing individual pieces of work. Outlines: • how the subject Orders should be used to assist in planning schemes of work; • requirements to report annually to parents on pupils' progress; • additional information available to support target setting for pupils whose performance is below age-related expectations. Summarises the range of approved qualifications available to pupils of secondary school age (p. 19).
Other requirements	Compulsory curriculum elements additional to the National Curriculum	Explains the requirement to provide: • religious education, the scope for parents to withdraw children from RE lessons, and the nature of the agreed syllabuses; • sex education, the need to 'encourage pupils to have due regard to moral considerations and the value of family life' (QCA/DfEE, 1999, p. 20), the scope for parents to withdraw children from all or part of the programme; • a programme of careers education in secondary schools.

Learning across the NC	The requirement to promote the spiritual, moral, social and cultural development (SMSC), PSHE and a range of skills across all aspects of the NC	Explains what each of the four elements of SMSC involves and indicates where explicit opportunities can be made to promote their development in pupils. Draws attention to the non-statutory programme of study for PSHE (p. 21). Identifies the need to develop in pupils the key generic skills they need as well as subject-specific skills. Defines six key skills to be developed throughout compulsory schooling and post-16: • communication; • application of number; • information technology; • working with others; • improving own learning and performance; • problem solving.
	The requirement to promote other aspects of the school curriculum	Outlines a range of thinking skills including information processing, reasoning, enquiry, creative thinking and evaluation skills. These skills enable pupils to develop their metacognitive skills, their ability to 'learn how' as well as 'learn what'. Discusses the need to prepare pupils for adult life by developing their financial capability, enterprise and entrepreneurial skills and undertaking work-related learning, and suggests where opportunities to do this occur in the curriculum. Identifies the need to enable pupils to understand their responsibilities for protecting the planet for the enjoyment of the citizens of the global community in the future is outlined within Education for sustainable development.
General teaching requirements	Inclusion: providing effective learning opportunities for all pupils	This section is statutory and is much enhanced in importance and scope compared with the access statements in the 1995 Orders. The section outlines three principles for ensuring that the curriculum is more inclusive of the needs of the diversity of pupils educated in maintained schools across the country. It identifies the need to: • set suitable learning challenges; • respond to pupils' diverse learning needs; • overcome potential barriers to learning and assessment for individuals and groups of pupils. Describes and exemplifies ways of achieving these goals. Subject-specific examples are included in the free-standing single subject Orders but not in the primary and secondary school handbooks.
	Use of language across the curriculum	A statutory requirement outlined in a statement of what teachers must do in the context of teaching their own subject to develop the pupils' language skills and their use of standard English.
	Use of information and communications technology across the curriculum	A statutory requirement for the development of secondary school pupils' use of the range of ICT tools across all aspects of the curriculum.

• Numbers refer to page numbers in the *Handbook for Secondary Teachers* (DfEE/QCA, 1999a)

Table 7.3.4 The structure of the subject Orders in the National Curriculum

Component	Status	Content	Commentary
Programme of Study for each Key Stage in which the subject is a compulsory part of the curriculum	**Statutory**	Knowledge, skills and understanding Breadth of study	What has to be taught by teachers and developed by pupils over the Key Stage The contexts, areas of study, pupil experiences and activities through which the knowledge, skills and understanding are to be taught and developed
Attainment Target(s) (found in fold-out section at the end of the subject Order(s))	**Statutory**	Statements of the knowledge, skills and understanding that individual pupils of different abilities are expected to attain by the end of each Key Stage, divided into eight level descriptions with an additional description of what constitutes exceptional performance in that subject	The vast majority of pupils at Key Stage 3 should be working within Levels 3–7. When statutorily assessed at the end of Key Stage 3 the majority of pupils will be expected to achieve Level 5 or 6 in the subject. For those subjects with a Key Stage 4 programme of study attainment at the end of the Key Stage will be assessed through GCSE, or another recognised national qualification.
During the Key Stage description	non-statutory	A summary of what the pupils will learn over the Key Stage	This statement explains links between the two elements in the Programme of Study and provides an overview of the range of experiences the pupils should receive in the subject over the Key Stage
Subject-specific marginal notes	non-statutory	Key information and definitions of terms used in the Programme of Study	The notes amplify certain points and terms that have a particular meaning when used in the Programme of Study
ICT opportunities (located in the margins)	non-statutory	Suggestions for the use of ICT within the Programme of Study for the Key Stage	Explains that pupils' ICT skills should be developed across all subjects in the curriculum and what they should be made aware of where ICT is particularly useful in individual subjects
Links with other subjects in the curriculum	non-statutory	Identifies where aspects of the knowledge, skills and understanding in one subject build on learning in another subject in the curriculum	This is a tool for effective cross-curricular planning. You need to be aware of links from your subject to others and also from other subjects to your own

Inclusion

Issues were raised at the time of both the 1994 review (Dearing, 1994) and the most recent review (1998–9) about whether the NC met the needs of all the pupils for whom it was intended including those with special educational needs, disabilities, English as an additional language and pupils from different ethnic and cultural backgrounds. The 1998–9 review took place in the wake of the inquiry into the murder of Stephen Lawrence and the subsequent publication of the McPherson report into the handling of the police inquiry. Concurrently there were growing concerns about the under-achievement of boys and pupils from certain minority ethnic groups; see Unit 4.4 for details. Widespread consultation and discussion resulted in the development of guidance called *Inclusion: providing effective learning opportunities for all pupils* (DfEE/QCA, 1999d, p. 32). This guidance summarises current thinking and good practice in inclusive education. For further discussion of 'inclusion' see Unit 4.6 on inclusion and special educational needs.

Optional national schemes of work

Another initiative from the government welcomed by teachers was the publication of Schemes of Work (SoW) at Key Stage 3 in all NC subjects, including Citizenship and religious education (DfEE/QCA, 2000). This publication followed a similar initiative for primary teachers of Schemes of Work for Key Stages 1 and 2 in all NC subjects. Primary teachers had been requesting this sort of guidance and support since 1989. These SoW are optional and exemplify how the NC programmes of study for 2000 can be translated into medium-term teaching plans to meet the needs of the majority of pupils in a class. The SoW suggest how to modify the plans for pupils making slower or faster progress than expected. It was intended that schools would draw on the published schemes and modify them to meet the particular needs of their pupils rather than adopt them wholesale.

Task 7.3.2

IMPLEMENTING THE CROSS-CURRICULAR DIMENSIONS OF THE NATIONAL CURRICULUM

1 Find out how your school experience school is implementing one (or more) of the following NC requirements:

- ICT across the curriculum (see Table 7.3.3, general teaching requirements);
- language across the curriculum (see Table 7.3.3, learning across the NC);
- the spiritual, moral, social and cultural dimension (see Table 7.3.3, rationale for the NC and learning across the NC);
- the six key skills (see Table 7.3.3, learning across the NC).

Select a topic on which to focus. This task can be tackled by talking to a member of staff and reading policy documents. We suggest you talk to your tutor about whom to approach and what you intend to do, and why. A deputy headteacher or other teacher with responsibility for the school curriculum might be a suitable interviewee. Arrange a time to talk to the teacher and agree how long you have for the interview. Collect as much information as you can, including copies of any policy documents. Read and review the information you have collected before the interview.

2 Talk to your subject mentor about the way in which the cross-curricular dimension you chose is put into practice in lessons in your subject.

3 Discuss with student teachers placed in other schools how their schools implement the cross-curricular aspects of the NC and the extent to which the approach taken is successful in practice. Assess the strengths and weaknesses of the different approaches.

5 Focus your lesson observations for one week on the opportunities that arise in those lessons to promote the cross-curricular dimension you chose.

6 Plan and teach a lesson in which one of your learning objectives relates to the cross curricular dimension. Evaluate how well you achieved that objective.

SUMMARY AND KEY POINTS

This unit has outlined the development of the National Curriculum for England and Wales since 1988. The period 1988–2000 saw many changes to the school curriculum and the work of teachers. Assessment has been a major area of development and discussion; further information on assessment is given in Units 6.1 and 6.2.

A further review of the NC is not planned. However, the proposals outlined recently by central government to reorganise secondary education may carry curriculum implications (Wintour, 2000, 2001). Individual subjects are to be reviewed in a rolling programme. Any revisions of curricula are intended to take account of subject monitoring and the need to update content. In 1999 the government indicated its awareness of the need to update the science curriculum and there will be a call for change to other Programmes of Study that no longer reflect current trends in the teaching and learning of the subject. The majority of teachers working in maintained schools today perceive the NC as having more benefits than drawbacks. This perception is very different from that held by teachers at the time of the introduction of the first ever government-initiated school curriculum in 1988.

You have the opportunity over your course of initial teacher education to test and evaluate the current National Curriculum, referred to as 'Curriculum 2000'. You should link your study of this topic to the competences/standards for your course.

FURTHER READING

Department for Education and Employment and Qualifications and Curriculum Authority (DfEE/QCA) (1999a) *The National Curriculum for England. Handbook for Secondary Teachers in England: Key Stages 3 and 4*, London: Stationery Office. (See also QCA website: http://www.nc.uk.net./about/about_ks3_ks4.html.)
This handbook is the compendium of all the NC subject Orders and guidance provided to teachers and managers in schools.

Department for Education and Employment and Qualifications and Curriculum Authority (DfEE/QCA) (2000) *A Scheme of Work for Key Stage 3* (in your subject), London: DfEE/QCA.
The schemes of work are available for all NC subjects (and also for religious education) at Key Stages 1 and 2 and Key Stage 3. Each scheme provides examples of how the NC requirements can be taught to pupils of a wide range of abilities.

Department of Education and Science and the Welsh Office (DES/WO) (1988) *National Curriculum Task Group on Assessment and Testing (TGAT Report)*, London: DES.
This report explains the rationale and the intended structure for assessment in the NC. The recommendations provide a basis for evaluating the current assessment arrangements used in schools.

Qualifications and Curriculum Authority and Department for Education and Employment (QCA/DfEE, 1999) *The Review of the National Curriculum in England. The Secretary of State's Proposals*, London: QCA.
The consultation version of the NC was sent into schools to seek teachers' opinions on the proposed changes. The document provides a rationale for the approach taken and enables you to see what changes were made before the Orders were published.

CHAPTER 8 **YOUR PROFESSIONAL DEVELOPMENT**

In this chapter we consider life beyond your student teaching experience. The chapter is designed to prepare you for applying for your first post and to make you aware of the opportunities available to further your education as a teacher after you have completed your initial teacher education course. It contains three units.

Getting a job at the end of your initial teacher education course is important, time-consuming and worrying for student teachers. Unit 8.1 is designed to help you at every stage of the process of getting your first post. It takes you through the stages of deciding where you want to teach, looking for suitable vacancies, sending for further details of posts that interest you, making an application, attending an interview and accepting a post.

Unit 8.2 considers the transition from student teacher to newly qualified teacher, immediate induction into the school and the job, ongoing induction throughout the first year, and your further professional development. Part of the unit focuses on the development of your professional portfolio, which you should start as a student teacher (see the introduction), and how this may be used to aid your further professional development. At the end of your initial teacher education course it is used to inform and illustrate your Career Entry Profile, which is mandatory for those of you gaining Qualified Teacher Status in England.

Unit 8.3 is designed to give you an insight into the system in which many of you will be working as teachers. We look briefly at the structure of the state education system in England and then at teachers' accountability: professional, moral and contractual. This leads into a slightly fuller consideration of the legal and contractual requirements and statutory duties that govern the work of teachers.

UNIT 8.1   **GETTING YOUR FIRST POST**

SUSAN CAPEL AND ALEXIS TAYLOR

INTRODUCTION

Obtaining your first teaching post may be one of the most important decisions of your life, so it needs to be taken carefully. Obtaining a post involves a number of stages, each of which is equally important. The stages are:

- deciding where you want to teach;
- looking for suitable vacancies;
- selecting a post which interests you and sending for further details;
- making an application;
- preparing for and attending an interview;
- accepting a post.

This unit should also be helpful if you have gained Qualified Teacher Status (QTS) through an employment-based route (the Graduate or Registered Teacher Programme (GRTP)), as you may, in future, wish to move from the school in which you undertook your initial teacher education. Before you apply for your first post you need to decide where you want to teach, prepare your curriculum vitae (CV), write a generic letter of application, contact potential referees to make sure that they are prepared to act for you and to confirm their address, and undertake a mock interview. This unit is designed to help you with that process.

OBJECTIVES

At the end of this unit you should:

- understand the procedure for and process of applying for your first teaching post;
- be able to make a written application which is received favourably;
- be prepared for an interview for a teaching post.

DECIDING WHERE YOU WANT TO TEACH

If you are committed to living in one place because, for example, you have family commitments, you need to consider the distance it is possible to travel to a job in order to determine the radius in which you can look for your first post. You need to think about the travel time to and from school, as you probably will not want a long journey in your first year of teaching when you are likely to be tired at the end of each day or when you have had school commitments in the evening.

For other student teachers, deciding where to apply is your first major decision. If you opt for a popular area it could be difficult to obtain a post. The reasons for popularity may be that there are few schools, turnover from schools is low, or there are a number of applications from student teachers at a local higher education institution. It is therefore worth considering if your preferred areas are popular areas and, if so, whether there are other areas to which you could go or whether you could be totally flexible as to where you teach. It is worth doing some research about other areas of the country rather than basing your decision on assumptions about certain areas.

Task 8.1.1

WHERE DO YOU WANT TO TEACH?

Think about where you would like to teach and how flexible you are able to be in where you can look for a post. List all areas you would consider working in and find out something about those areas. If you know anyone from the area, talk to them about it. Visit the area if at all possible to get a general 'feel of the place' and further information about the area.

Also think about the type of school in which you want to teach. There are different types of school. In most areas there are primary schools catering for pupils in Years 1–6 (ages 5 to 10) and secondary schools catering for pupils in Years 7–13 (ages 11 to 18), or in some cases Years 7–11 (ages 11 to 16), with pupils going to a sixth form college for Years 12 and 13. Other areas have middle schools catering for pupils in Years 4–7 (ages 8 to 11) or 5–8 (ages 9 to 12) and upper schools starting at Year 8 or 9 (age 12 or 13) and generally catering for pupils up to Year 13. In some areas middle schools operate on a secondary model, employing subject specialists; in others, on a primary model, employing class teachers; and in yet others they operate on both a primary and secondary model, with class teachers for the first one or two years and then subject specialists.

Schools can be either maintained or private. Maintained schools are funded through the Local Education Authority (LEA) and supported by services from the LEA. Other types of school include voluntary aided, e.g. some Church schools and special schools. Alternatively, if you have trained for the 11–18 age range, you may wish to teach in a sixth form college or further education college. Alternatively you may want to teach abroad, either in a paid or voluntary capacity, such as Voluntary Service Overseas (VSO). Some teaching jobs abroad require you to have teaching experience before you can apply.

You probably have a list of criteria for the type of school you would be happy to teach in. However, it is advisable not to close your mind to other options. During your school experiences you see or hear about a range of types of school and you may surprise yourself by enjoying teaching in a type of school that you had not previously considered.

Task 8.1.2

WHAT TYPE OF SCHOOL DO YOU WANT TO TEACH IN?

Think back to the types of schools you experienced/are experiencing during your initial teacher education. List the aspects you find positive about working in them and list the opportunities you were/are not able to experience in these different types of schools. List criteria for schools you would be happy to teach in. Find out about different types of school and discuss these with other student teachers or teachers in your school experience school who have gone to or taught in these different types of school. Find out what types of school there are in those areas in which you would like to teach. You can start by looking at the OFSTED database (http: www.ofsted.gov.uk), which lists all schools, or by looking at the *Education Authorities Directory and Annual* and the *Education Year Book* (see further reading at the end of this unit). If you visit the area(s) in which you would like to teach, try to arrange to visit some schools.

LOOKING FOR SUITABLE VACANCIES

The majority of advertisements for teaching posts are for specific posts in specific schools. Advertisements generally start around January or February. However, the majority of advertisements are around April or May because teachers who are leaving at the end of the academic year are not required to hand in their notice until the end of May. Independent schools often advertise earlier, from December onwards.

Teaching posts are advertised in a number of different places. Advertisements are generally placed in the **national press**, sometimes the **local press** (especially for part-time posts) and sometimes **sent directly to your institution**. The major source of information about teaching posts is the *Times Educational Supplement* (published every Friday). However, jobs are also advertised in:

- the *Guardian* (the Tuesday edition);
- the *Independent* (the Thursday edition);
- the *Daily Telegraph* (the Thursday edition) (mostly for jobs in independent schools);
- the *Teacher* (published weekly).

There are also advertisements in **religious** and **ethnic minority newspapers** such as:

- the *Asian Times*;
- *Catholic Times*;
- *Church Times*;
- *Jewish Chronicle*;
- the *Universe*;
- the *Voice*.

Most of these have online versions where jobs are listed.

Letters from headteachers are often sent to teacher education institutions. These give advance notice of posts about to be advertised and information about making applications.

LEAs sometimes advertise posts themselves. Sometimes subject inspectors or advisers send information to institutions that have courses offering that specific subject. Some LEAs produce lists of vacancies which they send on request; some send information and guidance about applications for posts to teacher education institutions. Some advertise for general applications to the LEA rather than to an individual school. Many LEAs produce recruitment literature, e.g. brochures and/or videos, which are designed to show what it is like to work for the authority. Practices vary; therefore check current practice in LEAs in which you might be interested.

A recent initiative in some LEAs has been the appointment of **Recruitment Strategy Managers** (**RSMs**). One of the roles of RSMs is to establish strategic recruitment (and retention) projects in response to teacher supply needs identified in their LEA. RSM coverage is not yet nation-wide, but, at present, eighty-one LEAs have an RSM available. A list of contact names is available from the Teacher Training Agency (TTA). You may wish to contact an RSM in an LEA in which you are interested in teaching, as they may be aware of local needs.

An increasing number of posts are being offered **online**, via agencies, with whom you can register. For student teachers registered on an initial teacher education course, such agencies match up preferences for posts (for example, location, type of school and type of contract) with vacancies at schools, and forward details of suitable posts to student teachers. One such initiative is the Student Teacher Employment Programme (STEP: www.stepjobs.com).

The procedures for applying for teaching jobs in Scotland and Northern Ireland are different. If you are interested in teaching in Scotland or Northern Ireland, you should obtain further information from your institution, or the Scottish or Northern Ireland Office (addresses are in Appendix 4).

SELECTING A POST WHICH INTERESTS YOU AND SENDING FOR FURTHER DETAILS

If an advertisement interests you then write for further details. Write briefly and to the point. For example:

Dear Sir/Madam (or name if given in advertisement)

I am interested in the vacancy for a (subject) teacher (quote reference number if one is given) at ABC School, advertised in (publication, e.g. the *Times Educational Supplement*) of (date) and would be grateful to receive further details of this post.

Yours faithfully (if you use Sir/Madam, or Yours sincerely if you use a name)

MAKING AN APPLICATION

As you read details of all posts for which you are interested in applying, underline key words, phrases and the requirements specified which indicate whether the post is suitable for you as a first post, e.g. whether you have the knowledge, skills, qualities and experience the school is looking for and whether the school meets some or all of your requirements.

If you decide to apply, remember that first impressions are very important and applications are the first stage in the selection process. You need to present yourself effectively on paper. Plan the content of your application before you complete an application form or CV or write a covering letter for a specific post. You use the same basic information for all applications. However, you cannot have a standard application form, CV or letter of application which you use for every application. Each application needs to be slightly different as you want to match your experience and qualifications to the requirements of the post, highlighting different points and varying the amount of detail you provide according to specific requirements of the post and the school. You should find it useful to look back at the key words, phrases and requirements you underlined in the details for the post. These help you to personalise the application. A personalised application shows that you have taken the time to find out about a specific post in a specific school, and should help your application to stand out from the others. An application which fails to explain why you are interested in the specific post in the specific school is unlikely to be considered further.

Thus, completing an application form for each post takes time. Two hours is probably the minimum time to complete an application properly without rushing it if you have prepared beforehand and have all the information available – longer if you have not. It is a good idea to keep all your information on a computer. This helps you to be able to customise your applications more easily (and enables you, if necessary, to develop your information and communications technology (ICT) skills).

Referees

When applying for teaching posts you are normally asked to supply the names and addresses of at least two referees. Before you complete an application, contact potential referees to make sure that they are prepared to act for you, to confirm their address (and other contact details, such as an email address), and find out if there are any dates when they are away and unable to respond should a request arrive.

Your first referee is normally someone associated with your teacher education course. Some institutions indicate who you should name as the referee, e.g. the course director or your personal tutor; others leave this to the student teacher. Check if there is one particular person who you should name as the first referee and, if not, decide who you would like this to be and then ask that person. This reference covers all areas of your work on the course and represents the assessment of a large number of staff, including lecturers, professional tutor and mentor. It is often helpful for the person compiling your reference to have additional information about you which might be included in a reference, e.g. other activities you are involved in. Therefore, check whether it would be helpful for your referee to have a copy of your CV.

Your second referee should be someone who knows you well and is able to comment on your character, qualities, achievements and commitment to teaching as a career. Your mentor (or other member of staff) at your final block school experience school may well be an appropriate person, or it may be someone with whom you have worked in a permanent or vacation job, someone from your degree course, your school or institution tutor.

It is not normal practice to include open testimonials with your application as schools or LEAs value confidential references more highly. Some LEAs have a policy of open references, i.e. the reference is shown to the applicant in certain circumstances. The referee knows this at the time of writing the reference.

Methods of application

Schools normally require job applicants to submit a letter of application and a completed application form or a CV.

Letter of application

A letter of application should state clearly your reasons for applying for the post, matching your qualifications, experience, particular skills and personal qualities to the post as described in the information sent to you from the school. The letter is normally between one and two sides of A4 in length, on plain white notepaper. A suggested format for a letter of application is given below.

Address
(at top right-hand side)

Date

Name of headteacher

Address

Dear Sir/Madam or Name of headteacher

Paragraph 1

In reply to your advertisement in (name of publication) of (date) I would like to apply for the post of (subject(s)) teacher (quote reference number if one is given) at (name of school).

Or

My University/College has informed me that, in September, you will have a vacancy on your staff for a teacher of (subject(s)) and I would like to apply for this post.

Paragraphs 2/3

This section should begin by explaining why you are applying for this particular post. It should then carefully match your qualifications, experience, particular skills and personal qualities to those required by the school, indicating what you could contribute as a teacher of the subject(s) specified.

Paragraphs 3/4

These might begin:

The enclosed curriculum vitae provides details of the content of my teacher education course. I would also like to draw your attention to . . . (here outline any special features of your course and your particular interest in these, anything significant about your teaching and any other work experience, anything else you have to offer above that required specifically by the post, including being able to speak a language other than English, extra-curricular activities, a second subject, skills in ICT, pastoral work, etc., which you wish the school to be aware of, and any other information about interests and activities related to the post or to you as a teacher, including additional qualifications, awards and positions of responsibility you have held).

If you are unavailable for interview on any days, this is the point to mention it. You might indicate this by including a statement such as 'It may be helpful to know that my examinations (or other event) occur on the following date(s) (quote actual dates). Unfortunately this means that I am not able to attend for an interview on those dates. I hope this does not cause inconvenience as, should you wish to interview me, I could come at any other time.'

Yours faithfully (or Yours sincerely, if you use the headteacher's name)
Name

Application form

The information required on an application form closely matches that identified for a CV (below). Read through an application form before you write anything on it. We recommend that you make a photocopy of the blank form and complete this in pencil as a practice before completing the original form. This both helps you focus on what you are going to write and enables you to see whether it fits into the space provided. Follow exactly any instructions given. Check that there is no missing information, dates or other detail, or questions which have not been answered. Do not leave any sections of the form blank. If there are sections that you cannot complete, write 'N/A' (not applicable). You might find it helpful to check your draft with your tutor.

One page of the form is often blank and in the space provided you are required to explain why you are applying for the post and to elaborate on the skills and experience that equip you for it. This section should be written in continuous prose as if it is a section of a letter, following the suggested format and containing the type of information given for a letter of application (above). It is usually acceptable to use additional sheets of paper and staple them to the form. This section requires information that would otherwise be included in a letter of application; therefore a letter of application with such an application form is normally very brief, indicating that you have included your application for the post of (subject) teacher as advertised in (publication). A longer letter of application would be needed if the application form does not include such a section.

CV

A CV should always be accompanied by a longer letter of application. A CV summarises your educational background, qualifications, teaching and other work experience, interests and activities and any other relevant qualifications and information. A sample format for a CV is provided below.

CURRICULUM VITAE

Name: Date of birth:
Term time address: Home address:
Telephone number: Telephone number:
email address: e-mail address:

(indicate dates when you are at your term time address and when your home address should be used)

Academic qualification(s): (your first degree and above, with subject, institution and class)

Professional qualification (for initial teacher education): if you are yet to qualify, write 'I am currently on a PGCE/BEd (or other) course and expect to qualify in July 200?.'

Previous relevant experience:
(provide only very brief details here to highlight the most important points to help the reader; expand on these later in the CV)

EDUCATION
(list institutions from secondary school on, in reverse chronological order)

Institution: Dates attended:
(you might want to include some detail about your degree and/or teacher education course, particularly emphasising those aspects of your course which match the requirements of the post)

QUALIFICATIONS
(list qualifications from O levels/GCSEs on, in reverse chronological order)

Qualification gained: Date awarded:
(with subject(s), grades or classification)   (or date to be awarded)

TEACHING EXPERIENCE
(list any prior teaching experience and the school experiences on your course, in reverse chronological order)

School and subject(s) taught: Year(s), length and focus of experience:

OTHER WORK EXPERIENCE
(list permanent full- or part-time jobs and holiday jobs separately, each in reverse chronological order)

Job: Dates (start and finish):
(include anything special about each job, particularly where it relates to children and/or teaching)

INTERESTS AND ACTIVITIES
(e.g. membership of clubs or societies, details of offices held, achievements, e.g. sport, music, hobbies; group these together if appropriate, with the most relevant first and, if giving dates, in reverse chronological order)

ADDITIONAL QUALIFICATIONS
(e.g. ability to use ICT, additional languages, music grades, coaching or first aid awards)

OTHER INFORMATION
(include anything else that you think is important here in relation to the post for which you are applying)

REFERENCES
First referee: Second referee:
Position: Position:
Address: Address:
Telephone number: Telephone number:
email address: email address:

Notes about applications

1   Applications should be laid out well and presented clearly, completed neatly, with legible writing and without using jargon. Check your application to ensure that there are no basic errors such as typing errors, mistakes in spelling, grammar or punctuation; and that the information is accurate and consistent. If there is time, it is worthwhile asking a colleague, friend or tutor to read through your final application. We recommend that you use black ink as applications are often photocopied for members of an interview panel.

2   Indicate clearly any dates when you will not be able to attend for interview, e.g. because you have an examination. Examinations must normally take precedence over interviews. However, holidays do not take precedence and most schools will not wait until you return from holiday to interview you; therefore do not book holidays at times when you are likely to be called for interview.

3   Remember that if you put down additional skills or experiences, e.g. that you can sing, you may be invited to use those skills in school, e.g. in the school choir. Therefore, do not make exaggerated claims about your skills or additional experiences.

4   Always send the original application, but keep a copy of every letter of application, application form or CV so that you can refresh your memory before an interview.

Task 8.1.3

YOUR CURRICULUM VITAE

Draft a specimen letter of application and CV and obtain and complete an application form. Ask your tutor to check these for you. Use these as the basis for all your job applications.

PREPARING FOR AND ATTENDING AN INTERVIEW

If you are offered an interview, acknowledge the letter at once, in writing if there is time, indicating that you are pleased to attend for interview on that date. If you are offered two interviews on the same day, you will probably have to choose which one you attend, unless they are at different times and close enough together to enable you to attend both. Write and decline the interview you decide not to attend.

If there is a problem with an interview date, e.g. it coincides with an examination, let the school know immediately.

Preparing for an interview

Prepare for an interview in advance. Read through the advertisement, job description and any other information about the school and post, again. Also try to find out if there is anyone at your institution or school experience school who knows the school. If possible, visit the school beforehand to find out more about it and about the local area. Most schools welcome this as long as you ask, as this enables them to arrange a suitable time. Do not just turn up at the school and expect to look around. Decide what to look for when shown around the school. If possible, talk to a newly qualified teacher in the school.

You might find it helpful to reflect on why you applied for this particular post, so that you can put across the relevant information convincingly at the interview. Read through your application again so that you can communicate effectively the information and evidence you consider to be relevant to the post. It also helps you to avoid any contradictions between what you say and what you wrote in your application, as each member of the interview panel has a copy of your application and so can compare answers. Prepare answers to the questions in the list on p. 376.

If you are not reading the *Times Educational Supplement* on a regular basis, we recommend that you do so before your interview so that you can talk about and answer questions on the latest educational issues and debates.

It is useful to have a portfolio of, for example, good lessons, worksheets, evaluations, review of resource(s), ICT skills. This is derived from the professional portfolio you have been keeping throughout your initial teacher education course (see Unit 8.2 for further information). From this professional portfolio you also develop your Career Entry Profile.

If you are learning to teach a subject which requires you to take a portfolio of your work, e.g. art or design technology, begin to prepare this early in the year, gathering examples of work from school when you are on school experience. Subject books addressing student teachers on initial teacher education courses often include advice on interviews.

Plan what you are going to wear to the interview as your appearance is important. Knowing something about the school is useful, e.g. if the staff dress formally, you should dress formally. If you are unsure, it is advisable to be conservative in your dress.

Attending an interview

It is difficult to generalise about interviews because these vary considerably. In many schools, all people invited to interview arrive at the school at the same time, are shown around the school, and sit and wait, while everyone is interviewed, for a decision to be made and for the successful candidate to be told. In other interviews, candidates are invited at different times so that they do not meet.

The format for interview days varies. It may, for example, comprise a tour of the school, an informal talk or interview with the head of department and/or a senior teacher, teaching a lesson, lunch and a panel interview. An example of an interview day is shown below.

Example interview day

9.15 a.m.	Arrive at school	At this stage you are normally welcomed, along with other candidates, by the headteacher and are given the schedule for the day, if this has not been sent to you in advance.
9.35 a.m.	Meeting with head of faculty and head of department	At this stage, information about the school and department is explained to you. For example: structure and organisation; curriculum; roles and responsibilities; assessment policies; examination results; procedures about school routines and expectations. You may well receive further

---

		documentation. If there is more information you would like to have, take the opportunity to ask questions.
10.00 a.m.	Coffee	This might be with other members of the department or staff. Again, use this as an opportunity to learn more about the school, department and post.
10.15– 10.45 a.m.	Tour of the school	You may well be escorted by a member of staff or by pupils. This provides an opportunity to take note of what may be your working environment. For example: the layout of the school and department; display work; facilities; the learning and working atmosphere in the lessons.
10.45– 12.30 p. m.	Teaching a lesson	There is normally a rota for this with other candidates. You will be prepared for this part of the interview in advance. It is not normal practice for this to be sprung on you without warning! See the section on teaching a lesson at interview, below, for further information.
12.30 p. m.	Lunch	This may well be in the school canteen with other members of the department. Again, use this period of the day as an opportunity to ask questions.
1.30 p. m.	Formal interviews	Candidates are interviewed individually, normally in alphabetical order. If you have a legitimate commitment (for example, a train to catch) and need to leave before your allocated time, it is best to say so, and the school is usually able to accommodate this request.

It is now regular practice for candidates to be asked to teach a lesson (or part of a lesson) as part of the interviewing process. If required make sure that you know the age and size of the class, what you are expected to teach, the pupils' prior knowledge, the length of the lesson, what resources and equipment are available, i.e. all the information you require before teaching any class. You should be told this in the letter of invitation to the interview. If not, telephone and ask. Plan this lesson carefully, giving attention to learning outcomes, purpose of content and activities, and resources. It is useful to have copies of the lesson plan available to give to those who are observing you. This is an opportunity to show the quality of your preparation and planning. Lessons taught as part of the interviewing process also provide you with the opportunity to demonstrate the level of your subject knowledge, so, again, prepare well, particularly if you have been asked to teach a topic with which you are not totally familiar. It is probably best to try to base your interview lesson on something that has been successful on a previous occasion with similar classes. The lesson is also an opportunity to show your enthusiasm for teaching and pupils' learning. Try to appear confident and relaxed, although those who are observing you will understand that you probably feel a little nervous!

It is a good idea to make an opportunity to talk briefly with relevant staff about the lesson; for example, how you feel it went, what the pupils learned, how you know that they learned this, and what you might change. Don't be anxious about mentioning if some things have not gone to plan. For example, your timing might have gone astray, or your instructions were not as clear as you had anticipated. Use the opportunity to show that you have realised this and analyse why it happened and how you might change this in the future. This demonstrates that you are reflective and thoughtful and serious about your own practice.

As the format for interview days varies so does the panel interview. In some interviews you are faced by a panel comprising anything between two to three and six to seven people; in others you have a series of interviews with different people. In either case these people normally include some of the following: the headteacher, a governor, another senior member of the school staff, the head of department and possibly an LEA subject adviser. The length of time for a panel interview can vary from about half an hour to one and a half hours.

An interview is a two-way affair. At the same time as being interviewed you are, in effect, interviewing the school and deciding if this is a school you could work in and, therefore, if this is a post for you. Therefore, take the opportunity to learn as much as you can about the school, the post and the working environment. This requires you to be alert to what is being said and to be prepared to ask as well as to answer questions at all times. If not included as part of the interview day, be firm in requesting an opportunity to look around the school prior to interview, including sitting in on a subject lesson if appropriate.

The initial impact you make is very important as interviewers tend to form an overall impression early. The interview starts as soon as you walk into the school, and you are assessed throughout the day. Your performance, including your verbal and non-verbal communication, in each activity is therefore important and could make the difference between being offered the job or not.

Particular attention is paid to the impression you create in the formal interview. For example, do not sit down until you are invited to do so, and then sit comfortably on your chair looking alert; do not sit on the edge of your chair looking anxious or slouch in your chair looking too relaxed. Look and sound relaxed and confident (even if you are not). Try to be yourself. Try to smile and to look at the panel during discussion. Do not talk too much. If you are unsure about how much information to give when answering questions, it is probably better to keep an answer brief and then ask the panel if they would like further information. Avoid repeating what you say but do not worry if you repeat information included in your application, as long as you do not contradict what you wrote. Interviewers have various degrees of specialist knowledge and understanding. Avoid jargon in explanations but assume interviewers have some knowledge and understanding of your subject area. Aim to provide a balanced picture of yourself but, on the whole, be positive and emphasise your strengths.

Interviewers are trying to form an impression of you as a future teacher and as a person, and have a number of things they are looking for. These include:

- your knowledge and understanding of your subject and your ability to teach it. Interviewers assess your ability to discuss, analyse, appraise and make critical comment about ideas, issues and developments in your subject and subject curriculum, your personal philosophy about and commitment to the teaching of your subject(s);

- your professional development as a teacher. This is based partly on your school experiences. Interviewers assess your ability to analyse observations of pupils' behaviour and development, your involvement in the whole life of the school on your school experiences, your development on school experiences, and your ability to discuss, analyse, appraise and make critical comment about educational issues;
- your ability to cope with the post. Interviewers assess how you would approach your teaching, e.g. your understanding of the different roles you are required to undertake as a teacher, how you have coped or would cope in a number of different situations, e.g. disciplining a difficult pupil or class, dealing with a difficult parent or with teaching another subject;
- your ability to fit into the school and the staffroom and to make contact with and relate to colleagues and pupils. Interviewers assess your verbal and non-verbal communication skills (your written communication skills have been assessed from your application);
- your commitment to living in that particular area and to the specific post. Interviewers assess the interest and enthusiasm you show for the post to try to find out if this is a post you really want or whether you see this post as a short-term stop-gap before you can find a post in an area where you really want to teach.

After introductions and preliminaries, most interviews focus on the information in your application, including your personal experiences, your education, qualifications, teaching skills gained from school experiences and other teaching and/or work experience, your interests and activities and other qualifications. You are normally also asked what you feel you can contribute to the school and why you are interested in and want this particular post, and general questions about professional or personal interests, ideas, issues or attitudes. Therefore, think about areas you want to emphasise or any additional evidence of your suitability for the post which you did not have room to include in your application. Draw on your experiences both from your teacher education course and school experience and from other experiences, e.g. other work with children, such as Camp America, Sunday school teaching, work in a youth club or with organised groups such as Boys' Brigade or Guides or voluntary work. These demonstrate your commitment to working with children.

You also need to show that you realise you still have things to learn (you should be able to talk about your weaknesses here) and that you are committed to continuing your development as a teacher. Depending on when your interview takes place, it might be possible for you to refer to your Career Entry Profile which indicates your strengths towards the end of your initial teacher education and also areas for development in your induction year. It is helpful to have a career plan, but not to appear so ambitious that you leave the school with the impression that you will leave at the first opportunity (you may want to think of committing yourself to two years in your first post, provided that you and the school are happy with your development).

Questions asked at interview vary considerably; therefore it is not possible for you to prepare precisely for an interview. However, it is helpful if you identify possible questions in your preparation and prepare some possible outline responses to such questions. It is useful to give a general response to the question, to show you understand some of the principles and issues, and also to refer to examples of your own practice. For example:

Interviewer: What are your views on differentiation?

Candidate: This is an important way of enabling all pupils to have equal access to the curriculum so that they learn as much as possible. There are a number of strategies that can be used; for example, differentiation by outcome or by task. During my last school experience I was teaching a Year 7 class about religious festivals. I did not want to give out several different worksheets as this might have embarrassed some children, so I made one worksheet which had some core tasks for all pupils and also some optional tasks, which involved different levels of work and different types of activities. I also developed differentiation through my use of questioning. . . .

Some questions which might be asked are given below.

Your commitment to teaching

Why did you choose teaching as a career?
Why did you choose to teach the secondary (middle/upper) age range?
Tell me something about your teacher education course.
Why did you choose this particular course?
Tell me something about your school experiences.
Which school experience was most successful/did you enjoy most and why?
What have been the most difficult aspects of your school experiences and why?
How do you know that a lesson is going well?
Recall a lesson that went well and/or one that went badly. Describe why this lesson went well or badly. How would you improve the lesson that went badly?
What do you consider to be your strengths and weaknesses as a teacher? How are you working to overcome your weaknesses?
Tell me about any other experiences of working with pupils which you think are relevant. What have you learned from these?

Your knowledge and understanding of your subject and subject application

What experience do you have of teaching your subject(s)?
Which aspects of your subject have you taught on school experience and to what years?
How would you introduce topic X to a Year 9 class?
How would you deal with, say, three boys misbehaving during a lesson in which there are safety implications?
Do you think that your degree subject prepares you to teach A level?
How has your development in your subject during your course contributed to your work in the classroom?
How do the theory and practice on your course relate?
How can you tell if pupils are learning in your subject?
Can you describe one incident where a pupil was not learning and what you did about it?
What experience have you had of setting targets for pupils?
What other subjects could you teach and to what level? What background/teaching experience do you have in these subjects?

Your views about education, philosophy of education and educational ideas

Do you view yourself as a teacher of children or of X subject?
Why should all pupils study X subject?
What do you think education is about (individual development or to acquire skills to get a job)?

What do you think the aims of secondary (middle/upper) education should be?
What type of school would you like to work in and why?
What are your views about streaming, setting or mixed ability teaching?
How did you set about planning differentiated learning for a class you have taught recently?
How do you think your subject can contribute to the education of all pupils?
What are your views about the way that the National Curriculum should develop?
What are your views on assessment?
Should pupils' achievements be based on test results or classwork/homework?

Your ability to cope as a teacher

What do you think are the qualities of a good teacher?
What are your strengths as a teacher at this stage in your career?
How would you maintain good discipline in the classroom?
What are your views about noise in the classroom and how would you keep it at an acceptable level?
How would you motivate a group of Year 9 pupils who do not have much interest in your subject?

Other roles you may be asked to undertake

What experience do you have of being a form tutor?
How do you feel about taking on the responsibilities of a form tutor?
How do you feel about taking extra-curricular activities after school, in the lunchtimes or on a Saturday morning?
What experience do you have of dealing with parents?

Your future development as a teacher

What are your targets for development during your first year of teaching?
How do you see your career developing?
How do you think you will go about achieving your career goals?
How long do you expect to stay in this school?
How do you aim to widen your experience as a teacher?

Other interests, activities, etc.

What has been your greatest/worst achievement to date?
What interests or hobbies do you have and how involved are you in these? Do you see yourself being involved with any of these at the school?
Have you taken any positions of responsibility in any organisations you belong to?

Other questions

At the end of the interview you may be asked:
If you were to be offered this post would you be in a position to accept it?

At some interviews you may be asked this question earlier. You can say that you decline the offer to respond at that point but will respond after the interview.

At the end of the interview you are normally asked if you have any questions. Asking one or two questions shows a genuine interest in the school and the post; therefore, do ask questions (not too many), if you have any. You are likely to forget the questions you wanted to ask if you are nervous; therefore, do not be afraid to take a checklist of questions with you to an interview. It is quite acceptable to refer to this during the interview itself. You may also wish, at this stage, to clarify issues that have come up during the interview day. You should enquire what arrangements there are for induction of newly qualified teachers in the school and what you might expect. However, do not ask questions just to impress. If all your questions have been answered during the course of the day and you do not have any questions, just say politely that all the questions you wanted to ask have been answered during the day (or in the interview).

At some point you may want to ask about your starting salary. In a private school and in some situations in the state sector you may have to negotiate your salary. In the state sector you are on a national rate of pay, but your starting point on the scale depends on your degree classification. Any previous relevant experience may also be taken into account. Student teachers with prior relevant experience may be offered different starting points on the scale in different schools and different LEAs. If you have left school, gone straight through a degree and then completed a teacher education course, you probably cannot negotiate a starting point on the scale. However, if you have previous relevant experience, you may want to negotiate your starting salary. If you feel you are in a strong position, you may want to negotiate your starting point on the scale during your interview and ask for confirmation of this before you accept a post. In other situations – e.g. if you feel you are not in a very strong position, but really want the post – it may be appropriate to discuss the starting salary at a later date. How you describe experience in an application and at interview, therefore, is very important as it may be used to support any claim for increments above the starting salary.

Task 8.1.4

MOCK INTERVIEWS

Arrange for a mock interview with your tutor or another student teacher. If possible, either have an observer or video the interview so that you and the interviewer can use this to analyse your verbal and non-verbal communication after the interview. If, on analysis, you or the interviewer feel that there is a great deal on which you can improve, arrange for another interview after you have worked at improving your weaknesses.

ACCEPTING A POST

Where all candidates are invited for interview at the same time, you may be offered a post on the same day as the interview. You are normally expected verbally to accept or reject the offer at that time. Schools will rarely give you time to think about an offer. Therefore it is important that you consider all the implications of accepting the post before you attend the interview. On rare occasions it may be that you feel you really need some time to think about the offer. You may want to ask if you can think about the offer overnight and telephone first thing in the morning. If your request is refused, you have to make a decision there and then or be prepared for the post to be offered to another candidate. Your decision depends on how much you want a particular job and how strong a position you think you are in.

If candidates are invited for interview at different times, you may have to wait for a few days before being offered a post. However, normally you do not know which format an interview is going to take until you arrive at the school, so you cannot rely on being able to do this.

It is normal practice to be asked to confirm your verbal acceptance of a post in writing. It is unprofessional to continue to apply for other teaching posts after you have verbally accepted a post, even if you see one advertised that you prefer.

Expenses (including basic overnight accommodation where necessary) are usually paid for attending an interview. However, rules vary between schools and LEAs and you might want to check in advance whether expenses are paid, whether receipts are needed and whether a claim for meals and/or overnight accommodation will be approved. You should receive a travel and expenses claim form with the letter notifying you of the interview or at the interview itself.

As you have access to children and young people, you are required to disclose all previous criminal convictions under the Rehabilitation of Offenders Act. After you have been offered a post you will be asked to complete a form detailing any criminal convictions and to give your consent to the school or LEA to verify your responses with the police.

You may also be asked to have a medical before you start a job. You will be sent the details of this from the school or the LEA.

If you are not offered the post

It is disappointing when a post is offered to another candidate. However, try not to think of this in terms of failure on your part. There may be many legitimate reasons why the post was offered to the other candidate in preference to you. For example, the other candidate might have relevant teaching experience (which you did not have) in an aspect of the curriculum required for the post. If you are not successful, build this into your learning experience. Most interview panels routinely offer feedback to candidates. If not, you can ask if this will be possible as it will help you identify strengths and areas to develop in preparation for your next interview.

SUMMARY AND KEY POINTS

There is no point in learning to become an effective teacher if you do not obtain a teaching post at the end of your teacher education course. This unit is therefore designed to help you realise that, just as with your teaching, you must prepare for obtaining your first post; you cannot leave it to chance or rely on your innate ability to perform well at interview. In this unit we have tried to lead you through the steps, skills and techniques you need to prepare actively for obtaining your first post. We hope it serves you well as you apply for your first post.

FURTHER READING

Crane, C.D. (1993) *The Key to your Success: Applying for a Secondary Post*, Weymouth: Education Appointments Council.
This book provides information and examples, where appropriate, about job selection, CVs, letters of application and interviews to help you in applying for jobs.

National Union of Teachers (annually) *Your First Teaching Post*, London: NUT.

> This guide is designed to answer some of your questions about where to look and what to look for in your first teaching post. It contains information supplied by education authorities and can be obtained from the NUT.

The Education Authorities Directory and Annual (annual), Redhill: The School Government Publishing Company Ltd.

The Education Year Book (annual), London: Longman.

> These books list all the LEAs in England and Wales, along with names, addresses and telephone numbers of secondary schools and sixth form colleges in their areas.

Times Educational Supplement First Appointments Supplement (annually, around the middle of January).

> This supplement is published yearly. It contains articles and features on processes and procedures to help you get your first post, and what to expect when you start your first post. It also contains many advertisements from LEAs about general applications.

ACKNOWLEDGEMENT

Although the contents of this unit have been updated considerably for this third edition of the book, we would like to acknowledge the work by Gay Humphrys at the University of Greenwich, published in a booklet entitled *Getting a Teaching Job*, sponsored by the Teaching as a Career Unit (TASC), which was used in preparing this unit for the first edition of the book.

UNIT 8.2 DEVELOPING FURTHER AS A TEACHER

SUSAN CAPEL AND ALEXIS TAYLOR

INTRODUCTION

The success of any school depends on its staff. However, although you have demonstrated successfully the competences/standards for the award of Qualified Teacher Status (QTS) at the end of your initial teacher education (ITE) course, you still have a lot to learn about teaching. Continuing professional development (CPD) helps you continue to learn and develop professionally throughout your career in order to increase your effectiveness. Induction is part of your CPD. Statutory induction arrangements were introduced in 1999 for England. In Scotland, teachers serve a two-year probationary period. Induction includes immediate induction into the post and ongoing induction throughout the first year. If you are teaching in England the agenda for ongoing induction should be derived largely from the issues identified by you in your Career Entry Profile. Thus, induction is the first part of your CPD. This can be shown as follows:

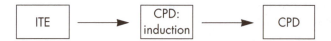

Although school managers should recognise your need for further professional development, you must take responsibility for your own professional development. Your Career Entry Profile is the beginning of active planning of your future career, identifying appropriate areas for development and activities and learning or experience to get you there. Professional accountability includes a commitment to keeping abreast of changes in education, in order to develop your knowledge and teaching skills.

This unit considers life beyond your student teaching experience. It considers the transition from student teacher to newly qualified teacher, induction into the school and the job and during the first year of teaching, and CPD beyond the first year. It also considers aspects of the work of the school that provide valuable developmental experiences.

OBJECTIVES

By the end of this unit you should:

- understand the need to undertake continuous learning and development;
- be beginning to recognise the induction and CPD opportunities available to you;
- be beginning to be able to set goals for your CPD early in your career.

PROFESSIONAL PORTFOLIO

You should develop, throughout your ITE course, a professional portfolio or portfolio of achievement. This portfolio contains evidence of your developing professional knowledge and judgement to complement your subject knowledge. Specifically, it documents your performance in relation to the competences/standards for the award of QTS, it documents other strengths and successes, it identifies areas for development, and it gives examples of your work as part of your ITE course (e.g. reports, observations on you made by teachers, lesson plans, assignments, examples of pupils' work, and notes and records contained in your diary of reflective practice). The diary of reflective practice is a record of the outcomes of tasks undertaken as you work through aspects of this book and other tasks undertaken as part of your course. It should help you to reflect on your school experiences and provide useful information for assignments undertaken.

Towards the end of your course you need to make sure that this information is gathered together. The evidence in the portfolio can be used to develop a portfolio to take to interview (see Unit 8.1 for further information about interviews). For those of you learning to teach in England it is also used to develop your Career Entry Profile which you take into your first teaching post to inform your induction and which you build on throughout your career.

Many ex-student teachers of ours have commented that they did not see the relevance of certain information, theories or activities while they were student teachers, but began to see their relevance as they developed as teachers. They then referred back to the notes they took or work they did as student teachers. Therefore, the information included in the portfolio is useful in its own right. However, many higher education institutions now recognise and accredit learning that has resulted from experience (this is called accreditation of prior experiential learning (APEL)) as entry to or exemption from part of a higher degree or professional qualification. In order to claim this exemption you must provide evidence. This is normally requested as a portfolio. Therefore, if you get into the habit of keeping your portfolio up to date, you will have evidence ready to hand for consideration for APEL for a further qualification.

Task 8.2.1

DIARY OF EFFECTIVE PRACTICE AND PROFESSIONAL PORTFOLIO

If you are reading this unit near the beginning of your course, start keeping a diary of reflective practice for tasks you undertake as you read through this book and as part of your ITE course. If you are near the end of your course and have not been developing a diary, collect together evidence from the tasks and assignments you have undertaken on your course. Reflect on and write down what you perceive to be your strengths and your weaknesses as a student teacher. Develop and implement a strategy for overcoming your weaknesses.

CAREER ENTRY PROFILE

All newly qualified teachers in England complete a Career Entry Profile (Teacher Training Agency, 1998). The purpose of the Career Entry Profile is to provide a summary of information about your strengths and priorities for your further professional development from ITE to your first teaching post, in relation to the standards required for gaining QTS. This information is intended to help you to build on your strengths and to target and address your development needs in your first year of teaching. It is designed to help you to take responsibility for your own professional development from as early as possible in your career, by establishing the practice of target setting and review, in order to provide a good foundation for appraisal and your CPD.

It is also designed to help your first teaching post school to deploy newly qualified teachers effectively, taking account of the strengths and development needs which were identified as priorities at the end of your ITE course. It enables the school to draw up an action plan for induction, which takes account of your own targets, targets identified by the school and any nationally identified objectives for induction. It also enables targeted monitoring and support to be provided during your induction.

The Career Entry Profile has three sections:

- Section A contains a summary of your ITE, including any distinctive features of your course (as agreed between you and your ITE provider);
- Section B identifies your strengths and priorities for your further professional development during induction (as agreed between you and your ITE provider);
- Section C identifies targets and an action plan for the induction period (as agreed between you and your first teaching post school).

Sections A and B are completed near to the end of your ITE course. Section C is completed in conjunction with the member of staff responsible for your induction in your first teaching post school.

TRANSITION FROM STUDENT TEACHER TO NEWLY QUALIFIED TEACHER

When you successfully complete your course and get your first teaching post you will probably feel immense relief at having 'made it'. You may feel very confident and believe that you are going to be able to solve any problem you are faced with, e.g. motivating an unmotivated pupil or class, or changing the teaching methods in the department so that much more active learning takes place. You may also fear failing in your new job. Different people have different fears, e.g. fear of not being able to control the pupils, of being thought to be lacking skill or ability, of not being accepted by other members of staff, of not liking the school or the people you work with. The transition from student teacher to newly qualified teacher is considered further in Capel, Leask and Turner (1997).

As the new person in a school and department, you may not be sure of how to behave or of the rules or procedures to follow. You will have some successes and some failures and will soon realise that you cannot solve every problem or change the world. As a result, your confidence may decrease and you may not be fully effective until you are settled in the school and the job. A well-structured induction programme should help you make this transition. A chapter on your immediate professional needs is included in Capel, Leask and Turner (1997).

INDUCTION

Induction can be divided into two main parts: immediate induction into the job, which gives you vital information to help you through the early days; and ongoing induction, which continues throughout the year, providing the link between ITE and CPD. We consider immediate induction first.

Immediate induction

The immediate induction programme applies only to the first few days and weeks of any job and focuses on general familiarisation and welfare aspects that all newly qualified teachers in that school need. Immediate induction should, therefore, help you to understand, as quickly as possible, how you fit into the school and the department, building on information gained previously from the literature, your interview and any further visits to the school after you were appointed. ACAS (1984) produced an induction checklist (summarised below) which you can use to check the content of any induction programme that you receive:

- reception, including completing paperwork required by the school, tour of the school, introducing you to key members of staff you have not previously met, management and administrative arrangements;
- layout of school, including cloakroom and toilets, first aid room, entrances and exits to be used, canteen, notice-boards;
- the school, including structure and departments, future developments, brief historical comments;
- the department, including its function, supervision, colleagues, and standard of work expected;
- conditions of employment, including contract of employment, reporting, salary and deductions, holidays, sickness and medical statements, sick pay, pension scheme;
- education, training and promotion, including school or LEA training schemes, policy on release for courses, assistance with fees, appraisal;
- safety procedures, including behaviour, fires, location of fire-fighting equipment, location of exits, use of extinguishers, first aid, how to get medical help;
- rules, regulations and procedures, including misconduct, disciplinary procedures, involvement of employee representatives, grievance procedures, appeals;
- employee involvement and communication, including employee representatives, dispute procedures, consultative arrangements, communication and briefing arrangements (e.g. morning staff meetings);
- physical facilities, welfare and employee benefits/facilities, including canteen facilities, protective clothing, lockers, medical services, suggestions scheme, sports/social facilities, telephone facilities, transport arrangements.

The immediate induction programme is supported in England by ongoing statutory induction throughout the equivalent of your first year of teaching, which is linked to your career-long CPD.

Statutory induction in England

Statutory induction arrangements were introduced in England for all those qualifying after May 1999. These arrangements apply to all newly qualified teachers working in posts that last for one term or more in a maintained school (although arrangements are also being implemented in many independent schools).

The arrangements aim to ensure that, as a newly qualified teacher, your professional development is secure, and that you are given adequate support. The statutory induction arrangements include an individualised programme and also assessment against the national Induction Standards (which build on the national standards for QTS, which you must demonstrate successfully at the end of your initial teacher education). You must complete successfully the requirements of the statutory induction in order to continue teaching in a maintained school or a non-maintained special school.

The induction period comprises three school terms. It is advisable to begin your teaching career and statutory induction period immediately after you finish your initial teacher education and gain QTS. The world of education is dynamic, not static, and things move on swiftly, with changes occurring constantly (for example, in subject knowledge, in curriculum development, in assessment, in teaching approaches), and a school making an appointment needs to consider the 'freshness' of your school experience. However, there is no time limit to when you start the statutory induction, although the induction period must be completed satisfactorily within five years of starting. For example, you may have commitments that prevent you beginning your teaching career immediately after your course (for example, family obligations or further study). In such cases, you are able to commence the induction as soon as you begin teaching in a maintained school. You may also take breaks between each of the terms. However, only appointments that last a term or more count towards your induction period. You would be wise to clarify at your interview the induction arrangements, especially if you are appointed to a position on a part-time basis. For example, if you are teaching two-and-a-half days a week, your induction period lasts six terms.

The induction period includes:

- a reduction in your timetable commitments. Normally, you will be expected to undertake teaching duties of 90 per cent of a full-time teaching load. Your non-contact time is, therefore, over and above what the school normally allocates. You should use this time wisely to focus on activities that are part of your induction programme;
- funding from the government Standards fund, from which your school meets the financial costs of your induction, probably including some release from teaching;
- a dedicated tutor throughout your induction programme in that school. This tutor has responsibility for implementing your programme;
- a programme that is planned to suit your needs. You work collaboratively with your induction tutor to ensure that your programme is appropriate. You are expected to play an active role in your own induction, and therefore need to develop skills of self-reflection, target setting and action planning. The starting point for your induction is section C of your Career Entry Profile, which identifies targets for your induction period, and specifies actions to achieve these, along with resources needed and colleagues to help you. Success criteria and review dates are also identified. The important principle is that your induction programme is individualised and that it should meet *your* needs in trying to demonstrate the national Induction Standards. When discussing section C of your Career Entry Profile with your induction tutor, try to think of what support you need to achieve your targets. For example, this could include collaborative work with other teachers in the department; visiting other schools for focused tasks; participation in formal training courses; or subject-specific tasks such as planning particular schemes of work or assessment activities;
- observation of your teaching. The first observation normally takes place in the first four weeks in post, then normally at least once each half-term. Your induction tutor and others undertake observation. Following each observation there is a collaborative review of your progress towards the Induction Standards, and your targets, programme and action plan are revised as necessary;
- formal assessment meetings with your induction tutor. These take place at least once each term. After each of the first two formal assessment meetings, your headteacher makes a report to the

Local Education Authority (LEA) (or the Independent Schools Council Teacher Induction Panel (ISCTIP), for independent schools). This report records your achievements in line with the national Induction Standards. If you are identified as needing further help to reach the national Induction Standards, the school will arrange for this;

- recommendation to the LEA and General Teaching Council (GTC). After the final assessment meeting your headteacher makes a recommendation to the LEA/ISCTIP, who decide whether you have successfully met all the requirements for the statutory induction. They inform your headteacher and the GTC of their decision.

Task 8.2.2

PREPARING FOR INDUCTION

Before you begin your first teaching post, find out what is expected of you by the end of your induction period by reading the national Induction Standards. Also, look back to your Career Entry Profile and match your strengths (identified in section A) and areas for development (identified in section B) against the national Induction Standards. This should help you to gain an idea of what you need to prepare for your discussions with your induction tutor when you are completing section C.

Arrangements outside England

Formal induction arrangements for Scotland and Northern Ireland are different from those for England. If you complete induction arrangements for Scotland or Northern Ireland, you are able to teach in a school in England. There are plans to introduce formal induction arrangements in Wales.

National basic skills tests

Basis skills are part of the government's agenda for professional training (DfEE, 1998c). National skills tests in numeracy, literacy and information and communications technology (ICT) are in the process of becoming a requirement for QTS in England. If you gained QTS between 1 May 2000 and 30 April 2001, you need to pass the *numeracy* test in order to complete your induction period successfully. It you are seeking to gain QTS after 1 May 2001 you need to pass the *numeracy* and *literacy* tests **before** you can be awarded QTS, register with the GTC and begin your induction period. The basis skills test in *ICT* is to be introduced at a later date (Teacher Training Agency, 2000a). You can find out more about the tests on the TTA website (www.canteach.gov.uk).

General Teaching Council (GTC)

The GTC was introduced in September 2000, and is the statutory professional body for teachers. It advises the government on a wide range of teaching and education matters, including recruitment, initial teacher education and induction, and professional development. One of its responsibilities is to maintain a register of all qualified teachers. Another of its responsibilities is to prepare a code of professional conduct and practice expected of registered teachers in England. It has the power to take a teacher off its register on the grounds of unacceptable conduct or serious professional misconduct or incompetence. It also hears appeals against decisions by LEAs in the case of a newly qualified teacher failing to pass the induction year.

GENERAL INDUCTION MATTERS FOR ALL NEWLY QUALIFIED TEACHERS

In our experience many newly qualified teachers report that school experience gave them an indication of the demands of teaching, but had not prepared them fully for the demands of a full-time post. They had felt that, as they would not be constantly observed, evaluated and assessed, stress and tiredness would reduce. However, they discovered that the first year of teaching was just as tiring and stressful as their school experience, if not more so.

In one way, being a newly qualified teacher in your first teaching post is not much different from being a student teacher: you are still a beginner, albeit a beginner with more experience. In other ways, however, your first teaching post is a very different experience from school experience as a student teacher. You may feel differently about yourself as a 'real' teacher. This may influence the way you behave. Further, staff and pupils may treat you differently as a full member of staff.

ITE courses cannot adequately prepare student teachers for all aspects of teaching in the time available. All newly qualified teachers still have a lot to learn and inevitably feel unprepared for some aspects of the teacher's role. It is likely that as a student teacher you do not undertake all the activities that teachers undertake, e.g. student teachers are unlikely to be involved with developing schemes of work for a year or a Key Stage, or with administering examinations. In your first year of teaching you undertake a greater range of responsibilities than as a student teacher, e.g. you have your own groups and classes and can establish your own procedures and rules for classroom management right from the beginning of the school year. You therefore undertake the full role of the teacher in your classroom.

During the first few weeks or first term in your new post, you probably find that you concentrate mainly on becoming confident and competent in your teaching so as to establish yourself in the school. You are busy getting to know your classes, planning units of teaching from the school's schemes of work, preparing lesson plans, teaching, setting and marking homework, undertaking pastoral activities with your form and getting to know the rules, routines and procedures of the school.

Over the course of the first year you face situations that you did not experience as a student teacher. This includes undertaking activities for the first time, e.g. discussing progress with pupils as part of their Record of Achievement, setting questions for examinations, undertaking supervisory duties, or sustaining activities that you have not had to sustain over such a long period of time previously, such as:

* planning and preparing material for a year to incorporate different material, teaching strategies and approaches to sustain pupil interest and motivation;
* adapting your planned unit of work to meet the needs of different groups of pupils. As you should be aware from your school experiences, you cannot plan one set of material and deliver it in exactly the same way to different groups of pupils. This adaptation requires careful planning and being able to think on your feet in order to meet the needs of particular pupils and classes;

- encouraging progress, target setting and maintaining learning over the period of a year;
- maintaining discipline over a whole year. This is very different from maintaining discipline over a short period of time on school experience. You cannot 'put up with' things that you may have been able to put up with for a relatively short period of time on school experience.

Although taking extra-curricular activities may be expected of you, we advise you not to take on too many (certainly not every lunchtime and evening as many physical education teachers do). In your first year you need to concentrate initially on developing into an effective teacher.

However, as a newly qualified teacher, you may not be expected to undertake the full range of roles and responsibilities of teachers, e.g. you may not be expected to deal with some of the more serious pastoral problems or to undertake the full range of administrative demands. Marland said that this:

> therefore confirms and contradicts the assertion that probationers are invariably thrown in at the deep end of teaching. They might be thrown in, but it is a rather smaller pool in which they have to swim, since most of the administrative and managerial responsibilities do not come their way. Nonetheless, to continue the metaphor, it is possible to drown in a very small pool and . . . the classroom is notoriously hazardous. The major consolation is that much of the classroom-based work will have been encountered during the teaching practice term.
>
> (1993, p. 191)

Thus, you may feel that teaching is more difficult than you first thought and realise that you still have a lot to learn. As a result, you may become frustrated, and have doubts about whether you can teach and what you are achieving with the pupils. You may need help and understanding from other members of staff to overcome these doubts and continue to develop as a teacher.

In England there are requirements for the induction period (see p. 384). There will be similar arrangements in place for many of you outside England. However, wherever you begin your teaching career, as a newly qualified teacher you should be allocated an experienced member of staff to act as a tutor during your first year of teaching. You may be given a lighter teaching load during your first year of teaching to enable you to spend time with your tutor and also to account for the fact that everything is new and takes you longer to do. You can draw on your tutor's experience to help you to answer the numerous questions you have as new situations arise, and to overcome problems with aspects of your teaching. Your tutor can help you to learn as part of your normal job, by identifying and using opportunities available in your everyday work to develop further your skills, knowledge or understanding. You may discuss a problem and then go away and try to put some of the suggested solutions into practice. Your tutor should observe a lesson, discuss it with you, give you feedback and constructively criticise your performance, suggesting alternative approaches if appropriate. This type of learning (often called coaching) is generally effective because you learn by doing, you get feedback on your performance and the learning is relevant. This is especially important in an activity or situation in which it is difficult to simulate the experience.

In an ideal world a tutor is proactive, making a conscious effort to look for opportunities for development. However, your tutor is busy and you spend much of your time in a classroom on your own with pupils; therefore there may be limited opportunities for coaching. You may therefore use coaching reactively by identifying areas where you feel you would benefit most from further development or where something has gone wrong. You can set up a situation where your tutor can help you address or correct that particular issue, e.g. ask your tutor to observe a lesson and comment on a particular aspect of your teaching; or observe a lesson taken by your tutor or another member of staff; or team-teach particular topics in which you lack confidence. A chapter on working with your tutor is included in Capel, Leask and Turner (1997).

Most other members of staff are helpful and understanding, especially if you establish good relationships with them. Relationships take time to develop and you need to be sensitive to the environment you are in. You will not get off to a good start if, for example, you sit in someone's usual chair in the staffroom, try to impress everyone with your up-to-date knowledge, ideas and theories, try to change something immediately because you think things you have seen in other schools could work better, ask for help before you have tried to solve a problem yourself or do not know when to ask for help, or do not operate procedures and policies and enforce school rules. If you do not operate procedures and policies or enforce school rules, you undermine the system and create tensions between pupils and teachers and between yourself and other members of staff.

However, as you settle into the job and work with your classes and learn the procedures, rules and routines, other staff may forget that you are new. As they become ever more busy with their own work as the term and year progress, they treat you as any other member of staff and do not offer help and advice. If you need support, approach staff and talk to them about your concerns and ask for help.

You may form a support group with other newly qualified teachers. You can share your concerns and problems, support and learn from each other and remind each other that, despite the amount you still have to learn, you also have much to offer and are enthusiastic.

CPD (BEYOND THE FIRST YEAR)

Successfully completing the statutory induction period does not mean the end of your learning; indeed, it marks the start of a new period of your career. There are several aspects of your CPD you need to consider in collaboration with colleagues.

Your own individual development needs

New teachers spend the first couple of years in teaching establishing themselves. However, you will increasingly wish to take on additional responsibilities and develop areas of expertise. Indeed, in the final assessment meeting of your induction period, you target areas for development for your second (and early) years of teaching. For example, you may wish to become involved in pastoral work or work placements, or even aspects of ITE. Your annual appraisal will help you to identify further training needs.

As you develop you will probably want to take on posts of responsibility, either within the department or within the school. It is important to recognise that, just as when you started your first post, when you take up a new post later in your career, you will go through a period of transition as you adjust to the new situation. You are likely to adjust more quickly if you have identified the range of new responsibilities required in the post, identified areas for development through reflection and planning as recorded in your professional portfolio, through the appraisal process or analysis of critical incidents, and undertaken appropriate CPD. Your Career Entry Profile should have been the beginning of a professional development scheme which you continue to work on throughout your career. There are many ways in which you can develop new areas of expertise (as well as improve on any areas of weakness), e.g. short or long courses, a higher degree or a further professional qualification, and being involved in development and change activities in the school. In England, all new heads of department and headteachers are required to undertake training for their responsibilities (see Teacher Training Agency, 1998).

Appraisal

Teacher appraisal is part of making explicit teacher accountability. Appraisal normally consists of observation of your teaching and an appraisal interview. The appraisal interview may start with discussion of your observed teaching performance. It may then progress to your performance in the job over the past year (particularly in relation to pupils' progress), your strengths, areas for development and professional development undertaken to address these. In doing this, there are a range of topics which may be discussed, e.g. your teaching, pastoral work, curriculum development work, management and administrative activities, and membership of committees and working parties. Your Career Entry Profile should be used to provide a focus for this discussion in your first appraisal. An appraisal interview should provide you with valuable dialogue, resulting in the identification and confirmation of areas for development and ways in which any identified needs might be met, e.g. by attending conferences, studying for a higher degree, further involvement in the school development plan, or other opportunities for CPD within the school.

Teacher appraisal is a crucial part of the school's performance management arrangements. Appraisal informs decisions about teachers' pay as well as their professional development, with excellent performers moving rapidly up to the payment threshold.

The priorities of the school

Involvement in development and change processes, most often through school development planning, is a valuable form of CPD. Following an inspection by OFSTED, all schools must produce a development plan to address issues raised in the OFSTED report. Further, you are more likely to effect change through being involved in this process. You are unlikely to effect change if you 'jump in with both feet' as a new teacher, because you are unlikely to understand the particular school context, its politics, rules, routines, procedures and policies and the reason that these are in place, or to have developed effective channels of communication and working relationships with established staff.

A school development plan enables a school to:

> organise what it is already doing and what it needs to do in a more purposeful and coherent way . . . it brings together, in an overall plan, national and LEA policies and initiatives, the school's aims and values, its existing achievements and its needs for development. By coordinating aspects of planning which are otherwise separate, the school acquires a shared sense of direction and is able to control and manage the tasks of development and change. Priorities for development are planned in detail for one year and are supported by action plans or working documents for staff. The priorities for later years are sketched in outline to provide the longer term programme.

> (Hargreaves *et al.*, 1989, p. 4)

School development plans should start from where the school is now, developing whole school, departmental and other plans covering all aspects of school life, e.g. teaching, curriculum and assessment, management and organisation, resources, staff development and finance. Development planning comprises four processes. These are:

audit: a school reviews its strengths and weaknesses;
plan construction: priorities for development are selected and turned into specific targets;
implementation: of the planned priorities and targets;
evaluation: the success of implementation is checked.

(Hargreaves *et al.*, 1989, p. 5)

This is illustrated in Figure 8.2.1.

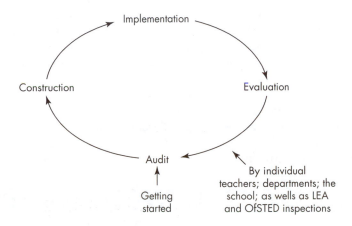

Figure 8.2.1 The planning cycle for school development planning
Source: Adapted from Hargreaves *et al.*, (1989, p. 50).

School development plans work best when all staff are involved. This requires consultation so that the views of all staff, including support staff, and any parent–teacher association are considered. To work best, everyone needs to know how they can contribute and what they are expected to do. Different processes and activities are shared out; for example, governors, the headteacher, senior managers, the CPD co-ordinator, curriculum leaders, departments and teams of staff may be responsible for different aspects of the plan. You may be involved at different stages of school development planning in a number of different ways, depending on the foci of the plan for any one year. Take the opportunity to be fully involved in all appropriate aspects of the plan in order to initiate development and change within the school and to further your professional development.

Professional development is part of your professional accountability as a teacher. You should therefore monitor your progress as a teacher and your professional development.

National training needs

The government in its Green Paper *Teachers Meeting the Challenge of Change* (DfEE, 1998c) clearly stated its intention to 'modernise the teaching profession' (p. 6), ready to 'advance with confidence into the 21st Century' (p. 13). This document sets out the government's future agenda for the teaching profession in terms of initial teacher education; recruitment; leadership; support for professional development; and enhancement of teaching and learning through, for example, the use of new technologies. As a reflective teacher you will be aware of national priorities as these will affect and influence your own priorities and those of your school and LEA.

Monitoring and evaluation

You should already be familiar with the process of monitoring and evaluating in your work with pupils, e.g. monitoring the attainment of pupils, evaluating the effectiveness of lessons or of different teaching strategies. In order to continue to learn in the teaching situation, as well as get the most out of your professional development activities, continue the active, reflective approach to learning which you developed during your ITE course. Monitor and evaluate your teaching and your development activities against specific objectives you have identified for development, as you would a lesson, and continue to question what you are doing and identify alternative approaches. Record your progress in your portfolio.

You can also benefit from discussing your development as a teacher and your professional development activities. You can, of course, do this informally, but appraisal gives you the opportunity to discuss it formally.

SUMMARY AND KEY POINTS

This unit has considered the sequence of development as a teacher through:

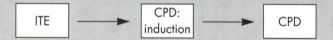

You are already on the professional development road and it is your professional responsibility throughout your career to seek opportunities for development. Your Career Entry Profile helps you to target and address your development needs and to build on your strengths in your first year of teaching. It also helps you to take responsibility for your own professional development from as early as possible in your career, by establishing the practice of target setting and review, in order to provide a good foundation for appraisal and your CPD. Your targets may include targets for wider aspects of your role as a teacher. For example, do you know what to do if a pupil has an epileptic fit or an asthma attack? Would you feel more in control if you knew how to deal with such situations in your teaching? If so, would you benefit from undertaking a first aid course (see, for example, St John Ambulance, 1999)? Similarly, although competence in ICT is a requirement if you are learning to teach in England (DfEE, 1998c), do you, for example, need to develop further the use of ICT in teaching and learning, or are there aspects that you need to update?

There are many areas in which you could probably benefit from education and training. For example, your career plan may be to progress to a management post. Although you may be identifying CPD needed to make such a move, you will want to ensure that you are fully established as a teacher first. It is important not to take on too much at once. Your first year of teaching is very demanding and therefore it is important that you pace yourself when planning for your further professional development.

FURTHER READING

Dean, J. (1993) *Managing the Secondary School*, London: Routledge.
   This book was written for people in management positions in secondary schools and therefore gives a broad perspective on the life of the school. For any new teachers looking to management as a possible career path, this text is very helpful in highlighting the range of managerial activities undertaken.

Department for Education and Employment (DfEE) (1998c) *Teachers Meeting the Challenge of Change*, London: HMSO.
   This booklet sets out the government's agenda for education in the twenty-first century and is useful in preparing you for some of the national priorities you will need to engage with during your early teaching career.

Dunham, J. (1995) *Developing Effective School Management*, London: Routledge.
   This book is designed to help teachers to identify and develop knowledge and skills to become effective middle managers. The first chapter addresses the importance of whole school management, and following chapters address different aspects of management, including effective management styles, management theories, the management of teams and meetings, key management skills, CPD, managing change, time management, stress management.

Hargreaves, D.H., Hopkins, D., Leask, M., Connolly, J. and Robinson, P. (1989) *Planning for School Development: Advice to Governors, Headteachers and Teachers*, London: DES.
   This short booklet provides information about school development planning, but should provide useful information for any planning process in which you might be involved and therefore should be of interest whether or not you are working on a school development plan.

Lawton, D. (1996) *Beyond the National Curriculum. Teacher Professionalism and Empowerment*, London: Hodder and Stoughton.
   This book explores issues relating to professionalism. It should help you to clarify your thoughts, principles and actions about your practice in your teaching career.

Leask, M. and Terrell, I. (1997) *Development Planning and School Improvement for Middle Managers*, London: Kogan Page.
   This book was written for teachers wanting to move to head of department/head of year positions in secondary schools.

Teacher Training Agency (TTA) (2000a) *An Introduction for Trainee Teachers to the Induction Period for Newly Qualified Teachers*, London: TTA.

Teacher Training Agency (TTA) (2000c) *Moving Forward: Support and Challenge in the Induction Period*, London: TTA.

These brief handbooks explain the principles and procedures for the statutory induction period in England.

Teacher Training Agency (TTA) (2000d) *QTS Skills Tests Information Booklet for Trainees*, London: TTA.

This handbook gives information about the requirements and procedures for national skills tests and complements other support material. Copies can be obtained from the TTA website (www.canteach.gov.uk).

UNIT 8.3 **ACCOUNTABILITY, CONTRACTUAL AND STATUTORY DUTIES**

MARILYN LEASK

INTRODUCTION

As a newly qualified teacher in the state system your work is controlled by the requirements of national and local government, school, subject, parent and pupils – so you are accountable to a whole range of interested parties for the quality of your work. To help you understand the context in which teachers work, we have provided a description of the system within which teachers in the state system operate.

OBJECTIVES

By the end of this unit you should:

- understand the structure of the state education system;
- be aware of the legal and contractual requirements that govern the work of the teacher.

WHERE DO TEACHERS FIT WITHIN THE EDUCATION SYSTEM?

The structure of the education system in England and Wales is set out in Figure 8.3.1 to show the relationships between classroom teachers and the rest of the education system.

The Secretary of State, ministers and staff at the DfEE do not usually have teaching experience. They are provided with professional advice by advisory bodies such as the Qualifications and Curriculum Authority (QCA) (previously the School Curriculum and Assessment Authority (SCAA)), which has some members with a wide range of expertise in the profession, and the Teacher Training Agency (TTA). However, Local Education Authority officers and professors and lecturers in education normally start their careers as classroom teachers.

Whilst the responsibilities within the school, listed in Figure 8.3.1, are shared out differently in different schools, the structure is usually similar, but the terminology used is in some cases different.

There are also numerous support staff whose contribution to school life is essential to the smooth running of the school: caretaker (school's premises' officer); nurse; secretarial staff; technical staff; cleaners; lunchtime supervisors; the bursar. Staff from other professions are also linked with the school, e.g. the education welfare officer, school psychologists, and some pupils have social workers who are responsible for overseeing their progress.

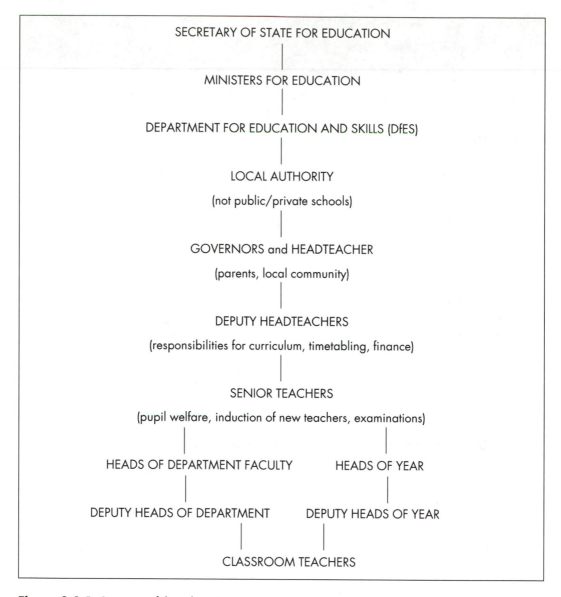

Figure 8.3.1 Structure of the education system

ACCOUNTABILITY

Within the structure of the education system and individual schools, teachers are accountable for what they do, and the Office for Standards in Education (OFSTED) plays a major part in monitoring the work in schools. As an individual teacher, though, you are also accountable – to parents, to colleagues, to pupils, to your employer.

Bush (in Goddard and Leask, 1992, p. 156ff.) identifies three ways in which a teacher experiences accountability. Bush calls these:

- Moral accountability;
- Professional accountability;
- Contractual accountability.

Moral accountability is related to your conscience about how you should carry out your work. You are 'morally accountable' to students, parents and society.

Your professional accountability relates to your responsibility to your colleagues and to the teaching profession, to do your work to the highest standard of which you are capable.

Contractual accountability is defined by legal requirements set down by your employer as well as in legislation passed by Parliament.

Whilst this may seem an oversimplification of a teacher's accountabilities, these three aspects provide a useful framework for developing your own understanding of your accountability. However, the way in which moral and professional accountability is personally perceived depends on the values of the individual teacher and on the standards they set themselves.

Task 8.3.1

MORAL ACCOUNTABILITY AND PROFESSIONAL ACCOUNTABILITY

Consider what being morally and professionally accountable means for you and for the way you approach your work. Discuss this with other student teachers or your tutor.

The following section sets out in some detail your legal duties, both contractual and statutory.

LEGAL DUTIES

You have various legally binding contractual responsibilities and statutory duties. In addition you also have, as do all citizens, 'common law duties', which means, among other things, that you have a duty of care towards other people. Teachers, again as citizens, are subject to criminal law. One aspect of criminal law you should note is that if you hit a pupil or if a pupil hits you this constitutes assault. It also is common sense to protect yourself against allegations by ensuring that you do not spend time alone in closed environments with individual pupils. Talk to your tutor about these issues and about practice in your school experience school.

CONTRACTUAL DUTIES

Your contractual duties are negotiated between you and your employer. In the case of teachers employed in state schools in England and Wales, the document that sets out teachers' contractual duties in England and Wales is *School Teachers' Pay and Conditions* which is produced by the DfEE and updated annually. Additional conditions may apply in individual schools. There may also be 'implied terms' to your contract, i.e. terms which are not written down, e.g. that you will behave in a manner befitting your role – some schools operate a dress code. You can obtain detailed advice from one of the teachers' unions. *The Headteacher's Guide to the Law* (annually updated, Croner) is recommended further reading for those with a particular interest in this area. In *School Teachers' Pay and Conditions*, guidelines are laid down for the exercise of your professional duties under the headings of teaching, other activities (which covers pastoral work), assessment and reports, appraisal, review, further training and development, educational methods, discipline, health and safety, staff meetings, cover (for absent colleagues), public examinations, management, administration and working time.

STATUTORY DUTIES

Statutory duties are those which the government has established through legislation. In Table 8.3.1, we provide a summary of those statutory duties of teachers in which you are most likely to be involved as a student and early in your career. A fuller version of the statutory duties of those involved in education is set out in the *Handbook for the Inspection of Schools, Part 6: The Statutory Basis for Education* (OFSTED, 1994a). We use this where information is provided covering the statutory duties of heads, governors and parents as later editions of the handbook are less detailed. Table 8.3.1 is taken directly from this handbook. In the handbook, the legislation related to each aspect is also listed. (You may find it useful to refer back to Table 5.4.2 which lists the criteria for judging teaching published by OFSTED in 2000.) Chapters on conditions of service, legal liabilities and responsibilities, child protection and other important aspects of a teacher's role can be found in Cole, 1999.

Task 8.3.2

STATUTORY DUTIES

As you read the list of statutory duties, we suggest you think carefully about the responsibilities you are taking on and that you summarise these and record them in your diary. All of these statutory duties are part of the teacher's job. As a student teacher you gain experience of most of the statutory duties during your school experience. However, three areas which are easily neglected are report writing (7.2), special educational needs (7.4) and appraisal (7.6.i). We suggest that you occasionally check back to this list to see that you are gaining the required experience, and that you ask if you are not.

Table 8.3.1 Statutory duties of teachers

(This summary is taken from the OFSTED handbook, 1994a)

5.1 Pupils' spiritual, moral, social and cultural development

The curriculum of a maintained school must promote the spiritual, moral, cultural, mental and physical development of pupils and of society; and prepare pupils for the opportunities, responsibilities and experiences of adult life.

. . . All pupils, unless withdrawn by their parents, must attend a daily act of collective worship.

5.2 Behaviour and discipline

The head is responsible for maintaining discipline taking the governors' views into account. . . .

Corporal punishment has been abolished for all pupils in maintained schools and for pupils in independent schools whose fees are wholly or partly met from public funds. Corporal punishment may be applied to privately funded pupils in independent schools with more than 50 boarders.

Child protection: parents, in effect, give schools the authority to act 'in loco parentis'. Schools should take independent action to deal with emergencies. They have a general duty to act independently in respect of suspected abuse at home.

Schools have a duty to protect children from harm. They are recommended to have designated teachers and procedures to notify Social Services Departments, NSPCC and police where they are concerned about a pupil's safety. The designated staff should be properly trained and be aware of the role of local Area Child Protection Committees.

5.3 Attendance

All schools must keep an attendance register in which pupils are marked present or absent at the beginning of each morning and afternoon session. Schools must distinguish in their attendance registers between authorised and unauthorised absences of pupils aged 5–16 and must publish rates of unauthorised absence in prospectuses and annual reports . . .

6 Subjects of the curriculum and other curricular provision

This section of the OFSTED report outlines the legislation behind the curriculum. Religious education and ten other subjects have to be taught – English, mathematics, science, technology, history, geography, a modern foreign language, art, music, physical education.

7.2 Assessment, recording and reporting

National Curriculum assessment

Schools are required to assess pupils in National Curriculum subjects at or near the end of each Key Stage for the purpose of ascertaining what they have achieved in relation to Attainment Targets for that stage . . .

Records

Schools must provide at least annually a written report to the parents of each pupil for their retention . . . The report must contain brief particulars of a pupil's progress in all subjects and activities studied as part of the school curriculum; details of a pupil's general progress; information on performance in all National Curriculum assessments and in public examinations; school and national comparative information about National Curriculum assessments and public examinations; an attendance record; and details of the arrangements under which the report may be discussed with teachers at the school.

continued

Table 8.3.1 continued

Provision of information
School must make available the results of pupils' achievements in examinations and ensure that they are published . . .

7.3.ii Equality of opportunity
Schools have a general duty to ensure that facilities for education are provided without sexual or racial discrimination.
Pupils are entitled to efficient full-time education suitable to their ages, abilities and aptitudes and any special educational needs they may have.

7.4   Provision for pupils with SEN
Where a pupil has been assessed as having special educational needs, a statement of needs must be prepared and maintained in accordance with its provisions.
All pupils in maintained schools should follow the National Curriculum to the maximum extent possible, but the application of its provisions may be disapplied or modified in relation to pupils with statements of special educational needs.

7.6.i Teaching and non-teaching staff
All qualified teachers, except those in non-maintained schools, employed full-time or at least 40 per cent full-time on contracts of not less than one year, are subject to appraisal of their performance on a two-year cycle . . .

7.6.ii Resources for learning
A learning authority shall not intentionally promote homosexuality or publish material with the intention of promoting homosexuality.
Licences are required for reprographics and recording of broadcasts.
School must use resources safely, especially low-level radioactive materials . . .

Source: Summarised from OFSTED (May 1994a) *Handbook for the Inspection of Schools, Part 6: The Statutory Basis for Education*, pp. 6–15; see also further OFSTED texts listed at the end of this unit.

SUMMARY AND KEY POINTS

As a student teacher, you need to be aware of the full range of a teacher's duties. Whenever you are working in a school, you are acting with the agreement and support of qualified teachers. When you take over their classes, you are responsible to them for upholding the legal duties which guide their work.

We recommend that you return to this unit from time to time as you become more familiar with the work of the teacher so that you can check your practice against the requirements. Students and teachers who are union members will find that advice is readily available from their union. The addresses of teachers' unions can be found in the *Education Year Book* which is available in many libraries.

FURTHER READING

Cole, M. (ed.) (1999) *Professional Issues for Teachers and Student Teachers*, London: David Fulton.
This text contains chapters on conditions of service, legal liabilities and responsibilities, child protection and other important aspects of a teacher's role.

Croner (updated annually) *The Headteacher's Guide to the Law*, New Malden: Croner Publications.
Croner produce a range of publications which provide up-to-date advice for headteachers and other staff.

Department for Education and Employment (updated annually) *School Teachers' Pay and Conditions*, London: HMSO.
The provisions in this document are based on the statutory conditions affecting the employment of teachers (in all sectors: primary, secondary, special) who are employed by Local Education Authorities or governing bodies of voluntary or most grant-maintained schools. It provides useful information about salary scales and conditions of work.

OFSTED (2000c) *Improving Schools – The Framework*, London: OFSTED.
Some OFSTED publications such as that above set out the statutory basis for the work of teachers. The main requirements affecting the work of beginning teachers have been summarised in this unit. We suggest that you become familiar with the latest OFSTED publications for your subject. The OFSTED website can be found through the search engine on the http://www.teachernet. dfee.gov.uk website. This site is intended to be an internet gateway for teachers.

Teacher Net on http://www.teachernet.gov.uk provides access to key resources and government documents.

CHAPTER 9 **AND FINALLY**

Throughout this book, we have mixed information and background with enquiries and tasks. The tasks are intended to provide opportunities to examine the practice of other teachers, of yourself and the organisation of schools. The tasks which focus on enquiries generate the data or ideas upon which an understanding of and an explanation for the complex world of teaching and learning in schools are built.

The relationship between explanation and practice is a dynamic one; explanations are needed to make sense of experience and inform practice. Some explanations will be your own, to be tried and tested against the theories of others, often more experienced teachers and educators. At other times you may use directly the explanations of others. Explanations in turn generate working theories, responsive to practice and experience. Theory is important; it provides a framework in which to understand the complex world of the classroom and to direct further research into improving the quality of learning. It provides, too, a reference point against which to judge change and development, both of yourself and schools. It is the encompassing of these ideas, the interplay of theory and practice, which underpins the notion of the reflective practitioner.

We ask you, as one last task, to consider the message in the following poem which we have occasionally found displayed on staffroom walls:

CHILDREN LEARN WHAT THEY LIVE

If a child lives with criticism,
  he learns to condemn,
If a child lives with hostility,
  he learns to fight,
If a child lives with ridicule,
  he learns to be shy,
If a child lives with shame,
  he learns to feel guilty,
If a child lives with tolerance,
  he learns to be patient,
If a child lives with encouragement,
  he learns confidence,
If a child lives with praise,
  he learns to appreciate,
If a child lives with fairness,
  he learns justice,
If a child lives with security,
  he learns to have faith,
If a child lives with approval,
  he learns to like himself,
If a child lives with acceptance and friendship,
  he learns to find love in the world.
        Dorothy Law Nolta (date unknown)

As a teacher you will have an impact – beyond what you will ever know – on people's lives and thus on the community and society. We hope that what your pupils learn from you will help them to make positive contributions to their world. We hope too that you will have helped pupils to build personal self-confidence and skills to cope with adult life and to become autonomous learners and caring members of society.

To achieve these goals, you can expect to need to carry on learning throughout your professional life. You will also need to balance society's continual demands on teachers with your personal needs and to lead a fulfilling life beyond school.

APPENDIX 1 **GLOSSARY OF TERMS**

All items with ★ are used with specific reference to England and are taken from: OFSTED (1994a) *Handbook for the Inspection of Schools, Part 6: The Statutory Basis for Education*, London: Office of Her Majesty's Chief Inspector of Schools.

All items with ★★ are taken from: Department for Education (1994c) *Code of Practice on the Identification and Assessment of Special Educational Needs*, London: DfE.

ACCAC	Awdurdod Cymwysterau, Cwricwlwm ac Asesu Cymru (Qualifications, Curriculum and Assessment Authority for Wales). The English equivalent is QCA (qv).
AEB	Associated Examining Board. Now part of AQA (qv).
★★**Annual review**	The review of a statement of special educational needs which an LEA must make within twelve months of making the statement or, as the case may be, of the previous review.
AQA	Assessment and Qualifications Alliance. An awarding body comprising C and G (qv), NEAB (qv) and AEB (qv), for GCSE (qv), GCE A and AS levels and GNVQs (qv). (http://www.aqa.org.uk)
Attainment Targets (ATs)	Objectives for each core and foundation subject of the National Curriculum, setting out the knowledge, skills and understanding that pupils of different abilities and maturities are expected to have by the end of each key stage in the subject. See also Level Descriptions and Programmes of Study.
Awarding body	There are now three awarding bodies, formed by merging a number of examination boards. These are:
	Assessment and Qualifications Alliance (AQA) (qv) (http://www.aqa.org.uk) Edexcel (qv) (http://www.edexcel.org.uk) Oxford and Cambridge Regional (OCR) (qv) (http://www.ocr.org.uk)
★**Banding**	The structuring of a year group into divisions, each usually containing two or three classes, on grounds of general ability. Pupils are taught within the band for virtually all the curriculum.
Baseline testing	The assessment of pupils in Year 1 and Reception classes for speaking, listening, reading, writing, mathematics and PSE (qv). (See the DfEE website.)

Basic curriculum

Religious education plus the three core subjects plus the foundation subjects of the National Curriculum. From August 2000 seven subjects at Key Stages 1 and 2 are compulsory. From August 2002 nine subjects at Key Stage 3 and five at Key Stage 4 are compulsory.

Beacon schools

Schools identified as representative of the best practice which can be disseminated to other schools. Such best practice might focus on a wide range of areas, including: individual curriculum subjects; assessment of pupils; school management; parent/community partnerships; special educational needs; gifted and talented pupils.

BEd

Bachelor of Education (a route to QTS (qv)).

BTEC

Business and Technician Education Council. Joined with London Examinations (qv) to form EdExcel Foundation (qv). The BTEC label is still used for certain purposes.

C and G

City and Guilds.

Career Entry Profile

A document to help newly qualified teachers and their first teaching post schools to identify and address targets, to target monitoring and provide support during induction. All ITT (qv) providers in England are required to provide newly qualified teachers with a Career Entry Profile produced by the TTA (qv).

CCW

Curriculum Council for Wales; now ACCAC (qv).

CDT

Craft, Design and Technology; a school curriculum subject.

Certificate of Achievement (COA)

An examination designed to give a qualification to pupils who may not gain a GCSE grade. Courses are available in many subjects. The COA is awarded at pass, merit and distinction corresponding to levels 1, 2 and 3 respectively of the NC. Details available from the websites of AQA, Edexcel or OCR (qv).

Citizenship

A compulsory element of the National Curriculum at Key Stages 3 and 4 from August 2002.

★Collaborative group

A way of working in which groups of children are assigned to groups or engage spontaneously in working together to solve problems; sometimes called co-operative group work.

★Combined course

A course to which several subjects contribute while retaining their distinct identity (e.g. history, geography and RE within combined humanities).

Community school

One of three categories of state school: Community, Foundation (qv), and Voluntary (qv) schools in England and Wales. Admissions and staff appointments controlled by LEA (qv).

★Comprehensive school

A secondary school which admits pupils of age 11 to 16 or 19 from a given catchment area, regardless of their ability.

*Continuity and progression	Appropriate sequencing of learning which builds on previous learning to extend and develop pupils' capabilities.
Core skills	Skills required by all students following a vocational course, e.g. GNVQ (qv).
*Core subjects	English, mathematics and science within the National Curriculum. Strictly speaking these are both core and foundation subjects.
Coursework	Work carried out by pupils during a course of study, marked by teachers and contributing to the final examination mark. Usually externally moderated.
CPD	Continuing professional development.
CRE	Commission for Racial Equality.
Criterion-referenced assessment	A process in which performance is measured by relating candidates' responses to pre-determined criteria.
Cross-curricular elements	These run across the whole curriculum and are not confined to one subject. Introduced in the National Curriculum in 1988 as dimensions, themes and skills. In National Curriculum 2000 these have been replaced by Careers; Citizenship; Personal, Social and Health Education; Key Skills; Thinking Skills.
CTC	City Technology College.
*Curriculum guidelines	Written school guidance for organising and teaching a particular subject or area of the curriculum (see National Curriculum Programmes of Study).
D and T	Design and Technology (in National Curriculum Technology).
Dearing Report	A review of the 'National Curriculum and its assessment' (1994). Recommended review of subject Orders and five-year moratorium on further change.
DES	Department of Education and Science (became DfE (qv)).
DfE	Department for Education (formerly DES (qv)), (became DfEE (qv)).
DfEE	Department for Education and Employment (formerly DfE (qv), DES (qv) and now DfES (qv).
DfES	Department for Education and Skills.
*Differentiation	The matching of work to the differing capabilities of individuals or groups of pupils in order to extend their learning.
*Disapplication	Arrangement for lifting part or all of the National Curriculum requirements for individuals or for any other grouping specified by the Secretary of State.

*EBD

Emotional and behavioural difficulties and disorders. Used with reference to pupils with such difficulties or schools/units which cater for such pupils.

EdExcel Foundation

An awarding body formed from BTEC (qv) and London Examinations (qv) (previously ULEAC (qv)). (http://www.edexcel.org.uk)

*Education Welfare Officer (EWO)

An official of the LEA concerned with pupils' attendance and with liaison between the school, the parents and the authority.

EOC

Equal Opportunities Commission.

ERA

Education Reform Act (1988).

*ESL

English as a second language.

Examination group

Public examination bodies which agreed to work together to provide a range of syllabuses for examination. These have been replaced by awarding bodies (qv).

*Exclusion

Under Section 22 of the Education (No.2) Act 1986 the headteachers of county, voluntary and maintained special schools are empowered to exclude pupils temporarily or permanently when faced with a serious breach of their disciplinary code. The Act sets out procedures relating to the three categories of exclusions: fixed-term, indefinite and permanent.

Flexible training programme (for QTS)

A flexible training programme, directed particularly to career-change/mature trainees, based on an individual needs analysis and individualised programme and centred on a modular approach, which can include distance learning on a part- or full-time basis.

Formative assessment

Assessment linked with teaching; describes pupils' progress and is used to identify the next stage of teaching and learning; it uses diagnostic approaches, employing a wide range of methods, including formal and informal methods.

*Forms of entry (FE)

The number of forms (of thirty pupils) which a school takes into its intake year. From this can be estimated the size of the intake year and the size of the school.

Foundation schools

One of three categories of state school: Community (qv), Foundation and Voluntary (qv) schools in England and Wales. Admissions and staff appointments controlled by the governing body.

Foundation subjects

English, mathematics and science are both core and foundation subjects. The remaining foundation subjects are: art, geography, history, modern foreign language, music, physical education, and technology. Not all foundation subjects are compulsory at all Key Stages.

*GCSE	General Certificate of Secondary Education. National external qualification usually taken at age 16 after a two-year course. This replaced GCE O level.
GMS	Grant-Maintained School. A grant-maintained school received funding direct from the DfEE (qv) and was not under LEA (qv) control. Now Foundation school (qv).
GNVQ	General National Vocational Qualifications.
Grade-related criteria	The identification of criteria, the achievement of which are related to different levels of performance by the candidate.
Graduate Teacher Programme (GTP) (for QTS)	An employment-based route to QTS (qv), which includes working as an unqualified teacher in a school, while receiving an individualised training programme.
*Group work	A way of organising pupils where the teacher assigns tasks to groups of children, to be undertaken collectively, although the work is completed on an individual basis.
HMCI	Her Majesty's Chief Inspector of schools in England.
HMI	Her Majesty's Inspectors of schools in England.
HOD	Head of Department.
*House system	A structure for pastoral care/pupil welfare within a school in which pupils are grouped in vertical units, i.e. sections of the school which include pupils from all year groups.
HOY	Head of Year.
IB	International Baccalaureate. A post-16 qualification designed for university entrance.
ICT	See Information and Communications Technology.
*In-class support	Support within a lesson provided by an additional teacher, often with expertise in teaching pupils with special educational or language needs, in the classroom.
Inclusion	Inclusion in education refers to the NC (qv) for England and Wales (DfEE/QCA, 1999a). Inclusion involves the processes of increasing the participation of pupils in, and reducing their exclusion from, the cultures, curricula and communities of local schools. Inclusion is concerned with the learning participation of all pupils vulnerable to exclusionary pressures, not only those with impairments or categorised as having special educational needs.
Independent school	A private school which receives no state assistance but is financed by fees. Often registered as a charity. See also public school.
Information and Communications Technology (ICT)	Computer hardware and software which extend beyond the usual word-processing, database, graphics and spreadsheet applications to include hardware and software which allow computers to be

networked across the world through the World Wide Web, to access information on the internet and which support other communication activities such as email and video-conferencing.

Information Technology (IT) Methods of gaining, storing and retrieving information through microprocessors. Covers a range of microcomputers, both portable and desktop; generic or integrated software packages, such as word processors, spreadsheets, databases and communication programmes, and interfacing equipment; input devices such as keyboards, overlay keyboards, specialised access switches and touchscreens; output devices such as monitors, printers and plotters; storage devices such as CD-ROM; and microelectronics control devices such as a floor turtle. Often encompassed within Information and Communications Technology (qv). IT is a compulsory subject in the National Curriculum for England.

*INSET In-service Education and Training. See CPD (qv).

*Integrated course A course, usually in a secondary school, to which several subjects contribute without retaining their distinct identity (e.g. integrated humanities, which explores themes that include aspects of geography, history and RE, for example).

**Integration Educating children with special educational needs together with children without special educational needs in mainstream schools wherever possible, and ensuring that children with special educational needs engage in the activities of the school together with children who do not have special educational needs.

IT See Information Technology.

ITT Initial Teacher Training.

Key Skills Of the National Curriculum for England: communication; application of number; IT; improving own learning and performance; problem solving and working with others. See also Thinking Skills.

*Key Stages (KS) The periods in each pupil's education to which the elements of the National Curriculum apply. There are four Key Stages, normally related to the age of the majority of the pupils in a teaching group. They are: Key Stage 1, beginning of compulsory education to age 7; Key Stage 2, 7–11; Key Stage 3, 11–14; Key Stage 4, 14 to end of compulsory education. The equivalent year groups are Years R (Reception), 1 and 2; Years 3–6; Years 7–9; Years 10 and 11. Post–16 is a further Key Stage.

*Language support teacher A teacher provided by the LEA or school to enhance language work with particular groups of pupils.

LEA Local Education Authority. LEAs have a statutory duty to provide education in their area.

*Learning support
A means of providing extra help for pupils, usually those with learning difficulties, e.g. through a specialist teacher or specially designed materials.

Level description
Of the National Curriculum for England. A statement describing the 'types and range of performance that pupils working at a particular level should characteristically demonstrate'. Level descriptions provide the basis for making judgements about pupils' performance at the end of Key Stages 1, 2, 3 and, where appropriate, 4. At Key Stage 4, national qualifications are another means of assessing attainment in the subject.

Levels of attainment
Eight different levels of achievement are defined within the National Curriculum Attainment Targets in England. These stop at KS3 (before 1995 there were ten levels, which continued until KS4).

London Examinations
An examining body previously known as ULEAC (qv), which joined with BTEC (qv) to form EdExcel Foundation (qv).

MEG
Midland Examining Group. Now part of OCR (qv).

Middle school
A school which caters for pupils aged from 8 to 12 or 9 to 13 years of age. They are classified legally as either primary or secondary schools depending on whether the preponderance of pupils in the school are under or over 11 years of age.

*Minority ethnic groups
Pupils, many of whom have been born in the United Kingdom, from other ethnic heritages, e.g. those of Asian heritage from Bangladesh, Pakistan, India or East Africa, those of African or Caribbean heritage, or of Chinese heritage. The groups are often closely associated with countries in the British (New) Commonwealth, although non-Commonwealth refugee pupils are also to be found in schools.

*Mixed ability group
Teaching group containing pupils representative of the range of ability within the school.

Moderation
An exercise involving teachers representing an examination group external to the school whose purpose is to check that standards are comparable across schools and teachers. Usually carried out by sampling coursework or examination papers.

*Module
A definable section of work of fixed length with specific objectives and usually with some form of terminal assessment. Several such units may constitute a modular course.

*National Curriculum (NC)
The core and other foundation subjects and their associated Attainment Targets, Programmes of Study and assessment arrangements of the curriculum in England.

National Induction Standards	Standards that all newly qualified teachers in England are required to demonstrate by the end of their induction period.
NCC	National Curriculum Council. Merged with SEAC (qv) to form SCAA (qv). Now QCA (qv).
NCVQ	National Council for Vocational Qualifications. Joined with SCAA (qv) in 1997 to form QCA (qv).
NEAB	Northern Examinations and Assessment Board (now part of AQA (qv)).
NFER	National Foundation for Educational Research. Carries out research and produces educational diagnostic tests.
***Non-contact time (NCT)**	Time provided by a school for a teacher to prepare work or carry out assigned responsibilities other than direct teaching.
Norm-referenced assessment	A process in which performance is measured by comparing candidates' responses. Individual success is relative to the performance of all other candidates.
Normative assessment	Assessment which is reported relative to a given population.
NQT	Newly Qualified Teacher.
NSG	Non-Statutory Guidance (for National Curriculum). Additional subject guidance for the National Curriculum but which is not mandatory; to be found attached to National Curriculum subject Orders.
NVQ	National Vocational Qualifications.
OCEAC	Oxford and Cambridge Examination and Assessment Council (now OCR (qv)).
OCR	Oxford and Cambridge Regional (a merger of MEG (qv), OCEAC (qv) and RSA (qv) examinations groups). (http://www.ocr.org.uk)
OFSTED	Office for Standards in Education. Non-ministerial government department established under the Education (schools) Act (1992) to take responsibility for the inspection of schools in England. OFSTED inspects pre-school provision, further education, teacher education institutions and Local Education Authorities (qv). Her Majesty's Inspectors (HMI) form the professional arm of OFSTED. See also OHMCI.
OHMCI	Office of Her Majesty's Chief Inspector (Wales). Non-ministerial government department established under the Education (schools) Act (1992) to take responsibility for the inspection of schools in Wales. Her Majesty's Inspectors (HMI) form the professional arm of OHMCI. See also OFSTED.
PANDA	Performance and Assessment Reports (used by OFSTED (qv)).

**Parent

This is defined in section 114 (1D) of the Education Act 1944, as amended by the Children Act 1989. Unless the context otherwise requires, parent in relation to a child or young person includes any person:

- who is not a natural parent of the child but who has parental responsibility for him or her,
- or who has care of the child.

Section 114 (1F) of the 1944 Act states that for the purposes of subsection (1D):

- parental responsibility has the same meaning as in the Children Act 1989, and
- in determining whether an individual has care of a child or young person any absence of the child or young person at a hospital or boarding school and any other temporary absence shall be disregarded.

**Parental responsibility

Under section 2 of the Children Act 1989, parental responsibility falls upon:

- all mothers and fathers who were married to each other at the time of the child's birth (including those who have since separated or divorced),
- mothers who were not married to the father at the time of the child's birth, and
- fathers who were not married to the mother at the time of the child's birth, but who have obtained parental responsibility either by agreement with the child's mother or through a court order.

See *Code of Practice on the Identification and Assessment of Special Educational Needs* (DfE, 1994c) for further details.

*Partnership teaching

An increasingly common means of meeting the language needs of bilingual pupils in which support and class teachers plan and implement together a specially devised programme of in-class teaching and learning. It is used as a criterion for the allocation of Section 11 grants. See also Support teacher.

*Pastoral care

Those aspects of a school's work and structures concerned to promote the general welfare of all pupils, particularly their academic, personal and social development, their attendance and behaviour.

PGCE

Post Graduate Certificate in Education. The main qualification for secondary school teachers in England and Wales recognised by the DfES (qv) for QTS (qv).

PICSI

Pre-Inspection Context and School Indicator (used by OFSTED (qv)).

★Policy	An agreed school statement relating to a particular area of its life and work.
PoS	Programmes of Study (of National Curriculum for England).
★Pre-vocational courses	Courses specifically designed and taught to help pupils to prepare for the world of work.
Profile	Samples of work of pupils, used to illustrate progress, with or without added comments by teachers and/or pupils.
Programmes of Study (PoS)	The subject matter, skills and processes which must be taught to pupils during each Key Stage of the National Curriculum in order that they may meet the objectives set out in Attainment Targets. They set out what pupils should be taught at each Key Stage and provide the basis for planning schemes of work.
★Project	An investigation with a particular focus undertaken by individuals or small groups of pupils leading to a written, oral or graphic presentation of the outcome.
PSE courses	Personal and Social Education courses. They are mainly concerned to promote pupils' personal and social development, and to help educate pupils for life outside and following school. See also PSHE courses.
PSHE courses	Personal, Social and Health Education courses. PSE courses with a specific additional health component.
★PTA	Parent–Teacher Association. Voluntary grouping of parents and school staff to support the school in a variety of ways (financial, social, etc.).
★PTR	Pupil:Teacher Ratio. The ratio of pupils to teachers within a school or group of schools (e.g. 17.4:1).
Public school	Independent secondary school not state-funded. See also independent school. So called because they were funded by public charity at their inception.
QCA	The Qualifications and Curriculum Authority. The QCA came into being in 1997 as a result of the Education Act 1997. Its remit is to promote quality and coherence in education and training. It brings together the work of NCVQ (qv) and SCAA (qv), with additional powers and duties that give it an overview of the curriculum, assessment and qualifications across the whole of education and training, from pre-school to higher vocational levels. QCA advises the Secretary of State for Education and Skills on all matters affecting the curriculum in schools, the assessment of pupils and publicly funded qualifications offered in schools, colleges and workplaces. The Welsh equivalent is ACCAC (qv).

*QTS	Qualified Teacher Status. This is usually attained by completion of a Post-Graduate Certificate in Education (PGCE) or a Bachelor of Education (BEd) degree or a Bachelor of Arts/Science degree with Qualified Teacher Status (BA/BSc (QTS)). The registered teacher training scheme is a route to QTS (qv) for people in posts as unqualified teachers and who have 240 credits at higher education levels. The final 120 credits at level 3 required for a degree can be accrued during the period of training. The Graduate Teacher Programme (qv) is an employment-based route to QTS (qv).
*Record of Achievement (ROA)	Cumulative record of a pupil's academic, personal and social progress over a stage of education.
Registered teacher training scheme	See QTS.
Reliability	A measure of the consistency of the assessment or test item; that is, the extent to which the test gives repeatable results.
RSA	Royal Society of Arts.
*SACRE	The Standing Advisory Council on Religious Education in each LEA to advise the LEA on matters connected with religious education and collective worship, particularly methods of teaching, the choice of teaching materials and the provision of teacher training.
SATs	See Standard Assessment Tasks.
SCAA	School Curriculum and Assessment Authority. Joined with NCVQ (qv) in 1997 to form QCA (qv).
*School Development Plan (SDP)	A coherent plan, required to be made by a school, identifying improvements needed in curriculum, organisation, staffing and resources and setting out action needed to make those improvements.
SCITT	School-Centred Initial Teacher Training. A distinctive route for teacher training based in and organised by schools.
SEAC	School Examination and Assessment Council. Merged with NCC (qv) to form SCAA (qv).
Section 11 staff	Teachers and non-teaching assistants additional to the school's staffing establishment whose specific function is to provide language and learning support for pupils of New Commonwealth heritage.
SEG	Southern Examining Group. Now part of OCR (qv).
*SEN	Special Educational Needs. Referring to pupils who, for a variety of intellectual, physical, social, sensory, psychological or emotional reasons, experience learning difficulties which are significantly

greater than those experienced by the majority of pupils of the same age. The Warnock Report (DES, 1978) envisaged support for very able pupils but they are excluded from the definition of SEN and support is rarely provided.

*Setting	The grouping of pupils according to their ability in a subject for lessons in that subject.
*Short course	A course in a National Curriculum foundation subject in Key Stage 4 which will not by itself lead to a GCSE or equivalent qualification. Two short courses in different subjects may be combined to form a GCSE or equivalent course.
Sixth form college	A post-16 institution for 16- to 19-year-olds. It offers GCSE, GCE A and AS level and vocational courses.
SLD	Specific Learning Difficulties.
SOA	Statements of Attainment (of National Curriculum subjects).
**Special school	A school which is specially organised to make special educational provision for pupils with special educational needs, and which is approved by the Secretary of State under section 188 of the Education Act 1993.
Specialist schools	Maintained schools in England can apply for specialist school status in one of the following areas: technology; languages; sports; arts. These schools are supported by government funding and, while teaching the National Curriculum, establish distinctiveness in their chosen area.
*Standard Assessment Tasks (SATs)	Externally prescribed National Curriculum assessments which incorporate a variety of assessment methods depending on the subject and Key Stage. This term is not now widely used, having been replaced by 'standard national tests'.
*Statements of Special Educational Needs	Provided under the 1981 Education Act to ensure appropriate provision for pupils formally assessed as having SEN (qv).
Statutory Induction	Introduced in 1999 in England, this provides an individualised programme for newly qualified teachers to monitor, support and assess their progress during their first year of teaching.
*Statutory Order	A statutory instrument which is regarded as an extension of an Act, enabling provisions of the Act to be augmented or updated.
*Streaming	The organisation of pupils according to general ability into classes in which they are taught for all subjects and courses.
Summative assessment	Assessment linked to the end of a course of study; it sums up achievement in aggregate terms and is used to rank, grade or compare pupils, groups or schools. It uses a narrow range of methods which are efficient and reliable, normally formal, i.e. under examination conditions.

Supply teacher	Teachers appointed by LEAs (qv) to fill vacancies in maintained schools which arise as a result of staff absences. Supply teachers may be attached to a particular school for a period ranging from half a day to several weeks or more.
★Support teacher	Teachers who give additional support for a variety of purposes, e.g. ESL (qv), general learning support for SEN (qv) pupils; most support is now given in-class although withdrawal (qv) does still occur.
★Teacher's record book	A book in which a teacher plans and records teaching and learning for his or her class(es) on a regular basis.
★Team teaching	The teaching of a number of classes simultaneously by teachers acting as a team. They usually divide the work between them, allowing those with particular expertise to lead different parts of the work, the others supporting the follow-up work with groups or individuals.
TES	*Times Educational Supplement.* Published weekly and contains articles on educational issues, information about developments in education, job vacancies, etc.
TGAT	Task Group on Assessment and Testing (of National Curriculum). Produced the *TGAT Report* (1988), which led to some of the assessment procedures for the NC.
Thinking Skills	Of the National Curriculum for England. Additional skills to be promoted across the National Curriculum (qv).
★Traveller education	The development of policy and provision which provide traveller children with unhindered access to and full integration in mainstream education.
★Travellers	A term used to cover those communities, some of which have minority ethnic status, who either are or have been traditionally associated with a nomadic lifestyle; includes gypsy travellers, fairground or show people, circus families, New Age travellers, and bargees.
TTA	Teacher Training Agency. Established in 1994, the TTA is responsible for teacher education and educational research in England.
★Tutor group	Grouping of secondary pupils for registration and pastoral care purposes.
ULEAC	University of London Examinations and Assessment Council (was LEAG) (of examination groups) (became London Examinations (qv)). Now part of Edexcel (qv).
Validity	A measure of whether the assessment measures what it is meant to measure – often determined by consensus. Certain kinds of skills and abilities are extremely difficult to assess with validity via simple pencil and paper tests.

Voluntary school	One of three categories of state school: Community (qv), Foundation (qv), and Voluntary schools in England and Wales. It receives financial assistance from the LEA, but is owned by a voluntary body, usually religious.
★Withdrawal	Removal of pupils with particular needs from class teaching in primary schools and from specified subjects in secondary schools, for extra help individually or in small groups. In-class support is increasingly provided in preference to withdrawal.
WJEC	Welsh Joint Education Committee (of examination groups).
★Work experience	The opportunity for secondary pupils to have experience, usually within school time, of the world of work for one or two weeks, during which a pupil carries out a particular job or range of jobs more or less as would regular employees, although with emphasis on the educational aspects of the experience. It may only take place after Easter in Year 10 (i.e. in the final year of statutory schooling).
World class tests	Devised by the government for gifted and talented pupils aged 9–13 years. (See QCA website.)
★Year system	A structure for pastoral care/pupil welfare within a school in which pupils are grouped according to Years, i.e. in groups spanning an age range of only one year.
Years 1–11	Year of schooling. Five-year-olds start at Year 1 (Y1) and progress through to Year 11 (Y11) at 16 years old. This comprises four Key Stages (KS) (qv): KS1 = Y1 to Y3; KS2 = Y4 to Y6; KS3 = Y7 to Y9; KS4 = Y10 to Y11.

APPENDIX 2 GUIDANCE FOR WRITING

SUSAN CAPEL AND JOHN MOSS

INTRODUCTION

In order to gain Qualified Teacher Status at the end of your initial teacher education course you are required to meet the competences/standards which apply to newly qualified teachers on your course. You are also required to complete and pass written assignments through which you demonstrate your ability to produce academic work worthy of a graduate or postgraduate qualification. These assignments are designed to encourage you to make connections between educational theory and practice. This is to ensure that when you complete your initial teacher education course you have begun to develop an understanding of:

- how to make use of educational theory and research to inform and improve your practice;
- how to develop your own theories about teaching and learning, reflecting on and evaluating established practice;
- how to develop and assess innovative practice in your own classroom;
- how to respond creatively and critically to local and national educational initiatives.

It is very likely that your education to date has provided you with many opportunities to find out what processes you need to work through in order to produce good written assignments. One literacy expert, Margaret Meek, has often argued that, if we want to know what literacy practices benefit our pupils, we should start by considering what works for us. Consequently, working on the assignments for your initial teacher education course also provides you with an opportunity to reflect on how you can support your pupils in undertaking the writing tasks you set them. If something helps you, it may well help them. Research on writing suggests that paying attention to the following issues is particularly significant.

UNDERSTANDING THE GENRE

Genre is the term used to define a type of text which has a set of agreed conventions. These conventions apply at different levels, including the kind of vocabulary and voice it is appropriate to use, the structure and organisation of sentences and paragraphs, and larger required structural elements. In academic writing these elements may include: an introduction; a literature review; the statement of a question or hypothesis to be investigated; a description and analysis of the methodology used; the presentation of data with an analysis of the data, comparing findings with established theory or positions; conclusions.

You bring preconceptions about academic writing from your earlier studies to assignments on your initial teacher education course. However, the genre 'essay' contains many 'subgenres', just as the genre 'novel' includes science fiction, romance and detective stories among many other kinds of novel. You should establish which of the elements of academic writing listed above (and others) the genre(s) you are expected to write in must contain.

For example, the expectations of different elements of your work may be as follows. The *introduction* should normally identify the focus of the assignment and outline the structure of what is to follow, i.e. the sequence in which material is presented in the assignment. It may include the *statement of a question or hypothesis*, explaining the scope of the investigation and the reasons for it. The *literature review* usually analyses the academic writing that is relevant to the topic, identifying common or contrasting views and current issues. The *description and analysis of methodology* explain how an issue was investigated, the reasons for this approach and the advantages and disadvantages of the methods chosen. The *data presentation and analysis* should enable a reader to see what is established fact in the work, where interpretation begins, and how and why that interpretation has been made. *Conclusions* should arise from the investigation and its results, and matters which are unresolved should be identified. Recommendations for future practice may be included if appropriate. There is a *bibliography* at the end of each assignment which lists all references used in the assignment.

Just as it helps your school pupils if you do this, it is good practice for your tutors to teach you explicitly what is appropriate. Some methods which may be used for this include modelling and providing examples of successful work. Good modelling involves a practical demonstration of how an assignment can be constructed, for example, by developing a plan or a paragraph on an overhead transparency. Formative feedback on plans or first drafts also helps writers to understand what is required of them, and consequently to improve. The assessment criteria for the assignment should be made explicit from the outset; these criteria should always make reference to the kind of writing that is expected as well as the required content. It will also help you as a writer if you are given more than one opportunity to write a particular kind of assignment, so that you develop experience in using the genre.

UNDERSTANDING THE PURPOSE AND MODE OF WRITING

Writing may, of course, have many different purposes. In the pupil National Curriculum for English, for example, these range from description and narration to argument and persuasion. The primary purpose of many written assignments in initial teacher education is to develop a capacity for *reflection*. This means that you are encouraged to use your writing to think about your experiences in school, your own teaching, your observations of, or discussions with, others, your analysis of school documents or activities or events that occur in school, and the content of lectures, seminars and academic literature, in order to reach a higher standard of awareness about your teaching and the ways in which pupils learn.

Reflection requires you to stand back from a specific lesson, observation, activity or event and question it. You draw on your knowledge about, and understanding of, the work of others, research and theory, and consider it in relation to the practice on which you are reflecting. Reflection is as integral to your teaching as your ability to manage a class and control pupil behaviour. It is a process which should continue into your first year of teaching and throughout your teaching career.

Evaluation of your teaching at the end of each lesson is an example of reflection. Evaluation can be carried out alone or with your tutor. When you evaluate a lesson, you question what went well as well as what did not go well, what might have worked better and what you might do next time which will enable you to improve what you are doing. As evaluation and reflection involve recall of what took place, you need to focus your evaluation and reflection in advance. So much is going on in a lesson that unless you select one or two things on which to focus you are unlikely to collect the detailed data necessary for an in-depth evaluation. You need also to write a few notes and identify points of relevance as soon as you can after the lesson or observation so that you record your perceptions when they are fresh in your mind. There are checklists, guidelines and series of appropriate questions included in many of the texts concerned with helping teachers to develop into reflective practitioners (see the further reading section at the end of Unit 5.4).

Your reflections can then be used as the basis for explicitly linking the work of others to your practice in your assignments. You should aim to show how the work of others, research and theory, informs your practice and vice versa, rather than leaving the two separate, isolated from and not informing each other. Reflection allows you to give your own opinions, but you should underpin these with reference to research and theory. An assignment title which requires you to reflect does not imply that you should not include theory; nor does it mean that you should not include references. Rather, the expectation is that you should include examples from practice to support or challenge the research and theory. When drawing on examples from your practice in assignments, you should not use the name of the school or any individual. All such references should be made anonymous.

Common pitfalls in reflective writing include: discussing the issues entirely at a theoretical level so that the work fails to engage with your practical experience in school; and discussing only practical experience without making any reference to the theoretical context in which your own work is inevitably set. To avoid these and other pitfalls, detailed preparation and planning, and thorough drafting and academic referencing are necessary. These processes take time in themselves, and writing is also often improved if there are time gaps between the different stages of its production. These gaps help you, as the writer of an assignment, to approach it as a reader will do, and to judge your work to date more objectively. It follows that an important first step is to plan how to pace your coverage of the planning, preparation and drafting stages indicated below, to allow you to meet the assignment deadline comfortably.

PREPARATION AND PLANNING

1 Identifying the title, focus and audience

Before you begin an assignment, you need to be very clear about what you are writing about, i.e. the title and focus of the assignment. You may be given a title or you may have to choose your own topic or focus. In either case, you should be very clear about the topic and focus before you start. It is often helpful to have a short title which clearly focuses on the issue you are going to address. The title can be written as a problem or a question and may be intentionally provocative. Phrasing the title in this way clarifies and reminds you of the focus when you are writing the assignment. Ask yourself: 'What am I seeking to find out by writing this assignment?'

You should also establish who the intended audience for the work is. Although many assignments in initial teacher education are primarily reflective, you may be asked to produce work which can benefit the schools in which you undertake school experience or your peers on your initial teacher education course. If there is an intended audience other than your tutor, as a monitor of your development as a reflective practitioner, this will influence how the assignment is written.

2 Collecting information

You should make a list of the sources of information that will help you to address the topic. You are used to identifying and collecting together relevant notes from higher education institution based sessions, books, and articles from journals. However, you should also collect together information from school, such as lesson plans and evaluations of lessons you have taught or observed, and records of observations or interviews conducted in school, so that your written work can refer to, and link, published sources and your developing practice in school.

Make sure that you are familiar with the library system at your institution. You will probably have an induction briefing about this. If not, find out what books and journals are available to support your course. Ask what databases for education are available (e.g. BEIndex (British Educational Index)) and find out how to use them.

DRAFTING

Drafting is given high status in the pupil National Curriculum for English. You should give it high status also. However, it is sometimes poorly interpreted as 'writing it out' and 'writing it out again with the spelling (and perhaps some "grammar") corrected'. In fact, effective drafting is a complex process involving several stages.

1 Gathering ideas

Brainstorm ideas and collect key points from your reading notes, seminar or lecture notes, teaching file and material from school. At this point, include everything you think of that appears to be even slightly relevant. A spider diagram (see Unit 5.2) or arrows may be used, perhaps at a second stage, to begin to group points and ideas. It is a good idea also to identify examples and illustrations and note them next to key points and ideas: this helps you to work out which points you have most to say about and whether others should be eliminated or need more research before you start writing.

2 Selecting and sequencing ideas in a plan

Produce a plan which supports visually the organisation of ideas in a way that is appropriate to the content and structure of the assignment. For example: flow charts are useful if the core of the assignment is concerned with a process; columns can be used to list pairs of contrasting points or ideas and illustrations; a matrix provides a means of charting complex matters in which combinations of factors need to be taken into account. At this stage, it is possible to check whether you have appropriate amounts of information for each stage of a process to be discussed, each side of an argument, or each combination of factors. You may consequently decide you need to research or develop your thinking about part of the subject matter. It can help to add numbers to diagrams of this kind as you work out the order in which you intend to deal with the material.

3 Drafting

Write parts of the assignment as fluidly as possible. Allow ideas to develop rather than stopping too often to check detail or refine wording. It is not necessary to write in sequence: in fact, it may help to work on the different main sections of the assignment concurrently. This can help you to work out what each section needs to include, and, for example, to sort out what belongs appropriately in the introduction and conclusion. If you have a section reviewing literature or discussing examples of practice, writing about one text you have read or lesson you have taught can help you to see how much space you have for each example, and so help you to balance the whole assignment. Clearly, using a word processor helps you to sequence and re-sequence the writing as it develops because you can move chunks of text so easily. The aim of this stage is a continuous draft.

4 Redrafting

This stage should involve careful checking of the structure and balance of the assignment. A good exercise is to make notes from your own writing, paragraph by paragraph. This draws attention to repetition, arguments which are left unsupported or incomplete, and the overall balance or imbalance in the work. Some questions to consider include: does the introduction cover what the reader needs to know about the context of the work? Are the arguments, illustrations and examples given appropriate space? Do the points in the conclusion really arise from the earlier discussion? Are there some unresolved issues which could only be addressed in another piece of work? Where you have used information selectively, is it clear that it has been selected from a larger set of information and for a particular reason? It may be appropriate to move or re-sequence whole paragraphs or larger sections of the text during this stage.

5 Editing and proofreading

Editing should always involve some consideration of what can be deleted from the work to improve it. Many assignments exceed word limits and you may be penalised for this. A GCSE English Chief Examiner once said how impressed he was by a candidate who had the courage to cross out a long paragraph from an answer in examination conditions – because the piece was better balanced and the arguments flowed better as a result, this action had made the answer worthy of an A★ grade rather than an A.

Proofreading, or checking for technical accuracy, is often enhanced by reading aloud, which forces you to slow down, and draws attention to matters such as overlong sentences and word omissions. Reading each paragraph in turn from the end of the assignment to the beginning can also help you to focus on technical accuracy rather than the development of the content. Spelling and grammar checkers in word-processing packages are useful tools, but remember, if this is appropriate, to use UK rather than US spelling which may be the preset option. Grammar checkers have a preference for active rather than passive constructions, which may not always be appropriate in academic writing. It is also easy to click on 'change' rather than 'ignore' by mistake, and vice versa, when working quickly, so a final read through is still needed. We know this does not always happen from the number of times we find 'offside' in assignments rather than 'Ofsted'.

Some other technical points to consider are as follows.

Academic writing is normally written mainly in the third person. However, if you are reflecting on your own practice you may want to use the first person – I – when referring to your own practice. This helps to distinguish your practice and thoughts from those of other writer(s) to whom you refer.

The first sentence of a paragraph usually identifies the main point of the whole paragraph; this is a useful signal for readers. Make sure that each sentence contains a main verb. You should use a new paragraph to mark the introduction of a new point or idea. It is important to use a variety of sentence structures. Words and expressions like 'however', 'nevertheless', 'on the other hand', and 'in addition' provide useful openings which help a reader to understand how sentences are related to each other.

The word 'the' tends to be overused. A statement that includes 'the' – e.g. 'the fact that' or 'the answer is' – is a categorical statement that portrays certainty or definitiveness which may not be appropriate. Words or phrases such as 'a', 'one of', 'there is a suggestion that', or 'one possible answer is' may be better instead because they are less definite. Another overused word is 'very', e.g. 'very large', when 'large' would do.

Choose your words carefully. Do not use slang, jargon, colloquialisms, abbreviations or words that need to be put into quotation marks, unless quoting somebody else. For example, the use of 'kids' is slang.

Be careful about punctuation, i.e. full stops, commas, colons, semicolons, dashes (e.g. for an aside) and brackets (e.g. for an explanation). By using punctuation appropriately, you help the reader to make sense of what you are saying. Under-use of commas is probably the most common error. Leaving out a comma can alter the meaning of a sentence. Dashes or brackets (normally curved brackets), used at the beginning and end of a phrase or clause, may help a reader to better understand the relative importance of different parts of a sentence.

Many writers make errors when using or omitting apostrophes. Remember that apostrophes are used to indicate possession or letter omission, but not plural nouns.

ACADEMIC REFERENCING

In academic writing, ideas, descriptions and explanations should not be taken for granted, even if everything you have read about the issue seems to provide a consensus. Ideas, assertions, descriptions, explanations or arguments should be supported by evidence from the work of others – from research and theory, appropriately referenced (e.g. you might say that 'the research undertaken by Bloggs (1997) suggests that . . . This supports/contradicts the findings of Smith (1994)'). However, alongside references to the work of others, research and theory from texts or articles, you should draw on your own teaching or observations in school, giving examples of activities or events you have observed or participated in to provide evidence from practice, where appropriate.

By 'the work of others' and 'theory' we mean explanations of teaching and learning, and descriptions of research, as well as any theories which have been developed from such work. You should use the evidence of others and your own evidence to advance your own understanding and formulate your own theories. Your own theories evolve by bringing your critical faculties to bear on the work of others and what has been happening in your teaching.

When referring to other research or to texts, a reference should always be given, together with a page number if quotations are used. It is important to show, by appropriate citation, what is your work and what is the work of others. Direct quotations should be used sparingly; otherwise they disrupt the flow of the assignment. Do not put in a quotation for the sake of it: only use quotations with a clear purpose. You need to explain whether a quotation is being used as evidence which supports or disagrees with your point of view. If you are not clear why you are using a quotation, it may be better to paraphrase the point.

References cited in the text must be included in a *bibliography* at the end of the assignment. Your higher education institution provides you with information about how to present your bibliography. This may be different from the way you were required to present bibliographies on your degree course. If you are not given information, ask the library which system is used in the institution to present bibliographies. Otherwise use a recognised system such as the Harvard system. Details of this should be available in the library.

STRATEGIES FOR MAKING NEUTRAL REFERENCE TO GENDER[1]

Your writing is governed by social customs and conventions. One such custom and convention in Britain is to make sure that there is no gender bias in your writing, that men and women are regarded as equal. This translates into not making assumptions that certain jobs (e.g. lawyer, doctor, lorry driver, primary teacher, nurse) are either male or female and, therefore, not using words such as 'he', 'him', 'his' to refer to someone in one of these jobs.

Thus, in your writing you need to avoid such gender bias. Three methods of overcoming the difficulty have been identified: (1) *avoidance*; (2) *disclaimer*; or (3) *inclusion*. Unless your higher education institution prescribes one method for you to use, you may use any of the three methods. Avoidance is probably the most popular and effective of these methods, and inclusion the least popular method.

1 Avoidance

'Avoidance' avoids using male or female words altogether when reference is made to a person who could equally be male or female. Some strategies for avoidance are shown below.

STRATEGY	EXAMPLE	
	Avoid this	*by writing this*
Change to plural	. . . when a teacher meets his class for the first time	. . . when teachers meet their classes for the first time
Change to an article	. . . so that every member of the group can give his opinion	. . . so that every member of the group can give an opinion
Recast the clause so that a different noun becomes the subject	If the student cannot understand his feedback . . .	If the feedback is difficult to understand . . .
Use neutral words like *the other, an individual, the author*	Each student must read what his partner has written	In pairs, each student must read what the other has written
Omit the male/female word	. . . working with each individual to ascertain her needs	. . . working with each individual to ascertain needs

2 Disclaimer

A disclaimer is a statement at the beginning of the assignment that you are using words like 'he', 'him' and 'his' throughout without wanting to convey gender bias. In other words you claim that the male words are to be read as neutral in their reference. Alternatively you might state that you are using 'she', 'her' and 'hers' throughout the assignment for some particular purpose, without wanting to convey gender bias. This might be appropriate, for example, when referring to primary teachers, as most primary teachers are female. Thus, the statement disclaims that any gender bias is intended. Without such a statement, you are likely to offend others. Even with a disclaimer, some readers may find this strategy offensive.

3 Inclusion

Some people prefer to get a round the difficulty by using the phrase 'he or she', or 'he/she' or 's/he'. If used occasionally, such phrases may be appropriate, but they affect the style and interrupt the flow of the assignment when used frequently. It may be best to avoid using this approach to avoid such difficulties.

CONCLUSION

To sum up, assignments set as part of your initial teacher education course require good academic writing, but are also designed to enable you to show that you are reflecting on the theory of teaching and are applying this to your own developing practice as a teacher, i.e. that you are developing as a reflective practitioner. You therefore need to combine good academic writing and evidence of reflection in your written assignments.

Teachers need good writing skills. You write on the board, you write notices, you send letters to parents, write reports and undertake numerous other written communications. Whatever your subject, you have a responsibility to promote in your lessons the development of literacy skills. Therefore, you need good spelling, grammar, punctuation, sentence construction and paragraph formation. If your writing skills are not as good as necessary to write effectively for a variety of audiences in school, you should ask for help during your time in initial teacher education. Higher education institutions can direct you to study support units and to self-study materials available on the internet.

Good luck with writing your course assignments and the written communications you make as part of your teaching.

NOTE

1 The section on strategies for making neutral reference to gender is adapted from a paper produced by the Department of Language Studies, Canterbury Christ Church University College.

FURTHER READING

Burchfield, R. (ed.) (1996) *The New Fowler's Modern English Usage*, Oxford: Clarendon.

Greenbaum, S. and Whituit, J. (1988) *Longman Guide to English Usage*, Harlow: Longman.

Palmer, R. (1996) *Brain Train: Studying for Success*, London: Spon.

Palmer, R. (1993) *Write in Good Style: A Guide to Good English*, London: Spon.

APPENDIX 3 **DISCIPLINE IN SCHOOLS (THE ELTON REPORT)**

Extracts from: Department of Education and Science and the Welsh Office (1989) *Discipline in Schools. Report of the Committee of Enquiry Chaired by Lord Elton*, London: HMSO, pp. 20–53.

RECOMMENDATIONS

3 Teachers

Teachers and their trainees should recognise and apply the principles of good classroom management.

4 Schools

R21   Headteachers and teachers should, in consultation with governors, develop whole school behaviour policies which are clearly understood by pupils, parents and other school staff.

R22   Schools should ensure that their rules are derived from the principles underlying their behaviour policies and are consistent with them.

R23   Schools should strike a healthy balance between rewards and punishments. Both should be clearly specified.

R24   Pupils should learn from experience to expect fair and consistently applied punishments for bad behaviour which make the distinction between serious and minor offences apparent.

R25   Headteachers and teachers should ensure that rules are applied consistently by all members of staff, but that there is flexibility in the use of punishments to take account of individual circumstances.

R26   Headteachers and teachers should avoid the punishment of whole groups.

R27   Headteachers and teachers should avoid punishments which humiliate pupils.

R28   Headteachers and staff should:

R28.1   be alert to signs of bullying and racial harassment;

R28.2   deal firmly with all such behaviour;

R28.3   take action based on clear rules which are backed by appropriate sanctions and systems to protect and support victims.

R29   Pupils should tell staff about serious cases of bullying and racial harassment of which they are aware.

R30   All parties involved in the planning, delivery and evaluation of the curriculum should recognise that the quality of its content and the teaching and learning methods through which it is delivered are important influences on pupils' behaviour.

R32 Schools should not use rigid streaming arrangements to group their pupils by ability. They should take full account of the implications for pupil behaviour when reviewing their arrangements for grouping pupils.

R33 Schools should:

R33.1 distribute their teaching and other resources equitably across the ability range;

R33.2 provide a range of rewards accessible to pupils of all abilities.

R34 Schools should make full use of off-site learning as a means of motivating their pupils.

R36.2 Schools should also provide personal and social education programmes outside the National Curriculum.

R37 Secondary headteachers and teachers should base pastoral systems on the strengths of the traditional integrated academic, welfare and disciplinary role of the teacher.

R38 Secondary headteachers and teachers should identify clear aims for the use of tutorial time. These aims should include reinforcing the school's behaviour policy.

R39 Headteachers and teachers should:

R39.1 recognise the importance of ascertaining pupils' views;

R39.2 organise systems for doing so and for taking the information gathered into account in the management of the school.

R40 Headteachers should ensure that there is regular and effective communication between their staff and support services, and that these services are given early warning of developing problems.

R41 Headteachers and teachers should ensure that pastoral care in schools is characterised by a healthy balance between challenge and support for pupils.

R46 Headteachers and teachers should recognise the importance of displaying pupils' work in creating an attractive environment, increasing pupils' self-esteem and fostering a sense of ownership of the premises.

R51 Headteachers and their senior management teams should recognise the importance of efficient and sensitive timetabling as a management tool which can be used to reduce problems of circulation, supervision and classroom management. The annual timetabling cycle should involve thorough consultation with staff.

R52.1 Senior staff should be visible and strategically placed during mass circulation periods between lessons.

R52.2 Headteachers and teachers when moving about the school should be aware of and take responsibility for pupils' behaviour.

R56.2 Headteachers should use . . . (for funding lunchtime supervision) funds to devise schemes which meet the needs of their schools and encourage participation by teachers.

R57 Headteachers and teachers should ensure that parents receive positive and constructive comments on their children's work and behaviour as a matter of course.

R58 When disciplinary problems arise, headteachers and teachers should involve parents at an early stage rather than as a last resort.

R59   Teachers should recognise that pupils' behaviour at home may differ markedly from their behaviour at school. They should take this into account when discussing pupils with their parents.

R60.1   Headteachers and teachers should develop an active partnership with parents as an aid to promoting good behaviour.

R60.2   They should ensure that their schools provide a welcoming environment for parents.

R61   Headteachers and teachers should develop policies to secure easy access to them by parents and good communications between them and parents which go beyond the provision of formal parents' evenings.

R62   Schools should ensure that:

R62.2   where significant numbers of parents use first languages other than English, communications are in these languages as well as in English.

R66   In appropriate cases, LEAs and headteachers should make time available for home visits by teachers, who should consult with the education welfare service and other agencies where necessary.

5 Parents

6 Pupils

R75   Headteachers and teachers should give pupils every opportunity to take responsibilities and to make a full contribution to improving behaviour in schools.

R76   Headteachers and teachers should encourage the active participation of pupils in shaping and reviewing the school's behaviour policy in order to foster a sense of collective commitment to it.

R77   The Secretaries of State, LEAs and schools should ensure that records of achievement give due weight to a wide range of achievements and personal qualities.

R79   Schools, LEAs and employers should increase their co-operation in developing means of increasing pupils' motivation, such as compacts.

R80   Pupil records should cover their pastoral as well as their learning needs. They should be in a format which could be adopted by schools and LEAs throughout England and Wales.

R83   All LEAs and schools should ensure that the special educational needs of pupils with emotional and behavioural difficulties are assessed and met.

R85   LEAs and schools should ensure that the learning needs of pupils involved in disruptive behaviour who may not be suffering from emotional and behavioural difficulties are properly identified as part of any plan for remedial action.

R89   Teachers should take account of the gender differences involved in pupils' behaviour, for example by not reinforcing attention-seeking and aggressive behaviour.

R90   Headteachers and staff should work to create a school climate which values all cultures, in particular those represented in it, through its academic and affective curricula.

R91   Teachers should recognise the potential for injustice and the practical dangers of stereotyping certain kinds of pupils as troublemakers.

R92   Teachers should guard against misinterpreting non-verbal signals and speech patterns of pupils from different cultural backgrounds.

R93   Teachers should avoid modelling any kind of insulting or discriminating behaviour.

R96   Teachers and parents should make active use of television as an educational resource, reinforcing the positive messages presented by programmes and encouraging children to become more discriminating and critical viewers.

7 Attendance

R99   Headteachers and teachers should make full use of education welfare officers to maximise attendance.

R100   Senior school staff should carry out frequent random attendance checks on individual lessons.

8 Police

R107   All LEAs and schools should recognise the practical and educational value of good relations with the police and promote the development of school–police liaison projects.

9 Governors

10 Local Education Authorities

11 The Government

APPENDIX 4 **USEFUL ADDRESSES**

Department for Education and Skills
Sanctuary Buildings
Great Smith Street
London SW1P 3BT

020 7925 5000
http://www.dfee.gov.uk

Wales Office Education Department
National Assembly for Wales
Cathays Park
Cardiff CF1 3NQ

029 2082 3207
http://www.wales.gov.uk

Scottish Executive Education Department
Victoria Quay
Leith
Edinburgh EH6 6QQ

0131 556 8400
http://www.scotland.gov.uk

Department of Education for Northern Ireland
Rathgael House
Balloo Road
Bangor
Co Down BT19 7PR

028 9127 9279
http://www.deni.gov.uk

The Qualifications and Curriculum Authority (QCA)
29 Bolton Street
London W1Y 7PD

020 7509 5555
http://www.qca.org.uk

Awdurdod Cymwysterau, Cwricwlwm ac Asesu Cymru
Qualifications, Curriculum and Assessment Authority
   for Wales (ACCAC)
Castle Buildings
Womanby Street
Cardiff CF1 9SX

029 2037 5400
http://www.accac.org.uk

Scottish Consultative Council on the Curriculum
   (Scottish CCC)
Gardyne Road
Broughty Ferry
Dundee DD5 1NY

01382 455053
http://www.sccc.ac.uk

Scottish Qualifications Authority (SQA)   0131 663 6601
Ironmills Road   http://www.sqa.org.uk
Dalkeith
Midlothian EH22 1LE

Northern Ireland Council for the Curriculum, Examinations   028 9026 1200
and Assessment (NICCEA)   http://www.ccea.org.uk
29 Clarendon Road
Belfast BT1 3BG

Teacher Training Agency (Enquiries)   01245 454454
PO Box 3210   http://www.teach.org.uk
Chelmsford
Essex CM1 3WA

Office for Standards in Education (OFSTED)   020 7421 6800
Alexandra House   http://www.ofsted.gov.uk
33 Kingsway
London WC2B 6SE

Estyn Her Majesty's Inspectorate for Education and Training in   029 2032 7496
Wales (OHMCI)
Anchor Court,
East Moors Industrial Estate
Ocean Park,
Cardiff CF24 5JW

ASSESSMENT BODIES

In England there are now three unitary awarding bodies, formed by merging a number of examination boards. They are:

Assessment and Qualifications Alliance (AQA)   01483 566506
Stag Hill House   http://www.aqa.org.uk
Guilford
Surrey GU2 7XJ

EdExcel   020 7393 4500
Stewart House   http://www.edexcel.org.uk
32 Russell Square
London WC1B 5DN

Oxford and Cambridge Regional (OCR)   01223 552552
1 Regent Street   http://www.ocr.org.uk
Cambridge
Cambridgeshire CB2 1GG

Other awarding body:

The Welsh Joint Education Committee (WJEC)   029 2026 5000
245 Western Avenue   http://www.wjec.co.uk
Cardiff CF5 2YX

(Awarding bodies provide copies of syllabuses, past examination papers, and reports by subject. Some also produce support materials, particularly for teaching GCE A level.)

SUBJECT ASSOCIATIONS

Council of Subject Teaching Associations
The Niven Suite
The Mansion
Ottershaw Park
Surrey KT16 0QQ

For subject associations please refer to: *The Education Authorities Directory and Annual* (see below), or consult appropriate staff.

OTHERS

Equal Opportunities Commission   0161 833 9244
Overseas House   http://www.eoc.org.uk
Quay Street
Manchester M3 3HN

Commission for Racial Equality   020 7828 7022
Elliott House   http://www.cre.gov.uk
10–12 Allington Street
London SW1E 5EH

National Society for the Prevention of Cruelty to Children   020 7825 2500
42 Curtain Road   http://www.ncpcc.org.uk
London EC2A 3NH

Health and Safety Executive   0114 289 2345
Broad Lane   http://www.hse.gov.uk
Sheffield S3 7HQ

Voluntary Service Overseas   020 8780 7200
317 Putney Bridge Road   http://www.vso.org.uk
London SW15 2PN

Health Development Agency   020 7222 5300
Trevelyan House   http://www.hda.org.uk
30 Great Peters Street
London SW1P 2HW

For further addresses please refer to: *The Education Authorities Directory and Annual* (published annually), The School Government Publishing Company Ltd. This is available from most public libraries.

This directory includes addresses of government departments, including the Stationery Office (for government publications), Public Offices, LEAs, examinations organisations, schools, teachers centres, further education colleges, English language schools, recognised education and educational associations, teachers unions, subject associations, institutes/colleges of higher education, university departments of education, establishments for pupils with special learning needs, social services departments, educational psychology services, careers centres, public library authorities and other organisations concerned with education, and educational publishers and equipment suppliers in England, Wales, Scotland, Northern Ireland, Channel Islands and Isle of Man.

BIBLIOGRAPHY

ACAS (1984) *Advisory Booklet Number 7: Induction of New Employees*, London: HMSO.

Adams, C., Brown, B.B. and Edwards, M. (1997) *Developmental Disorders of Language,* London: Whurr.

Addison, N. and Burgess, L. (2000) *Learning to Teach Art and Design in the Secondary School: A Companion to School Experience*, London: RoutledgeFalmer.

Adey, P. (1992) 'The CASE results: implications for science teaching', *International Journal of Science Education*, 14, 137–146.

Adey, P. (2000) 'Science teaching and the development of intelligence' in M. Monk and J. Osborne (eds) *Good Practice in Science Education*, Buckingham: Open University Press.

Adey, P. and Shayer, M. (1994) *Really Raising Standards*, London: Routledge.

Adey. P., Shayer, M. and Yates, C. (1989) *Thinking Science*, London: Macmillan.

Aldrich, R. and White, J. (1998) *The National Curriculum beyond 2000: The QCA and the Aims of Education*, London: Institute of Education.

Anderson, J.R., Reder, L.M. and Simon, H.A. (1996) 'Situated learning and education', *Educational Researcher,* 25, 5–11.

Atkinson, J.W. (1964) *An Introduction to Motivation*, Princeton, NJ: Van Nostrand.

Ausubel, D.P. (1968) *Educational Psychology: A Cognitive View*, New York: Holt, Rinehart and Winston.

Balderstone, D. and King, S. (1997) 'Preparing pupils for public examinations: developing study skills' in S. Capel, M. Leask, and T. Turner (eds) *Starting to Teach in the Secondary School: A Companion for the Newly Qualified Teacher,* London: Routledge.

Ballard, R. and Kalra, V.S. (1994) *The Ethnic Dimensions of the 1991 Census: A Preliminary Report,* Manchester: University of Manchester, Manchester Census Group.

Barnard, N. (2000) 'Tests are so, so, so boring Mr Blunkett', *Times Educational Supplement*, 18 August.

Barnes, D. (1976) *From Communication to Curriculum,* Harmondsworth: Penguin Education.

Barnes, D., Britton, J., Rosen, H. and the LATE★ (1972) *Language, the Learner and the School* (revised edn), Harmondsworth: Penguin Education (★LATE is the London Association of Teachers of English).

Barnes, D. *et al.* (1987) *Learning Styles in TVEI: Evaluation Report No. 3,* Leeds: Manpower Services Commission, Leeds University.

Batchford, R. (1992) *Values: Assemblies for the 1990s,* Cheltenham: Stanley Thornes.

BECTa (2000) *A Preliminary Report for the DfEE on the Relationship between ICT and Primary School Standards,* Coventry: BECTa.

Bee, H. (2000) *The Developing Child* (9th edn), London: Allyn and Bacon.

Bennett, N. and Dunne, E. (1994) 'How children learn: implications for practice' in B. Moon and A. Shelton-Mayes (eds) *Teaching and Learning in the Secondary School*, London: Routledge, pp. 50–56.

Biggs, J.B. (1978) 'Individual and group differences in study processes', *British Journal of Educational Psychology*, 48, 266–279.

Biggs, J.B. (1987) *Student Approaches to Learning and Studying*, Hawthorne, Victoria: Australian Council for Educational Research.

Biggs, J.B. (1993) 'What do inventories of students' learning processes really measure? A theoretical review and clarification', *British Journal of Educational Psychology,* 63, 3–19.

Black, P. and Wiliam, D. (1998) *Inside the Black Box*, London: King's College.

Blamires, M., Brookes, H., Lacey, R. and Roux, J. (2000) *Communication Difficulties, the Classroom and Curriculum*, London: Special Educational Needs Joint Initiative and Training (SENJIT), Institute of Education, University of London.

Bleach, K. (2000) *The Newly Qualified Secondary Teacher's Handbook*, London: David Fulton.

Bloom, B.S. (ed.) (1956) *Taxonomy of Educational Objectives. Handbook 1: Cognitive Domain*, London: Longman.

Boaler, J. (1997) *Experiencing School Mathematics: Teaching Styles, Sex and Setting*, Buckingham: Open University Press.

Bourne, J. and Moon, B. (1994) 'A question of ability?' in B. Moon and A. Shelton-Mayes (eds) *Teaching and Learning in the Secondary School*, London: Routledge, pp. 25–37.

Bourne, R., Davitt, J. and Wright, J. (1995) *Differentiation: Taking IT Forward*, Coventry: National Council for Educational Technology.

Bramall, S. and White, J. (eds) (2000a) *Why Learn Maths?* London: Institute of Education, University of London.

Bramall, S. and White, J. (2000b) *Will the New National Curriculum Live up to its Aims?* Impact: No 6 in series of policy discussions. London: Philosophy of Education Society of Great Britain.

Brandeth, G. (1981) *The Puzzle Mountain*, Harmondsworth: Penguin.

Briggs, A. (1983) *A Social History of England*, London: Book Club Associates.

British Stammering Association, *A Chance to Speak: Teachers' Information Pack* (Video and leaflets). Information from the Association website. www.stammering.org

Brown, A.L. (1994) 'The advancement of learning', *Educational Researcher*, 23, 4–12.

Bruner, J. (1966) *Towards a Theory of Instruction*, New York: W.W. Norton.

Bruner, J. (1983) *Child's Talk: Learning to Use Language*, Oxford: Oxford University Press.

Bull, S. and Solity, J. (1987) *Classroom Management: Principles to Practice*, London: Croom Helm.

Bullock Report (1975) *A Language for Life*, London: HMSO.

Burchfield, R. (ed.) (1996) *The New Fowler's Modern English Usage*, Oxford: Clarendon.

Buzan, T. (1984, 1995) *Use Your Memory*, London: BBC Books.

Cains, R.A. and Brown, C.R. (1998) 'Newly qualified teachers: a comparative analysis of the perceptions held by BEd and PGCE-trained primary teachers of the level and frequency of stress experienced during the first year of teaching', *Educational Psychology*, 18 (1), 97–110.

Canter, L. and Canter, M. (1977) *Assertive Discipline*, Los Angeles: Lee Canter Associates.

Capel, S. (1994) 'Help – it's teaching practice again!' Paper presented at the 10th Commonwealth and International Scientific Congress, Victoria, BC, Canada.

Capel, S. (1996) 'Changing focus of concerns for physical education students on school experience', *Pedagogy in Practice*, 2 (2), 5–20.

Capel, S. (1997) 'Changes in students' anxieties after their first and second teaching practices', *Educational Research*, 39 (2), 211–228.

Capel, S. (1998) 'A longitudinal study of the stages of development or concern of secondary PE students', *European Journal of Physical Education*, 3 (2), 185–199.

Capel, S., Leask, M. and Turner, T. (eds) (1997) *Starting to Teach in the Secondary School: A Companion for the Newly Qualified Teacher*, London: Routledge.

Carter, T. (1986) *Shattering Illusions: West Indians in British Politics*, London: Lawrence and Wishart.

Centre for Science Education, Sheffield (1992) *Active Teaching and Learning Approaches in Science*, London: Collins Educational.

Centre for Studies on Inclusion in Education (CSIE) (2000) *Index for Inclusion: Developing Learning and Participation in Schools*, Bristol: CSIE with CEN (University of Manchester) and CER (Christ Church University College, Canterbury (T. Booth, ed.).

Child, D. (1993) *Psychology for Teachers* (5th edn), London: Cassell.

Child, D. (1997a) 'Learning theories and practice' in D. Child, *Psychology and the Teacher* (6th edn), London: Cassell.

Child, D. (1997b) *Psychology and the Teacher* (6th edn), London: Cassell.

Chyriwsky, M. (1996) 'Able children: the need for a subject-specific approach', *Flying High*, 3, 32–36 (Worcester: The National Association for Able Children in Education).

Coard, B. (1971) *How the West Indian Child is Made Educationally Sub-normal in the British School System*, London: New Beacon Books.

Cockburn, A.D. (1995) 'Learning in classrooms' in C. Desforges (ed.) (1994) *An Introduction to Teaching: Psychological Perspectives'*, Oxford: Blackwell.

Cockburn, A.D. (1996) 'Primary teachers' knowledge and acquisition of stress relieving strategies', *British Journal of Educational Psychology*, 66, 399–410.

Cole, M. (ed.) (1999) *Professional Issues for Teachers and Student Teachers*, London: David Fulton.

Coles, A. and Turner, S. (1995) *Diet and Health in School Age Children*, London: Health Education Authority. A briefing paper.

Cooper, P. and Ideus, K. (1996) *Attention-Deficit/Hyperactivity Disorder – A Practical Guide for Teachers*, London: David Fulton.

Cowie, H. and Sharp, S. (1992) 'Students themselves tackle the problem of bullying', *Pastoral Care in Education*, 10 (4): 31–37.

Cox, M. (1999) 'Motivating pupils through the use of ICT' in M. Leask and N. Pachler (eds) (1999) *Learning to Teach Using ICT in the Secondary School: A Companion to School Experience*, London: Routledge.

Crane, C.D. (1993) *The Key to Your Success: Applying for a Secondary Post*, Weymouth: Education Appointments Council.

Crook, D., Power, S. and Whitty, G. (1999) *The Grammar School Question: A Review of Research on Comprehensive and Selective Education*, London: Institute of Education. A monograph in the series 'Perspectives on Education Policy'.

Cruikshank, D.R. (1990) *Research that Informs Teachers and Teacher Educators*, Bloomington, Ind: Phi Delta Kappa.

Curtis, S.J. (1967) *History of Education in Great Britain*, Foxton, Cambs: University Tutorial Press.

D'Arcy, J. (1989) *Stress in Teaching: The Research Evidence*, Belfast: Northern Ireland Council for Educational Research, Occasional Paper Number 1.

Daugherty, R. (1995) *National Curriculum Assessment: A Review of Policy 1987–1994*, London: Falmer Press.

Davies, F. and Green, T. (1984) *Reading for Learning in Science*, Edinburgh: Oliver and Boyd.

Davies, N. (2000) *The School Report: Why Britain's Schools are Failing*, London: Vintage Books.

Davis, B. and Sumara, D.J. (1997) 'Cognition, complexity and teacher education', *Harvard Educational Review*, 67, 105–121.

Dean, J. (1993) *Managing the Secondary School*, London: Routledge.

Dearing, R. (1994) *The National Curriculum and its Assessment. Final Report*, London: School Curriculum and Assessment Authority (The Dearing Report).

Dearing, R. (1996) *Review of Qualifications for 16–19 Year Olds (Full Report)*, London: School Curriculum and Assessment Authority.

de Bono, E. (1972) *Children Solve Problems*, London: Penguin Education.

Department for Education (DfE) (1994a) *Pupil Behaviour and Discipline*, Circular 8/94, London: DfE.

Department for Education (DfE) (1994b) *Bullying: Don't Suffer in Silence. An Anti Bullying Pack for Schools*, London: DfE.

Department for Education (DfE) (1994c) *Code of Practice on the Identification and Assessment of Special Educational Needs*, London: DfE.

Department for Education and Employment (DfEE) (1997a) *Targets to Action: Guidance to Support Effective Target Setting in Schools*, London: Standards and Effectiveness Unit, DfEE.

Department for Education and Employment (DfEE) (1997b) *Excellence in Schools*, London: DfEE.

Department for Education and Employment (DfEE) (1997c) *Guaranteeing Standards: A Consultation Paper on the Structure of Awarding Bodies*, London: DfEE.

Department for Education and Employment (DfEE) (1998a) *Target Setting in School*, Circular 11/98, London: DfEE.

Department for Education and Employment (DfEE) (1998b) *Teaching: High Status, High Standards. Requirements for the Award of Qualified Teacher Status'*, Circular 4/98, London: DfEE. See the DfEE website (www.open.gov.uk/dfee) and the Teacher Training Agency.

Department for Education and Employment (DfEE) (1998c) *Teachers Meeting the Challenge of Change*, London: HMSO.

Department for Education and Employment (DfEE) (1998d) *University for Industry: Engaging People in Learning for Life (Pathfinder Prospectus, the Learning Age)*, London: DfEE.

Department for Education and Employment (DfEE) (1998e) *Extending Opportunity: A National Framework for Study Support*, Sudbury: DfEE Publications Office.

Department for Education and Employment (DfEE) (1998f) *Initial Teacher Training National Curriculum for the Use of Information and Communications Technology in Subject Teaching*, London: DfEE.

Department for Education and Employment (DfEE) (1999) *Youth Cohort Study: The Activities and Experiences of 16 year olds: England and Wales 1998*, London: Stationery Office. Issue 4/99, March – Statistical Bulletin.

Department for Education and Employment (DfEE) (2000) *Consultation Draft of the Special Educational Needs Code of Practice*, London: DfEE (July). See the DfEE website: www.dfee.gov.uk

Department for Education and Employment and Qualifications and Curriculum Authority (DfEE/QCA) (1998) *Education for Citizenship and the Teaching of Democracy in Schools: Final Report of the Advisory Group on Citizenship, 22 September 1998*, London: QCA.

Department for Education and Employment and Qualifications and Curriculum Authority (DfEE/QCA) (1999a) *The National Curriculum for England. Handbook for Secondary Teachers in England: Key Stages 3 and 4*, London: Stationery Office. (See also QCA website: http://www.nc.uk.net./about/about ks3_ks4.html)

Department for Education and Employment and Qualifications and Curriculum Authority (DfEE/QCA) (1999b) *Citizenship: The National Curriculum for England*, London: Stationery Office.

Department for Education and Employment and Qualifications and Curriculum Authority (DfEE/QCA) (1999c) *The National Curriculum for England. Science: Key Stages 1–4*, London: DfEE

Department for Education and Employment and Qualifications and Curriculum Authority (DfEE/QCA) (1999d) *Inclusion: Providing Effective Learning Opportunities for all Pupils*, London: DfEE/QCA,

Department for Education and Employment and Qualifications and Curriculum Authority (DfEE/QCA) (2000) *A Scheme of Work for Key Stage 3 (in your subject)*, London: DfEE /QCA.

Department for Education and Employment and Qualifications and Curriculum Authority (DfEE/QCA) (2001) *Guidelines for Teaching Pupils with Learning Difficulties*, London: DfEE.

Department of Education and Science (DES) (1967) *Children and their Primary Schools*, London: HMSO (The Plowden Report).

Department of Education and Science (DES) (1978) *Special Educational Needs*, London: HMSO (The Warnock Report).

Department of Education and Science (DES) (1985a) *Education for All: The Final Report of the Committee of Inquiry into the Education of Children from Ethnic Minority Groups, Cmnd. 9453*, London: HMSO (The Swann Report).

Department of Education and Science (DES) (1985b) *Better Schools, Cmnd. 9469*, London: HMSO.

Department of Education and Science and the Welsh Office (DES/WO) (1988) *National Curriculum Task Group on Assessment and Testing (TGAT Report)*, London: DES.

Department of Education and Science and the Welsh Office (DES/WO) (1989) *Discipline in Schools. Report of the Committee of Enquiry Chaired by Lord Elton*, London: HMSO (The Elton Report).

Department of Health (1989) *The Diets of British Schoolchildren. Sub-committee on Nutritional Surveillance. Committee on Medical Aspects of Food Policy*. Report on Health and social subjects, No. 36, London: HMSO.

Desforges, C. (1995) *An Introduction to Classroom Teaching: Psychological Perspectives*, Oxford: Blackwell.

Dewey, J. (1916) *Democracy and Education*, New York: Free Press.

Dickinson, A. (1991) 'Assessing, recording and reporting children's achievements: from changes to genuine gains' in R. Aldrich (ed.) *History in the National Curriculum*, London: Kogan Page, pp. 66–92.

Dickinson, A. (1998) 'History using information technology: past, present and future', *Teaching History*, 93, 16–20.

Doise, W. (1990) 'The development of individual competencies through social interaction' in H. Foot, M. Morgan and R. Shute (eds) *Children Helping Children*, Chichester: Wiley.

Donaldson, M. (1978) *Children's Minds*, Glasgow: Collins/Fontana (also London: Croom Helm).

Donaldson, M. (1992) *Human Minds: An Exploration*, London: Allen Lane.

Driver, R. (1983) *The Pupil as Scientist*, Milton Keynes: Open University Press.

Driver, R. (1994) 'The fallacy of induction in science teaching' in R. Levinson (ed.) *Teaching Science*, London: Routledge.

Driver, R. and Bell, J. (1986) 'Students thinking and learning of science: a constructivist view', *School Science Review*, 67 (240), 443–456.

Dunham, J. (1995) *Developing Effective School Management*, London: Routledge.

Dyer, C. (1994) 'Law Society warns solicitors to stamp out race discrimination', *Guardian*, 14 September, p. 7.

The Education Authorities Directory and Annual (annual), Redhill, Surrey: School Government Publishing Company Ltd.

The Education Year Book (annual), London: Longman.

Eggleston, J. (1985) *Education for Some*, Stoke-on-Trent: Trentham Books.

Elliott, J. (1998) *The Curriculum Experiment: Meeting the Challenge of Social Change*, Buckingham: Open University Press.

Entwistle, N.J. (1981) *Styles of Learning and Teaching*, Chichester: Wiley.

Entwistle, N.J. (1993) *Styles of Learning and Teaching* (3rd edn), London: David Fulton.

Equal Opportunities Commission (EOC) (2000) *Facts about Women and Men in Great Britain, 1999*, Manchester: EOC. These data are on the EOC website: www.eoc.org.uk

ERA (1988) *Education Reform Act, 29 July 1988; Section 1, 2, Aims of the School Curriculum*, London: HMSO.

Erikson, E.H. (1980) *Identity and the Life Cycle*, New York: W.W. Norton.

Fielding, M. (1996) 'Why and how learning styles matter: valuing difference in teachers and learners' in S. Hart (ed.) *Differentiation and the Secondary Curriculum: Debates and Dilemmas*, London: Routledge.

Fitzgerald, R., Finch, S. and Nove, A. (2000) *Black Caribbean Young Men's Experiences of Education and Employment,* Report Number RR186, London: DfEE.

Flavell, J.H. (1982) 'Structures, stages, and sequences in cognitive development' in W.A. Collins (ed.) *The Concept of Development: The Minnesota Symposia on Child Psychology,* vol. 15, pp. 1–28.

Fontana, D. (1993) *Managing Time*, Leicester: British Psychological Society Books.

Franklin, G. (1999) 'Special educational needs and ICT' in M. Leask and N. Pachler (eds) *Learning to Teach Using ICT in the Secondary School: A Companion to School Experience*, London: Routledge.

Freud, S. (1901) *The Psychopathology of Everyday Life*. Republished in J. Strachey (ed.) (1953) *The Standard Edition of the Complete Psychological Works of Sigmund Freud, Vol. 6,* London: Hogarth.

Gagné, R.M. (1977) *The Conditions of Learning*, New York: Holt International.

Gardner, H. (1983) *Frames of Mind*, London: Heinemann.

Gardner, H. (1993a) *Frames of Mind* (2nd edition), London: Fontana.

Gardner, H. (1993b) *Multiple Intelligences: The Theory in Practice*, New York: Basic Books.

Gardner, H. (1994) 'The theory of multiple intelligences' in B. Moon and A. Shelton-Mayes (eds) *Teaching and Learning in the Secondary School*, Milton Keynes: Open University Press.

Gardner, H., Kornhaber, M. and Wake, W. (1996) *Intelligence: Multiple Perspectives*, Fort Worth, Tex.: Harcourt Brace.

Gardner, M. (1965) *The Annotated Alice,* Harmondsworth: Penguin.

George, D. (1992) *The Challenge of the Able Child*, London: David Fulton.

Gessell, A. (1925) *The Mental Growth of the Preschool Child*, New York: Macmillan.

Gilham, B. (ed.) (1986) *The Language of School Subjects*, London: Heinemann.

Gillborn, D. and Gipps, C. (1996) *Recent Research on the Achievement of Ethnic Minority Pupils*, London: HMSO (OFSTED: views of research).

Gillborn, D. and Mirza, H.S. (2000) *Educational Inequality: Mapping Race, Class and Gender; A Synthesis of Research Evidence*, London: OFSTED. See the OFSTED website: www.ofsted.gov.uk

Gingell, J. and Brandon, E.P. (2000) *In Defence of High Culture*, Oxford: Blackwell.

Gipps, C. (1995) 'Principles of assessment', unpublished lecture, Institute of Education, University of London, 7 February.

Goddard, D. and Leask, M. (1992) *The Search for Quality: Planning for Improvement and Managing Change*, London: Paul Chapman.

Goleman, D. (1995) *Emotional Intelligence,* New York: Bantam.

Good, F. and Cresswell, M. (1988) *Grading the GCSE,* London: Secondary Examinations Council.

Gould, S. J. (1984) *The Mismeasure of Man*, London: Pelican.

Graduate Teacher Training Registry (GTTR) (2000) *Annual Statistical Report 1999 Entry*, Cheltenham: GTTR.

Great Britain (1996) *Education Act, Elizabeth II 1996, Chapter 56,* London: HMSO.

Great Britain, Education and Employment Committee of the House of Commons (1999) *School Meals: 1st Report*, London: Stationery Office.

Greenbaum, S. and Whituit, J. (1988) *Longman Guide to English Usage,* Harlow: Longman.

Greenhalgh, P. (1994) *Emotional Growth and Learning*, London: Routledge.

Hall, D. (1996) *Assessing the Needs of Bilingual Pupils*, London: David Fulton.

Hallam, S. (1996) *Grouping Pupils by Ability*, Viewpoint, No. 4 (July), London: Institute of Education, University of London.

Hallam, S. and Toutounji, I. (1996) *What Do We Know about the Grouping of Pupils by Ability? A Research Review*, London: Institute of Education, University of London.

Handy, C. (1993) *Understanding Organisations* (4th edn), London: Penguin.

Hargreaves, A. (1984) *Improving Secondary Schools: Report of the Committee on the Curriculum and Organisation of Secondary Schools*, London: ILEA.

Hargreaves, D.H., Hopkins, D., Leask, M., Connolly, J. and Robinson, P. (1989) *Planning for School Development: Advice to Governors, Headteachers and Teachers*, London: DES.

Harlen, W. (1995) 'To the rescue of formative assessment', *Primary Science Review,* 37 (April), 14–15.

Hart, K. (1981) *Children's Understanding of Mathematics*, London: Murray.

Hart, N.I. (1987) 'Student teachers' anxieties: four measured factors and their relationship to pupil disruption in class', *Educational Research,* 29, (1), 12–18.

Hart, S. (ed.) (1996) *Differentiation and the Secondary Curriculum: Debates and Dilemmas*, London: Routledge.

Harter, S. (1985) 'Competence as a dimension of self-evaluation: toward a comprehensive model of self-worth' in R.L. Leay (ed.) *The Development of the Self,* Orlando, Fla: Academic Press.

Hay McBer (2000) *Research into Teacher Effectiveness: A Model of Teacher Effectiveness*, London: DfEE.

Haydn, T., Arthur, J. and Hunt, M. (eds) (1997) *Learning to Teach History in the Secondary School: A Companion to School Experience*, London: RoutledgeFalmer, pp. 176–180. (Note: a second edition is to be published in 2001.)

Haydon, G. (1997) *Teaching about Values: A New Approach*, London: Cassell.

Haydon, G. and Lambert, D. (1992) *Professional Studies: Tutor Support Pack*, London: Institute of Education, University of London.

Haylock, D. (2001) 'Assessment' in A. Cockburn (ed.) *Teaching Children 3–11: A Students' Guide*, London: Paul Chapman.

Head, J., Hill, F. and Maguire, M. (1996) 'Stress and the post graduate secondary school trainee teacher: a British case study', *Journal of Education for Teaching*, 22 (1), 71–84.

Health Education Authority (1998) *Health Survey for England: The Health of Young People, 95–97: A Survey Carried out for the Department of Health,* London: Stationery Office. See Department of Health website for details, tables and summary: http://www.doh.gov.uk/dhhone.htm

Her Majesty's Inspectorate (HMI) (1977) *Curriculum 11–16*, London: Department of Education and Science.

Her Majesty's Inspectorate (HMI) (1978) *Mixed Ability Work in Comprehensive Schools*, London: HMSO.

Holt, J. (1964) *How Children Fail*, New York: Pitman.

Hopkins, D. (1993) *A Teacher's Guide to Classroom Research* (2nd edn), Milton Keynes: Open University Press.

Humphrys, G. (1993) *Getting a Teaching Job 1994*, London: University of Greenwich.

ICAN: 'I Can' is a charitable organisation for people with speech and language difficulties. Their website is: www.ican.org.uk

ILEA (1984) See Hargreaves, 1984.

Institute of Policy Studies (1994*) Entry to the Legal Profession: Discrimination: A Report,* London: Institute of Policy Studies.

Jennings, A. (1995) 'Discussion' in J. Frost (ed.) *Teaching Science*, London: Woburn Press.

Kerry, T. (1999) *Learning Objectives, Task Setting and Differentiation*, London: Hodder and Stoughton.

Keys, W., Harris, S. and Fernandes, C. (1996) *Third International Mathematics and Science Study – First National Report – Part 1. Achievement in Mathematics and Science at Age 13 in England*, London: National Foundation for Educational Research.

King, S. (1996) *Classroom Observation*, London: Institute of Education, University of London. A booklet in the series 'Occasional papers in Teacher Education and Training', available from Academic Services, Initial Teacher Education, Institute of Education, University of London, 20 Bedford Way, London WC1H OAL.

Klein, G. (1993) *Education towards Race Equality*, London: Cassell.

Kohlberg, L. (1976) 'Moral stages and moralization: the cognitive-developmental approach' in T. Lickona (ed.) *Moral Development and Behaviour: Theory, Research, and Social Issues*, New York: Holt, Rinehart and Winston.

Kolb, D.A. (1976) *The Learning Style Inventory: Technical Manual,* Boston, Mass.: McBer and Co.

Kolb, D.A. (1985) *The Learning Style Inventory: Technical Manual* (revised edn), Boston, Mass: McBer and Co.

Kozulin, A. (1998) *Psychological Tools. A Sociocultural Approach to Education,* Cambridge, Mass.: Harvard University Press.

Kramarski, B. and Mevarech, Z.R. (1997) 'Cognitive-metacognitive training within a problem-solving based Logo environment', *British Journal of Educational Psychology*, 67, 425–445.

Kyriacou, C. (1989) 'The nature and prevalence of teacher stress' in M. Cole and S. Walker (eds) *Teaching and Stress*, Milton Keynes: Open University Press.

Kyriacou, C. (1997a) *Effective Teaching in Schools: Theory and Practice* (2nd edn), Cheltenham: Stanley Thornes.

Kyriacou, C. (1997b) *Essential Teaching Skills* (2nd edn), Cheltenham: Stanley Thornes.

Kyriacou, C. (2000) *Stress-Busting for Teachers*, Cheltenham: Stanley Thornes.

Kyriacou, C. and Stephens, P. (1999) 'Student teachers' concerns during teaching practice', *Evaluation and Research in Education*, 13 (1), 18–31.

Lambert, D. (1991) 'Assessment: a view from the receiving end', in *Geography Assessment Supplementary Pack*, Cambridge: Cambridge University Press, p. 30.

Lambert, D. (1994) *Differentiated Learning*, London: Institute of Education, University of London. A booklet in the series 'Occasional Papers in Teacher Education and Training', available from Academic Services, Initial Teacher Education, Institute of Education, University of London, 20 Bedford Way, London WC1H 0AL.

Lambert, D. (1999) 'Assessing and recording pupils' work' in S. Capel, M. Leask and T. Turner (eds) *Learning to Teach in the Secondary School: A Companion to School Experience* (2nd edn), London: Routledge, pp. 283–323.

Lambert, D. and Balderstone, D. (2000) *Learning to Teach Geography in the Secondary School: A Companion to School Experience*, London: RoutledgeFalmer, pp. 271–288.

Langford, P. (1995) *Approaches to the Development of Moral Reasoning*, Hove: Erlbaum.

Lave, J. and Wenger, E. (1991) *Situated Learning: Legitimate Peripheral Participation*, Cambridge: Cambridge University Press.

Lawton, D. (1989) *Education, Culture and the National Curriculum*, Sevenoaks: Hodder and Stoughton.

Lawton, D. (1996) *Beyond the National Curriculum. Teacher Professionalism and Empowerment*, London: Hodder and Stoughton.

Leask, M. (ed.) (2001) *Issues in Teaching with ICT*, London: RoutledgeFalmer.

Leask, M. and Pachler, N. (eds) (1999) *Learning to Teach Using ICT in the Secondary School: A Companion to School Experience*, London: Routledge.

Leask, M. and Terrell, I. (1997) *Development Planning and School Improvement for Middle Managers*, London: Kogan Page.

Leask, M., Dawes, L. and Litchfield, D. (2000) *Keybytes for Teachers*, Evesham: Summerfield Publishing. This is a text and CD-ROM for teachers wishing to practise basic ICT skills.

Lloyd-Jones, R. (1988) *How to Produce Better Worksheets*, London: Hutchinson Education.

McCarthy, B. (1987) *The 4MAT System*, Barrington, Ill.: Excel.

McClelland, D.C. (1961) *The Achieving Society*, Princeton, NJ: Van Nostrand.

Macdonald, B. (2000) 'How education became nobody's business' in H. Altricher and J. Elliott (eds) *Images of Educational Change*, Buckingham: Open University Press, pp. 20–36.

McGregor, D. (1960) *The Human Side of Enterprise*, New York: McGraw-Hill.

Maitland, I. (1995) *Managing your Time*, London: Institute of Personnel and Development.

Marks, J. (1994) 'Methods of assessment: value for money', in B. Moon and A. Shelton-Mayes (eds) *Teaching and Learning in the Secondary School*, London: Routledge.

Marland, M. (1993) *The Craft of the Classroom*, London: Croom Helm.

Marland, M. (1997) *The Art of the Tutor: Developing your Role in the Secondary School*, London: Croom Helm.

Maslow, A.H. (1970) *Motivation and Personality* (2nd edn), New York: Harper and Row.

Maybin, J., Mercer, N. and Stierer, B. (1992) 'Scaffolding learning in the classroom' in K. Norman (ed.) *Thinking Voices: The Work of the National Oracy Project*, London: Hodder and Stoughton.

Mercer, N. (1994) 'Classrooms, language and communication' in B. Moon, and A. Shelton-Mayes (eds) (1994) *Teaching and Learning in the Secondary School*, London, Routledge.

Miller, O. (1996) *Supporting Children with Visual Impairment in Mainstream Schools*, London: Franklin Watts.

Milner, D. (1975) *Children and Race*, Harmondsworth: Penguin Education.

Mitchell, R. (1994) 'The communicative approach to language teaching: an introduction' in A. Swarbrick (ed.) *Teaching Modern Languages*, London: Routledge, pp. 33–42.

Montgomery, D. (1996) 'Differentiation of the curriculum in primary education', *Flying High*, 3, 14–28 (Worcester: National Association for Able Children in Education).

Mortimore, P. and Whitty, G. (1997) *Can School Improvement Overcome the Effects of Disadvantage?* London: Institute of Education, University of London.

Morton, L.L., Vesco, R., Williams, N.H. and Awender, M.A. (1997) 'Student teacher anxieties related to class management, pedagogy, evaluation, and staff relations', *British Journal of Educational Psychology*, 67, 68–89.

Mosston, M. and Ashworth, S. (1994) *Teaching Physical Education* (4th edn), New York: Macmillan College Publishing.

Munn, P., Johnstone, M. and Holligan, C. (1990) 'Pupils' perceptions of effective disciplinarians', *British Educational Research Journal,* 16 (2), 191–198.

Murphy, P. (ed.) (1999) *Learners, Learning and Assessment,* London: Paul Chapman.

Myers, K. (ed.) (1987) *Genderwatch!* Cambridge: Cambridge University Press.

Myers, K. (1990) *Sex Discrimination in Schools,* London: Advisory Centre for Education.

Myers. K. (ed.) (1996) *School Improvement in Practice: Schools Make a Difference Project,* London: Falmer Press.

National Association for Special Educational Needs (UK) (NASEN) (2000) *Specialist Teaching for Special Educational Needs and Inclusion.* Policy Paper 4 in the 'SEN Fourth Policy Options' series, London: NASEN. See the NASEN website (http://www.nasen.org.uk)*;* select book list, then policy options.

National Audit Office (NAO) (2001) *Tackling Obesity in England: A Report (HC220),* London: Stationery Office. See the NAO website: www.nao.gov.uk

National Commission for Education (1993) *Learning to Succeed: A Radical Look at Education Today,* London: Heinemann.

National Council for Educational Technology (1994) *Information Technology Works! Stimulate to Educate,* Coventry: National Council for Educational Technology.

National Foundation for Educational Research (NFER) (1996) *Cognitive Abilities Test,* Windsor: NFER–Nelson.

National Union of Teachers (annually) *Your First Teaching Post,* London: NUT.

Naylor, S. and Keogh, B. (1999) 'Constructivism in the classroom: theory into practice', *Journal of Science Teacher Education,* 10 (2), 93–106.

Newbold, D. (1977) *Ability Grouping: The Banbury Inquiry,* Windsor: NFER–Nelson.

Nicholls, G. (1995) 'Ways pupils learn' in S. Capel, M. Leask and T. Turner (eds) *Learning to Teach in the Secondary School: A Companion to School Experience,* London: Routledge.

Norman, K. (ed.) (1992) *Thinking Voices: The Work of the National Oracy Project,* London: Hodder and Stoughton.

Novak, J.D. and Gowin, D.B. (1984) *Learning How to Learn,* Cambridge: Cambridge University Press.

Office for National Statistics, 1 Drummond Gate, London SW1V 2QQ. The website address is: *www.statistics.gov.uk*

Office for Standards in Education (OFSTED) (1993a) *The New Teacher in School: A Survey by Her Majesty's Inspectorate in England and Wales, 1992,* London: HMSO.

Office for Standards in Education (OFSTED) (1993b) *Achieving Good Behaviour in Schools. A Report from Her Majesty's Chief Inspector of Schools,* London: HMSO.

Office for Standards in Education (OFSTED) (1994a) *Handbook for the Inspection of Schools, Part 6: The Statutory Basis for Education,* London: OFSTED.

Office for Standards in Education (OFSTED) (1994b) *Mathematics Key Stages 1, 2, 3 and 4,* London: HMSO.

Office for Standards in Education (OFSTED) (1996a) *Promoting High Achievement for Pupils with Special Educational Needs in Mainstream Schools,* London: HMSO.

Office for Standards in Education (OFSTED) (1996b) *The Implementation of the Code of Practice for Pupils with Special Educational Needs: A Report from the Office of Her Majesty's Chief Inspector of Schools,* London: HMSO.

Office for Standards in Education (OFSTED) (1996c) *Subjects and Standards. Issues for School Development Arising from Ofsted Inspection Findings, 1994–5,* London: HMSO.

Office for Standards in Education (OFSTED) (1998) *Judging Attainment: An Occasional Paper on the Relationship between Inspectors' Judgements and School Results,* London: OFSTED (June). Published with *Update* 26.

Office for Standards in Education (OFSTED) (1999) *Inspecting Schools: The Framework,* London: OFSTED (effective from January 2000). The OFSTED website address is: http://www.ofsted.gov.uk

Office for Standards in Education (OFSTED) (2000a) *Progress in Key Stage 3 Science,* London: OFSTED.

Office for Standards in Education (OFSTED) (2000b) *The Annual Report of Her Majesty's Chief Inspector of Schools, 1998/99*, London: OFSTED. The OFSTED website address is: http://www.ofsted.gov.uk

Office for Standards in Education (OFSTED) (2000c) *Improving Schools: The Framework*, London: OFSTED.

Ogborn, J., Cress, G., Martins, I. and McGillicuddy, K. (1996) *Explaining Science in the Classroom*, Buckingham: Open University Press.

O'Hear, P. and White, J. (eds) (1991) *A National Curriculum for All: Laying the Foundations for Success*, London: Institute for Public Policy Research.

Olweus, D. (1993) *Bullying at School*, Oxford: Blackwell.

Organisation for Economic Co-operation and Development (OECD) (1994) 'Risk of failure in school', *Innovation in Education*, 67 (February), 1.

Owen-Jackson, G. (ed.) (2000) *Learning to Teach Design and Technology in the Secondary School: A Companion to School Experience*, London: RoutledgeFalmer.

Pachler, N. with Williams, L. (1999) 'Using the internet as a teaching and learning tool' in M. Leask and N. Pachler (eds) *Learning to Teach Using ICT in the Secondary School: A Companion to School Experience*, London: Routledge.

Palmer, R. (1993) *Write in Good Style: A Guide to Good English*, London: Spon.

Palmer, R. (1996) *Brain Train: Studying for Success*, London: Spon.

Parekh, B. (2000) *The Parekh Report: A Review of the Future of Multi-ethnic Britain*, London: Profile Books (for the Runnymede Trust).

Partnership with Parents (1998) *Dealing with Dyslexia in the Secondary School*, Shepway Centre, Oxford Road, Maidstone, Kent ME15 8AW. (Tel: 01622 755515)

Pateman, T. (1994) 'Crisis, what identity crisis?', *First Appointments Supplement, Times Educational Supplement*, 14 January, 28–29.

Patmore, M. (2000) *Achieving QTS: Passing the Numeracy Skills Test*, Exeter: Learning Matters, 2000. University of Exeter for the Teacher Training Agency. Contains practice questions, model answers and complete mock test.

Perrott, E. (1982) *Effective Teaching*, London: Longman.

Piaget, J. (1932) *The Moral Judgment of the Child*, New York: Macmillan.

Piaget, J. (1954) *The Construction of Reality in the Child*, New York: Basic Books.

Plato (1955) *The Republic*, translated by H.D.P. Lee, Harmondsworth: Penguin.

Postlethwaite, K. (1993) *Differentiated Science Teaching: Responding to Individual Differences and Special Educational Needs*, Milton Keynes: Open University Press.

Postlethwaite, K. and Denton, C. (1978) *Streams for the Future? The Long-term Effects of Early Streaming and Non-streaming: The Final Report of the Banbury Enquiry*, Banbury: Pubansco.

Qualifications and Curriculum Authority (QCA) (1998) *Maintaining Breadth and Balance at Key Stages 1 and 2*, London: QCA.

Qualifications and Curriculum Authority (QCA) (2000) *Research into the Dip in Performance in English of Children Entering Key Stage 3 (secondary school for most)*. Report commissioned by QCA and carried out by the University of Cambridge Local Examination Syndicate Evaluation Team. The QCA website address is: http://www.qca.org.uk

Qualifications and Curriculum Authority and Department for Education and Employment (QCA/ DfEE) (1999) *The Review of the National Curriculum in England. The Secretary of State's proposals*, London: QCA.

Qualifications and Curriculum Authority and Department for Education and Employment (QCA/DfEE) (2000) *Assessment and Reporting Arrangements*, London: QCA/DfEE.

Rampton, A. (1981) *West Indian Children in our Schools (Interim Report of the Committee of Inquiry into the Education of Children from Ethnic Minority Groups)*, London: HMSO.

Reeve, P. (1992) 'The average child', unpublished dissertation, De Montfort University, Bedford.

Riding, R.J. and Cheema, I. (1991) 'Cognitive styles – an overview and integration', *Educational Psychology*, 11, 193–215.

Riding, R.J. and Rayner, S. (1998) *Learning Styles and Strategies*, London: David Fulton.

Rieser, R. and Mason, M. (1992) *Disability Equality in the Classroom A Human Rights Issue* (2nd edn), London: ILEA/Disability Equality.

Ripley, K., Daines, B. and Barrett, J. (1997) *Dyspraxia: A Guide for Teachers and Parents*, London: David Fulton.

Robertson, J. (1989) *Effective Classroom Control: Understanding Pupil–Teacher Relationships*, London: Hodder and Stoughton.

Robertson, J. (1996) *Effective Classroom Control* (3rd edn), London: Hodder and Stoughton.

Robinson, K. (Chair) (1999) *All Our Futures: Creativity, Culture and Education. Report of the National Advisory Committee on Creative and Cultural Education*, London: DfEE.

Rodwell, L. (2000) '10 foods that may prevent cancer', *Choice*, 29, 10 (October), 80–1.

Rogers, C. (1982) *A Social Psychology of Schooling: The Expectancy Process*, London: Routledge and Kegan Paul.

Rogoff, B. (1990) *Apprenticeship in Thinking: Cognitive Development in Social Context,* Oxford: Oxford University Press.

Rowe, M.B. (1972) 'Wait-time and rewards as instructional variables', paper presented at the National Association for Research in Science Teaching, Chicago, April.

Rutter, M., Maughan, B., Mortimore, P. and Ouston, J. (1979) *Fifteen Thousand Hours: Secondary Schools and their Effects on Pupils,* London: Open Books.

Ryan, A. (2000) 'Comment', *Independent,* 9 November.

St John Ambulance (1999) *Emergency Aid in Schools* (7th edn), St John Supplies, Priory House, St John's Lane, London WC1M 4DA (Tel: 020 7235523).

Scarman, Lord (1982) *The Brixton Disorders 10–12 April, 1981,* Harmondsworth: Penguin.

Schneede, U. (1973) *Surrealism*, New York: Abrams (one of many books on Dali).

School Curriculum and Assessment Authority (SCAA) (1997) *Target Setting and Benchmarking in Schools: A Consultation*, London: SCAA (now the Qualifications and Assessment Authority, QCA).

Selinger, M. (1999) 'ICT and classroom management' in M. Leask and N. Pachler (eds) (1999) *Learning to Teach Using ICT in the Secondary School: A Companion to School Experience*, London: Routledge.

Selman, R.L. (1980) *The Growth of Interpersonal Understanding*, New York: Academic Press.

Shemilt, D. (1984) In-service training course for history teachers, Eltham, London, July.

Short, G. (1986) 'Teacher expectation and West Indian underachievement', *Educational Research*, 27 (2), 95–101.

Skinner, B.F. (1953) *Science and Human Behaviour*, New York: Macmillan.

Smith, D. and Tomlinson, S. (1989) *The School Effect: A Study of Multiracial Comprehensives*, London: Policy Studies Institute.

Smith, C.J. and Laslett, R. (1993) *Effective Classroom Management: A Teacher's Guide*, London: Routledge.

Smith, K. (1999) 'Quality assessment of quality learning in quality teaching: an integral part of teachers' professional knowledge. How can teacher preparation meet the challenge?' Paper presented at the 24th Annual Conference of the Association for Teacher Education in Europe, Leipzig. Enquiries to Kari Smith Oranim, Academic College of Teacher Education, Israel. Email: Kari@mofet.macam98.ac.il

Smith, R. and Standish, P. (eds) (1997) *Teaching Right and Wrong: Moral Education in the Balance*, Stoke-on-Trent: Trentham.

Smithers, R. (2000) 'Class notes', *Guardian Education*, supplement to *Guardian*, October 31, para. 3 (or read at: www.guardianunlimited.co.uk/archive/).

Snow, C.P. (1960) *The Two Cultures and the Scientific Revolution*, Cambridge: Cambridge University Press (The Rede Lecture, 1959).

Stobart, G. and Gipps, C. (1997) *Assessment: A Teacher's Guide to the Issues*, London: Hodder and Stoughton.

Stoll, L. and Fink, D. (1996) *Changing our Schools,* Buckingham: Open University Press. See 'Teachers as learners', particularly pp. 152–157.

Stone, M. (1981) *The Education of the Black Child in Britain: The Myth of Multicultural Education,* London: Collins/Fontana.

Stones, E. (1992) *Quality Teaching: A Sample of Cases,* London: Routledge.

Stradling, R., Saunders, L. and Weston, P. (1991) *Differentiation in Action: A Whole School Approach for Raising Attainment,* London: HMSO.

Sutton, C. (ed.) (1981) *Communicating in the Classroom,* London: Hodder and Stoughton.

Sutton, R. (1991) *Assessment: A Framework for Teachers,* London: NFER-Nelson.

Swann Report: see DES, 1985a.

Taher, A. (2000) 'Stuff of dreams', *Guardian Education,* supplement to *Guardian,* 7 November, 10–11.

Tanner, J.M. (1990) *Foetus into Man,* Cambridge, Mass.: Harvard University Press.

Tarrant, G. (1981) 'Social studies in the primary school: the place of discussion', *Social Studies Teacher,* 13 (3), 63–65.

Teacher Training Agency (TTA) (1998) *Career Entry Profile for Newly Qualified Teachers,* London: TTA.

Teacher Training Agency (TTA) (2000a) *An Introduction for Trainee Teachers to the Induction Period for Newly Qualified Teachers,* London: TTA.

Teacher Training Agency (TTA) (2000b) *Computerised Skill Tests in Literacy, Numeracy and ICT: Guidance for Trainee Teachers,* London: TTA. See the TTA website: www.teach-tta.gov.uk

Teacher Training Agency (TTA) (2000c) *Moving Forward: Support and Challenge in the Induction Period,* London: TTA.

Teacher Training Agency (TTA) (2000d) *QTS Skills Tests Information Booklet for Trainees,* London: TTA.

Thacker, J. (1995) 'Personal, social and moral education' in C. Desforges (ed.) *An Introduction to Teaching: Psychological Perspectives,* Oxford: Blackwell.

Tikly, C. and Wolf, A. (2000) *The Maths We Need Now: Demands, Deficits and Remedies,* London: Institute of Education, University of London.

Times Educational Supplement (*TES*) *First Appointments Supplement* (annually, around the middle of January) London: TES.

Topping, K.J. (1992) 'The effectiveness of paired reading in ethnic minority homes', *Multicultural Teaching to Combat Racism in School and Community,* 10 (2), 19–23.

Townsend, S. (1982) *The Life of Adrian Mole,* London: Methuen.

Trend, R., Davis, N. and Loveless, A. (1999) *QTS Information Communication Technology,* London: Letts Educational.

Turner, A. and DiMarco, W. (eds) (1998) *Learning to Teach Science in the Secondary School: A Companion to School Experience,* London: Routledge.

Turner, S. (1995) 'Simulations' in J. Frost (ed.) *Teaching Science,* London: Woburn Press.

Underwood, J. (1998) 'Making groups work' in M. Montieth (ed.) *IT for Learning Enhancement,* Exeter: Intellect.

Vygotsky, L. S. (1962) *Thought and Language,* Cambridge, Mass.: MIT Press.

Vygotsky, L.S. (1978) *Mind in Society: The Development of Higher Psychological Processes,* London: Harvard University Press.

Vygotsky, L. S. (1986) *Thought and Language* (revised edn), Cambridge, Mass.: MIT Press (A. Kozulin, ed.)

Warnock, Report, The. See DES (1978).

Warnock, M. (1998) *An Intelligent Person's Guide to Ethics,* London: Duckworth.

Warren, A., Brunner, D., Maier, P. and Barnett, L. (1998) *Technology in Teaching and Learning: An Introductory Guide,* London: Kogan Page.

Waterhouse, P. (1983) *Managing the Learning Process,* Maidenhead: McGraw-Hill.

Watkins, C. (1998) *Learning about Learning*, Coventry: National Association for Pastoral Care.

Weiner, B.J. (1972) *Theories of Motivation*, Chicago, Ill.: Markham.

Weiner, G. (1995) 'Ethnic and gender differences' in C. Desforges (ed.) *An Introduction to Classroom Teaching: Psychological Perspectives*, Oxford: Blackwell.

Wellington, J. (ed.) (1986) *Controversial Issues in the Curriculum*, Oxford: Blackwell.

Wersky, G. (1988) *The Visible College: A Collective Biography of British Scientists and Socialists of the 1930s*, London: Free Association Books.

Which? (1998) 'From chalk to fork: schools teaching about food', *Which? Health*, October.

Which? (2000) 'Obesity', *Which? Health*, June, 20–23.

White, J. (1998) *Do Howard Gardner's Multiple Intelligences Add Up*? London: Institute of Education, University of London. In the series 'Perspectives on Education Policy'.

White, R.T. and Gunstone, R. (1992) *Probing Understanding*, London: Falmer Press.

Whitehead, R.G. (Chairperson) (1991) *Report on Health and Social Subjects No. 41. Dietary Reference Values for Food Energy and Nutrients for the United Kingdom: Report of the Panel on Dietary Reference Values of the Committee on Medical Aspects of Food Policy*, London: HMSO for the Department of Health.

Whylam, H. and Shayer, M. (1978) *CSMS Reasoning Tasks: General Guide*, Windsor: National Foundation for Educational Research.

Willson, M. and Williams, D. (1996) 'Trainee teachers' misunderstandings in chemistry: diagnosis and evaluation using concept mapping', *School Science Review*, 77 (280), 107–115.

Wineburg, S. (1997) 'Beyond breadth and depth: subject matter knowledge and assessment', *Theory into Practice*, 36, 4 (Autumn), 255–261.

Wintour, P. (2000) 'Blair plans schools revolution', *Guardian*, 9 September, 1, para. 1.

Wintour, P. (2001) 'Blair offers new school revolution', *Guardian,* 9 February, 1. See also pp. 12–13.

Wood, D. (1988) *How Children Think and Learn*, Oxford: Blackwell.

Wragg, E. (ed.) (1984) *Classroom Teaching Skills*, London: Croom Helm.

Wragg, E. (1993) *Classroom Management*, London: Routledge.

Wragg, E. (1994) *An Introduction to Classroom Observation*, London: Routledge.

Wragg, E.C. and Wood, E.K. (1989) 'Teachers' first encounters with their classes' in E.C. Wragg (ed.) *Classroom Teaching Skills*, London: Routledge.

Wright, C. (1994) 'Black children's experience of the secondary system' in B. Moon and A. Shelton-Mayes (eds) *Teaching and Learning in the Secondary School*, London: Routledge.

Wringe, C. (1988) *Understanding Educational Aims*, London: Unwin Hyman.

NAME INDEX

Adams, C. 228 with Brown, B.B. and Edwards, M.

Addison, N. 161–2, 252 with Burgess, L.

Adey, P. 62, 163, 168–72, 176, 239; 253 with Shayer, M.; 168 with Shayer, M. and Yates, P.

Aldrich, R. 337, 340 with White, J.

Allsop, T. 27

Anderson, J. 237, 239 with Reider, L.M. and Simon, H.A.

Arthur, J. 217 with Haydon, T.

Ashworth, S. 113, 273–4, 277 with Mosston, M.

Atkinson, J. 105

Ausubel, D. 243

Awender, M.A. 32 with Morton, L.L.

Balderstone, D. 217, 258 with Lambert, D. 324; with King, S.

Ballard, R. 181 with Kalra, V.

Barnard, N. 307

Barnes, B. 272–3

Barnes, D. 261

Barnett, L. 37–47 with Warren, A.

Barrett, J. 228 with Ripley, K.

Batchford, R. 7

BBC, *see* British Broadcasting Corporation

BECTA (British Educational Technology Association) 41, 42, 46; *see* NCET

Bee, H. 238, 248

Beer, S. 11

Bell, B. 242 with Driver, R.

Bell, J. 284

Bennett, N. 261, 267 with Dunne, E.

Biggs, J. B. 247

Black, P. 305, 307, 312 with Wiliam, D.

Blamires, M. 228 with Brookes, H., Lacey, R. and Roux, J.

Bleach, K. 24, 27

Bloom, B. S. 94

Boaler, J. 132

Bourne, J. 133 with Moon, B.

Bourne, R. 146 with Davitt, J. and Wright, J.

Bramall, S. 16, 214–5, 335, 344–6 with White, J.

Brandeth, G. 165

Brandon, E. 342 with Gingell, J.

Brittain in Klein, G. 182

Brookes, H. 228 with Blamires, M.

Brown A. L. 237, 241

Brown, B.B. 228 with Adams, C.

Brown, C.R. 34 with Caines, R.A.

Bruner, J. 239, 241

Brunner, D. 37, 47 with Warren, A.

Bullock Report 240

Burchfield, R. 426

Burgess, L. 161–2, 252 with Addison, N.

Bush, T. 396

Buzan, T. 81, 87

Caines, R.A. 34 with Brown, C.R.

Calhoun, E, 276 with Joyce, B.

Canter, L. 75, 124, 126

Canter, M., 124, 126 with Canter. L.

Capel, S. 32, 33; with Leask, M. and Turner, T. 8, 124, 383, 389

Carter, T. 182

Centre for Studies on Inclusion in Education 219

Centre for Science Education (Sheffield) 264, 267

Cheema, I. 245, with Riding, R.J.

Child, D. 36, 104, 115, 147, 174, 248, 267

Chyriwsky, M. 243

Coard, B. 182

Cockburd, A.D. 34, 63, 267

Cohen, L.75 with Manion, L. and Morrison, K.

Cole, M. 27, 400

Coles, A. 155, 157, 158, 159 with Turner, S.

Coles, M.J. 276 with Robinson, W. D.

Collins, J. 46 with Hammond, M. and Wellington, J.

Connolly, J. 393 with Hargreaves, D.

Cooper, P. 230

Cowie, H. 209 with Sharp, H.

Cox, M. 42, 46
Crane, C.D. 379
Crawley, T. 17 with Stephenson, P.
Croner, 397, 400
Crook, C. 46
Crook, D. 130 131, 146, 175 with Power, S. and Whitty, G.
Curtis, S.J. 8

D'Arcy, J. 34
Daines, B. 228 with Ripley, K.
Daugherty, R. 316
Davies, F. 258 with Green, T.
Davis, B. 237 with Sumara, D.
Davis, N. 130, 189, 201
Davis, N. 37, 47 with Trend, R. and Loveless, A.; 47 with Somekh, B.
Davitt, J. 146 with Bourne, R.
Dawes, L. 37 with Leask, M. and Litchfield, D.
De Bono, E. 173–4, 176
Dean, J. 34, 393
Dearing, R. 143, 318, 319, 350, 352, 359
Demarco, W. 157 with Turner, A.
Dennison, B. 276 with Kirk, R.
Denton, C. 132 with Postlethwaite, K.
Department for Education (DfE) 116, 126, 300
Department for Education and Employment (DFEE) 62, 132–3, 143, 145, 157, 161, 185, 187, 203, 205–7, 214, 216, 218, 220–1, 226, 228,294, 302–6, 312, 322, 325–6, 333–5, 341, 344, 355–61, 386, 392–3, 400
Department of Education and Science (DES) 130, 131, 183, 188, 194, 333
Department for Education and Science and the Welsh Office (DES/WO) 88, 116, 120–1, 123–5, 127, 288, 305, 313, 315, 344, 361
Department of Health 151, 156
Desforges, C. 16, 61, 63, 202, 217, 267
DES/WO see Department for Education and Science and the Welsh Office
Dewey, J. 331, 332, 337
Dickinson, A. 287, 298
Dillon, J.T. 284
Dockerill, J. 276 with McShane, J.
Doise, W. 241
Donaldson, M. 174–6, 239
Drever, E. 284 with Munn, P.
Driver, R. 242, 252, 287 with Bell, B.
Dunham, J. 393
Dunne, E. 36, 261, 267 with Bennett, N.
Dwyer, C.D. 47 with Sandholtz, J. H.
Dyer, C. 194

Education Act (1996) 203

Education Act (1997) 349
Education Authorities Directory and Annual 380
Education Reform Act (ERA) 13, 131–2, 203, 313, 318, 347
Edwards, M. 228 with Adams, C.
Eggleston, J. 193
Elliott, J. 307
Elton Report 88, 116, 120–1, 123–5, 127, 427
Entwistle, N. 115
Equal Opportunities Commission (EOC) 189, 190
Erikson, E. H. 238

Fernandes, C. 169 with Keys, W.
Fielding, M. 246
Finch, S. with Fitzgerald, R. 183
Fink, D. 64 with Stoll, L.
Fisher, R. 16, 276
Fitzgerald, R. 183 with Finch, S. and Nove, A.
Flavell, J.H. 239
Fontana, D. 32, 36
Francis, 117
Freud, S. 238
Frobisher, L. 27 with Monaghan, J., Orton, J., Roper, T. and Threfall, J.
Frost, J. 217

Gagne, R.M. 236, 243
Gardner, H. 132, 162, 176, 235; 163 with Kornhaber, M and Wake, W.
Gardner, M. 340
George, D. 232
Gessell, A. 237
Gilham, B.258
Gillborn, D. 108, 194 with Gipps, C.; 108, 183, 185, 194, 202 with Mirza, H.A.
Gingell, J. 342 with Brandon, E.
Gipps, C. 108, 183, 187–8, 194, 303, 305, 311, 321 with Gillborn, D.; 322–3 with Harlen, W.; 314, 325 with Stobart, G.
Goddard, D. 8, 409 with Leask, M.
Goleman, G. 235
Gould, S. 175, 182
Gowin, D. 258 with Novak, J.
Graduate Teacher Training Registry (GTTR) 154
Great Britain Education and Employment Committee of the House of Commons 156, 158
Green, T. 258 with Davies, F.
Greenhalgh, P. 138
Griffin, C. 276 in Jarvis, P.
Gunstone, R. 258 with White, R.T.

Hall, D. 225
Hallam, S. 132, 146 with Toutounji, I.

Hammond, M. 46 with Collins, J.
Handy, C. 36
Hargreaves, D. H. 294, 390–1, 393 with
　　Hopkins, D., Leask, M., Connolly, J. and
　　Robinson, P.
Harlen, W. 310, 312
Harris, S. 169 with Keys, W.
Hart, K. 169
Hart, N.I. 32
Hart, S. 146
Harter, S. 238
Hay McBer 16, 65, 76, 87, 121, 127, 281
Haydon, G. 125; 217, 349 with Lambert, D.
Haydon, T. 217 with Arthur, J. and Hunt, M.
Haylock, D. 291, 308
Head, J. 34
Headington, R. 312
Health Education Authority 155
Her Majesty's Inspectorate , 131, 163
Hill, F. 34
Holford, J. 276 in Jarvis, P.
Holligan, C. 24, 27 with Munn, P. and Johnstone,
　　M.
Holt, J. 311
Hopkins, D. 64, 284; 275 with Joyce, B; 393 with
　　Hargreaves, D.
Howe, M.J.A. 27
Humphrys, G. 380
Hunt, M. 217 with Haydon, T.

Ideus, K. 230 with Cooper, P.
ILEA 270

James, M. 325
Jarvis, P. 276 with Holford, J. and Griffin, C.
Jennings, A. 216
Johnstone, M. 24, 27 with Munn, P. and Holligan,
　　C.
Joyce, B., 276 with Calhoun, E. and Weil, M.

Kalra, V.S. 181 with Ballard, R.
Keogh, B. 242 with Naylor, S.
Kerry, T. 143,146
Kettle, C. 62, 74
Keys, W. 169 with Harris, S. and Fernandes, C.
King, S. 58–9, 64; 324 with Balderstone, D.
Kirk, R. 276 with Dennison, B.
Klein, G. 179, 181–4, 194–9, 202, 213
Kohlberg, L. 238
Kolb, D.A. 246
Kornhaber, M. 163 with Gardner, H.
Kozulin, A. 240
Kramarski, B. 239 with Mevarechz, R.
Kress, G. 102 with Ogborn, J.

Kyriacou, C. 17, 24, 27, 37, 61, 76, 102, 115; 32
　　with Stephens, P.

Lacey, R. 228 with Blamires, M.
Lambert, D. 146, 290, 292; 217, 258 with
　　Balderstone, D.; 125 with Haydon, G.
Langford, P. 203, 204, 217
Laslett, R. 117, 120, 127 with Smith, C.J.
Lave, J. 237 with Wegner, E.
Lawton, D. 305, 342, 346, 393
Leask, M. 46, 262 with Capel, S. and Turner, A.;
　　8, 124, 383, 396 with Goddard, D.; 37 , 47
　　with Dawes, L. and Litchfield, D; 393 with
　　Hargreaves, D.; 40, 43, 47, 227, 229, 232, 265
　　with Pachler, N.; 393 with Terrell, I.
Lewis, I. 284 with Munn, P.
Litchfield, D. 37 with Dawes, L. and Leask, M.
Loveless, A. 37, 47 with Trend, R.

MacDonald, B. 307
MacGillicuddy, K. 102 with Ogborn, J.
Mager, R. 76, 277
Maguire, D. 40
Maguire, M. 34
Maier, P. 37, 47 with Warren, A.
Maitland, I. 36
Manion, L. 75 with Cohen, L.
Marland, M. 17, 24, 27, 89, 388
Martins, I. 102 with Ogborn, J.
Maslow, A.H. 106, 109
Mason, M. 233 with Reiser, R.
Matheson, D. 17 with Grosvenor, I.
Maughan, B. 159, 178 with Rutter, M.
Maybin, J. 241
McCarthy, B. 246
McClelland, D.C. 105
McGrath, M. 17
McGregor, D. 105
McGuiness, C. 277
McNamara, E. 17
McShane, J. 276 with Dockerill, J.
Mercer, N. 241 with Maybin, J.
Mevarech, Z.R. 239 with Kramarski, B.
Miller, O. 232
Milner, D. 182
Mirza, H.A. 108, 185, 187–8, 194, 201 with
　　Gillborn, D.
Mitchell, R 243
Modood 188 in Gillham, D. and Mirza, H.A.
Monaghan, J. 27 with Frobisher, L.
Moon, B. 133 with Bourne, J.
Morrison, K. 75 with Cohen, L.
Mortimore, P. Foreword, 159, 178; 284 and
　　Whitty, G.

Morton, L.L. 32 with Vesco, R., Williams, N.A. and Awender, M.A.
Mosston, M. 113, 271–2, 275, 277; with Ashworth, S.
Munn, P. 24, 27 with Johnston, M. and Holligan, C. ; 284 with Drever, E.; 284 with Lewis, I.
Murphy, P. 305, 312
Myers, K. 178, 180

National Audit Office 155
National Commission on Education 193, 310
National Council for Educational Technology (NCET) 41, 47; see also BECTA
National Union of Teachers 380
National Association for Special Educational Needs (NASEA) 226
National Foundation for Educational Research 173
Naylor, S. 242 with Keogh, B.
Newbold, D. 132
Nicholls, J. 7
Nolta, D.L. 402
Norman, K 240, 249
Novak, J.D. 258
Nove, A. with Fitzgerald, R. 183

Office for National Statistics 181
O'Hear, P. 214 with White, J.
OFSTED 110, 127, 132, 183, 207, 232, 280, 311, 315, 322, 398–9, 400–1, 404
Ogborn, J. 102 with Kress, G., Martins, I. and MacGillicuddy, K.
Olweus, D. 110
Organisation for Economic Cooperation and Development (OECD) 178
Orton, J. 27 with Frobisher, L.
Ouston , J. 159, 178 with Rutter, M.
Owen-Jackson, G. 157, 164

Pachler, N. 40, 43–7, 227, 229, 232, 262, 265 with Leask, M.; 44 with Williams, L.
Palmer, R. 426
Papert, S. 47
Parekh, B. 180
Partnership with Parents 233
Pateman, T. 33
Patmore, M. 171
Peddiwell, J. 8; see Goddard, D. and Leask, M.
Perrot, E. 94, 102
Piaget, J. 237
Plowden Report 131
Postlethwaite, K. 107, 132; with Denton, C.
Powers, S. 130–1, 146, 175 with Crook, D.

Qualification and Curriculum Authority (QCA)

62, 143, 157, 161, 203, 205–7, 214, 216, 218, 220–1, 226, 228, 294, 302, 306, 315, 334–6, 341, 344, 355–61
Queensland Department of Education 284

Rampton, A. 183
Rampton Report 183
Rayner, S. 249 with Riding, R.
Reder, L.M. 237, 239 with Anderson, J. R. and Simon, H.A.
Reiser, R. 233
Riding, R. J. 242–5; 249 with Rayner, S.
Ringstaff, C. 47 with Sandholtz, J. H.
Ripley, K. 229
Robertson, J.24, 27, 97, 99, 102, 119
Robinson, K. 163
Robinson, P. 393 with Hargreaves, D.
Robinson, W.D. 276 with Coles, M.J.
Rodwell, L. 155
Rogers, C. 106, 108
Rogoff, B. 237, 241
Roper, T. 27 with Frobisher, L.
Roux, J. 228 with Blamires, M.
Rowe, M. 62
Rutter, M.159, 178 with Maughan, B., Mortimore, P. and Ouston, J.
Ryan, A. 289–90

Scarman, Lord 183
School Curriculum and Assessment Authority (SCAA) 145
Scottish Consultative Council on the Curriculum (SCCC) 76, 285
Selinger, M. 43
Selman, R. L. 238
Shaffer, R.H. 17
Sharp, H. 209 with Cowie, H.
Shayer, M. 171; 162, 168, 172 with Adey, P.; 168 with Adey, P. and Yates, C.; 168 with Wylam, H.
Shemilt, D. 291
Short, G. 180
Simon, H.A. 237, 239 with Anderson, J.R.
Skinner, B. 106
Smith, C. J. 117, 120, 127 with Laslett, T.
Smith, D. 178, 183 with Tomlinson, S.
Smith, K. 251
Smith, R. 217 with Standish, P.
Smithers, A. 194
Snow, C.P. 162
Somekh, B. 47 with Davis, N.
St John Ambulance 17, 392
Standish, P. 217 with Smith, R.
Stephens, P. 32 with Kyriacou, C.

Stephenson, P. 17 with Crawley, T.
Stierer, B. 241 with Maybin, J.
Stoll, L. 64 with Fink, D.
Stones, E. 236, 243
Stradling, R. 143 with Saunders, L. and Weston, P.
Stobart, G. 314, 325 with Gipps, C.
Sumara, D. J. 237 with Davis, D.
Sutton, C. 260, 267
Sutton, R. 317
Swann, Lord 183, 188, 194

Taher, A. 184
Tanner, J. 151, 159
Tarrant, G. 216
Task Group on Assessment and Testing (TGAT) 288, 305, 313, 315, 348
Teacherline 17
Teacher Training Agency (TTA) 37, 171, 382, 390, 393–4
TGAT; see Task Group
Threfall, J. 27 with Frobisher, L.
Tikly, C. 344 with Wolf, A.
Times Educational Supplement 312, 380
Thacker, J. 217
Tomlinson, S. 178, 183 with Smith, D.
Topping, K.J. 241
Toutounji, I. 132, 146, with Hallam, S.
Townsend, S. 147
Trend, R. 37, 47 with Loveless, A. and Davis, N.
TTA; see Teacher Training Agency
Turner, A. 8, 124, 383, 389 with Capel, S. and Leask, M. ; 157 with Demarco, W.
Turner, S, 155, 157–9, 217

Underwood, J. 311

Vesco, R. 32 with Morton, L.L.
Voice Care Network 28
Vygotsky, L. 240, 250

Wake, W. 163
Warnock, M. 206
Warren, A. 37, 47
Waterhouse, P. 30
Watkins, C. 256
Weil, M. 276 with Joyce, B.
Weiner, B.J. 105
Weiner, G. 202
Wellington, J. 46, 216
Wenger, E. 237 with Lave, J.
Werskey, G. 182
Weston, P. 147 with Stradling, R.
Which 156, 157
White, J. 163; 214 with O'Hear, P.; 337, 340 with Aldrich, R.; 16, 214–5, 335, 344–6 with Bramall, S.
White, R.T. 258 with Gunstone, R.
Whitehead, R.G. 148–51
Whitty, G., 146, 175 with Crook, D.
Whylam, H. 168 with Shayer, M.
Wiliam, D. 305, 307, 312 with Black, P.
Wilkin, M. 27
Williams, L. 44 with Pachler, N.
Williams, N.A. 32 with Morton, L.L.
Willson, M. 258
Wineburg, S. 310
Wintour, P. 133
Wolf, A. 344 with Tikly, C.
Wood, D. 241
Wood, E.K. 61,120 with Wragg, E.C.
Wragg, E. C. 50, 64, 87, 93, 95, 101, 285; 61, 120 with Wood, E.K.
Wright, C. 184, 193
Wright, J. 146 with Bourne, R.
Wringe, C. 337

Yates, P. 168 with Adey, P. and Shayer, M.
Yin, R. 285
Youth Cohort Study 185, 187–8

SUBJECT INDEX

A level; *see* General Certificate of Education Advanced Level

ability: of pupils 105–7; range in the classroom 32, 107; selection by 333

able pupils 232

abstract thought 171; see also formal operations; stage theories of development

academic work/writing 418, 423, 425; see also assignments

ACAS 384

accommodation (in stage theories of development) 238

accountability 21–2, 286–7, 301–3, 305, 313, 321–2, 390–1, 395, 397; contractual 362; moral 362; professional 362, 381, 391; see also assessment; external assessment; public examinations

accreditation of prior experiential learning (APEL) 382

achievement 104, 108, 124–5, 185–94, 344; aspects 293–4; ethnicity 180, 187–8; gender differences 186, motivation 105, 107; public examinations 185–6, 190–1; 189–91; social class 186, 189–91; *see also* motivation

action planning 385

action research 278–84

active learning 93, 126, 234, 250–67, 383; advantages of 265; methods 267; *see also* experiential learning

adaption 238; *see also* stage theories of development

ADD: *see* attention deficit disorder

ADHD: *see* attention deficit hyperactivity disorder

administration 33, 388, 390; of examinations 387

adolescence 128, 142, 153, 158, 238

Adrian Mole 147

Advanced Level (of GCE): *see* General Certificate of Education

Advanced Level Information System 301; Advanced Level Information System plus 301

Advanced/Subsidiary Level (A/S): *see* General Certificate of Education

advertisements for jobs 365–6, 371; *see also* first post

affection needs of pupils 106

affiliation needs of pupils 106

aims: 143–6, 203, 207; academic 331; common conception of 336; of the curriculum 345; to develop individual 331–2, 336; different levels of 336; differentiation in 143, 334; of education 326–37, 338, 343; influences on teaching 329; justification of 333, 345; lessons 69; and means 214; moral 344; of the National Curriculum 205, 334, 336, 343, 346; nature of 329; personal 331; relationship to curriculum 343–5; school 328, 341, 343, 349, 390; social 344; for the good of society 331–2, 336; tensions between different aims 328; values in 335; variety of 329, 331, 333; vocational 331; *see also* areas of experience; moral development

anti-racism 183, 185, 212; and National Curriculum 194; *see also* diversity; discrimination; Equal Opportunities; Personal, Social and Health Education; racism

anti-racist policy 341; *see also* Equal Opportunities

anti-sexist policy 341; *see also* Equal Opportunities

anxiety: *see* stress

appearance: of teacher 89, 97–8; *see also* teacher presentation

application form (for a job) 367, 369, 371; *see also* first post

applying for a job 362–3, 371; *see also* first post

appraisal 4, 383, 389–90, 392;

areas of experience 163; *see also* curriculum; intelligence

arriving late for lesson 120

Art and Design 153, 161–2

AS (Advanced Supplementary) level; *see* General Certificate of Education Advanced Supplementary Level

ASD: *see* autistic spectrum disorder
Assertive discipline 124
assessment 69, 105, 165–9, 210, 286–312, 360, 399; Australia 302–3; changes as a result of review of the National Curriculum 351; commercial tests 301; competence based 319–20; context 169, 282; cost 306; course work 306; criterion referenced 107–8, 290–1, 314–16, 319–20; diagnostic 300–1; -driven curriculum 348; eleven plus 130; entry to secondary school 224; formative 104, 115, 133, 236–7, 286, 289–90, 298, 304–5, 307, 310–11, 314–15; high and low stakes 293, 307, 321; holistic 162, 252; integrity 307–8; ipsative (value-added) 291; Key Stage 3 315–16; lesson planning 288; managing 308–9; modular 318–19; national tests 286, 315–16, 348, 350–2; norm-referenced 107–8, 175, 290–1, 303, 314–16; objectives 293–4; oral 306; overcoming potential barriers to 357; practical 306; pre-National Curriculum 295–7; principles 286; of pupils by pupils 113; pupil's view 299; purposes 298–304; range 298; reporting 290, 295, 297, 399; special educational needs 300–1; summative 133, 286, 289–90, 302, 304–5, 307, 313–25; synoptic 319; targets 354; teacher 319, 348, 350–1; of teaching 33; teaching and learning 293–4, 298, 304, 314–15; tiered 315–16; vocational courses 319–20; *see also* accountability; achievement; differentiation; external lesson planning; motivation; level descriptions; public examinations; reliability; questioning; SATs; validity; norm referencing; pupil grouping; intelligence quotient (IQ); national testing; special educational needs; Task Group on Assessment and Testing
Assessment of Performance Unit 182
assignments 382; guidance for writing 418–26; drafting/redrafting 422; editing 420; proof-reading 422; use of quotations 423–4
assimilation (in stage theories of development) 238
asthma 158
atmosphere: *see* classroom atmosphere
Attainment (in National Curriculum): Levels 302, 305, 312; Targets 305, 316, 347, 349, 351–2, 356, 358
attendance 399
attention deficit disorder (ADD) 230
attention deficit hyperactivity disorder (ADHD) 230
attention: gaining pupils' 79–83, 90–1, 93; pupils not paying 120; seeking by pupils 118
attitude: 184, 253; of class 121; development of in

pupils 331; of pupils to school 103; of teachers 103
attribution theory (of motivation) 105, 107; *see also* motivation
authority of teacher 100, 119–20
autistic spectrum disorder (ASD) 229
Awarding Bodies (public examinations) 322

banding: *see* grouping of pupils; mixed ability
baseline testing 301
basic skills; *see* skills
behaviour: disorder 229; management of pupils' 82, 84–5, 88, 103, 120–1, 126, 235, 399; policy 124–5; of pupils 100, 103, 106, 108, 110, 112, 116–27, 375, 419; of teachers 103, 108, 268; *see also* code
behavioural learning theories (of motivation) 106, 235
behaviourist theory 235
beliefs: differences 336
bell shaped curve 314; *see also* norm referencing
bias 52, 183, 197–8; *see also* prejudice; racism; stereotyping
bibliography (in assignments) 424; *see also* assignments
bicycle for postmen 173
black pupils 179; *see also* equal opportunities; ethnicity; minority ethnic group
Bloom's taxonomy 94
body language 121
body mass index 155: *see also* diet, growth and development
boredom: of pupils 104, 114, 118, 121
brainstorm 244, 256
breadth of study (of the National curriculum) 347, 358
breakfast and academic performance 151: *see also* diet; growth and development
British Educational Index (BEIndex) 420
Britishness 180–1
Bruner 239, 241
Bullock Report 240
bullying 117, 123–5

calculators 171
Career Entry Profile 2, 4, 362, 372, 375, 381–3, 385–6, 389–90, 392
careers: choice 157, 344; education and guidance 344, 356; *see also* motivation
caring: by teacher 98, 101–2
case studies (of pupils) 137–9; *see also* action research
CASE: *see* Cognitive Acceleration in Science Education

CASK model 269
Certificate of Secondary Education (CSE) 316
certificates 109
cheating 210
Children Act 184
citizens 335
citizenship 205, 213, 328, 336, 341, 344–5, 354, 359; *see also* moral education, PSHE
class (social) 103, 128, 183; achievement 183
class size 271
classroom: assistants 30; atmosphere 92, 110, 119, 121; climate 101–2, 125; displays 59–60; environment 101; interaction 1, 118; management 9–10, 22–3, 42, 77, 88, 97, 103, 116, 118–21, 123, 126, 271, 387, 419; observation 50–64; routines 77; *see also* behaviour; equipment; gender; movement; observation; pupil talk; routines
Clause 28 328
clothes worn by teachers 98
coaching 388
code: of conduct (for behaviour) 119–20, 126, 332, 341; of ethics 204–5; of Practice for special educational needs 128, 218, 221, 232; of professional conduct and practice 387; *see also* behaviour; rules; special educational needs
cognition 160–1, 170, 228, 235; *see also* cognitive development; situated cognition
Cognitive Abilities Test 175, 301
Cognitive Acceleration in Science Education (CASE) 168, 172, 239, 253; *see also* cognitive; thinking
cognitive: conflict 167, 172, 241; development 128, 160–77, 234–8; development in Art and Design 162; measuring 172; 174–5; model of 171–2; theories of 235; 237–40; *see also* Cognitive Acceleration in Science Education; development; metacognition; stage theories of development
collaborative work (of teachers) 385
Commission for Racial Equality 101
commitments outside teaching 363, 385;
committee duties 33, 390
common-sense 167; *see also* logic
communal constructivism 48
communication: as a key skill 294, 357; between pupils 89; between teachers and pupils 89–102; channels of 390; effective 97; multimedia 263–4; non-verbal 88–90, 95, 97–8, 100–1, 108, 110, 374–5; pupils with special educational needs 227–8; pupil teacher 57–8, 63; verbal 88–90, 95, 97–8, 100, 108, 374–5; written 375, 425; *see also* body language; contact time; DARTs; language; pupil talk; overhead

projector; questioning; social constructivist theory; skills; voice; writing on board
comparison: avoiding 122
competence based assessment ; *see* assessment
competition between schools 328
comprehensive schools: *see* schools, types of
computers 265; *see also* ICT; information processing theory
concept development 236, 240, 243–4; *see also* cognitive development; stage theories; information processing theory
concept map 244, 256–8; *see also* scaffolding, structuring
concept of education 332
concrete operational thinking 238–46; *see also* stage theories of development
conditioned learning 160
conference attendance 390
confidence: of pupils 335; of teacher 91, 98, 100–1, 374, 383, 387
conflict: with pupils 32; role 33
confrontation with pupils 122–3
consistency 122
constructivism 237, 240–2
constructivism 48, 235, 237, 240, 242
contact time with pupil 63; *see also* communication
context in which working 338, 345, 390
continuing professional development (CPD) 4, 33, 270, 362, 375, 377, 381–94
continuity 258
contractual requirements of teachers 362, 395–401; *see also* accountability
control: in the classroom 32, 97, 100, 117, 123–4, 383, 419; of education 327–8
co-operative learning 252; *see also* active learning; learning
core subjects 315–16
counsellor 124
coursework (of GCSE) 317–18
CPD; *see* continuing professional development
CPD co-ordinator 391
creaming 130
Creative and Cultural Education 163
criminal convictions (of teachers) 379
criteria: setting of 113
criterion referenced assessment: *see* assessment
critical incidents 211–12
critical thinking 244
critical thinking 244–5
criticism: of pupils by teacher 110–12, 122; of your teaching 388
cross-curriculum issues: *see* curriculum
CSE: *see* Certificate of Secondary Education
cultural differences 101, 128, 178, 336, 342; diet

and health 158; IQ 174–5; spiritual, moral and cultural differences (of ERA) 128, 203; Two Cultures 162; *see also* cultural, ethnicity; achievement

cultural: background 359; celebration of 182; diversity 178–202; groups 334; heritage 335; traditions 327

culture 342–3: influence of 103; of a society 342

curriculum 8–10, 347; *2000* 128, 355–60; activities 350; aims of 214, 344–5, 354, 356; broad and balanced 183, 215, 353; common 340; compulsory 340, 356; content 331, 338; context 345; core 340; cross curriculum issues 157–8, 344, 360; development 390; entitlement 184, 349, 351, 356; formal 338–41, 344–5; hidden 338, 340–1; informal 338, 340–1, 344–5; leader 391; load 207; place of subjects 214–15; planning 171; national policy on school curriculum 326; optional parts 340; planned 338; planning 171, 342; priorities for whole curriculum 354; purposes of 356; reflecting aims 326; role in education 338; sabre-toothed 8; school 326, 335, 356, 338–46; as a selection from culture 342–3, 345; spiral 241; subject 326, 335, 339–41, 344–5; theories 342; values of the whole curriculum 354, 356; whole 347, 349, 354; *see also* areas of experience; National Curriculum; pastoral curriculum

curriculum vitae (CV) 363, 366–7, 369–71; *see also* first post

DARTs: *see* Directed Activities Related to Texts

data analysis 57, 165, 169

data protection act 280, 283

deafness: *see* hearing impairment

Dearing: Review of the National Curriculum (1994) 350, 352–3

deep learning: *see* learning

delegating 30, 32

demands of job 34

department 391

Department for Education and Skills (DfES) 395

describing: use of in teaching 30,

design and make (in Design and Technology) 164

Design Technology 164, 173, 351, 353, 356

detention 123

development needs of teachers 392; *see also* continuing professional development

development: of autonomy 335; of co-operation 341; of consideration for others 341; of critical thinking 332; cultural 334–5, 349, 357, 359, 399; emotional 147, 235; enterprise skills 335; identity 335, 344; innovation skills 335; of

integrity 335; intellectual 344; mental 147, 334, 349; normal 147; of personal qualities 331; personal and social 125; of pupils 125, 375; rationality 332, 335; social 335, 344, 357, 359; spiritual 334–5, 349, 357, 359, 399; stages of 237; *see also* Bruner; cognitive development; growth and development; learning; moral development; Piaget; PSHE

Dewey 332

DfES; *see* Department for Education and Skills

diabetes 158

diagnostic assessment 300–1

diary of reflective practice 2, 4, 362, 381

diet 128, 148, 151, 155–8; healthy eating 148; and intelligence 151; in the National Curriculum 157; *see also* school meals; growth and development

differentiation 105, 107–8, 128–46, 375; aims 143–5; between groups 144; between individuals 144; ICT 146; planning for 135–7, 141; stimulus-task-outcome 139–43; by task 139–41; *see also* learning; mixed ability; pupil grouping

Directed Activities Related to Texts (DARTs) 258–62

disabilities 359; *see also* special educational needs

discipline 30, 32, 91–3, 116, 123–124, 253, 375, 388; self-discipline 125; *see also* misbehaviour

discrimination 179–80, 183, 185, 271, 344; overt 184; *see also* attitudes; bias; prejudice

discussion 93, 96, 215–17, 252, 269; *see also* active learning; communication; language; motivation

disruption: disruptive behaviour 32, 120

diversity 128, 178–202, 212–13, 328

Driver 242, 252; *see also* constructivism

dyslexia 228–9

dyspraxia 229

eating habits 155–6; *see also* diet; growth and development

eating: *see* diet

EBD: *see* emotional and behavioural difficulties

economic: understanding 344; and industrial understanding (cross-curricular theme) 344; status of pupils 103

economically competitive 328

Education Act 1944 131, 175, 326, 347

Education Act 1980 156

Education Act 1981 221

Education Act 1996 203, 205

Education Act 1997 349

Education Authorities Directory and Annual 365

Education Reform Act (ERA) (1988) 286, 302,

313, 326, 347, 349–50, 356; *see also* author index

education social worker 124

education system 327: decentralised 327; national 327; state controlled/funded 327; structure of 362

education welfare: officer 124; service 124

Education Year Book 365

education: ideas 376 (for assignments 420); as indoctrination 332; value of 332; value-laden 327; views about 376; *see also* aims

educational psychologists 124; *see also* special educational needs

educational: issues 375; performance 103

effective learning 88, 102, 109, 116, 126; *see also* teaching and learning

effort by pupils 105, 107–8, 118

eleven plus 130, 151

Elton Report (the) 88, 116–17, 120, 123–7, 427–30

emotional and behavioural difficulties (EBD) 118, 226, 229–30

emotional development; *see* development

emotional: intelligence 235; well-being 335, 344

employment (pupil) 103, 191–3, 335, 345

enactive representation (stage theories of development) 239

encouragement of pupils 113

energy: use of 29

English 176, 354; as an additional language 225, 359; profile components of National Curriculum 291; pupils use of standard 357

enjoyable activities (as rewards for pupils) 109; *see also* motivation

entering the classroom 120

entitlement: *see* curriculum entitlement

environment: factor in intelligence 171; education about 344; respect for 335–6; values 206

equal opportunities 178–80, 183, 333, 401; policy 194–5, 199, 328

equipment 117, 120; respect for 120

ethics 204–5, 283; *see also* code

ethnic: background 359; group 334; *see also* minority ethnic group; multicultural society

ethnicity 128, 200; reporting 154, 179; setting and streaming 200; teacher response to 197

eugenics 182

European Computing Driving Licence 37

European Schoolnet 44, 48

evaluation: of your teaching 33, 75, 278, 392, 418, 420 *see also* action research, observation

examinations: administration of 387; board 339; pupils with special educational needs 226;

public 313–25; *see also* assessment; General Certificate of Education; General Certificate of Secondary Education; public examinations

exceptional performance 358

expectation theory (of motivation) 106, 108; *see also* motivation

expectations: of pupils by teachers 106; of teachers 118; *see also* expectation theory; motivation

experiences of pupils 103, 327, 335

experiential learning 31, 246, 252, 271; *see also* active learning; cognitive development; intelligence; ways pupils' learn

explaining to pupils 30, 93, 100, 236, 402

extension: papers for SATs 316; work 84; *see also* level descriptors, levels; assessment, tiered

external assessment 313–25, 352; purposes 320–1; setting and marking papers 323; *see also* assessment; examinations; General Certificate of Education; General Certificate of Secondary Education; public examinations

extra-curricular activities 35, 388

extrinsic motivation; *see* motivation

eye contact 95, 100–1, 121

facial expression: of teacher 89, 97, 99; *see also* teacher presentation

failure by pupils 104–6, 113

fairness: by teachers 112

family background: influence of 103; *see also* growth and development

feedback: on assignments 419; external 113; to pupils 88, 103–4, 113–15; on your teaching 35, 388; *see also* assignments

firmness: of teacher 101

first aid 392

first post 362–80

flow charts 420

form tutor 33, 115, 124, 198, 387

formal assessment meetings 385; *see also* induction

formal operational thinking 238; *see also* stage theories of development

formative assessment; *see* assessment

foundation: GCSE paper 316–17; school 130; subject 164

Freud 238

further education college 364;

further professional development; *see* continuing professional development

Gagne 235

GCE A Level: *see* General Certificate of Education Advanced Level

GCE O Level: *see* General Certificate of Education Ordinary Level

GCSE: *see* General Certificate of Secondary Education

gender 128, 178–80, 183, 196, 271, 311, 334; differences in achievement 183; differences in growth 148–53; employment 191–3; grouping in class 311; influence of 103; IQ 175; neutral reference to in assignments 424–5; setting and streaming 200; teacher response to 196; *see also* equal opportunities

General Certificate of Education Ordinary Level (GCE O Level) 316

General Certificate of Education: Advanced Level (GCE A Level) 286, 313, 318, 353; 'A2' 318–9; Advanced Subsidiary Level (A/S) 286, 318, 353; grade boundaries 314–16; teaching GCE 322–3

General Certificate of Secondary Education (GCSE) 286, 289, 301, 313, 316–18, 351, 353, 358; course work 317–18; differentiation 316; grade boundaries 314–16; grade limits 316; grade parity 317; short course 351; teaching GCSE 322–3; unclassified grade 317

General National Vocational Qualification (GNVQ) 319–20, 351

General Teaching Council (GTC) 20, 386–7

genetic: factor in intelligence 161, 171

genre (in writing) 418–19; *see also* assignments

Gestalt Theory 235

gesture: use of 89, 97, 99

Global School House 45

GNVQ: *see* General National Vocational Qualification

Golda Meir 251

government 124, 327, 352–3; control of education 328; intervention in education 347

government Standards fund 385

governors 124, 330, 354, 374, 391

grades 109; *see also* GCSE, GCE and marking

graduate or registered teacher programme (GRTP) 363

grammar and punctuation 418, 423; *see also* assignments

Group Education Plan: *see* Individual Education Plan

group: management skills 116; work 341 *see also* classroom management; work 125

grouping pupils; banding 200; by age 152; by performance 152; setting 108; streaming 108; 112; bottom stream 112; *see also* ability; mixed ability class; pupil grouping

growth and development 128, 147–53, 229; effect of family size 151; growth spurts 151; height and weight 148–53; intelligence 151; physical 147–53, 334–5, 349; effect of social class 151–2;

differences between urban and rural pupils 151; *see also* body mass index; cognitive development; development; moral development

guided discovery 254

habits 253; *see also* routines

Hay McBer Report 121

head of department 33, 374, 390

head teacher 390–1; guide to the law 397

Health Education Authority 155

health: education 344; healthy lifestyle 335 and safety 14–15, 71

healthy eating: *see* diet

hearing impairment, support for pupils 219, 231

hierarchy of needs theory (of motivation) 106, 109; *see also* motivation

high stakes assessment: *see* assessment

higher degree 382, 390

higher order skills 240, 253, 305; *see also* assessment; formal operational thinking; thinking

history of education 333

holistic problem solving 173

home/family influence on teachers 34,

homework 30, 95, 107, 112, 326, 387

house points 109

iceberg metaphor 11

iconic representation (stage theories of development) 239

ICT: *see* information and communications technology

IEP: *see* Individual Education Plan

ILEA: *see* Inner London Education Authority

imagination 161–2

immigration 180–1

inclusion 128, 357, 359; definition 219; principles of 220; *see also* special educational needs

inclusive education 359

independent schools council teacher induction panel (ISCTIP) 386; *see also* induction

Index for Inclusion (in special educational needs) 219

Individual Education Plan (IEP) 222, 300

individual needs of pupils 102, 103

induction 362, 378, 381, 383–6, 388; immediate 384; programme 383; statutory (in England) 381, 384–6; year 375

information and communications technology (ICT): 37–48, 263, 265, 309; classroom management 42; ethics 39; just in time learning 37; Key Skill 294; motor skills 153; National Curriculum for student teachers 39–40; projects

44–5; pupils' use of 357–9; research evidence 41–2; skills audit 39; skills of teachers 367, 372, 386, 392; in subjects 40; *see also* computers; information technology; Key Skills; national basic skills tests for teachers

information processing 235, 237, 242–5; theory 235

information technology (IT) 351, 357; *see also* skills, information and communications technology

initial teacher education 392

Inner London Education Authority (ILEA) 294

in-service training and professional development: *see* continuing professional development

inspection 280; *see also* OFSTED

instructions to pupils 100, 258–9

integration 333

intellectual skills 237

intelligence 128, 132–3, 160–3, 176; emotional 235; late developers 175; linguistic 162–3; logico-mathematical 162–3; multiple intelligences 128, 132, 160, 162–4, 177, 235; *see also* cognitive; cognitive development; growth and development; IQ tests; learning theories; special educational needs

intelligence quotient (IQ) tests 162–3, 171, 174–5, 246; non-verbal 175; spatial 175; training for 175; verbal 175; *see also* intelligence

interaction with pupils 30, 88

interactive whiteboard 38

internet 354, 366; *see also* websites

interview for a teaching post 4, 362–3, 371–8, 382; dress for 372; format of 372–4; impression 374; questions you may be asked 375–7; *see also* first post

intrinsic motivation; *see* motivation

investigational work 269

ipsative assessment; *see* assessment

IQ: *see* intelligence quotient

Japan 132

job vacancies 363, 365–6; *see also* first post

Key Skills 294, 306, 357, 359; *see also* skills

Key Stage 3: assessment 315–16; dip in pupil's performance 315; *see also* SATs

Key Stages (of the National Curriculum) 347–8, 351, 354, 356, 358–9

knowledge, skills and understanding (in the National Curriculum) 331, 347, 358

knowledge: theories of knowledge acquisition 237; recall 305; *see also* growth and development; high order skills

Kolb 246

language 160, 171, 196; impairment 227–8; and learning 240–1; 258–63; of pupils 92, 357, 359; of the teacher 89–90, 92–3, 240; *see also* DARTs; intelligence; Intelligence Quotient; special educational needs; stage theories of development

LEA; *see* Local Education Authority

leadership: development in pupils 335; in the teaching profession 392

league tables 317, 321, 353

learning society 133

learning: 25–6, 278; across abilities 134; active engagement in 93; activities 237; approaches 247; challenges 335, 357; commitment to 335, cognitive 237; deep 247, 250; difficulties and pupil grouping 133; by discovery 251; diverse needs 357; experiential 269; enhancement of 89, 392; higher order 240, 305; models of 256, 288; outcomes 373; personal theories of 235; potential barriers to 357; pupil 340; rote 172, 254–5; styles and strategies 235, 245–7, 258–62, 269; surface 247, 250; superficial 247; and teaching 236–37; theories of 1–2, 235–49, 418; types of 236–7; *see also* active learning; stage theories of development; teaching and learning; teaching for understanding

leaving the classroom 120

legal requirements of teachers 362

legislation 328

lesson: content 143–5; changing activities (transitions) 58; cycle 73–4; ending 58; evaluations 288, 303; first lessons with a class 50; inclusion of co-operative work 341; management 126; objectives 293, 298, 311; pace 121; plan 30, 35, 382, 387, 420; planning 29–32, 65–76, 80–1, 88, 96, 100, 118, 120, 126, 144, 258, 288, 310–11, 373; preparation 29, 32–5, 88, 101, 120, 126, 387; presentation 88; sequence and flow 55; starting 53–4; *see also* aims; assessment; curriculum; lesson planning; objectives; planning loop; reflection; target group

letter of application for a job 363, 366–8, 371; *see also* first post

Level (of the National Curriculum): of achievement/attainment 347, 353, 356; descriptions 298, 302, 351, 353, 356, 358; descriptors 298; attainment levels 302, 305, 312; statements 348; *see also* attainment; levelling; levels of achievement/attainment; SATs

levelling 316; *see also* Standard Assessment Tasks

Lewis Carroll 340

library system 420

lifestyle: diet 155–8; healthy 157–8;

Listening 259–60; by pupils 96; listening skills (to pupils) 88–9, 95–7, 101–2, 104; *see also* communication; DARTs; language

literacy 352–4; of teachers 386, 425; *see also* national basic skills tests for teachers; national literacy strategy

Local Education Authority 124, 328, 364–7, 374, 378–9, 384, 386–7, 390, 392, 395

local management of schools 347

logic 160, 165–8; *see also* intelligence; Intelligence Quotient

logical reasoning 160

long term memory 242–3

McPherson report 359

management: role 390, 393; of school 341

managing behaviour: *see* behaviour

manner: of teacher 95

mannerisms: of teacher 89, 97–8; *see also* teacher presentation

marking 30, 95, 103, 107, 299–300, 308–9, 312, 350, 387; external 352; grade boundaries 314–5; *see also* assessment; General Certificate of Education; General Certificate of Secondary Education; external examinations

mathematics 132, 162, 168, 170–1, 176, 243; *see also* numeracy

matrix 420

maturation 237

media interest (in education) 354

medical (for teaching post) 379

memory 242; short term 242–3

mental development *see* development; *see also* cognition; cognitive development; stage theories of development

metacognition 235, 239, 253, 300, 306

Middle Years Information System (MIDYIS) 301

minority ethnic group 179, 193, 212–13, 359; *see also* critical incidents; employment; ethnic background

misbehaviour 88, 103, 110, 112, 116–23, 253; *see also* behaviour; discipline

mixed ability 107–8, 128–32; mathematics teaching 132; *see also* differentiation; grouping of pupils; pupil grouping; teaching styles

mixed: age class 152; sex groups 334; *see also* grouping of pupils; pupil grouping

MLD: *see* moderate learning difficulty

modelling 419

moderate learning difficulty (MLD) 226

modern foreign languages 243

modification of work for pupils: *see* differentiation

modular courses 318–19

monitoring pupil progress; *see* formative assessment

mood of class 121; *see also* classroom atmosphere

moral development 128, 160, 171, 203–16, 237, 334–5, 344, 349, 357, 359, 399; and aims 207–9; critical incidents 211–12; discipline 207, 210; National Curriculum 205; OFSTED 207; school curriculum 207; *see also* citizenship; development; ethics; logical reasoning; PSHE; religious education; values; ways pupils' learn

moral: accountability 396–7; standards 328; training 332

motivation 32, 42, 88, 103–16, 122, 124, 126, 161, 235, 247, 252–3, 298, 307, 311, 383, 387; extrinsic 104–5, 247, 252; intrinsic 104–5, 247, 252; theories of 104–9; *see also* active learning; learning approaches

motor skills: *see* psychomotor skills

movement: of pupils in class 117, 120; of pupils around the school 31, 341; of teacher in class 99–100

multicultural: education 182, 213; response of National Curriculum to 194; society 333, 342; 345; *see also* ethnicity; racism; Swann Report

multidisciplinary assessment (of pupils with special educational needs) 224–5; *see also* statementing

multimedia projectors 38; hyperstudio 47

multiple intelligences 235; *see also* intelligence

names of pupils 81–2

Nathan's story 250–1

national basic skills tests for teachers (in England) 386

National Curriculum 288, 290, 294, 298, 305, 326, 328, 339–40; 347–61; administrative arrangements 350; aims of 334, 336, 343, 346; assessment of 360; common requirements 349; content 347; framework 347; intentions 349; nature 347; order (statutory and non-statutory) 344; 349–50, 354–5, 357–8; overload in 350; place of in whole curriculum 354; rationale 356; review of 350, 352–3, 359–60; scope 347, 356; statutory content 350, 357, 358; structure 356; subject order 350, 354, 356; subject task group 354; *see also* aims; attainment; cross-curricular themes; curriculum 2000; level; national assessment/tests; subject

National Forum (National Curriculum) statement of values 206, 213–14

National Foundation for Educational Research (NFER) 175, 301; *see also* assessment

national identity 354

national Induction Standards 384–6; *see also* induction
national literacy strategy 352
national numeracy strategy 352
national priorities for training 392
national testing 350; *see also* assessment; league tables
national training needs 392
National Vocational Qualification (NVQ) 319–20, 351
naturalistic intelligence 163; *see also* intelligence
negative comment: *see* criticism
new technologies 392; *see also* ICT; IT
newly qualified teacher: transition to 381, 383
newspapers (for job advertisements) 365; *see also* first post
NFER: *see* National Foundation for Educational Research
noise in the classroom 117, 120–1
norm referenced; *see* assessment
normal development; *see* development
norms of society 213
numeracy 352–4; of teachers 386; test for new teachers 171; *see also* national basic skills tests for teachers; national numeracy strategy
nutrition: *see* diet
NVQ: *see* National Vocational Qualifications

obesity 155–8; *see also* diet; growth and development
objectives 32, 69, 268, 293, 298, 311; *see also* lesson objectives
observation 278, 275, 282; analysing data from 57, 165; lessons 50–64, 196; participatory 51–2; perception 162; planning observations 52–3; of pupils 101, 104, 114–15; purpose 51; schedules 54–64, 281; systematic 51–2; tasks 53–64; of other teachers 1–2, 50–64, 96, 421; of your teaching 33–5, 382, 385, 388–90; *see also* classroom
OFSTED 33, 132, 194, 207, 364, 390, 396; inspecting special educational needs 221, 231; *see also* author index; PICSI
open enrolment 347
operations (in stage theories of development) 238
organisation in the classroom 30, 88, 101; *see also* classroom
overhead projector 263–4

PANDA: *see* Performance and Assessment Data
paperwork 32
parents 33, 171, 326, 328, 338, 354, 356, 375
parent-teacher association 391
pastoral: activities 387; casework 125; curriculum 125, 341; management 125; role 124–6, 338, 387, 389; work 389–90
patience in teaching 91
pattern: *see* problem-solving
pause: use of in teaching 91, 95
pay/salary 378, 390
payment threshold 390
pedagogy 236, 270, 402
peer: group influences 103; tutoring 241
pendulum 165–8; *see also* logic
perceiving (learning strategy) 246
percentage 168
perception 242
Performance and Assessment Data (PANDA) 304
performance management 390
personal and social education 125; *see also* citizenship; personal, social and health education
personal, social and health education (PSHE) 156–7, 198–9, 205, 341, 344, 351, 354, 357; guidance for teaching 157; *see also* citizenship; development (moral)
personality theory 235
personality: of teacher 1, 98, 117; theories 235
philosophy of education/teaching 1–2, 4, 376;
physical development: *see* growth and development; pupils
physical education 153, 157, 351, 353, 356
physiological needs of pupils 106
pi 168; pi chart 292
Piaget 235, 237–40; *see also* stage theories of development
PICSI: *see* Pre-Inspection and Contextual School Indicators
planning: 65–76, 80; loop (lesson) 288; *see also* learning models, lesson, reflection, schemes of work
Plato 333
pleasure: of pupils as motivation 104; *see also* motivation
Plowden Report 131
poise of teacher 99
policy documents 341, 360; *see also* behavioural policy; school policy
politics 326–8
population: changes 180–81; growth 181; ethnic mix 180–82
portfolio 372, 392; of achievement 382; *see also* professional portfolio
post of responsibility 389
post-16 education 199–200, 13, 318–20, 357
posture: of teacher 89, 97, 99–100; *see also* teacher presentation

praise 88, 91–2, 95, 97, 101, 104, 106, 108–13, 115, 122–3; *see also* motivation; reinforcement; reward

Pre-Inspection and Contextual School Indicators (PICSI) 322

prejudice 179–80; and insularity 185; *see also* bias; discrimination; racism; stereotyping

preparation for adult life 334, 357

probationary period 381

problems: dealing with 35, 118; *see also* behaviour management

problem-solving 160, 173, 240, 252, 294; *see also* active learning

procedures in school 383, 387, 389

processing (as learning strategy) 246

product analysis (Design Technology) 164

professional: accountability 268, 396–7; judgement 10–11; knowledge 10–11, 270, 278; portfolio 2, 4, 362, 382, 389; *see also* portfolio

professionalism 20–1, 402

Programme of Study (of the National Curriculum) 316, 339, 347–50, 353–4, 356–60

programme of work 67 *see also* lesson planning, scheme of work

progression 69, 128, 134–5, 152, 315; *see also* assessment; lesson planning

projects with ICT 44–5; *see also* information and communications technology

proportion 168, 170; *see also* ratio; pi

PSHE: *see* Personal, Social and Health Education

psychoanalytic approach to personality 238

psychology and learning 234, 237

psychomotor skills 152–3

public examinations 286, 313–25, 350; *see also* assessment; awarding bodies; examinations; General Certificate of Education; General Certificate of Secondary Education; league tables; publication of results

publication of results 347, 352; *see also* league tables; public examinations

punishment 88, 112, 114–15, 119, 122–3; physical punishment 123; *see also* sanction

Pupil Performance Information 321; *see also* PANDA

pupil: all-rounders 172; background case studies 137–9; differences 128–233; diversity 61; frustration 122; grouping 108, 128–46, 151–2, 174–5, 199–200, 302; interest in a subject 103, 387; misconceptions 242; progress 388; prior knowledge 242–3, 287; questioning 61; ranking 303–4; relationships 151; response time 62; self esteem 307; special needs 218–33; statementing 223–5; supporting 141–3; talk 117, 120–1, 237, 240–1; under-achievement 178; understanding 122; work 120–1 *see also* achievement; cognitive development; development; diet; differentiation; growth and development; observation; special educational needs; stage theories of development; ways pupils' learn

pupils' names: knowing 101, 114; use of 92

qualification: approved 356; recognised national 358; of teachers 375, 382, 390; *see also* General Certificate of Education Advanced Level; General Certificate of Education Advanced Subsidiary Level; General Certificate of Secondary Education; General National Vocational Qualification; National Vocational Qualification

Qualifications and Curriculum Authority (QCA) 334, 353–5, 395

qualified teacher status (QTS) 362–3, 386, 418

quality of life 332

questioning/questions 61–3: closed-questions 61–2, 94–5; gender 201; open-questions 61–2, 94–5; pupils 61; use of in teaching 30, 90, 92–6, 100; wait time to respond 62; *see also* pupil; teacher

Race Relations Act 184

racial harassment 117, 123–4

racism 183, 185, 271; 'prejudice plus power' 185; *see also* anti-racist policy; bias; equal opportunities; prejudice, stereotyping

ratio 168–9; *see also* proportion; pi

reading for meaning 260–1; *see also* study skills; Directed Activities Related to Texts

rebuke: to pupils 93

recall 140, 165, 167, 255; *see also* learning (rote); study skills

record keeping 69, 399

Record of Achievement 387

recruitment of teachers 392

Recruitment Strategy Manager (RSM) 365–6

referees (for a teaching job) 363, 367, 370; *see also* first post

reference (for a teaching job); *see* first post; referees

referencing 423; *see also* assignments

reflection 2, 4, 236, 246, 256, 284, 327, 385, 389, 392, 402, 418–20;

reflective practitioner 1–2, 374, 392, 402, 420, 425

reflex actions 160

register 399

registered teachers (in England) 387

Rehabilitation of Offenders Act 379

reinforcement 106, 253; by teacher 106, 109, 119, 124; *see also* praise; reward relationships: help pupils to form 335; with pupils 92, 102; with other teachers 389–90

reliability 286, 291, 306, 313, 322; *see also* assessment

religious: beliefs 327; education 205, 347, 349, 351, 356, 359; groups 334

repetition: use of 92

reporting: by pupils 261–2; to parents 302; *see also* assessment

reprimand of pupils 122

research 50–64, 418–20, 423; by teachers 234–5; guide for teachers 64; *see also* action research; classroom; NFER; observation

resource units (bases) in schools 226; *see also* special educational needs

respect: disrespect 121; of pupils for property and equipment 120

responsibilities: of adult members of society 332, 334–5; of pupils 113, 124; of teachers 8–28, 30, 33, 387–9;

reward 73, 103, 109, 112, 114–15, 119, 341; *see also* praise; reinforcement

role: ambiguity 33; conflict 33, 35; of teacher 8–28, 100, 377, 387–8; overload 33, 35; play 35, 269

rote: *see* learning; routines

routines 77, 79–87, 253; in the classroom 30, 35, 118; of school 387, 390; *see also* learning

Royal Society of Arts 316

rules 383: for behaviour 30, 119–20, 126; school 117, 387, 389–90; *see also* behaviour; code of conduct

safety 90, 100, 117, 120, 384; of pupils 106

sanction 73, 341; *see also* punishment

satisfaction: of pupils 104

SATs: *see* Standard Assessment Tasks

scaffolding 235, 241–2; *see also* concept map; structuring

schemata (stage theories of development) 238, 243

schemes of work 65–76, 158, 347, 355–6, 359, 387; optional national 359

School Action Plus (for special educational needs) 223–4

School Curriculum and Assessment Authority (SCAA) 354, 395

school development planning 390–1

school experience 19

school policies 203; discipline 207; equal opportunities 194–5, 199; special educational needs 220–6

School Teachers' Pay and Conditions 397 *see also* pay

school: curriculum 335, 338–6; effective 123, 352; effectiveness 178; efficiency 304; ethos 103, 203, 331; free school meals 156; leaving age 133; ; meals 156; meals service 156; organisation 331, 341; policy 124, 389–90; politics 390; standards for school meals 156; structure 395–6; system 331; values 335; whole school issues 354; *see also* curriculum; schools types of

schools 'make a difference' 178

schools, types of 130, 364; boys 333; comprehensive 130–3; Foundation 130; girls 333; grammar 130–1, 151, 146, 326, 333; independent 130, 365; maintained 347, 360, 364, 384; middle 364; primary 353, 364; private 364, 378; religious foundation; 333–4; secondary 364; secondary modern 175, 326, 333; single sex 334; secular schools 333; special 226; sports college 328; technical 175, 326, 333; technology 328; upper 364; voluntary-aided 364; *see also*; further education college; *see also* the glossary; sixth form college

science 153, 157, 162, 165–8, 176; eugenics 182

seating arrangements in the classroom 96

Secondary School Regulations for England 1904 340

secondary schools, numbers of 130

Secretary of State for Education and Employment 352

selection: *see* pupil grouping

self and values 206

self-actualisation of pupils 106

self-esteem: of pupils 106, 118, 124, 235, 335–6, 344, 402

self-management techniques 35

self-presentation of teacher: *see* teacher presentation

SEN: *see* special educational needs

SENCO: *see* special educational needs co-ordinator

senior managers 391; *see also* head of department; head teacher

sensory motor stage: 238 *see also* stage theories of development

setting; *see* grouping of pupils

Sex Discrimination Act 184

sex education 349, 351, 356

sexism 185, 198–9

sexual morality 214

sexuality 147

short term memory 242–3

silence: in the classroom 79, 90; of teacher 92

Simple Minds 287

simulations 217, 244

situated cognition 237

sixth form college 364; *see also* schools, types of
skills: 357; application of number (by pupils) 357;
basic 352–4; creative thinking 335, 357;
enquiry 357; improving own learning and
performance (by pupils) 357; information
processing 357; metacognitive skills 357;
physical 335; practical 345; problem solving (by
pupils) 335, 357; reasoning 357; thinking
rationally 335; thinking skills 357; working
with others (by pupils) 357; *see also* Key Skills
smile 109
social class: *see* class
social constructivist theory 235, 237, 240–2, 271
social interaction 118
society 328; *see also* multicultural society
society and values 206, 213
special educational needs (SEN) 128, 147, 175,
218–33, 333–4, 359, 400; categories 219; four
stages of statementing 222; helping special
educational needs pupils learn 226–7;
Individual Action Plan 222; legislation 221;
National Curriculum 220; Multidisciplinary
assessment 224–5; revised code of practice 218,
221; public examinations 226, 321; School
Action Plus 223–4; *see also* code; differentiation;
inclusion
special educational needs co–ordinator (SENCO)
220, 222, 224
special units (in schools) 226
spider diagram 256–7, 420
staffroom 375
stage theories of development 237–40, 246
standard assessment data 113
Standard Assessment Tasks (SATs) 301–2, 305,
315–16; differentiated papers 316; levelling 316;
extension papers 316; *see also* assessment; level
descriptors; levelling
standard of work 108
standards 305; of education 347, 356; raising 353
standards for the award of QTS 326
state: control 327; funded 327
statementing 223–5; *see also* special educational
needs
Statements of Attainment 298, 348, 351; *see also*
level descriptors
statutory duties of teachers 362
statutory order (of the National Curriculum): *see*
National Curriculum
Stephen Lawrence 359
stereotypes 108
stereotyping 182, 184, 197; *see also* bias; prejudice,
racism
stimulus–task–outcome: *see* differentiation
streaming of pupils: *see* grouping of pupils

stress: causes of 34; coping with 34; prevention 32,
34; of teaching 29, 32
structuring topics 244; *see also* concept map;
scaffolding
Student Teacher Employment Programme (STEP)
366
Student teacher: phases of development 22–7; role
and responsibilities 18–28; self image 22–4
study skills 253, 324
subject: adviser/inspector 365, 374; aims 344;
application 376; association 351, 354; content
340; contribution to overall aims 346; core 344,
349–53; foundation/non-core 344, 349–50,
352–4; knowledge 10–2, 100, 236, 374, 376,
382; monitoring 360; in the national
curriculum 348–9; order (in the national
curriculum) 350; place in the whole curriculum
338–9, 345; *see also* aims; curriculum; National
Curriculum
success: of pupils 30, 103–10, 113
summative assessment; *see* assessment
supervisory activities/duties 30, 387
support staff 223, 391, 395
support: supporting pupils 101; for teachers 35,
118, 123, 126, 389, 392
supporting learning: *see* concept map; scaffolding,
structuring topics
surface learning: *see* learning
sustainable development 335, 357
Swann Report 183
swearing 81–2
syllabus 339; *see also* curriculum; subject
symbolic representation (stage theories of
development) 239

talk: *see* communication; language; pupil talk
target group 133, 145; *see also* grouping of pupils;
pupil grouping
target setting 321, 356, 385, 388, 392
Task Group on Assessment and Testing (TGAT)
288, 305, 313, 315–6, 348, 350–1
tasks for pupils: challenging 105; difficulty of
104–5, 107, 118
tasks: time engaged on 30
Teacher Training Agency 366, 386, 395; *see also*
author index
teacher: ability to cope 376; adaptability 387;
asking questions 61–3; association 353–4;
effective 1, 103; enthusiasm 97–9, 103, 375;
expectations 271, first encounters with classes
50; goals 310; interests 375, 377; movement in
class 59; presentation 88–90, 97–102;
reactions/response 118, 121; relationship with
pupils 77; response to cheating 210; role and

responsibilities 8–28; status 119; strengths 35; time with pupils 63; wait time for response 61; weaknesses 35; *see also* behaviour (of teacher)

TeacherNet 4, 6

teachers work 362

teaching abroad 364

teaching and learning: effective 12, 23–4, 26, 101, 116, 244, 268, 279–81; enhancement of 392; framework for 326; process 1–2

teaching: assessment expectations of 303; commitment to 376; competently 119, 387; concepts 250; for understanding 165–8, 287, 310–11; enhancement of 391; externally assessed courses 322–3; healthy eating 155–8; improving 234; load 388; methods 66, 254, 269, 340, 383; models 311; monitoring of 392; objectives 311; procedures 1; routines 77, skills 1, 32; strategies 2, 103, 215–17, 234–5, 387, 392; style 1, 50, 103, 114, 116, 119, 215–17, 234–8, 268–77; techniques 1, 95; using past examination papers 324; *see also* discussion; public examinations; thinking

teams of staff 391

TGAT: *see* Task Group on Assessment and Testing

The Republic 333

theories of learning: *see* learning

theory 1–2, 382, 418–20, 423; and practice 1, 4, 418; *see also* learning theory; theory of motivation; personality theory; stage theories of development

theory *x* and theory *y* (of motivation) 105, 107; *see also* motivation

thinking 161–2, 253, 294; *see also* CASE; higher order skills; stage theories of development

tiered assessment; *see* assessment

time: use of in the classroom 29–32, 326; use of own time 30, 86; management 29–33, 35; travel 363; waste of 31

Times Educational Supplement 365, 372

timetable 340–1, 345; commitments 385

tiredness 29, 35, 363

transfer from primary to secondary 224

transfer of learning 239–40; *see also* metacognition

trial and error 167

tuck shops 156

Two Cultures 162

types of schools: *see* schools, types of

under achievement/performance 113, 178–80, 183, 301, 307, 359; contributing factors 178; boys 180, 183; minority ethnic pupils 182–3; *see also* pupils; English as additional language

unit of work 67, 387; *see also* scheme of work

validity 286, 291, 305, 313, 322; consequential 311

value added 301

value added assessment (ipsative); *see* assessment

values 128, 203–16, 332; assessing what is valued 293; OFSTED reporting on 207; own 125, 327, 336; of pupils 118; school 335; social 335; statement of values 206

variables 165–8, 177

vending machines 156

verbal-imagery (styles of learning) 245

video 44, 264

Virtual Teacher Centre 42

visual impairment 231–2

visualisation 35

vocabulary: of teacher 96, 110, 418; *see also* assignments; language

vocational: A Levels 319–20; courses and examinations 286, 315, 319–20; assessment 320; opportunities 353; qualification 351; *see also* public examinations

voice: pitch of 91; projection of 90–1; speed of 91; tone of 95; use of 89–90, 99, 100; volume of 90–1,

Voluntary Service Overseas (VSO) 364

Vygotsky 240–1, 250

warning of pupils 122

Warnock Committee 333

Warnock Report 206

Ways pupils' learn 234–49; *see also* cognitive development

WebQuest 44

websites 37, 44–8; *see also* internet

whiteboard; *see* interactive whiteboard

whole class teaching 132

whole-part-whole teaching 109–10, 113

wholist-analytic (styles of learning) 245

wide ability: *see* mixed ability; pupil grouping

work experience/placement 353, 389

workload: of teacher 33

worksheet design 264

writing (of teachers) 419; purposes of 419; skills 425; *see also* assignments

writing on board 263–4;

Year 11 Information System (YELLIS) 301

YELLIS: *see* Year 11 Information System

Youth Cohort Study 185–8

zone of proximal development 240